THE GR

Egypt

Travel Publications

Hannay House, 39 Clarendon Road
Watford, Herts WD17 1JA, UK
☎ 01923 205 240 - Fax 01923 205 241
www.ViaMichelin.com
TheGreenGuide-uk@uk.michelin.com

Manufacture française des pneumatiques Michelin
Société en commandite par actions au capital de 304 000 000 EUR
Place des Carmes-Déchaux – 63 Clermont-Ferrand (France)
R.C.S. Clermont-Fd B 855 200 507

© Michelin et Cie, Propriétaires-éditeurs, 2002
Dépôt légal avril 2002 – ISBN 2-06-100066-5 – ISSN 0763-1383
Printed in France 03-02/1.1

Typesetting: le Sanglier, à Charleville-Mézières
Printing and binding: IME, à Baume-les-Dames

Cover design: Carré Noir, Paris 17ᵉ arr.

THE GREEN GUIDE:
The Spirit of Discovery

The exhilaration of new horizons, the fun of seeing the world , the excitement of discovery: this is what we seek to share with you. To help you make the most of your travel experience, we offer first-hand knowledge and turn a discerning eye on places to visit.

This wealth of information gives you the expertise to plan your own enriching adventure. With THE GREEN GUIDE showing you the way, you can explore new destinations with confidence or rediscover old ones.

Leisure time spent with THE GREEN GUIDE is also a time for refreshing your spirit and enjoying yourself.

So turn the page and open a window on the world. Join THE GREEN GUIDE in the spirit of discovery.

Contents

*Like all pharaohs,
Senusret I lived on
after his death.*

*The lush greenery
of the Dakhla oasis
in the heart of the desert.*

Sights

Advice for readers:

The Sights section of this guide is divided into five geographical regions: Alexandria, the Mediterranean Coast and the Delta; Cairo and its Environs; The Oases and the Desert; The Sinai and the Red Sea; The Nile Valley and its Ancient Sites. Within each of these sections, the towns and sites described are arranged in alphabetical order, although visitors may come across different spellings of these place names around the country. As a general rule, signs for major towns and cities in Egypt are in English; those for smaller settlements are referred to by a transliterated form (not always consistent) of the Arabic name. Consequently, Cairo and Alexandria will always be signposted by their English name, and not as El-Qâhira or El-Iskandariya, and Rosetta will be referred to by its Arabic form, Rashid. As a final point, we have used the most common English name for towns and cities in the main body of the guide in cases where more than one option exists.

*The tomb of Queen Nefertari,
in the Valley of the Queens,
is one of the most beautiful in Egypt.*

*A selection of colourful
headgear in one
of the country's many souks.*

Maps and Plans

Road Maps

A detailed map of Egypt is useful for following the itinerary of an organised tour, and essential if you are planning on hiring a car and setting out independently.

Michelin map no 954 (North-East Africa) has the advantage of placing Egypt in its geographical context, and covers the length of the Nile as far as Lake Victoria. Major routes are shown on this map, although its large scale (1:4 000 000) precludes smaller roads, particularly those in the north of the country. The following maps have been used by the author of this guide and are recommended to readers:

• Maps and tourist information published by the **Egyptian Tourist Authority**; these are on sale around Europe and in Egypt.
• The 1:1 000 000 scale map produced by **Freytag & Berndt** covers the entire country (this map is not available locally and will need to be purchased prior to arrival).

The following maps are available in Egypt:

• Cairo Tourist Map, with a scale of 1:20 000, produced by the **Cairo Engineering and Manufacturing Co.**
• The Egypt New Communications map, with a scale of 1:500 000, published by the **Middle East Publishing Co. MapMakers.**
• the **Shell** Road Atlas of Egypt, with a scale of 1:1 000 000.
• The **Lehnert & Landrock** map of Egypt, with a scale of 1:950 000.

This Egypt Green Guide also contains a comprehensive selection of maps and plans, a list of which can be found on page 7.

MUHAFAZAT / GOVERNORATES

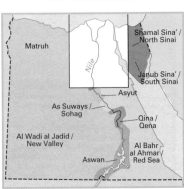

1 Ad Daqahliyah / Dakahliya
2 Al Gharbiyah / Gharbiya
3 Al Iskandariyah / Alexandria
4 Al Isma'iliyah / Ismailiya

5 Al Minufiyah / Monofiya
6 Al Qalyubiyah / Kalyobiya
7 Ash Sharqiyah / Sharkiya

8 Bur Sa'id / Port Said
9 Dumyat / Damietta
10 Kafr ash Shaykh / Kafr El-Sheikh

Main Maps

Town/City Maps

Museum Plans

Site Plans

Regional Maps

Key

Selected monuments and sights

◉➡	Tour - Departure point
⬒	Mosque
⛪ ✝	Catholic church
✡	Synagogue
⬛	Building
■	Statue, small building
✝	Calvary, wayside cross
◎	Fountain
●▪◄	Rampart - Tower - Gate
⋈	Château, castle, historic house
∴	Ruins
‿	Dam
☼	Factory, power plant
☆	Fort
∩	Cave
⊓	Prehistoric site
▼	Viewing table
⑈	Viewpoint
▲	Other place of interest

Special symbols

☾	Hospital
⸙	Palm grove
◭	Pyramid

Sports and recreation

🐎	Racecourse
≋ ≋	Outdoor, indoor swimming pool
⚑	Trail refuge hut
□■■□	Cable cars, gondolas
□+++□	Funicular, rack railway
🚂	Tourist train
◆	Recreation area, park
🎭	Theme, amusement park
🦌	Wildlife park, zoo
❋	Gardens, park, arboretum
🐦	Bird sanctuary, aviary
🚶	Walking tour, footpath
☺	Of special interest to children

Abbreviations

M	Museum
POL.	Police station
T	Theatre
U	University

	Sight	Seaside resort	Spa
Highly recommended ★★★		☆☆☆	‡‡‡
Recommended ★★		☆☆	‡‡
Interesting ★		☆	‡

Additional symbols

i		Tourist information
═══	═══	Motorway or other primary route
❶	❶	Junction: complete, limited
▭	▭	Pedestrian street
ⁱ════ⁱ		Unsuitable for traffic, street subject to restrictions
▭▭▭	----	Steps - Footpath
🚂	🚃	Train station - Auto-train station
🚌		Coach (bus) station
•—•—		Tram
⊙		Metro, underground
♿		Access for the disabled
✉		Post office
☎		Telephone
⊠		Covered market
℧		Quarry
✕		Mine
B	F	Car ferry (river or lake)
🚢		Ferry service: cars and passengers
⛴		Foot passengers only
Bert (R.)...		Main shopping street
AZ B		Map coordinates

Hotels and restaurants

20 rooms: Number of rooms:
375£/250£ high season/low season
100$/70$

    No credit cards accepted

    Without air-conditioning

MEDITERRANEAN SEA

**ALEXANDRIA,
THE MEDITERRANEAN COAST
AND THE DELTA**

Mersa Matruh ⚐

Rashid

Damiette

ALEXANDRIA

El Mansura

Damanhûr

Tanta

Tanis

El-Alamein

Wadi el Natrûn ▲ Deir Suriâni

Zagazi

CAIRO

SAQQARAH ▲

GIZA

**CAIRO AND
SURROUNDING AREA**

Dahshûr

El-Lis

Tomb of Si-Amun ▲

Maidûm

El-Faiyum

Beni Sue

Siwa ✿

G. Dakrur ✳

Bahr Yousouf

▲ Baharîya

**THE OASES
AND THE DESERT**

El Minya

Tûna el Gabal ▲

Beni Hasa

Tell el-Amarna ▲

White Desert

▲ Farâfra

Asyut

Deir el-Hagar ▲

Necropolis of El Bagawât ▲

El Kasr ●

Temple of Hibis ▲

Dâkhla

Khârga ✿

Dûsh ●

Tropic of Cancer

LIBYA

NILE

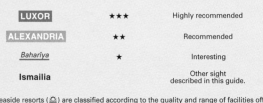

LUXOR	★★★	Highly recommended
ALEXANDRIA	★★	Recommended
Baharîya	★	Interesting
Ismailia		Other sight described in this guide.

Seaside resorts (⚐) are classified according to the quality and range of facilities offered.

Principal sights

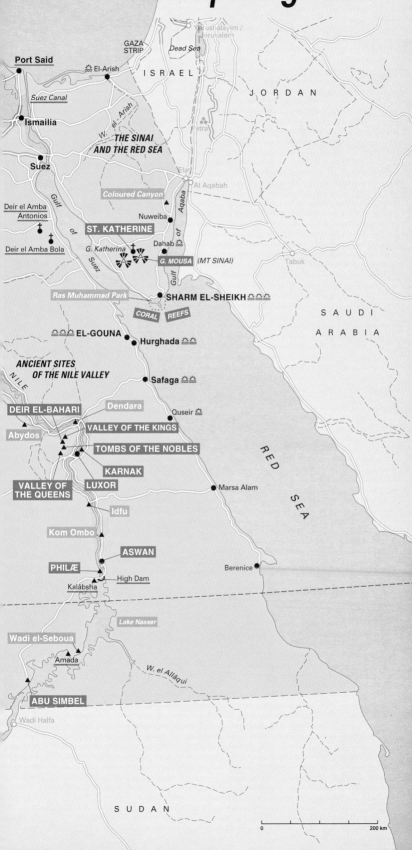

Driving tours and Places

For descriptions of these tours, turn to the Practical Information section.

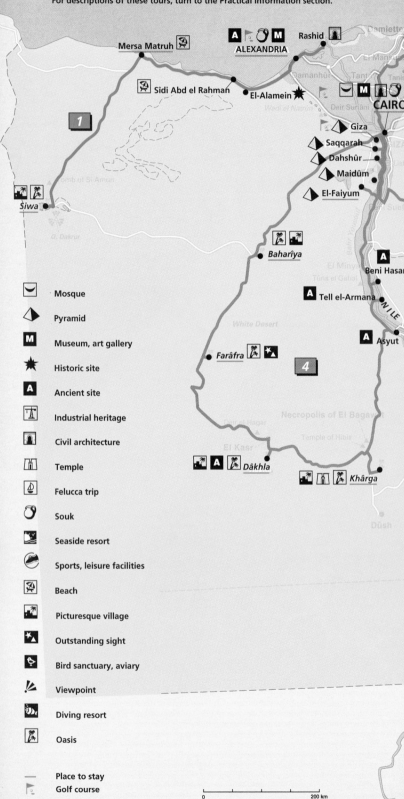

Legend

- ⌣ Mosque
- ◁ Pyramid
- **M** Museum, art gallery
- ✴ Historic site
- **A** Ancient site
- ⊤ Industrial heritage
- ⌂ Civil architecture
- ⊓ Temple
- ⚲ Felucca trip
- ○ Souk
- ⛱ Seaside resort
- ⊘ Sports, leisure facilities
- ⚑ Beach
- ⌨ Picturesque village
- ★ Outstanding sight
- ◆ Bird sanctuary, aviary
- ⚶ Viewpoint
- ⊛ Diving resort
- ⌨ Oasis
- — Place to stay
- ⚑ Golf course

Mersa Matruh · Sîdi Abd el Rahman · El-Alamein · ALEXANDRIA · Rashid · CAIRO · Giza · Saqqarah · Dahshûr · Maidûm · El-Faiyum · Siwa · Baharîya · Farâfra · Dâkhla · Khârga · Beni Hasan · Tell el-Armana · Asyut

0   200 km

to stay

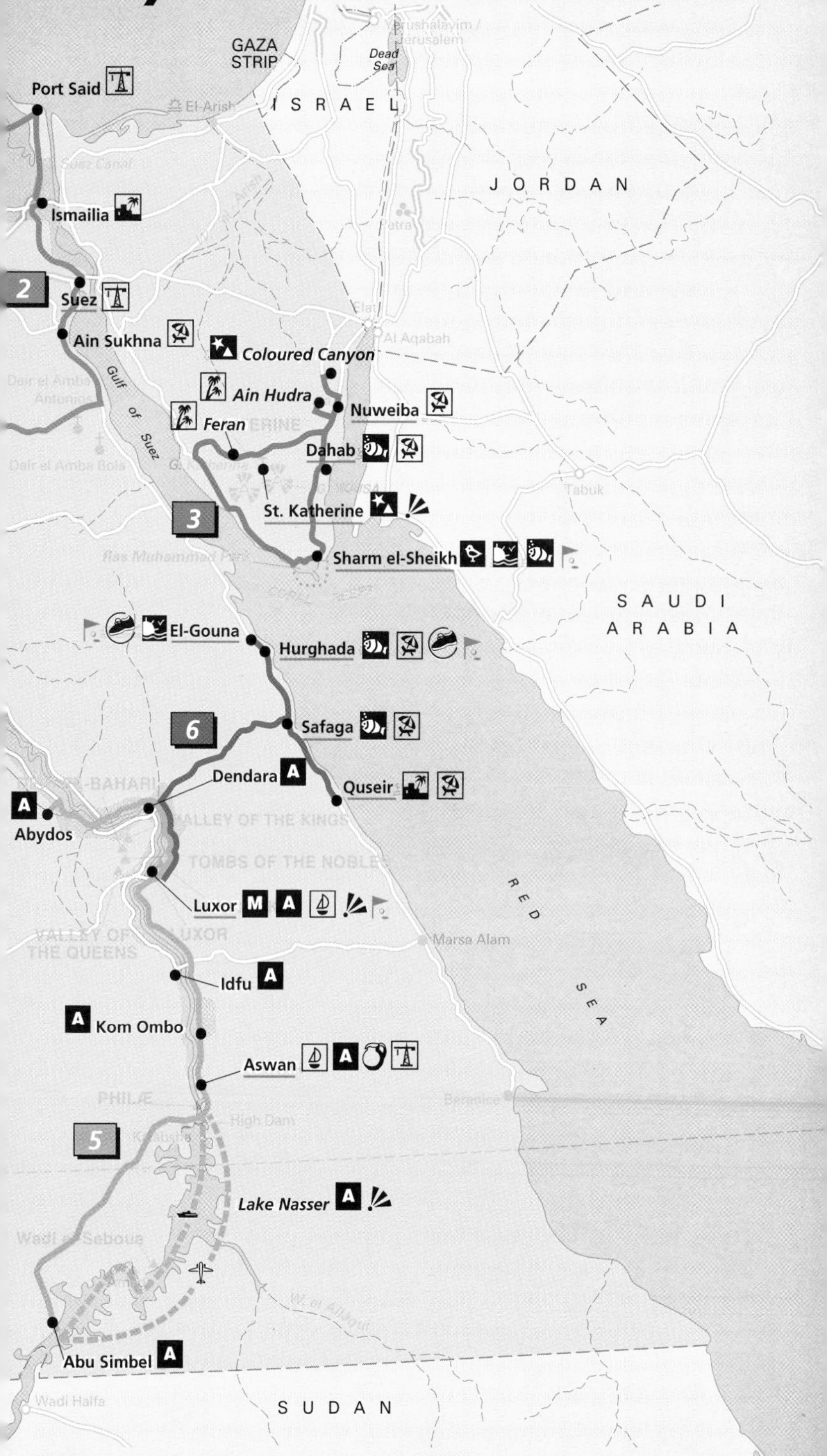

Port Said

Ismailia

2 Suez

Ain Sukhna

★ *Coloured Canyon*

Ain Hudra

Feran — Nuweiba

Dahab

3 St. Katherine

Sharm el-Sheikh

El-Gouna

Hurghada

6 Safaga

Dendara A

Abydos

Quseir

A Luxor M A

A Idfu A

A Kom Ombo

Aswan

5

Lake Nasser A

Abu Simbel A

SUDAN

GAZA STRIP

I S R A E L

JORDAN

Dead Sea

SAUDI ARABIA

RED SEA

1	From the Mediterranean to the Desert	**4**	The Oasis Route
2	Pyramids and Modern Towns	**5**	Ancient Ruins along the Nile
3	Gebels and the Gulf Coasts	**6**	From the Nile to the Red Sea

Relief

MEDITERRANEAN

0 |___|___|___| 150 km

Libyan Plateau

Mersa Matruh ○

Rashid ○
ALEXANDRIA ○
Damanhûr ○

○ El-Alamein

Wadi el Natrûn

Qattara *Depression*

LOWER

Birket el-Qarur

Wadi el-Rayan

Siwa ○
Siwa

G. Ghorâbi
316 △

Bawîti ○

Bahariya

White

Desert

Farâfra ○
Farâfra

△
332

469
△

El Kasr ○ 439
△

Dâkhla ○ Mût

LIBYA

1000
△

Gilf Kebir   Tropic of Cancer

Plateau

1082
△

△
Jabal Arknu
1436

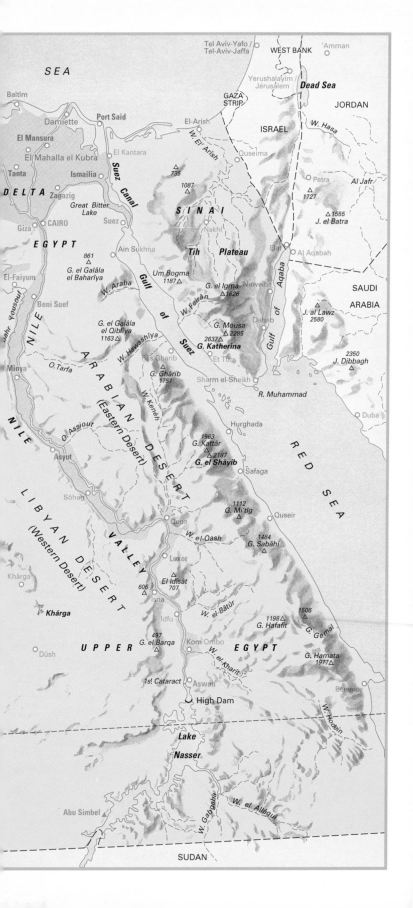

Practical Points

Planning your Trip

useful addresses

EGYPTIAN TOURIST OFFICES

United Kingdom – Egyptian State Tourist Office, Egyptian House, 170 Piccadilly, London W1V 9DD ☎ (020) 7493 5282.

United States – New York: Egyptian Tourist Authority, Suite 1706, 630 Fifth Avenue, New York, NY 10111 ☎ (212) 332 2570; egyptoursp@aol.com; **Chicago**: Egyptian Tourist Authority, Suite 829, 645 N. Michigan Ave, Chicago, IL 60611 ☎ (312) 280 4666; **Los Angeles**: Egyptian Tourist Authority, Suite 215, 8383 Wiltshire Blvd, Beverly Hills, CA 90211 ☎ (323) 653 8815; egypt@etala.com.

Canada – Suite 250, 1253 McGill College Avenue, Montreal, H3B 2Y5 ☎ (514) 861 4420; eta@total.net

EGYPTIAN EMBASSIES AND CONSULATES

United Kingdom – Embassy: 26 South Street, London W1Y 6DD ☎ (020) 7499 2401/7499 3304; etembuk@hotmail.com; **Consulate**: 2 Lowndes St, London SW1X 9ET ☎ (020) 7235 9777; Egyptconsulate@netscapeonline.co.uk.

Ireland – Embassy: 12 Clyde Road, Ballsbridge, Dublin 4 ☎ (01) 660 6566/660 6718; embegypt@indigo.ie.

United States – Embassy: 3521 International Center, Washington DC 20008 ☎ (202) 895 5400; egypt-embassy@usa.net; **Consulates**: New York: 1110 Second Avenue, New York, NY 10022 ☎ (212) 759 7120; egyptcg@aol.com; **Chicago**: Suite 1900, 500 N. Michigan Ave, Chicago, IL 60611 ☎ (312) 828 9162/3/4; **San Francisco**: 3001 Pacific Ave, San Francisco, CA 94115 ☎ (415) 346 9700; egypt@egy2000.com; **Houston**: Suite 2180, 1990 Post Oak Blvd, Houston, TX 77056 ☎ (713) 961 4915/6.

Canada – Embassy: 454 Laurier Avenue, East Ottawa, Ontario K1N 6R3 ☎ (613) 234 4931; **Consulate**: **Montreal**: 1 Place Ville Marie, Montreal, Quebec H3B 4S3 ☎ (14) 866 8455.

Australia – Embassy: 1 Darwin Avenue, Yarralumla, 2600 Canberra, ACT ☎ (02) 6273 4437/8; **Consulates**: **Sydney**: 112 Glenmore Road, Paddington, Sydney, 2021 N.S.W. ☎ (02) 922 3177/99; **Melbourne**: 124 Exhibition St, 9th floor, Melbourne, 3000 Victoria ☎ (03) 9654 8869/8634.

WEBSITES

www.fco.gov.uk – The British Government's Foreign and Commonwealth Office website provides up-to-date information on travel around the globe.

www.state.gov – American visitors should check the US State Department website for travel advice to the Near and Middle East.

www.sis.gov.eg – The website of Egypt's Ministry of Information.

www.touregypt.net – The official site (in English) for Egypt's Ministry of Tourism, providing comprehensive information on all aspects of the country.

www.egypttoday.com – The Internet version (in English) of the respected monthly magazine.

climate

Weather – With the exception of December and January, when the weather can be changeable, the weather in Egypt is likely to be hot and sunny. Autumn is considered the most pleasant season in which to visit the country.

Climate variations – Apart from the Mediterranean coast, Egypt's climate is subtropical desert in type. As a result, most of the country is dry and hot during the daytime in summer (which lasts between five and seven months) and relatively cool at night. Outside Cairo, which, like most major cities, is often shrouded in a carpet of smog, visitors can expect cloudless blue skies. As a general rule, the difference in temperature between day and night is significant; this phenomenon is most noticeable in desert areas, where variations can be extreme, with biting cold giving way to unbearable heat within a short space of time.
In the spring (between March and May), the weather can be unsettled. When the stifling *khamsin* blows from the south, the country is almost brought to its knees by the heat; the *sobaa* is equally unforgiving and can reduce visibility to zero. Rainfall varies considerably from one region to another: compare Aswan (which receives a pitiful 10mm/0.5inches of rain every five years) and Cairo (just a

MINIMUM/MAXIMUM TEMPÉRATURES IN °C												
	Jan	Feb	March	April	May	June	July	Aug	Sept	Oct	Nov	Dec
Alexandria	9/18	9/19	11/21	13/23	16/26	20/28	22/29	23/30	21/29	18/27	14/27	11/20
Aswan	8/23	9/26	13/30	17/36	21/40	24/42	24/42	24/42	22/39	19/37	16/32	10/26
Cairo	9/19	9/20	11/23	14/28	17/32	20/34	21/35	22/35	20/32	18/30	14/21	10/21
Dakhla	4/21	6/24	9/28	14/33	20/40	22/39	23/40	23/40	21/36	17/33	12/28	7/23
Hurghada	9/20	10/20	13/23	16/26	20/29	23/31	25/32	25/33	23/30	21/28	15/25	11/22
Luxor	5/23	7/25	10/29	15/35	21/39	22/40	23/41	23/41	21/39	17/35	12/29	8/25

couple of days' rain a year), with Alexandria, where the winter can at times be wet. Localised climate changes over the past few years, including torrential rain in certain parts of the country, have been blamed on the construction of the Aswan High Dam.

formalities

VISAS AND PASSPORTS

Unless you're a resident of an Arab country, you will need a visa to enter Egypt. These can either be obtained from an Egyptian Consulate within 24 hours (photo required) or immediately upon arrival at Cairo Airport (no photo required). If you decide upon the latter, buy the necessary stamps from the Thomas Cook office (E£15) before passing through customs. Visitors must be in possession of a passport that is valid at least six months beyond your return date. As a general guideline, a single-entry Tourist Visa costs around E£85, and a multiple-entry Business Visa E£185. Both of these are valid for three months and cover a stay not exceeding one month. Visas at Cairo airport must be paid for in cash.

Identification – You will be asked for your passport by hotels, exchange offices, when buying tickets for travel around the country, and at police checkpoints in the deserts and on the Sinai Peninsula.

Advice – You are advised to photocopy the relevant pages in your passport before leaving home. If your passport is stolen, ask for a police statement from the nearest station and make your way to the relevant consulate with this form and a photocopy of your passport.

CUSTOMS ALLOWANCES

You are allowed to enter Egypt with 1 litre of alcohol, 1 litre of perfume and 200 cigarettes (plus 25 cigars). Once in the country, you have 30 days in which to buy duty-free goods in shops belonging to the Egypt Free Shops Company. Although you are only allowed to bring a maximum of E£1 000 into Egypt, there is no limit to the amount of foreign currency you can bring into the country.

VIDEOS AND MOBILE PHONES

When you land at the airport, you will need to register your video recorder (after customs), which will involve the entry of the serial number in your passport; the purpose of this is to prevent travellers from selling their video cameras in Egypt. You won't have any problem with your mobile phone as there is good reception throughout the country, with the exception of Siwa.

DRIVING LICENCES

An international driving licence is required if you wish to drive in Egypt. To obtain one, contact your nearest driving licence centre (your regular licence, a photo, proof of domicile and a stamped-addressed envelope are normally required). If you are wary about driving on Egyptian roads you may wish to hire a car with a chauffeur, an option that is not as expensive as you might think.

STUDENT CARDS

The International Student Identity Card (ISIC) offers discounts of up to 50% on entry to museums and archaeological sites, in addition to reductions on some rail journeys. If you don't have a card (and you think you're entitled to one), apply to the Medical Scientific Centre (103, Mathaf al-Manial, Rodan, Cairo) with a valid card from your own country or a letter from your university (in English).

INOCULATIONS

Although no compulsory vaccinations are required by the Egyptian health authorities, it is advisable to be protected against diphtheria and hepatitis A and B. Yellow fever is not endemic in Egypt. If you are planning a trip where standards of hygiene are likely to be poor, you are also advised to be protected against typhoid. For further information on the above, contact your local doctor or travel centre. Some airlines such as British Airways also operate a medical service for travellers.

Our advice – If you are diabetic or likely to require injections, bring a supply of single-use syringes. Also ensure that you have medication for any ongoing conditions.

INSURANCE

Travel insurance is essential for any visit to Egypt. Nowadays, there are numerous policies available for travellers ranging from single-trip insurance to annual cover.

A standard policy will cover all your medical expenses (subject to a small excess), repatriation in the event of serious injury or illness, as well as insurance for luggage, delay etc. Most tour operators will be happy to take care of this for you but it is always worth shopping around. If you're travelling to Egypt on a scuba-diving holiday, make sure your policy covers you for this.

Travelling to Egypt

by ferry

Since the suspension of the Brindisi-Alexandria and Athens-Alexandria ferries, there are no passenger services currently operating between Europe and Egypt.

by plane

FROM THE UK

Both British Airways and EgyptAir operate direct flights between the United Kingdom and Egypt.

British Airways – Waterside, PO Box 365, Harmondsworth, UB7 0GB, England; ☎ (0845) 77 333 77; www.british-airways.com. BA operates daily direct flights from London Heathrow to Cairo and a thrice-weekly service to Alexandria on its subsidiary carrier, British Mediterranean.

EgyptAir – Egypt's national airline operates daily flights from London Heathrow to Cairo and one flight a week from Manchester to Cairo and Heathrow to Luxor respectively.
London: 29/31 Piccadilly, London WIV 0PT ☎ (020) 7734 2343 or 7734 2395; www.egyptair.com.eg

Travel agencies – A number of travel agents in the UK and North America (including some of the tour operators listed opposite) are able to book flight-only arrangements to Egypt. In the UK, these include companies such as Trailfinders (www.trailfinders.com), Flightbookers (www.ebookers.com) and STA Travel (www.statravel.com). Details on many of these companies can be found in the weekend travel sections of national newspapers.

FROM NORTH AMERICA

EgyptAir has direct flights from Cairo to New York, Los Angeles and Montreal.
New York office: 720 Fifth Avenue, New York, NY 10019 ☎ (212) 581 5600 or 1-800 344 6787 (toll-free).
A number of North American airlines including Air Canada

(www.aircanada.ca), Delta (www.delta.com) and American (www.aa.com) also operate services to Cairo on a code-share basis with another airline. Another option is to fly to Europe with one of any number of carriers, then take a connecting flight for the final leg to your destination in Egypt.

CHARTER FLIGHTS

A number of major tour companies operate charter flights from the UK to Cairo, Alexandria, Luxor, Hurghada and Sharm el-Sheikh. These are particularly popular over the winter months. During the low season, prices can drop by between 40% and 60%.

organised tours

The majority of tourists to Egypt are booked on tours arranged by tour operators in their respective countries. For most travellers a visit to the pyramids and a cruise along the Nile between Luxor and Aswan will be the highlight of their trip, the latter option allowing the country to be explored at a leisurely pace and in a fair degree of comfort and even luxury. Itineraries that include Cairo, the Sinai, the oases and Abu Simbel are also becoming increasingly popular with visitors. For those who prefer a little more adventure, several specialist companies now offer cruises on Lake Nasser, 4WD safaris in the Libyan Desert, diving in the Red Sea and hiking in the country's *gebels*. The following is a far from exhaustive selection of tour operators.

UNITED KINGDOM

Abercrombie & Kent – 56 Sloane Square, London SW1W 8AX ☎ (020) 7559 8755; www.abercrombiekent.co.uk
Swan Hellenic – 77 New Oxford St, London WC1A 1PP ☎ (020) 7800 2200; www.swanhellenic.com
Cox & Kings – Gordon House, 10 Greencoat Place, London SW1P 1PH ☎ (020) 7873 5000; www.cox-kings.co.uk

Bales Worldwide – Junction Road, Dorking, Surrey RH4 3HL.
☎ (0870) 241 3208;
www.balesworldwide.com

Page & Moy Holidays – 136-140 London Road, Leicester LE2 1EN
☎ (08700) 106 400;
www.page-moy.co.uk

Hayes & Jarvis – 152 King St, London W6 0QU ☎ (0870) 898 9890;
www.hayesandjarvis.co.uk

Kuoni – Kuoni House, Dorking, Surrey RH5 4AZ ☎ (01306) 747 002;
www.kuoni.co.uk

Thomas Cook Holidays – Numerous offices around the UK ☎ (08705) 666 222; www.thomascook.co.uk

British Airways Holidays – 17 Coningsby Rd, Peterborough PE3 8SB ☎ (0870) 443 4448;
www.baholidays.co.uk

Peltours – Sovereign House, 11/19 Ballards Lane, London N3 1UX
☎ (020) 8343 0590; www.peltours.com

Soliman Holidays – 162 Hammersmith Road, London W6 7JP ☎ (020) 7370 5159;
www.solimantravel.co.uk

ADVENTURE TOURS

Explore Worldwide – 1 Frederick St, Aldershot, Hampshire GU11 1LQ
☎ (01252) 760 000; www.explore.co.uk.

Guerba –Wessex House, 40 Station Rd, Westbury, Wiltshire BA13 3JN
☎ (01373) 826 611; www.guerba.co.uk

The Imaginative Traveller – 14 Barley Mow Passage, Chiswick, London W4 4PH. ☎ (020) 8742 8612;
www.imaginative-traveller.com

UNITED STATES

Abercrombie & Kent – 1520 Kensington Road, Suite 212, Oak Brook, Illinois 60523 ☎ 1-800 323 7308;
www.abercrombiekent.com

Travcoa – 2350 S.E. Bristol, Newport Beach, CA 92660 ☎ 1-800 992 2003;
www.travcoa.com

Maupintour – 1421 Research Park Drive, Lawrence, KA 66049 ☎ 1-800 223 7460; www.maupintour.com

Overseas Adventure Travel – 347 Congress St, Boston, MA 02210 ☎ 1-800 955 1925; www.oattravel.com

Homeric Tours – 55 East 59th St, 17th floor, New York, NY 10022; ☎ 1-800 223 5570; www.homerictours.com

CANADA

Adventures Abroad – 2148-20800 Westminster Highway, Richmond, British Columbia V6V 2W3; ☎ 1-800 665 3998; www.adventures-abroad.com

Nouvelles Frontières - Vacances – 1180 Drummond Street, Montreal H3G 2S1; ☎ (514) 871 3060;
www.nouvelles-frontieres.com /www.newfrontiers.com

what to take

CLOTHING
Given the hot climate, your best option is to take light-coloured clothes made from natural fibres, although make sure you pack a sweater for the occasional cool evening. Although you may prefer to wear shorts during the day, you will not be allowed into religious sites unless you're wearing long trousers; these have the added benefit of offering protection against mosquitoes in the evening.

ACCESSORIES
A good money belt, preferably one that is tucked out of sight, is advisable for valuable items such as passports, travellers' cheques, credit cards, airline tickets etc. A small rucksack is useful for excursions, as are essential items such as a hat, sunglasses, plenty of sunscreen, a Swiss army knife and a small torch, which will come in very handy inside tombs and mastabas. Make sure you also have a ready supply of film for cameras and videos, and floppy disks for digital cameras. Film for videos and slides can be purchased at tourist sites but is generally exorbitant in price and is not stored in ideal conditions because of the heat. Remember that at most major sites you will need to buy a permit to use your camera and video. In Egypt, electrical current is 220V. Visitors from North America are likely to need a converter.
Wearers of contact lenses should take the precaution of bringing their own solution with them as dust and sand are a permanent feature of travel around Egypt.
Ballpoint pens are very useful as gifts for small children, and a supply of coins and small denomination notes will come in handy on those occasions when a *baksheesh* is required.

MEDICATION
You may wish to carry an emergency medical kit with you that includes basic supplies such as plasters, aspirin and/or paracetamol, antiseptic cream, tablets to combat diarrhoea , and a mosquito repellent.

Travelling in Egypt

useful addresses

Foreign embassies in Egypt

United Kingdom – 7 Ahmed Ragheb St, Garden City, Cairo ☎ (02) 794 0850/52/58; www.britishembassy.org.eg; e-mail: information.cairo@fco.gov.uk

Ireland – 3 Abu el-Fida St (7th floor), Zamalek, Cairo; postal address: PO Box 2681, Zamalek, Cairo ☎ (02) 735 8264 or 735 8547; irishemb@rite.com

United States – 5 Latin America St, Garden City, Cairo ☎ (02) 797 3300; www.usembassy.egnet.net; e-mail: consularcairo@state.gov

Canada – Arab African International Bank Building, 5 Midan al Saraya al Kobra, Garden City, Cairo; postal address: PO Box 1667, Cairo ☎ (02) 794 3110; www.canada-eg.com

Australia – World Trade Center (11th floor), Corniche el Nil, Boulac, Cairo ☎ (02) 575 0444; cairo.austremb@dfat.gov.au

Consulates

United Kingdom – 3 Shira Mina, Roushdi, Alexandria ☎ (03) 546 7001/2; britconsul@dataxprs.com.eg

Ireland – 36 Shira Kafr Abdou, Roushdi, Alexandria ☎ (03) 546 4686 or 546 9883.

Tourist offices

The addresses and phone numbers of tourist offices are listed in each chapter in the Sights section of this guide.

emergencies

Health

Problems that may affect visitors to Egypt include heatstroke, heat exhaustion, stomach upsets and insect bites. If you need to obtain medical attention during your stay, your embassy and/or consulate should have a list of recommended doctors in major towns and cities around the country. The following list details some of the best private hospitals in Egypt (visitors are advised to avoid public hospitals):

Cairo – Anglo-American Hospital, Gezira: ☎ (02) 340 61 62/65.

Cairo – Misr International Hospital, Doqqi ☎ (02) 360 82 81.

Cairo – Hayat Medical Center, 5 Sheraa Menès el Korba, Heliopolis ☎ (02) 290 70 17.

Cairo – Nile Badrawi Hospital, El Nil Corniche ☎ (02) 363 86 88.

Alexandria – Smouha Medical Centre ☎ (03) 420 26 52.

Luxor – Luxor Hospital ☎ (095) 37 20 25.

Bilharzia is a serious illness contracted by bathing in fresh water, particularly in the Nile and the Delta region; the disease is less prevalent in the country's oases. If you have recently swum in a river, lake or stream and are experiencing symptoms of fever, digestive problems and headaches, you should consult a doctor or visit the nearest hospital as soon as possible. Pharmacies are also able to treat minor medical problems such as the frequent stomach bugs that often afflict tourists, and usually have a ready supply of medicines, many of which can be obtained over the counter without a prescription.

Emergency numbers

Police: ☎ 122. Tourist Police: ☎ 126. Ambulance: ☎ 123. Fire Brigade: ☎ 125.

money

Currency

The unit of currency in Egypt is the Egyptian pound (E£), *guinay* in Arabic. One pound is divided into 100 piastres (pt), or *'irsh* in Arabic. Notes come in the following denominations: 1, 5, 10, 20, 50 and 100 Egyptian pounds (E£); and 10, 25 and 50 piastres. Coins have values of 5, 10, 20 and 25 piastres. Banknotes are in Arabic on one side and English on the other.

Our advice – We recommend that you carry small denomination notes with you although these are harder to come across than you might think. These can then be handed out as a *baksheesh* (tip) or to pay for minor expenses as you travel around. Taxi-drivers are notorious for not having any change, so try and pay for your fare with the exact money if possible. The most commonly accepted foreign currency is the US dollar, so it can be useful to have a small supply with you, especially $1 bills.

Entering Egypt – Visitors are allowed to bring a maximum of E£1 000 into the country. Having said this, it is difficult to find Egyptian currency abroad, although you may wish to try the Bank of New York (bankofny.com) in both London and New York, which acts as an agent for the Misr Exterior Bank.

Leaving Egypt – Visitors leaving the country can take no more than E£20 with them. At Cairo airport you can either change excess currency at the bank (you may be asked for exchange receipts) or buy some last-minute gifts at the duty-free shop.

As a guideline, in march 02 the exchange rate for the Egyptian pound was as follows: E£6.11 to £1; E£4.25 to $1; E£3.2793 to 1.

CHANGING MONEY

Currency – Although most foreign currencies can be exchanged in Egypt, the US dollar is by far the most widely accepted. Money can be exchanged at banks, offices of Thomas Cook and American Express, and exchange bureaux at major hotels.

Travellers' cheques – These are the safest way of carrying funds and are easy to replace should you lose them (remember to keep the cheque numbers separate from the cheques themselves). American Express, Thomas Cook, Visa and Travelex are all able to supply travellers' cheques, in addition to Citicorp in Canada. For further information, contact your nearest bank or exchange office. You are likely to have to pay a small commission charge when exchanging travellers' cheques in Egypt, so it is worth asking what this fee is before signing your cheques to avoid any unwelcome surprises.

CREDIT CARDS

These can now be used almost everywhere in Egypt with the exception of the oases, although it might be wise to check with individual hotels/restaurants/tour operators etc before making a reservation. Visa and MasterCard are the most widely accepted.

Cash machines – Automatic distributors are now a common feature in major cities such as Cairo, Alexandria, Luxor, Aswan and Sharm el-Sheikh, although less so in smaller towns and in the oases, and non-existent in Siwa. To withdraw money over the counter in a bank, you will need to show your passport.

Lost/stolen cards
Emergency numbers:
MasterCard/Visa – ☎ (02) 357 11 48.
Diner's Club – ☎ (02) 357 11 48.
Amex – ☎ (02) 570 34 11.

getting around

BY PLANE

The majority of domestic scheduled flights are operated by Egyptair and its subsidiary, Air Sinai. Fares are generally high and it is advisable to book well in advance in high season. As an example, a Cairo-Aswan return flight will cost in the region of $335.

BY BOAT

If you haven't pre-booked a Nile cruise on one of the enormous floating hotels that operate on the river before arriving in the country, you may be able to book a trip through a local tour operator in either Cairo or Luxor *(for a list of reliable agencies, see LUXOR – Directory)*. Another option is to take a trip by traditional **felucca**, particularly from Aswan *(see LUXOR – Directory)*, which can be for just a few hours or a few days. If taking one of these trips, ensure that any valuables you carry with you are safe at all times. Daily ferry services also operate between Hurghada and Sharm el-Sheikh *(see the Directories under these resorts)*, and the ports of Nuweiba and Aqaba, in Jordan *(see NUWEIBA – Directory)*.

BY BUS

Travelling around Egypt by bus can be quite a memorable experience! A short journey on the slow and suffocatingly hot buses in the country's major cities is an experience that most visitors may not wish to repeat, although this contrasts dramatically with the air-conditioned comfort of services operated by private companies (West Delta Bus Company, East Delta Bus Company and Superjet) between major towns and cities. Tickets for these long-distance services should be purchased at bus stations either on the day of departure, or a few days in advance, particularly in high season.

Cairo – There are plans to relocate the city's bus stations, although for the time being there are four main terminals as follows: the **Turgoman** bus station, for services to Alexandria, Mersa Matruh, Luxor, Aswan, Sharm el-Sheikh, Dahab, Nuweiba, Hurghada, Safaga and Quseir; the bus terminal at **Midan Ulali** (near Midan Rameses), for routes to Suez, Ismailiya, Port Said, and towns in the Delta region; the **Ahmed Helmy** terminal (just to the north of Rameses railway station), for buses to El-Minya and Asyut; and the **Abbassiyya** bus station, which links Cairo with resorts on the Sinai Peninsula.

Alexandria – The city's bus station is located alongside the Sidi Gaber railway terminus. Services operate to Cairo and Mersa Matruh.

Luxor – The bus terminal situated behind the Temple of Luxor is the departure point for long-distance routes to Cairo, Hurghada, Suez and Aswan.

Aswan – Aswan's bus station is on Sheraa Abtal al-Tahrir, from where services run to Luxor, Cairo and (in theory) to Abu Simbel.

Hurghada – The Superjet terminal is in the Dahar *(downtown)* district, near the mosque; that of its competitor, the Upper Egypt Company, is also in the downtown area, albeit slightly to the south. Both serve Suez, Luxor and Cairo.

Sharm el-Sheikh – The East Delta Bus Company terminal is located behind the Mobil petrol station between Sharm el-Sheikh and Naama Bay. The company operates services to Suez and Cairo.

By train

On the whole, travelling by train is an excellent means of getting from Cairo to Alexandria, Luxor and Aswan. For the latter two cities, it is best to take the comfortable overnight sleeper service, on which breakfast is served before arrival. Tickets for these trains should be booked in advance. Apart from these routes, the train is not a terribly practical or pleasant option, unless you're on a tight budget, as travel is slow and the standard of the carriages often leaves a lot to be desired.

The slow trains operating from Cairo to destinations in Middle Egypt are quite an experience and live up to their name, stopping at regular intervals en route. Comfort would not appear a major priority on board although you can choose from three classes: first class (reclining seats or couchettes); second class (padded seats, some carriages with air-conditioning); and third class (wooden benches). In general, fares for these routes are low.

By taxi

Taxis are ideal for getting around any large Egyptian town or city, but can also be useful for excursions to nearby sites and even for long journeys if your preference is to avoid public transport. Taxis are rarely fitted with a meter that works, but bear in mind that a vehicle without a meter (albeit one that doesn't work!) is not a proper taxi. Irrespective of the journey you're undertaking, make sure that you agree a price before you set out, and only pay the driver once you've reached your destination. Be prepared to bargain hard, particularly in Luxor and Aswan, where drivers are more streetwise, and be wary of taxi-drivers offering a "special price" – these are usually far from it. Don't forget that Egyptian towns and cities are generally overrun with taxis so if you have an uncomfortable feeling about a particular driver or vehicle, try somebody else.

Taxi colours – Every governorate in Egypt has different coloured taxis: orange and white in Ismailiya; light blue and white in Damietta, Luxor, Mersa Matruh and Sharm el-Sheikh; navy blue and white in Port Said; black and white in Cairo; maroon and white in El-Mansura; orange and black in Alexandria; green and white in Rosetta; and all white in Aswan.

Collective taxis – These taxis provide an alternative means of transport for travellers on inter-city routes, and are both inexpensive and practical, although space is at a premium – don't be surprised if conditions are somewhat cramped for the entire journey. Their drivers normally ply their trade close to bus stations, but only leave once they're full – out of season this can take some time after the driver has announced where he's heading. In terms of price, it's pretty straightforward as it's the same fare for everyone. The most popular vehicles used as collective taxis are Peugeot 504s. Potential users should also be aware that the accident rate for this means of transport is relatively high.

Microbuses – These are slightly larger than collective taxis and give the impression of accommodating far more passengers than you would have thought possible! They operate on the same principle as collective taxis, the only difference being that the destinations they serve are generally further afield.

Hitchhiking

Hitchhikers are rarely seen in heavily populated parts of the country. The same is true in Egypt's more isolated areas although, conversely, you're more likely to catch a lift in these regions. If you're hoping for a free ride, bear in mind that most drivers are likely to ask hitchikers for a contribution towards fuel costs.
If you're a single woman, our advice is not to even think about trying to hitch because of the obvious dangers involved.

By car or motorbike

If you're planning on driving in Egypt, particularly in Cairo and Alexandria, you'll need to be bold, have a sense of adventure, and have eyes in the back of your head! The general caution and courtesy that we normally take for granted in Europe or North America seem to be absent from Egyptian road etiquette, with the result that Egypt has one of the highest death rates of anywhere on the planet. Although it's true that the authorities are keen to improve the country's appalling road safety record, the general attitude of those behind the wheel comes as something of a shock to Westerners. On the positive side, slight improvements have been made over the past few years, including the propensity of drivers to stop more

frequently at red lights. It should be added, however, that more often than not this is because a policeman is on duty nearby, rather than as a result of a change in overall driving behaviour.

Road network – Although Egypt has very few motorways, its road system is well developed, with numerous dual carriageways (two lanes in each direction). The speed limit on these is 100km/hr (62mi/hr); on other main roads the limit is 90km/hr (56mi/hr). At police checkpoints you will need to show both your passport and your international driving licence – if you fail to do so you will be fined $100 on the spot (payment is required immediately). Petrol is generally inexpensive (E£1 per litre). Outside the main towns and cities you are strongly advised to fill up whenever you see a petrol station just to be on the safe side.

If you are planning to travel by motorbike in Egypt it is best to bring your own because of the unreliable nature of bikes locally.

Car hire – If you do decide to hire a car to visit various parts of the country, bear the following points in mind: 1) never assume that you have the right of way; 2) pedestrians seem as oblivious to danger as motorists; 3) make sure the car horn is working properly as it is an essential accessory when driving here; 4) you are strongly advised not to drive at night; 5) if you have an accident, head directly to the nearest police station to report the incident.

The following list details reputable car hire companies in Cairo:

Avis – Cairo International Airport ✆ (02) 291 42 88 (ask for Avis); 16 Mamal as-Sukkar, Garden City ✆ (02) 356 24 64; Nile Hilton ✆ (02) 576 64 32; Meridien Heliopolis ✆ (02) 290 50 55.

Hertz – Cairo International Airport ✆ (02) 291 42 88 (ask for Hertz); Rameses Hilton ✆ (02) 574 44 00; 195 Sharia, 26 July St, Mohandissen ✆ (02) 303 42 41.

Budget – Cairo International Airport ✆ (02) 265 23 95.

Chauffeured vehicles – A safer and more pleasant way of experiencing the country, although this comes at a price. The car-hire companies above are able to offer this service, although you should ensure that you confirm exact rates before setting off, in addition to any incidental expenses such as daily accommodation and food allowances for your driver.

OTHER MEANS OF TRANSPORT

Horse-drawn carriages – A useful way of getting around during the day, and a romantic option at night. Calèches are particularly popular in Luxor, Aswan and Edfu. As with any other form of transport, make sure you fix the price beforehand.

Camel rides – Somewhat touristy, but fun all the same. These days you're more likely to take one for the experience rather than getting from A to B. Easy to find near to archaeological sites.

Bicycles – Cycling is ideally suited to oases such as Siwa, as well as to Luxor and the sites in the surrounding area; bikes can also be rented in Aswan and Hurghada. As a general rule this mode of transport is only a feasible option in smaller towns, and should not even be contemplated in larger cities such as Cairo or Alexandria.

TRAVELLING INDEPENDENTLY

Anyone travelling around the country under their own steam, whether it be by hire car, taxi or private minibus, should, however, be prepared for a number of difficulties along the way. The benefits of independent travel include a freedom to roam at will, although in Egypt this comes with certain provisos as permits are needed for access to certain areas such as the Red Sea coast beyond Marsa Alam. The Sudanese border, parts of the Sinai and several sections along the Suez Canal are also out of bounds. If you attempt to enter these areas and are caught the police will confiscate your passport. A number of intercity routes, in particular the road between Hurghada and Luxor, can only be undertaken in convoy and under military escort. These convoys depart at specific (albeit rarely adhered to) times and only stop at pre-arranged places to enable passengers to stretch their legs and get something to drink. In the oases, the Fayum region, Middle Egypt and the Sinai you will be stopped at various checkpoints and asked to provide details of your itinerary, including where you are planning to stay. The purpose of these security measures is to provide protection for travellers to these outlying areas. Any requests for specific authorisations should be made to the Ministry of the Interior: 110 Qasr el-Aini St, Cairo ✆ (02) 354 83 00.

opening times

GOVERNMENT OFFICES, BANKS AND EXCHANGE BUREAUS

Most offices and shops are closed on Friday, the day of prayer. Banks are generally open from 8.30am-2pm Sunday to Thursday, although in major cities some remain open all day and even into the evening. As a guideline, opening hours for exchange offices are 8.30am-noon and 4-8pm Monday to Thursday, although exchange desks in major hotels tend to stay open longer. During the holy month of Ramadan, banks are open from 10am-1.30pm.

SHOPS AND RESTAURANTS

Shops – Shops are usually open Saturday to Thursday 9am-6pm (9pm in summer) and until noon on Fridays; some close on Sundays. During Ramadan, shops tend to close at 3.30pm and reopen from 8-11pm.

Restaurants – These are often open all through the day and evening, although some close for the whole of Ramadan or only open after sunset.

communications

POST

Postage rates – A postcard or letter not exceeding 15g in weight costs E£1.5 to send to anywhere in Europe, although delivery time can vary between six days and two weeks.

Poste Restante – If you are aware of your movements ahead of time, poste restante can be a useful service, even though the advent of e-mail has had a drastic effect on the numbers of travellers now using it. Mail should be addressed as follows: your name, c/o Poste Restante, Main Post Office, the name and postcode of the town or city, Egypt. To obtain mail, you will need to show your passport and be patient, as service can be intolerably slow. Mail is occasionally held under the initial of your first name, so it is worth asking for both names to be checked when making your initial enquiry.

TELEPHONES

Calling Egypt – When calling Egypt from abroad, dial the appropriate international access code ("00" from the UK; "011" from the USA and Canada), followed by "20" (the code for Egypt), the area code (minus the first "0"), and finally the number of the person you are calling.

Main Egyptian dialling codes – Cairo (02), Alexandria (03), Ismailiya (064), Hurghada (065), Port Said (066), El-Arish (068), Sharm el-Sheikh (069), Luxor (095) and Aswan (097). Mobile phone networks include Mobinil (012) and Clic (010).

Phoning within Egypt and abroad – Given the extortionate rates often charged by hotels, the cheapest option is to buy a phonecard; these can be used in public phones often operated by private companies, hence the different colour schemes on Egyptian phone boxes. Please note that if you purchase a phonecard from one specific company, this will have to be used at a phone operated by the same supplier, e.g. Menatel (green and yellow cabins) or NilePhone (red and white booths). Shops selling phonecards for these companies normally display the appropriate logo outside their premises. Telephone exchanges are best avoided as they are often full to overflowing and you're likely to waste a considerable amount of time getting to the front of the queue. If you have to use one, try to avoid the evening, however, when the crowds are likely to be even worse.

Provided you have an international roaming facility, your mobile phone should work without any problem in Egypt. To avoid any nasty surprises on your return, check with your mobile supplier before leaving home about rates for both making and receiving calls within the country.

The **international access code** for calls made abroad from Egypt is 00.

E-MAIL

Now that the Internet has become commonplace in even the most remote parts of the planet, you can access and send e-mails from anywhere in the world provided you have an account with one of the major web servers such as Hotmail, mail2web etc. If you're on business and have a laptop with a built-in modem, just dial up your account from a fixed line (bear in mind that in some parts of the country this can prove difficult). The other option is to head for an Internet café, a phenomenon that has taken off in Egypt over the past few years, particularly in major towns, cities and resorts. A few of these are listed under the Directories for a number of cities and resorts in this guide, although you may wish to consult www.netcafeguide.com for an up-to-date listing of cybercafés in the areas you are likely to be visiting.

public holidays

The main Egyptian public holidays are religious in nature and correspond to Islamic or Coptic celebrations. The Islamic calendar changes by 10 to 12 days every year, so it is difficult to provide a precise list of dates in advance. The main public holidays are as follows:

Christmas – 7 January.

Epiphany – 19 January.

Aid el-Adha (commemorating the sacrifice of Abraham) – 23 February 2002, 12 February 2003.

Ras as-Sana (Hegira New Year) – 15 March 2002.

Easter – March-April.

Sham en-Nessim (spring festival) – corresponding to Easter Monday.

Celebration of the liberation of the Sinai – 25 April.

Labour Day – 1 May.

Mouled el-Nabi (anniversary of the birth of the Prophet Muhammad) – 25 May 2002.

Festival of the 1952 Revolution – 23 July.

Armed Forces Day – 6 October.

Ramadan – In 2002, Ramadan starts on 5 November and continues until **Aid el-Fitr** (the festival signalling the end of the holy month) on 5 December 2002.

annual events

Cairo Book Fair – End of January. This major fair, held at the city's exhibition centre, is an opportunity for authors and publishers to meet the general public, and to publicise and discuss their work at a range of conferences and lectures.

Aid al-Adha – During this festival to commemorate the sacrifice of Abraham, sheep are sacrificed in public as a sign of redemption. For specific dates, refer to the Public holidays section above.

Cairo Biennial Visual Arts International Festival – March-April. The works of some 250 artists from 50 countries are exhibited at this leading festival.

Al-Nitaq Festival – Mid-March to mid-April. This arts festival devoted to contemporary Egyptian art is staged across several galleries in the centre of Cairo.

Gourna Festival – End of March. This highlight in the Sufic music calendar takes place on the west bank of the Nile, in Luxor.

Arab Film Festival – End of March. This gathering brings together young Arab directors living outside and within the Arab world who deal with controversial issues in their work.

Festival of Music – 21 June. This annual event has become popular in Cairo, where hundreds of amateur musicians take to the streets of the city.

National Film Festival – Late-June to early-July. This Cairo-based festival is an opportunity for cinema-goers to view films produced in Egypt during the previous year.

Citadel Music Festival – Mid-August. This lively event is characterised by an interesting blend of Arab and Western music. The festival gets under way at Cairo's citadel, and continues at several theatres in the city.

Ismailiya Festival – End of August. This folk dance festival is held every year in Ismailiya, on the banks of the Suez Canal.

Cairo Experimental Dance Festival – Beginning of September. This popular festival attracts numerous dance companies from within and outside the Arab world. It is likely that the event will soon be moved to a permanent home in Beirut, in the Lebanon.

Alexandria International Festival – Mid-September. This celebration of international cinema attracts entrants from some 20 countries, who come to Alexandria in the hope of carrying off one of the country's leading film awards.

Rally of Egypt – October. One of the leading 4WD car rallies on the international circuit. The race starts and finishes against the magnificent backdrop of the Giza pyramids.

Festival of Arab Music – Beginning of November. This important gathering, attracting performers from 15 countries, is mainly held at the Cairo Opera.

Cairo International Film Festival – Late-November or early-December. An opportunity for the inhabitants of Cairo to watch uncensored films from around the world in cinemas across the city.

Aid el-Fitr – This three-day festival, held at the end of the ninth month of the Ramadan calendar, celebrates the end of this holy month. For specific dates, refer to the Public holidays section above.

Hotels and Restaurants

HOTELS

In general, visitors to Egypt will choose from one of two options: either a group tour booked through a travel agent or tour operator, or an independent trip with a partner, spouse or a small group of friends. For those on an organised package, everything is likely to be taken care of, including accommodation, meals and excursions. Travellers on these tours tend to stay in first-class hotels offering excellent service and a range of facilities, have lunch in typical restaurants close to the sites visited, dine at their hotel, and have just a small amount of free time at the end of the afternoon and in the evening to explore the towns and cities in which they are staying. Visitors often combine this type of land tour with a luxurious cruise on the Nile lasting from a few days to a week.

For those visitors who prefer a more independent approach, it is advisable to book accommodation for the first and last nights of the trip at least. If you have a good idea of your itinerary, it is also sensible to book as far ahead as possible to get the accommodation of your choice rather than accepting what's left if you leave things until the very last minute. This is particularly important in high season, as the more comfortable hotels in the major cities and resorts tend to fill up with tour groups. Nor should you be surprised if you find that the room rate for Egyptians, or foreigners living in Egypt, is half of that quoted to tourists, because of the two-tier pricing policy that is often in place in hotels around the country. If you're prepared to be more adventurous and wait until you arrive at a new destination to get a room, be prepared to bargain, particularly out of season, when hotel rates drop considerably.

HOTEL CATEGORIES

The star rating system listed below is that outlined by the Egyptian Ministry of Tourism:

One- and two-star hotels – This category can also include a number of hotels as yet without a star rating, where the level of facilities and comfort is comparable to one- and two-star hotels. Hotels of this type are generally inexpensive, lacking in creature comforts but with an acceptable level of cleanliness and hygiene. The quality of accommodation can vary, although you'll most certainly be staying in a more typical Egyptian environment, far removed from the more standardised hotels belonging to the major international chains that are now commonplace around the country. Depending on where you are, you may find yourself paying very little for a decent room in an unclassified hotel,

but upwards of E£50 for a room with no frills or private bathroom in a two-star hotel. Wherever you end up, make sure you ask to inspect the room before accepting it to check that it has hot water, a door that locks properly, and that the sheets are clean; if you are travelling independently and are on a tight budget, it can be a good idea to bring a sheet sleeping bag with you on your travels. In this category, you will also find that very few rooms have their own bathroom and you will be using shared facilities along the corridor.

Three- and four-star hotels – In terms of comfort, there is a marked difference between hotels in this category and those in the one- and two-star bracket. Furthermore, some of the four-star hotels in Egypt are on a par with their five-star counterparts, with the exception of a swimming pool, which sways the balance in the rating system. If you're turning up on spec, the same rules apply: ask to see the room and bargain if you can, but be wary of the supplements that are sometimes added by hotels in these categories, such as compulsory breakfast, a 5% government tax and a 12% service charge. At this level, you can expect your own bathroom, air-conditioning and a TV. Given the speed at which prices change in Egypt, it is difficult to give an average price for a room in this category, although expect to pay more in the more popular tourist destinations such as Cairo, Alexandria, Luxor, Aswan and the resorts along the Red Sea. It is also worth remembering that most hotels in this category will only accept payment in Egyptian pounds although some will accept credit cards.

Five-star hotels – Dozens of lavish new establishments have sprung up across the country in the past decade and most are comparable with their counterparts anywhere in the world, with superb facilities, a high level of comfort and obliging staff. Having said this, if you are travelling independently and are planning to stay in this standard of hotel in Egypt, be prepared to pay room rates of between $ 150-$ 250 for more than your fellow guests who have booked as part of a package.

EATING OUT

The initial comments in the Hotels section also hold true for eating out in Egypt. In hotels booked solid by tour operators, groups will generally eat Western-style cuisine, supplemented by a few Egyptian specialities such as *fuul* (a purée of brown broad beans seasoned with cumin), *tahina* (a sesame paste with olive oil and a pinch of red chilli pepper), *baba ghanoug* (a highly seasoned aubergine and garlic dish), *koftas* (meatballs), and kebabs (diced pieces of veal or beef marinated in oil, herbs and spices and grilled on skewers). In these hotels, salads will have been carefully washed with treated water to reduce the risk of guests succumbing to stomach bugs, although in the first few days of a holiday these are more often than not the result of a change in climate rather than anything else. Beyond the confines of Egypt's major hotels, visitors will soon realise that it is possible to eat both well and cheaply, although certain precautions and commonsense are required. In terms of its cuisine, Egypt has been influenced over the centuries by many of its Eastern Mediterranean neighbours, in particular Greece, Turkey, Syria and the Lebanon. One example of this is the tradition of *meze*, a selection of small dishes is served at the beginning of a meal in similar style to Spanish tapas. Given the country's extensive coastlines, it is hardly surprising that fish and seafood appear frequently on Egyptian menus. The ports of Alexandria and Port Said, in particular, are both renowned for the quality of the prawns and fish caught in the Mediterranean; these are usually either grilled or baked in the oven.

Vegetarians will also find a good choice of dishes, especially in Cairo and along the Nile Valley, with dishes such as *taamiya* or *falafels* (balls made from white broad beans mixed with onion, parsley and coriander and then fried) and *mahchis* (vegetables such as courgettes, aubergines, peppers and tomatoes) stuffed with rice, onions and spices. In these areas meat figures predominantly in the day-to-day diet, with veal, chicken and pigeon all popular. Egyptian desserts are also worthy of their reputation, particularly pastries, which are often generously coated in sugar and honey. As in most places around the world, fast food from the West has become extremely popular in Egypt, particularly with the young who are keen to take on board the latest food trends from the West. Many of these culinary imports have subsequently been adapted by Egyptians to suit their own tastes.

Hygiene – A few basic precautions are essential for every visitor to Egypt. Always wash your hands before a meal; only drink mineral water, sodas or beer (if buying bottled water in small shops or off the street, make sure the cap has not been tampered with); refuse the offer of ice cubes, including in alcoholic drinks (unless you know they have been frozen from mineral water); steer clear of raw foods and ask for meat and fish that is well cooked; be especially wary with salads, raw vegetables and fruit (never eat a fruit that has already been peeled, for example).

Make sure you drink plenty of non-alcoholic liquids, as dehydration is one of the major causes of stomach upsets ; have more sugar than normal at breakfast or in your tea or coffee; add more salt to dishes than you generally would at home; and ensure that you get plenty of vitamin C.

recommendations in this guide

We have travelled the length and breadth of Egypt to provide you with recommendations for hotels and restaurants that meet our stringent criteria for comfort, a relaxed atmosphere and quality of service. All have been individually visited and carefully selected and we are sure that these will enhance your trip to this fascinating country. Specific details on them, as well as a comprehensive listing of bars, local tour operators and a whole host of other practical information, can be found in the Directory section of individual towns and cities within this guide. It goes without saying that in a country as large and diverse as Egypt standards vary and options for accommodation and eating out in the villages of the country's oases will compare unfavourably with the larger cities and the glitzy resorts of the Red Sea. Nonetheless, we have attempted to list hotels and restaurants in every place of interest to travellers around the country, with the one proviso that they meet our basic criteria. Obviously, things change and some details may have altered since our most recent visit, in particular with regard to prices, but if you have any comments or suggestions on hotels, restaurants etc that we have included in this guide or . would like to recommend somewhere that is not, please let us know – we would be delighted to hear from you!

USING THE DIRECTORIES

The Directory sections in this guide are found under the entries dedicated to Egypt's main towns, cities, resorts and

sites of historical and archaeological interest and include a wealth of practical information for visitors. Prices are given either in Egyptian pounds (E£) or US dollars ($) – the larger the hotel, the more likelihood you'll find the rate in the latter, although your bill will almost certainly be detailed in local currency. For some hotels we have specified two rates: the lower rate is the low-season tariff (which in most areas extends from May to August), the higher price is the rate for high season (September to April).

Categories – In every Directory, hotels and restaurants are classified into three price categories (Budget, Moderate and Expensive) which can fluctuate according to the region in which they are located. As an example, an "Expensive" hotel in one of Egyptís oases may be the same price as a "Moderate" hotel in Cairo or in a cosmopolitan resort such as Sharm el-Sheikh.

As the name suggests, the **"Budget"** category is for those with limited funds but who nonetheless expect a hotel that is clean, even if the facilities are on the basic side. Generally these hotels have one or two stars, although occasionally we have included a hotel without a star rating. It is, of course, possible to find hotels that are cheaper in price than those we have specified but these have been omitted because of their failure to meet our basic requirements in terms of cleanliness and comfort.

The **"Moderate"** category is likely to appeal to those on a slightly larger budget who are looking for a hotel offering greater comfort and better facilities, usually with a swimming pool and its own restaurant. These hotels generally have better locations than those in our "Budget" selection and fall into the three- and four-star category, and occasionally the lower end of the five-star range.

For those visitors who prefer more luxurious levels of comfort and facilities in addition to impeccable service, we recommend our **"Expensive"** category, which includes a selection of Egypt's most exclusive hotels. It should be noted that many of Egypt's top hotels

(particularly those which are part of recognised international chains) cater mainly to groups and as such are missing from our list as they are often fully booked well in advance and are lacking the special touches, individuality and service associated with the country's most exclusive establishments, several of which are housed in former palaces.

ACCOMMODATION

Hotels – In this guide you will find a huge choice of hotels to suit all tastes and budgets. In the more upmarket hotels you will be asked for a credit card number when making a booking and will have to hand over your passport when you check in. Those hotels that do not accept credit cards may ask for an advance in cash, although this is rare. Unless specified otherwise, the room rate will include breakfast, government tax and service. Almost every hotel in the "Moderate" and "Expensive" categories will have its own swimming pool and restaurant, both of which are normally open to non-guests, although a charge is usually levied for use of hotel pools. This option is particularly useful for those staying in a more budget-orientated hotel as, with the exception of the Red Sea and the Mediterranean, it is often difficult to find somewhere to swim in Egypt. Whatever you do, do not swim in the Nile or any of the country's other rivers and lakes as the risk of contracting bilharzia is high.

Youth hostels – In total, Egypt has 15 youth hostels, although none of these are listed in the Directories in this guide as they are often quite remote, are difficult to find, often lack the requisite cleanliness and peace and quiet for inclusion, and because they rarely accept couples. However, if you are keen to stay in Egyptian youth hostels, we recommend that you contact or write to: The Egyptian Youth Hostels Association, 1 Sheraa Al-Ibrahimy (south of Midan Tahrir), Garden City, Cairo ✆ (02) 354 05 27; fax (02) 355 03 29.

Camp sites – These are rare in Egypt and when they do exist, facilities are usually extremely basic. If you are planning to bring a tent, however, it is worth knowing that several hotels around the country, particularly those in the oases and in the area around Nuweiba and Dahab, allow travellers to camp in their grounds for a nominal fee. Camping in the wild is either not recommended or prohibited – expect to be fined if you are caught breaking this law. Contact tourist offices for information on local camp sites.

RESTAURANTS

In order to cater for all gastronomic tastes, we have selected a range of restaurants that specialise in typical Egyptian fare or serve international cuisine for those visitors who prefer to stick to Western food. Don't forget that if you're not staying at a particular hotel you can still eat at its restaurant. Depending on your choice, prices can vary from just a few Egyptian pounds to several hundred. Wherever you eat, however, always check your bill, and if itís in Arabic, make sure you ask the waiter or manager to explain it to you if there's anything you're unsure about.

Other options for a quick bite to eat include the snack bars and small restaurants that line many Egyptian streets, the ubiquitous fruit and vegetable stalls that add a vibrant splash of colour to the country's souks, and the pastry shops and cafés that are an important part of everyday life in Egypt.

If you do buy something from a street stall or local restaurant, use your commonsense and judgement in deciding what and where to eat, as although much of the food on display may appear extremely tempting, it may not be as fresh as you think, and may cause you more problems than you bargained for.

Ideas for your Visit

CHOOSING A BASE

If you have booked a package holiday with a tour operator, your decision has already been taken care of and will undoubtedly include stays in one or more of the most popular destinations around the country, perhaps in addition to a Nile cruise lasting from a few days to a week. For those visitors who are planning an independent itinerary, your choice is an extensive one and can be tailored to your specific needs.

The driving tours described below have been designed to enable you to make the most of your time, taking into account local sights of interest, journey times and accommodation options.

places to stay

The towns, cities and resorts listed below would make an ideal base for anything from three days to a week.

ALEXANDRIA (3 DAYS)

From the outset you will be pleasantly surprised by the atmosphere of this relatively unknown Mediterranean port. The best way of embarking upon a tour of this lively city is on foot or by horse-drawn carriage along the lengthy Corniche. The most interesting section is between the Qaitbey Fort and the recently built Bibliotheca Alexandrina, the modern version of the mythical Alexandria Library, upon which, along with Alexander the Great and Cleopatra, the renown of this sophisticated city has been based. After this refreshing breath of sea air, why not dine on excellent grilled fish before ending the day with a stroll along the city's shopping streets, which remain busy late into the evening. The next day can be devoted to the city's archaeological sites, including the catacombs, Pompey's Pillar and the Roman amphitheatre, followed by an opportunity to delve into the evocative world of Alexandria's souks. To finish off your day, pop into one of the old-fashioned cafés that are such a characteristic feature of the city centre. Your third and final day could start with an hour or two taking in the treasures of the Greco-Roman Museum. Then, before heading back to Cairo or inland towards the oases, maybe relax in the sun at one of the beaches at the eastern end of the Corniche or head for Abukir for a seafood lunch on a terrace overlooking the Mediterranean.

ASWAN (4 DAYS)

The wonderful light and air will strike you as soon as you set foot in Aswan, beautifully situated on the banks of the Nile, which is lined here by the attractive, leafy Corniche. One of the best introductions to this enchanting town is via a felucca trip on the river, taking your time to enjoy the magnificent setting with Aswan on one side of the river and an almost deserted west bank opposite. Once back on dry land, end your day by exploring Elephantine and Kitchener Islands on foot.

The cool of the following morning will be a perfect time to visit the Temple of Philae, one of the highlights of any trip to Egypt. This magnificent structure has been rebuilt on an island between the two dams and is reached by motor boat. After a well-earned rest by the pool, spend the evening exploring the most attractive and most atmospheric of all the souks in Egypt. You could devote your third day to a trip by plane or bus 253km/158mi south to Abu Simbel to visit the two unforgettable temples that grace the modern-day shores of Lake Nasser. Make sure you stay to enjoy the magnificent sunset here, when the surrounding area turns a deep red as the sun disappears slowly to the west. Back in Aswan enjoy a drink and a meal in a Nubian restaurant, where you'll have the chance to admire a display of traditional Nubian dance. On your final day in Upper Egypt, spend the morning at the Nubian Museum, of great interest both for its memorable exhibits and the architecture of the building itself. The rarely visited but spectacular Temple of Kalabsha is also a must, impressive in its construction and the solitude of its situation. A visit to Aswan would not be complete without a chance to admire the famous High Dam.

Hurghada (3 days)

A three-day stay on the west coast of the Red Sea involves rest, relaxation and the opportunity to enjoy the diving and sports facilities of this world-renowned resort. Most people who make their way to Hurghada have not come to visit any archaeological sites, although through your hotel it is easy to organise an excursion to Mons Porphyrites, where a Roman temple stands proudly against a stunning backdrop of uninhabited *gebels*. Hurghada's main attractions are its beaches and the underwater world of the Red Sea, which attracts scuba-divers from far and wide. The Red Sea has some of the planet's finest coral reefs, with myriad species of multicoloured fish, particularly in the waters of the Strait of Gubal. If you prefer to admire this underwater extravaganza from more comfortable surroundings, why not take one of the mini-submarine trips that can be booked in the resort. Three days may not be enough, but it will give you the chance to try your hand at most of these activities, plus perhaps an hour or two of water-skiing and a trip by microlight.

Cairo (5 days)

The urban chaos and frenetic atmosphere of Egypt's capital city will come as a profound shock to most visitors to the city and the initial temptation may be to spend as little time as possible here. However, it is worth persisting and allowing yourself to become gradually acclimatised to the noise and pollution, as Cairo has a wealth of artistic and historical treasures. The most popular attraction is undoubtedly the Egyptian Museum, an excellent introduction to the history of the pharaohs; its collections span the entire length of Ancient Egyptian history, from the Old Kingdom to the Greco-Roman period. After visiting the museum, experience the buzz of modern Cairo with a stroll through the lively, commercial district around Midan Tahrir. On your second day, visit the world-famous pyramids at Giza, one of the Seven Wonders of the Ancient World, situated to the west of the city; afterwards continue on to Saqqara, where the pyramids are smaller and less impressive but nonetheless contain magnificent funerary decoration. After the frenetic sightseeing of the previous two days, start your third day with a visit to the city's historic heart, the Coptic Quarter. After a gentle stroll through this area, head for the Oum Kalsoum Museum, then visit the citadel to enjoy some memorable views of the city. Now would be a good time to explore Islamic Cairo, after which you can delve deep into the colourful Khan el-Khalili souk, where you may be tempted to sit in a café and smoke the traditional *shisha* or hookah pipe. Head back to the Islamic district on the fourth day and visit some of its old mosques like the sumptuously decorated Al-Azhar Mosque and the grandiose Ibn Tulun Mosque. For your last day in Cairo, you have a choice: explore the suburb of Heliopolis, the southern and northern cemeteries, better known as the "City of the Dead", or perhaps return to explore a site or museum in more detail. But make sure you don't leave Cairo without visiting the Museum of Islamic Art, one of the city's highlights.

Luxor (6 days)

Luxor is the most visited city in Egypt, with a wealth of ancient sites dating back to pharaonic times. Your first port of call here should be the Temple of Karnak, the hypostyle hall of which is one of the most breathtaking sights in the country, with 134 colossal columns forming an unforgettable forest of stone and creating an overall impression of surreal beauty. You may wish to follow this visit with a stroll along the Corniche and a felucca ride on the river; in the late afternoon the sunset over the Theban mountains on the west bank of the river is truly magnificent. On your second day in Luxor, make the most of the cool early morning and cross the Nile for a full day's sightseeing on the west bank. In this stark desert landscape, a number of sites and monuments provide an unforgettable insight into the beliefs and traditions of the Ancient Egyptians: visit some of the

impressive mortuary temples, as well as the site of Deir el-Bahri and its splendid Temple of Hatshepsut. Back in Luxor, spend the evening exploring the town's souk, taking time to soak up the lively and colourful atmosphere. On your third day, head out to the Valley of the Kings, where the underground rock-tombs of the New Kingdom pharaohs house impressive paintings and low reliefs, illustrating the funerary beliefs of the Ancient Egyptians. The decoration in the tombs focuses on the afterworld, depicting the Pharaoh's journey to the kingdom of Osiris and his dialogue with the gods. In the afternoon, take a leisurely stroll around the colourful houses of the village of El-Qurna and visit the Valley of the Queens, including the tomb of Nefertari, probably the most beautiful of all Ancient Egyptian tombs.

The next day you may wish to get up early and take a hot-air balloon ride over the Nile Valley and the foothills of the Libyan mountains. As you look down upon the valley, it is easy to understand why the Nile was referred to by the Ancient Egyptians as "a gift of the gods"; without the river, there would have been no Egyptian civilisation. In the afternoon, take a cycle ride through the banana and sugar-cane plantations outside the city. On your fifth day, head north to visit the magnificent Temple of Hathor at Dendara, but make sure that you are back in time to attend the unforgettable sound and light show at the Temple of Karnak. On your last day, spend some time relaxing and strolling around the city, perhaps indulging in some last-minute shopping, before visiting the Luxor Museum of Ancient Egyptian Art, home to a collection of statuary, steles and other items discovered in the temples and tombs of Thebes. An evening visit to the superbly illuminated Temple of Luxor will bring your stay to a memorable end.

SHARM EL-SHEIKH (4 DAYS)

Many visitors consider Sharm el-Sheikh to be the most attractive of the coastal resorts in Egypt, with the spendid sweep of Naama Bay just outside the town and a good choice of both public and private beaches. The resort is situated on the southern tip of the Sinai Peninsula and is one of the most important centres for scuba-diving in the world, as well as being an excellent base for excursions into the mountainous interior of the Sinai. On your first day, head towards the magnificent Naama Bay to relax on the beach, perhaps taking time to learn the rudiments of scuba-diving. In the evening you may wish to return here to enjoy the nightlife on offer in this popular resort.

After a late night, a lazy morning may well be in order, folowed by a relaxing afternoon on the beach. After a relatively inactive day, this evening would be a good time to join an organised excursion to Mt Sinai, where visitors can climb the mountain by camel from one of the hotels near the Monastery of St Catherine. The advantage of this night-time ascent is the splendid sunrise from the summit and the magnificent panoramic view over the rocky mountains stretching to the east. Back in Sharm el-Sheikh at the end of the morning, you will appreciate the beach and the cool sea breeze all the more after your excursion into the hot and arid landscapes of the gebels.

On the fourth day, make your way to Ras Mohammed National Park, home to a number of species of migratory birds. Here you can either swim or go scuba-diving in one of the most beautiful sites in the Red Sea.

driving tours

The driving tours described below are marked on the map of the same name at the beginning of the guide.

We have compiled six different itineraries for travellers who prefer to explore Egypt under their own steam, rather than as part of an organised tour. Travelling independently in Egypt requires a certain amount of patience and a definite sense of adventure, mainly because of the time-consuming process of taking different methods of public transport and having to search out your own accommodation, which can be frustrating at times, not because the areas crossed are dangerous in any way. However, the advantages of travelling independently far outweigh the disadvantages: you will see parts of Egypt often neglected by tourists, and as a result will gain a clearer understanding of the country, its people and customs, as well as visiting the sites and monuments for which the country is famous.

1 – From the Mediterranean to the Desert

1 262km/788mi round trip from Alexandria, followed by a 112km/70mi round trip to Rosetta – Only one good tarmac road leads from the Mediterranean city of Alexandria south-west across the desert to the small oasis town of Siwa, where the Berber population for centuries lived an isolated existence cut off from the rest of the world. The road cuts across the desert, initially passing several apparently empty holiday villages, before reaching El Alamein, where Montgomery defeated Rommel, and a couple of seaside resorts which are mainly popular with Egyptians. From Mersa Matruh, the temperature starts to rise as the road crosses the uniformly flat desert to Siwa. The hustle and bustle of Alexandria seem light years away as the road enters the oasis, where only the call of muezzin interrupts the peace and quiet of the small town. Once back in Alexandria, head east along the coast to the pleasant palm-lined town of Rosetta, with its old Ottoman houses.

Recommended method of transport: hire car with driver, or air-conditioned bus; by taxi or train to Rosetta.

2 – Pyramids and Modern Towns

806km/503mi, departing from Cairo – The pyramids of Ancient Egypt are scattered to the south of Cairo along the Nile at Giza, Saqqara, Dahshur and Meidum. A visit to all of these sites will provide a comprehensive introduction to these Ancient monuments, which are among the oldest in the world. An excellent road then leads across the valley of the Arabian Desert to the Coptic monastery of St Antony before following the Gulf of Suez north to the town of Suez, where you can admire one of the most remarkable achievements of the modern age: the Suez Canal. Further north, the road leads to the small town of Ismailiya, built alongside the canal, and then to the prosperous duty-free port of Port Said.

Recommended method of transport: hire car with driver or taxi from Cairo to Beni Suef, bus from Beni Suef to Suez and Suez to Port Said; return to Cairo by train.

3 – Gebels and the Gulf Coasts

646km/403mi, departing from Sharm el-Sheikh – The many delights of the Red Sea can be enjoyed in Sharm el-Sheikh, the focal point of this circular itinerary. After heading north past the small seaside resorts of Dahab and Nuweiba, the landscape changes as the road leaves the sparkling blue of the sea for the more arid backdrop of the Ain Hudra oasis and the Coloured Canyon. It is worth taking time to explore this little-visited geological feature before continuing west to the Monastery of St Catherine and Mt Sinai. You will undoubtedly want to spend time in the small village of St Catherine, both to visit the monastery and to climb Mt Sinai, an ascent traditionally attempted at night so that you can enjoy what many consider to be the highlight of the trip: the stunning sunrise over the immense solitude of the Sinai mountains. As you carry on west towards the Gulf of Suez, you will pass through the attractive and lush Feran oasis which is still inhabited by Bedouins. The road then follows the Gulf of Suez back south to the resort of Sharm el-Sheikh, where you may wish to scuba-dive or snorkel in the waters of the magnificent Ras Mohammed Park reserve.

Recommended method of transport: by taxi (if you're part of a small group), or by bus. Ask your hotel in Sharm el-Sheikh to arrange this excursion for you.

4 – The Oasis Route

1 674km/1 046mi, departing from Cairo – With the notable exception of the Nile Valley, Egypt is an arid country. However, its parched desert landscapes are occasionally broken by the welcome sight of palm groves announcing the existence of an oasis town. The oases of Bahariya, Farafra, Dakhla and Kharga are linked by an excellent road and are well worth a visit. The monotony of the road is relieved by the ever-changing landscapes of the deserts, by the greenery of their oasis towns and by the unusual light that is a feature of the Great Sand Sea which extends to the south-west of the country. The road follows the old caravan routes across the desert, where the views across the arid landscape are majestic in their simplicity, changing colour constantly throughout the day and culminating in the magnificent reds and oranges of a desert sunset. At night the sky takes on the appearance of an unforgettable velvet backdrop punctuated with thousands of bright stars. Eventually the road leaves the desert and enters the Nile Valley. Stict its magnificent Ancient sites such as Tell el-Amarna and Beni Hassan north of Asyut and the pyramids south of Cairo. Recommended method of transport: hire car with driver, or air-conditioned bus, as far as Asyut; return from Asyut to Cairo by train.

5 – ANCIENT RUINS ALONG THE NILE

976km/610mi round trip from Luxor, followed by 328km/205mi round trip to Abydos – Most tourists visiting Egypt for the first time will probably take a cruise along the Nile, and it is true to say that a cruise from Luxor to Aswan in Upper Egypt is one of the most fascinating travel experiences in the world. Many of the most important Ancient ruins in Egypt are found in Luxor and its surrounding area; Aswan is better known for its gentle pace of life and dramatic Nubian landscapes, where traditional white-sailed feluccas glide gently along the Nile. In this part of the country the comfort of a luxury cruise boat is perhaps the best environment in which to learn about Ancient Egyptian civilisation, while appreciating the wonderful scenery along the banks of the river. Sites to the south of Aswan popular with tourists include the temples on the shores of Lake Nasser, such as those at Abu Simbel. From Luxor it is also possible to visit the temples at Dendara.

Recommended method of transport: fast boat, plane or bus from Aswan to Abu Simbel and back; taxi or train from Aswan to Luxor; taxi from Luxor to Abydos and back.

6 – FROM THE NILE TO THE RED SEA

724km/452mi round trip from Luxor – Once you have visited Luxor and the royal valleys, it is relatively easy to get to the Red Sea, on the far side of the Arabian Desert separating the coast from the Nile. Four resorts are dotted along the west coast of this magnificent expanse of water, each with its own character and particular attractions. Hurghada, the largest and most popular of the resorts, is renowned for its diving sites. North of Hurghada, El-Ghouna, although tiny in comparison, is blessed with a delightful marina and has a distinctly upmarket feel, in keeping with its peaceful, tranquil setting. To the south, the new resort of Safaga is the port used by pilgrims making their way to Mecca in Saudi Arabia; the town is also known for its pleasant breeze which attracts windsurfers to the area. Further south still, Quseir retains some of the atmosphere of an East African port with vestiges of its traditional coral architecture.

Recommended method of transport: bus or taxi from Luxor to Hurghada, usually as part of a convoy; by taxi from one resort to another along the coast.

Sport

scuba-diving

The Red Sea is one of the most popular areas in the world for snorkelling and scuba-diving, with a choice of resorts dotted along the African coast, from Marsa Alam to Safaga, Safaga to Hurghada and Hurghada to El-Ghouna. The southern tip of the Sinai Peninsula on the opposite coastline is perhaps even better known, with a string of diving sites extending from Ras Mohammed National Park to Tiran Island, and even as far as the Gulf of Aqaba. For further information and advice on diving and diving courses, contact the British Sub Aqua Club at Telford's Quay, South Pier Road, Ellesmere Port, Cheshire CH65 4FL ☎ (0151) 350 6200; www.bsac.org.

fishing

Lake Nasser has been attracting an increasing number of fishing enthusiasts in recent years. Although the leisure fishing industry in Egypt is in its infancy, it is gradually becoming more organised. Nature-lovers will be pleased to hear that fish are returned to the water alive once they have been caught. Generally, there is no fishing in July and August because of the intense heat.

African Angler – For further information, contact Abercrombie & Kent in Cairo ☎ (02) 394 77 35.

Bohayrat Orascom – For information on crocodile safaris, contact this company's office in Aswan on ☎/fax (097) 31 40 90.

horse riding

Horse riding is available in the coastal resorts of the Sinai Peninsula, at the foot of the pyramids at Giza and on the west bank of the Nile at Luxor; horses can generally be hired by the hour, half-day or full day. For further information, consult the Directory sections of the relevant town in this guide. Organisations that offer safaris usually offer horse riding as well. The stables in Giza are situated close to the Great Sphinx near the ticket office.

tennis and squash

A number of the more expensive hotels in Egypt have their own tennis courts for use by guests. In Cairo, players can also hire the courts at the tennis club situated close to the Nile.

Squash is becoming increasingly popular in Egypt, which explains the presence of several top Egyptian players on the international circuit. For further information on facilties, please contact one of the clubs listed below:

Gezira Sporting Club – Sheraa Saray al-Gezira, Zamalek ☏ (02) 735 60 00.

Heliopolis Sporting Club – Sheraa al-Sayyid al-Mirghany, Heliopolis ☏ (02) 417 00 61.

Zamalek Sporting Club – Sheraa Sitta wi-Ashrin Yulyu, Mohandissen ☏ (02) 302 63 00.

sailing and windsurfing

The Egyptian coastline is not ideal for sailing and windsurfing, although a number of hotels in Hurghada offer these sports as part of their overall activities. Safaga, south of Hurghada, is one of the main resorts for windsurfing and funboarding on the Red Sea. The Asian side of the Gulf of Suez is beginning to take advantage of the strong winds that are a feature of this area: Moon Beach, in particular, is developing a growing reputation for both sailing and windsurfing. To the south of the Sinai Peninsula, Sharm el-Sheikh and Dahab are the most popular resorts for these activities.

golf

Golf is becoming increasingly popular among wealthy Egyptians and has enjoyed something of a boom in recent years. The country now has 16 golf courses, notably in 6 October City (to the west of Cairo), Giza (at the Mena House Oberoi Hotel), Alexandria, Luxor, Hurghada, El-Gouna, Sharm el-Sheikh and Taba. The largest club in the Near East is the recently opened Al-Suleimaniya Golf Club in the north of Cairo, which has 27 holes and covers an area of 840ha/2 075 acres, located close to the desert road linking the city to Alexandria.

Visitors who are interested in playing should contact their hotel reception desk, which will be happy to provide information on the nearest course and to organise transport for you.

Shopping

In addition to the main shopping areas in Egyptian towns and cities, we have also included a number of specific shops and boutiques selling typical Egyptian products in the Directory sections of this guide.

souks

Souks are a typical feature of many Egyptian towns and cities. The word translates literally as "market" or "bazaar" and refers to a collection of stalls and small shops which may cover an area of several blocks depending on the size of the town or city they are in.

The largest souks, such as those in Aswan, Luxor, Cairo (the fascinating Khan el-Khalili souk) and Alexandria, are described in the relevant chapters of the guide; information on smaller souks in provincial towns, the oases and coastal resorts can be obtained from relevant tourist offices. Markets away from the major tourist centres are usually fairly modest in size, and sell mainly food and traditional clothing. These are generally the best places in town to buy fresh fruit and vegetables and are well worth a visit in their own right for their colourful stalls and lively atmosphere. Larger souks tend to be more specialised, with the bazaar at Alexandria selling mainly fabric and the one in Cairo focusing on leatherwork, although they also sell a wide range of typical souvenirs for tourists.

typical souvenirs

CLOTHES, JEWELLERY AND PERFUME

Traditional costumes – The word *gallabiyya* refers to a long, hoodless robe worn by the majority of Egyptians living outside the major cities; in Europe it is perhaps better known by the term djellaba, a word used to describe a similar robe worn in North Africa. Although you're unlikely to purchase one of these to wear for everyday use back home, the *gallabiyyas* sold to tourists in Egyptian souks and hotel boutiques make elegant, practical dressing gowns or beach robes, with styles that range from simple designs to stunning robes ornately embroidered with pearls.

Cotton garments – Egyptian cotton enjoys a worldwide reputation and is of a very high quality. Shops in Cairo, in particular, sell a wide range of reasonably priced, good-quality shirts, T-shirts and trousers, although counterfeits of top brand names are common in Port Said.

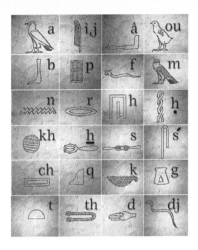

a	i,j	â	ou
b	p	f	m
n	r	h	ḥ
kh	ẖ	s	s'
ch	q	k	g
t	th	d	dj

Among the most popular souvenirs on sale in Egypt are T-shirts embroidered with a name spelt out in hieroglyphs. Most cruise ship boutiques sell these personalised T-shirts, which make an unusual and distinctive gift for friends and family back home.

Jewellery – Gold and silver souvenirs are reasonably priced in Egypt and are on sale in expensive jewellery shops, specialist boutiques in major hotels, souks such as the Khan el-Khalili souk in Cairo, as well as in the capital's Islamic district. If you are travelling in Egypt on an organised tour, you will more than likely be taken to a large jewellery store in Luxor or Cairo by your guide, who along with the travel agent organising the tour, will receive a commission for his efforts. Jewellery stores usually offer a wide choice, ranging from a simple profile of Nefertiti, an *ankh* cross or a blank cartouche on to which your name can be engraved, to valuable bracelets, necklaces and brooches studded with semi-precious stones. A number of jewellery stores are also able to produce tailor-made items on request.

Gold is sold by weight, so visitors thinking of buying an expensive piece of jewellery are advised to consult the *Egyptian Gazette* for the current gold rate. Armed with this information, you should be able to negotiate a better price during the bargaining process, bearing in mind, of course, the value added by the artisan's craftwork.

Perfume – The Khan el-Khalili souk in Cairo has a number of small stalls and shops where pure essences can be bought by the ounce; these are sold in attractive glass containers which come in a range of colours. Cheaper diluted perfume and fragrant perfumed oils are also on sale here, as well as in the local shops. Perfume-sellers are renowned in Egypt for their impressive selling techniques.

FOOD

Spices – Many of the souks in Egypt have a vast array of colourful spices that often bear little resemblance to the same spices sold in shops and supermarkets back home, and are of a far superior quality. These can make ideal gifts although it's best to check that you are legally allowed to bring them into your own country. The only spices that may not be worth buying are saffron (which is, in fact, often turmeric), used in Egypt to colour dishes rather than flavour them, and curry powder, which has very little taste. The best places to shop for spices are the souk in Aswan and a section of the Khan el-Khalili souk in Cairo *(see CAIRO – Directory)*.

Condiments – Local specialities such as *tahina* and *sahlab* can be bought from grocery shops and supermarkets in most major towns and cities around the country. *Tahina* is sold in concentrated form in small pots, and should be diluted with hot water before use.

OTHER TYPICAL SOUVENIRS

Papyrus – Although some painted "papyrus" sold in Egypt are actually made from banana or maize leaves, these souvenirs only cost a few pounds. If, however, you're interested in buying a hand-painted product on genuine papyrus (albeit not an antique) things become a little more difficult as price is not a sufficiently reliable indicator that the product is genuine.

To determine whether an article is genuine or fake, look to see if the motif is completely printed (in which case the article is fake). Also check if the paper tears when it is rolled or lightly crumpled (also a sign that it is fake), if your fingers are slightly ink-stained after touching the paper (it could be genuine), and if when placed against a black background you can see through the papyrus (genuine papyrus is fairly thick and not transparent). A reliable but expensive place to purchase papyrus is the Papyrus Institute in Cairo, which is run by Dr Ragab and is on the west bank of the Nile, 500m/550yd south of Midan al-Gala.

Antiques – Although excellent bargains can occasionally be found, visitors should be under no illusions. Only real antique experts and wealthy collectors will feel completely at home in the Egyptian antiques market.

As far as antiques from pharaonic Egypt are concerned, the rules are simple: it is illegal to leave the country with artefacts dating from this period. The antiques that we are refering to are more the "modern" type of antiques, such as the kind that can be found in the Attarine souk in Alexandria or in Sheraa Hoda Sha'rawy in Cairo, and a pleasant couple of hours canbe spent strolling through these districts and exploring antique shops.

PRACTICAL SOUVENIRS

Carpets – The Bedouins sell highly decorative *kilims* in desert areas, often with motifs inspired by everyday life. Carpets and rugs are also on sale in a number of outlets known as "carpet schools" close to Giza and Saqqara: it is worth knowing that the children who work here are often badly exploited and very rarely receive any kind of education. In contrast, the Ramses Wissa Wassef Art Center *(see SAQQARA)* teaches the craft of carpet-making to children, who also attend lessons in other subjects. As a result, the carpets produced here are more expensive, but the technical and artistic quality is of a higher standard.

Metalwork – Several souks sell a range of copper and brass objects ranging from simple ashtrays to ornate teapots. In the souk in Cairo, a number of these articles are certified as dating from the Mameluke period, although such claims should be taken with a pinch of salt.

Leatherwork – Like cotton, leather is reasonably priced in Egypt, although the quality can sometimes be poor. If you are interested in buying leather, the best approach is to choose your leather first and then have the article made for you. Khan el-Khalili souk in Cairo specialises in this.

Basketwork – Visitors who travel through the oases will find attractive souvenirs made from plaited palm leaves, including small boxes, baskets, hats and trays. Such items can also be found in the souks of the major cities.

Glass – The art of glass-blowing is an old tradition in Egypt, with the result that a vast array of colourful carafes, glasses, cups and jugs are on sale around the country. Visitors are spoilt for choice in the larger souks, where the choice is huge, with something for every taste and budget.

Local Customs

bargaining

Throughout the guide, and especially in the Directory sections, readers are reminded that the art of bargaining is part of everyday Egyptian life. Although there is a limit to where visitors can haggle over prices – obviously don't try out your bargaining skills in pharmacies, department stores, trains or buses – the ability to haggle over the price you are willing to pay is a useful skill in the many souks and souvenir shops around the country, as well as in taxis, which never use their meters. Bargaining is a local tradition, almost a game, which follows certain rules. You should bear in mind that prices are always negotiable and that they have been inflated with this ritual in mind. Visitors react differently to this ritual, depending on their personality; some take to it like a duck to water, others find the whole process excruciatingly embarrassing.

Tactics – If you are interested in an object, first of all say that you think it is too expensive (it undoubtedly is!). Move on to look at something else before casually coming back to the one that genuinely interests you. The vendor knows the game that you are playing and understands that you are inviting him to negotiate a price for this. Wait until he lowers his offer first, even if you have to leave his shop before he does so – don't worry, he'll come after you! You can then make a lower offer, although bear in mind that any price you quote that is close to half of his will be considered insultingly low. If you then stick to your price he will eventually offer his "lowest price", which is still higher than yours. If the article that you are intending to buy is fairly expensive, you may well be invited to have a cup of tea with the vendor. Once you have completed this ritual drink, stick to your price and be ready to leave if it is not accepted. This is the most important moment of the negotiating process; either the vendor will lower his sights and accept your price or you will have to go and try your luck elsewhere. It should be added that to indulge in this exercise for something worth just a few pounds is hardly worth it and could give offence.

baksheesh

Baksheesh, which means tip, is one of the first words visitors are likely to learn in Egypt. Although in theory paid in return for a service, a *baksheesh* is often requested even when no service has been provided! Visitors travelling around Egypt as part of an organised tour will frequently be confronted with children begging for a *baksheesh* around the main sites, the custodians of which are also likely to demand a *baksheesh*, usually in return for showing visitors a particularly good spot for a photo; a *baksheesh* is also expected in public toilets. Visitors travelling independently should be prepared for more hassle, as they're unlikely to have a guide with them as protection against this. When deciding whether or not to part with a *baksheesh*, bear in mind that locals with little money think of Westerners as coming from rich countries, which is generally true, and that Egyptian employees see a *baksheesh* as a supplement to their meagre salary, which it is. Occasionally a *baksheesh* can solve a problem which seemed to have no solution: it can open a site which was previously shut, procure you a good room in a hotel or help you obtain reliable information when moving on from one town to the next. However, care should be taken not to confuse a *baksheesh* with a bribe – the offer of payment to speed up officialdom is likely to have the opposite effect.

Advice – Visitors are advised to be consistent in their policy of handing out *baksheesh*, as by offering money to all and sundry you are doing little more than perpetuating an irritating system. Instead, focus on the main purpose of the *baksheesh*: that of thanking someone for a service rendered. If someone does perform a genuine service for you, by all means give them a few pounds in return. On the other hand, someone who grabs your suitcase and carries it for a few yards might be better thanked with a smile. Be aware that by accepting a custodian's offer to show you around a site, you are implicitly agreeing to accept their service and in such circumstances it is normal to thank them financially. It is often a good idea to carry a ready supply of 25pt, 50pt and E£1 notes on you separately from the rest of your valuables and larger bills; by doing so you will be able to offer a *baksheesh* without worrying about revealing all your cash.

women travelling alone

Egypt is a conservative country, where the role and status of women are very clearly defined. Although a certain amount of emancipation may be in evidence for women in the major cities, it is certainly not commonplace for the majority of the female population. However, it is easy to overlook the fact that thousands of women in Egypt do actually work, often holding positions of responsibility, and that women have recently obtained the right to leave the country if they so wish without the written authorisation of their husband. Divorce laws have also recently been changed in favour of women. Without going into the complex status of women in any great depth, we have included below some useful tips on acceptable behaviour for women travelling in Egypt on their own.

Many Egyptians have a stereotypical image of the Western woman, often promoted by satellite television channels, in the same way as Westerners may have preconceived ideas of life in Egypt. Our purpose here is not to pass judgement on Egyptian society, but to provide advice for those visiting the country.

Advice – Women travelling alone should take care to behave modestly in public. Make sure that you dress appropriately (no mini-skirts or shorts), and that you cover your head when visiting mosques. Never smoke in the street and ignore any verbal harassment that you encounter (in the event of a serious problem, approach another woman or a police officer). Make sure that you never sit in the front of a taxi next to the driver (he'll think that you're making advances) and always sit in one of the first two carriages of the Cairo metro, which are specifically reserved for women.

Further Reading

reference

How to Read Egyptian Hieroglyphics: A step-by-step guide to teach yourself – Mark Collier and Bill Manley (British Museum Press 1998)
A Dictionary of Egyptian Gods and Goddesses – George Hart (Routledge 1986)
British Museum Dictionary of Ancient Egypt – Ian Shaw and Paul Nicholson (British Museum Press 1997)

history

The Egyptians – Cyril Aldred, Aidan Dodson (Thames and Hudson 1998)
The Complete Temples of Ancient Egypt – Richard H Wilkinson (Thames and Hudson 2000)
The Complete Valley of the Kings – Nicholas Reeves, Richard H Wilkinson (Thames and Hudson 1996)
The Complete Pyramids – Mark Lehner (Thames and Hudson 1997)

The Egyptians – Barbara Watterson (Blackwell Publishers 1998)
The Oxford History of Ancient Egypt – edited by Ian Shaw (Oxford University Press 2000)
Ancient Egypt: the Great Discoveries – Nicholas Reeves (Thames and Hudson 2000)
Tutankhamun – TGH James (Tauris Parke 2000)
Egypt After the Pharaohs – Alan Bowman (British Museum Press 1996)
Coptic Egypt – Barbara Watterson (Scott Academic Press 1989)
A History of the Crusades – Steven Runciman (Penguin Books 1991)
The Rise of Modern Egypt – George Annesley (Pentland 1994)
Cairo: the City Victorious – Max Rodenbeck (Picador 1999)

travel

A Thousand Miles up the Nile – Amelia Edwards (Darf 2001)
Flaubert in Egypt – Gustave Flaubert (Penguin Books 1996)
Letters from Egypt – Florence Nightingale, Anthony Sattin (Ed) (Parkway Publishing 1998)
Egyptian Diaries – Jean Francois Champollion, Peter Clayton (Introduction) (Gibson Square Books Ltd 2001)

literature

EGYPTIAN AUTHORS

The Days – Taha Hussein (American University in Cairo Press 1997)
The Cheapest Night – Yousouf Idris (Lynne Rienner Publishers 1989)
Arabian Nights and Days – Naguib Mahfouz (Doubleday 1995)
Woman at Point Zero – Nawal el-Sadawi (Zed 1998)

FOREIGN AUTHORS

Death on the Nile – Agatha Christie (Harper Collins 2001)
Oleander, Jacaranda – Penelope Lively (Penguin Books 1995)
Moon Tiger – Penelope Lively (Penguin Books 1987)
The Levant Trilogy – Olivia Manning (Penguin Books 2001)
The Map of Love – Adhaf Soueif (Bloomsbury 2000)
In the Eye of the Sun – Adhaf Soueif (Bloomsbury 1999)
The Pharaoh's Shadow – Anthony Sattin (Indigo Paperbacks 2001)
The Alexandria Quartet – Lawrence Durrell (Faber and Faber 2001)
The English Patient – Michael Ondaatje (Picador 1997)

Cinema

Egypt has been the setting for a number of famous films, a selection of which are listed below:

The Sinai: *The Ten Commandments* (1956) by Cecil B de Mille, with Charlton Heston, Yul Brynner and Edward G Robinson. Views of the Sinai from a distance.

Alexandria: *Cleopatra* (1963) by Joseph L Mankiewicz, with Elizabeth Taylor and Richard Burton. Shot entirely in a studio in Hollywood.

Luxor, **Aswan** and **Abu Simbel**: *Death on the Nile* (1978) by John Guillermin, with Peter Ustinov, Mia Farrow and Jane Birkin. In the book, Hercule Poirot never even made it as far as Luxor, but in the film the boat follows the Nile from Aswan to Abu Simbel, via Karnak, providing some magnificent scenery for Agatha Christie's novel.

Cairo and **Tanis**: *Raiders of the Lost Ark* (1981) by Steven Spielberg, with Harrison Ford. The site of Tanis owes much to the imagination, and many of the street scenes set in Cairo were actually shot in Tunisia!

Cairo: *Sky of Hell* (1954) by Youssef Chahine, with Omar Sharif. This Egyptian film introduced the world to the future star of *Lawrence of Arabia*.

Cairo and **Luxor**: *The Spy Who Loved Me* (1977) by Lewis Gilbert, with Roger Moore. A typical James Bond film, with the usual action and excitement, set in the land of the pharaohs.

Cairo: *Ruby Cairo* (1993) by Robin Clifford, with Andie MacDowell and Liam Neeson. A rather clichéd film.

Cairo and the **Libyan Desert**: *The English Patient* by Anthony Minghella, with Ralph Fiennes, Kristen Scott-Thomas and Juliette Binoche.

Glossary

Although English is widely spoken and understood in most hotels and restaurants in Egypt, it may be useful to learn a few words and phrases in Arabic.

TERMS OF ADDRESS

Good morning: sabah al-kher;
reply: sabah al-nour
Good evening: missa al-kher;
reply: missa al-nour
Hello: salam aleikoum;
reply: wa 'aleikoum es salam
Please: lao samaht
Thank you: shokran
No, thank you: la' shokran
How are you? Ezzayyak? (to a man);
ezzayek? (to a woman)
Excuse me: assef (male): asfa (female)
It doesn't matter: maalesh
If God is willing: incha Allah
Goodbye: ma 'es salama.

USEFUL WORDS AND PHRASES

Yes: aywa; no: la'a
Here: hena; there: henak
How much? Kam?
It's too expensive: ghali 'awi
All right: meshi
I don't agree: ma yenfash
Maybe: yemken
It's possible: momken
Right: yemin; left: shemal
Good: helou; bad: wahesh
That's enough: kefaya
Open: maftouh; closed: ma'foul
Today: en-nahârda; tomorrow: bokrâ
Pound (money): guinay; 50 piastres:
noss guinays
Old town: el medina el'adima
Post office: bôstâ
Police station: 'esm el bôlis
Hospital: moustashfa
Embassy: safâra; passport: bâsbor
I don't understand: ana mish
fahem (m), ana mish fehla (f)
I don't have any money: ma'andish
felous
I'm ill: ana ayyan
Do you speak English? betetkallem
inglezi?
I would like to change money: aïz
aghâyyâr felous
Could you tell me the way to Hotel...?
Momken t'ewarri-ni at-tariq le
fondoq...?
Do you have any spare rooms? Fih
ôda fâdia?
May I visit the mosque? Momken
'azour el-guema'?
Where can I leave my bike (horse)?
Fen a'aggar 'agala (hossân)?

IN RESTAURANTS

Restaurant: mât'âm
Menu: kart
Bill/check: hissab
Plate: tâbâ'
Knife: sekkina

Fork: shôka
Salt: malh
Pepper: felfel
Sugar: sokkar
Bread: aïsh
Meat: lahma
Fish: samak
Vegetables: khôdâr
Salad: sâlâtâ
Mineral water: mâyya maadanyya

TRAVEL

Aeroplane: tâyyâra
Boat: merkeb
Train: 'atr
Car: ârabeya
Bus: ôtobis
Railway station: mahatta
Bus station: mahattat el-ôtobis
Where is the bus station? Fen
mahattet el-ôtobis?
Which is the bus for Aswan? Any
ôtobis yerouh Aswan?
How much is it to Aswan? Be kam at-
tazkâra li Aswan?
When does the bus to Aswan leave?
Emta i'oum el ôtobis li Aswan?
How many buses a day are there to
Aswan? Kam ôtobis fil yom yirouh
Aswan?
Can you wait for me? Moumken
t'estanna-ni?
Stop here: Bess hena.

DAYS OF THE WEEK

Monday: (yom) el-etnen
Tuesday: (yom) el-talat
Wednesday: (yom) el-'arba
Thursday: (yom) el-khamis
Friday: (yom) el-goma'a
Saturday: (yom) el-sabt
Sunday: (yom) el-had
Yom means day and does not have to
be used.

NATIONALITIES

I am British: ânâ ingleezi (m),
ingleeziah (f).
I am American: ânâ amreeki (m),
amreekiah (f).
I am Australian: ânâ ustrâli (m),
ustrâlîah (f).
I am Canadian: ânâ kanadî (m),
kanadîah (f).

NUMBERS

1: wahed; 2: etnen; 3: talata;
4: ârbâ'a; 5: khamsa; 6: setta;
7: saba'a; 8: tamanya; 9: tesa'a;
10: 'ashara; 20: ashreen;
30: talateen; 40: arba'een;
50: khamseen;
100: meyya;
200: miten;
300: toltomeyya;
400: robb'omeyya;
500: khomsomeyya;
1 000: elf.

Insights and Images

Egypt Today

Egypt as a nation began to embrace modernity in the late 19C, since when, with the exception of religious fundaments, many facets of Egyptian life have experienced dramatic change. Politics, the economy and cultural life have all witnessed marked upheaval, numerous conventional ideas have been challenged, and even the social emancipation of women has become a subject of great topical interest.

Egyptian Society

Egypt finds itself at the crossroads of three continents, at the centre of the Arab world, and halfway between a wealthy north and a poorer south. In addition, because of its geo-political and intellectual standing, it also exercises considerable influence across the Middle East.

When asked to define their country, many Egyptians proudly state: *"Masr, oum el dunya"*, "Egypt is the mother of the world".

Modern Government

In 1952, the revolution led by Nasser installed a Republican regime and removed from power the dynasty founded by Mohammed Ali. Four presidents have since assumed the role of Head of State: Mohammed Naguib, Gamal Abdel Nasser – the *Raïs* (literally "The Boss") elected by referendum in June 1956 – Anwar el-Sadat, and Hosni Mubarak. The latter has been President of the Arab Republic of Egypt for the past 20 years, and was re-elected for a third term in October 1999.

The President Mubarak.

The People's Assembly, which has an absolute majority, appoints the president for a mandate of six years and has its decision ratified by referendum. The president holds executive power and appoints and dismisses ministers in accordance with the Constitution of 1956. Legislative power consists of two chambers: the People's Assembly (444 members elected by direct universal suffrage, in addition to 10 appointed by the president) and the Consultative Assembly, or *Al Choura*.

The multi-party system was established by Sadat, although it is still forbidden to create a party based on religious principles. The head of the majority National Democratic Party, which was created in 1978, is President Mubarak. A state of emergency has existed in Egypt since the death of Sadat in 1981.

The Economy

Under the impetus of the IMF and the World Bank, Egypt has instituted a number of reforms, although its population growth prevents it from overcoming its economic and social problems. According to the World Bank, 23% of the country lives below the poverty line and, despite undeniable efforts, the unemployment rate remains above 20%, with an illiteracy level close to 40%.

This painting on a building in the village of El-Qurna shows that the owner has completed a pilgrimage to Mecca.

A closer inspection of its main sources of income (tourism, earnings from the Suez Canal, and oil) gives Egypt the appearance of a country with independent financial means. The export of its main industrial products (oil, cotton and textiles) brought in a revenue of 7.26 billion dollars in 2000, compared with 5.24 billion the previous year. The recent discovery of extensive natural gas reserves will undoubtedly inflate these figures in the years to come. On the other hand, imports, mainly in the form of manufactured goods, rose to $17 billion in 2000 against $15.16 billion in 1999, representing a deficit against exports of 42.7%. In 1999, the country's GDP was $91.3 billion , with growth estimated at 3.9%, and a stable inflation rate of around 3%. In 1993, the government launched a programme of privatisations, but of the 92 planned for 2000, only a dozen have been pushed through. Despite its liberal economic policy, the government has delayed a number of key reforms; one of the consequences of this is an increase in poverty over the past decade.

Religion

Islam is the State religion in a country where 90% of the population are Sunni Muslims and 10% are Christians, predominantly Copts. Egypt is the ninth largest Muslim country worldwide, a long way behind Indonesia, Pakistan and India. The Al-Azhar mosque-university, built in Cairo in 970, is the highest religious authority for the Sunni Islamic faith. The *ulemas* (doctors of law) of the Muslim world come here to study the doctrine of an Islam that is moderate, and devoid of both racism and fanaticism.

Muslims must respect the five pillars of Islam:
1. The *shahada* or profession of faith: there is no other God than Allah and Muhammad is his prophet.
2. The *salat* or prayer, five times a day.
3. The *zakat* or provision of alms to those in need.
4. The *siyam* or fast, during the month of Ramadan.
5. The *hadj* or pilgrimage to Mecca, for those able to do so.

Christians in Egypt are referred to as Copts. Originally, the Arabic word *qibt* was an abbreviation of the Greek term *aegyptios*, meaning "Egyptian". The Copts are, in fact, Egyptians who refused to convert to Islam during the Muslim conquest and who established a national church in defiance of Byzantium. Nowadays, they constitute the largest Christian community in the Arab Orient. They speak Arabic, although the Coptic language is used during religious services.

Ethnic Groups

The largest ethnic group in the country has lived along the banks of the Nile for several millennia and represents 80% of the population. Its physical features resemble those of Egyptians from the Pharaonic Period. Other ethnic groups include the Bedouins of the Sinai, who originated from Arabia, and the Bedouins of the Libyan Desert, who have settled between Alexandria, the Libyan border and the oases; the inhabitants of the Siwa claim to have Berber origins. The Nubians occupy the south of the country and are characterised by their dark skin and fine features. Their lands to the south of Aswan have almost completely disappeared as a result of the construction of the High Dam.

Friday prayers at the Sayyidna el-Husayn mosque in Cairo.

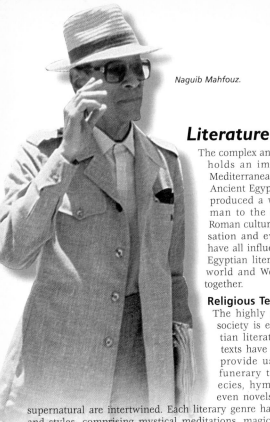

Naguib Mahfouz.

Literature

The complex and original literature of Egypt holds an important place in Eastern Mediterranean culture. The civilisation of Ancient Egypt used the written word and produced a wide range of texts linking man to the divine world. The Greco-Roman culture, centuries of Islamic civilisation and even the British occupation have all influenced the peculiar nature of Egyptian literature, in which the Islamic world and Western society are brought together.

Religious Texts

The highly religious nature of ancient society is evident in the earliest Egyptian literature. Although few written texts have survived, those that remain provide us with a rich literature of funerary texts, lamentations, prophecies, hymns, narratives, stories and even novels in which the real and the supernatural are intertwined. Each literary genre has its own traditions, themes and styles, comprising mystical meditations, magic and mythology, as well as humour and satire, demonstrating that Egyptian writers were able to portray their contemporary world with great success.

Myths and Legends

Certain works of literature developed the themes of the traditional Egyptian myths, in the form of occasionally complex narratives. Spread by travelling narrators who performed these works as songs, they were then transcribed in written form on to papyrus.

The Tale of the Shipwrecked Sailor (12th Dynasty) recounts the adventure of a king's envoy shipwrecked on an island after a violent storm. He confides his misfortune to a snake, who predicts a happy ending for him; soon after, a ship arrives and the marooned sailor is saved. This tale, typical of narratives where animals are endowed with human qualities, is later found in Classical Mediterranean literature and in Arab works from the areas bordering the Red Sea.

The Tale of the Two Brothers (19th Dynasty) relates the quarrel of the brothers Anubis and Bata. Anubis's wife tells him that Bata is in love with her and as a result Bata exiles himself, placing himself under the protection of the gods. The moral of this tale, written in a very pure, poetic style, was to have a major influence on future Eastern literature.

Modern Literature

For the first few centuries of Islamic civilisation, Damascus and Baghdad were the centres of the Arab literary world, rather than Cairo. Following the golden age of the Abbasid period there was even a sharp reduction in creative activity in Egyptian literature. At the beginning of the 19C, Egypt opened its doors to the West, firstly as a result of Napoleon's Egyptian campaign, which sparked a cultural renaissance, and secondly during the reign of Mohammed Ali, who sent a number of professors to Europe. Since then, intellectual life in Egypt has built upon this literary nahda (renaissance), which is particularly noticeable in the poetry of Mahmoud Sami al-Baroudy, Ahmed Shawqi and Hafiz Ibrahim.

Contemporary Works

The novella and novel were not used in Arabic literature until just before the outbreak of the First World War. Zaynab (1914), written by Mohammed Hussein Haykal, is considered to be the first real Arabic novel because of its tragic vision of the world. Other writers depicted the dual character of Egypt in the first half of the 20C: its respect for tradition and its fascination with the West. Some of these writers, such as the brothers Mohammed and Mahmoud Taymur and Mahmoud

Kamil, used a realist style to achieve this. Before the Second World War, two important figures in Egyptian literature emerged: Tawfiq al-Hakim and Taha Hussein. The latter, blind from a young age, wrote a largely autobiographical body of work, which included his novel Al-Ayyam (The Days) (1929), in which he expresses the values and concerns of the underprivileged, as well as women's refusal to submit to men. In Diary of a Country Prosecutor (1937),

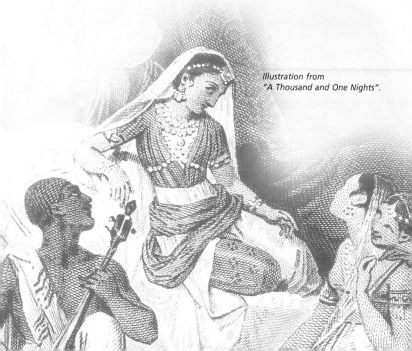

THE BOOK OF THE DEAD
This collection of funerary texts, which appeared during the New Kingdom, was inspired by the Coffin Texts. These literary works, which accompanied the dead body that they protected, were characterised by their content – a collection of prayers and incantations – and their use of papyrus.

It was Karl Richard Lepsius who gave the generic name Book of the Dead to this collection, after Champollion referred to it as "a funerary ritual". The texts would perhaps be more aptly named The Chapters of Coming Forth by Day, as the main purpose of the texts was to encourage the deceased to leave their tomb during the day to return to earth.

Al-Hakim embraces similar themes, describing the aspirations and disillusions of the fellah peasant class. Although he was a British writer, Lawrence Durrell has become inextricably associated with contemporary Egyptian literature. The Alexandria Quartet (1960), inspired and heavily influenced by his long period of residence in the city, turns to psychoanalysis and to the ambiguous erotism that marked the spirit of the time, both in Egypt and Europe.

New Developments

Often compared to the French writers Balzac and Zola, Naguib Mahfouz is considered to be the most important Egyptian writer of the second half of the 20C. The leading exponent of the new wave of social realism, Mahfouz paints a critical portait of his country's society while at the same time probing the transformations taking place within it. After writing a series of psychological stories, such as Palace Walk (1956), and other novels in which he describes the despair of the human condition, the author returned to the traditional narrative techniques of Arab literature in Arabian Nights and Days (1982), a work which starts where A Thousand and One Nights, one of the masterpieces of world literature, finished. Mahfouz received the Nobel Prize in 1988.

Although less well known abroad, other Egyptian writers of note include Albert Cossery, Yousouf Idris, Gamal Ghitany, Nasr Abou Zeid and Édouard Al-Kharrat.

Illustration from "A Thousand and One Nights".

A musician from the Nile region.

Music

The once proud city of Cairo has gradually disappeared over the years, its glorious past crumbling to dust along with its old stones and ancient buildings. Nowadays, the high-rise towers of the city's new districts and unbridled construction projects are as much a part of the city as the traffic pollution and desert dust. However, although the peaceful green city of the past may have been replaced by the noisy chaos of the largest city in Africa, the same love for music still remains.

A Musical Mosaic

Different types of music can be heard in the city's hotels and nightclubs, on the radio and even in taxis. The popular and urban *shaa'biya* differs from the *sa'idiya* from Upper Egypt, the Nubian *nuybiyya* and the *sharqiya* which accompanies Eastern dance. Egyptian youngsters listen to *shabâbiyya*, also known as *gîl al-gedid*, which is a kind of Egyptian pop music. The nahda, for many years a symbol of the renaissance of Arab music, now only exists on old vinyl LPs and in the novels of Naguib Mahfouz.

A Legendary Figure

The voice of Oum Kalsoum (1900-75) can still be heard throughout Cairo. Already popular during the reign of King Farouk and subsequently the figurehead of Nasser's Egypt, the singer was unique in her ability to perform the traditional Arabic *tarab* (an expression of elation which builds into a crescendo of ecstasy). A legendary figure, Oum Kalsoum introduced a new type of classical song which replaced the traditional *wasla*, a combination of Arabic song accompanied by musical instruments. From 1926, this doyenne of Egyptian music worked with a number of famous composers such as Muhammad Abd al-Wahâb, who was responsible for the modern reform of Egyptian song, and Abd el-Halim Hafez, whose film scores are renowned throughout the country.

Between Tradition and Modernity

The *takht* was originally a small instrumental ensemble comprising an *oud* (lute), a *nây* (a long reed flute), a *qânun* (zither) and a *riqq* (tambourine); over the years, this ensemble developed into a large typically Oriental orchestra, with several rows of violins, an organ, a guitar and a double bass. Light music (*gîl al-gedid*) has also evolved and is now dominated by the sounds of electric instruments.

Oum Kalsoum, the voice of Egypt, in 1936.

Only the percussion instruments, namely the tabla and daraboka, remain largely unchanged from days gone by. Large advertising hoardings all over Cairo promote the stars of the latest Lebanese-Egyptian sounds, with singers such as Amr Diab, Mohammed Mounir (of Nubian origin) and Medhat Salah featured alongside female stars such as Ghada Ragab, Asalah, Latifa and Anoushka. Echoes of the sharqi, an Eastern dance developed in Ottoman palaces and made famous by Fifi Abdo, the last great Egyptian dancer, among others, live on in the musical comedies performed around the city.

Belly dancers were so-named by Napoleon's troops.

A dance festival at Al-Ghuri mausoleum in Cairo.

Sufi Singers

The art of the Arab world was primarily focused on language and writing; as a result it is not surprising to see rural Egyptians still attached to the poetry of their ancestors. One of the key person-alities of popular tradition in Upper Egypt is the *munshed*. Whereas the classical musical traditions of the country are disappearing, this professional reciter is one of the last remaining performers of the *inshad*, a religious song inspired by the Sufi tradition. The munshed moves from village to village, keeping the Sufi rituals alive through a combination of poetry and slang. Two particularly well-known Sufi stars are Ahmad al-Tûni and Sheikh Yasin al-Tûni, both from the village of Hawatka, near Asyut in Middle Egypt. Their shows attract an audience of several thousand people who are inspired by the pure emotion of the *sultana*, a type of Arabic song.

Music on the Nile

Another type of celebratory music originating from Upper Egypt is the *sa'idiya*, per-formed by famous musicians of the Nile. These travelling artists play the *rababah*, a viol-shaped instrument made from coconut and two horse-hair strings, and are the last bards of Egypt.

In the same way as old folk stories used to be told in cafés, these musicians recount the stories of the Hilalian chanson de geste cycle, which date back to the 10C. Some of the stories may have been slightly modernised: young women are nowadays described as sweet as fizzy lemonade rather than strawberries or pomegranate juice!

A Cultural Melting Pot

Each type of popular music tells the story of the history and geography of the coun-try in its own way. Egypt has a broad and diverse range of musical influence – Muslim, Christian, Arabic, Nubian, Turkish, Bedouin and even Western – all of which form a rich musical tapestry. In Upper Egypt, for example, group song and dance is often accompanied by a clapping of hands, a gesture which expresses the soul of the south where Africa and Asia meet. Here, the Nubian community, which has been dispersed since the construction of the Aswan Dam, attempts to preserve its traditions which are in danger of being destroyed through the creation of Lake Nasser and the modernisation of Cairo. It was in this part of Egypt that the *tan-bùra*, the African and Nilotic lyre depicted on the low reliefs of Ancient Egypt, evolved. The tortoise shell originally used as a resonance chamber has been replaced by a metal plate to create an instrument known as the *semsemiyya*, now seen all along the Red Sea, from the Yemen to the Suez Canal.

Porte cinq *(1983)*
by Nader Galal.

Cinema

Throughout the 20C cinema has acted as a barometer for Egypt's cultural, social and political life, acting as a symbol of the country's modernity and having a unifying effect on the Arab-speaking world as a whole. Its stars are known from the Atlantic Ocean to the Persian Gulf and because of this the Egyptian dialect is the most widely understood by Arabs from all countries.

Origins

In 1896, a film produced by the Lumière brothers was shown in Alexandria to enthusiastic acclaim. Twenty-six years later Mohamed Bayoumi directed the first Egyptian short film, entitled *Barsoum Looks for a Job*. However, the real origins of Egyptian cinema can be traced to the work of a woman, Aziza Amir, who in 1927 directed and performed in Leila, co-directed by Wedad Orfi and Stéphane Rosti; this film was to have a profound influence on the world of Egyptian cinema. In 1928, *A Kiss in the Desert*, by Ibrahim and Badr Lama, led to an interest in exotic adventure films, while *Zaynab* (1930) by Mohamed Karim depicted the world of rural Egypt.

From Silent Movies to Song

The White Rose (1933) by Mohamed Karim brought musical comedy to the big screen and filming to the banks of the Nile. Having captured the interest of the Arab world, film production steadily increased and in 1935 the growing popularity of the industry was marked by the construction of the Misr film studios. The following year, *Wedad*, by Fritz Kramp and featuring the star Oum Kalsoum, represented Egypt at the first Venice Film Festival. This marks the beginning of the Misr Film school which produced directors of international renown such as Ahmed Badrakhan, Kamal Selim and Salah Abu Seif. The production of comedies, melodramas, and historical and religious films gradually transformed Egypt into the Hollywood of the East.

The 1940s and 1950s were the golden years of Egyptian cinema. Films were mass produced in two to three weeks, and followed an often-identical storyline. Musical stars of the time included Leila Mourad who, in 1942, played in *Leila* directed by Togo Mizrahi, and Farid al-Atrache, who starred in *Victory of Youth* by Ahmed Badrakhane. A censorship code was introduced in 1947, based on the model of the Hays Code established in the United States.

Youssef Chahine.

From Escapist Cinema to Social Commentary

The history of Egyptian cinema turns a page with the filming of *Willpower* by Kamal Selim in 1939. This film, produced in an age of national fervour, focused on social conflict and brought with it a new tone of realism to Egyptian cinema.

In 1952, during the Nasser revolution, new archetypes were to emerge which favoured the realistic trend of film-makers such as Salah Abu Seif, Henri Barakat, Atef Salem, Kamal el-Cheikh and Tewfik Saleh. The work of Youssef Chahine showed instinctive promise, even in his early films, and Omar Sharif played in his *Sky of Hell* before he became an internationally recognised star. However, although these were important films, they also represented a small proportion of the film industry which for the most part catered for the public's taste for escapism, to the

Painted cinema posters are a familiar sight in Cairo.

delight of directors and distributors. In the 1960s cinema was one of the sectors of society most influenced by the socialism of Nasser's regime. One exception was *The Mummy* (1969), Chadi Abdel Salam's masterpiece, which adopted pharaonic history as its subject.

Cinema reflected the social problems and contradictions which were rocking a dominantly rural society desperate for modernisation, and it is perhaps through the exploration of the role of women that this modernity was most obvious. A number of films of the period dealt with themes such as the equality of the sexes, the working woman and a woman's right to choose her own husband. Souad Hosni and Nadia Lotfi were important figures of this movement, whereas Faten Hamama, who for years had played a series of roles as a young, submissive woman, could suddenly be seen rebelling and demanding a divorce in *I Demand a Solution* by Said Marzouk (1974).

After the Arab defeat by Israel in 1967 and the death of Nasser in 1970, Sadat came to power, bringing change to the political climate. With denationalisation at the forefront of the political agenda, the law of market forces crept into Egyptian cinema, and the new generation of film-makers who had trained at the Institute of Cinema in Cairo now had to rely on their own abilities in order to survive. Ali Badrakhan, Mohamed Radi, Ali Abdel Khalek and Samir Seif were some of the new names who were happy to fill this void.

A Tentative Coming of Age

The boldest films of the 1970s were the work of an experienced film-maker, Youssef Chahine. Risking censorship, he pursued his career with unfailing enthusiasm and in 1997 his film *Destiny* won a prize at the Cannes Film Festival. His followers included Yousri Nasrallah, director of *The Town* (1999), who soon proved to be the leading director of the new generation.

In 1981, the assassination of Sadat by a group of fundamentalists provoked a feeling of unease in the country which was also reflected in the films of the time. Cinema reacted with mockery, a form of expression popular with Egyptians and much used by the comedian Adel Imam. *The Lawyer*, by Rafaat al-Mihi, is one of the most representative films of this decade, which saw the emergence of directors such as Mohamed Khan, Khairi Beshara, Atef el-Tayeb and Daoud Abdel Sayed. Through the talents of actors and actresses such as Ahmed Zaki, Nour el-Cherif, Mervat Amin, Naglaa Fathi, and Yousra, these film-makers depicted the difficult daily grind of their compatriots. Whereas this last generation of film directors denounced the workings of the growing fundamentalist movement, as witnessed in *Closed Doors* by Atef Hatata, a recent wave of comedy films uses a more light-hearted approach to diffuse the tense atmosphere.

Although Egyptian cinema has temporarily run out of ideas and is desperately searching for solutions to its crisis, the number of cinemas in the country continues to grow and new multi-screen complexes are being built in its wealthier areas to replace the dilapidated cinemas of the past. The Egyptians' eternal passion for the silver screen remains intact.

Omar Sharif.

17C reliquary in Coptic and Arabic.

Writing and Language

Arabic, the official language of Egypt, is spoken by a billion people and is the most important of the world's Semitic languages. It was used centuries before the arrival of Islam, although at the time of the Arab invasion of Egypt, the Egyptian people spoke Coptic, which nowadays is used only for church services. During the first half of the 7C, the Koran was written in Arabic by the Prophet Muhammad (Mahomet).

With its close links to Islam, Arabic is the religious language of all Muslims, with all prayers and the Koran being recited in the language. The expansion of Islam over the centuries has ensured the survival and development of Arabic and it was the Koran that was used as a reference when the grammatical rules of Classical Arabic were first established.

Literary Language

As is the case in all Arabic-speaking countries, the language is used in literature, education, in newspapers and on television. The considerable development of the media and the increasing numbers of people attending school and university have led to a wide diffusion of this literary language, which now has a growing influence on the different Arabic dialects.

Dialects

The Egyptians speak a dialect which is very close to Arabic, often taking its roots from Classical Arabic, while not necessarily following its syntax and grammar to the letter. Understood throughout the Arab and Muslim worlds, mainly as a result of its cinema, television and song, it is also present in literature, with contemporary authors using it in their works.

This dialect exists alongside other regional dialects and it is often pronunciation which allows inhabitants of the Delta to be distinguished from those of Upper Egypt. On the Egyptian-Sudanese border, the Nubians speak a number of different Kushite languages, such as *Kenuzi* and *Fadicha* (very close to Sudanese). Nomads from the Libyan desert who have settled along the Mediterranean coast west of Alexandria use a form of Arabic spoken in Libya, while in the Siwa Oasis the locals speak *siwi*, a Berber dialect from North Africa which has been strongly influenced by Arabic. However, Arabic remains the main language of use between these different ethnic peoples.

Variations of "How are you?" in different Egyptian languages:

"*Kaïf el hal?*" (standard Arabic)
"*Ezzaïk?*" (spoken Egyptian)
"*Meska gna?*" (Nubian)

Written Language

In the same way as hieroglyphs had religious significance for the Ancient Egyptians, so the writings of the Koran are considered to be the "word of God" for Muslims. According to Islam, the writing of the Koran is sacred, having been directly dictated to Muhammad by God. This work is revered, even when it cannot be read or understood, as is the case in non-Arabic speaking countries where the Koran is still taught in its original Arabic form.

Arabic, like Hebrew, has evolved from the Phoenician alphabet and is read and written from right to left. The alphabet has 28 letters, the shape of which changes according to whether the letter stands alone or is placed at the beginning, middle or end of a sentence. There are only three long vowels (a, i, ou), and short vowels are not written, except in the Koran and books which teach the language.

Calligraphy of the word **"dream"** by Ahmad Dari.

Calligraphy

It is thought that the development of Arabic calligraphy is linked to the fact that any portrayal of the human figure is forbidden by Islam. Although no verse of the Koran actually stipulates this, Islamic tradition quite clearly forbids any kind of representation; the purpose of this ban was to eliminate the last surviving totemic practices rejected by Islam.

Calligraphy was considered to be a major art, with highly respected artists carefully copying out the Koran and skilfully making the most of the artistic possibilities of the Arabic letters. As the same letter could be written differently depending on its position, artists competed to create the most inventive calligraphy, playing with the different compositions at their disposal.

In order to eliminate difficulties associated with reading Kufic letters – a rigid, angular written form of Arab-Muslim calligraphy, named after the town of Kufe, in Iraq – Ibn Mukla, the Abbasid Grand Vizier of Iraq, established a number of rules which developed into the six styles known as *Aklam-i sitta:*

Kûfi
Thuluth
Naskhi
Anadalûsi-maghribi
Riqâ
Diwâni
Tâliq (or Farsi).

"God is with those who fear him and with those who do good".

In cursive writing, characters are linked to each other. Arabic writing is remarkable for its ability to be expressed in a number of different forms. In the manuscripts of the Koran or other prayer texts, the language is written in a highly decorative way, whereas in architecture, the writing itself becomes part of the decor: there is not a mosque, palace or tomb in the Islamic world that has not had its surfaces embellished in some way with Arabic calligraphy. The language is written in ink on paper, but also lends itself perfectly to marble, stucco or wood.

Arabic calligraphy, which can be considered as the basis of the "arabesque" style, has a huge variety of decorative styles, from the Kufic style to the modern calligramme, and a large number of artists have become famous throughout the Arab world for their aesthetic interpretations of the Arabic alphabet.

Street scene in Esna.

Urban and Rural Life

In the Egypt beyond the major archaeological sites, visitors will discover a daily life in which tradition and conservatism are still strong, but which is nevertheless becoming increasingly attached to modern values. The country's somewhat disconcerting towns and cities often present an image of organised chaos in contrast to the seemingly gentle pace of a rural life that has existed for thousands of years. Although every province has its own individual character, the whole country has a deep sense of community, from the poorest districts of Egypt's large cities, where the greatest aspiration is to climb up the social ladder, to the smallest plots of land where peasants remain the trustees of traditional values.

Towns and Cities

Egypt's noisy, crowded towns and cities continue to develop at a frantic pace. Nowadays, it is not uncommon to see two or three storeys added to already completed buildings, while shanty towns continue to be established and developed in the suburbs; an example of this is the City of the Dead in Cairo, which is inhabited by thousands of people. Streets have become besieged by cars, lorries, countless taxis, an ever-increasing number of minibuses, as well as the more traditional sights of carts pulled by donkeys, street-peddlers hawking their wares and a throng of pedestrians.

Quality of life is not the same for everyone, however, as alongside employees, civil servants and workers (the latter engaged in a continual struggle for their daily survival), a new middle class has developed which has profited from the country's economic expansion; these privileged few live in luxury apartments, own several cars and travel abroad. This social divide resulting from the *infitah* – the economic liberalisation policy launched in 1975 – has failed to prevent Egyptians from facing up to their problems with humour, with the press becoming increasingly fond of caricatures that relay their concerns and expectations.

The Countryside

Egyptian *fellah* (peasants) lead tough, austere lives. The entire family works in the fields, a situation that indirectly leads to a high level of illiteracy in rural areas. Children lead animals to the fields, pick cotton, and gather *berseem* (Egyptian clover) for their cattle, while the women wash dishes and clothes in the Nile or in the closest canal. A typical peasant's house generally consists of two rooms: one for the numerous members of the family, the other for their animals. Over the years, the traditional dried-mud houses with their typical rural architecture have disappeared, replaced by others built of brick or breeze blocks.

Souks

These typical markets, generally found in narrow streets and alleyways, are a maze of tiny shops spilling out onto the pavement and selling goods of every description; over the years they have become a popular attraction for tourists. In the Khan el-Khalili souk, in Cairo, which is renowned for its colourful displays, several "districts" stand side by side (a sight repeated elsewhere in the country, particularly in Alexandria and Aswan). Distinct areas are set aside for different products, and although jewellers and perfume merchants are found here, it is the sellers of spices, fragrances and colourful fabrics that tend to take centre stage. Depending on the town;

Sugar cane juice: a popular Egyptian drink.

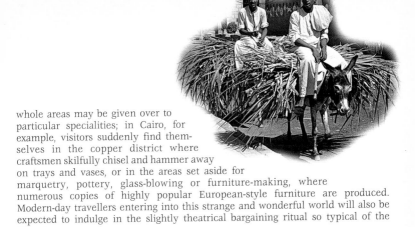

whole areas may be given over to particular specialities; in Cairo, for example, visitors suddenly find themselves in the copper district where craftsmen skilfully chisel and hammer away on trays and vases, or in the areas set aside for marquetry, pottery, glass-blowing or furniture-making, where numerous copies of highly popular European-style furniture are produced. Modern-day travellers entering into this strange and wonderful world will also be expected to indulge in the slightly theatrical bargaining ritual so typical of the Orient.

Traditional Trades

In the middle of the hustle and bustle and congestion in Cairo and other towns and cities around Egypt, a whole range of traditional and often unusual trades are still plied. Wander around the streets of any sizeable town and you will undoubtedly come across sellers of *fuul* (boiled beans), pastries, lemonade and spectacles, the ubiquitous shoe-shiners, potters, barbers who often work crouched on the ground, knife-grinders and bakers. Although a dying breed, public scribes can still be seen on Egyptian streets, an activity that survives due to the illiteracy levels in the countryside.

Café Life

These days, Egyptian public opinion is to a large extent forged in the country's cafés. The men who frequent them come here to drink tea or coffee, smoke the *shisha* (hookah pipe), discuss current affairs, and play dominoes or trictrac. Cafés are the epicentre of daily life, to such an extent that they are an essential stop on the campaign trial of any candidate standing for election; failure to do so would be a sure way of losing considerable numbers of votes! Cafés, therefore, act as important meeting-points for men to catch up with old friends or to discuss business affairs. They are male bastions where women never venture unaccompanied.

Festivals

Every Egyptian respects and celebrates Muslim festivals. *Aïd el-Fitr* closes the period of Ramadan, while *Aïd el-Adha* commemorates Abraham's sacrifice and is celebrated at the end of the pilgrimage. The festivals known as *moussem* are also linked to the Hegira calendar; the two most important are the New Year and the *Mouled el-Nabi*, the anniversary of the birth of the Prophet. On these special days, confectioners erect colourful tents on pavements and sell small sugary figures such as the famous multi-coloured dolls.

For the vast majority of the population, excursions are restricted to visits to family and an annual picnic on the day of *Sham el-Nessim*, an Egyptian festival dating back to the time of the Pharaohs, when the whole of Egypt heads for the banks of the Nile, the country's canals or the coast, to eat raw salted fish (*fessikh*) with onions.

The hookah pipe (shisha) – a familiar sight in the country's cafés.

A souk in the Fayum,
the "orchard of Egypt".

Egyptian Cuisine

Tourists travelling around Egypt on an organised tour are unlikely to sample traditional cuisine, and those visitors travelling independently are likely to exercise caution because of Western concerns about hygiene. However, trying local dishes can be one of the highlights of a holiday and Egyptian food has much to offer. If you receive the honour of being invited to visit an Egyptian family, such is their desire to offer a warm welcome that you are likely to be offered a table full of delicious and varied dishes.

Vegetarian Dishes

The ever-popular *fuul* is a purée of brown broad beans seasoned with cumin; it is often served at breakfast, but can be eaten at any time of day. *Taamiya* are balls made from white broad beans mixed with onion, parsley and coriander and then fried. *Bissara*, which can be eaten either hot or cold, is an alternative version of the above, with *molokheya* (see *Soups* below) added to the puréed white beans. *Aats* is a soup made with white lentils.

Stuffed Vegetables

Mahchis are vegetables (courgettes, aubergines, peppers, tomatoes) or vine or cabbage leaves which have been stuffed with rice, onions, spices and occasionally chopped meat.

Meat Dishes

Grilled meats include *kebabs* (diced pieces of veal or beef marinated in oil, herbs and spices) and meatballs *(koftas)*; chicken kebabs *(shish kebab)* and grilled veal cutlets are also popular. With the exception of the "festival of the sheep", very little lamb is eaten in Egypt. Among the most widely consumed fried dishes are chicken breasts, breaded veal fillets and a range of offal. In the street, shops sell sandwiches of chicken liver and *shawerma* (meat grilled under a low heat, cut into thin slices and served with tomatoes and onions). *Basterma* is a fillet of beef coated in spices and then sun-dried; it is then cut into thin slivers and eaten either raw or pan-fried with eggs. A perhaps less appetising dish is *kawera* (boiled tripe served with bread and rice), which is vaunted as being a "man's dish" with aphrodisiac properties. Egypt's main speciality is pigeon stuffed with wheat *(hamam mahchi bel frick)*, served with *kishk* (see *Soups* below). All types of poultry can be stuffed; at celebratory meals when poultry is served (turkey at Christmas or goose at Sham el-Nessim), this stuffing is enhanced by dried fruits. Macaroni is generally prepared with alternating layers of pasta, bechamel sauce and minced meat in an onion and tomato sauce. The aubergine-based Greek dish, moussaka, has also become popular in Egypt, where it is known as *messa'a*.

Soups

Meat stock, with flour and milk added, is used as a base for one particular soup known as *kishk*, served on a bed of rice. Vegetable soups include *molokheya*, which can be best described as a watercress soup flavoured with garlic.

Fish

Fish comes from the Nile, the Mediterranean and the Red Sea and can be either grilled or fried. Sham el-Nessim (spring festival) is the traditional time to enjoy *fessikh*, a salted and dried fish served with onions and decorated with boiled egg.

Salads

Salad is traditionally served with every dish, and can vary from raw vegetables to dishes that resemble purées or sauces. *Tahina* is a sesame paste with olive oil and a pinch of red chilli pepper; the basic constituents of the highly seasoned *baba ghanoug* are aubergine and garlic; *hummus* is a mixture of chickpeas, sesame purée and garlic. Mention should also be made of *mekkhallel*, vegetables marinated in vinegar.

Pastries

Egyptian pastries are usually oozing with honey or syrup and are served for dessert or as an accompaniment to tea. The most common are *konafa*, long strands of vermicelli-like pastry stuffed with currants, almonds and coconut; *baclawa*, a flaky pastry dessert made with raisins, pistachio and almonds; *basboussa*, a semolina and coconut-based delicacy; and *oum ali*, a pastry with almonds and raisins which is cooked in milk and flavoured with cinnamon.

Drinks

Egyptians drink tea *(shay)* throughout the day. It is served very sweet and in a simple glass that is almost too hot to handle. When served with mint it is known as *shay bel nanaa*. Coffee *(ahwa)* is drunk from small cups and has different names according to its level of sweetness: if you prefer it without sugar, ask for a *sadah*; a *mazbout* has some sugar added; while a *ziaada* is for those with a very sweet tooth. Some people add brandy to their coffee, in which case it becomes known as a Turkish coffee.

Karkadé is a decoction of hibiscus flowers served hot or ice-cold, and heavily sugared, while the hot aniseed-based drink, *yansoun*, is for many the perfect end to a busy day. In addition, a wide variety of fruit juices are available everywhere, ranging from the exotic mango and guava to orange, lemon, strawberry and banana. A visit to Egypt would not be complete without trying the exquisite sugar cane juice *(assir assab)* on sale in small shops and in souks. The cane is crushed in front of you and its juice served immediately (refuse any offer of juice that is not fresh as it oxidises very quickly).

Although not always easy to find, beer is the alcoholic drink most readily available, with two Egyptian labels, *Stella* and *Saqqarah,* dominating the market. The cheapest and most widespread of the two is the basic Stella beer (ask for a *local Stella*).

For a long time Egyptian wine was considered of very average quality, although this situation has improved in recent years. The country's two leading brands, Obélisque and Gianaclis, each produce reds, whites and rosés: those under the Obélisque label include the Rouge des Pharaons, Blanc d'Alexandrie, and Rosetta; Omar Khayyam, Cru des Ptolémées and Rubis d'Égypte all come under the Gianaclis label. Unfortunately, wines are not always stored in the best possible conditions, so visits and tasting can be disappointing, particularly as the wines themselves tend to be on the expensive side.

As for other types of alcohol, these are generally best avoided!

Egyptian spices: a feast for the senses.

Geography

The Arab Republic of Egypt occupies a predominantly desert landscape covering an area of 1 001 449km²/386 659sq mi. Of this, just 5% is habitable, an area mainly corresponding to the 39 000km²/15 050sq mi of cultivated land.

The fertile banks of the Nile River near Luxor.

Regions

The country stands at a latitude of between 22° and 32°N and a longitude of between 24° and 37°W, and straddles the continents of both Africa and Asia, including the Sinai Peninsula on the eastern side of the Suez Canal. At its widest, Egypt spans a distance of approximately 1 200km/800mi east to west, while from north to south it extends 1 080km/675mi. It shares its borders with Sudan to the south, Libya to the west, and Israel (and the Gaza Strip) to the east.

To the north, the country has 995km/622mi of Mediterranean coastline, with a further 1 942km/1 214mi along the Red Sea, to the east. The country can be divided into four distinct areas: the Nile Valley, along which the majority of Egypt's cultivated land is situated and which can be subdivided into three zones (Lower Egypt, Middle Egypt and Upper Egypt); the Libyan Desert (or Western Desert); the Arabian Desert (or Eastern Desert); and lastly, the desert-like Sinai Peninsula.

View of Cairo.

Nile Valley

Covering an area of 33 000km²/12 750sq mi – less than 4% of Egypt's total surface area – the valley extends from the south of the country to the north, from Lake Nasser, which straddles the Sudanese border, to the Delta, where the Nile flows out into the Mediterranean. In total, 90% of the Egyptian population live along this thin fertile strip of land. The Nile Delta covers some 23 000km²/8 880sq mi and stretches along the Mediterranean for a distance of 250km/156mi. Along its course the river flows through arid desert plateaux with cliffs reaching heights of 200-300m/650-1 000ft.

Libyan Desert

The Libyan Desert is an extension of the Sāhara and occupies an area of 680 000km²/262 550sq mi (68% of Egypt's total surface area). This vast basin of sand dunes consists of a limestone plateau at 300m/984ft, dotted with depressions and oases. The oasis of Siwa, to the west, and the Natrun Valley, to the east, demarcate the northern extension of the Libyan Desert, as it enters its coastal plain. A loop of oases descending from Bahariya to Kharga in the desert's central and southern sections provide welcome relief in this otherwise barren landscape.

A bale of cotton, a familiar sight in the Egyptian souks.

Arabian Desert

Considerably smaller in size – 225 000km²/86 900sq mi or 23% of the country's area – than its western counterpart, the Arabian Desert is characterised by a long chain of mountains with a succession of desolate *gebels*, some of which extend to heights of 1 500m/4 900ft. This rocky landscape bereft of oases is dissected by valleys formerly used by caravans and which now offer the only road links between the Nile Valley and the Red Sea.

Sinai Peninsula

This extension of the Arabian Desert is a triangular peninsula covering an area of 61 000km²/23 550sq mi, and acts as a transition point between Africa and Asia. The granite mountains to the south rise up between the gulfs of Aqaba and Suez, culminating in Mount Catherine (2 637m/8 649ft), which stands alongside Mount Sinai (2 285m/7 495ft). The wide Tih Plateau occupies the central section of the peninsula. A vast desert-like coastal plain, created by erosion over the centuries, stands to the north.

Population

Egypt has a total population of 66 900 000, a figure that represents one-quarter of the Arab world; of this total, 40% live in urban areas. Cairo alone accounts for 9 600 million inhabitants, although some unofficial estimates give a figure of 16 million. In certain parts of the capital, population density is as high as 31 000 inhabitants per km²/80 290 inhabitants per sq mi, against a natural average of 1 096 per km²/2 839 per sq mi in populated areas; when the entire country's surface area is taken into account, this figure falls to just 65 per km²/168 per sq mi. The Mediterranean city of Alexandria is Egypt's second largest urban area with a population of around 5 million. Other smaller cities include El-Mansura, Zagazig and Tanta, all of which are situated in the Delta region; Beni Suef, Asyut, Damanhur, El-Minya and Medinet el-Fayum, in Middle Egypt; and Aswan, in Upper Egypt.

Population growth continues unchecked in Egypt, with an estimated annual increase of 2.2%. As a result, Egypt is a predominantly young country, with 35% of the total population under the age of 15.

COMBATTING THE DESERT

Agriculture employs 51% of the country's active workforce and acts as the backbone of the Egyptian economy. Under Nasser, land was redistributed, resulting in the allocation of an average of 0.5ha (approximately 1 acre) of farmland to every peasant *(fellah)*. Since the time of Mohammed Ali, Egypt's main export crop has been cotton, which, if specialists are to be believed, is the best in the world. Other important crops include sugar cane, developed by Ismail Pasha, corn, rice and wheat; the production of these crops is on the increase, with national self-sufficiency the ultimate goal. Fruit production also continues to increase year on year. In order to expand areas under cultivation, President Mubarak has introduced several extensive irrigation programmes across the country, including the spectacular "Southern Valley" initiative, 70km/44mi west of Abu Simbel.

A Bedouin in the White Desert.

As a result of the Aswan High Dam, fishing can now take place all year.

The Nile, Source of Civilisation

As Herodotus wrote in his *Histories*, "Egypt is a gift of the Nile". Indeed, without the River Nile, Egypt as we know it would not have existed, as this desert country was only able to sustain life as a result of the abundant alluvium deposited when the river flooded. The Nile, which dissects the country from south to north, was so essential that the Ancient Egyptians believed that it had its origin in the "primordial waters" of Nun, for them the source of all creation. Incarnated by Hapy, an androgynous god with a papyrus headdress, the Nile was firstly called "the sea", then "the large river", and finally *Neilos* by the Greeks, although the origin of this word is uncertain. The flooding of this extraordinary river has shaped the destiny of an entire people and had a strong influence on its remarkable civilisation.

An Interminable African River

The Nile is generally considered to be the third longest river in the world, after the Amazon and the river network formed by the Mississippi and Missouri, extending over a course of 6 671km/4 169mi. The source of the White Nile is in Burundi, at the heart of the high plateaux of Africa, just north of the equator. The river then crosses Rwanda and runs into Lake Victoria, bordered by Tanzania, Kenya and Uganda. From here, it cuts through Uganda and enters the Sudan Basin, where, at Khartoum, its waters meet those of the Blue Nile, which has its source close to Lake Tana in Ethiopia. It is from the Sudanese capital that the Nile develops its full majesty, increasing in size from cataract to cataract, traversing the Sahara Desert before dispersing into the immense delta which separates Cairo from the Mediterranean.

A Fertile Land

Agriculture was Ancient Egypt's most valuable resource. The Nile made the earth of the pharaohs' land fertile, the combined result of the water it carried across the land and the alluvium which it deposited. Flooding lasted from July to October, during which time the Nile fed a fertile stretch of land along the course of the river (which in places extended to a width of 20km/12.5mi). This supply of alluvium enabled the inhabitants to grow cereals, flax, fruit trees, vines, papyrus and vegetables. However, the fertility guaranteed by the Nile was dependent upon the annual inundation. If the floods were too strong or too weak, the prosperity of the country was destroyed, and famine, which was endemic beyond the Nile Valley, occurred. To overcome this problem, the Pharaoh set up national wheat reserves during prosperous years and officials calculated the tax that would be paid by the *fellahin* (peasants).

White sails and blue water at Aswan.

A traditional felucca on the Nile.

The Modern Nile

From Abu Simbel to the Giza pyramids, the Nile heavily influenced the life of the *fellahin* and the Pharaoh's prestige through the magic of its repeated flooding. Although it never failed to regenerate this long oasis bordered by temples and cities, the river only provided one harvest a year. Nowadays the flooding of the river is a thing of the past. As a result of the large Aswan Dam opened in 1971, *fellahin* are now able to produce two or even three annual harvests, yet the agricultural landscape and techniques remain largely unchanged. As in the past, fields are ploughed by animals and the water from the irrigation canals is extracted by pump, even if diesel oil and electricity have replaced the traditional *noria* (water-wheel), Archimedes screw and *shaduf* (bucket attached to a pole and balanced with a counterweight). As a result of the dam, the country can attempt to cope with its demographic explosion: the surface area suitable for cultivation, which was originally 6 million *feddans* (3 million hectares/7 million acres), has been doubled and can now feed the country's population. However, progress comes at a price. The poetic mystery linked to the floods has disappeared and the Nile no longer turns red as it used to when full of alluvium during the periods of flooding. Instead, the river has turned grey and around Cairo and downstream of the city it is no more than an ordinary polluted river.

Sails in the Desert

Some of the former mystery of the Nile has nevertheless survived, as those who have seen feluccas sailing on the river at Luxor and Aswan will testify. These charming sailing boats chart their course along the river, occasionally troubled by the enormous cruise ships that constantly ply back and forth between the two towns. In former times, the river provided the only means of communication in this desert country; the first vessels on the river in Antiquity included fishing boats made of papyrus and larger boats made from sycamore wood, which transported the stones used in the construction of pyramids and temples. Yet it is the felucca (from the Arabic *faluwa*, meaning small cargo vessel) which symbolises the Nile. It is well worth travelling to Luxor or Aswan just to see the armada of these little boats on the river. The memory of watching the sun set on the horizon of Upper Egypt as you sit beneath the silent white sail of a felucca is perhaps longer lasting than any visit to an ancient tomb.

WATER HYACINTH

Originally from South America and used from the beginning of the 20C as a decorative plant, the water hyacinth *(Eichhornia crassipes)* is one of the indicators of the deteriorating water quality of the River Nile. This fast-spreading plant, with white or purple flowers, has colonised large sections of the river and is responsible for the blockage of nearly 80% of the river's irrigation canals, mainly in the Delta. It represents a serious economic threat because of its huge evaporation capacity in a country where water is as valuable as gold. In addition, the plant is home to a snail which carries bilharzia, a parasitic illness caught through bathing in contaminated waters.

Hoopoe.

Fauna and Flora

From the aridity of its vast tracts of desert to the fertile banks of the Nile, the flora and fauna of Egypt has markedly changed since the Pharaonic Period. In former times, the country's appearance was more akin to that of a savannah, where lions, cheetahs and leopards roamed, and elephants and gazelles drank from the waters of the Nile, which in turn was home to a large population of crocodiles and hippopotami. With the passing of time, these animals migrated south as the deserts advanced and civilisation progressed. Despite this exodus, Egypt still retains a rich array of often discreet wildlife that can be observed by those able to explore beyond the country's most popular tourist centres.

Wildlife along the Nile Valley

While the donkey (domesticated by Egyptian peasants *(fellahs)* because of its indefatigable nature), is without doubt the animal most visible along the Nile, the valley is also home to numerous other species. Of the valley's bird population, some species are common to Egypt; others migrate to the country from the harsh European winter and the western parts of Asia. The cattle egret, the small white wader with its yellow beak, the hoopoe, with its amazing silhouette, and the ibis are common visitors to cultivated land, as is the garden bulbul, recognisable by its reedy song. Along the banks of the river, note the pied kingfisher, which delights observers with its aerial acrobatics, the Nile Valley sunbird with its colourful plumage, and the red-breasted barn swallow. Birds that are rare or harder to spot include the black-shouldered kite, a small bird of prey that is now well acclimatised to Delta conditions, and the attractive sultan's moorhen, characterised by its blue-tinged plumage and red feet. The river's reed beds provide a habitat for the clamorous reed warbler, the grey heron and the spur-winged plover. Mention should also be made of the white pelican, the spoonbill, the stork and the pink flamingo.

The valley's farmland shelters one of the Nile's most fearsome creatures, the black-necked cobra. Although you are unlikely to come across this extremely poisonous snake, particular caution is required if strolling along the valley's irrigation canals after dark. As for the Nile monitor lizard, this large, impressive reptile tends to find shelter in heavy vegetation along the banks of the river.

Desert Animals

The camel is a constant feature of Egypt's desert landscape. This surprisingly fast animal, used to the drought conditions of these areas, is the only animal able to digest the thorns of the acacia, and for centuries has been the constant companion of the Bedouin. The hostile desert environment does, in fact, conceal a few rare addax, the antelope most suited to the desert, although currently threatened with extinction, and even wolves, several of which come to water on the shores of Lake Nasser at nightfall. The fennec, or desert fox, wild dogs, the hyena and even the jerboa all manage to survive amid these vast landscapes, which initially

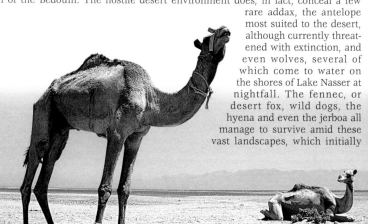

appear hostile to any other wildlife apart from insects and snakes. If you venture into the desert make sure you are accompanied by a guide and are wearing appropriate footwear, as the stones and rocks along your path can conceal a dangerous scorpion or viper.

Flora

Several species of trees and bushes are endemic to the area between the river and the edge of the desert, including the acacia. A number of varieties of this tree fill the air with their delicate scent from dusk onwards, including the Nile acacia and the mimosa. Throughout the valley, the spaces left by former plantations are now the habitat of tamarisks, the giant eucalyptus, flamboyants, casuarinas, bougainvillaea and sycamores; the outlying areas of the Nile are home to plantations of banana trees,

groves of palm trees, mangoes and oranges, as well as fields of sugar cane. However, by far the most typical tree in Egypt is the date palm. This prolific species, which is pollinated by hand in the spring, is grown for its different varieties of fruit, which are ready for harvesting in November. Once the tree is too old to produce dates, its trunk is cut into planks that are used in construction or as crossing points over irrigation canals. A more discreet climbing shrub, Egyptian jasmine, with its large white or yellow flowers, has long been the backbone of Egypt's perfume industry; its delightful scent pervades the air at dusk. This plant has a reputation of being the best in the world for perfume-making and perpetuates a tradition that dates back to ancient history. Recipes for processing its essence have been discovered in the tombs of the pharaohs.

Date palm, the best examples of which are found in the oases.

Lotus flower.

Pharaonic Egypt

The first person to study the history of Ancient Egypt was a priest called Manetho, who lived during the reign of the first two Ptolemies. He divided his work, the Aegyptica, into 31 dynasties and translated the names of the pharaohs into Greek. Adapted and revised over the centuries, Manetho's chronology remains an important reference for contemporary historians.

The Great Sphinx stands guard over the pyramids at Giza.

Origins

At the end of the Neolithic Period, Egypt was divided into two areas of civilisation: the kingdom to the north (Lower Egypt) was dedicated to Osiris, whose son Horus was incarnated by the king wearing a red crown; the kingdom to the south (Upper Egypt), whose king wore a white crown, was dedicated to Seth. After the unification of these two kingdoms by the early Egyptian ruler Narmer, the two crowns were combined to form the double *pschent* crown. Henceforth, Upper and Lower Egypt would form a single nation, a moment that marks the beginning of Egyptian history.

Old Kingdom

From the beginning of the 3rd Dynasty the capital of Egypt was Memphis, hence the term Memphite Empire, sometimes used to describe the Old Kingdom. Although isolated in the middle of nomadic peoples and far from Mesopotamia, Egypt's influence was already far-reaching and trade expeditions were made to Libya, Nubia, the Sinai, the Lebanon and Syria. The history of the Old Kingdom is also indelibly linked with its classical art, which reflects a rich and dazzling civilisation. Little is known about this civilisation beyond the fact that its kings established an elaborate system of centralised state control which guaranteed the security of the country. The successful kings of this period included Djoser, supported by his vizier (Imhotep); Sneferu, who formed a powerful army despite the fact that he had no expansionist plans; and Khufu (Cheops), who was responsible for the construction of the largest of the Giza pyramids. From the 5th Dynasty onwards public officials became more prominent in political and religious affairs; from the 6th Dynasty the monarchic centralisation of the state began to

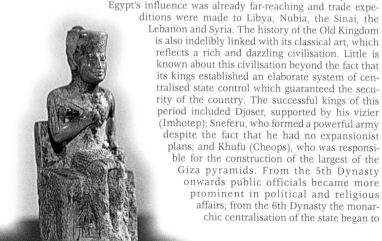

The tiny statuette of Khufu, the Pharaoh who built the largest pyramid at Giza.

Ra, the Heliopolitan sun-god.

weaken. The nomarchs who represented the king consulted him less frequently in the everyday running of their nome, and gradually Egypt began to disintegrate.

First Intermediate Period

This anarchy led to a period of crisis. In the south, the nomarchs reigned as kings; in the north, the Delta was partly invaded by conquering armies from Asia, and the capital, Memphis, crumbled. If Manetho is to be believed, the 7th Dynasty had approximately 70 kings over a period of 70 days! For around 50 years, the nomarchs of Herakleopolis (near Asyut) managed to impose some hegemony on this disorder, but it was Intef I, a nomarch from Thebes (Luxor), who declared himself king and founded the 11th Dynasty. The Thebans eventually emerged victorious from this conflict and Mentuhotep II succeeded in reunifying the country.

Middle Kingdom

The reunification of Egypt led to a period of opulence. In order to assert his authority, Mentuhotep II replaced the hereditary nomarchs with submissive state officials. A new period of centralisation began with Amenemhat I (12th Dynasty) who, although he made Thebes the capital of the country, decided to reside to the south of Memphis. He involved his son, Senusret I, in the day-to-day running of the country and proved himself to be an able administrator, introducing political and religious reform while at the same time developing the country's literature. His successors, Senusret I and Senusret II, continued in this vein, consolidating relations with the outside world and developing the Fayum region. Amenemhat III, who was said to be respected as far as Byblos, the capital of Phoenicia (modern-day Lebanon), colonised part of Nubia by building fortresses on the present-day border. However, the economic situation of the country suddenly worsened, the power of the State dwindled and a new period of chaos began.

Second Intermediate Period

The country remained divided for approximately 250 years. The exact reasons for this division, as well as much of the history of this period, are unknown, although what is certain is that during this time the crown of Egypt was disputed by a multitude of kings. During this period of unrest the Hyksos from Asia began to infiltrate the country, part of a larger movement of peoples which saw the Hittites settle in Anatolia and the Kassites in Babylon. The Hyksos settled in the Delta and imposed two successive dynasties on Egypt (15th and 16th Dynasties), both of which were contemporary with the 17th Dynasty. The latter preserved national traditions and patiently endured foreign rule until the reign of Kamose, who proved himself to be a great military leader. Aided by determined generals, he repelled invaders, pushing them back as far as Palestine, and led Egypt into a period of renewal.

A Period of Prosperity

After 1 000 years of splendour undimmed by constant upheavals, Egyptian civilisation was to enjoy five centuries of prosperity. The expulsion of the Hyksos was followed by an unprecedented military policy which pushed the boundaries of territory controlled by Egypt as far as the Euphrates to the north and the fourth cataract to the south. This expansion was as much preventive as colonialist in nature and hid the growing importance of religion in the affairs of the State. It was this increasing dominance of religious affairs, coupled with a succession of coups d'état, that brought about the decline and destruction of the New Kingdom.

Foundation of the New Kingdom

The task of rebuilding the country after the Second Intermediate Period fell to Ahmose, the first Pharaoh of the 18th Dynasty, and his immediate successors. It is conceivable that Ahmose – whose name translates as "renaissance" – may well be the same ruler as Kamose, the last Pharaoh of the Second Intermediate Period, although this is uncertain. Whatever his origins, Ahmose introduced a policy of foreign conquests and the establishment of an Egyptian protectorate in Phoenicia; internally Thebes remained the country's capital and a reorganisation of the state administration was introduced. Furthermore, his theocratic government granted a substantial amount of power to the high priests of Amun.

The young Tutankhamun.

Reigns of Splendour

Supported by the high priest of Amun, Hatshepsut, the widow of Thutmose II, acted as regent to Thutmose III and eventually assumed full pharaonic powers. She adopted the male attributes of the Pharaoh and seized power from the deceased king's natural son, who was forced to wait 22 years before ascending to the throne. Thutmose III reigned over one of the most glorious periods in Egyptian history, readopting the policy of territorial expansion started by his predecessors and abandoned by Hatshepsut, consolidating Egyptian domination, and suppressing revolts in Asia through the famous victories of Megiddo and Qadesh. An unequalled strategist and experienced warrior, Thutmose III was also a prolific builder and an educated man of letters. Egypt now experienced a period of peace. Amenhotep II, less intellectual than his father but said to be endowed with extraordinary physical strength, maintained firm control over Asia. He was succeeded by Thutmose IV, an exceptionally pious king, and by the calm and diplomatic Amenhotep IV, who enjoyed a peaceful reign over a country at the height of its influence.

The magical site of Abu Simbel, which now stands on the banks of Lake Nasser.

The Amarna Period

On her husband's death, the wife of Amenhotep III, Queen Tiy, acted as regent for her young son. Following the death of Ramose, vizier during the reign of Amenhotep III and the regency of Queen Tiy, the young king Amenhotep IV took the name Akhenaten. Through this act the state god Amun was replaced with the god Aten, unleashing a period of revolutionary reform and resulting in the establishment of a new city, Akhetaten, which became home to the Pharaoh and his wife Nefertiti. The main purpose of this act was to break the influence of the Amun clergy, who had created a State within a State; its effect was to mark an end to political and religious certainties. The impact of Aten worship, which is so spectacular in art, is also noticeable in literature and the economy. However, the idealist Akhenaten neglected his borders and abandoned part of his Asian empire to the Hittites.

After the brief reigns of the young Tutankhaten – who changed his name to Tutankhamun under pressure exerted by the clergy – and of Ay, Horemheb ascended to the throne and set about reorganising the State, erasing any trace of the Amarnian schism.

Ramesside Rule

Towards the end of his life, Horemheb, who had no heirs, appointed a former military colleague by the name of Paramessu as his vizier and prince regent. Paramessu, who, like Horemheb, was not of royal blood, took the name of Rameses I, founding the Ramesside dynasty, which established its capital at Piramesse, in the Delta.

Rameses I's military background was to strongly influence the spirit of the 19th Dynasty. During the reign of Sety I, the Egyptians made important conquests in Asia, while Sety I's successor, Rameses II, probably the most famous of the Pharaohs, won renown through the Second Battle of Qadesh against the Hittites. Although the battle was inconclusive, it enabled the Pharaoh to reduce the number of Asian rebellions over the course of several military campaigns and heralded a new period of peace and stability for Egypt. It is also probable that it was during the reign of Rameses II that Moses, who had received an Egyptian education, led the Exodus of the Jews from the Delta to Israel.

Signs of Decadence

Trouble over the succession broke out during the reign of Sety II, who was challenged by a rival ruler in the south. The reign of Rameses III, an intelligent and determined leader, was characterised by administrative reform and fierce resistance to the threats posed by the Libyans and Philistines; however, his was to be the last of the great Egyptian reigns. Under his successors, royal prestige was gradually eroded and internal struggles, conspiracies and corruption weakened royal power and strengthened the role of the high priests. Insecurity was rife by the reign of Rameses XI, who died leaving no heirs.

Third Intermediate Period

For 400 years, Egypt gradually fell apart. Initially, both Smendes and Psusennes I seemed to possess the resolve required to pull the country together, though neither was able to do so and the situation gradually worsened. Thebes and Tanis fought over the title of capital and Sheshonq I took advantage of the dispute, installing a Libyan tribe on the throne which, although powerful, was soon to prove anarchic. This period was followed by the reign of the Egyptianised Kushite kings, from Nubia, who gradually increased their sphere of influence until their Pharaoh, Taharqo, controlled much of the country, albeit under the control of Assyria, which pillaged Thebes.

The Colossi of Memnon, near Luxor.

Above: the site of Philae; left: a relief of Cleopatra at Dendera.

Twilight Years

Egypt experienced a brief respite during the reigns of the Saite kings of the 26th Dynasty. However, the decline of the Egyptian civilisation was well underway and the country's earlier splendour was soon to be little more than a memory. After the "African" kings, the Persians, Greeks and Romans all left their own mark on the once glorious civilisation of the Pharaohs.

From the Saite Kings to the Late Period

The Saite Dynasty had its origins in the 26th Dynasty, with Saite, in the Delta, as its main centre of power. The Saite kings originally accepted Assyrian suzerainty and it was the Assyrian king Ashurbanipal who placed Nekao I on the Egyptian throne. Supported by his protector and assisted by conscripts and mercenaries, his son Psamtek I undertook the reconquest of Upper Egypt. He succeeded in reuniting the country, reviving its economy and stimulating trade beyond its borders. During this renaissance, an important development saw the king encouraging the settlements of Greeks in the Delta in order to limit the authority of the Libyan chieftainships in the north. Psamtek I's successors continued to reorganise the country's administration and strengthen the Egyptian army. Then, during the reign of Psamtek III, the Persians defeated King Croesus of Lydia, seized Babylon and turned their attention to Egypt.

The Persian Occupation

King Cambyses of Persia defeated Psamtek III's army at the Battle of Pelusium (south-east of present-day Port Said) in 525 BC : for the second time in its history, Egypt was defeated and subsequently invaded by foreigners. The Persian king, who reigned over Iran, Anatolia and the Babylonian empire, subsequently transformed Egypt into a province, although it is not thought that he committed the atrocities described by Herodotus. After the defeat of Darius I at Marathon, in Greece, the Egyptians attempted a number of uprisings and the 28th and 29th Dynasties finally succeeded in temporarily freeing themselves from Persian control. Under the 30th Dynasty, Nectanebo I and Nectanebo II even managed to repel their enemies and revive the country's great building traditions. Unfortunately, Persian strength was such that Egypt succumbed yet again. By now the country had run out of strength and did not attempt to hide its enthusiasm when Alexander the Great, the king of Macedonia, defeated Darius II and entered Egypt.

A Greek Colony

From this moment on, Ancient Egypt would never again achieve political autonomy and no other native dynasty would henceforth be included on the historical table drawn up by Manetho. Welcomed as a liberator, Alexander the Great skilfully made the most of the Greek presence that had existed in Egypt since the Saite period, immediately showing an enthusiasm for Egyptian religion and demonstrating that he would respect its national customs. Pre-occupied by his conquests which would take him as far as India, he entrusted the administration of this new colony to the satrap Ptolemy; when Alexander died aged 33, Ptolemy continued to govern Egypt on behalf of Phillip III and Alexander IV. In 305, he declared himself king under the name of Ptolemy I Soter and founded the Ptolemaic Dynasty. Under

his reign and that of his successors, Greek civilisation was to have a profound influence on Egypt, mixing Greek mythology with local traditions. Fifteen Ptolemies revived and maintained the protocol of the Ancient pharaohs, although they should perhaps be seen as kings of Alexandria rather than pharaohs of Egypt. Only two rulers were to resurrect some of Egypt's former splendour: Ptolemy III and Cleopatra VII. The latter, who inherited a weakened state threatened by the Roman domination of the Mediterranean, threw all her energies into saving her kingdom. The suicide at Alexandria of her lover, Mark Antony, who had placed Egyptian interests over those of Rome, sounded the death knell for Cleopatra, whose tragic end is well documented. Her son Caesarion, whose father was Julius Caesar, never ascended to the throne and was assassinated while still an adolescent on the orders of Octavian.

A Roman Colony

While annexing Egypt, Octavian granted the country special status, distinguishing it from other conquered territories which were usually reduced to provinces of the Roman Empire. Egypt became one of the major bread baskets for Rome, while remaining the personal property of Octavian because of its strategic geographical position. Although provinces were usually represented by a procurator, in Egypt this position was held by a prefect. The country was at that time predominantly rural, with just one major city, Alexandria, one of the great Greek cities of the Mediterranean. A number of revolts took place during the reigns of Caligula, Vespasian, Antoninus and Marcus Aurelius, but a more serious uprising occurred under Gallienus, when the population of Alexandria, weary of the religious upheaval of the period, elected their prefect, Emilian, as their own emperor. In 292, Alexandria was taken by Diocletian, who set about persecuting Egypt's Christian population. Religious freedom was subsequently granted to Christians in 313 by Constantine, who incorporated the country into his empire. In 384, Theodosius issued an edict which forced the closure of all pagan temples. After his death Egypt was absorbed into the Byzantine Empire. The country continued to be plagued by religious conflict during this period (395-642) and as a result put up very little resistance to the Arab invasion of the country. Umar, the second successor to Mohammed, seized Egypt in the 7C, opening a new chapter in the country's history.

The northern section of Dendara, with the Roman mammisi to the left and the ruins of the entrance pylon to the right.

Muslim Egypt

The 12C mosque of Abu el-Haggag built inside the Temple of Luxor.

The most significant event of the early Middle Ages in Egypt – since 395 a colony of the Byzantine Empire – was the Arab conquest. Following these invasions, a Muslim community quickly developed in the country and Islam spread across the kingdom. In parallel with this, the Coptic Church was encouraged to forge greater autonomy in order to bring down the Byzantine hierarchy.

The Arab Conquest

After two and a half centuries of Byzantine domination and exhausted by its rivalry with Sassanid Persia, Egypt was unable to withstand the Arab invasion brought about by the call of the Prophet Muhammad. After conquering Mecca in 630, Islam spread quickly in the Middle East and within 15 years had reached Mesopotamia, Syria, Palestine and Egypt.

640 – Capture of the "Babylon of Egypt" (Cairo) by Amr (a general under Umar), who took Alexandria two years later.

Umayyads (661-750)

After the death of Muhammad in 632, the caliphs transferred their capital from Medina (Arabia) to Damascus (Syria), where the Umayyad Dynasty was founded. Under this dynasty, Arab-Muslim expansion reached its zenith. Egypt became an Arab protectorate, administered by a governor.

Abbasids (750-868)

The descendants of Al-Abbas, Muhammad's uncle, were Sunni Muslims who founded the Abbasid Dynasty and made Baghdad (Iraq) their capital in 762. Arabic, which had been the official language since 706, was adopted throughout the empire.

846 – Abandoned by central government, Egypt comes under the control of the Turkish generals of the caliphs of Baghdad.

Tulunids (868-905)

A Turkish officer from Cairo, Ahmed ibn Tulun (835-84), took control of his province and founded the Tulunid Dynasty, making Egypt an independent Muslim state for the first time. A royal city was established on the site of present-day Cairo. The dynasty failed to survive the assassination of the founder's son.

Ikhshidids (934-69)

In an attempt to block Fatimid expansion, a Turkish governor by the name of Mohammed ibn Turhdj, often referred to as El-Ikhshid, founded a new dynasty. The Ikhshidid Dynasty proved unable to withstand the Fatimid invasion.

Fatimids (969-1171)

The Shiite caliphs of the Fatimid dynasty, descendents of Fatima, Muhammad's daughter, took control of North Africa in 910. This dynasty, its wealth derived from its profitable commercial policies, showed considerable tolerance towards Egypt's population, which at that time was mainly Christian and Sunni Muslim.

969 – Foundation of Cairo by Gohar, a general under Caliph El-Muizz.

970 – Foundation of the Al-Azhar Mosque, the oldest Islamic university.

Ayyubids (1171-1250)

In 1171, the vizier Salah al-Din al-Ayyubi (Saladin) overthrew the last Fatimid sultan and founded the Ayyubid Dynasty, which reigned in Cairo on behalf of the Abbasid caliphs. It re-established the Sunni doctrine and unified Egypt and Syria. In order to develop a resistance to the Mongol threat of Genghis Khan, the last Ayyubid sultan enrolled an army of Turkish slaves (*mamluk* in Arabic).

The sultan Saladin captured Jerusalem and defeated the crusaders.

1174 – Saladin becomes the undisputed ruler of Egypt.

1187 – Saladin captures the city of Jerusalem, which had been occupied by the Franks since 1099. He dies in 1193, having brought Egypt back into contact with other Muslim lands.

1249 – The king of France, St Louis, lands at Damietta during the Seventh Crusade and is imprisoned at El-Mansura, in the Delta; the sultan El-Salih is killed in combat. St Louis is forced to pay a huge ransom to free his army.

Mamelukes (1251-1517)

After their victories against the crusaders, the Turkish mercenaries assassinated El-Salih's successor and took control of the country. The regime of the Mameluke sultans can be divided into the Bahri or Turkish Mamelukes (1251-1381) and the Circassian Mamelukes (1382-1517). They established a strong, warrior-like administration in Egypt; its hierarchy was based on rivalries between the emirs, and its prosperity guaranteed by the trade of goods between the East and West. Their internal squabbles and the discovery of the Cape of Good Hope brought about their gradual decline in the face of the Ottoman threat.

1260 – The Mamelukes crush the Mongol army in Palestine, after the latter's victories in Iraq and Syria, and are consequently hailed as the saviours of Islam.

1291 – Capture of Acre, which signals the end of the Frankish Empire in Syria.

1453 – The capture of Constantinople by the sultan Mohammed II, known as "the Conquerer", marks the end of the Byzantine Empire; the Ottomans begin to advance towards the Near East.

Ottoman Egypt (1524-1767)

The powerful Ottoman Empire brought Egypt under its control in 1517, when the Turks defeated the Mamelukes in Cairo. The Caliphate was transferred to Istanbul, Egypt became an Ottoman province and the Mamelukes were integrated into the ruling elite. In the 17C and 18C, a series of setbacks in Europe and internal revolts sparked the decline of the Ottoman Empire. This was to have a negative effect on Egypt's cultural and political life, as well as its economy. The sultan's authority weakened largely as a result of his distance from Cairo and the negligence of many of the pashas, while political confusion allowed the Mamelukes to take advantage of the situation and regain power.

1524 – Suleiman the Magnificent, known in the East as Suleiman the Legislator, is appointed a pasha in Egypt; he adminsters the country but does not have Turkish troops at his disposal.

Mamelukes (1767-1805)

Once again, the Mamelukes became masters of Egypt. On this occasion, however, their reign was short-lived, and political intrigues and instability soon plunged Egypt into civil war.

1798 – On 21 July, Napoleon defeats the Mameluke troops at the Battle of the Pyramids. The French occuptation lasts until 1801. The Mamelukes are unable to take power again and, despite British support, surrender to a newcomer, Mohammed Ali, who finally establishes Egyptian national unity.

Napoleon at the foot of the pyramids on 21 July 1798.

Modern Egypt

Sadat (left) and Nasser (right).

Egypt's modern history has been particularly turbulent. Before becoming a free and powerful country respected by the West and other Arab powers alike, the country was part of the Ottoman Empire, came under the rule of the Mamelukes for a second time, and was briefly occupied by Napoleon's troops.

A Modern Pharaoh

In 1805, Mohammed Ali, a commander in the Ottoman army's Albanian division, imposed his authority on Cairo, later assassinating the Mameluke governors in his citadel in 1811. As viceroy and master of Egypt, he crushed the fundamentalist Wahhabis of Saudi Arabia, conquered the Sudan and founded Khartoum, subsequently emancipating the country from Turkish domination. Having imposed absolute power, he then garnered the support of France for the recognition of hereditary rights. The pasha devoted his energies to the modernisation of the country and the reform of its administration, as well as to the revitalisation of industry and agriculture, and improvements in public health. His successors, Mohammed Saïd Pasha and Ismail Pasha, opened up the country to European influences. However, as a result of debt the latter was eventually forced to hand over control of the country's finances to an Anglo-French condominium. The British navy took advantage of the ambitions for financial freedom promulgated by Colonel Orabi, the Minister for War, to land in Egypt in 1882.

British Rule

Once they had put an end to the condominium, the British took control of Egypt (France abandoned any claim to the country in March 1899 after its defeat at Fashoda). Under the despotism of Lord Cromer, the British developed agriculture but restricted industrialisation and learning, in so doing alienating the majority of Egyptians. Lord Kitchener promulgated a new constitution that was more favourable to the population, although this coincided with the outbreak of the First World War, during which the country became a British protectorate. When, in 1922, Fouad I exchanged his title of sultan for that of king of Egypt, the country obtained the independence demanded since 1918 by the Wafd, the nationalist party of Saad Zaghloul. However, London continued to manage the country's economy, perpetuating the contradictions existing inside Egypt.

Although in a weakened position, the Wafd was recalled to power in 1951 by King Farouk in order to remedy a catastrophic political situation mainly caused by the presence of British troops along the Suez Canal. However, the poorly led Wafd was to collapse, riots became commonplace, and the throne faltered.

The new Biblioteca Alexandrina.

Abu Simbel, saved from the waters of Lake Nasser by UNESCO.

Gamal Abdel Nasser

On 23 July 1952, the "free officer movement" overthrew King Farouk; his son, Fouad II, who was just six months old, ascended to the throne for a few short months. In 1953, a Revolutionary Command Council, comprising Nasser and Sadat, abolished the monarchy, proclaimed a republic and appointed General Naguib as president. In 1956, his prime minister, General Nasser, deposed him and became head of State. The immediate withdrawal of finance for the Aswan High Dam by the United States resulted in a split with the West, a situation symbolised by the nationalisation of the Suez Canal, which was to result in the infamous crisis *(see PORT-SAID)*. The popularity of Nasser, who became known as the Boss *(Raïs)*, was now at its height. He founded the only political party, the National Union, and in 1958, upon the initiative of Damascus, established the United Arab Republic (UAR), bringing together Egypt and Syria, with Cairo as its capital. In the same year, an agreement was signed in Moscow for the construction of the high dam. In 1961, following the promulgation of a land reform creating a maximum land ownership threshold of 40ha/100 acres, Nasser imposed his administrative and economic policies on Syria, which immediately withdrew from the alliance. By reorganising the State apparatus, nationalising its industry, and depossessing its ruling classes, the president radicalised his position internally and founded the Arab Socialist Union (ASU). Triumphantly re-elected in 1965 on the back of indisputable economic success, Nasser suffered a severe setback during the 1967 war against Israel, and although he resigned from power the same year, he was immediately recalled by the Egyptian people. His death on 28 September 1970 resulted in scenes of collective grief throughout the country.

Anwar el-Sadat

Vice-president under Nasser, Sadat would quickly strengthen the Muslim character of the regime, abandon the socialism of his predecessor, reconcile Egypt's differences with the West and expel Russian advisers from the country. The ASU was disbanded, and new parties came to the fore. Although the 1973 conflict with Israel did not result in victory, it gave confidence to the army and enabled the president to seek peace with Israel. In 1979, he signed the Camp David agreements allowing Egypt to recover its territories in the Sinai – accords that won Sadat the Nobel Peace Prize in 1978 and the rejection of his Arab partners. On the economic front, his liberalisation programme *(infitah)* launched in 1975 resulted in rampant inflation and violent riots. He was assassinated on 6 October 1981 by an Islamic commando. Although viewed as a scheming politician by his people, Sadat is nowadays seen as a visionary who ensured that Egypt avoided the fate that has befallen modern-day Syria.

Hosni Mubarak

Vice-president under Sadat, Mubarak was elected with 98% of the vote. He immediately confirmed the Camp David accords, promised greater democracy and attempted to forge closer links with fellow Arab states which had suspended Egypt's membership of the Arab League in 1978 *(see CAIRO)*. An admirer of Nasser and a loyal supporter of Sadat, the president obtained the total return of the Sinai, and developed an enviable reputation as a vital negotiator on the Palestinian question. Under his leadership, Egypt has gradually developed a production-based economy, and has succeeding in controlling the influence of conservative Islamists.

Traditions of Ancient Egypt

Our knowledge of the Egypt of the pharaohs is still in its infancy. Although the main events of the country's ancient history are well documented and widely studied, our analysis of Egyptian civilisation has raised more questions and enigmas than it has produced concrete facts. Indeed, our continuing fascination with Egypt is due largely to the mysterious nature of its myths, traditions which probably originated from the Ancient Egyptians' obsession with immortality.

The Pharaohs

Statue of Djoser.

The word pharaoh, which refers to the kings who ruled Ancient Egypt, sums up the grandeur of this marvellous civilisation. The Egyptian compound *per-aâ* translates as the "great house". In the Bible, this was literally transcribed into Hebrew as *par'oh*, from which came the Greek Φxpxw *(pharao)*, and hence the word pharaoh.

God and King

The phrase *per-aâ* was originally used to describe both the royal palace and the people who occupied it; around the time of the Armana period this meaning changed to signify the royal sovereign. However, it was not until the 22nd Dynasty that the word was commonly adopted as a title accompanying the name of the king of Egypt; it was Sheshonq I, the Shishak of the Bible, who was first addressed in this way. Although the general custom has been for modern historians to give this name to kings preceding Sheshonq, this is, in fact, erroneous.

The Pharaoh was considered by his subjects to be both god and king. This dual role was already discernible during the Old Kingdom, as the sovereign was at that time described as the "son of Ra", the sun-god. According to this theology, the god Amun-Ra came down to earth and took the form of the king in order to marry the queen and produce an heir to the throne who was divine in essence.

Religious and Temporal Power

The Pharaoh's primary role as the representative of the gods was to maintain order on earth, and therefore the unity of Egypt, in the name of the creative powers. For this reason, the divine nature of his birth – so often depicted in the reliefs and paintings adorning Egyptian tombs and temples – was reinforced by the almost magical force of the rites practised during his enthronement. Such rites hark back

to Ancient Egypt, when the sun was said to have given birth to the gods and created order in the world. The Pharaoh was responsible for this order and for ensuring that chaos did not break out on earth; this explains his theoretical authority over the priests who performed daily worship in the name of his supernatural power, considered essential for the survival of the universe.

The Pharaoh was often represented as a victorious warrior.

The sovereign exercised both religious and direct temporal power over the society he ruled. He controlled the resources necessary to maintain power and wielded absolute authority over his subjects in Egypt, as well as the entire population of the world, of which he was theoretically the ruler. He was the sole commander of the army and was also responsible for dispensing justice. The Pharaoh's total superiority required an iron rule, as the slightest weakness provoked thoughts of independence. Towards the end of the reign of Pepy II in the 6th Dynasty, for example, the authority of the Pharaoh had declined in society to the extent that the nomarchs were able to take the title of vizier and put an end to centralised power.

After his death "His Majesty" returned to Ra, thereby emphasising the celestial dimension of his earthly mission. Only he and his family went to heaven or "flew away", to use the expression adopted by the funerary rites. However, throughout his reign this living god remained a man whose mission consisted of safeguarding his society. This role was passed to the Pharaoh's heir upon his death.

A Symbol of Glory

The Pharaoh had many names and attributes. Primarily he was known as Horus, the falcon-god – who was the first king of Egypt according to theology – in order to ensure his reincarnation. He was also given the *Nebty* name, made up of the names of Wadjyt, the cobra goddess, and Nekhbet, the vulture-goddess, who represented the kingdom of the north (Lower Egypt) and the south (Upper Egypt) respectively. His birth name, preceded by the phrase "king of Upper and Lower Egypt" was also accompanied by the title "son of Ra", which can be seen in hieroglyphs on the cartouches of ancient monuments. The Pharaoh's throne name and birth name are usually the two names depicted in an oval frame or cartouche on ancient monuments; the cartouche was first used by Huni in the 4th Dynasty.

Visitors to ancient sites and museums will find it relatively easy to identify the Pharaoh as he is the most important of all those represented, and is always depicted as much larger than his subjects. He usually wears the crown of Lower or Upper Egypt (or both), while his headdress is often adorned with the *uræus*, or raised cobra, the incarnation of Wadjyt and symbol of his royal power. Occasionally he will be represented holding the royal regalia of the crook and flail. If these attributes are not enough to identify him, two details are reserved for Pharaoh alone in the many paintings or sculptures that can be admired in Egypt, namely the bull's tail which hangs from his loincloth, and the false beard worn only by gods.

The gold funerary mask of Tutankhamun.

The Pyramid of Khafra at Giza.

The Pyramids

The first dictionary definition of the word "pyramid" refers to the large monument used as a tomb for the Pharaohs of Egypt; the explanation of a polyhedron and its geometric conditions usually follows. It was, in fact, the Egyptians who created this geometric form, whose name was later to be adopted by analogy to define a polyhedron with triangular-shaped plane faces culminating in a common apex. However, even though the pyramids of Egypt have been accorded greater importance, just above the Mexican monuments of the same shape to which they have subsequently given the same name, nobody knows for certain the exact origin of the term.

A Perfect Shape

Whether stepped or totally smooth, the purpose of a pyramid was to enable the soul of the deceased to ascend to heaven. As such, with the embalmed body of the Pharaoh enclosed within its depths, it served purely as a funerary monument. This unique structure was part of a larger architectural complex comprising an upper and lower temple linked via a covered passageway; this complex corresponded to the various stages of the funereal ceremony reserved for royalty.

The earliest tombs were mastabas which, with their sloping sides and flat tops, resembled the mud-brick benches found outside Egyptian peasants' houses. In time the mastaba was replaced by the pyramid. The brilliant Imhotep, the vizier and architect to King Djoser, was the first person to build a true vertical pyramid over a royal sarcophagus. This decisive step forward in Egyptian history took place at Saqqara, where the Step Pyramid erected can be interpreted as a superposition of mastabas. However, the most accomplished expression of pyramid building can be seen on the Giza plateau, where the Great Pyramid of Khufu (Cheops), the only one of the Seven Wonders of the Ancient World to have survived the ravages of time, stands alongside the pyramids of Khafra (Chephren) and Menkaura (Mycerinus).

An Enduring Image

What was the pyramid supposed to signify? One theory is that it represented the convergence of the sun's rays descending upon the earth. Whatever its true mythological significance, and despite numerous fanciful interpretations, the underlying purpose of the pyramid was to protect the tomb of the Pharaoh within it and to elevate him to his eternal home.

The Great Pyramid of Khufu, the largest pyramid ever built, is an overwhelming sight. Confronted by a structure of such power and grandeur, it is natural to ask how the Egyptians were able to build such a tour de force, especially given the fact that they did not use the wheel. Given the lack of documents from the period, it is thought – and this is the most generally accepted explanation – that the Egyptians made use of mud-brick ramps to erect these seemingly eternal monuments.

In texts from Ancient Egypt, the pyramid is referred to by the term *mer*. Herodotus, the Father of History, employed the word *puramous*, the name of a cake made from wheat and honey with a similar shape. It is also probable that Greek mathematicians subsequently used this term when describing Egyptian funerary monuments. More recently, Maspero thought that the origin of the term was to be found in *pri-em-ous*, which Egyptian geometricians employed to define one of the sides of the pyramid. However, the exact provenance of this quasi-magical word will probably remain unknown.

The Step Pyramid of Djoser at Saqqara.

The Long Line of Pyramids on the Nile

Egypt's 87 pyramids are scattered along the left bank of the Nile, in the north of the country, in an area extending 160km/100mi, from Giza (to the west of Cairo) to El-Lâhun (to the south-east of El Faiyûm). Despite their differing dimensions, materials and, in some instances, overall shape, they all follow a precise, astrologically calculated orientation. Having made their first appearance at the end of the 3rd Dynasty under the Old Kingdom, this type of construction continued to be built until the 12th Dynasty, during the Middle Kingdom period. The last great pyramid was that of Amenemhat III, located at Hawara. However, even though several smaller structures of the same type continued to be built beyond this time, the pyramid was to subsequently disappear, to be replaced by the large walled tombs favoured during the New Kingdom.

The Great Sphinx stands guard over the Pyramid of Khafra.

Mummies

Although the Egyptians appear to have been obsessed with death, it was precisely because they were so impassioned with life that they wanted to ensure their existence in the next life. It is also because the myth of Osiris (the god of the dead) dictated that it was only possible to come back to life if the body was well preserved after death. Consequently, a

An anthropoid sarcophagus has the same shape as the body it contains.

quite extraordinary funerary rite, known as mummification, was developed. Nobody could remain indifferent to the desire to preserve existence beyond life in order to ease the perilous journey to the unknown. The mummies thus created have survived several millennia and various civilisations, enabling us to develop a clearer understanding of the beliefs held by the descendants of Ra.

Laid to Rest Amid Gold and Stone

Within the pyramid or mastaba, the mummy was laid to rest in a sarcophagus or wooden coffin. Coffins and sarcophagi were decorated, and became anthropoid during the New Kingdom. During the latter period, it was also the practice to enclose coffins one inside the other before placing them in a rectangular granite or basalt sarcophagus. Although the majority of sarcophagi were made of stone, some were cast with several kilos of gold. The sarcophagus or coffin was the true resting place of the dead, attested to by the fact that it was given the name *nebankh*, meaning "lord of life"; its religious purpose was to provide a "house" for the deceased and ensure their well-being in the afterlife.

The Concept of Eternal Life

The tombs were fitted out with everything necessary to sustain life on the final journey. This included furniture, the presence of servants in the form of *shabti*, the food necessary for day-to-day life, and the representation of feasts – at which the entombed could participate – on the walls. However, in order to enjoy these benefits, it was vital that the body remained intact; it was therefore necessary for it to be mummified. Once the body was embalmed, the mummy had to undergo the Opening of the Mouth ceremony, a ritual which restored life to the deceased. Only then could the soul re-enter the body and access the eternity granted it by Osiris.

Under the Sands of Egypt

It is thought that the idea of mummification came to the Egyptians after they noticed that a body dried naturally when buried in the desert, as the hot sand absorbed the body's humidity. Given their belief in the hereafter, little more incentive was required to encourage the Egyptians to mummify their dead, in so doing improving upon the work of nature. Tombs were often damp and the risk of decomposition threatened the intact state of the body. Consequently, mummification presented itself as an obvious solution. The process required the use of an artificial technique, on the one hand to dehydrate the body, and on the other to envelop it. It was from the Thinite Period onwards, coinciding with the 1st and 2nd Dynasties, that the first known attempts were realised.

The Jackal-god

The process was so jealously guarded that no complete description exists today of the technique employed by the *hery seshta* (embalmers) under the high protection of Anubis, the jackal-god to whom the paternity of mummification is attributed. However, a wealth of information is provided by the mummies themselves. Three types of mummification were used, the most developed and expensive technique lasting 70 days.

After death the body was taken to a tent known as the "Place of Purification". First of all, the brain was extracted through the nostrils using a hook, and the cranial cavity was cleaned with palm wine before being filled with a sterilising liquid resin. Through an incision on the left side, the incision-maker would then slice through the diaphragm, removing all the internal organs with the exception of the heart, and fill the abdomen with bags of incense, gum, spices (myrrh, cinnamon) and natron (sodium carbonate). This desiccating agent was then used to cover the entire body before it was sewn up. Thirty-five days later, with the dehydration process complete, the natron was removed. During the course of the following 30 days, the body was bandaged up, while prayers were recited and amulets and embalming spells were placed between the linen wrappings held together by liquid resin. The final act saw the mummy placed in a sarcophagus, at which point the funeral ceremony could begin.

A Mine of Information

Modern science allows mummies to be analysed without the risk of damaging them. A single sample of tissue or skin removed almost surgically is able to provide a wealth of information. In particular, it is possible to determine the age of a Pharaoh at the time of death, the relationship between royal mummies, as well as details such as the living conditions of the Egyptians, their illnesses, and the operations performed at the time. We know, for example, that the Egyptians suffered from rheumatism, arthritis and arteriosclerosis, that they were familiar with dental fillings (using a mineral cement) and trephination, and that pharaohs were not systematically circumcised. Hopefully the future will bring with it further revelations, and may explain the astonishing presence of tobacco and cocaine in certain mummies. Will this perhaps be the key enabling historians to establish a maritime link between the Old and New Worlds?

It appears that the Egyptians were not the first to practise the science of mummification. The first people to mummify their dead lived on the coast of Chile, in South America, some 7 000 years ago.

This artificial method of preservation would seem to have been introduced by the Chinchoro Indians, albeit using different techniques.

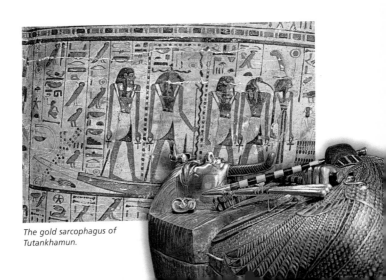

The gold sarcophagus of Tutankhamun.

Anubis.

Gods

What is particularly striking upon arrival in Egypt is the number of tombs and temples, both divine and funerary. This profusion is the physical reflection of a civilisation marked by a religion which lasted for almost 3 500 years. Although many aspects of this religion remain unclear, it continues to appeal to our imagination and intrigue our curiosity. Of prime importance among Ancient Egypt's rich religious tapestry, the subject of gods remains one of its most characteristic features, given that practically no texts exist to explain the theology of this magnificent civilisation.

The Creation of the World

According to the Ancient Egyptians, the world was created by Nun, the god who personified the "primordial waters" inhabited by chaos. This creative power enabled light to pour forth from the waters, thus creating order in the world, pushing Nun to the edges of the universe and begetting the early gods. In Heliopolis, where the clergy initiated the solar character of the Egyptian monarchy, the story of this creation told that Atum, the son of Nun, gave birth to nine gods. This ennead included Shu and Tefnut, Geb and Nut, who gave birth to the sun, as well as Isis and Osiris, who have left us a legend of major importance in the history of Egyptian mythology.

The Power of Worship

The belief in this creation of the world sustained the entire political organisation of Egyptian religion. Religion was deeply embedded in both society and politics and permeated all aspects of life. As initial order was not guaranteed, it was essential to ensure that the balance of society was maintained through the worship of a founding god in order to keep chaos at bay. Each sunrise symbolised the rebirth of the world, and the gods, whose representative was Pharaoh, had to be appeased in order to maintain the harmony of the universe. This was the role of worship. This is why the god's mission on earth had to be affirmed in the temples each day, and why great care involving washing, dressing and perfuming was taken of the god's statue every day. It is why offerings were made to the statue every morning and why the statue was purified every evening with incense and the sprinkling of holy water. It also explains the importance of festivals and rituals in keeping alive the legends which were the basis of Heliopolitan mythology.

The Hierarchy of the Clergy

The servants of god, who were obliged to follow very strict rules of ascetism, either inherited their role or were nominated by the Pharaoh. The priests (or "divine fathers" as they were known) worked in the temples; their main mission was to perpetuate the established order. They alone were authorised to see the image of the god, which they visited each morning in order to wake him after a night of inactivity. The priestly organisation was divided into the upper and lower clergy. The first group included the "prophets" *(hem netjer)*, who interpreted the oracle of

A procession of gods accompanies the deceased on his journey to eternal life.

the god; the second consisted of the priests responsible for maintaining the instruments of the cult: the "lector priests" who recited the hymns and the "hour priests" who determined the time of the ceremonies. A number of women served as priestesses to the goddess Hathor, and there was also occasionally a *hemet netjer*, the female equivalent of the prophet title. Musicians, singers and other women priestesses took part in processions.

A Diverse Polytheism

The gods of Ancient Egypt can be counted in their hundreds. They include creator gods, local gods and protective genies, in addition to numerous gods organised into a confused hierarchy marked by myriad differences. Some of these took human form, while others were represented by animals or plants, albeit still in an anthropomorphic manner. The name or appearance of a god could vary from one sanctuary to another. In addition, the cosmogony evolved over the years depending on the theological model in force at the time. There were, however, a series of "primary" gods along the entire stretch of the Nile Valley, who can be fairly easily identified on tombs and temples situated close to the banks of the river. The following four pages will help visitors to identify these main gods.

The Ordinary People

The general population did not have access to the theological subtleties of the religion practised in the temples. In addition to the major places of worship, there were local sanctuaries dedicated to secondary gods or to derivative forms of the principal gods. Ordinary people visited the temples, left offerings and prayed in their houses, but also adopted more superstitious practices often linked to magic. Amulets protected them from illness, incantations attracted love, cures guaranteed a good harvest and magic spells kept the evil eye away. Gradually, small gods and genies grew in number, in time removing the ordinary people from the unicity of state pantheism. As a result, by the time Theodosius closed the temples of the Nile Valley in AD 384, Egyptian religion had dissolved into idolatry and demonism.

The goddess Hathor protected many temples, which were often decorated with Hathor-headed capitals.

Identifying
the Egyptian gods

Amun

A god who appears in many different forms, Amun is usually represented as a human figure wearing a loincloth and double-plumed crown. He is also often depicted with a ram's head.

Anubis

One of the most important funerary gods, Anubis guarded the necropolises from the wild dogs that roamed around them, hence his portrayal as a man with a dog's head, usually black in colour. His human body is represented either standing or lying down.

Aten

Easily identified, this deity is represented by the sun, usually as a disc radiating sun rays. These rays end in hands which transmit vital energy.

Bastet

Originally represented as a lioness – and therefore much feared – this goddess was gradually tamed to become a smiling cat, an animal much admired by the Egyptians. She is often shown holding a sistrum, a musical instrument dedicated to Hathor.

Bes

The deformed, grotesque features of this god leave no room for doubt; Bes is immediately recognisable. The grimaces of this bearded dwarf-god with his protruding tongue provoked laughter, which had the effect of frightening away evil spirits.

Chou (Shu)

This man with raised arms supports the sky-goddess Nut. Portrayed either kneeling or standing, he is also often represented with a lion's head or wearing a headdress in the form of a plume.

Hathor

Often confused with Isis, Hathor is depicted in several forms. The goddess is symbolised by a cow and is distinguished by the first of her attributes, maternity. She is often portrayed with a solar disc between her horns and sometimes as a woman with cow's ears.

Horus

This name is used for a number of gods, so complex is Egyptian mythology. The best known is the falcon-headed god, Horus, the god of the sky (the other well-known Horus is the son of Isis and Osiris). His eyes represent the sun and the moon.

Isis

Undeniably the most popular of the Egyptian gods, this goddess can be recognised by the throne which she carries on her head (the hieroglyphic sign for her name is a throne). From the New Kingdom onwards, she was depicted wearing a solar disc between cow horns, similar to Hathor.

Khepri

Depicted with a scarab in place of his head, or in the form of a scarab, this god was identified with the sun god Ra. Priests took the verb *kheper*, which means "to come into existence", for his name and chose the scarab *(kheprer)* as his symbol.

Khnum

God of fertility and fecundity, Khnum is portrayed with the head of a ram, an animal often associated with water cults. In Aswan, where he was worshipped, a live ram was used to represent this "lord of the cataract".

Khons

There are two mummiform images of this god. In the first, the god is represented as a hawk-headed figure with a moon headdress; in the second as a youth with a headdress of a full moon and a crescent moon. In the second representation, youth is symbolised by a lock of hair.

Maat

The ostrich feather which decorates her headdress makes this goddess, the daughter of Ra, easy to recognise. The feather is used both as a hieroglyph and as an instrument to write the name of this attractive, but formidable young goddess.

Min

Although depicted as a mummy, this fertility god is represented with an erect phallus (the term ithyphallic is used to describe this image) and as a result is easily recognised. Like Amun, he wears a double-plumed headdress.

Montu

This fearsome god of war is, like Horus, represented with a falcon's head. However, while the sky-god wears the *pschent* headdress bearing the crowns of Upper and Lower Egypt, Montu's headdress is crowned with a solar disc and two feathers.

Mut

The vulture hieroglyph depicted this goddess. She is represented either as a vulture, or as a female figure with a vulture headdress crowned with the *pschent*. The goddess was also sometimes represented in other forms, depending on her role.

Neith

This goddess has the most complex imagery in terms of her iconography, which often changes according to her role and the region. However, she is usually shown wearing a close-fitting garment and the crown of Lower Egypt; her symbols are a shield and two arrows.

Nekhbet

The emblem of this goddess is the vulture, like Mut. Nekhbet is often depicted on bas-reliefs in the form of a vulture, with wings outstretched above the Pharaoh. Unlike Mut, she wears only one crown, that of Upper Egypt.

Nephthys

A stylised mansion under a bowl crowns the headdress of this goddess often depicted in tombs with her sister, Isis. This unusual image corresponds to the hieroglyphs for her name.

Nut

A naked woman arched over the earth is the most striking image of Nut, the sky-goddess. Her feet stand to the east, and her hands are to the west, both touching the earth. Her body, studded with stars, symbolises the vault of the sky.

Osiris

This well-known legendary god is recognised by his *atef* crown, which is topped by a small solar disc and flanked by two ostrich feathers. Osiris is usually depicted as a mummy, his hands protruding through the bandaging to hold a flail and sceptre.

Ouadjit (Wadjyt)

A rearing cobra, associated with the red crown of the pharaoh, represents this goddess of Lower Egypt, who was also occasionally portrayed as a lion. Known as an uræus, this cobra may be shown alone or as part of a crown.

Ptah

This mummiform god has a shaven head or wears a tight-fitting skull-cap. Only his hands protrude from his wrappings to hold a staff that combines the *was* sceptre (of the gods) and the *djed* pillar (of archaic origin).

Ra (Re)

The most important god of all, Ra absorbs the other gods to the point of being almost polymorphous. He is the source of all creation and is always associated with the solar disc, as the sun is omnipresent.

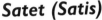

Satet (Satis)

The wife of the god Khnum wears the white crown of Upper Egypt with antelope horns on either side of it. Like her husband, she is a water-deity, the guardian of the source of the Nile who reigned from above the first cataract.

Sekhmet

One of the lioness-goddesses of the Egyptian pantheon. "She who is powerful" was much feared throughout the kingdom.This female figure with a lioness's head was originally the goddess who protected regions where the rivers were frequented by lions.

Serket

"The one who causes the throat to breathe" was believed to give protection against venomous bites, and is often portrayed with a scorpion on her head. The protector of the dead, she is also referred to as Selkis and Selket.

Seth

Considered to be the force of evil because of his murderous role in the Osiris legend. This god of Upper Egypt is usually depicted as a mysterious animal, with a long nose and straight, tall ears.

Sobek

God of the water who makes the land fertile, Sobek is represented by a crocodile, a male figure with a crocodile's head, or a man wearing a crocodile skin. Although crocodiles are no longer found in the Nile north of Aswan, this was not always the case.

Thoth

This god is depicted in the form of two animals. He is sometimes portrayed as a baboon, usually shown seated next to a scribe, and sometimes as a male figure with the head of an ibis.

Thoeris (Taweret)

This benevolent goddess was associated with protection, despite her rather disturbing appearance. She is represented by a hippopotamus with a swollen belly and lion paws and is often a rather heavy figure (the adjective "heavy" was symbolised by a hippopotamus hieroglyph).

Hieroglyphs

The term "hieroglyphic writing" is used to denote the "sacred writing" of the Ancient Egyptians. In more practical terms, hieroglyphs are the characters used in one of the forms of writing of Ancient Egypt, although by extension, the term is often employed to refer to any form of writing that uses ideograms. Since the end of the 17C, the word hieroglyph, in the figurative sense of the term, has also come to refer to a form of writing that is impossible to decipher. Yet, thanks to the French Egyptologist, Jean-François Champollion, who succeeded in solving the mystery of the Rosetta Stone, the enigma which surrounded hieroglyphs has been removed and they have become one of the vital keys to Egyptology.

Hieroglyphs were used to relate the history and myths of Ancient Egypt.

A Sense of Aesthetics

A visit to the monuments of Ancient Egypt quickly reveals the extent to which hieroglyphic writing is profoundly aesthetic. Engraved on the walls of temples, on columns and on obelisks, these perfectly sculpted signs are harmoniously set out

A fragment of the Rosetta Stone.

both horizontally and vertically according to the artistic whim of the lapidary (engraver), who would have arranged them according to the form of architecture and to avoid any ungainly empty spaces. A visit to an Ancient Egyptian tomb will reveal walls covered in hieroglyphs, while museums displaying archaeological exhibits will undoubtedly display steles and statuary bearing their unmistakable form. These ornamental inscriptions are everywhere, for the simple reason that from the palette of King Narmer to the island of Philae, in other words from the oldest to the most recent hieroglyph, a period of some 3 000 years elapsed.

A World Dominated by Stone

Ancient Egypt used three types of writing: hieratic (using cursive signs written from right to left, in columns and then in lines); demotic (even more cursive in nature, and also written from right to left and in linear form); and hieroglyphic. Only the latter was used throughout Egyptian Antiquity, practically without any variation except when analysed from a graphic viewpoint. The use of hieroglyphs was reserved for inscriptions on stone, mainly incised in the stone, either in relief or hollowed out, although on occasion they were produced in painted form. Depending on the period and the aesthetic effect required, their appearance varied between stylised, realist and archaistic, and could be further embellished by inlaid molten glass.

The Path to Extinction

With the closure of temples in the 4C AD, the three types of Egyptian script died out, to be replaced by Greek characters. In fact, it was the Greeks themselves who gave their name to the oldest type of Egyptian writing, which they called *hieroglyphika grammata*. Moreover, from the 3C BC onwards, hieroglyphs were practically no longer used; as a result nobody was able to understand them and they became unintelligible.

Champollion and the Renaissance

In 1822, basing his research on work by the Englishman, Thomas Young, and the Swede, Johan David Åkerblad, the French Egyptologist Champollion succeeded in deciphering a block of basalt discovered at Rosetta (in the Nile Delta) in 1799 bearing three types of script: Greek, demotic and hieroglyphic. He was thus able to establish that hieroglyphs were just as much ideographic as they were phonetic, and embarked upon the compilation of a dictionary which, because of his death, was sadly never completed.

General Pictorial Principles

Each sign represented an object, which was drawn by a scribe or lapidary. This was a simple exercise when the object was a concrete one, for example a scarab or the sun, as it is today when all we have to do is click on the printer icon on our computer screen in order to print a document. However, the principle became somewhat more complicated when attempting to depict something more abstract, such as love or the verb "to give birth". Without entering into a complex analysis of the hieroglyphic system (which would require a work on its own) it can safely be said that the system made use of both homophony and rebuses. In these instances the sign is no longer used for its direct meaning, but for the sound it represents; a sound could also be symbolised by several signs. As an example, a hoe, which is pronounced *"mer"*, could on the one hand be used simply to describe a hoe, or on the other to refer to the homophonic term *mer*, meaning love. In other words, it was the particular situation that dictated usage. Moreover, a graphic rebus could be interpreted as an abstraction. To express the verb "to give birth", a drawing may have shown a kneeling woman with the head of a child below. If the rebus is homophonic, signs corresponding to the sounds that make up the chosen term are used; by combining these phonograms it is possible to form an expression or a sentence. Having said this, we have, in fact, lost the true pronunciation of Egyptian words.

The Development of Egyptology

Egyptology is a relatively young science. Before the middle of the 19C, when the term was first coined, Egypt was observed and described rather than studied. With the Egyptologists an era of investigation and analysis was born, inspiring a new generation of specialists to leave for Egypt with all the enthusiasm of

A bust of Champollion at the French Institute of Oriental Archaeology, Cairo.

medieval knights searching for the Holy Grail. A century and a half later, the enthusiasm of these experts remains unchanged.

Early Inroads

Before the end of the 18C, European knowledge of Egypt came from a few scant Ancient texts. The first scholar to describe this distant country was the Greek historian Herodotus (5C BC), the "father of history", who published fascinating and occasionally exaggerated descriptions of the country *(Histories)*. He was followed by Diodorus Siculus (1C BC) *(Bibliotheca Historica)*, and soon after by Strabo, who visited the banks of the Nile and whose descriptions are of fundamental importance to our understanding of the country *(Geography)*. Sadly, just a few segments remain of the history of Egypt *(Aegyptiaca)* compiled by the Egyptian priest Manetho (3C BC), who divided the sovereigns of Egypt into dynasties and who Hellenised their names. Ancient Egypt also proved to be of major interest to Arab scholars during the Middle Ages.

True Beginnings

Although the German Jesuit Athanasius Kircher made an attempt to decipher hieroglyphs in the 17C, it was not until Napoleon's military expedition to Egypt in 1798 that the science of Egyptology was born. Napoleon took with him an entourage of some 150 scholars and artists, including Dominique Vivant-Denon, the future founder of the Louvre Museum. These experts embarked upon an extensive project compiling information on the flora, fauna and history of Egypt, the results of which were published between 1809 and 1828 under the title *Description de l'Égypte*. The 20 volumes of this work were the direct result of the aims of Napoleon, who had since become emperor, and were strongly influenced by the encyclopaedists of the previous century. The work was one of the first to introduce the world to the historical and geographical richness of the country, which Napoleon was battling to free from Ottoman domination. Although Napoleon's expedition was curtailed by the British, these French scholars were allowed to continue their work until 1802.

The Rise of Egyptomania

In 1822, Jean-François Champollion's success in deciphering hieroglyphs encouraged historians of all backgrounds to show an interest in the hitherto unknown Egyptian civilisation. Legions of scholars, often insufficently equipped, flooded into Cairo and to the banks of the Nile, eager for new discoveries and revelations, bringing in their wake the first tourists, who were attracted by the exoticism of Egypt, so rich in history. The country also had an impact on artistic style in Europe: the "Egyptian style" was evident in the Empire and Regency styles in Paris and London respectively. In Britain, the artist Thomas Hope moved away from the use of picturesque Hellenistic styles to create a feeling of Antiquity, and instead designed divans in the shape of crocodiles and sofas in the shape of sphinxes! Soon, Orientalist artists would seize upon this success and create unusual paintings in the Romantic style.

Europe's growing fascination with Egypt was largely due to the untiring work of pioneers such as Mariette, Maspero, Petrie and Borchardt, who promoted the study of the new science of Egyptology with energy and enthusiasm.

Of Treasures and Men

Egyptology proper could be said to have begun with the Prussian Lepsius who visited a number of sites as far south as the Sudan between 1842 and 1845. From this moment on, the systematic and analytical search for material enabled a greater understanding of the history of Ancient Egypt. It was thanks to Petrie that the objectives of archaeology in Egypt were established on a firm foundation, although it was around the same time that a number of European diplomats pillaged the larger sites, either for personal gain or on behalf of their governments. Egyptology gradually recovered from these excesses, partly as a result of the extraordinary discoveries which raised public awareness of Egypt's rich heritage, but also as a result of the many salvage operations which took place during the 20C. Other lesser-known treasures also played their part; had it not been for the study of history, religion, texts and language, as well as the use of innovative conservation techniques, this science would have introduced the world to magnificent objects without allowing us to understand them.

An Egyptian Miracle

From the first digs led by Mariette to the saving of Aswan under the aegis of UNESCO in 1968 and the recent salvaging of fragments of colossuses from the waters off Alexandria, methodical and enthusiastic archaeologists have excavated, analysed and then reconstructed a huge number of splendid monuments and artefacts whose existence could barely have been imagined as recently as two centuries ago. This "renaissance" is also the result of years of diligent work by unknown specialists: behind these spectacular discoveries lies the patience of archaeologists and restorers without whom the riches of ancient Egyptian art would have remained hidden for ever. Each statue, artefact and temple visited in Egypt today has benefited from the enthusiasm of these anonymous experts.

The Temple of Philæ,
by David Roberts (1839).

The Great Explorers

The heroes of *The Mystery of the Large Pyramid* by Edgar P Jacobs and Steven Spielberg's Indiana Jones have given archaeologists a glamorous image. Although exaggerated, it is true that those who venture into the unknown in search of awe-inspiring ancient monuments require an adventurous spirit and perhaps a dose of carefree recklessness. In the past, the "curse of the pharaohs" was evoked to explain the sudden deaths of a number of archaeologists, helping to create a stereotypical image of the great explorers who revealed to the world monuments and sites that had in theory been consigned to eternal silence. Nonetheless, the boundless curiosity demonstrated by these explorers of the unknown is worthy of our utmost admiration.

Giovanni Battista Belzoni (1778-1823)

Born in Padua, the son of a Roman barber, Belzoni was first and foremost an adventurer. Nonetheless, he produced a number of beautiful life drawings and was responsible for various archaeological discoveries, including the tomb of Sety I in Luxor, the opening of the pyramid of Khafra (Chephren) in Giza, and the temple at Abu Simbel. In 1816, while he was working for the British Consul General in Cairo, he offered his employer a huge statue of Rames II, which was immediately sent to London.

Auguste Mariette (1821-81)

An employee of the Egyptian Antiquity Department at the Louvre Museum, Mariette became perhaps the greatest of the leading Egyptologists. Sent to Cairo in 1850 to purchase some Coptic manuscripts, he became interested in Egyptology while walking in Saqqara, where he discovered the Serapeum the following year. He was involved in numerous archaeological digs right up to his death and founded two major institutions: the Egyptian Antiquities Service in 1859, and the Bulaq Museum in 1863, which formed the nucleus of the Egyptian Museum in Cairo. "Mariette Pasha" started the archaeological digs at Saqqara, Tanis, Abydos, Giza and Luxor, excavated the temples of Edfu and Dendera, and discovered the famous statues of Khafra, Sheikh El-Beled and the seated Scribe.

The statue of Mariette in Boulogne-sur-Mer.

Gaston Maspero (1846-1916)

In 1880, a year before the death of Mariette, this archaeology professor came to Cairo and took over from his distinguished colleague as the Head of the Egyptian Antiquities Service. He is remembered particularly for two discoveries: the inscriptions in the pyramids of the 5th and 6th Dynasties, and the royal mummies of Deir el-Bahri (including that of Rameses II). He founded what was to become the present-day French Institute of Oriental Archaeology (IFAO) and explored the temples in Nubia. He was also responsible for the excavation of the Sphinx at Giza and the temple at Luxor, and devoted much of his time and energy to restoration work.

William Matthew Flinders Petrie (1853-1942)

The founder of the Egyptian Research Account, which became the British School of Archaeology in 1906, Petrie arrived in Egypt at the same time as his colleague Maspero. A key figure in the world of scientific Egyptology, Petrie introduced statistical methods and was responsible for excavating a large number of sites, includ-

Howard Carter, Lord Carnarvon and his daughter, Lady Evelyn Herbert, discovering the treasure of Tutankhamun.

ing Tanis, El Fayum, Tell el-Amarna, Luxor, Memphis, Heliopolis, Nagada and Medum. His experience and precision were the basis of archeaological techniques which, although perhaps not spectacular, were based on tried and tested principles which have gained widespread acceptance and are still used today. Petrie was also responsible for the notions of typology and stratigraphy.

Ludwig Borchardt (1863-1938)

This German Egyptologist first set foot in Egypt in 1895 and founded the German Institute of Archaeology in Cairo in 1907. An architecture specialist, he led a number of digs, the most famous of which was the workshop of the sculptor Thutmose in Tell el-Amarna. There he discovered one of the most famous and most beautiful busts in the history of art, that of Queen Nefertiti, which is now on display in the Egyptian Museum in Berlin.

Howard Carter (1874-1939)

Carter's discovery of the tomb of Tutankhamun in 1922 has given him a prominent place in the history of Egyptology. Born in London, he worked as a draughtsman at Beni Hasan and Deir el-Bahri before becoming Inspector of Monuments for Upper Egypt in 1899, then Inspector of Antiquities of Lower Egypt in 1903. Four years later, he was appointed by Lord Carnarvon to copy the paintings in the Valley of the Kings. Evidence that he came across by chance led him to the discovery of the most sensational of all the tombs opened in Egypt. Shortly after the tomb was opened Lord Carnarvon died, soon followed by Georges Bénédite and Arthur Mace, who were also present at the opening of the tomb. There was much talk at the time of the "curse of Tutankhamun"; we now know that it can be dangerous for those in poor health to enter too quickly a tomb which has been sealed for a long time, because of the build-up of bacteria and mould.

Ahmed Fakhry (1905-73)

Born in the Fayum, Fakhry is one of the great Egyptian Egyptologists, along with Selim Hassan, Kamal el-Malakh and, more recently, Ali Radwan. Having studied in Cairo, Berlin, Brussels (with the Belgian archaeologist Jean Capart) and Liverpool, Fakhry made his name on a number of excavation projects in the oasis of the Libyan desert, as well as at Giza. He remains best known for his work on the rhomboid pyramid of Dahshur between 1951 and 1955, where he excavated the reliefs of the temple of the valley.

Jean-Yves Empereur (1952)

Empereur, the Director of Research at the Centre National de la Recherche Scientifique and founder of the Alexandria Study Centre, has recently been in the news as a result of his discovery of colossal remains in the Bay of Alexandria. Underwater excavations are now part of modern archaeology and Empereur's project hopes to rebuild one of the seven wonders of the Ancient World, the recently discovered Pharos of Alexandria (pharos = lighthouse).

ABC of Architecture

Main Types of Columns

A column consists of a vertical shaft (comprising either a circular section or a polygon of more than four sides) with a base and capital.

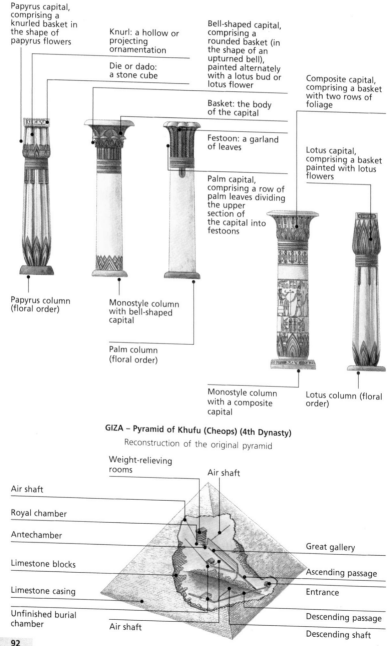

Papyrus capital, comprising a knurled basket in the shape of papyrus flowers

Knurl: a hollow or projecting ornamentation

Die or dado: a stone cube

Bell-shaped capital, comprising a rounded basket (in the shape of an upturned bell), painted alternately with a lotus bud or lotus flower

Composite capital, comprising a basket with two rows of foliage

Basket: the body of the capital

Festoon: a garland of leaves

Lotus capital, comprising a basket painted with lotus flowers

Palm capital, comprising a row of palm leaves dividing the upper section of the capital into festoons

Papyrus column (floral order)

Monostyle column with bell-shaped capital

Palm column (floral order)

Monostyle column with a composite capital

Lotus column (floral order)

GIZA – Pyramid of Khufu (Cheops) (4th Dynasty)

Reconstruction of the original pyramid

Weight-relieving rooms

Air shaft

Air shaft

Royal chamber

Antechamber

Limestone blocks

Limestone casing

Unfinished burial chamber

Air shaft

Great gallery

Ascending passage

Entrance

Descending passage

Descending shaft

DEIR EL-BAHARI – Temple of Mentuhotep II (11th Dynasty)
Reconstruction

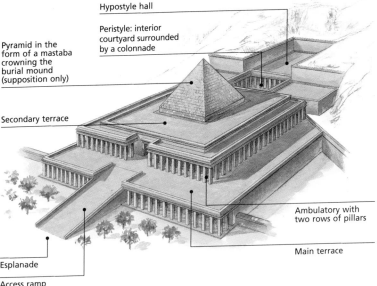

Hypostyle hall

Peristyle: interior courtyard surrounded by a colonnade

Pyramid in the form of a mastaba crowning the burial mound (supposition only)

Secondary terrace

Ambulatory with two rows of pillars

Main terrace

Esplanade

Access ramp

LUXOR – Great Temple (18th and 19th Dynasties)
Reconstruction of the temple entrance

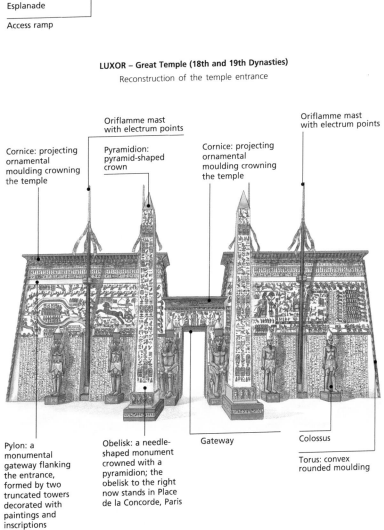

Oriflamme mast with electrum points

Oriflamme mast with electrum points

Cornice: projecting ornamental moulding crowning the temple

Pyramidion: pyramid-shaped crown

Cornice: projecting ornamental moulding crowning the temple

Pylon: a monumental gateway flanking the entrance, formed by two truncated towers decorated with paintings and inscriptions

Obelisk: a needle-shaped monument crowned with a pyramidion; the obelisk to the right now stands in Place de la Concorde, Paris

Gateway

Colossus

Torus: convex rounded moulding

ABU SIMBEL – Temple of Rameses II (19th Dynasty)
Reconstruction of the façade

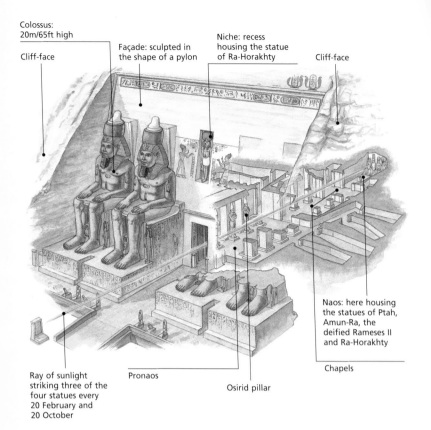

Colossus:
20m/65ft high

Cliff-face

Façade: sculpted in
the shape of a pylon

Niche: recess
housing the statue
of Ra-Horakhty

Cliff-face

Naos: here housing
the statues of Ptah,
Amun-Ra, the
deified Rameses II
and Ra-Horakhty

Chapels

Ray of sunlight
striking three of the
four statues every
20 February and
20 October

Pronaos

Osirid pillar

Valley of the Kings – Tomb of Sety I (19th Dynasty)

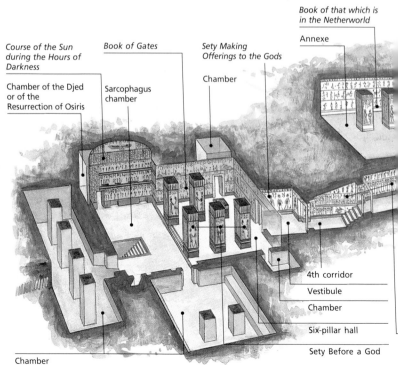

*Book of that which is
in the Netherworld*

Annexe

*Course of the Sun
during the Hours of
Darkness*

Book of Gates

*Sety Making
Offerings to the Gods*

Chamber

Chamber of the Djed
or of the
Resurrection of Osiris

Sarcophagus
chamber

4th corridor

Vestibule

Chamber

Six-pillar hall

Sety Before a God

Chamber

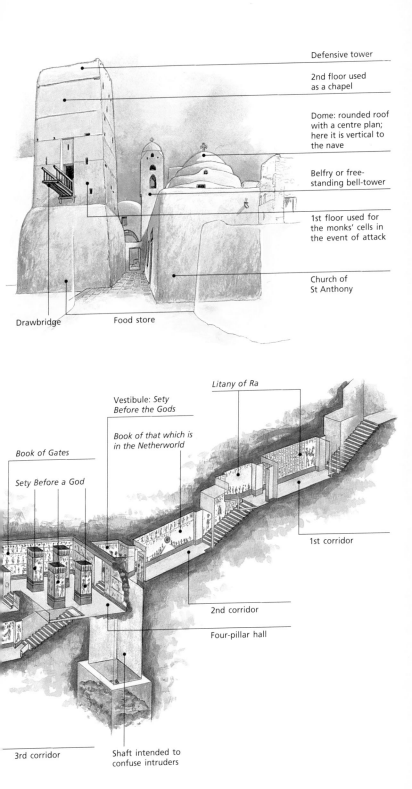

ARABIAN DESERT – Monastery of St Anthony (6-12C)

Defensive tower

2nd floor used as a chapel

Dome: rounded roof with a centre plan; here it is vertical to the nave

Belfry or free-standing bell-tower

1st floor used for the monks' cells in the event of attack

Church of St Anthony

Drawbridge

Food store

Litany of Ra

Vestibule: *Sety Before the Gods*

Book of that which is in the Netherworld

Book of Gates

Sety Before a God

1st corridor

2nd corridor

Four-pillar hall

3rd corridor

Shaft intended to confuse intruders

Book of the Opening of the Mouth

CAIRO – Al-Azhar Mosque (14-18C)

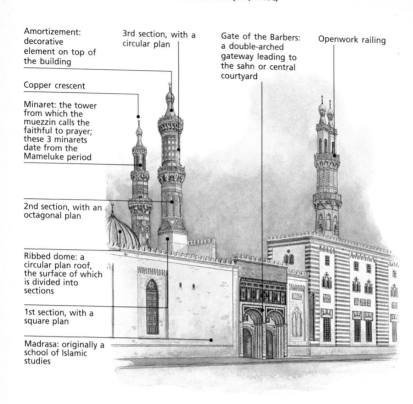

Amortizement: decorative element on top of the building

3rd section, with a circular plan

Gate of the Barbers: a double-arched gateway leading to the sahn or central courtyard

Openwork railing

Copper crescent

Minaret: the tower from which the muezzin calls the faithful to prayer; these 3 minarets date from the Mameluke period

2nd section, with an octagonal plan

Ribbed dome: a circular plan roof, the surface of which is divided into sections

1st section, with a square plan

Madrasa: originally a school of Islamic studies

ALEXANDRIA – Fort Qaitbey (late 15C)

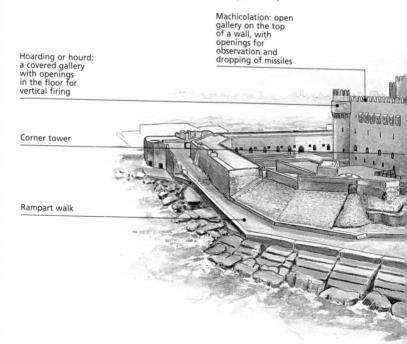

Machicolation: open gallery on the top of a wall, with openings for observation and dropping of missiles

Hoarding or hourd: a covered gallery with openings in the floor for vertical firing

Corner tower

Rampart walk

CAIRO – Mosque of Mohammed Ali (mid-19C)

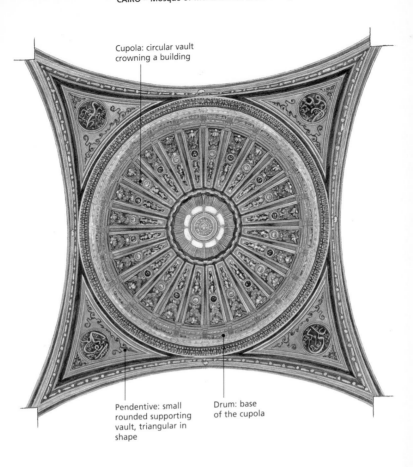

Cupola: circular vault crowning a building

Pendentive: small rounded supporting vault, triangular in shape

Drum: base of the cupola

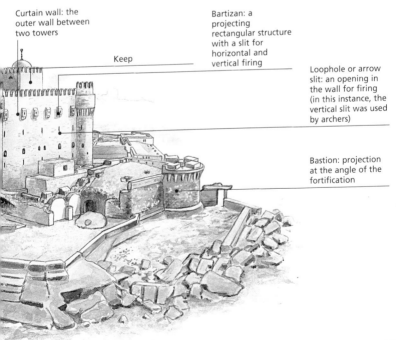

Curtain wall: the outer wall between two towers

Keep

Bartizan: a projecting rectangular structure with a slit for horizontal and vertical firing

Loophole or arrow slit: an opening in the wall for firing (in this instance, the vertical slit was used by archers)

Bastion: projection at the angle of the fortification

Egyptian Art

Egyptian art is particularly striking for its coherence of style. For over 3 000 years the Egyptian civilisation adhered to the same aesthetic ideals and dedication to a timeless art. Far from following the precepts of "art for art's sake", Egyptian art is the result of a strong belief in a cosmic order, and, as such, speaks to us in a universal language.

A fishing scene, a familiar sight in private tombs.

Pepy I.

Thinite Period

The first examples of Egyptian art can be traced back to around 3 000 BC, a period which also saw the first use of hieroglyphs. The conventions of Egyptian art were gradually laid down in the three centuries of the Archaic period, during which the creation of elaborate tombs formed the basis of funerary architecture, and the first masterpieces of royal sculpture were carved. Even votive figurines sculpted at this time bear witness to the nascent development of a studied naturalism.

Old Kingdom

During this period, which lasted for 500 years, Egyptian art quickly reached its zenith in all fields, developing the finer points of its formal style. Most of the art of this period, with very few exceptions, was funerary art. The Old Kingdom is considered to be the Golden Age of Egyptian Art and the artistic reference for subsequent generations.

Architecture

Royal tombs were buried in mounds during Protodynastic times and then in mastaba tombs during the Thinite period. The first example of a pyramid dates back to the reign of Imhotep (3rd Dynasty). The pyramid attained unparalleled proportions from the 4th Dynasty onwards, although its basic structure and purpose remained unchanged – the funerary complex acted as a link between the world of the living and that of the dead and was dependent on rituals reserved for the Pharaoh. A typical layout consisted of a port linked to the Nile, and a valley temple, from which an ascending causeway led to a cult temple built in front of the east side of the pyramid. The funerary complex proper contained a small pyramid, the queens' pyramids, pits housing the royal barks, and tombs of important functionaries.

The cross-legged scribe, a common theme in private funerary art.

The wall of Djoser's funerary complex in Saqqara.

The religious and private buildings of the time have not survived; new temples were subsequently constructed over the original buildings and the houses failed to withstand the test of time. Pyramids were usually built on isolated, new land; stone was used for the Pharaoh's pyramid, whereas mastabas for other individuals were built of mud brick, a distinction which was to remain unchanged for centuries. During this period, architectural decoration saw the development of an early type of column, either grooved or decorated with plants, but the most important new features to emerge were the cornice, the gargoyle and the kheker frieze.

Sculpture

The 3rd Dynasty also marked the beginning of a new era in sculpture. The archaic style of earlier works disappeared and the canons for the portrayal of human figures became fixed, initially in the remarkable royal statuary of the period, and later in the representation of individuals.

One single principle dominated royal sculpture – the representation of the role of the individual rather than the individual themself. Only when this principle had been abided by would the artist then turn his attention to personal features that would distinguish a king from his predecessors. Artistic conventions governed the king's pose, royal attributes and the type of material used, and served to convey his divine nature. Seven poses have been recorded, of which the two most common depict the king either seated on his throne or standing, with his left foot thrust forward. The attributes used to identify the king are also strictly codified: his headdress could be a crown, a nemes headcloth or, more unusually, a wig, which was always crowned by the uræus (royal cobra); he could be portrayed dressed in either a knee-length robe or a three-panelled loincloth, and could wear a false beard and carry royal emblems, such as the crook and the flail.

Private sculptures were not bound by these codes and are therefore more realistic, even showing a certain naturalism from the 4th Dynasty onwards. Like the royal sculptures, these are frontal portraits, but they differ in their focus on the physical features of the deceased, who may be represented in a number of different poses.

Reliefs and Paintings

The increasing use of stone in architecture favoured the development of low-relief sculpture, the conventions of which were determined at the time of the Narmer Palette (Protodynastic period): the shoulders and eye were depicted frontally, whereas the face and legs were shown in profile; the same decorative processes were used for both reliefs and paintings. The most common depicted the king in the upper register, larger in size than other figures shown, either alone or opposite the gods; the lower register consisted of the repetition of a number of identical figures. Gradually, as the decorated area grew in size, compositions of groups appeared. However, not a single scene of this period relates the story of a precise historical event, and on the whole the narrative is limited to rituals relating to the king's jubilee and conversations with the gods.

Private reliefs depicted funerary cults but could also portray scenes from everyday life, with gifted sculptors producing very detailed tableaux. Furthermore, mastabas were adorned with rich decoration which was full of life, and which led to the creation of the "coloured mosaic" technique.

Middle Kingdom

The realism of the Old Kingdom was abandoned during the decadence of the First Intermediate Period, an era characterised by the disappearance of royal art. This period of crisis was subsequently followed by the Middle Kingdom, during which royal art reappeared, although for a time this echoed the "provincial" trends of the Intermediate Period. During the 12th Dynasty a new lease of life for royal art revived the classical styles that had previously disappeared.

Architecture

The Middle Kingdom did not have the necessary wealth to build monuments to rival the stature of the pyramids at Giza. An unusual mortuary temple in Deir el-Bahri copies the pyramid style, but differs from the traditional pyramid in its addition of terraces, as well as a broad

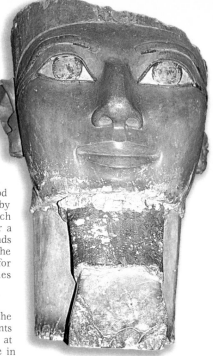

Queen Hatshepsut.

open-air avenue. The kings of the following dynasty built pyramids and iathor on two of its sides, was fully developed during the following period. In private architecture, the nobility of the period began to hollow out cave tombs for themselves.

Sculpture, Reliefs and Paintings

The sculpture of the period is characterised by its powerful, schematic style, which moves away from the detail of the Old Kingdom. During the reign of the Senusret pharaohs the quality of art improved in both sculpture in the round and reliefs, with artists surpassing Old Kingdom works in their realism and attention to detail. The tombs of this period are also decorated with paintings of a previously unattained quality and bear witness to a profound attachment to colour and freedom.

New Kingdom

The Second Intermediate Period halted the evolution of art for almost two centuries. However, this period is followed by almost five centuries of artistic development during which art rediscovered its former splendour and experienced a period of flourishing creative activity.

Architecture

During the New Kingdom, the pyramid was replaced by the hypogeum. Kings and queens were buried in private tombs, and from Thutmose I to the Ramesside rulers, these tombs were cut in the rock of the Valley of the Kings. The temple of Hatshepsut, built against the cliff face at Deir el-Bahari, adopts the same principle of openness initiated by Mentuhotep II. The kings of this period built prolifically at Karnak, Thebes (Luxor) and in the Nile Valley, erecting

Osirid statue of Senusret I.

obelisks, avenues of sphinx, and the first pylons ever built. Sadly, the buildings constructed by Amenhotep IV are barely known, as little has survived of his new town, Akhetaten. However, we do know that he built on a large scale, a tendency later adopted by the Rameses, who created the typical temple structure comprising a pylon, a courtyard, hypostyle halls and a naos flanked by chapels. Their taste for the colossal can also be seen in their underground temples, the most impressive of which is undoubtedly the Great Temple of Rameses II carved into the rock at Abu Simbel.

Sculpture

Prior to the artistic development initiated under Hatshepsut during the 18th Dynasty, the tendency in sculpture was to copy the art of previous dynasties. During the reign of Hatshepsut's successor, Thutmose III, artists achieved technical perfection and remarkable aesthetic synthesis, producing a coherent classical style which was to survive until the reign of Amenhotep III. This idealism gradually faded and royal sculpture moved away from the traditional timeless canons to portraits in which individual anatomical features are represented. The Amarnian revolution of Amenhotep IV pushed this artistic style to its climax. Suddenly sculptures became exaggerated in style, almost to the extent of being caricatures of their subject. This unusual and unique "expressionist" style, which was used for both royal and private sculpture, was perhaps the most splendid in the 3 000 years of Ancient Egyptian art, but came to an abrupt end. Despite the counter-reformation which followed, the artistic style of Amenhotep IV's reign had a strong influence on the works of Tutankhamun. Academicism reasserted itself during the reign of Sety I, but hints of the expressionist style show how the art of the Rameses benefited from this liberation of form. The New Kingdom period drew to a close with the inventive spirit and profusion of works produced during the reign of the Rameses pharaohs.

Reliefs and Paintings

The artistic development that took place in sculpture can also be seen on the walls of tombs and temples, albeit in a more complex form. Initially, the human figure was depicted according to the classical canons favoured by the first kings of the 18th Dynasty. Soon, however, artists began to paint more lively scenes, freeing themselves from the rigidity of composition which had been dominant until that time; the majority of the Theban tombs bear witness to this golden age of art. Under Amenhotep III, this style developed to create a painted narrative which gradually evolved into a subjective style that found its full expression under Amenhotep IV. By now, art had been liberated from the constraints of tradition; paintings of this period often represent simple everyday scenes in which the subjects are shown pursuing ordinary activities such as fishing or eating. However, despite this movement away from traditional rules, artists never completely freed themselves from what has been called their "aspective" vision of things – where the spectator is forced to stand at right angles to the painting being viewed – and this rigid structure was to remain in place until the Greek period.

Following this important evolutionary period, low reliefs and painting would remain influenced indefinitely by a taste for movement and nature. This was in turn adopted by the Baroque style of the Rameses pharaohs, although work produced during their reigns would never equal the pictorial apotheosis of Amenhotep III and Amenhotep IV.

The Amarnian art of Akhenaten.

Ptolemaic reliefs at Kom Ombo.

Late Period

After a return to sobriety during the Third Intermediate Period, the Late Period saw the appearance of unusual artistic trends introduced mainly by non-Egyptian kings. This period of diversity can be divided into sub-periods, ranging from the Saite period to the Persian occupations; however, with the odd exception it can be said that the decline of Egyptian art had already set in. It was to last for almost 1 000 years.

Architecture

The Kushite kings of the 25th Dynasty built mainly between the third and fourth cataracts. Their temples were inspired by those in Thebes and contain elegant bell-shaped columns, known as "Taharqo columns", which demonstrate how this dynasty was successful in assimilating Egyptian styles. Sadly, little of architectural significance remains from the period of the Saite kings, as the monuments which they erected in the Delta, much admired by Herodotus, have been destroyed. Subsequently, the reputation of Nectanebo I was established by his construction of a number of large monolithic chapels in this region. Persian activity on Egyptian soil decreased at this time; only one temple was built under Darius, in the Kharga oasis.

Sculpture, Reliefs and Paintings

The term Late Period carries with it a pejorative note that cannot be applied to the skilled work of the sculptors of this period. Although Late Period art shows a certain reserve not present in New Kingdom works, it does demonstrate a high level of technical skill, benefiting from the use of bronze as a medium for statuary, following the cire perdue or lost wax technique. Eclecticism dominated: in royal sculpture the classical style, mixed with a hint of African exoticism, can be seen, while in contrast a blunt realism is evident in private sculpture. This is followed by a period of academicism, revived by Psamtek I, and subsequently refined by a hitherto unseen polished quality and the so-called "Saite" smile, later transferred to Greek art by the 30th Dynasty, the last that can really be described as Egyptian. This style is essentially neo-Classical, as demonstrated by the Avenue of Sphinxes at the temple of Luxor.

Greco-Roman Period

Statues were carved from Greek marble in Alexandria...

Alexander the Great was the catalyst for the final decline of Egyptian art. Hellenistic influence was felt as far as the Nile, although Egyptian traditions continued to be respected until the Roman period, resulting in a mix of artistic styles.

Architecture

The Ramesside temple plan was codified by the Ptolemies for reasons of ritual: a huge pylon opened onto a porticoed courtyard, with a hypostyle hall with composite columns closed by a screen-wall leading into a succession of rooms towards the naos, which was still surrounded by chapels. Although the Egyptian spirit survived in this grandiose design, the outer walls were decorated with hieroglyphs explaining the ceremonies which took place in the sanctuary. By this period there was almost no mention of the divine nature of the Pharaoh. The Ptolemies were prolific builders and were responsible for works at Philae, Kom Ombo, Dendera, Esna and Edfu. The Romans also built temples dedicated to local gods in Nubia and completed already existing structures, such as the magnificent Kiosk of Trajan at Philae.

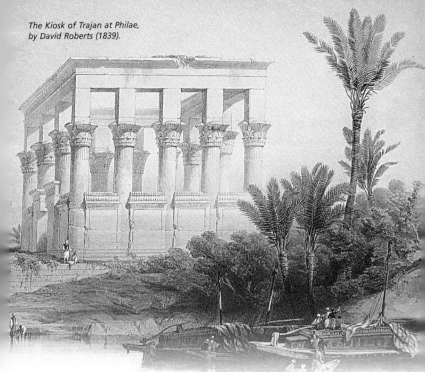

The Kiosk of Trajan at Philae, by David Roberts (1839).

Sculpture

Egyptian art survived most strongly in sculpture, rivalling new artistic ideas emanating from Greece, and resulting in the coexistence of Ptolemaic (Egyptian) and Alexandrian (Hellenistic) art. The Ptolemaic style was one of compromise: the body was frontal, hieratic and therefore typically Egyptian, whereas the face was Greek. The Alexandrian style produced statues associated with the new cults, modelled in transparent folds, as well as an enormous quantity of statuettes in erotic poses. The Romanisation of works was not particularly successful; although a Latin influence can be detected in the treatment of hair, for example, and Egyptian techniques survived through the treatment of hard stone, little innovative work was produced.

Reliefs and Paintings

...while granite was still the medium of choice in Aswan.

Low-relief sculpture did not respond well to the mixed artistic style which developed in architecture and sculpture. This can be explained by the fact that Egyptian artists, who demonstrated an unsurpassed creativity of form over a period of 3 000 years, were unable to assimilate the fundamental changes introduced by the Greeks. In the tomb of Petosiris at Tuna el-Gebel, Egyptian art appeared to be able to withstand the Greek style, but this period coincided with the pre-Alexander era. Subsequently, Ptolemaic art saw the domination of Greek processes, such as the portrayal of musculature and the modelling of the surface to accentuate the effects of light and dark, thus completely engulfing Egyptian philosophy and invention.

It was in painting that new methods were most visible. Funerary art was based mainly on the notion that it was necessary for the body to be preserved in its entirety in order for the deceased to attain eternal life. Funerary masks, of which the gold mask of Tutankhamun is the most famous example, had changed little over the centuries. This ritual was now the subject of a new artistic trend which adapted the sculpted mask to create painted portraits, such as those seen in the Fayum. In this way the Egyptian tradition contributed to the art that was developing along the Mediterranean coast and in the Near East; this art form would finally come of age in the religious icons of the Byzantine age.

A Lexicon of Egyptology

Akh – One of the three spiritual elements of man (along with the ba and the ka) inherent to the celestial kingdom and therefore of a supernatural nature. After death, the deceased rejoined his akh, which was then successfully reunited with his ba and ka and considered to be unchanging for eternity. The akh was represented by a crested ibis.

Amulets – These small decorative objects were believed to protect both the living and the dead. Made from semi-precious stones (rarely gold), or more commonly from faience or glass paste, the most common types of amulet included the djed pillar, the heart, the wedjat-eye and hieroglyphic signs. The most popular form was the scarab.

Ankh Cross – This ideogram was believed to transmit the life force. The gods are often depicted holding the ankh cross in their hand or offering it to the Pharaoh. The cross was subsequently adopted by the Coptic Church and referred to as the crux ansata. Nowadays it is the most popular piece of jewellery sold as a souvenir in Egypt.

Ba – Another of the spiritual elements of man, roughly corresponding to our conception of the human soul. The ba, represented by a bird which from the 18th Dynasty onwards had a human head, lived on after death.

Canopic Jar – A vase containing the viscera of a mummy, the lid of which bore a representation of one of the four sons of Horus: a man's head (Imsety) for the liver; a dog's head (Duamutef) for the stomach; a hawk's head (Qebehsenuef) for the intestines; and a baboon's head (Hapy) for the lungs.

The Pharaoh Sneferu, depicted under his cartouche.

Cartouche – An elliptical outline containing the name of the Pharaoh (usually the last two names), which symbolised the universality of his reign.

Colossus – A large royal statue, the size of which demonstrated the divinity of the Pharaoh.

Crowns – There were five types of crown: the white crown of Upper Egypt (hedjet); the red crown of Lower Egypt (deshret); the double crown of Upper and Lower Egypt (skhemty or pschent); the crown of Amun; and the atef crown with a papyrus plume on either side. The blue helmet known as the khepresh can also be considered a royal crown, but the nemes (a piece of cloth worn over the hair and falling over the shoulders) is a headdress.

Djed – A symbol in the form of a pillar which eventually became the attribute of Osiris.

Hypogeum – A tomb cut in the rock. Particularly popular during the New Kingdom, when it was eventually adopted as the traditional tomb for kings and queens of that period, replacing the pyramids and mastabas used by earlier eras.

The ankh cross, the hieroglyph for which signifies "life".

Hypostyle – This adjective is used to describe halls whose ceilings are supported by columns. Large temples usually had three hypostyle halls.

Ka – A spiritual element with no equivalent in modern culture and therefore almost impossible to translate. The ka can be thought of as the lifeforce which was believed to accompany the individual from birth to death and which enabled survival in the afterlife. This is, however, only one aspect of this complex element.

Lotus – There are three species of Nile water lily. The blue lotus (Nymphæe cœrulea) is most frequently represented in the art of Ancient Egypt, while the white lotus (Nymphæe lotus) is less common and can be identified by its more rounded petal.

Mammisi – This word was used by Champollion to describe the small buildings which stood in front of the temple pylons. This type of building was used to celebrate the birth of the divine child and was only constructed during the Late Period.

Mastaba – This rectangular structure, comprising a burial chamber accessible via a burial shaft and surmounted by a serdab and a chapel, was the most common type of tomb in the Memphis region. Mastabas grouped together formed a necropolis arranged around the pyramids.

Naos – In Egypt, the naos is the shrine in the temple housing the statue of the god. The term is also used more generally to refer to the inner and central sections of the temple.

Necropolis – A vast underground or open-air cemetery, often situated to the west of the site (the Amenti believed by the Egyptians to be inhabited by the dead). Necropoli were built on the edge of the desert to avoid flooding by the Nile.

Nome – A word of Greek origin describing an administrative region in Ancient Egypt known as a sepat. In total, there were 38 nomes during the Old Kingdom and 42 when the country was subsequently divided into Upper and Lower Egypt.

Nomarch – The head of a nome exercised enormous administrative, military and religious power and as a result represented a real threat to a weak Pharaoh (the nomarch of Thebes founded the 11th Dynasty). The position became hereditary during the 5th Dynasty.

Ostracon – A shard of pottery or fragment of rock on which the Egyptians noted accounts or jottings. The use of an ostracon was cheaper than papyrus, which was expensive and difficult to find.

Palette – A stone object initially used to grind make-up. Palettes later acquired votive characteristics and were decorated with carvings to commemorate major events. The term is also used to refer to a scribe's palette.

Papyrus – This aquatic plant once grew profusely in Egypt, especially in the Delta. Its bark was used to make articles such as loincloths, sails, ropes, sandals and even rafts, but it is best known for its transformation into a paper-like writing material. The State had a monopoly on the production of this material, which was replaced in the Middle Ages by parchment.

The Pharaoh Awibra Hor, represented below his ka (two raised arms).

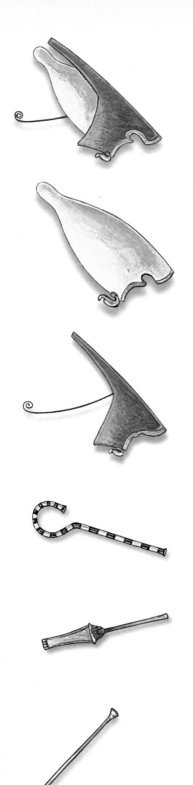

Sacred Lake – A number of temples had a large pool, usually rectangular in shape, within the temple precinct. This lake symbolised the primordial waters which gave birth to the god Ra and was directly linked to the Nile or to ground water, and so never dried out. Priests performed their ritual cleansing in the lake.

Scarab – This beetle symbolised "being" and "becoming". Used as an amulet, it was placed on the mummy's chest to defend the soul of the deceased before the court of Osiris and was even worn by the living, who hoped to receive the breath of life that it symbolised.

Sceptres – The Egyptians had several different insignia for royalty. These included the "fly whisk" or flail (nekhakha); the was sceptre, a long cane crowned with the head of a greyhound; the crook (heka); and the wadj sceptre, a long cane in the form of a papyrus-shaped column. The sekhem sceptre was used by individuals as a mark of authority.

Scribe – The scribe was responsible for writing official documents and was required to follow a protracted apprenticeship. He was more than a mere draughtsman and was highly respected for his intellectual status. On occasion he was even called upon to act as ambassador or vizier.

Serapeum – The name given to the temples of Serapis during the Ptolemaic period.

Serdab – The serdab was a small room in the mastaba housing one or several funerary statues. It was connected to the chapel by a narrow slit enabling incense smoke to reach the statues.

Shabti – This word is used to describe the statuettes which accompanied the deceased in order to carry out menial corvée labour in the afterlife. In the Middle Kingdom, the deceased was provided with a single shabti, although the number of figurines had increased by the New Kingdom, when the quantity and quality of shabtis served to demonstrate the wealth of the deceased.

From bottom to top: the nekhakha flail; the aba and heka crooks; the red crown of Lower Egypt; the white crown of Upper Egypt; the double crown of Upper and Lower Egypt; and the atef crown.

*Painting in the tomb of
Queen Nefertari.*

Sphinx – The statue of the sphinx defended the entrance to temples and places of worship. This mythical beast with the head of a man and the body of a lion is known by its Greek name; the Egyptians referred to it as shesep ankh, meaning "living statue". The oldest, largest and best known is the Great Sphinx of Giza. During the New Kingdom avenues of sphinxes were built in front of temple entrances.

Stele – A monolithic monument bearing inscriptions or carved decorations. The most common are the funerary steles, but others in the form of false doors can also be found at the entrance to mastaba tombs.

Vizier – After the Pharaoh, the vizier held the most important post in the State. According to an ancient formula he was "chief of all the king's works, the eyes and ears of the king". His string of other titles included "royal chancellor of Lower Egypt".

Wedjat – The eye of the falcon-god Horus is represented by a painted eye depicted above a falcon's head and was used as a symbol of good health. It is often found painted in tombs and is a popular form of amulet.

Terms not included in this lexicon may be found under Elements of Architecture or Traditions of Ancient Egypt.

A papyrus copy of "Ducks in Marshland", a painting from the palace in Tell el-Amarna.

Coptic Art

Coptic art appeared during the last years of the Pharaonic era. This artistic style flourished predominantly before the birth of Islamic art in Egypt, and remained distinctive from both earlier and later styles. It developed during the Early Christian period, at a time when Egypt was dominated by a heterogenous paganism still influenced by Pharaonic beliefs, and took its inspiration directly from the Greco-Roman art present along the banks of the Nile. The style developed initially in this region, among both pagans and early Christian communities, and later, from the 6C, exclusively among the latter. Its importance gradually declined after the Arab conquest.

The White Monastery (Deir el-Abiad) at Sohag.

7C fresco.

Architecture

In the first few centuries of the Christian era, Coptic monks and anchorites established monasteries and hermitages in remote areas, often moving into pharaonic monuments and transforming them into churches or hermit cells. These buildings were frequently destroyed by Bedouin tribes and have been modified and rebuilt over the centuries, so that those still standing rarely retain their original structure. However, it is often possible to make out their Christian architecture which, with its geometric exterior, rounded angles and domes, blends harmoniously with the surrounding desert environment. The earliest examples of this architecture to have survived were usually triple-aisled basilicas with a trefoil apse, preceded by a narthex and adorned with Hellenistic capitals. Although the Arab invasion brought about restrictions and slowed down the development of Coptic architecture, the Coptic community continued to build churches and monasteries until the 12C.

The Monastery of St Bishuy (Deir Amba Bishuy) in Wadi Natrun.

Painting

It seems likely that the Fayum portraits – pagan works of art with a strong Hellenistic style – had a profound influence on the development of Coptic frescoes and icons, which were created using similar techniques.

Coptic monasteries, pillaged and destroyed on countless occasions over the centuries, have retained few of these frescoes. Those that do remain, none of which date from before the 5C, demonstrate a marked Byzantine influence, especially in their iconology, although their composition and treatment bears witness to a much more flowing style. From the time of the Arab invasion, frescoes were decorated with ornamental motifs, while still retaining their distinctive Coptic style. Frescoes from this period reveal large uniform areas of colour, with no gradation, and are defined by simple lines.

Coptic painting concentrated almost entirely on portraiture, producing a large number of icons: religious paintings on wood panels. Bearing the same characteristics as Coptic frescoes, these works of art are marked by the expression of a firmly held faith. Byzantine influence can be detected in the hieratic postures of the subjects, although the simply painted, very spiritual faces with their large, staring eyes show striking similarities with the Fayum portraits. Most of the icons to have survived either date from before the 8C or after the 17C. The lack of artistic works from the intervening period can be explained by negligence as much as deliberate destruction: icons were often damaged by candle soot or by the faithful writing messages directly on the icon itself, as was often the custom.

Sculpture

The Copts considered statues to be a form of idolatry and as a result destroyed large numbers of pharaonic works. Although they produced some clumsily carved statues of their own, most of their sculpture was of capitals and friezes following the Hellenistic model, as well as low reliefs and palaeo-Christian steles engraved with praying figures and *crux ansata* (hieroglyphs representing life). The execution of these works is crude, as Coptic art was primarily concerned with ideas and not with achieving perfect artistic proportions. The highly decorative and generally geometric reliefs are softened by the addition of natural floral and stylised animal ornamentation.

Textiles

The full genius of Coptic art is perhaps best revealed in its famous textile work. The originality of the Coptic style was to weave its motifs onto the textiles, a technique not employed during pharaonic times, when motifs were either embroidered or painted directly onto the material.

The geometric patterns and floral designs visible in the sculpted decoration of churches can also be seen on these textiles, the oldest of which date from the 4C, as well as in pagan subjects which bear witness to continuing Hellenistic influence. As was the case with painting, the illusion of relief was initially represented by hachures (shading); this technique was gradually abandoned and was eventually replaced by the use of flat surfaces. From the 5C onwards, Christian subjects and motifs were used against a backdrop of scenes inherited from pagan mythology. The textiles used could either be single-colour (black, violet or purple) or multi-coloured (a maximum of 12 colours).

Coptic art continued to flourish after the Arab invasion, although more complex motifs, such as interlaces, were adopted. Coptic textiles continued to demonstrate originality up to the 12C and remained relatively unaffected by the monotony of the Umayyad naturalistic motifs or the highly decorative Fatimid style. This fact can perhaps be explained by the emphasis of Coptic art on the importance of ideas rather than form.

The Monastery of St Catherine, shown at the foot of Mt Sinai.

Islamic Art

More than anywhere else in the Islamic world, Cairo possesses a superb and unique range of Islamic architecture. This is largely due to the fact that each family that ruled over Egypt left its distinctive mark on the mosques and palaces of the city, with the result that the history of Islamic art can be divided roughly into as many periods as there were dynasties. Elaborate and detailed Islamic art is above all the expression of a community life whose rules are laid down by the Koran. Rejecting any representation of God and the prophets, this learned art developed an incomparable decorative stylisation, creating magnificent buildings which evoked the presence of the Creator.

Al-Azhar Mosque in Cairo, founded by the Fatimids; the minarets date from the Mameluke period.

Tulunids (868-905)

The Umayyad dynasty, based in Damascus, was succeeded by the Abbasid dynasty, who made Baghdad their capital. A Turkish officer, Ahmed Ibn Tulun, was authorised by the Caliphate to invade Egypt, where he founded the Tulunid dynasty and established a royal city on the site of present-day Cairo. Only one mosque, named after Ahmed Ibn Tulun and designed by a Copt, remains from this period. This architectural jewel bears witness to a national autonomy with growing ambitions.

Fatimids (969-1171)

The Fatimid dynasty founded the city of Cairo and brought about true Egyptian independence. This dynasty demonstrated a real love of luxury, perhaps as a result of increasing competition with its rival Baghdad. Textiles and ceramics dating from this period are richly decorated and convey an accomplished technical mastery. Sumptuous earthenware pieces of all shapes and sizes are adorned with mainly floral motifs, although geometric and human designs are also represented.

A number of Fatimid mosques can still be seen in Cairo. These are classical in form, with a central courtyard surrounded by arcades and a portico facing the direction of Mecca. The sculptures and carvings in these mosques are magnificent works of art, in which finely carved geometric motifs are set against an architectural framework inspired by Persian models, with a large dome built over an octagonal drum. The overall construction makes splendid use of the diversity of architectural lines, creating a dazzling mosaic of overlapping diamonds, squares and stars.

However, the iconographic repertoire is not limited to the decorative use of stone. Fatimid Egypt has also left fine examples of wood carvings, once used to adorn the Caliph's palace, many of which can now be admired in the Museum of Islamic Art in Cairo. These carvings not only make full use of interlacing, foliage and polygons, but also present a fascinating array of representational scenes. In these lively images artists have created a series of evocative tableaux depicting a range of everyday activities, such as hunting, fishing, dance and music, in which both human figures and animals are represented in a refreshingly natural style.

A mashrabiya screened balcony.

Ayyubids (1171-1250)

The Ayyubid dynasty was founded by Saladin, who imposed the Sunni doctrine on Egypt. This period saw the introduction of new architectural forms and the construction of Syrian-style monuments, such as the mausoleum or *khanqah*, the monastery-mosque. These buildings were decorated with finely carved geometric figures, always presented in a symmetrical fashion; however, despite the abundance and quality of the decor, there was a move away from luxurious art under the Ayyubids. Syrian influence was apparent in the copperwork of the time: a number of Damascene pieces bear witness to the technical ability of the craftsmen, who hammered designs of gold or silver thread onto the metal surface of their artistic creations.

Mamelukes (1251-1517)

The Mamelukes presided over what was undoubtedly the richest artistic period in medieval Egypt. They brought great wealth to the city of Cairo, which soon became an important centre of intellectual and artistic activity. The many splendid monuments built at this time include madrasas (religious colleges), mausoleums, caravanserais, *khanqahs*, mosques, hospices, monasteries and public fountains. In Cairo, minarets soared and high quality materials were used in the construction of religious buildings; impressive domes and portals were built, façades were adorned with stone stalactites, and interiors were lavishly decorated. The 14C and 15C were the golden years of Islamic architecture in Cairo. Mosaics, carved wood, festooned Gothic arches, earthenware tiles and polychrome marble decor all give the impression of a spontaneous outpouring of artistic creation, whereas in fact the opposite was true. These works were composed according to precise techniques which created perfect harmony between the massive size of the building and the exquisite delicacy of its decor.

The late 15C and early 16C saw a gradual downturn in artistic virtuosity. Skilled work was still produced, and even attained a high level of technical ability, but a certain mannerism can also be detected in the decoration of the period, marking the end of Mameluke artistic originality.

A final architectural feature to make its appearance prior to the Ottoman period of Egyptian history was the mashrabiya. These elegant screened balconies, which enabled women to look out of the building without being seen, were added to many of the private residences built under the Mameluke sultans, especially in the cities of Cairo and Rashid. Their delicately carved Lattia-work can still be admired in several districts of both cities today.

Alexandria,
The Mediterranean Coast
and the Delta

Alexandria★★

Alexandria's history is indelibly linked with that of its founder, Alexander the Great. During Antiquity the city became known for its art and philosophical thinking, and succeeded Athens in terms of influence around the Mediterranean; sadly, this splendour was not to last. However, after a decline spanning over a thousand years it was to regain its former glory under Mohammed Ali in the 19C. Today, the country's second largest city has also developed into the most popular resort in Lower Egypt.

Location
225km/140mi NW of Cairo, to the NW of the Delta, on the northern shore of Lake Maryut. Access: by plane from Cairo on Egyptair; by car along the desert road; on bus services operated by Superjet and West Delta (E£20/E£30; journey time: 2hr 30min), by direct train (E£18; 3 departures daily; journey time: 2hr 30min); or by collective taxi (E£10). Ferry services no longer operate to Alexandria from Europe.

ALEXANDRIA(S)
Towns named after Alexander during his Asian conquests include one in the Caucasus, another in Western Pakistan and one in Mesopotamia. An Alexandropolis exists in Parthia (nowadays Iran), while Sogdiana (modern-day Uzbekistan) has a city by the name of Alexandresketa.

Name
The city was founded by Alexander the Great (356-323 BC), who built around 70 towns and cities during his lifetime.

Transcription: الإسكندرية

Famous People
Following his posting to the British Embassy in Cairo, the English poet and novelist Lawrence George Durrell (1912-90) spent three years in Alexandria from 1957-60, during which time he wrote the four famous novels that became known as *The Alexandria Quartet*.

History
Alexandria succeeded Memphis as the capital of Egypt from the reign of Ptolemy I onwards. Rome would subsequently strip the city of this title.

background

The city of Alexander – By 331 BC, Alexander III, or Alexander the Great, the king of Macedonia, had developed plans to build a city on the site of *Rê-Qedet*, a stronghold built under the pharaohs as a defence against pirates and frequented by Phoenician mariners. Following the oracle's

Alexandria's Corniche is the perfect place for a stroll or a quiet read.

official recognition of Alexander as the son of Amun at Siwa *(see SIWA)*, the latter founded the city of Alexandria, which he would never see; he died at Babylon in 323 BC.

A Greek plan – The plans for the city are attributed to Deinocrates of Rhodes, whose design incorporated a grid system of streets cut by two main axes, 30m/100ft wide, running east-west and north-south. This huge project was started under Alexander, but was only completed during the reign of Ptolemy II. Two ports were created as part of the plan: one to the east, the other to the west, separated by a causeway 1 239m/4 064ft long, known as a Heptastadion (or "seven stades"), each 177m/580ft in length.

A period of expansion – Ptolemy came to the throne following the death of Alexander. The city developed during his reign, a process continued under Ptolemy II, who oversaw further expansion, resulting in the city's becoming the largest port in the Mediterranean and the world's most important trading centre. Alexandria became the channel for the export of Egypt's riches, in so doing ensuring its own fortune. Rome would have to reach its peak in order to break its dominance.

A cosmopolitan, intellectual city – In order to enhance the royal nature of their residences and in keeping with their lofty ambitions, the first two Ptolemaic rulers invited a number of scientists, philosophers and poets from the Greek world to their new city, which the writers of the time described as being of exceptional beauty. Demetrios of Phaleron, the founder of the Bibliotheca Alexandrina, the physician Herophilus, the mathematician Euclid and the artist Antiphilos, among others, all travelled to Alexandria, which soon developed into a melting-pot of civilisations. In addition to the majority of Greeks and Egyptians, Alexandria also attracted Phoenicians, Jews and mercenaries; this multi-cultural mix would soon lead to the birth of the first native Alexandrians. Control of these diverse groups was to prove difficult, particularly given the Ptolemies' greater emphasis on administration rather than authority. Dissension would ultimately result in their downfall, although their disappearance in no way lessened the status of this proud and important city.

Second only to Rome – Following the rise of Augustus, Alexandria lost its title of capital and as a sign of its decline its library was razed to the ground. Despite the tidal waves that destroyed its low-lying districts, the city continued to develop its trade, although this period saw a rise in friction between Egyptians, Greeks and Jews. From the 3C, Alexandria was a hotbed of pillage and repression, a situation worsened by the external wars that weakened and finally crushed Rome's power base, and the persecutions suffered by the early Christians. Yet, Alexandria managed to absorb these setbacks and the destruction of many of its monuments to such an extent that when Amr, general to the Caliph Umar, entered the city in 642, he encountered opulence that filled him with awe. The Arab conquest would bring further ruin upon the city, particularly following the suppression of trade with the East. In 875, Ahmed ibn Tulun destroyed its walls, which he considered too large. Slowly, the flame in the city was extinguished, a decline which culminated in the collapse of its famous lighthouse following an earthquake in 1303.

Mohammed Ali and Alexandria's renaissance – Empowered by the knowledge acquired during Napoleon's Egyptian expedition, the country's new leader chose Alexandria as his maritime and commercial base; he also lived in the city for a time and built a palace here. Alexandria enjoyed a resurgence, its port became active once more – mainly a result of the cotton trade – and an arsenal was established; the Al-Mahmoudieh Canal, linking it with the Nile and providing the city with drinking water, was also dug. Ismail Pasha also opened a railway between Cairo and Alexandria and numerous European buildings began to be erected in the city.

> The city's largest burial ground, or necropolis, was situated outside the walls to the west. It is currently being excavated by the French archaeologist, **Jean-Yves Empereur**.

AN ANCIENT WONDER
In the 3C, Philon of Byzantium drew up a list of the Seven Wonders of the World *(de septum orbis miraculis)*. These included the Pharos of Alexandria, built by Sostratus of Knidus around 300 BC on the island of Pharos, linked by the Heptastadion to terra firma. *(Drawing from the work of H. Thiersch)*.

> **BIBLIOTHECA ALEXANDRINA**
> Following the razing of the Bibliotheca under the Romans, it was rebuilt in the Serapeum, only for its contents to be burned once more by Umar. The fire was so intense that it is said that its heat provided hot water for the city's 4 000 baths for 183 days.

GETTING ABOUT

By taxi – Taxis are numerous and can be hailed from the street. Meters are generally for show only – fares are negotiated according to distance (between E£3-E£5 in the city centre; E£10-E£15 to the Montazah Gardens).

By collective taxi – For 25pt, these often-packed taxis will get you around the city quickly. However, if you don't speak Arabic it can be difficult to find out which way you're going! Let the driver know when you want to get out.

By tram – From the Ramla terminus, next to Midan Saad Zaghloul: yellow trams head to the west of the city and blue ones to the east. Yellow trams (15pt): nos 14, 15 (Abu Abbas Mosque and Qaitbey Fort), no 16 (Pompey's Pillar); blue trams (20pt): nos 1 and 2 (towards Montazah), nos 3 and 7 (Sidi Gaber North), nos 4 and 6 (Sidi Gaber South), and nos 5 and 8 (San Stefano).

By bus – Three useful bus routes depart from Midan Orabi: no 231 (Qaitbey Fort), no 260 (Abukir via the Corniche) and no 221 (the village of Mamoura). This option is often less practical than the tram.

By horse-drawn carriage – An attractive way of getting around the city, although progress by *calèche* can be slow, especially during the holidays when traffic is heavy. If the roads are quiet, make sure you follow the famous Corniche. Rates start from E£5, are negotiable, and are calculated according to the distance covered.

INTERNET CAFES

Zawia – *62, Shira Safia Zaghloul (close to Midan Saad Zaghloul). Open 10am-1am.* A useful address for checking e-mails. E£5/hour.

Net Serve – *678, Shira El-Horriya. Open 10am-2am.*

Compu-Net – *36, Shira Mostafa Kamel. Open 10am-2am.*

WHERE TO STAY

• *Budget*

Amoun Hotel – *32, Midan El-Nasr –* ☎ *(03) 481 82 39 – 100 rooms: E£146.* Basic and reliable, but the type of hotel where most people tend to spend just the one night. No alcohol.

Semiramis – *180, Shira 26 July (next to Midan Saad Zaghloul) –* ☎ *(03) 484 68 37 – 40 rooms: E£110.* An ideal location and the best option for those on a tight budget, despite rooms that are not always spotless. The superb views from the restaurant on the top floor extend across the bay.

Al-Madina Almonawara Hotel – *Shira El-Mousher Ahmed Ismaiel (close to Gaber station) –* ☎ *(03) 545 30 09 – 60 rooms: E£85.* A hotel with a good location and the same prices for Egyptians and Europeans. No alcohol.

Holiday Hotel – *6, Midan Orabi –* ☎ *(03) 480 15 59 – 40 rooms (28 with bathrooms): E£60.* basic, but adequate hotel for budget travellers.

Marhaba Hotel – *1, Midan Orabi –* ☎ *(03) 480 95 10 – 33 rooms (21 with bathrooms): E£58.* Basic, even stark levels of comfort, but a bed for the night. The bar serves wine and beer.

Hotel Canal de Suez – *Shira El-Borsa El-Kadina –* ☎ *(03) 480 83 73 – 50 rooms (13 with bathrooms): E£30..* Very basic, but expectations tend to go out of the window at this price!

• *Moderate*

Sofitel Cecil – *Midan Saad Zaghloul –* ☎ *(03) 483 71 73 – 83 rooms: $135.* The reputation of the Cecil, which was opened in 1929, was built up by its early well-heeled European guests. It has since been adequately refurbished and retains some of its former charm. The rooms overlooking the sea provide superb views of the bay. Casino.

Paradise Inn Metropole Hotel – *52, Shira Saad Zaghloul –* ☎ *(03) 482 14 65 – 66 rooms: $125.* The former Metropole has been given a complete facelift, but still retains its quiet, relaxing atmosphere. Impeccable service and wonderful attention to detail. Ask for a room at the back, overlooking the Mediterranean.

The opulence of the past can still be seen in Alexandria.

Windsor Palace – *On the corner of Shira El-Shohada and the Corniche –* ☎ *(03) 480 87 00 – 80 rooms: $140.* This rival to the Cecil was opened in 1907 and had a major overhaul in 2001, which saw the refurbishment of its predominantly white and gilded decor. An elegant hotel with impeccable service.

Helnan Palestine Hotel – *Montazah Palace Gardens –* ☎ *(03) 547 40 33 – 222 rooms: $215/$262.* This charming, comfortable hotel stands by the sea, inside the Montazah Gardens. Private beach where bikinis can be worn.

Sheraton Montazah – *Montazah Corniche –* ☎ *(03) 548 12 20 – 312 rooms: $320.* Facilities here include a secluded pool and private beach.

Hotel Mercure – *303, Shira El-Gueish –* ☎ *(03) 588 09 11 – 55 suites: $300/$325.* On the Corniche, between the Montazah Gardens and the city centre. The Mercure has a slightly isolated position, but offers the comfort you would expect from this worldwide hotel chain.

Renaissance Hotel – *544, Shira El-Gueish –* ☎ *(03) 549 09 35 – 171 rooms: $235.* This hotel overlooking the sea to the east of the city centre along the Corniche *(entrance to the rear on Khaled Ebn el-Walid St)* has an attractive pool on the upper terrace with views across the bay.

Landmark Hotel – *163, Shira Abd el-Salam Aref –* ☎ *(03) 588 05 00 – 142 rooms: $45/$90.* Set back slightly from the Corniche but with a small pool on the 9th floor. A good fallback if other hotels are full.

• *Expensive*

El-Salamlek Hotel – *Montazah Palace Gardens –* ☎ *(03) 547 79 99 – 14 suites: $350 to $1 850; 6 rooms: $305.* Situated at the heart of the gardens, this former outbuilding of King Farouk's palace has not needed a great deal of work to transform it into an exclusive hotel. Although lacking a pool, the magical nostalgia of its royal days still pervades the building, in which the service and setting are in keeping with its luxury rating. Yacht excursions can be organised by the hotel.

WHERE TO EAT
• *Budget*

Corfou – *Just before the Qaitbey Fort (look for the sign with a rudder on it). Open noon-midnight.* ⊿ This restaurant on the second floor of Alexandria's Greek maritime club is renowned for its fish, although meat also features on the menu. Views overlooking the bay and a private beach open to everyone (E£20).

Elite – *43, Shira Safia Zaghloul. Open 8am-midnight.* ⊿ ⊠ This simply furnished café-restaurant was opened in the 1950s and was a popular haunt frequented by Dalida. Owned by the legendary Madame Christina, a local Greek personality, the Elite serves dishes including chicken and squid to a background of jazz. Whisky and vodka are served here.

Kadoura – *47, Shira 26 July. Open 24hr a day.* Somewhat canteen-like in appearance, but serving excellent cuisine. Choose your fish or seafood on the ground floor, decide how you want it cooked, then sit down to a starter of salad and *tahina*. Drinks (water or lemonade) are included. Note the unusual way in which the waiters clear the tables here!

Taverna – *Midan Saad Zaghloul (behind the Trianon).* ⊿ The best sandwiches in town on the ground floor (E£3.5) washed down perhaps by a delicious strawberry fruit juice. The small restaurant on the first floor serves simple but tasty local dishes.

• *Moderate*

Trianon – *Midan Saad Zaghloul.* This cosy, old-fashioned restaurant with its wood panelling dates from 1903. The atmosphere is enlivened at 8pm every evening by the resident pianist. Traditional dishes such as quail and grilled pigeon are served here.

Tikka Grill – *The first building by the sea after the monument to the Unknown Soldier in the direction of the Qaitbey Fort.* An ideal position, and popular with the local jet-set who come here to enjoy good, albeit less-than-inspiring cuisine. We recommend the jumbo prawns and the puri bread, which the Tikka Grill claims to be an exclusive speciality.

Samalemak – *42, Shira Qasr Ras and Tin El Anfoushi. Open 3pm-1am.* A popular local fish restaurant.

TEA-ROOMS

Trianon – *Midan Saad Zaghloul.* A pleasant setting in which to enjoy excellent pastries, such as *oum ali* (with hazelnuts) and *mehalabia* (with pistachios), ice-cream (particularly the chocolate-flavoured *mou*), or a glass of chilled curdled milk. Alcohol served from 11am-1am.

Délices – *46, Shira Saad Zaghloul. Open 7am-midnight.* ⊿ Despite the occasional surly service, the Délices remains one of Alexandria's institutions. Opened in 1901, the decor is simple, the pastries exquisite (crystallised dates and the "surprise" cake) and the fresh fruit juices delicious.

BARS AND CAFÉS

Cap d'Or – *4, Shira Abib (near Shira Saad Zaghloul). Open 9am-4am.* ⊿ Opened by Greeks in 1890 and now run by Egyptians, this pleasant bar is popular with locals and Europeans alike. Fish is the house speciality – but at a price!

Riviera – *146, Shira 26 July (Corniche). Open 24hr a day.* ⊿ Eat outside on the terrace in fine weather to the sounds of Egyptian music. Make sure you try the rice pudding and the delicious *sahlab*.

exploring Alexandria

Seafront and City Centre★
Egypt's second largest city extends along a magnificent avenue over 20km/12mi in length, yet it extends inland for no more than 3km/1.8mi. Here, the traditional face of Egypt – the pharaohs' pyramids and funerary temples, the feluccas of Aswan and Luxor, and the sweltering heat of Cairo – have been left behind, to be replaced by the European atmosphere of the impressive **Corniche★★** with its pleasant beaches and imposing buildings.

An old-fashioned air – Two seawalls enclose the **Eastern Harbour** with its flotilla of fishing boats. This area stretches from the old Qaitbey Fort to the New Library – two contrasting images that embody modern-day

> **TOURIST OFFICE**
> On the corner of Shira Saad Zaghloul and Midan Saad Zaghloul ☎ *(03) 484 33 80.* Open daily 8am-6pm. Tourist police office on the first floor. Another tourist office is located at Misr railway station ☎ *(03) 492 59 85.*

View of the New Library, situated on the seafront.

Alexandria. The centre of the city stands to the south of this impressive crescent-shaped port area, in particular on either side of Shira Saad Zaghloul. The square of the same name is considered to be the hub of this lively city.

> **EASTERN HARBOUR**
> The sunset over the harbour is particularly impressive. This port stands on the site of the former *portus magnus* guarded by the lighthouse which once stood on the present site of the Qaitbey Fort.

Along the seafront, the impressive, recently restored buildings from Alexandria's so-called Golden Age stand defiant, endowing the Corniche with its characteristic Art Deco air; the residences around the French Consulate and the monument to the Unknown Soldier (erected by the city's Italian colony in 1938 in homage to Ismail Pasha) in Midan Orabi act as reminders of Alexandria's 19C splendour, despite the fact that they have seen better days. Around **Midan Saad Zaghloul**, the Cecil Hotel, a favoured residence of Somerset Maugham and the British Secret Service and mentioned in Lawrence Durrell's *The Alexandria Quartet*, stands alongside old-fashioned tea-rooms where pashas would have made the acquaintance of Greek ladies.

In summer and during the Aid el-Adha festival, Midan Zaghloul is transformed into a seething mass of young children eating candyfloss and ice-cream, teenagers enjoying tours of the square on horseback, adults chanting festive songs to the accompaniment of tambourines, young lovers trying to find a quiet bench to sit on, and older generations quietly enjoying this lively scene.

> **SAAD ZAGHLOUL SQUARE**
> Also known as Mahattet al-Rami or "the sand terminus", this square is the starting-point for any visit of the city.

Souks and shopping streets – Shira Saad Zaghloul and Shira Satiyyah Zaghloul to the south of the square are home to myriad boutiques and shops, some of which spill out onto the pavement. In the evening, all of Alexandria seems to converge on this area, which also includes Midan Ramla, with its busy tram terminus.

Shira Satiyah Zaghloul leads to Midan Gomhuriyya, dominated by the Mahattet Masr station, the city's main railway terminus. A souk specialising in food is located in a maze of narrow streets on the other side of the square, where stalls of fish and spices stand shoulder to shoulder with fruits and vegetables. The nearby **Attarine souk** to the north specialises more in second-hand goods *(Shira Masguid el-Attarine)*. In the past it was possible to find some real treasures from the glorious days of Alexandria's past. Nowadays, however, stallholders have become far more shrewd and you will need to exercise your best bargaining skills to buy at a reasonable price the furniture and objets d'art of varying levels of quality on display here.

Head along Saad Zaghloul as far as Midan Tahrir, which was developed by Mohammed Ali in 1830 (his statue graces the centre of the square). To the west, two avenues *(Nokrashi and Faransa Streets)* lead to the souks in the **Anfushi district**. The first is lined by cafés and displays a huge range of food, domestic appliances and utensils. The affectionately known **"stampede of women"** *(Zan'et el-Sittat)*, a market tucked away in a covered alleyway, specialises in haberdashery and sells everything from buttons to bags; the **fabric market** adjoining Zan'et el-Sittat *(open daily 11am-9pm)*, which is particularly busy on a Thursday, displays clothes as well as a huge choice of fabrics. If you're looking for fish, make sure you visit the fish market, which is open early in the morning next to the Qaitbey Fort.

Mosques – Although the Greek and French presence has had a marked effect on Alexandria's history, the city remains profoundly Muslim. This is especially noticeable in the **Anfushi** district, nestling between the two ports *(the Western Harbour is off-limits to the public)*. The whitewashed **Abu Abbas el-Mursi** mosque was built in 1767 on the site of an earlier mosque, above the tomb of the pious Abu Abbas, a 13C Muslim saint from Southern Spain. The **Ibrahim Terbana** mosque, dating from the mid-17C, and crowned by a splendid minaret, stands slightly to the south. Architectural features from Antiquity are visible in the **Shorbagi** mosque *(Shira Nokrashi)*, the façade of which is made up of exposed red and black bricks bound with white mortar; this style is typical of the Delta region and can also be seen at Rosetta.

Montazah Gardens – *At the eastern end of the Corniche, 20km/12mi from the city centre. Entrance fee: E£3.* King Farouk's former estate has been transformed into a public park, while the eclectic **El-Montazah Palace** *(closed to the public)* has been a presidential residence since the 1952 revolution. The **Salamlek Pavilion** above it was built in 1892 by the Khedive Abbas II, the grandson of Ismail Pasha, and is now a hotel. A small bay next to the park to the east has a beach *(E£5)* which is popular with Europeans.

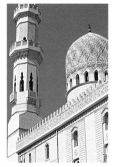

Standing slightly back from the Corniche, the Abu Abbas el-Mursi mosque attracts thousands of faithful during Ramadan.

worth a visit

Qaitbey Fort★

Open daily 9am-5pm. E£15 (9am-4pm); E£20 (4pm-5pm); camera permit E£10; video permit E£150. The Naval Museum is currently closed. See the ABC of Architecture in the Insights and Images section of this guide.

Built in the late-15C by Sultan Al-Malik Nasy Qaitbey – who also built a citadel with the same name in Rosetta – this fort, which is currently undergoing restoration, was partially built with blocks of stone from the city's Ancient lighthouse. The west terrace, a fine example of Arab defensive architecture, commands a delightful **view**★ of the bay. In recent times the fort has become the site of extensive

> **THE PHAROS OF ALEXANDRIA**
> The Qaitbey Fort stands on the site of Pharos Island, on which the city's famous Hellenistic lighthouse once stood, at one end of the impressive Heptastadion.

The Qaitbey Fort at the end of the promenade was transformed into its modern-day appearance by Mohammed Ali.

underwater research. The ground floor of the fort houses a somewhat neglected **museum** devoted to the city's underwater discoveries *(open daily 9am-midnight; E£1; camera permit E£5)*. Exhibits include the skeleton of a whale washed up at Rosetta in 1936.

Anfushi Necropolis

Open daily 9am-5pm. E£15; students E£8; camera permit E£5; video permit E£150.

Although smaller in size than the catacombs at Kom el-Shugafa, this necropolis dates from the 3C and 2C BC and therefore predates the latter. Two of the five underground vaults, comprising two tombs with a shared atrium, are open to the public. The decoration on the walls is an attempt to imitate architecture known at the time, with scenes in a mixture of Greek and Egyptian styles characteristic of the Ptolemaic period. In vault no 2, for example, the mythological scenes are heavily Hellenised, with Osiris *(on the staircase)* no longer presiding over the funerary tribunal; instead, he is shown welcoming the deceased and offering him a vase of lustral water.

> **T**he Ras el-Tin Palace
> *(closed to the public)*
> stands between the
> Qaitbey Fort and the
> Anfushi Necropolis. Built
> by Mohammed Ali, it
> was used by King Farouk
> during the revolution and
> is now the headquarters
> of the Admiralty.

UNDERWATER DISCOVERIES

In the past few years the world's press has shown increased interest in Alexandria's ancient history, mainly as a result of the recent underwater excavations carried out by the French archaeologist **Jean-Yves Empereur**, which have uncovered spectacular Ptolemaic remains at the foot of the Qaitbey Fort. In October 1995, some 3 000 statues, sphinxes and other architectural artefacts were discovered, significantly enhancing hitherto hypothetical research on Alexandria's Pharos. Finds included a colossal statue in four pieces of either Ptolemy I or II, sculpted from Aswan granite. Weighing 23t in total, this impressive statue measures 10m/32ft, not taking into account its legs.

In addition, **Frank Goddio**, a French diver and treasure-hunter, has unearthed the remains of two cities which have been dated to a period before the foundation of Alexandria, and which were submerged following an earthquake. This discovery was made off the coast of Abukir at a depth of just 6m/20ft. The first, Menouthis, was a sacred city dedicated to Isis and Serapis; the second, Heraklion, the gateway to Egypt, has only been referred to in texts by Herodotus and Strabo.

Kom el-Shugafa Catacombs★

Open daily 9am-5pm. E£12; students E£6; camera permit E£5; video permit E£150.

The "Mound of Shards" – These catacombs were discovered by accident in 1900 when (according to records) the ground collapsed beneath the hooves of a donkey in the middle of one of the city's working-class districts. Dating from the 1C and 2C AD, this Roman necropolis comprises six vaults on three floors, with a depth of 35m/115ft (the lowest floor is under water). The decoration in the tombs is one of the finest examples of the combined Greco-Roman and Egyptian styles.

Niches and sarcophagi – *Access via a spiral staircase.* The two immediate impressions upon the descent into the vaults are the astonishing structure of its tombs, which occupy every available inch of space, and the temperature inside them, which remains constant all year round. A rotunda provides access to a triclinium (a funerary dining room reserved for the family of the deceased), and from there, via a staircase, to the **main tomb**, preceded by an antechamber, the entrance of which is flanked by the statues of the owners of the tomb (note their Greco-Roman hairstyles). The decoration in the chapel is proof that despite the date of the tomb, some Alexandrians continued to believe in the religion of the pharaohs. Yet, despite the fact that the sarcophagi

Kom el-Shugafa remained in use until the 4C. As a result, additional niches had to be dug in the rock to house sarcophagi and funerary urns.

sculpted in the rock are indeed Greek (with garlands and bunches of grapes from Dionysus, the god of the Resurrection), several of the surrounding low-reliefs are typically Egyptian in subject matter (Osiris, an Apis bull, Horus, Thoth and Anubis); others are clearly Hellenistic (Athena's shield, Medusa and Hermes).

The rotunda also leads to tombs of a later date, as well as to the **Caracalla tomb**, so-called because it served as a refuge for Christians fleeing the persecutions of this particular Roman emperor. Access between this tomb and the others referred to above was established by those who originally plundered the catacombs. The stuccoed walls are painted with barely visible scenes, yet manage to demonstrate once more the co-existence of two visions of the divine world, side-by-side rather than merged into a hybrid style.

Pompey's Pillar and Serapeum★
Open daily 9am-5pm. E£6; students E£2; no charge for cameras or videos.

A case of mistaken identity – The highest column in the Greco-Roman world (30m/98ft) stands in the southern section of the city. Ancient texts recounted that Caesar erected the column in memory of Pompey, Sulla's former lieutenant, following the latter's assassination by Ptolemy XIII as soon as he had set foot on Egyptian soil after his defeat at Pharsalus. However, the inscription on the west side of its base attributes it to the Emperor **Diocletian**, who lived more than three centuries after Caesar. Despite the fact that its correct title should be "Diocletian's Column", the name of Pompey has been for ever associated with it.

The column's role – The column was originally used to support a statue of the Emperor Diocletian, who ruled the Roman world from AD 284-305. It was, in fact, a dedicatory column, similar to that of Trajan in Piazza Venezia in Rome, but was to assume a role that its architect could hardly have expected, namely as a seamark for mariners sailing into Alexandria. In 391, the area around the column was completely destroyed by Christians whose intention was to eradicate the worship of Serapis; however, the column of the emperor who had ordered persecutions against them was to be spared from destruction.

The **two sphinxes** placed in front of the column were unearthed nearby at the beginning of the 20C.

Serapeum – Barely a single trace remains of the Great Temple of Serapis erected by Ptolemy I, subsequently enlarged by Ptolemy III and rebuilt by Hadrian. What is known, however, is that an annexe of the Bibliotheca Alexandrina was housed here after the fire that destroyed this library, an event that was the result of the burning of the Egyptian fleet by Caesar. This annexe was said to have contained over 700 000 rolls of papyrus texts.

The column and one of the two sphinxes, both of which are carved from pink Aswan granite.

ALEXANDRIA

0 _____ 1000 m

QAITBAY

AQUARI

BEACH

Sh. 26 JULY

ANFUSHI
BEACH

ANFUSHI

Abu
Abbas el-Mursi

Anfushi
Souq

FISI
MARI

Sh. Ras el-Tin

Ras el-Tin
Palace

Anfushi

AL-JUMRUK

Terba

Shorbagi

Zan'et el
el Sittat

28

AL-MANSHIYY

MARITIME
STATION

Sh. el-Nasr

Sh. Ibrahim al-A

Sh. al-Bab al.

al.

WESTERN   HARBOUR

Tir'al

al-Mahmdiy

Sh. al-Max

al-Amer

31

18

MINIA
AL-BASAL

Sh. Ibn Sahlan

Rashid

Rida

al-Max

Sh.

Sh.

A

B

V

X

Y

A

B

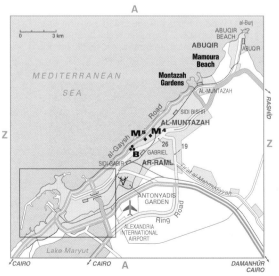

MEDITERRANEAN
SEA

al-Burj

ABUQIR
BEACH

ABUQIR

ABUQIR

Mamoura
Beach

Montazah
Gardens

AL-MUNTAZAH

RASHID

Road

SIDI BISHR

AL-MUNTAZAH

M⁵ M⁴

al-Gaysh Road

26

19

B

GABRIEL

Tir al-Mahmudiyah

SIDI GABIR

AR-RAML

ANTONYADIS
GARDEN

Ring   Road

ALEXANDRIA
INTERNATIONAL
AIRPORT

Lake Maryut

CAIRO   CAIRO

A

DAMANHÛR
CAIRO

Z

Z

0 ___ 3 km

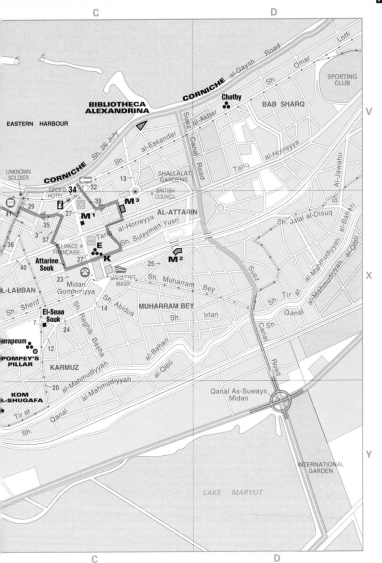

All that remains from the famous sanctuary are column shafts, a few foundations, a nilometer and underground passageways. It is said that the inside of the temple was covered with precious metals in order to reflect light from the rising sun onto the colossal statue of the god.

ANCIENT ALEXANDRIA: THE CAESARIUM

Of the buildings that were known to have existed in Cleopatra's Alexandria but have since disappeared, the temple built by the queen for the worship of Mark Antony is known to have been situated just south of Midan Saad Zaghloul. Octavium, who defeated him at Actium, completed the construction of the sanctuary and dedicated it to imperial worship. He had two obelisks of Thutmose III brought from Heliopolis, in Cairo, to flank the entrance.

Nothing remains of this temple which stood alongside the sea, and which was probably Greek in style. It must have appeared as a majestic portico to sailors over whom it provided symbolic protection. As for the two Egyptian obelisks, sculpted in Aswan 2 000 years before the birth of Alexandria, one is now in London, the other in New York.

Kom el-Dik Roman Amphitheatre★

Open daily 9am-5pm. E£6; students E£3. Camera permit E£10; video permit E£150.

This 4C amphitheatre was uncovered in 1963 by the Polish Mediterranean Archaeology Centre following the demolition of a Napoleonic fort in order to make way for blocks of apartments. Arranged in a semicircle, its 12 marble tiers were surrounded by a wall 8m/26ft high. Numerous ancient texts refer to the existence of several companies of actors in Alexandria, stylised representations of whom can be seen in the Greco-Roman Museum. Here, as is the case all over Alexandria, excavations are continuing to unearth the remains of baths and villas.

A panther, peacock, parrot, moorhen and turtledove grace the floor of the dining room in the Villa of the Birds.

Villa of the Birds – *E£6; students E£4.* This Roman villa was covered by Byzantine buildings at the end of the 5C, but was restored by the American Center for Egyptian Research and opened in January 2001. The pavement is decorated with exquisite **mosaics**★★ mostly dating from Hadrian's reign. The essentially animalistic theme, detailed in fine colours and with remarkable naturalism, stand out against an *opus sectile* comprising geometric forms made up of small black and white squares. This "carpet" style was a popular feature of Alexandrian villas.

Fine Arts Museum

18, Shira Menashe (near the railway station). Open daily except Fri 9am-1pm and 5-7pm. No charge.

Pride of place in the museum is given to modern and contemporary Egyptian art, with rooms devoted to the Alexandrian artist Mohammed Naghi (1888-1956) and to the Wanely brothers. Artists such as Ahmed Sabry and Yussuf Kamel, who belong to the first generation of modern Egyptian painters, are also strongly featured.

This impressive white marble amphitheatre could seat some 8 000 spectators.

Works by several foreign artists who spent time in Alexandria, such as the Greek Enrico Brondani, the Italian Cléa Baddaro, and the Frenchman, André Lhote, are also on display. Several Orientalist canvases and paintings by foreign artists who have visited Egypt are also exhibited inside the museum; these include works by the French artist **Émile Bernard**, who spent six years in the country.

Cavafy Museum

4, Shira Sharm el-Sheikh (near Shira Nabi Daniel). Open daily except Mon 10am-3pm. E£8.

The Greek poet Constantine Cavafy (1863-1933) was born in Alexandria and spent his lifetime in the city. The museum dedicated to the man considered to be the greatest modern Greek poet is housed in the apartment in which he spent the last 25 years of his life. Two of the rooms have been conserved in their original state, while another is devoted to the writer Stratis Tsirkas.

Greco-Roman Museum★★

5, Shira El-Mathaf. Open daily 9am-4pm (closed Fri from 11.30am-1.30pm). E£20; students E£10. Camera permit E£10; video permit E£150.

Collections – This museum is housed in a neo-Classical building and was established in 1892 by the Italian archaeologist Giuseppe Botti who, along with Evaristo Breccia and Achille Adriani, was responsible for the principal excavations undertaken in Alexandria in the late 19C and early 20C. Despite being mainly centred on discoveries and treasures from the city itself, the collection is also enhanced by donations and legacies from elsewhere, and although the main focus is on the Greco-Roman period, exhibits from the Delta, the Fayum and Middle Egypt are also on display.

Statuary – Very few **portraits** of **Alexander the Great** still exist, yet the museum has no fewer than eight of them on display: two in marble and one in granite *(Room 6)*; a further four in marble *(Room 16a)*; and one in terracotta *(Room 18a)*. Works discovered in the Serapeum include the granite **Apis bull**★ *(Room 6)*, dedicated by Hadrian, which bears witness to the continuity of worship to this pharaonic god, as well as marble and alabaster **busts of Serapis** *(Rooms 6 and 7)*, the trepan-worked hair and beards of which show clear evidence of their Greek manufacture. Also particularly worthy of note are a colossal statue of Rameses II *(Room 7)*, found in Abukir; a head of Caesar *(Room 14)*; Aphrodite *(Room 16a)*; and a bronze **head of Hadrian**★ with glass eyes *(Room 23)* discovered at Qena.

Mosaics – The superb mosaic of **Berenice**★ *(Room 6)*, the wife of Ptolemy III, is signed by an artist known as Sophilos. The queen is crowned with the prow of a warship, leading to the long-held belief in her as the personification of the city.

Funerary Art – Room 8 contains a number of mummies and funerary masks, including an interesting Fayum portrait, as well as a painted plaster mask from the Roman period. A fine example of a **Roman sarcophagus**★, carved from Carrara marble, is on display in Room 17; the reliefs on the coffin depict an episode from the life of Ariadne, who is shown asleep, and then surprised by Dionysus and his retinue of bacchantes. The island of Naxos where the scene is played out is suggested by the prow of a ship.

The Fayum – Exhibits discovered in Theadelphia, one of the Ptolemaic cities in this region, are displayed in Room 9. The city's **temple**★ has been completely reconstructed in the garden.

Ceramics – Several Greek vases are displayed in Room 18 alongside oil lamps, a selection of crockery and several small statues. The earthenware statues in Room 20, including one of an actor wearing an evocative mask, are also worthy of particular note.

MAJOR WORKS
Given that the museum covers a relatively short period of time in the history of the Ptolemies and Rome, we have selected the most important and representative works on display rather than providing a lengthy inventory of every exhibit in every room.

The 4C **headless statue**★★ of an unidentified person in Room 17 is one of the most important porphyry statues from the Ancient World. Constantine, Diocletian and even Christ have all been suggested as possible subjects.

A mosaic representing a meal on the banks of the Nile is on display in Room 17.

TANAGRA

Another major attraction in the museum is the collection of small statues of **Tanagra**★★ in Room 18a. These terracotta figurines were made between 330 BC-200 BC, and take their name from the town in Ancient Boeotia, in Greece. They represent graceful young women, standing and clothed in delicate *chiton* tunics. Those on display in the museum were all discovered in Alexandria.

"Demetrios disposed of huge financial resources with which to assemble, if possible, every book in the world" *(The Letter of Aristeas).*

SHIP BOOKS

It would seem that in order to build up the collection of books in the Ancient library, ships entering the port would be searched in an attempt to find books of any description that would then be brought to the library, and either confiscated or copied.

The Greek physician Galen referred to these books as "ship books".

Make sure you take the time to enjoy Alexandria's friendly atmosphere in between visits to its excellent museums and archaeological sites.

Painting – The museum's major work is a **wall fresco**★ *(Room 17)*, thought to date from between 2C BC and the 3C AD, which was taken from a tomb in the city. It portrays a rural scene in which cattle can be seen working a waterwheel alongside a child playing a pan-pipe.

Decorative Arts – Glass was one of Alexandria's artistic specialities. In recognition of this, Room 22 brings together a rich collection of **millefleurs**★. These polychrome examples of decorative glass bear witness to the great skill of the city's glassworkers who were able to produce these works by superimposing coloured layers fired just once in the oven. In the same room, note also the impressive ducks dating from the 2C, while the 1C Dionysus-inspired silver goblet encrusted with gold is the undisputed highlight of Room 3.

Coins – The 255 revolving panels in Room 24 display a superb collection of Greek, Roman, Byzantine and Islamic **coins**★★. Several of these are exceptionally rare, such as the silver coins from the last Pharaonic Dynasty, which were used to pay mercenaries *(panel 19)*; the coins stamped with the effigy of Alexander the Great *(panels 36-43)*; those *(panel 88)* bearing that of Cleopatra VII (note the hooked nose); and that of Marcus Aurelius, the reverse side of which reveals a representation of Alexandria's Pharos *(panel 119)*.

Architecture – A number of interesting archaeological fragments have been laid out in various parts of the museum, including Coptic low reliefs from Middle Egypt exhibited in Rooms 1 and 2.

Bibliotheca Alexandrina★★★

Opening times and conditions not available at the time of publication.

A legacy of knowledge – At the beginning of the 3C BC, **Demetrios of Phaleron**, an Athenian statesman and pupil of the philosopher Theophrastus, founded the Bibliotheca Alexandrina, in all likelihood at the instigation of Ptolemy I. *The Letter of Aristeas*, the oldest known document detailing its creation, teaches us that from its conception the library was of universal importance.

Demetrius purchased books from Athens and Rhodes, and received, collected, archived and wrote works which developed rapidly into a tour de force of literature and knowledge. He accumulated Egyptian papyrus texts as well as Greek works, as his intention was to create a depository of information from the world ruled over by his new king. The collection was an eclectic one, covering medicine, astronomy, history, traditions, religion, the study of languages, myths and legends, science, literature, and translation. The library was considered to be a great centre of research, with in excess of 500 000 books, all of which were listed and indexed, in addition to those housed in the Serapeum.

The New Library – This large glass building along the Corniche has been built in the shape of a solar disc on the site of its predecessor in the former royal district. Designed by

the Norwegian firm of architects, Snohetta, this modern structure covers a surface area of some 45 000m²/484 335sq ft, laid out on 11 storeys (eleven of which have been set aside for reading rooms). The side of the building facing the sea is a huge mass of glass, while the side overlooking the city is an immense wall of Aswan granite covered with script written in ancient and modern languages.

More than just a library – Along with its capacity for 3 000 readers, the New Library or Bibliotheca Alexandrina will also house several museums, schools of science and information, and a planetarium, as well as a conference centre in an annexe. In addition, the library will have considerable audio-visual and multimedia resources at its disposal, alongside its initial collection of 500 000 (rising to between 4 and 8 million) works, brought together with the help of UNESCO. These works will come from a number of different countries, including Italy, France, Germany, the United States, Greece and Turkey, and from various associations established around the world. This is in addition to its comprehensive Egyptian and Arab collections from institutions within the country and around the Middle East, such as the microfilmed 11C-18C manuscripts from the libraries of mosques. Numerous contributions have also been received from countries within the Arab world such as Iraq, Oman and Saudi Arabia. Spain has also made a significant donation, with exhibits from the library at El Escorial (outside Madrid) and those in the former Moorish cities of Seville, Cordoba and Granada. However, quite apart from this impressive list, the major attraction of this new institution is its multilingualism, as although Arabic, French and English are the library's official languages, the research system will operate in Arabic and will transcribe all non-Latin characters in order to respond to requests made in Russian or Japanese, for example.

The aim of the New Library is to provide every available piece of information to researchers worldwide.

Chatby Necropolis

Port Said Road. Open all year 9am-4pm; E£8; students E£4. Tipping recommended.

The late-4C BC vaults discovered here (crowned on the surface by funerary monuments) are considered to be the oldest of all the tombs discovered in Alexandria, and as such house the remains of the very first Alexandrians. ▶

THE TOMB OF ALEXANDER THE GREAT

One of the many enigmas connected with Alexander – and there are many – is the question of where the tomb of this great Macedonian king is actually located. As early as 1889, the German archaeologist Henrich Schliemann, who discovered Mycenae and what was presumed to be Troy, arrived in Alexandria with this aim in mind, only to give up his quest because of administrative problems. The Greek Stelios Coumoutsos, an archaeology enthusiast, would continue the search, which led him to carry out excavations (albeit in vain) in the area near Shira Nabi Daniel. The most promising lead was followed up by Achille Adriani, who believed the tomb of Alexander to be the alabaster tomb in the Latin Cemetery because of its Macedonian style and the fact that it was the tomb of an important citizen. Analyses carried out have yet to confirm this hypothesis.

To add to the confusion are apparent discoveries at various points between the Siwa Oasis and Syria, in addition to Ancient texts that indicate three tombs: one at Memphis, the two others in Alexandria! The search goes on…

> **MUSTAFA KAMEL NECROPOLIS**
> *Shira El-Moaskar ar-Romani. Open 9am-4pm; E£20; students E£10.* The tombs in this burial site are decorated in grandiose Doric style.

Royal Jewellery Museum★

Shira Ahmed Yehia. Open daily 9am-4pm (closed Fri 11.30am-1.30pm). E£20; students E£10. Camera permit E£10; video permit E£150.

This museum opened in 1986 and is housed inside an attractive villa built in 1919 for Fatma Ali Heider Fadel by an Italian architect and ceramicist. The jewels on display belonged to the family of Mohammed Ali. The full ▶ splendour of this period can be seen in the diadems (including one with 2 159 diamonds), the sets of jewellery, sceptres from this dynasty, and even the chess board decorated with enamel and 425 diamonds.

> **WORTH SEEING**
> The friezes bearing motifs of animals and nature in the bathroom and the sculpture by Jean-Baptiste Carpeaux in the stairwell.

Mahmoud Said Center for Museums

6, Shira Mohammed Said, Gianaclis. Open daily 9am-6pm except Mon. E£13. Cameras and videos prohibited.

Opened in 2000, this centre occupies the residence of Mahmoud Said (1897-1964), who curtailed his 50-year career as a judge to devote his energies to his passion for painting. The building houses the Mahmoud Said Museum, containing several interesting portraits; the Egyptian Modern Art Museum, an eclectic collection of regularly rotated modern and contemporary art; and the Seif and Adham Wanely Museum.

ROOM 3
Note the portrait of Sayed Darwish, a popular and well-known singer from Alexandria whose songs protested at the presence of the British in Egypt.

Seif and Adham Wanely Museum – Seif (1906-79) and Adham (1908-59) were brothers born in Alexandria. The works of the former, initially a portrait artist who was later attracted by abstract arts, are the more interesting. *The Black Bird* (1957, *Room 5*) along with several other canvases bear witness to the influence of the School of Paris on his prodigious talent.

outskirts

Abukir

25km/15mi E of the centre of Alexandria and 5km/3mi E of the tourist village of El-Mamoura. Access: by taxi (the easiest option) or by bus (nos 260 and 261) from Alexandria.

Modern-day Abukir has little to attract visitors unless you are looking for peace and quiet (in which case avoid Fridays!) and good seafood. In the evenings you may even catch the sound of melodies sung by fishermen as they work.

FISH AND SEAFOOD
Make sure you avoid the enticements of restaurant touts encouraging you to eat at the so-called "Dead Sea" Beach, where prices tend to be outrageous. Your best bet at Abukir Beach is the **Zephyron** restaurant, with its pleasant terrace, where you can enjoy excellent fish (particularly sea bass and sea bream) and seafood (crabs and sea urchins) for E£40. Trips (E£100) operate from the beach to the lighthouse on Nelson's island.

Historical notes – In 244 BC, the hair Berenice offered to the gods for the safe return of her husband Ptolemy III from his campaign in Assyria was said to have transformed itself into stars. Abukir is the former Canope, which was dedicated to Serapis and became a town of leisure under the Romans. It was also the scene of three battles: the first, in August 1798, resulted in **Nelson's** crushing victory over the French fleet led by Admiral Brueys; the second, in 1799, saw Napoleon defeat the Turkish army which had come ashore with help from the English fleet; while the third, in 1801, saw the English general, Abercromby, inflict a further defeat on French troops under the command of General Friant.

Beaches

Alexandria's coastline attracts few tourists, who are more tempted by the Red Sea. Westerners tend to be wary about swimming between the Eastern Harbour and Montazah as this area is reserved for men and children only. Visitors are advised to head for the expensive **Mamoura Beach**, 1km/0.6mi E of Montazah (*double entry fee: park E£3; beach E£3; beach chair E£3; parasol E£7*). To avoid confusion, when the red flag is flying, swimming is permitted; when the black flag is out, it's not.

Damietta

This active, prosperous town is known throughout Egypt as a centre for the manufacture of furniture. Sadly, Damietta has lost many of its features of historical interest, although it stands in a pleasant position on a loop of the Nile. By contrast, the nearby resort of Ras el-Barr has grown in popularity in recent times, attracting thousands of annual holidaymakers.

Location
194km/121mi NE of Cairo and 58km/36mi W of Port Said, at the mouth of the eastern branch of the Nile, on a strip of land just north of Lake Manzala. Access: by East Delta Company bus from Cairo (departures every hour from 6am to 6.30pm).

Name
The first name given to the town was Tamiathis, although no historical traces remain from the period prior to the Crusades. Damietta has retained its European name, although in Arabic it is known as Dumyat.

Transcription: دمياط

Famous People
Better known by the name Saladin, the sultan Salah al-Din al-Ayyubi (1138-93), the champion of the counter-Crusade and a model of rectitude, fortified the town in order to protect one of the main access routes to Cairo.

> **SALADIN**
> This great conquerer founded the Ayyubid Dynasty, which overthrew the Fatimids in Egypt in 1171.
> In 1187, Saladin recaptured Jerusalem from the "infidels" and fought against the 3rd Crusade led by Philippe Auguste of France and Richard the Lionheart.

background

Under siege – Following its submission to the forces of Roger I of Sicily in 1155 during the Second Crusade, Damietta was retaken by **Saladin** before suffering further attack by Amaury I of Jerusalem in 1169. The town, which was already known for its flourishing textile trade, was besieged once more in 1218 by Jean de Brienne, the king of Jerusalem, as part of the Fifth Crusade. Sacked the following year, the town was abandoned in 1221 by the crusaders who were encircled during their march towards Cairo and who ceded Damietta in exchange for their freedom. The crusaders were to return to the town in 1249 during the Seventh Crusade.

Recapture – On this occasion, an army formed in answer to a call by Pope Innocent IV and under the command of the French king, **St Louis** (Louis IX), seized the port of Damietta. Louis' aim was to conquer Egypt, but following the rout of his army at Mansura, he was taken prisoner in 1250. To secure his freedom and to enable him to continue on his route to the Holy Land to preserve the lands conquered by the Franks, a huge ransom was paid and the town handed over.

Demolition – Sadly, Damietta's woes were far from over following the payment of a ransom by Queen Marguerite. In 1251, the Mameluke Turks, who had just overthrown the Ayyubid Dynasty, concluded that the town was far too vulnerable; as a result, its fortifications were demolished and its harbour closed by the sultan Baïbars. These events were to leave the town in total ruin.

Rise from the ashes – The town was to experience a ► new lease of life mainly due to the manufacture of luxurious brocades and *tiraz* (ceremonial linen robes embellished with silk), for which Damietta developed an enviable reputation throughout the Orient. From being completely deserted, the town gradually redeveloped close to its original site on a strip of land to the north of Lake Manzala, which is still occupied to this day. It is

> **A NATION OF PIGEON FANCIERS**
> Ever since the Mameluke sultans used the pigeon post, the Egyptians have been keen pigeon-lovers. Nowadays, the town cemetery hosts a weekly pigeon market.

> **A**lthough the Abu el-Maati Mosque, which was converted into a cathedral by Saint Louis, no longer exists, the **El-Bahr Mosque** (whose name translates as "the river"), is currently being restored alongside the Nile.

somewhat unfortunate, however, that modern Damietta exudes the air of a slightly run-down town that has been unable to maintain and display its historic monuments to maximum effect.

outskirts

ZEHERIS
A type of felucca with a low draught, the *zeheri* is unique to Damietta and is perfectly suited to the shallow waters of the lagoon.

Lake Manzala
◀ *To the SE of the town, between Damietta and Port Said.* This irregular body of water covering a surface area of 1 800km²/695sq mi is separated from the Mediterranean by a narrow spit of land providing a link between Damietta and Port Said. The lake's water level is constantly changing, resulting in the fluctuation of its southern shore. Marshy areas covered with deposits of alluvium and tells *(see TANIS)* indicate the position of ancient sites. This shallow lake is renowned for its fish stocks.

THE MOUTH OF THE NILE
After a journey of 6 671km/4 169mi, by which time it has lost two-thirds of its volume through evaporation and irrigation, the river has shrunk to a narrow channel at its mouth, marked by a small red lighthouse.

Ras el-Barr
◀ *13km/8mi N of Damietta.* This large seaside resort nestles in a pleasant location between the Mediterranean and the eastern branch of the river. Apart from its beaches, the main point of interest here is the meeting of the muddy waters of the Nile with those of the Mediterranean, a sight only otherwise visible at Rosetta. This small town has developed a Western appearance with its streets running at right angles and brightly coloured modern buildings. Ras el-Barr is primarily a summer resort which takes on a sleepy feel over the winter months.

The ferry at Ezbet el-Borg.

DAMIETTA'S SECOND PORT
The town's industrial port, located 4km/2.5mi north of Damietta, and to the south of Ras el-Barr, specialises in the import of wood to supply the local furniture industry.

Nearby, on the right bank of the river, stands the old port of Damietta, **Ezbet el-Borg**. Despite its modern appearance, the port's origins date back many centuries, although hardly any of the old *mashrabiya* screened windows, embellished with elegantly worked metal grilles, remain. As a result of its concentration on coastal and inshore shipping, it no longer rivals the larger ports of Alexandria and Port Said, although its flotilla of attractively decorated sky-blue fishing boats is a delightful sight.

A small ferry operates a free service between the two towns.

El-Alamein

El-Alamein, which stands alongside the Mediterranean on the edge of the Libyan Desert, takes us back to one of the most remarkable military episodes to have occurred on North African soil during the Second World War. Although far from spectacular, the site is a fascinating stopping-point along the coast road to the Siwa oasis.

Location
106km/66mi W of Alexandria to the NE of the Qattara depression. Access: by road only from Alexandria, either by car, taxi (E£100 round trip) or West Delta bus.

Name
For military historians the name El-Alamein is synonymous with a classic type of desert warfare which saw the coming of age of the caterpillar tank, invented by the Americans to avoid sinkage into the sand.

Transcription: العالمين

Famous People
The battle of El-Alamein is the tale of two strong-willed military leaders: on the one hand the British general, Montgomery (1887-1976), or "Monty" as he was better known, and on the other the German field-marshal, Rommel (1891-1944).

History
The battle of El-Alamein raged between October and November 1942, following the military offensive led by Rommel in Libya.

> **MINES**
> Swimming is generally prohibited in the coastal waters around El-Alamein because of the risk posed by unexploded mines on the sea-bed.

background

Geo-political context – Following Japan's entry into the war in December 1941, an event that diverted considerable Commonwealth reinforcements from Egypt (including the Australian divisions recalled in May 1942), the preservation of the Mediterranean supply route from Great Britain became a major preoccupation for the Allies. During the course of 1941, Rommel, as head of the **Afrika Korps**, had already consolidated the German position on the border between Egypt and Libya, and an initial conflict (Operation Crusader) with the **8th Army** resulted in the German army's withdrawal to the west of **Tobruk** in December of that year.

Rommel's counter-offensive – In May 1942, taking advantage of the vast area in which the 8th Army was forced to commit its troops, Rommel launched his tanks on the British forces commanded by General Ritchie. The assault by the combined German and Italian troops

> Rommel's defeat at El-Alamein signalled the beginning of the end for the Axis powers in North Africa. However, the military leader known as the "Desert Fox" would become a legendary figure in the history of modern warfare because of his daring and astute tactical awareness.

General Montgomery.

was such that the British, supported by the French under General Koenig, were pushed back to **El-Alamein** on 7 July. The following month, Montgomery received the command of the 8th Army, which he reorganised while Rommel was consolidating his position close to Sidi Abd el-Rahman.

The battle – With 230 000 troops and 1 030 tanks at his disposal (against the combined German forces of 100 000 men and 500 tanks), Montgomery decided to attack on the evening of 23 October. Following an intense artillery bombardment, he engaged his infantry in a pincer movement along the coast to the north and halfway towards the Qattara depression to the south. Having taken control of Kidney Hill (to the south of Sidi Abd el-Rahman) he mounted a decisive attack on 2 November with the support of his tanks. Despite the intervention of Hitler, who ordered Rommel to maintain his position whatever the cost, the latter retreated behind what was left of his army at Tobruk. From now on, the fighting moved west towards Libya, and then Tunisia.

> Universally recognised as a great strategist and leader of men, **Montgomery** accepted the surrender of German forces in the north at Lüneburg on 4 May 1945. He received a peerage the following year, in so doing becoming the first Viscount Montgomery of Alamein.

worth a visit

Military Museum
West of the village. Open in summer 8am-6pm (1pm Fri); in winter and during Ramadan 8am-3pm; E£5; camera permit: E£10; video permit: E£25.

This museum is of interest to those with a passion for military history, in particular the famous battle that took place nearby.

Exterior – Exhibits outside the museum include a collection of tanks and cannons, including the famous American Sherman tank, 300 of which were used to support Montgomery.

Interior – The museum is divided into rooms dedicated to individual countries (Italy, Egypt, Germany and Great Britain), each displaying collections of uniforms and weaponry. In the Egyptian Room note the green flag bearing a crescent and three stars (symbolising Egypt, the Sudan and Turkey) that flew above the country at the time.

El-Alamein War Cemetery
250m/275yd E.

With its long lines of graves (815 of which bear the words "unknown soldier"), the British cemetery is a particularly moving sight. A total of 7 367 men from the countries of the Commonwealth are buried here, including soldiers from India. The cemetery also houses the tombs of French and Greek soldiers.

The imposing monument of the Italian Military Cemetery.

German and Italian Cemeteries
8km/5mi and 12km/8mi W.

Both of these cemeteries overlook the sea in tranquil surroundings where the only sound is that of the wind blowing in from the sea.

outskirts

Sidi Abd el-Rahman
23km/14mi NW of El-Alamein.

◄ This village has developed around a mosque built to venerate a saint held in the same esteem as the Prophet Muhammad by the Bedouins. The people who have been resettled here by the Egyptian govenrment belong to the local Morabite tribes.

> **T**he dozens of private holiday villages built recently between Alexandria and El-Alamein have had a considerable visual impact on this hitherto wild and unspoilt coastline.

The **beach** at Sidi Abd el-Rahman is considered by many Egyptians to be the best along this stretch of coastline and has become a fashionable summer resort, making it likely that the 190km/119mi of coastline between here and Ras el-Hekma to the west will soon fall prey to property and leisure developers.

Mersa Matruh☼

This Mediterranean resort is popular with Egyptians who come here to enjoy its delightful beaches, considered to be among the best in the country. For most foreign visitors, however, Mersa Matruh has few attractions and as such is merely a staging post on the road to the Siwa oasis.

Location
On the Mediterranean coast towards the Libyan border, 595km/372mi NW of Cairo, 291km/182mi E of Alexandria and 305km NE of the Siwa oasis. Access: by bus services operated by Superjet and the West Delta Company from Cairo (journey time: 5hr) or Alexandria (4hr); by plane on Egyptair; or by road. The train is best avoided.

Name
During the Greco-Roman period the city was known as *Parætonium*. It was from here that Alexander the Great set off to Siwa, where he was officially recognised by the oracle as the son of Amun.

Transcription: مرسى مطروح

Famous People
Queen Cleopatra and Mark Antony came to Mersa Matruh to pursue their love affair away from the glare of Alexandrian society. During her war against Octavian (the future Augustus), Cleopatra established her battle headquarters in the port area of the city.

background

Cleopatra VII – Six Cleopatras preceded the most famous of the Egyptian queens to carry this name. Born in 69 BC, this daughter of Ptolemy XII Auletes (who was also known as the "flute player") initially shared the throne with her two brothers – whom she married one after the other in accordance with the rite established by the Ptolemaic dynasty – until their premature deaths, after which time this last descendant of the pharaohs ruled alone. In 47 BC, her brother and husband, Ptolemy XIII, who had had his rival **Pompey** murdered after the latter had taken refuge in Egypt, drowned in the Nile at the age of 16 during his battle against **Julius Caesar**. Her second brother and husband, Ptolemy XIV, was poisoned and died at the age of 14.

Alignment with Rome – Ptolemy XIV was just 11 years of age when he married his sister. However, this young regent would be swept aside by Julius Caesar, whose

CHANGING MONEY
If you're heading for Siwa, you are well advised to get hold of some money here, as there are no banks in the oasis. The National Bank of Egypt *(located on El-Matar Street, west of Iskendariyya Street, near the Corniche)* has a cash dispenser which accepts both Visa and MasterCard.

DREAM OR REALITY?
Both on the screen and in books Cleopatra has always been depicted as the incarnation of beauty. However, at an exhibition at the British Museum in London, an expert claimed that this beauty was "a myth and that evidence supported this". Given that Octavian destroyed most of her statues, the claim is difficult to substantiate, but one thing is beyond doubt: whether she was ugly or beautiful, Cleopatra still holds an undeniable fascination.

Even Asterix and Obelix succumbed to the charm of Cleopatra!

The Roman world was divided between three triumvirs: Mark Antony in Greece, Lepidus in Africa and Octavian in the West. This triumvirate followed on from that of Caesar, Pompey and Crassus.

conquest of the Orient was already in full flow. Having been the mistress of Pompey, Cleopatra fulfilled the same role for Caesar himself, bearing him a son by the name of Caesarion. In 45 BC, she followed the great emperor to Rome, but a year later he was assassinated by Cassius and Brutus, the latter his adopted son. The Queen of Egypt returned to Alexandria, where she soon ◄ became involved in a love affair with Mark Antony, with whom she lived for 10 years. Following the suicide of Mark Antony, defeated by Octavian at Actium in 31 BC, Cleopatra vainly attempted to seduce the victor, before committing suicide herself the same year.

A determined queen – Cleopatra's life has provided writers with a perfect storyline which combines love, power and adventure, but which ultimately ends in tragedy. Yet it is important to place the life of this woman, who was considered to be frivolous, and even cruel, in nature, within the troubled context of the time: namely the twilight period in the history of Pharaonic Egypt and the dawn of the Roman Empire. At the age of 17, Cleopatra inherited a kingdom whose economy was in severe crisis and which effectively was living on borrowed time. Despite this, she stubbornly refused to relinquish her authority, preferring instead to ally herself with the new leaders of the Ancient World. Until her death, she continued to demonstrate unprecedented willpower and strength, culminating in her suicide by ◄ deadly snakebite.

Unlike her predecessors, who were content with the title of "Kings and Queens of Alexandria", Cleopatra preferred the grander title of "Queen of Egypt". Ultimately her country and its people would tire of this indefatigable monarch, who nonetheless fought hard for her own immortality.

exploring Mersa Matruh

The town

Iskendariyya Street, which runs at right-angles to the Corniche, offers the best options for a drink or a bite to eat; those looking to buy arts and crafts, the Libyan mar- ◄ ket (Libya souk) specialises in imported products from Egypt's western neighbour and other parts of North Africa. Apart from tourism, the town's two major sources of income are watermelons and natural sea sponges.

ROMMEL MUSEUM
Open 9am-3pm in winter, 8am-2pm in summer. E£5. This small cave at Rommel's Beach served as the Desert Fox's headquarters during the Battle of El-Alamein. Its exhibits include Rommel's greatcoat (donated by his family), photos and maps.

Beaches

Mersa's 5km/3mi-long crescent-shaped bay is renowned for its calm waters and magnificent turquoise colour. Visitors should be aware that this beach is out of bounds after sunset.

Rommel Beach – *3km/2mi NE.* Named after the German field-marshal who came here to swim every morning, this beach is recommended for Western women.

Beau Site Hotel Beach – *See below.* This attractive beach is open to non-guests. Sun-loungers (E£3/day) and para-sols (E£12/day) are also available for hire.

LOCAL TRANSPORT
These beaches are accessible by collective taxi or minibus (E£3 to Agiba) from the main bus station (near the railway station), or alternatively by donkey-drawn cart (E£3 to Rommel Beach).

Cleopatra's Bath – *14km/9mi NW.* Legend has it that Queen Cleopatra and Mark Antony came here to swim in this natural pool. Today, the current is too strong to swim in safety.

Agiba Beach★ – *26km W.* This spectacular small cove, whose name translates as "Miraculous" is by far the best in the area.

directory

WHERE TO STAY

Mersa Matruh has a number of hotels, although most offer poor value for money. These are generally full in summer and closed in winter.

• *Moderate*

Beau Site Hotel – *West of the Corniche.*
☏ *(046) 493 20 66 – 174 rooms: E£350/E£687.* The resort's "cosmopolitan"

resort is somewhat expensive, but has a private beach.

WHERE TO EAT

• *Budget*

Gaby – *On the Corniche.* This pizzeria facing the bay serves a variety of pizzas (E£8-E£12) and grilled meats.

Rashid

The famous Rosetta Stone, which provided the key to deciphering Egyptian hieroglyphs, was discovered in Rashid (Rosetta). The city, a long-time rival of Alexandria, and sometimes referred to as "the city of a million palm trees", is known for its attractive and unique Ottoman architecture. Rashid is now a busy food-processing centre.

Location
220km/137mi N of Cairo, 56km/35mi E of Alexandria, on the left bank of the western branch of the Nile, 12km/7mi S of the Mediterranean. Access: by taxi, train or minibus from Alexandria station, via Abukir (change minibus where the bus crosses the track); the return journey to Alexandria is direct.

Name
The Arabic name *Rashid* comes from the Coptic *Rikhit*.
Transcription: رشيد

Famous People
When he arrived in Egypt for the first time in 1828, Jean-François Champollion (1790-1832) had already decoded the stone which was to make the name Rosetta world-famous.

The Rosetta Stone was actually discovered by Captain Pierre Bouchard, a member of Napoleon's expedition.

background

The Ottomans – Around 870, the Abbasid Caliph Ibn Tulun founded the town on a site which had been inhabited since prehistory. The town reached its zenith in the 17C, when trade between Constantinople and Egypt was at its peak. Prosperous until the beginning of the 19C, when it was Egypt's most important port, Rosetta's fortunes declined dramatically after the development of Alexandria by Mohammed Ali.

A legendary stone – In 1799, while carrying out consolidation work on the fort in Rosetta, a French engineering officer, **Pierre Bouchard**, uncovered a basalt slab bearing three scripts (Greek, Demotic and hieroglyphic). Following the announcement of his find in the French armed forces gazette, the discovery was sent to Cairo where Napoleon, aware of its scientific importance, had a number of mouldings made from it. The stone dates from 196 BC and was once part of a stele describing honours granted to Ptolemy V.

Local specialities include palm hearts, bought fresh from the market which runs along the banks of the Nile and its shipyards.

The key to ancient Egypt – The stone was moved to London, where it attracted much curiosity, as well as competition between scholars, as Egyptologists realised that by comparing the three scripts they could unravel the meaning of Egyptian hieroglyphs which had not been understood since before the Christian era. The Englishman **Thomas Young** and the Swede **Johan David Åkerblad** were able to identify the royal names in the Demotic text and ascertained that the letters of the name "Ptolemy" were found in the three texts. Young then established that the hieroglyphic script contained an alphabet and followed grammatical rules.

The final translation – However, it was not until 1822 that the text was finally deciphered. A 32 year-old Frenchman, **Jean-François Champollion**, who was convinced that Coptic was a late evolution of the language of the Ancient Egyptians, concentrated his research on a text discovered a year earlier in the temple of Isis at Philae, in Aswan. He soon understood that the hieroglyphs on the stone were a translation of the Greek text (and not the other way around), and that they were both ideographic and phonetic. He was then able to draw up a list of the signs and their Greek equivalents. From this moment on, hieroglyphs were no longer seen as decoration but became an important key to understanding the Ancient Egyptian civilisation, much of which had been shrouded in mystery for over 1 500 years.

exploring Rosetta

Ottoman Houses★

Four houses are open to the public (museum closed). Open all year, 9am-3.30pm. E£12; students E£6; camera permit E£5; video permit E£10. Ticket office in front of the museum gardens in Hureya Square.

The two main characteristics of the houses in Rosetta are their height (three, or even four floors) and the decorative use of black and red bricks fixed with a white mortar. The *mashrabiya* on the 23 houses bought by the Egyptian Antiquities Service are also worthy of note.

Abu Shahin Mill – The 19C stables are supported by columns with Greco-Roman capitals.

Ramadan House – The 18C former residence of an unpopular governor is devoid of furniture and has an underground passage which enabled the governor to escape in the event of a rebellion. Sadly it failed in its goal, as he was eventually hanged! The layout of the house is typical, with a ground floor where goods were stored, a first floor used by the men, and second and third floors used by the women. The third floor also had a *hammam* with an ingenious water-heating system.

Azouz Hammam – This 18C and 19C *hamman* was open to the public until 1982; it was used by men for four days of the week, by women for two, and closed on Fridays. Such establishments became redundant once houses were built with private bathrooms. The water tanks, positioned on the upper terrace, were supplied with water from the Nile.

Galal House – This 18C house belonged to a French general, Jacques-François Mino, who married an Egyptian woman by the name of Zubayda and converted to Islam.

The brightly coloured dome above the massage room of the Azouz Hammam, once open to the public.

worth a visit

Qaitbey Fort

3km/1.8mi N. Open all year, 9am-4pm. E£12; no camera permit required; video permit E£12.

The Rosetta Stone was discovered in the south-west tower of this fort, then known as St Julian Fort. The fortress was built by the Sultan Al-Malik Nasr Qait Bey in 1472.

Tanis★

Tour groups rarely disturb the silence that pervades Tanis, yet it was here that one of the most magnificent treasures of Ancient Egypt was discovered. Despite its rather bleak location amid a lunar-type landscape, Tanis has managed to retain its powerful charm of bygone days.

Cartouche – Rameses II

Location
130km/81mi NE of Cairo and 60km/37mi S of Damietta on the right bank of the Bahr Saft, a secondary branch of the Nile which flows into Lake Manzala. No direct access from Cairo; travel by train to Zagazig or Faqus, then take a taxi to San el-Hagar (1hr).

Name
The Greeks gave Tanis the name Djanet; in Arabic the town is known as San el-Hagar – *hagar* meaning "the stones" – as at one time the site saw use as a quarry. The prefix *San* derives from the Coptic word *Tjaami*, the direct translation of Tanis.

Transcription: تانيس

Famous People
Although Indiana Jones undoubtedly painted a fresh gloss on the story of the Ark of the Covenant or "Lost Ark" in which the Hebrew people transported the Tables of the Law, reality owes more to the French archaeologist Pierre Montet, who discovered the royal necropolis in 1939. His work led to a better understanding of a period hitherto relatively unknown.

> **A**lthough Steven Spielberg's *Raiders of the Lost Ark* was not actually filmed here, Tanis was the setting for Harrison Ford's first adventure as Indiana Jones.

History
"The forgotten capital of the Delta", Tanis was the residence and the place of burial for pharaohs during the Third Intermediate Period under the 21st and 22nd Dynasties. The town was also the capital of the 14th *nome* of Lower Egypt.

background

Origins – Like other archaeological sites in the Delta region, the monuments at Tanis pose a number of problems with regard to dating.

By the time of Rameses II (19th Dynasty), Tanis was already an important hub in trade between Egypt and the Near East, so much so that this famous pharaoh established a royal residence here. In 1069 BC, one year after the founding of the 21st Dynasty, the city experienced phenomenal growth, which continued until the advent of the Ptolemies in 306 BC. In fact, the "Tanite kings" transferred their capital from Piramesse, Rameses II's capital 20km/12mi to the south-east, in order to create "a new Karnak". It was Smendes II, the vizier of Lower Egypt, founder of the 21st Dynasty and first Tanite king, who turned Tanis into the capital of an Egypt which at the time was experiencing serious division (the 20th Dynasty continued to rule Upper Egypt under Herihor).

Disappearance – So what caused the demise of this city, which was of great importance in the 1C BC, but little more than a small town a century later? It would appear that a change in the course of the Nile, along with catastrophic flooding from the Mediterranean, was the catalyst for this sudden change of fortune, although it is unlikely to be the sole reason, as political and religious events may well already have reduced Tanis to an extremely minor role. An earthquake in AD 20 was also to have a devastating effect on Tanis. The town fell into total disrepair and was subsequently abandoned, a situ-

A CASE OF MISTAKEN IDENTITY
It was long thought that Tanis had been built by Rameses II (19th Dynasty), but we now know that the city was constructed out of materials taken from the town of Piramesse. This explains why hieroglyphs referring to this pharaoh have been discovered here.

EXCAVATIONS
Auguste Mariette carried out initial work here in the second half of the 19C, to be followed by William Petrie (1883-86) and Pierre Montet (1929-51). Work was continued by Jean Yoyotte in 1964, and by Philippe Brissaud in 1985.

ation that still existed five centuries later. Like other Delta towns, Tanis was gradually covered with silt and was even used as a quarry. Singled out during the Napoleonic invasions, it was widely pillaged until Auguste Mariette ensured its preservation following an initial series of excavations in the 1860s.

THE HYKSOS

Tanis has in times past been linked to Piramesse (or *Per Rameses*), an ancient Egyptian harbour-town built on the site of **Avaris**, the capital of the Hyksos. Even if this link is false, these invaders have nevertheless been directly associated with Tanis and are often mentioned in the same breath. The fact that Avaris has been located at Tell el-Dab'a *(see below)*, to the south-east of Tanis, further strengthens this association. The end of the 12th Dynasty heralded the beginning of the Second Intermediate Period, characterised by the first foreign invasion from Asia by the Hyksos ("rulers of foreign lands" in Egyptian). The "invasion" was in essence the gradual infiltration and integration of Semitic and Indo-European nomads; they initially colonised the western part of the Delta and established their capital at Avaris around 1720 BC, before founding the 15th and 16th Dynasties, which reigned from 1640-1532, in **Memphis**. The rulers of the 17th Theban Dynasty, the contemporaries of the Hyksos, were their vassals. The supremacy of the Hyksos in Egypt was to last barely a century.

worth a visit

RUINS AND NECROPOLIS★

Open all year 7am-5pm. E£20; photographic equipment E£5; videos E£25. (NB: times and sections open to the public may vary according to excavations.)

Of all the tells indicating the site of a major town in Antiquity, this one is by far the largest (30ha/74acres). Three main groups of ruins are visible (the great temple, the royal necropolis and the east temple), although it it hard to imagine that these were part of one of the most majestic cities of all Ancient Egypt. Despite being off the beaten track, and although lay visitors may have difficulty in interpreting the ruins, the site has retained a magical air.

The views of the site from the excavation centre and to the west towards the village of San el-Hagar are particularly attractive.

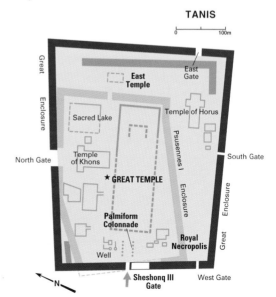

TANIS

Great Temple★

Bordered to the south by the wall built by Psusennes I and to the north by the main line of defence, the Great Temple of Amun is built on an east-west axis for a length of almost 400m/1 300ft. Today, this temple erected by Rameses II is no more than a chaotic pile of granite, as its stonework has long since been extracted for the production of lime. However, the colossal statues, pieces of obelisk and large blocks bear witness to the former splendour and glory of the site.

Sheshonq III Gate – The first ruin visible upon entering is a monumental gate without foundations, flanked by triads and colossi representing Rameses II. These blocks, which have been re-used, bear various legible inscriptions.

Palmiform Colonnade – The colonnade bears the names of Rameses II and Sheshonq III, the sovereign of the 22nd Dynasty established at Bubastis, in the Delta. This dynasty originated from Libyan mercenaries, whose head, Sheshonq I, overthrew Psusennes II, the last Tanite king.

Temple – The broken obelisks are succeeded by fragments of wall and statues. Rameses II is omnipresent here, both in the inscriptions and on the colossal sandstone statues recumbent on the ground. Further along, the actual sanctuary is difficult to recognise as it consists of nothing more than scattered blocks. It was here, on this desolate site, that Rameses II signed a treaty with the Hittites after the memorable **Battle of Qadesh**, an impressive portrayal of which can be seen on the walls of the Great Temple at Abu Simbel.

In 1948, a rectangular sacred lake, measuring 50m x 60m (164ft x197ft) was cleared to the north-east of the temple.

Royal Necropolis

Treasure – Situated to the south of the Sheshonq III gate between the enclosure wall built by Psusennes I and the Great Temple of Amun, the necropolis discovered by Montet in 1939 was filled with an incredible array of jewels and funerary objects that have mercifully been spared the pillaging suffered by other tombs. On display in a special room (*first floor, Room 2*) at the Egyptian Museum in Cairo, this **treasure** is only surpassed by that of Tutankhamun.

Tombs – These subterranean sepulchres dating from the 22nd Dynasty do not have a superstructure. The tomb of Psusennes I contained seven intact sepulchres, including the hawk-headed silver coffin of Sheshonq II. The burial chamber of Sheshonq III is decorated with scenes from the *Book of the Dead*.

East Temple

Situated within the main wall, this temple illustrates the phenomenon of usurpation which often complicates the task of dating monuments. The temple's **10 palmiform columns** bear the markings of Rameses II (19th Dynasty) and Osorkon II (19th Dynasty), although these, in fact, are earlier and originally date from the Old Kingdom. Quite simply, the columns have been re-used.

outskirts

Tell el-Dab'a

20km/12mi SE of Tanis. Tell el-Dab'a stands on the road linking Faqus and Tanis, and contains impressive vestiges from the 15th, 16th, 19th and 20th Dynasties. Following excavations carried out by the Austrian archaeologist, Manfred Bietak, it is now thought that this site was once the site of Avaris, the former capital of the Hyksos, as well as that of Piramesse; the former stood to the south of the site, the latter to the north. According to the Egyptian historian **Manetho**, it was Salitis, the king of the Hyksos, who founded Avaris, establishing a garrison of 240 000 men. The founder of the 28th Dynasty, Ahmose, subsequently seized the town (between 1550 and 1525), forcing the Hyksos to flee.

> **DÉJÀ VU!**
> On leaving Cairo airport, you may have noticed an obelisk on the road into the city. This column originates from this temple, and was one of nine erected here by Rameses II.

This remarkable gold necklace weighing over 6kg/13lb was among the jewellery discovered by Montet in the tomb of Psusennes I.

> **"STELE OF THE 400"**
> Discovered at Tanis, this stele dates the capture of Avaris by the Hyksos to 1720 BC. After their occupation of the Delta, they seized Memphis in 1675.

Wadi el-Natroun

The fertile depression of Wadi Natrun, covering a distance of approximately 30km/18mi, lies on the edge of the Libyan Desert, close to the motorway linking Cairo and Alexandria. This small valley has been farmed since Antiquity and has been a monastic centre since the early 4C. It is now home to four Coptic monasteries.

Location
94km/58mi NW of Cairo, 131km/82mi SE of Alexandria, at the NE tip of the Libyan Desert. Access: by the desert road linking Cairo and Alexandria (turn left after the resthouse and pass through the village of Bir Hooker); and on bus services from Cairo operated by the West Delta Company (E£20/30), then by taxi from the village.

Name
Wadi Natrun literally translates as "valley of salt". During the Pharaonic period, natron (hydrated sodium carbonate) was extracted here and used in the mummification process. The natron was harvested in March from deposits from two salt lakes in the area.

Transcription: وادى النطرون

> **NATRON**
> Today, natron is used by the chemical industry in the manufacture of glass and for whitening linen.

Famous People
The first Christians of Egypt owed much of their teaching to the philosopher Philo Judaeus (c 13-54), whose neo-Platonic ideas influenced many of the spiritual beliefs of this young community.

background

> **T**he Greek *Aegyptios* has its roots in the Ancient Egyptian *Hout-ka-Ptah*, the Egyptian name of the first capital Memphis, which translates as "it was here that the god Ptah created the world".

Origins of the word Copt – The word "copt" comes from the Arabic *qibt,* an abbreviated form of the Greek *Aegyptios*. Pronounced *Egoptos*, the word has given us "Egypt"; pronounced *Goptos*, it has given us "Copt". In other words, the Coptic Church is none other than the Egyptian Church, the origins of which are apostolic.

Origins of Christianity in Egypt – According to the historian Eusebius of Caesarea, Christianity was brought to Egypt in 42 AD by St Mark the Evangelist, who travelled to Alexandria to found a bishopric. St Mark is considered to be the first Patriarch of Egypt, in the same way that Peter is considered to be the founder of the Catholic Church in Rome.

worth a visit

> It is customary to remove your shoes before entering a church. If you are wearing shorts, you will be provided with a tunic.

Deir es-Souriani★
Closed for the 50 days before Orthodox Easter. No charge.

Foundation – The Monastery of the Syrians was founded in the 6C. Following the theological disagreement between Orthodox and Giainite Christians over the human nature of Christ (a theory disputed by the Giainites), the monastery was occupied by Syrian Giainite monks in the 8C.

Church of the Virgin★ – This church, which is crowned by cupolas and still retains elements of its 10C architecture, is adorned with striking Byzantine **frescoes★★** discovered under four layers of paint. One of these dates from the 9C and represents the Virgin with the archangel Gabriel, Isaiah, Moses, Ezekiel and Daniel. The choir lies transversally to the nave, in typical Syrian style; it is preceded by a wooden iconostasis dating from 926, and is decorated with 11C-12C frescoes. The *Annunciation* and *Nativity* can be seen in the semi-dome to the south, the *Dormition* to the north and the *Assumption* to the west.

> **WORTH SEEING**
> Between the choir and the *haikal* (the main sanctuary) stands a splendid wooden door dating from the 10C. The door is inlaid with ivory and comprises 42 panels representing Christ and the Virgin, alongside the most important personalities of the Coptic and Syrian patriarchate (first row) and a complex array of crosses (second row).

The Tree of St Ephraem – The tamarind tree growing next to the 13C Cave Church is supposed to have taken root during a meeting between St Ephraem and

The monks of Wadi Natrun dedicate themselves to a life of prayer and contemplation.

St Bishuy. Although the two men did not speak the same language, it is said that St Bishuy was suddenly able to express himself in Syrian and that St Ephraem's stick miraculously took root at the same moment.

Deir Amba Bishuy

Next to Deir es-Souriani. Open all day; church open 9am-5pm only (8am-8pm in summer). No charge.

Foundation – St Bishuy, who was born in the Delta around the year 320, is said to have been commanded by an angel to withdraw to the Scetis Desert (the old name for Wadi Natrun). There he attracted a community of anchorites and founded a monastery which was later attacked by Bedouin tribes on five separate occasions.

Church – Nothing remains of the original church. The present 9C building has a complex layout, with a narthex, central and side aisles, inner and outer choirs and three sanctuaries.

Defensive tower – This 5C tower leads to a terrace which has a lovely view of the desert and surrounding farmland.

Deir el-Baramus

10km/6mi N. Open 10am-4pm (6pm in summer); closed for the 50 days before Easter. No charge.

Foundation – The Monastery of Baramus, or Monastery of the Romans, is thought to be the oldest of the monasteries in Wadi Natrun. It was founded by St Macarius around the year 330, before the foundation of Deir Abu Makar.

Church of the Virgin – Built between the 9C and 11C, this church was inspired by the church at Deir es-Souriani. Beautiful 13C-14C **frescoes**★ can be seen in the central nave depicting, from east to west, the *Annunciation*, the *Visitation*, the *Nativity*, the *Baptism of Christ*, the *Wedding at Cana* and the *Entry of Christ into Jerusalem*. A door from the Fatimid period leads to the *haikal*, the main sanctuary, also decorated with frescoes from the same period, one of which portrays the *Sacrifice of Abraham*.

Defensive tower – This tower dates from the 7C.

Deir Abu Makar

20km/12mi SE. By appointment only (☎ (02) 577 06 14).

Foundation – St Macarius the Great, who was born in the Delta around the year 300, was a camel driver who came to Wadi Natrun to gather natron. A pious man, he decided to live in the solitude of the desert, where he attracted so many disciples that a monastic community grew up around him. He left this monastery and retired further into the desert, but was again followed by his disciples; the monastery of St Macarius was subsequently founded on this spot.

Church of St Macarius – Although built over foundations which date back to 330, the present church dates from the 11C and 12C. Certain sections, however, such as the walls of the central sanctuary, date back to the 7C. The relics of St Macarius, one of the most important figures in the Coptic Church, rest in this church, the walls of which are adorned with fragments of old frescoes.

MONASTIC TRADITIONS
Coptic monks dress in long black robes and wear a skull cap embroidered with 13 crosses. Of these, 12 represent the Apostles, while the 13th symbolises Christ. During ordination the prayer of the dead is read, after which monks are considered to belong to eternity rather than to this world. Parish priests, on the other hand, are able to marry and lead normal lives while carrying out their religious duties.

There are no statues in Coptic churches, only icons and *patée* or *ansata* crosses. As the Passion of Christ is only evoked and not depicted, there are no sculpted images of the Crucifixion.

Zagazig

The town of Zagazig, nowadays the capital of Lower Egypt, was established in the middle of the 19C from camps set up to house workers building a dam on a branch of the Nile. Modern Zagazig is an industrial and business centre which is home to the remains of Bubastis, the former site of the cat-goddess Bastet.

Location
85km/53mi N of Cairo on the Bahr Muweys, a branch of the Nile. Access: by train from Cairo (hourly from 6.20am to 6.30pm; journey time: 1hr 30min); by bus from Cairo on services operated by the West Delta Bus Company (hourly from 6am to 6.30pm; journey time: 2hr).

Name
The town takes its name from the *zagazoug* fish that once inhabited an old branch of the Nile.

Transcription: الزقازيق

> "Some 700 000 men and women make their way to Bubastis for the festival of the cat-goddess, where they celebrate with great sacrifices and consume more wine than the rest of the year."
> Herodotus

◄ Famous People
Bastet's soul still lives on in Zagazig even if her temple has long since disappeared. This cat-goddess was well loved, particularly because of her maternal and protective instincts.

Although she appeared late in the history of Ancient Egypt, Bastet was particularly venerated during the 22nd Dynasty, quite simply because its pharaohs came from *Per-Bastet*, the "House of Bastet" (also known as *Bubastis* in Greek, and *Tell Basta* in Arabic).

worth a visit

Orabi Museum
Open all year 8am-5pm (1.30pm Fri). £E5.
The museum's modest collection contains archaeological finds discovered in the surrounding region.

Tell Basta
SE of Zagazig. To reach the site, take a taxi from the railway station (15min). Archaeology enthusiasts will be familiar with this town by its more common Greek name of Bubastis, used by the historian Herodotus. This ancient site was dedicated to the feline goddess Bastet, and, according to the Father of History, was the highest in Egypt.

BASTET
It would appear that Bastet was initially possessed with a fiery and evil temperament. Her admirers gradually transformed her into a gentle cat-goddess, transferring her less endearing qualities to Sekhmet, another lion-goddess.

Site – It is hard to imagine that what nowadays amounts to no more than a few unimpressive stone blocks strewn among the sparse ruins here were once the capital of the 12th nome of Lower Egypt during the 28th Dynasty, 3 500 years ago, and that this city was to become the capital of Egypt under the 22nd and 23rd Dynasties! The excavations carried out by the Egypt Exploration Fund at the end of the 19C, under the supervision of the Swiss Egyptologist Henri Édouard Naville, which unearthed blocks engraved with cartouches of **Khufu** and **Khafra**, have confirmed that the site was active from the 4th Dynasty onwards. Traces of the 6th, 7th, 18th, 19th, 20th and 22nd Dynasties have also been found here, the latter often being referred to as the "Bubastic Dynasty". Excavators have also discovered thousands of

THE ORIGINS OF THE CAT
It is thought that the cat, formerly called *myou* by the Egyptians, arrived in Europe from Egypt via Greece. Originally hunted for its fur, the cat became domesticated from the 11th Dynasty. From then on it is frequently represented in poses of submission and tenderness.

◄ statuettes and mummies of cats (the cat cemetery and underground galleries are located 200m/250yd to the north, towards Zagazig).

Fragments of mosaic also bear witness to a Roman presence here. The town was subsequently inhabited by the Copts, before being abandoned, as was the case with Tanis, the other major Ancient city in the Delta region.

The Great Temple – The site of the temple proper remains difficult to ascertain for any non-specialist, making it hard to identify individual features such as the peristyle court, the jubilee chapel or the hypostyle hall. Although it is impossible today to imagine the temple's exact form, its importance is without question: it was situated at the very heart of Bubastis, with an east-west orientation, and flanked by two canals lined with trees. One unusual aspect was that the town overlooked the temple rather than the other way round. Putting a date on the temple poses a number of difficulties given that many of its features were re-used. In principle, its foundation preceded the reign of Rameses II (19th Dynasty); it was subsequently appropriated and enlarged by Rameses II, Osorkon I (21st Dynasty) – who also seized the ancient Bastet temple – and by Nectanebo II (30th Dynasty).

The double row of pillars visible on the opposite side of the road belonged to a temple dedicated to Pepy I (6th Dynasty).

THE "ZAGAZIG TREASURE"
In 1906, during the construction of a railway, workers here discovered gold and silver tableware from the 19th Dynasty that is now displayed in museums in Berlin, New York and Cairo (Egyptian Museum). This find was probably part of the temple's collection.

outskirts

Bilbeis
25km/15mi S of Zagazig. This agricultural settlement on the southern edge of the delta is located on the old caravan trade route between Cairo and the Sinai. A former important stronghold, Bilbeis has preserved the old Amir El-Geich mosque, founded in the 7C and modified in the 16C, as well as a 13C dam built during the reign of the Mameluke sultan, Baibars.

"THE ORIENTAL", THE CRADLE OF THE ARABIAN HORSE
The governorship of the Lower Egypt region, of which Zagazig is the capital, is known as "The Oriental" (or *Al-Sharqiyah* in Arabic).
The province, whose emblem is the Arabian horse, is well known for its cotton, soya and rice, but has a worldwide reputation for the quality of its stud farms. It provides 85% of Egyptian thoroughbreds, the only horses that King Solomon would ride, and which the sacred prophets never referred to as mere "animals". Here, the thoroughbred is considered close to man, as not only is it a beautiful, elegant and faithful beast, it is also a friend, created by the "Southern wind" and blessed with spirituality. It is for this reason that in times gone by, the Egyptian horse would sleep in the tent with the family rather than outside in the open air.

Every year,
from 2-9 September,
the **Arabian Horse** Fair
is held at an equestrian
centre in the province.

Cairo
and its Environs

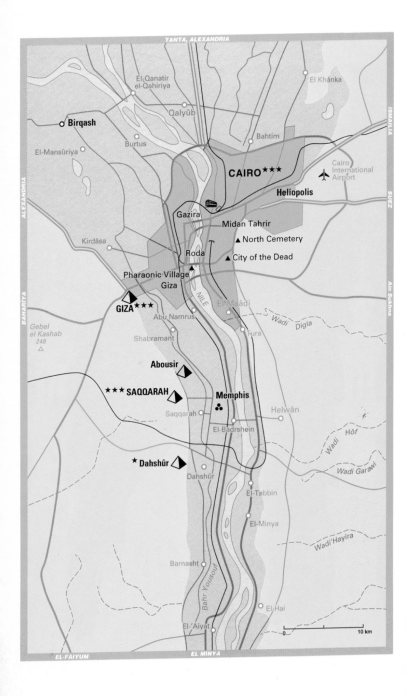

TANTA, ALEXANDRIA

El-Qanatir
el-Qahiriya

El Khânka

○ **Birqash**

Qalyûb

El-Mansûriya

Burtus

Bahtim

Cairo
International
Airport

CAIRO★★★

Heliopolis

Gazira

Kirdâsa

Midan Tahrir

▲ North Cemetery

Roda

▲ City of the Dead

Pharaonic Village

Giza

El-Maâdi

GIZA★★★

Abu Namrus

Wadi Digla

Gebel
el Kashab
248
△

Shabramant

Tura

Abousir

★★★ **SAQQARAH**

Memphis

Saqqarah ○

Helwân

El-Badrshein

Wadi Hôf

★ **Dahshûr**

Dahshûr

Wadi Garawi

El-Tebbin

El-Minya

Wadi Hayira

Barnasht

Bahr Yousouf

El-Hai

El-'Aiyat

0   10 km

EL-FAIYUM   EL MINYA

ALEXANDRIA

BAHARIYA

ISMAILIA

SUEZ

Ain Sukhna

Cairo★★★

On first impressions, the capital of Egypt is an unfathomable, frenetic city that appears to be expanding at an unstoppable rate. Yet, within this seemingly suffocating urban chaos, some 19 million inhabitants go about their daily lives, making Cairo the largest city on the African continent and in the Islamic world. Its maze of narrow streets and densely populated old quarters, overlooked by many of Cairo's 400 minarets, provide a stark contrast with the towers and apartment blocks of its modern districts. Scratch the surface of this metropolis, however, and discover a city that is the embodiment of Egypt and its momentous history.

Location

On the banks of the Nile, S of the Mediterranean, 225km/140mi SE of Alexandria, and 130km/81mi W of Suez. Access: from Europe and the USA by air on both scheduled and charter flights; from other Egyptian cities by plane, bus or train, and from smaller towns by bus only. ►

Cairo is situated 20km/12mi south of the point where the Nile splits into its two main branches, one towards Damietta, the other towards Rosetta.

Name

It was at the time of the construction of the city under the Fatimids that Cairo was named *El-Qahira*, "the Victorious One", as a result of the ascendancy of the planet Mars *(el-Qaher)* during this period. In Heliopolitan mythology, the two rivals gods Seth and Horus confronted each other on the right bank of the Nile, opposite what is now the island of Roda, at a place named *Kher-Aha*, or "the place of combat". ►

Transcription: القاهرة

Other names given to the city include *Oum el-Dounia*, the "mother of the world", and *Masr* (Egypt), so indelibly linked is the image of the city with that of the nation.

Famous People

Natives of Cairo synonymous with the city's modern history include the Khedive Ismail Pasha (1830-95); the winner of the Nobel Prize for Literature, Naguib Mahfouz (b 1912); the former Secretary-General of the United Nations, Boutros Boutros Ghali (1922); the actor Omar Sharif; and the singer Yolande Gigliotti, better known as Dalida. Although born in Alexandria, the architect Hassan Fathy (1900-89) spent much of his life in Cairo and is indelibly linked with the city.

At first glance Cairo appears to be a city that never seems to sleep!

background

The only vestige of this city, which was important primarily for the influence of its clergy, is an obelisk dedicated to Senusret I, situated in the working-class district of Matareya.

◄ **Heliopolis** – This, the 13th nome of Lower Egypt, is now a suburb of Cairo: excavations here have revealed traces of a settlement and necropolis from the Predynastic period. From the early days of the Old Kingdom, the site was a cult centre which saw the first known sun temple and which was home to the Great Ennead of Heliopolis, the nine Egyptian deities who participated in the creation myth. The buildings of the city were later used by the Arabs in the construction of Cairo itself.

Babylon – The walls of a Roman garrison established here under Emperor Augustus in 30 BC can still be seen in the Coptic Quarter; it was he who referred to this site as the "Babylon of Egypt". In 640, this by then Byzantine fortress was taken by **Omar**, the second successor to Muhammad. It was Omar's general, Amr Ibn el-As, who refused to demolish the camp because a dove had made its nest in his tent. Consequently, the camp remained and expanded.

969, the birth of Cairo – The garrison gradually prospered and became embellished with mosques until 870, when **Ahmed ibn Tulun**, the founder of the Tulunid Dynasty, enlarged *Masr* in *Al-Qataï*, a royal city which was subsequently razed by the caliphs of Baghdad in the year 905.

The city was divided into two districts: Masr el-Qahira and Masr el-Attika, in other words Cairo and Old Cairo.

◄ It was above these ruins that **Gohar**, a general under the Fatimid caliph El-Mouizz, established a city that would rival the Baghdad of the Abbasids. So it was, in 969, that the city of Cairo *(El-Qahira)* was born. From this time on, the Fatimids made Cairo their capital and set about its development, building a number of mosques (including that of Al-Azhar) and monumental gateways, and developing several districts.

Growth and prosperity – Sultan Salah al Din al Ayyubi (1138-93), or **Saladin**, the future vanquisher of the Christian crusaders, was the first ruler within the Ayyubid Dynasty. It was he who was to bring together the city's two distinct quarters as one and enclose it inside a protective wall. This new city was dominated by a citadel on the Moqattam Hill which was to become the residence of his successors. Despite the outbreaks of plague and murderous intrigues of the time, Cairo was to enjoy one of its most magnificent periods since the reign of the Mamelukes. Splendid new buildings sprang up everywhere and a sense of well-being pervaded the city – it was against this backdrop that *The Thousand and One Nights* was set. In 1524, Suleiman the Magnificent sent his vizier, Ibrahim, to Cairo, but by this time Egypt had already been a province of the Ottoman Empire for seven years. This event saw the city and, in turn, the country fall into a state of lethargy, which would last until the arrival of Napoleon three centuries later.

In 1811, Mohammed Ali had 500 Mamelukes killed during a banquet held at the citadel. Legend has it that just one person survived this terrible slaughter.

◄ **Cairo in the 19C** – Although French influence was only to last a total of three years, it had the effect of waking Egypt from its slumber and was to propel the country into a new era; it was **Mohammed Ali** who hoped to learn from this experience. Elected Pasha of Cairo in 1805 (his title became hereditary and remained in place until 1952), he rid the city of the Mamelukes and then embarked upon the development of modern Cairo through a programme of expansion, the cleaning up of its streets, the establishment of schools and the construction of the alabaster mosque on the Moqattam Hill.

European involvement in the Orient – With his penchant for French culture, **Ismail Pasha**, the grandson of Mohammed Ali, was to open up his city and his country to European influence. One example of this was the creation of wide Parisian-style avenues, the establishment of new residential quarters, the transformation of the island of Gezira into a park, and the opening of the city's opera house – all this to impress his royal guests who had travelled to Egypt for the official opening of the Suez Canal!

This urban momentum spread across the Nile, cutting the city in two: the old city to the east, the European section to the west.

directory

INTERNET

Most of Cairo's indoor shopping malls now have at least one Internet bar or café.
Nile Hilton Cybercafé – *In the hotel's shopping arcade. Open 10am-midnight (closed Fri noon-2pm).* Plenty of terminals for rent at a pro-rata rate of E£12/hr.

GETTING AROUND

On foot – Walking is by far the best way of getting to grips with the centre of Cairo and the Islamic section of the city. However, negotiating traffic can be a problem as there are no pedestrian crossings, so extreme caution is required. Beyond the centre you'll need to resort to some form of transport as the outskirts cover a vast area.

By taxi – Cairo seems to be literally swarming with black and white taxis. Meters are rarely used so the fare is based on the distance covered. As most taxi-drivers do not speak English, specify the closest well-known monument to your destination. As a general rule of thumb, expect to pay around E£20 round trip from Old Cairo to the Pyramids or from the Egyptian Museum to Khan el-Khalili. A trip to Saqqara will set you back E£75, including waiting time once you're there. A one-way trip to the airport is likely to cost in the region of E£50. Also be aware that it costs more to take a cab from outside your hotel; if you walk a few yards and hail one from the street you'll save yourself a few pounds.

By microbus – These cost between 25pt and E£1 from Midan Rameses to the Pyramids and more if you're heading out of the city. More practical than buses and quite an experience – provided you can get on!

By metro – The fastest way around Cairo. The two lines cross the city: line 1 from Helwan to El-Marg; line 2 from Shobra el-Kheima to Giza (the district, not the pyramids). Tickets cost 50pt-70pt. Station names do not necessarily correspond with the areas they serve: as an example Mubarak is the stop for Midan Rameses, while Sadat is the stop for Midan Tahrir.

By bus – 25pt-50pt, depending where you're going. Best avoided unless you're with a local. Getting on and off is a feat in itself, as is trying to find where they're heading (most signs are in Arabic), plus the heat is often stifling. An airport bus (white with blue and red stripes) provides a link with Midan Rameses and Midan Tahrir: E£2 plus 50pt per case. The stop for the airport is behind the Egyptian Museum.

By horse-drawn carriage – These operate between the Corniche and the Cairo Tower via the Qasr el-Nil bridge. Cost: approx. E£50 round trip.

TOURIST OFFICES

The main office is at 5, Sheraa Adly, near Midan Al-Opera – ☎ *(02) 391 34 54). Open 8.30am-8pm (5pm during Ramadan).* The staff here are both friendly and efficient. Another office can be found at the airport, although the welcome is generally not as warm.

WHERE TO STAY

• Budget

Mayfair Hotel – *29, Sheraa Al-Aziz Osman* – ☎ *(02) 340 71 15 – 35 rooms: E£60* 🖪 Not too far from the centre and relatively quiet, plus a terrace. Clean rooms, almost all with a balcony.

Hotel El-Hussein – *Khan el-Khalili, next to the famous Fishawi's Café* – ☎ *(02) 591 80 89 – 56 rooms: E£90.* 🖪 One of the few hotels inside a souk, with appropriate noise levels! The view from the restaurant is quite memorable and goes some way to making up for the quality of the food!

Fontana Hotel – *Midan Rameses* – ☎ *(02) 592 23 21 – 80 rooms: E£98.* 🖪 Basic and clean, with a cafeteria on the terrace with good views of the square.

Windsor – *19, Sheraa Alf-Alfy (near Midan Orabi)* – ☎ *(02) 591 52 77 – 51 rooms: $51.* The lift and pleasant bar are two of the opulent reminders of the former British Officers' Club, which once existed here. All the rooms are different, and vary in size.

Cosmopolitan – *1, Sheraa Ben Taalab, near Sheraa Qasr el-Nil* – ☎ *(02) 392 36 63 – 84 rooms: $59.* 🖪 An ideal location and the most expensive option in this price range. The hotel occupies an impressive Art Deco building and has retained the character of its rooms.

• Moderate

Concorde – *146, Sheraa El-Tahrir* – ☎ *(02) 336 11 94 – 72 rooms: $75/$85.* A family atmosphere, plus a good location and an English bar.

Maadi Hotel – *Maadi Entrance, Maadi* – ☎ *(02) 358 58 58 – 147 rooms: $90.* A reasonable option to the south of the city. The hotel has a small pool with delightful views overlooking the Nile.

Flamenco – *2, Sheraa El-Gezira, Zamalek* – ☎ *(02) 340 08 15 – 157 rooms: $70/$98.* Half of the rooms have balconies with Nile views. The service here is generally impeccable.

Marriott Hotel, Cairo

Sofitel – *Corniche, Maadi* – ☎ *(02) 526 06 01* – *173 rooms: from $160-$215*. To the south of the city, away from the main sights *(shuttle bus to the centre available)*. One of the hotel's main attractions is its magnificent terrace pool with views to the Pyramids across the Nile.

Sheraton Cairo – *Midan Al-Galaa, Doqqi* – ☎ *(02) 336 97 00* – *660 rooms: $255*. Slightly away from the city centre on the "wrong" bank of the Nile, but with spacious bedrooms and excellent service.

Meridien Cairo – *Corniche, Roda* – ☎ *(02) 362 17 17* – *1 000 rooms: $280*. A white building in the shape of an arc in which every room has a view of the Nile (perhaps the best of any in the city), although some rooms could do with a little attention. This hotel has recently been joined by another from the same chain which is even taller and has an even better position.

• Expensive

Cairo Marriott – *33, Sheraa Saraya el-Gezira, Zamelek* – ☎ *(02) 735 88 88* – *1 124 rooms: from $220-$350*. Still worthy of its reputation as the best hotel in Cairo. A veritable palace with service to match.

WHERE TO EAT

• Budget

Kochary – *Midan Tahrir*. Inexpensive with fast service. An ideal place to stop after a visit to the Egyptian Museum.

Al Américaine – *44, Sheraa Talaat Harb*. An excellent option for breakfast *(E£12)*, a quick bite to eat at lunchtime *(E£23)* or just a drink.

Fatatri El-Tahrir – *166, Sheraa El-Tahrir (overlooking the square of the same name). The* place to eat Egyptian pizzas! The decor isn't much to write home about but it's always busy.

Felfela – *Sheraa Hoda Sha'rawy*. A traditionally decorated and popular Cairo eatery renowned for its *fuul*, *taamiya* and stuffed pigeon *(average cost: E£30)*. You'll need to be patient as it's often full.

• Moderate

Café Riche – *17, Sheraa Talaat Harb. Open 8am-1am*. Formerly the haunt of Egyptian intellectuals, the Café Riche dates from 1908, when it existed as a theatre, and is now considered a historic monument. The restaurant, which opened in 1942, serves Egyptian and international cuisine (allow E£40).

Naguib Mahfouz Coffee Shop – *5, Sheraa El-Badestane, Khan el Khalili*. Part of the Oberoi chain. Excellent Lebanese kebabs *(E£40)*, lentil soup *(E£10)*, rice pudding *(E£11)*, as well as the strawberry fruit juice which is a particular favourite of the winner of the Nobel Prize for Literature, after whom the shop takes its name.

Cento – *100, Sheraa El-Hegaz, Heliopolis. Open 1pm-10pm*. French and international cuisine. Budget E£50 per person on dinner-dance nights *(8pm-midnight)*.

Le Pacha 1901 – *Sheraa Saray El Gezirah, Zamelek*. A selection of restaurants and a piano bar on board a paddle-steamer. Pleasant atmosphere.

BARS AND CAFÉS

Pub 28 – *Open noon-2am. 28, Shagarit Al-Durr, Zamelek*. ⌁ The style is Oriental and the music very varied. Food is also available here.

Stella Bar – *Sheraa Hoda Sha'rawy, near Midan Talaat Harb*. ⌁ It may look closed but don't be put off by first impressions. A pleasant bar for a refreshing beer in the centre of Cairo. Women will need to be accompanied by a man in order to get in.

Fishawi's – *Khan el-Khalili. Open 24hr a day*. ⌁ This centrally located Cairo institution is a real must, if only to admire its opulent mirrors. No alcohol is served here, so why not try a hot *anise*, or perhaps try your hand at smoking a *shisha*.

Al-Horreya – *Midan Al-Falaky, near Sheraa Talaat Harb*. ⌁ A timeless atmosphere in which to enjoy a cool beer.

TEA-ROOMS

Groppi – *Midan Talaat Harb. Open 7am-1pm*. This famous patisserie, with its wonderful choice of pastries, has barely changed since it opened in 1891. The company has another shop in Heliopolis *(Roxy, El-Ahram)*.
A wonderful choice of pastries.

PASTRY SHOPS

El-Abd – *42, Sheraa Talaat Harb*. Another good address for pastries (takeaway only).

DINNER CRUISES ON THE NILE

The Pharaohs – *Dock: 138, Sheraa El-Nile, Giza (near the zoo)* – ☎ *(02) 570 10 00*. Two boats decorated in pharaonic style offer Nile dinner cruises and performances of Oriental and Sufic dance. Cruises operate at the following times: 8pm *(E£100)*; 10pm *(E£112)*. A drinks-only cruise *(E£29)* operates every Friday (5.15pm-7pm). Reservations essential; boarding 30min prior to departure.

CINEMAS

Several cinemas show films in English. Consult the *Egyptian Gazette* or the *Al-Ahram Weekly* for listings.

Renaissance – *Corniche, World Trade Center, Boulaq* – ☎ *(02) 578 49 15*. A new cinema with digital sound.

El-Tahrir – *122, Sheraa Tahrir, Doqqi* – ☎ *(02) 335 47 26*.

The Pharaohs cruise boat.

Horreyya I and II – *Sixth floor; Horreyya Shopping Mall, Sheraa Al-Ahram, Heliopolis.* **Metro** – *35, Sheraa Talaat Harb* – ☎ *(02) 393 75 66. 1950s-style, but a bit run-down.*

NIGHTCLUBS

Not an Egyptian speciality although they do exist. The best night is Thursday, as Friday is a holiday.

Crazy House Disco – *Cairo Land, near the Southern Cemetery* – ☎ *(02) 366 10 82. E£25 (E£50 Thurs). The only way of getting here is by taxi (E£10 from the city centre).*

El Gato Negro – *32, Sheraa Jeddah, Doqqi* – ☎ *(02) 361 68 88. E£20.* The current place to be seen in Cairo.

SHOPPING

You'll find everything from papyrus to *shishas* (water pipes) to jewellery on sale in the city's boutiques, malls and souks. The **Nile Hilton** mall, near the Egyptian Museum, is particularly recommended.

Khan el-Khalili Souk – This huge bazaar sells the usual souvenirs but delve deeper and you'll find scarves, shirts, perfume, fabric, jewellery and food. Whatever you do, make sure you visit the spice section *(from Sheraa El-Azhar head along Sheraa Muizz li-Din Allah, then turn left just before the Barsby Mosque)*, with its mind-boggling selection, including saffron, which in Egypt provides colouring rather than flavour. *Karkadé* is also on sale here.

Misr Tulun – *Open Mon-Fri 10am-5pm. Opposite the Ibn Tulun Mosque.* A specialist shop selling oases arts and crafts such as clothes, textiles, pottery and dolls.

The British occupation – In 1882, British troops set foot in Egypt, at a time when Cairo was beginning to attract foreign investment and its very first tourists. However, under the khedives Tawfiq and Abbas II, the city's inhabitants saw themselves practically barred from several districts within their own city. A wave of anglophobia ensued, a situation worsened by the questionable personality of Lord Cromer, in effect the ruler of the country, and the political events which would ultimately lead to the British protectorate (1914-52).

"Egypt for the Egyptians" – In the period between the World Wars, Cairo's population tripled from one to three million, mainly as a consequence of a massive exodus from the countryside. The city expanded into the desert while districts such as Zamalek, Gezira and Heliopolis retained their air of exclusivity. In 1945, the **Arab League** was established at the instigation of Egypt and a climate of insecurity took root in the city; martial law was also imposed in response to the riots and attacks that erupted around Cairo. The former Fatimid city deteriorated into no more than a slum, and the homeless began to settle in the Mameluke cemeteries now known as the City of the Dead. On 23 July 1952, the Free Officer Movement, under the command of Nasser, came to power. Three days later King Farouk abdicated, to be replaced by his son, Fouad, barely six months old. On 18 June 1953, Naguib became the first President of the Republic. In 1954, his Prime Minister, General **Gamal Abdel Nasser**, deposed Naguib and inherited the title of Head of State.

> **C**airo mainly developed as a result of a Belgian, Baron **Édouard Empain**, who created the city's tram system and set out plans for Heliopolis.

exploring Cairo

Islamic Cairo has over 800 monuments, many of which have no signs to indicate their presence. As a result it is easy to get lost around this part of the city, with its maze of narrow streets. To help with orientation, we have organised descriptions around key buildings which can then be used as reference points.

Saad Zaghloul.

AROUND AL-AZHAR

Al-Azhar Mosque★★

In founding this mosque in 970, the Fatimids created the very first Islamic university. This institution is still in existence today and claims to be the world's oldest seat of learning. Its sheikh is the supreme religious authority in Egypt and also acts as the head of numerous Azhari institutes across the country.

The "Resplendent" – *See ABC of Architecture in the Insights and Images section of this guide. Only part of the mosque is open to the public. E£12.* This alternative title for the mosque originates from Fatima ez-Zahra, the daughter of the Prophet. This impressive monument has been restored and modified over the centuries and consequently is an amalgam of several different architectural styles. The mosque has been a cradle of the Sunni doctrine in Egypt since the time of Saladin (12C).

Access to the **central courtyard★★** *(sahn)* is via the **Barber's Gate**, built by Qaitbey in 1469, but whose double doors date from the 18C. Its arched porticoes, of Persian design, support a wall of blind niches and are the only feature to remain from the Fatimid period. The huge prayer room, covering an area of some 3 000m?/32 300sq ft, stands directly opposite, on the east side of the mosque.

The al-Taybarsiyya madrasa, to the right of the entrance corridor, houses a mihrab (a niche indicating the direction of Mecca) dating from 1310 and flanked by small porphyry columns.

Its nine bays contain eight arcades of columns arranged at right angles to the **mihrab★** (this distribution was inspired by the Great Mosque of Kairouan, in Tunisia), which does not occupy the far end of the room because of successive enlargements. The mosaics on this mihrab, the oldest example of its kind in Egypt, comprise superb star-shaped and geometric motifs.

In total, the mosque has five minarets, each erected by a different sultan. The oldest (14C), on the front side, is the furthest set back; the one dominating the entrance was built by Qaitbey in the 15C; the tower crowned by two amortizements was added a century later.

Students from every corner of the Islamic world come to study at the university. They then return to their own country as representatives of the official beliefs of Islam.

The university – Reorganised in 1961, it now consists of a modern university, made up of nine faculties (including, since 1962, one for female students), alongside the traditional Islamic institution.

From Al-Azhar to Bab al-Futuh

Khan el-Khalili★★★ – This district dates back to the 13C and is home to one of the best-known *souks* in the Middle East. It stretches from an area between Sheraa Muizz li-Din Allah and the Sayyidna al-Husayn Mosque.

This immense bazaar, with its unique atmosphere and narrow alleyways fronted by shops selling items of every description, attracts vast numbers of visitors and is best visited in the evening. Its arts and crafts, particularly copper, wood, leather and carpets, are a major attraction,

This mosque-university has defended and encouraged Islam and the cultural values of the Arab world for over a thousand years.

To get to the Khan el-Khalili souk, just utter the words "al-Husayn" to your taxi-driver.

as is the section between Sheraa Muski and the Al-Hussayn Mosque, considered the secular heart of the *souk*, where the Orient of legend seems to have survived.

Sheraa Muizz li-Din Allah – This street skirts the Khan el-Khalili district as far as the Bab al-Futah Gate. Six monuments along or close to this thoroughfare are worthy of note.

Al-Qalaoun Mausoleum★★ – *On the left side of the street, just beyond Khan el-Khalili.* E£6. Built in 1729 by the sultan of the same name, this monument also comprises a mosque and a madrasa. Its **façade**★ is crowned by elegant merlons and is somewhat surprisingly embellished by paired diagonal arches distinctly Christian in appearance. The **minaret**, with its two square and one cylindrical storeys, bears witness to its Mameluke origins. Inside, a corridor ornamented with blind arches provides access (to the left) to the madrasa (the mihrab of which is adorned with sculpted marble panels) and the **mausoleum**★★ (to the right), one of the most beautiful in Cairo and one of the best introductions to Islamic art. The tomb of Sultan El-Mansur Qalaoun is surrounded by a carved wooden screen. The niche of the mihrab is decorated with superb mosaics and flanked by porphyry columns. In the vestibule, note the Moorish arches with their lacework archivolts.

Al-Barquq Madrasa – *On the left side of the street, just after the An-Nasir Mausoleum (early 14C).* E£6. This Islamic college was erected at the end of the 14C. Its distinctive façade is pierced by a mosaic-adorned doorway, further embellished with black and white marble; a magnificent dome devoid of any ornamentation; and a three-tiered minaret crowned by a dome supported by small columns.

Beshtak Palace – *Just after the madrasa, on the right-hand side of the street. Currently closed.* This palace dates from the 1340s and contains an outstanding reception hall (*qa'a*), 25m/82ft in height, divided into one central section (*durqa'a*) and several side rooms.

Al-Aqmar Mosque – *Further along the same street, on the right.* The **façade**★ of this Fatimid mosque dating from 1125 was the first to be built entirely of stone. The craftsmanship is superb, and incorporates the first examples of stalactites, a decorative theme enthusiastically adopted by the Mamelukes. The interior and the minaret are not original.

Beit al-Suhaymi★★ – *Turn right into Darb al-Asfar. Closed for restoration.* The residence of the Sheikh of Al-Azhar was built in 1648 and enlarged in the late 18C. Magnificently decorated with marble, faïence and wood, it constitutes a fine example of domestic Egyptian architecture. Daylight from an inner garden is filtered into the house through decorative *mashrabiya* screens.

CAFÉS
One of the best places for a tea or coffee is the somewhat old-fashioned *Fishawi's* – a veritable Cairo institution just one block from Midan al-Husayn. Such is its popularity that often the only tables available here are outside. Be warned that many shops and cafés are closed on Sundays.

Once inside this mausoleum, crowned by an imposing cupola rebuilt in 1903 in imitation of the mosque in Jerusalem, the exuberance of the stucco decoration, polychrome marble and fine interlacing work is immediately striking. This impression is softened by the gentle light filtering through the building's stained glass.

Beyond the palace, on a corner on the right, note the Abdel al-Rahman Khatkhoda School, built in 1744. This institution, Arab-Turkish in style, provides "water to the thirsty and spiritual sustenance to the ignorant".

Al-Hakim Mosque – *At the end of the street. E£6. The mosque can also be seen from the ramparts (see below).* Built between 990 and 1013, this is one of the few Fatimid mosques to have retained its original layout of a large courtyard surrounded by colonnades and a prayer hall with five aisles. The monumental façade of imposing walls crowned by merlons is flanked by minarets bearing lofty domes. The section beneath these domes is known as *mibkhara* (or "perfume-burner"). Two small but elegant ablution fountains are visible in the courtyard.

Bab al-Futuh★ – *Tour of the ramparts: E£6.* The impressive and imposing "Gate of Conquests" demarcates the northern extremity of the ramparts raised by the Fatimids in the 11C, and is flanked by two round towers. At the time of its construction, the road running beneath its barrel vault was 5m/16ft below its current level.

Sayyidna al-Husayn Mosque – *Access for Muslims only.* Back towards Al-Azhar, this late-19C mosque, visible slightly to the east of the Khan el-Khalili souk, has incorporated the 12C Bab el-Akhdar Gate in addition to a 13C minaret. A room supposedly closed to the public houses one of Islam's most sacred relics: the head of al-Husayn, the grandson of the Prophet, who was killed by the Umayyads at the Battle of Kerbala in 680.

From Al-Azhar to Bab Zuwalya

Return to Sheraa Al-Azhar and cross the bridge to Sheraa Muizz li-Din.

The stalls of the souk extend as far as Bab Zuwalya, on the site of the old silk market. Nowadays, traders here tend to sell household items and inexpensive clothing, including a wide selection of *galabiyyas*.

Wikala al-Ghuri – *Between the Al-Azhar Mosque and Sheraa Muizz li-Din. Open 8am-midnight. E£6.* A *wikala* was a caravanserai used for commercial purposes, in which the ground floor served as a warehouse. This one dates from 1505 and is the best preserved in Cairo, with attractive *mashrabiyas* around the courtyard.

Al-Ghuri – *At the entrance to Sheraa Muizz li-Din*. This area stretching across both sides of the street is home to the madrasa and mausoleum of the penultimate Mameluke sultan, Qansuh al-Ghuri. The former *(on the right)* dates from 1503, the latter from 1504. The sultan was defeated at the age of 78 in Syria by the Turks, although his body was never found; soon after Egypt would come under Ottoman control. As a result his mausoleum contains the remains of his successor, Tumambey. The main features of interest here are the mosaics in the prayer room and in the *iman* of the madrasa, as well as the 65m/213ft climb to the top of the minaret.

House of Gamal al-Din al-Dahabi – *Head down the street and turn left into Haret ar-Rum*. This fine example of domestic Ottoman architecture dates from the middle of the 17C. The courtyard, its fountain, and the *mashrabiyas* on the balcony are worthy of particular note.

Al-Mu'ayyad Mosque★★ – *At the end of the street, on the right. E£12, plus a baksheesh for access to the minaret*. Also known as the "Red Mosque", this Mameluke building is the last example of an enclosure mosque. Embellished with stalactites and black and white marble, the entrance gateway frames a splendid lime-tree wood **door**★ clad in plates of chased bronze. The two sections measure 5.9m/19ft in height and were originally used in the Al-Husayn Mosque.

Head through a domed vestibule to reach the courtyard (similar in style to that of the Al-Azhar Mosque) and a mausoleum in the form of a square chapel also crowned by a cupola with pendentive supports. The mosque *(to the right)* is divided into three rows; the arches, divided into small bays, are surprisingly elegant given their large span. The coffered ceiling is magnificently worked, and decorated with gold and silver. Seven ogival niches covered with marble are built into the wall of the **mihrab**★, which is entirely decorated with polychrome marble and embellished with inlaid mother-of-pearl and ivory; note also the finely crafted *minbar* (a stepped chair from which the sermon is read).

Bab Zuwaylah★ – Contemporary with the north doors *(see Bab al-Futuh above)*, this door is the only surviving example from the original 11C ramparts. It was also the site of public executions; in 1811, some 500 Mamelukes were killed here by Mohammed Ali, their heads subsequently displayed on their own lances.

The two, triple-tiered **minarets** dominating it *(access via the mosque)* rise to a height of 50m/164ft.

AROUND THE CITADEL

Citadel★★

⊙ *Open daily 8am-5pm (6pm in summer); museum closes at 4.30pm. E£20. Sheraa Salah Salem. Entrance on the east side, opposite the car park. Access: by taxi from the city centre (E£5) or by bus (no 174 from Midan Rameses).*

SUFIC DANCE
Every Wednesday and Friday evening *(9pm in summer; 9.30pm in winter)* a display of Sufic dance is performed in the **Al-Ghuri Mausoleum**. Because of its popularity, it's best to arrive at least an hour before the start to be sure of a seat.

The mosque's two minarets provide stunning views of Cairo's skyline.

▶ **T**wo monuments opposite Bab Zuwalya are also worthy of note: to the left, the **As-Salih Tala'I Mosque** (1160); and opposite, the **Radwan Bay Wikala** (1650), Cairo's last covered market, also known by the name Al-Khiyyamiyya or "the bazaar of the tent canvas-makers". Nowadays, ceremonial fabric is on sale here.

The impressive view of Islamic Cairo from the terrace of the Mohammed Ali Mosque.

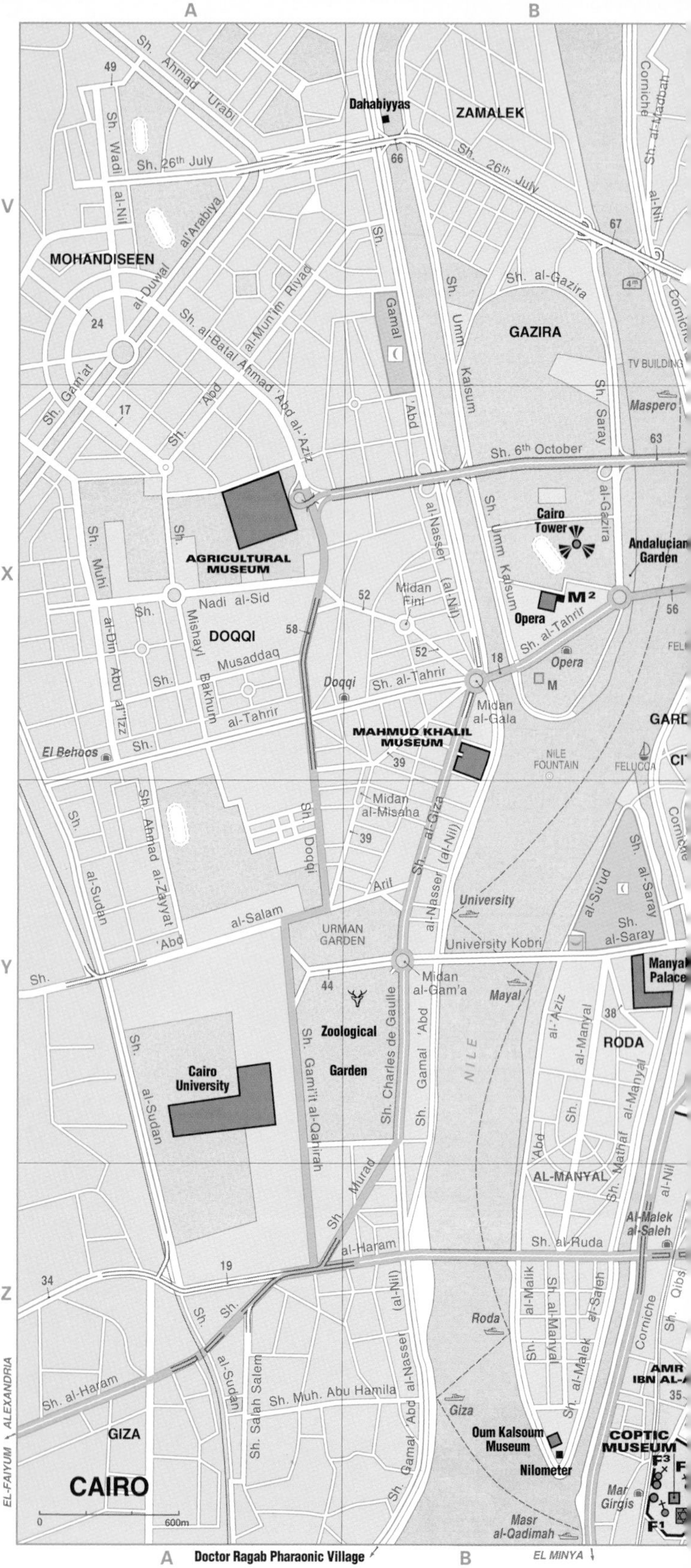

A   B

Sh. Ahmad 'Urabi

Dahabiyyas   ZAMALEK

Sh. Wadi al-Nil

49

66

Sh. 26th July

Sh. 26th July

V

67

MOHANDISEEN

al-Duwal al-'Arabiya

Sh. al-Munʿim Riyad

Sh. al-Batal Ahmad Abd al-'Aziz

Gamal

GAZIRA

Sh. al-Gazira

4th

24

Sh. Gamʿat

17

Abd

Sh.

Gamal Kaisum

Sh. Saray

TV BUILDING

Maspero

Sh. 6th October

63

Sh. Muhi

al-Din Abu al-'Izz

Bakhnum

Mishayi

Sh.

al-Nasser (al-Nil)

Sh. Umm Kalsum

al-Gazira

Cairo Tower

Andalucian Garden

X

AGRICULTURAL MUSEUM

Nadi al-Sid

DOQQI

52

Midan Fini

M²

Opera

56

FEL

58

Musaddaq

al-Tahrir

Doqqi

52

18

Sh. al-Tahrir

Opera

M

GARD

El Behoos

Sh.

Sh. al-Tahrir

Midan al-Gala

MAHMUD KHALIL MUSEUM

CI

Sh. Ahmad al-Zayyat

Sh. al-Sudan

'Abd

al-Salam

Doqqi

39

Midan al-Misaha

39

'Aril

Sh. al-Giza (al-Nil)

NILE FOUNTAIN

FELUCCA

Corniche

University

al-Suʿud

Sh. al-Saray

Y

URMAN GARDEN

University Kobri

Manyal Palace

44

Midan al-Gamʿa

Mayal

Sh. al-Saray

38

RODA

Cairo University

Sh. Charles de Gaulle

Sh. Gamʿit al-Qahirah

Zoological Garden

Sh. Gamal 'Abd

Mayal

al-'Aziz

al-Manyal

N I L E

Sh. al-Sudan

Sh. Murad

AL-MANYAL

Abd

Sh. Mathaf

al-Nil

Al-Malek al-Saleh

19

al-Haram

Sh. al-Ruda

Z

34

Sh.

al-Sudan

Sh. al-Nasser (al-Nil)

Roda

al-Malik

Sh. al-Manyal

Sh. al-Saleh

al-Mathaf

Corniche

Sh. Qibs

AMR IBN AL-ʿA

35

Sh. al-Haram

Sh. Salah Salem

Sh. Muh. Abu Hamila

Giza

COPTIC MUSEUM

GIZA

Sh. Gamal 'Abd al-Nasser (al-Nil)

Oum Kalsoum Museum

Nilometer

F3

F

CAIRO

0   600m

Masr al-Qadimah

Mar Girgis

F1

EL-FAIYUM / ALEXANDRIA

A   Doctor Ragab Pharaonic Village   B   EL MINYA

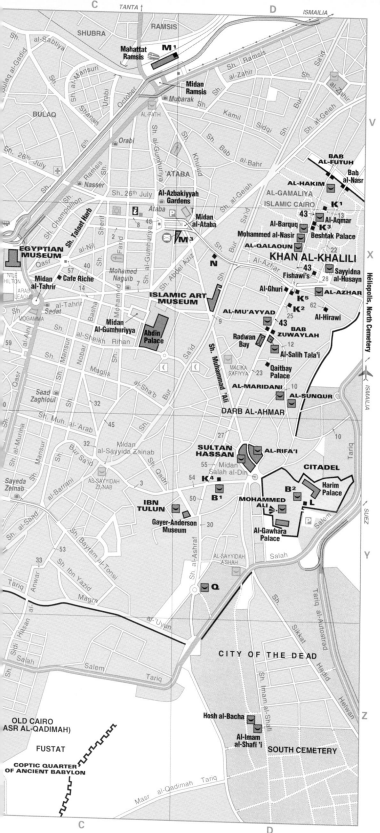

TANTA ↑
RAMSIS
ISMAILIA
SHUBRA
Sh. al-Sabtiya
al-Gadid
Sh. al-Mansuri
Mahattat
Ramsis
M 1
Midan
Ramsis
Sh. Ramsis
Sh. al-Zahir
Sh. al-Zahir
Mubarak
Sh. Kamil
Sidqi
BULAQ
Sh. Shanab
Orabi
Sh. al-Bahr
Sh. al-Geish
V
AL-FATH
Sh. 26th July
6th
Sh. al-Gumhuriyya
Sh. Khulid
Sh. Bab al-Bahr
Ramsis
Nasser
'ATABA
BAB
AL-FUTUH
Bab
al-Nasr
Sh. Champollion
Sh. 26th July
Al-Azbakiyyah
Gardens
AL-HAKIM
AL-GAMALIYA
ISLAMIC CAIRO
K 1
22
Ataba
Midan
al-Ataba
Said
43
13
Al-Aqmar
K 3
EGYPTIAN
MUSEUM
M 3
Sh. Abdel Aziz
Al-Barquq
Mohammed al-Nasir
Beshtak Palace
X
NILE
HILTON
Midan
al-Tahrir
Cafe Riche
57
40
Mohamed
Naguib
N
Al-Azhar
AL-QALAOUN
KHAN AL-KHALILI
43
Sayyidna
al-Husayn
Sh. Talaat Harb
Qasr
Sherif
Farid
14
Fishawi's
28
MOGAMMA
Sadat
al-Tahrir
ISLAMIC ART
MUSEUM
Al-Ghuri
K 5
AL-AZHAR
K 2
62
59
Midan
Al-Gumhuriyya
al-Sheikh Rihan
Abdin
Palace
AL-MU'AYYAD
9
43
Al-Hirawi
BAB
ZUWAYLAH
Radwan
Bay
12
Sh. Mansur
Nabawi
Maglis
Sh. al-Sha'b
Bur
Said
MALIKA
SAFIYYA
Al-Salih Tala'i
Qaitbay
Palace
23
Saad
Zaghloul
32
Sh. Muh. al-'Arab
AL-MARIDANI
AL-SUNQUR
10
DARB AL-AHMAR
Sh. al-Muniru
Bur Said
Mansur
45
32
Midan
al-Sayyida Zainab
10
Tariq
Sayeda
Zeinab
AS-SAYYIDAH
ZEINAB
3
SULTAN
HASSAN
AL-RIFA'I
CITADEL
Sh. al-Saad
al-Barrini
Sh. Qadri
55
Midan
Salah al-Din
K 4
B 2
Harim
Palace
Sh. Ibn Yazid
33
Sh. Ibn Anwar
53
54
50
IBN
TULUN
B 1
MOHAMMED
ALI
L
Salem
Gayer-Anderson
Museum
30
Al-Gawhara
Palace
Tariq
Magra
al-'Uyun
AL-SAYYIDAH
'ASHAH
Salah
Y
SUEZ
Sh. al-Ashraf
Q.
Tariq
Salah
Salem
Tariq al-Autostrad
Sikket
Hadia
Heliopolis, North Cemetery
ISMAILIA
CITY OF THE DEAD
Sh. Imam al-Shafi
Tariq al-Autostrad
Heliwan
OLD CAIRO
ASR AL-QADIMAH)
FUSTAT
Hosh al-Bacha
Z
Al-Imam
al-Shafi 'i
SOUTH CEMETERY
COPTIC QUARTER
OF ANCIENT BABYLON
Masr al-Qadimah
Tariq
C
D

CAIRO

An imposing fortress – Completed in 1183 during the reign of **Saladin**, the Cairo Citadel occupies an outcrop on the Moqattam Hill, overlooking the city. Surrounded by sturdy walls and towers, it was erected to withstand attacks from Christian crusaders and to provide protection for a royal residence. The first sultan to live here was Al-Kamil, Saladin's nephew. The citadel was constantly modified and was subsequently enlarged by the Turks in the 16C. Following an explosion, Mohammed Ali razed the old palaces and built a mosque on the site.

Mohammed Ali Mosque★ – *See also ABC of Architecture in the Insights and Images section of this guide. South wall.* Designed on the model of Ottoman mosques in Constantinople, this mosque is entirely covered with alabaster, hence its alternative name of the "Alabaster Mosque". The forecourt is enclosed by colonnades and has an ablution fountain crowned by a neo-Ottoman dome at ▶ its centre.

The interior is lavish – perhaps overly so – in its decoration, a feature that compares unfavourably with the decorative finesse of Mameluke buildings. To illustrate this, marble and gilded work compete with Persian rugs and coloured light effects beneath the 52m/170ft central cupola. The two minbars (stepped chairs) are interesting: one is carved from cedar and covered with gold; the other is alabaster and was a gift from King Farouk in 1939.

Al-Gawhara Palace – *To the south.* Built by Mohammed Ali in 1814 to receive important dignitaries, the palace now houses a small museum containing a collection of royal furniture *(currently closed).*

Al-Nasr Mohammed Mosque★ – *To the east.* Built in 1335, this mosque is the only Mameluke building within the walls, although the interior is in a poor state of repair; this contrasts with the exuberant external decoration, particularly that of the **minarets**★★, in which the architectural splendour of the Mameluke period finds its true expression. The taller of the two minarets, rising above an impressive portico, consists of three tiers. The sculpted square section is entirely covered with arabesques, rosettes and interlacing, as well as calligraphy, particularly beneath the stalactite-adorned railing which crowns this section.

Joseph's Well – *Skirt the mosque to the south.* This well, apparently of ancient design, was uncovered during the reign of Saladin just a few metres from the Moqattam Tower. Before its official, biblical designation in the 17C, it was simply known as the "spiral well", because of the spiral staircase dug 89m/292ft into the rock.

Harim Palace – This palace (1827) was the residence of Mohammed Ali and his family. It stands behind the equestrian statue of Ibrahim and on the other side of the tanks and planes displayed as a reminder of Israeli-Arab wars. The building is now home to a military museum *(currently closed)* displaying exhibits that include a model of the city, uniforms, and an impressive collection of shields and knives.

At the foot of the Citadel

Al-Maridani Mosque★ – *Sheraa Al-Tibbana.* The predominant aspect of this mosque, built in 1340 by Emir Al-Tounbougha el-Maridani, is its astonishing variety of styles. A doorway of green and white marble leads to a porticoed courtyard with an ablution fountain at its centre, originally from the Sultan Hussan Mosque. The prayer hall, eight columns of which date from the Ptolemaic period, is enclosed by an openwork screen, a unique feature in Cairo. Note also the **mihrab**★, a colourful mosaic of mother-of-pearl, red stone and blue enamel, and the sculpted stalactites on the minaret.

Al-Sunqur Mosque★ – *On Sheraa Bab al-Wazir, to the south.* Easily recognisable by its cylindrical minaret, the balconies of which seem to be supported by stalactite sculptures, this mosque was built in 1346 by the emir who ultimately gave it its name. It was restored after the

It is best to start your visit along the southern wall.

CLOCK TOWER
This small tower stands to the north-west of the courtyard and was a gift from King Louis-Philippe of France to Mohammed Ali in 1846. From all accounts it has never actually worked!

ABLUTION FOUNTAINS
Their presence in the courtyards of mosques is explained by the fact that Muslims must wash their hands, face, forearms, ears, neck and feet, as well as rinse out their mouth and nostrils three times a day and before each session of prayer, in order to ensure a state of purity.

Continue your visit along the north wall.

QAITBEY PALACE
This palace *(in the street behind the mosque)* was the residence of one of the greatest Mameluke sultans.

One of the 70 enamelled lamps (michkats) which once hung from the vault of the east iwan in the Sultan Hassan Mosque.

earthquake by an Ottoman officer, Agha Moudtahfizan. Its main attractions are its *minbar*, with its polychrome marble sides, and, most notably the **Iranian earthenware blue tiles**★ dorned with floral motifs, which were used to decorate the south *iwan* of the prayer hall upon its restoration in 1651. It is from these tiles that the building has acquired its more popular name, the "Blue Mosque".

Mosque-Madrasa of Sultan Hassan★★★ – *Midan Salah el-Din. Open 8am-5pm (6pm in summer). E£12; students E£6.* This magnificent religious building is unquestionably one of the masterpieces of Islamic architecture and a symbol of the great power of the Mamelukes at the time. It is also unique in that it stands alone at the foot of the citadel, rather than being hemmed in by other buildings.

The bare surfaces of its impressive façade, dating from 1539, come as something of a surprise. The explanation lies in its location, opposite the fortress, and the desire of the architect to replicate the same austerity and power – a goal he achieved through thick projecting cornices and a triple-balconied **minaret**★, 86m/282ft high (the tallest in Cairo); the second minaret was added later. The overall effect is of a fortress built to defend the faith.

The central **sahn**★★, or main courtyard, is cruciform in shape; this plan incorporates four *iwan* and madrasas corresponding to the four theological schools (Hanafi, Maliki, Shafi'i and Hanbali). An impressively large **ablution fountain**★ at its centre is surmounted by a spherical dome resting on slender marble columns (in former times, the dome was painted blue and its string course was gilded). To the east, the *iwan*★, attractively ornamented with quotations from the Koran, houses an immense platform, known as a *dikka*, which enabled the iman's assistants to officiate when the crowd of faithful was too far away from the *minbar* (note the fine bronze-plated door). Behind the *qibla*, which served to indicate the direction of Mecca, the *iwan* opens onto the tomb of the sultan. This monumental mausoleum is crowned with an impressively proportioned cupola adorned with stalactites. The catafalque contains the remains of the sultan's son, and not those of the sultan himself.

Al-Rifa'i Mosque – *Midan Salah el-Din. Open 8am-5pm (6pm in summer). E£12; students E£6.* Standing to the right of the Sultan Hassan Mosque, this building dates from 1912 and was designed as a pastiche of the Mameluke style. It houses the tombs of Kings Fouad and Farouk, as well as the cenotaphs of Princess Taoufida Hanem, the daughter of Ismail Pasha, and the last Shah of Iran.

Sheraa Mohammed Ali – This is the alternative, and more popular name for Sheraa Al-Qala, which leads to the Islamic Art Museum (see Worth a Visit) from Midan Salah el-Din. The street was laid out by Ismail Pasha and lined by Ottoman buildings such as the Malika Safiyya Mosque (1610). Nowadays it is known for its shops selling musical instruments and is a pleasant setting for an evening stroll.

From Salah el-Din to the Ibn Tulun Mosque
To reach this famous mosque, head along Sheraa Al-Salbiyya which runs from south of Midan Salah el-Din and passes by several smaller, yet nonetheless interesting buildings.

Sabil-Kuttab of Qaitbey★ – Built in 1479, this building was the first in the city to have a *sabil* or public drinking fountain *(ground floor)*, and was the home of the first Koranic School *(first floor)* to exist separately from a religious complex. This type of edifice became common during the Ottoman period and under Mohammed Ali. It was completely restored following the 1992 earthquake.

A second floor was added in the 1930s and 40s. Plans are also afoot to build a library here.

Mosque and Khanka of Shaykhu – The mid-14C mosque and hostel were built by the emir of the same name, the commander-in-chief of the Mameluke army under Sultan Hussan. They stand on opposite sides of the street and together form an imposing architectural ensemble.

Mosque of Ibn Tulun★★★ – *Open 8am-6pm. E£6. Entrance on the east side.* In 879, 90 years before the official existence of Cairo, the emir **Ahmed ibn Tulun**, the founder of the Tulunid Dynasty, constructed this universally renowned masterpiece, which is considered to be the oldest existing example of Islamic art in Egypt.

The mosque, built of brick and rendered with plaster, is lined on three sides by a walled enclosure *(ziyada)*, so only one façade is accessible to the faithful. Upon entering the *sahn* or **central court**★★★, the initial impression is one of great grandeur. The surrounding doorways consist of a succession of arches, with the areas between pierced by windows reproducing the same form. Although the Byzantine decoration on the friezes and archivolts is of interest, attention is drawn to the **intrados**★★ or inner section of the arches. Here, the first sculpted (rather than moulded as was previously the case) decorative features are visible, in the form of interlacing and geometric motifs.

The prayer hall is divided into five aisles separated by pillars adorned with engaged columns. Six mihrabs have been incorporated into the far wall; the main one is crowned by a small wooden cupola. The late-13C *minbar* is a superb example of decorative carpentry, although part of its inlaid marble and ebony has since disappeared. The **minaret** *(accessible to the general public)* on the other side of the court, is the only feature of the mosque to be built from stone, and was probably added by Sultan Hassan +X9+.

Gayer-Anderson Museum – *On the SE side of the mosque. Open daily 8.45am-4pm (closed Fri noon-1pm). E£16. Camera permit E£10; video permit E£25.* In the 1930s and 40s, Robert Gayer-Anderson, a British major and member of the Egyptian Civil Service, decided to restore these two mansions, linked by a passageway on the third floor. The buildings, also known as the House of the Cretans *(Beit el-Kretleya)* comprise an unusual mixture of recesses, landings and galleries, as well as a terrace with views of the Ibn Tulun Mosque. The furniture and decor is highly eclectic, so much so that it is rare to find such a variety of styles. A scene from the James Bond film, *The Spy Who Loved Me*, was shot in the large Persian reception room.

THE MOSQUE
The Arabic word *masqid* translates as "a place of prostration", and *gami'* as "a meeting place." A mosque is not a sanctuary in the Christian sense of the word, since God is not present. A mosque also acts as a religious school and a place of study, and is where the Muslim faithful assemble for prayer five times a day.

ABLUTION FOUNTAIN
The large fountain built by Sultan Hussan at the centre of the mosque's central court *(sahn)* is crowned by a bare cupola.

A MINI-ZIGGURAT
The helicoidal shape of the minaret is unique in Egypt, giving it the appearance of a miniature Tower of Babel.

Robert Gayer-Anderson purchased these adjoining 16C-17C mansions in 1935 in order to refurbish and furnish them in the Oriental style that he favoured.

The grandiose, yet sober Ibn Tulun Mosque takes its inspiration from the old Abbasid mosques in the Iraqi city of Samarra.

VISA EXTENSIONS
These can be obtained from counter no 42, on the first floor of the Mogamma building *(open daily except Fri 8am-2pm)*.
The area in and around Midan Tahrir is popular with professional **touts** *(kheraty)* intent on encouraging you to book their preferred hotel or tour, or persuade you to shop in a "recommended" boutique. The best way of dealing with them is a firm "no thank you".

Old-style service at the Café Riche.

RAMESES II
A granite statue of this great Pharaoh still stands incongruously at the base of one of the square's flyovers. Brought here in 1955 from Memphis, the statue is now suffering the effects of four and a half decades of urban pollution.

A permanent exhibition of **Oriental weaponry** will soon open to the public inside the palace.

AROUND MIDAN TAHRIR
The centre of the city is mainly concentrated around three squares: Rameses, Tahrir and Gumhuriyya. This is the modern section of Cairo, developed from the 19C onwards, and as such (with the notable exception of the Egyptian Museum) contains few sights of historical significance or interest to the visitor.

City Centre
Midan Tahrir – *Metro: Sadat.* The vast Liberation Square was modified following the 1952 revolution to present a contemporary vision of a renascent Egypt. To the north-west is the **Egyptian Museum** *(see Worth a Visit)*, to the west the Nile Hilton and the headquarters of the Arab League, and to the south the "**Mogamma**", an imposing 14-storey office block built in 1950 in austere Soviet style. The east of the square signals the start of two streets, Qasr al-Nil and **Talaat Harb**, the latter linking up with Midan Orabi and often referred to as "Sheraa Soliman Pasha".

This bustling commercial district is home to numerous banks, airline companies, travel agencies, hotels and inexpensive restaurants, yet it is in this area (particularly in Midan Talaat Harb) that visitors are able to gain an insight into the Art Deco architecture of 1920s Cairo; classic examples of this are timeless institutions such as the Groppi tea-room and the Café Riche, both of which are popular with locals and visitors alike and which convey the wonderful atmosphere of this golden era of Egyptian life.

Midan al-Ataba – *Metro: Ataba.* As its Arabic name indicates *(ataba* means "threshold"), this square acts as a transition point between modern Cairo, with its contemporary tower blocks, and medieval Cairo, its skyline dominated by Mameluke and Ottoman minarets. It is fronted by several sights of interest, including the **Postal Museum**, on the south-west side *(open 9am-1pm except Fri; 13pt)*, a must for stamp collectors and pigeon fanciers; and the **meat market**, to the east, hidden behind a building with green shutters (this market is only recommended for those with a strong stomach!).

The **al-Azbakiyyah Gardens**, to the north-west of the city, are a former oasis of greenery in Cairo's European quarter. These gardens were originally laid out by Napoleon Bonaparte, before being transformed by Mohammed Ali and Ismail Pasha. Nowadays the park is a shadow of its former self, a victim to the city's pollution and dust. Napoleonic enthusiasts will be interested to know that General Jean-Baptiste Kléber was assassinated here in 1800, three months after he had captured Cairo for the French, who were forced to leave Egypt the following year.

◄ **Midan Ramsis** – *Metro: Mubarak.* The square is an important intersection for Cairo's flyovers and major roads and as such is bombarded night and day with traffic from every corner of the city. This quasi-gridlock situation is not helped by the presence of the capital's main railway terminus, **Rameses Station** *(Mahattat Ramsis)*, at its centre, absorbing and disgorging tens of thousands of passengers every day. Yet, strange though it may seem, this apparent blot on the urban landscape is not lacking a certain charm, perhaps the consequence of the carefree excesses that have categorised this chaotic city for centuries.

The station is home to the **Egyptian National Railways Museum**★ *(open 8.30am-1pm except Mon; E£1.5; E£3 on Fri and public holidays)*, with its fine collection of locomotives and carriages. The exhibits on display paint a nostalgic picture of the country's railway network, the origins of which date back to 1862.

Midan al-Gumhiriyya – *Metro: Muhammad Nagib.* Midan al-Gumhiriyya or Republic Square resembles a large esplanade that is nowadays traffic-free. Separated ◄ from Midan Tahrir by the Bab al-Luq district, the square is dominated by the **Abdin Palace**, a former royal residence built in 1863 by the French architect, Rosseau.

ALONG THE NILE

A long corniche road built by Nasser half a century ago runs along the right bank of the river. At dusk, a stroll through Garden City, between the Egyptian Museum and the island of Roda, is popular with locals, who come here to sit quietly and watch the illumination of the Nile as night falls over the rooftops of Cairo.

Gazira

This residential island in the middle of the Nile, 4km/2.5mi long and 800m/880yd wide, is spanned by the 6 October Bridge and presents the appearance of an oasis of greenery in a concrete desert. The district of Zamalek, known for its soccer team and its smart residential areas, occupies the north of the island, while the south section is dominated by verdant parks and playing fields.

The Cairo Tower offers one of the best viewpoints in the city. For a clear view, your best bet is in the early morning or late afternoon.

Cairo Tower – *Metro: Opera.* ⌾ *Open 9am-midnight. E£10; video permit E£10.* This 185m/607ft tower, its concrete shaft culminating in a characteristic lotus-shaped crown, was erected in 1961 from American compensation for the non-participation of the United States in the construction of the Aswan High Dam. The building provides visitors with one of the best **views**★★ of the city.

Opera House – *Metro: Opera. Cultural complex and park open daily except Mon 10am-1pm and 5pm-9pm. E£10.* The perfectly maintained Opera building was financed by the Japanese and opened in 1993. It is built in the style of traditional Muslim architecture and offers a varied programme of performances throughout the year.

Andalucian Garden – *Metro: Opera. 63pt.* This narrow park alongside the Nile at the end of the Tahrir Bridge was formerly known as the "Maspero Garden", after the famous French Egyptologist.

> **CONTEMPORARY ART**
> The Opera complex includes a **Museum of Modern Art** *(same admission times and charges)*, displaying a collection of modern works by less well-known Egyptian artists.

CAIRO – A CONSTANT CACOPHONY

Whether you're wandering around the old Coptic quarter, the Islamic part of the city at the foot of the citadel, the modern district of Midan Tahrir or the Boulaq and Choubra neighbourhoods to the north, you'll be hard pressed to escape Cairo's incessant cacophony of sound. Five times a day, the habitual background sounds of car horns and bus engines are pierced by the voice of the *muezzin*, magnified through the city's 18 000 loudspeakers, calling the faithful to prayer. Throughout the day, the streets are a continual throng of humanity, including itinerant sellers, bicycle delivery boys, and carts pulled by donkeys slowly negotiating a path through the traffic. Radios blare out Oriental music everywhere you go – competition for merchants attempting to flog their wares to passers-by. Contrast this scene with the river bank, where fisherman, seemingly oblivious to this frenetic urban scene just a stone's throw away, calmly cast their nets into the water from their flimsy craft, under the relaxed gaze of young lovers and families out for a stroll along the Nile in search of a modicum of peace and quiet.

Mohandiseen and Doqqi

Half a century ago, this section of the left bank was virtually desert, but rampant urban development has seen the erosion of these natural landscapes, to be replaced by myriad new districts of characterless concrete. Within this context, the **floating houses** or *dahabiyyas* moored along the Sheraa al-Nil – to the north of the 15 May Bridge and facing the Zamalek district – take on greater visual significance, adding a touch of colour to a generally drab scene.

Agricultural Museum★ – *Sheraa Wizarit al-Zira'a. Metro: Doqqi, then head north along Sheraa al-Doqqi. Open daily except Mon 9am-2pm. 31pt.* This museum was opened in 1938 in the grounds of the Ministry of Agriculture. Despite its old-fashioned air, it contains interesting displays relating to the history of rural Egyptian life and agriculture, including peasant scenes and authentic collections of farming tools and machinery.

> **DAHABIYYAS**
> Nowadays, these floating houses provide accommodation for employees of the nearby British Council. In the inter-war period, they were used as casinos, cabaret clubs and – contrary to what the city's guides and authorities tell visitors – brothels.

The royal pavilion of the Manyal Palace used by the family of Prince Mohammed Ali combines an eclectic mix of Arabian styles.

Mahmud Khalil Museum★★ – *Sheraa al-Giza. Open daily 9.30am-6pm. E£25; students E£5.* It comes as something of a surprise to see works by Rodin, Millet, Utrillo, Sisley, Lautrec, Degas, Moreau and Rubens along the banks of the Nile, yet this museum, housed in a former residence of President Sadat, contains what is widely considered to be the best collection of its kind in the Middle East. The works here by Gauguin, Picasso and Corot are quite magnificent.

Giza

Although the part of Giza which is home to the pyramids is dealt with separately in this guide, the district running alongside the Nile contains two sights of potential tourist interest.

Zoological Garden – *Entrance on Sheraa Charles-de-Gaulle (the extension of Sheraa al-Giza). Open 9.30am-6pm. 31pt; camera and video permits E£20.* Sadly, a lack of funds has had serious consequences for the city's zoo, which is over a hundred years old. This in turn has affected the conditions in which its bears, lions and other animals are now kept – a great shame given the attractive surroundings in which it is located. Despite the overall neglect, the zoo attracts a steady flow of visitors, particularly on Fridays.

Doctor Ragab Pharaonic Village – *Ya'Qub island, to the south.* 🎥 *Open daily 9am-9pm (4pm in winter). E£74.* The village's re-creation of daily life under the pharaohs at times borders on the amusing, although it does include an interesting **reproduction** of Tutankhamun's tomb.

Roda

This residential district is slightly smaller than Gezira and lacks the latter's leafy character. The two main features of interest here are the Manyal Palace and the Nilometer.

Manyal Palace – *Metro: al-Sayyida Zeinab, then follow the Corniche, before crossing the branch of the Nile to the palace, on Sheraa al-Saray. Open daily 9am-4pm. E£5; camera permit E£10; video permit E£100.* This palace was built at the beginning of the 20C by Prince Mohammed Ali Tawfiq and converted into a museum in 1995. It comprises several buildings within a luxuriant garden and bears witness to the prince's opulent lifestyle.

Nilometer – *Metro: al-Malik al Salih, then cross the branch of the Nile as far as the southern tip of the island. E£6.* Known in Arabic as *el-Miqyas*, meaning "measure", this nilometer was erected in the early 8C and redeveloped three centuries later. Its equipment (a column upon which graduations are marked) enabled forecasts to be made as to whether the annual harvest would be a good one. An optimum reading of 16 would result in widespread rejoicing.

OLD CAIRO

The capital's oldest district is situated a little under 5km/3mi south of Midan Tahrir and just a stone's throw from the banks of the Nile. To Egyptians this area is known as *Masr al-Qadima* and to Europeans as the "Coptic Quarter". Its vestiges date back to the Roman period, a time when all that existed on the vast tract of land now occupied by modern Cairo was Heliopolis and the "Babylon of Egypt".

The Coptic Quarter of Ancient Babylon

Historical outline – The Coptic Christian community is an integral part of Egypt's identity and not a minority aspect of it. Originally from Alexandria and subsequently persecuted by the Romans, the Copts *(see Wadi Natrun regarding the provenance of the term)* and their Christian beliefs spread along the Nile until Constantine proclaimed Christianity as the official religion of the Roman Empire in AD 313. Organised during the 4C by, among others, St Pachomius, the Copts established themselves both in the desert and in this "Babylon of Egypt", which suffered further oppression at the hands of the Byzantines, before being "liberated" by **Omar**, the second successor to Muhammad.

Roman remains – The wall of the *Qasr esh-Shama* (the "Fortress of the Beacon") demarcated the perimeter of the Coptic Quarter. The Roman settlement established here by the Emperor Augustus in 30 BC was then rebuilt in AD 98 under Trajan. The two large **round towers** denote the site of the district's west wall and date from the period of Trajan's rule. The remains of Roman walls are also visible slightly to the north of St George's Church as well as to the south-east of the quarter.

Coptic Museum★★ – *See Worth a Visit.*

Church of the Virgin★ – *Access through the Roman towers. No charge. Visitors are asked not to visit during services on Fri (8am-11am) and Sun (7am-10am).* Better known as "the Suspended", this religious building probably dates back to the 4C, particularly the earliest section to the south-east; the basilical church standing today originates from the 6C. It was destroyed by a governor around the year 840, rebuilt, transformed into a mosque, and consecrated as a Christian church once more in the 10C. Inside, the central nave is separated from two side aisles by a rows of columns removed from ancient buildings; the nave is itself divided into two parts by three columns. The marble **pulpit**★★, the finest in Egypt, is supported by 15 small columns grouped (with one exception) into twos: each pair is different from the next. The marble slabs on display here are embellished with mosaics and low reliefs. Three sanctuaries to the rear of the church are hidden by cedar **iconostases**★ inlaid with ebony and ivory; the most elegant of these, in the centre, dates from the 13C.

Church of St George★ – *Access through the small door to the north of the Roman towers.* This relatively recent building (mid-19C) stands on the site of an early church erected in 684. The present church, which is used for Greek Orthodox worship, contains little of architectural or historical note for visitors.

Access to the following sights is via the underground staircase to the north of the preceding two entrances. Follow the narrow street, then turn right.

Church of St Sergius – *Open 8am-4pm.* This church, nestling in the very heart of old Cairo, is dedicated to Sergius, a soldier under Emperor Maximian who was martyred in Syria in AD 296. It stands on the supposed site of a stopping-point of the Holy Family as they fled the persecutions of King Herod *(the reliquary crypt is closed to the public).* The building was founded at the beginning of the 5C, altered in the 8C following a fire ordered by a Umayyad caliph, and restored in the 10C and 11C; it has a basilical layout with three naves preceded by a transversal narthex. Noteworthy features include the 12 Corinthian columns representing the Apostles, and a 12C-13C **iconostasis** superbly ornamented with inlaid ebony and ivory.

In the distant past, the Nile flowed at the foot of these towers, the foundations of which are 6m/20ft below street level. Today, the river is 400m/440yds away.

"THE SUSPENDED" The church was given this nickname (*El-Mouallaqa* in Arabic) because it was built on top of two bastions in the Roman wall, in other words above the level of the Nile. This fragile arrangement prevented cupolas from being added to the church.

THE HOLY FAMILY IN EGYPT If the Holy Family did travel through Egypt, they would have entered the country at Rafah. Their probable itinerary would have been El-Arish to El-Qantara, then across the Delta, before reaching the "Babylon of Egypt". From here, they would have headed into the Libyan Desert as far as El-Minya and then Dairut (Deir el-Muharraq), before arriving at Asyut, via Mir.

One of the characteristic features of the Church of the Virgin is the conspicuous absence of domes.

Church of St Barbara – *Continue along the narrow street and turn left. Open 8am-4pm.* This church is of lesser interest but was nonetheless founded in the late 7C and rebuilt the following century; it was significantly modified at a later date. Note the impressive marble pulpit and the 13C iconostasis.

Ben Ezra Synagogue – *Head back along the street, ignoring the street taken on the way here, then turn left.* The former Church of St Michael dates from the 8C but was converted into a synagogue at the end of the 9C. Three hundred years later, Rabbi Ibrahim ben Ezra undertook the complete overhaul of the building, which is the oldest Jewish place ◄ of worship in Egypt.

Around the Coptic Quarter of Ancient Babylon
Two years after **Omar** captured the Byzantine fortress, his general, Amr ibn el-As, founded Fustat and had a mosque erected on the site.

Fustat
Follow Sheraa Mary Girgis, which runs alongside the Coptic Quarter to the north. The first street on the right (Sheraa Ain as-Sirah) leads to the site.

A deserted site – E£6. Since the early 20C this vast city within a city has been a huge archaeological excavation site, although much of it has since been built over. Fustat was originally divided into different ethnic areas, and a stroll through the district reveals the remains of a muddled system of narrow streets, in addition to the remnants of dwellings and old wells. It is also known that Fustat had its own cisterns, water pipes and sewers. The city declined, and was then abandoned during the second half of the 11C, some two hundred years after Ahmen ibn Tulun founded Al-Qatai, the city that would become known as Cairo.

Amr Ibn al-As Mosque★ – *To the north of the Coptic Quarter, beyond the bus station. Entrance by the minaret. E£6.* Although the Ibn Tulun Mosque (879) is the oldest intact example of Islamic architecture in Egypt, the Ibn el-As Mosque retains a few features *(south of the east iwan)* from the original structure, which was built in 642. The building was enlarged in the 9C to meet the needs of a growing population, but was significantly modified in the 15C and, more recently, in 1983. As a result, none of the features of Omar's modest thatch-covered mud-brick building are still recognisable.

CITY OF THE DEAD
These unusual cemeteries are situated in Heliopolis, in the eastern part of Cairo. Dominated by the Moqattam Hill and bordered by the Sheraa Salah Salem, the street running past the Citadel, these two burial grounds (Northern and Southern) are a forest of tombs, domes and minarets. Due to the severe housing problems in central Cairo and the lack of suitable space for construction work, these have developed into shanty towns occupied by a population nowadays numbering hundreds of thousands.

Southern Cemetery
Despite being in a poorer state of repair than its northern counterpart, the Southern Cemetery contains a number of interesting monuments along its busy streets, all of which are easily accessible by bus or taxi. When visiting either cemetery, visitors should take care not to display visible signs of wealth, should request permission to take photographs, and should ensure that they leave well before dark as it is easy to get lost in the labyrinth of alleyways.

Mausoleum of the Abbasid Caliphs – *Just north of the Southern Cemetery, 100m/110yd to the east of Midan al-Sayyida Nefisa.* Contrary to its title, this mausoleum is the ◄ resting place for the remains of the caliphs' descendants.

Mausoleum of Imam al-Shafi – *On the street of the same name, 1.5km/1mi south of Midan al-Sayyida Aisha.* The 13C tomb of this *imam*, housed inside a 19C mosque, is located in an area of the cemetery rarely visited by tourists, and is a popular place of pilgrimage for Muslims

THE STORY OF MOSES
It is said that the building stands on the spot where a pharaoh's daughter found Moses in a basket made of bulrushes, after he had been abandoned on the banks of the Nile.

SHOPPING
Several families of artisans living close to the mosque and Coptic Quarter have a range of pottery fired in nearby kilns for sale. You'll find just about everything you could possibly imagine here, from sections of water pipe to huge flowerpots. If you're looking for a small souvenir which is typical of this district, then this is likely to be your best bet.

City of the Dead – one of Cairo's enduring images.

The mausoleum houses four wooden **sarcophagi**, each exquisitely crafted with the arabesques and geometric designs so typical of the art of the Ayyubid Dynasty.

Hosh al-Bacha – *To the north-west of the mausoleum.* The little-known sepulchre of the entire family of Mohammed Ali (with the exception of Pasha Tawfiq, who is buried in the Northern Cemetery), dates from 1820. It is an irony of history that the Mamelukes assassinated by Mohammed Ali *(see Background)* are also buried here, albeit beneath simple stone tombs topped by turbans. ▶

MOQATTAM HILL
The recently restored **Al-Guyushi Mosque** *(closed to the public)* is visible on top of the hill, next to the Mohammed Ali Fort. Built in 1085, it was one of the first buildings to employ stalactites as a decorative feature.

THE LIVING AND THE DEAD

Cairo's endemic problems of overpopulation and acute housing shortages have reached such a crisis point that over the past three decades hundreds of thousands of the city's inhabitants have been forced to live above and alongside the dead in the city's Northern and Southern Cemeteries. By tradition even the most humble tomb contained a room where friends and family of the deceased could come to pray, share a meal or even spend the night. Yet, today, these cemeteries have a permanent population of people who have made their home amid the tombstones and established their own city. The situation has become so worrying that the City of the Dead is now experiencing serious overcrowding.

Northern Cemetery

This second cemetery is spread out along and to the right of Sheraa Salah Salem heading towards Heliopolis, and has a larger number of interesting monuments, all of which are easily accessible on foot or by taxi.

Qaitbey Mosque★★ – *The easiest way of walking to the mosque is from Midan al-Husayn, near the Al-Azhar Mosque. From here, head along Sheraa Al-Azhar, and then Sheraa Gohar al-Qa'id, which leads directly to the Northern Cemetery. To help you recognise the mosque, look at the illustration on the back of an Egyptian £1 note. E£6.* The mosque is one of the most breathtaking expressions of 15C Islamic art in Egypt. Firstly, admire the **minaret★★**, 40m/131ft high, on which the transitions between the square, octagonal and cylindrical sections are the most successful of any example visible in Cairo, a feat achieved by the play of light and shade. Before entering, cast an appreciative eye up at the **dome★**, with its exquisite curves and delicate filigree of star-shaped polygons. The dome also bears the date of the building: 1474.

In the interior, the central enclosure or *sahn*, superbly paved in former times, is bathed in exquisite, gentle light. Access to the tomb, the graceful **cupola★** of which is adorned with a combination of star-shaped and floral interlacing, is through a door to the left of the south *iwan*. A block of granite bearing footprints attributed by legend to the Prophet Muhammad, stands alongside the sultan's catafalque, which is protected by a fine wooden enclosure.

Khanqah of Al-Ashraf Barsbay★ – *To the north. A tip* ▶ *should be given to the custodian.* This convent built in 1432 is lacking the refinement of the Qaitbey Mosque but is crowned by a beautiful **dome** embellished with interlacing and geometric forms. Inside, the wooden **minbar★** is inlaid with ivory and bone; the tomb is superbly decorated with marble and mother-of-pearl.

Khanqah of Ibn Barquq★ – *To the north. Open 8am-5pm. E£6.* This mosque-convent, comprising a *sabil-kuttab (see Sabil-Kuttab of Qaitbey)* with a fortress-like appearance, dates from 1411. The minarets, classical in structure, rise up 50m/164ft; the upper balcony of the north minaret provides an impressive view of the City of the Dead. The two imposing domes decorated with chevrons were among the first to be built in stone rather than brick and flank a smaller dome overlooking the mihrab. ▶

Heliopolis

Beyond the City of the Dead, Sheraa Salah Salem becomes Sheraa Al-Oruba, an expressway leading to the airport through the suburbs of Madinet Nasr and Heliopolis.

SAFETY AND SECURITY
If you're planning to visit this sensitive site you are advised to hire the services of a guide or to ask one of the cemetery's residents if they will escort you around (for a fee, of course!). The City of the Dead is an area best approached with both tact and discretion. With this in mind you are advised not to take any photos as any attempt to do may be considered offensive and disrespectful to those who live within its boundaries.

The term **khanqah** is used to describe a convent inhabited by mystics who have decided to retreat from the outside world. *Khanqahs* were often part of a larger religious complex.

The central court is surrounded by porticoes and is adorned with an ablution fountain (rebuilt in concrete). The two main features of note are the polychrome marble **minbar** and the wooden **screens** at the entrance to the tombs.

The monument to the Unknown Soldier of the 6 October 1973 War, in the sprawling new town of Madinet Nasr, faces the balcony on which President Sadat was assassinated by extremists on the same day, 18 years later.

To get to Heliopolis, either take a taxi (E£30-E£40), catch bus no 356 from Midan Abdel Moniem Riad, behind the Egyptian Museum, or jump on a tram from Midan Rameses (25pt).

New Heliopolis – Ancient Heliopolis has long disappeared, to be replaced by a new town that is now a fashionable suburb of Cairo and the headquarters of the presidential office. The brainchild of this ambitious project, started in 1905, was a Belgian baron, **Édouard Empain** (1852-1929), whose dream was to create a perfect town of wide, leafy avenues lined by sumptuous villas and private mansions. Today, several remnants of this entrepreneur's unusual vision of the Orient can still be seen.

October 6 War Panorama – *Sheraa Al-Oruba. Closed Thursday. E£8.* This large circular memorial houses a giant fresco celebrating Egypt's "victory" in the war against Israel in 1973.

Baron Empain's Palace – *Sheraa Al-Oruba. Closed to the public.* This pastiche of a Khmer temple was built of reinforced concrete in 1905 and can be seen on the road to the airport. Although now derelict, this palace was once as sumptuous a building as existed at the time.

Egyptians call this suburb *Masr al-Gedida*. Originally the area favoured by Egypt's wealthy, the district has been transformed almost beyond recognition since 1950, when the elegant villas began to be replaced by apartment blocks.

worth a visit

EGYPTIAN MUSEUM★★★
Midan Tahrir. Metro: Sadat. Open daily throughout the year 9am-4.45pm (3pm during Ramadan); closed 11.15am-1.30pm Fri. E£25; students E£13; camera permit E£10 (no flash photography); video permit E£100.

Background
Birth of a collection – In 1858, the French archaeologist Auguste Mariette founded a small antiquities museum in Boulaq. Soon swamped with artefacts, the collection was moved to Giza in 1890, to an annexe in the palace of the Khedive Ismail Pasha. As the museum's collection continued to grow under the management of Maspero and Jacques de Morgan, among others, the decision was taken to build a museum in Cairo with the sole purpose of housing and exhibiting the collection, which was still in its infancy.

Expansion – New discoveries, purchases, gifts and legacies continued to swell the museum collection over the years, so that it is perhaps more accurate to talk about a series of separate collections rather than one single collection. This is certainly the case with the treasures of Tutankhamun, the New Kingdom mummies, the jewellery from the royal tombs at Tanis and the funerary objects from Sennedjem's tomb in Deir el-Medina, although part of the latter is now on display in the Ägyptisches Museum in Berlin and the Metropolitan Museum of Art in New York.

If you're not part of a group, avoid visiting the museum at 9am. The best time is generally in the afternoon, when the museum is less crowded.

The Egyptian Antiquities Service, founded in 1835, had previously gathered together a collection of artefacts in an attempt to foil treasure hunters. This first collection was presented by the government to the Archduke Maximilian of Austria as a gift.

An Overview of Ancient Egypt

Al-Mathaf – A total of 120 000 items are exhibited in the Egyptian Museum, which is known to locals as *Al-Mathaf*; the museum houses double this number in its reserve collections. Nowhere else in the world is it possible to gain under one roof such a comprehensive overview of the art produced by a single civilisation.

Collections – The collections span the whole of Egyptian history and are more or less arranged in chronological order. The museum is broadly divided into two sections: sculpture is exhibited on the ground floor, with funerary objects on the first floor. Both floors are further divided into galleries housing the collections, some of which are arranged according to theme (coins, jewellery etc).

The Egyptian Museum is an old institution and as such is perhaps not as well organised as some of its more modern counterparts : lighting and ventilation are poor and the labels on exhibits are often not up to date. However, despite not always being displayed to maximum effect, the sheer number of magnificent artefacts more than compensates for any shortcomings the museum may have.

Main exhibits – It is, of course, impossible to describe the museum's entire collection in this guide. We have therefore selected a representative sample of the major items on display, in addition to pieces that have a particular association with the main historical and artistic periods of Ancient Egypt.

Visitors are advised to either follow the selection described below or to spend time viewing some of the thematically grouped collections. Whichever way you approach your visit, avoid the temptation of trying to take in too much – an exhausting task – and instead limit yourself to a small collection of exhibits.

As in all major museums, exhibits may occasionally be removed for restoration or sent to other museums around the world for temporary exhibitions. Items may also be replaced by items from the museum's reserve collection. As a result, some of the exhibits described below may not be on display to the general public.

Old Kingdom

Statue of King Djoser★★ – *Room 48, 3rd Dynasty*. This statue of King Djoser was discovered at Saqqara. Even during this early period it is apparent that art was expected to fulfil a function rather than focus on aesthetic ideals. The primary role of royal sculpture was to represent the divine nature of the king. The Pharaoh is portrayed sitting on his throne, his left hand on his knee, his right arm across his chest, wearing a royal crown or headdress (here it is the *nemes* headcloth), a false beard and a ceremonial robe. This is one of the most typical poses employed in royal sculpture, and is never used for ordinary individuals, making the king instantly recognisable and clearly differentiating him from any of his subjects. This statue is the oldest life-size sculpture in Egyptian art.

VISITING THE MUSEUM
Our description of the museum follows the major historical divisions of Egyptian history and the collections of the museum. Visitors are advised to visit the rooms in a clockwise direction, rather than in numerical order.

FUTURE PROJECTS
The Egyptian Museum is in a state of constant restoration, repair and reorganisation. As a result, there has been much talk of transferring the collection to a Museum of Civilisation to be built in Gezira, although no date for this has yet been confirmed.

The Narmer Palette★, which dates from the Predynastic period, can be seen in Room 43. King Narmer, who unified Upper and Lower Egypt, is portrayed slaying an enemy on one side of the palette. This symbolic theme of order triumphing over chaos is taken up time and time again throughout Egyptian history.

Opened in 1902, this neo-Classical-style building is the work of the French architect, Marcel Dourgnon.

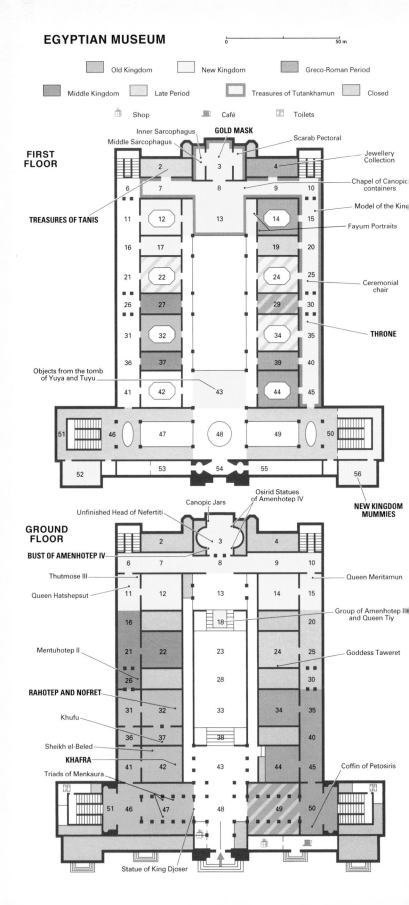

EGYPTIAN MUSEUM

0   50 m

Old Kingdom   New Kingdom   Greco-Roman Period

Middle Kingdom   Late Period   Treasures of Tutankhamun   Closed

Shop   Café   Toilets

FIRST FLOOR

Inner Sarcophagus
Middle Sarcophagus
GOLD MASK
Scarab Pectoral
Jewellery Collection
Chapel of Canopic containers
Model of the King
Fayum Portraits
Ceremonial chair
THRONE

TREASURES OF TANIS

Objects from the tomb of Yuya and Tuyu

GROUND FLOOR

Canopic Jars
Osirid Statues of Amenhotep IV
Unfinished Head of Nefertiti
BUST OF AMENHOTEP IV
Thutmose III
Queen Meritamun
Queen Hatshepsut
Group of Amenhotep III and Queen Tiy
Mentuhotep II
Goddess Taweret
RAHOTEP AND NOFRET
Khufu
Sheikh el-Beled
KHAFRA
Coffin of Petosiris
Triads of Menkaura

NEW KINGDOM MUMMIES

Statue of King Djoser

Triads of Menkaura★★★ – *Room 47, 4th Dynasty*. These triad statues represent the Pharaoh Menkaura flanked to his right by the goddess Hathor and to his left by the personification of a nome, carved out of schist. The king stands in another typical pose of royal sculpture, with his left foot thrust forward, his arms hanging alongside his body and his fists clenched. He wears a three-panelled loincloth, the crown of Upper Egypt and a false beard. His face bears a hint of a smile, unlike the earlier statue of Djoser. Both expressions were subsequently used by later Egyptian artists.

Head of Userkaf★ – *Room 47, 5th Dynasty*. Very few statues have survived from this dynasty. Discovered in Abusir in 1957, this perfectly executed head is a fine example of the sculpture of the period. Note the eyes, elongated by a thick line of make-up shown in relief. The Pharaoh wears the crown of Lower Egypt, while the false beard has been replaced by a thin moustache.

Khafra★★★ – *Room 47, 4th Dynasty*. This seated statue gives an impression of both strength (in the treatment of the arms and naked torso) and serenity (in the calm expression on the face), and moves away from the earlier, more rigid archaistic style. A Horus falcon embraces the back of the head (on the back of the *nemes*), emphasising the king's divinity. The statue is sculpted from diorite, which shines with natural light. In this way, the Pharaoh radiated light physically as well as spiritually.

*One of the **Triads of Menkaura** discovered in the Pharaoh's valley temple in Giza in 1908.*

OLD KINGDOM RELIEFS

In the funerary architecture of the Old Kingdom entire walls were covered with sculpted reliefs, which always followed the same simple conventions. In the portrayal of human figures, shoulders and eyes were depicted frontally, whereas the face and legs were in profile. Figures were represented either standing (men often with their legs apart) or sitting. The Pharaoh was always the focal point, larger in size than the other figures, usually walking, with his right arm raised, brandishing a weapon. Reliefs also featured scenes taken from daily life, alongside representations of the deceased who was shown taking part in everyday tasks.

Khafra – the Pharaoh is represented here wearing a loincloth and a nemes headdress crowned with the uraeus.

Sheikh el-Beled★★ – *Room 42, 5th Dynasty*. Private tombs often housed statues of the deceased. This realistic statue carved in wood bears witness to the artist's skill in capturing individual details that could not be represented in royal sculpture: note the signs of age, the shape of the body and the encrustation of the eyes – in quartz, rock crystal and black pigment – all of which help to

*It was Mariette's workers who nicknamed this statue **Sheikh el-Beled** ("the headman of the village"), because of its resemblance to their own village headman.*

build a strong image of this priest known as Ka-aper. A similar statue of **a bust of a man** with an asymmetrical face can be seen in the same room.

Seated Scribe★ – *Room 42, 5th Dynasty*. This statue is less famous than its contemporary in the Louvre Museum in Paris. The statue is carved in a cross-legged, seated position, the typical attitude used to portray scribes. Tomb-owners often chose to have themselves portrayed in this position because of the respect and admiration afforded to scribes at the time.

> **W**hile the face is carved in some detail, the body is represented in a simplified form.

ENIGMA

A glass case in Room 31 displays what the German archaeologist Hermann Junker called "replacement heads", more commonly known as "reserve heads", which date from the 4th Dynasty. Although the convention of the time was for the entire body to be represented, these limestone sculptures are of the head only, with no headdress. Another unusual feature of the statues is the fact that their ears appear to have been torn off. Experts are still unsure as to the purpose of these statues. Junker suggested that they may have been intended to replace real heads of mummies that had decomposed; others have put forward the theory that they are artists' moulds, the ears of which were broken when the plaster was removed.

> **T**he statue of Ty *(Room 32, 5th Dynasty)* is also well worth seeing. It is similar in style and shows the same treatment of the muscles. Food offerings would be left for the statue, which was discovered in the famous mastaba of Ty *(see SAQQARAH)*.

Statues of Ranefer – *Room 31, 5th Dynasty*. There were often many different statues of the deceased in their tombs, all of which usually followed the same stereotypical representation. However, these two almost identical statues both show the same concern for realism in the portrayal of their subject.

Rahotep and Nefret★★★ – *Room 32, 4th Dynasty*. The statue of this couple is one of the best examples of private sculpture of the period. Although the bodies are fairly stiff in form, the faces have been sculpted with striking individuality – the man has brown skin, while the woman is white, a feature that was to last for some time in both sculpture and reliefs.

Maidum Geese★ – *Room 32, 4th Dynasty. See MAIDUM*.

Pepy I★ – *Room 32, 6th Dynasty*. This statue is made from copper leaf, as bronze was unknown in Egypt at the time. Like much of the statuary dating from the 6th Dynasty, it is Mannerist in style, with huge eyes and a bulky, exaggerated physique.

> **T**he dwarf Seneb *(Room 32, 4th Dynasty)* was a wealthy man. In Egyptian eyes, his physical deformity was no obstacle to becoming a high-ranking court official. Seneb sits in the traditional scribe's position and is represented with his wife and children, who are of "normal" size.

Khufu★★ – *Room 37, 4th Dynasty*. The only surviving statue of this Pharaoh, who was responsible for the largest of all Egyptian pyramids, is this tiny ivory figurine, just 7.5cm/2.95in tall. The Pharaoh is represented in a typical pose and holds the flail, one of the royal emblems.

> **T**he statuette was discovered by Petrie in 1923 in Abydos, in a temple dedicated to the god Khentimentiu.

Middle Kingdom

Mentuhotep II★★ – *Room 26, 11th Dynasty*. This is the only statue to have survived intact from the 11th Dynasty. It is typical of the style of the period, with staring eyes, horizontal eyebrows and a sturdy build which was inherited from the First Intermediate Period; this is a significant departure from the more detailed physique of the Old Kingdom.

Queen Nefret – *Room 26, 12th Dynasty*. This statue clearly demonstrates the differences between the 11th and 12th Dynasties, as by the 12th Dynasty royal sculpture had become more realistic and natural in style.

Ten seated statues of Senusret I★ – *Room 22, 12th Dynasty*. These almost identical statues stand apart from the realism shown in other works of the period. However, although they are idealised portraits, it is possible to recognise the face of Senusret, with his straight nose, smiling mouth and round chin.

> **T**hese statues provide an insight into the highly perfected "mass-produced" art of this dynasty.

Senusret III★ – *Room 21, 12th Dynasty*. The finely rendered features of this statue, such as the tense line of the mouth, bear witness to the stresses of kingship at this time. The idea of royalty has modified somewhat by this period: the Pharaoh is perhaps slightly less divine and is represented with his hands placed religiously on his loincloth.

MIDDLE KINGDOM RELIEFS AND PAINTING

A diverse range of reliefs has survived from the Middle Kingdom, including examples of both flat and raised reliefs from the 11th Dynasty, which show a high degree of artistic skill. Faces are usually angular and carved in an expressive style; a characteristic detail is the flat-chested portrayal of women. During the 12th Dynasty, reliefs were used almost exclusively for the decoration of steles, and so it was mainly in painting that artists expressed themselves. Bright, varied colours were used to create paintings that are more natural than realistic in style. Movement is represented and relief provided by the use of shade. This sense of the pictorial reached its zenith in goldwork, creating magnificent forms and colours for the decoration of royal tombs.

The **Statue of Mentuhotep II,** *discovered by Carter in Deir el-Bahri in 1900.*

Sphinx of Amenemhat III★ – *Room 16, 12th Dynasty*. The exhibits in this room were discovered by Mariette in Tanis. During the reign of Amenemhat III, son of Senusret III, art continued to emphasise personal features, as can be seen in the slight kink given to the Pharaoh's nose. The king's power and authority are emphasised by the lion's mane, which in this example replaces the more usual *nemes* headcloth.

New Kingdom

Queen Hatshepsut★★ – *Room 11, 18th Dynasty*. In contrast to the virile, masculine style of the Middle Kingdom, this statue is an excellent example of the more feminine approach in New Kingdom sculpture. The 18th Dynasty was characterised by the number of child-kings who ascended to the throne, which in turn strengthened the queens' role. Hatshepsut's reign marked the beginning of the true New Kingdom style, as portrayed by this masterpiece of classicism, with its stylised, smooth face and strongly carved eyes and mouth.

Thutmose III★★ – *Room 11, 18th Dynasty*. Although he is considered to have been the greatest warrior in Egyptian history, none of the statues of Thutmose III demonstrate any sign of an aggressive personality. This is characteristic of the homogenous style of the period that was to last until the reign of Amenhotep IV. The only individual traits detectable on the statues of Thutmose III, whose reign was one of the longest in Egyptian history, are facial features such as a faint smile and a straight or hooked nose.

Thutmose III holding *nou* vases★ – *Room 12, 18th Dynasty*. This marble statuette represents the pharaoh praying while at the same time holding *nou* vases thought to have been used as containers for wine or milk. This ex-voto piece depicts the king in the same gentle style as the superb crystalline limestone **head of Thutmose III**★, part of a bust which is now exhibited in the Metropolitan Museum in New York.

Aset, mother of Thutmose III – *Room 12, 18th Dynasty*. The king's mother is shown in a typical royal pose: seated and holding a floral sceptre. She is wearing a three-segmented wig crowned with a cap studded with two tall feathers; wigs of the time were made either from real hair or from plant fibres and did not necessarily indicate that the head had been shaved.

Chapel of the Goddess Hathor – *Room 12, 18th Dynasty*. This shrine contains a statue of the goddess Hathor discovered in Deir el-Bahri. Thutmose III is depicted on the walls of the shrine, as is the goddess, who appears in the form of a cow. Hathor is also represented suckling the Pharaoh Amenhotep II on the front of the shrine.

Coffin of King Smenkhkara★ – *Room 3, 18th Dynasty*. The coffin of the official successor to Amenhotep IV, the gold mask of which has been partly damaged, is a magnificent work of art studded with lapis-lazuli, enamel, turquoise, glass paste and cornelian.

Bust of Amenhotep IV★★★ – *Room 3, 18th Dynasty*. Although found in Karnak, this fragment of an Osirid statue already shows many of the features typical of Amarnian art. The Amarnian style takes its name from the site of Tell el-Amarna, where Amenhotep IV – later to

DIVINE BLOOD

It was essential for the Pharaoh to marry a daughter of the king because of her royal blood. As a result a number of monarchs were forced to marry their sister or half-sister. Hatshepsut married her half-brother Thutmose III, who died at a young age. Hatshepsut then became regent to the illegitimate Thutmose III before claiming the title of queen for herself.

Other exhibits worthy of attention in Room 12 include the **statuette of Tjay**★, **Amenhotep, son of Hapu**, the **Expedition to the Land of Punt**★ from the temple of Hatshepsut at Deir el-Bahri, and the **block statue of Senenmut** depicting a seated man – a traditional symbol of resurrection.

*This head of **Queen Hatshepsut** belonged to an Osirid statue from the temple of Deir el-Bahri.*

NEW KINGDOM RELIEFS AND PAINTING

From Hatshepsut's reign onwards, paintings and reliefs appeared in the decor of private tombs, and used the same classical style observed in sculpture. Figures are depicted in sober dress and postures, with graceful lines and serene expressions, features seen in both private and royal art. This idealised style came to an end during the reign of Amenhotep III, when the first signs of the Amarnian style can be seen. Suddenly, sculptures became exaggerated and almost caricatural in style, provoking a subsequent reaction and a return to a purer, academic style. This was followed by the generally convex relief of the Rameses pharaohs, with the exception of Rameses II's reign, when flatter relief was the norm. The art of this period demonstrates an occasional over-emphasis of decoration and unrealistic representations, which both bear witness to the Amarnian heritage of this period and the almost Baroque nature of its art.

become Akhenaten – founded his new capital. The artistic style that was to evolve at Tell el-Amarna was the most unrealistic in the history of Ancient Egypt. The Osirid statues depict the Pharaoh standing, holding the royal emblems of the crook and flail, his feet together and arms crossed over his chest.

Osirid statues of Amenhotep IV★★★ – *Room 3, 18th Dynasty.* Although these two statues are sculpted in traditional pose, the Pharaoh is no longer represented in mummiform fashion like most Osirid statues: in one of the statues he is naked; in the other he wears a loincloth, showing that he is alive. With its half-closed eyes, long ears, thick lips, long chin, protruding belly and wide, asexual hips, this statue breaks with the classical style that dominated the period leading up to Amenhotep IV's ascension and marks the beginning of a new artistic trend in line with Akhenaten's philosophical revolution.

Stele of the royal family★ – *Room 3, 18th Dynasty.* This stele, from Tell el-Amarna shows that Akhenaten's art is not only new in style but also in subject-matter. For the first time, the royal family is depicted in an intimate family scene, with the Pharaoh sitting opposite his wife, the couple's eldest daughter, Meritaten, between them, and the younger daughters seated on their mother's lap. The poignant tenderness of the scene is also felt in the portrayal of **Akhenaten embracing one of his daughters**, proof of ◄ the spiritual dimension of the Armanian revolution.

Canopic jars★★ – *Room 3, 18th Dynasty.* The splendid female heads depicted on the lids of these jars bear witness to the finesse of Amarnian art. After its initial emphasis on unrealistic figures, the Amarnian style became more serene, reflecting the stable atmosphere of the last years of Akhenaten's reign.

Amun and Mut★ – *Room 8, 18th Dynasty.* These two monumental sculptures destroyed by tomb-robbers demonstrate the painstaking care taken by restorers. They also provide proof that Akhenaten's cult of Aten was overturned by his successors – who reinstated Amun as the official state god – and that the Amarnian style continued to influence Egyptian art despite the advent of the counter-reformation.

NEFERTITI

In Room 3 note the unfinished bust of **Nefertiti**★★, a masterpiece of purity; a **royal female head**; and the **bust of a princess**, the synthesis of the spirit of the Amarnian reform.

OSIRID STATUES

Although his iconographic language is new, Amenhotep IV uses the traditional form of the Osirid statue. A new type of statue would have been less effective in communicating the Pharaoh's revolutionary language, while the re-use of a traditional statue made his new message more effective.

Bust of Amenhotep IV
Is the androgynous appearance of this bust due to a physical deformity of the Pharaoh or to symbolic mysticism?

Bust of Rameses II★ – *Room 9, 19th Dynasty*. This portrait of a young Rameses II bears two characteristics which are typical of its period: the round wig and the tunic with multiple folds and flared sleeves. Amarnian influence can be detected in the elegant features and calm, meditative gaze of the subject. ▶

Sety I★ – *Room 14, 19th Dynasty*. Many of the typical features of Ramesside art can be discerned for the first time in this alabaster statue of Sety I. Despite a prevailing academicism, the art from his reign began to look back to the Amarnian period for inspiration.

Queen Meritamun★★★ – *Room 15, 19th Dynasty*. This sculpture is one of the masterpieces of Ramesside art. The queen – whose identity was not confirmed for many years and who was referred to as simply as "the white queen" – looks down, in a gesture of piety. With its charming smile and almost intact polychromy, this statue is one of the most entrancing works ever produced during the Ramesside period. The queen's beauty is emphasised by her jewellery: two round earrings, a wide necklace and a double bracelet. She wears a rosette on each breast, while her headdress is crowned with a cap encircled by a frieze of *uraeus* adorned with solar discs. ▶

Late Period

Goddess Taweret★★★ – *Room 24, 26th Dynasty*. Much of the art of the Late Period shows a strong classical influence, although the period is also characterised by its range of artistic styles, due as much to previous artistic trends as to external influences. This superb green schist statue dates from the reign of Psammtek I and is highly polished, a typical feature of this dynasty. The statue originally stood in an enclosed naos, which would have had a single opening through which the faithful would whisper their prayers to the goddess. ▶

Isis, Hathor and Osiris★ – *Room 24, 26th Dynasty*. In addition to the polished finish of this period, these statues also have the typical almond-shaped eyes and gentle smile of the dynasty's later works. This smile corresponds to the Saite period and was subsequently described as the "Saite smile" until Roman times.

Montuemhat – *Room 24, 26th Dynasty*. The Nubian features of this mayor of Thebes and prophet of Amun are a reminder that important court officials of the time were often of direct Kushite descent.

First-floor Collections

Objects from the tomb of General Mesehti★ – *Room 37, 11th Dynasty*. Figurines of servants known as *shabti* first appeared in tombs during the 6th Dynasty, becoming livelier in style during the First Intermediate Period and disappearing altogether after the 12th Dynasty. These small models served the same purpose as paintings and carved reliefs in later tombs, and provided a three-dimension portrayal of similar scenes. ▶

Jewellery Collection★★★ – *Room 4*. The technical perfection of Egyptian goldwork can be appreciated through these magnificent artefacts discovered in a number of different tombs. Particularly worthy of note are the **Head of the Falcon Horus**★★ *(6th or 12th Dynasty)*; the **Diadem of Sat-Hathor-Yunet**★ *(12th Dynasty)*, which belonged to a daughter of Senusret II; the **Necklace of Nefruptah**★ *(12th Dynasty)*, with its chain of amazonites and cornelians linked by two gold falcon heads; and the **Pectorals of Mereret** *(12th Dynasty)*, the cloisonné work of which is especially striking. Among the **Treasures of Dush** (2C), discovered in a jar in the Kharga oasis, note the two bracelets and a long necklace comprising 187 gold platelets.

Treasures of Tanis★★★ – *Room 2, 21st and 22nd Dynasties*. This exceptional collection contains masks, jewellery, amulets, weapons, dishes and gold sandals and is only eclipsed in opulence by the Tutankhanum collection. This magnificent artistic ensemble will be of particular interest to those who have visited the site of Tanis.

In Room 14 note the **Coronation of Rameses III** *(20th Dynasty)*, in which the Pharaoh is depicted flanked by the gods Horus and Seth, here symbolising order and anarchy.

MUSICAL ATTRIBUTES
Meritamun is holding a *menat* in her hand. This cult object, which made a noise when shaken, was linked with the worship of Hathor. Earrings were first depicted in the New Kingdom and were traditionally worn by chantresses.

OTHER HIGHLIGHTS
Thes include the moulding of the **Rosetta Stone** *(Room 34)*, the **Statue of King Khasekhemwy** *(Room 43, 2nd Dynasty)*, the **Group of Amenhotep III and Queen Tiy**★★ *(atrium, 18th Dynasty)*, and the **Coffin of Petosiris**★★ *(Room 50, Ptolemaic Dynasty)*.

The soldiers of **Mesehti's Army of Pikemen and Archers** are portrayed with wide, staring eyes, a typical feature of the 11th Dynasty.

The gold **Head of the Falcon Horus** *was once part of a bronze statue from Hierakonpolis in Upper Egypt.*

This elegant gold broad collar set with enamel and pearls is just one of many fascinating items discovered at Saqqara.

New Kingdom Mummies★★★ – *Room 56; entrance to the right of the east staircase; special ticket: E£50 (no photos). Guides not admitted.* These 11 mummies were hidden in a "royal" cache in the tomb of Queen Inhapy by priests from the 21st Dynasty in order to protect them from tomb-robbers. The most famous of the mummies is that of **Rameses II**, badly damaged by fungi and subsequently restored in 1976 by the Museum of Mankind in Paris; it has been preserved through sterilisation with gamma rays. This room was temporarily closed to visitors in 1981 by President Sadat, who considered the exhibition of the mummies to be disrespectful. It is now kept at a constant temperature of 22°C and was re-opened to the public in 1995. The **Coffin of Rameses II**★ *(Room 50)*, which once contained his mummy, can be seen in the next room. The painted coffin is made of wood and represents the Pharaoh in the attitude of Osiris.

Objects from the tomb of Yuya and Tuyu★★ – *Room 43, 18th Dynasty.* Objects on display from this tomb include beautiful funerary masks made from gilded cartonnage and semi-precious stones (the eyes are blue glass and quartz), a chariot, chairs, sarcophagi, jewels and chests; one of these, made from gilded wood, is studded with ebony, ivory and faience and was used for jewellery.

Egyptian faience has little in common with the true polished faience which comes from Faenza, in Italy. The material used here is crushed quartz which has been glazed with an alkaline veneer.

Objects from the tomb of Sennedjem★ – *Room 17, 19th Dynasty.* This interesting group of funerary objects includes the outer sarcophagus of Khons; the illustrations on the sides are taken from the *Book of the Dead.* Note also the *shabti* container in the form of a shrine.

The extensive collection of coffins on this floor *(Rooms 41 to 11)*, includes the *Silver Coffin of Psusennes I*★ *(Room 11)*, the models of the tomb of Meketra *(Room 27)*, and the *Book of the Dead of Maiherpri*★ *(Room 17).*

Treasures of Tutankhamun★★★

Rooms 3, 7 to 10, 13, 15, 20, 25, 30, 35, 40 and 45. 18th Dynasty.

A remarkable collection – The tomb of Tutankhamun was opened on 29 November 1922 by the British Egyptologist **Howard Carter**. It took a period of 10 years to make a full inventory of the tomb's contents: the sorting and restoration of the 171 objects in the antechamber alone required two years of painstaking work. The collection shown here consists of a total of 2 099 objects. Fortunately, the contract between Lord Carnarvon, the financial backer of the excavation project, and the Egyptian government guaranteed the latter exclusive rights to the archaeological finds. One important object is not on display in the museum, as the outer sarcophagus, with its outer coffin and mummy, has been left in the tomb.

This tomb *(no 62)* is situated just below the tomb of Rameses VI in the Valley of the Kings near Luxor.

The main components of this priceless collection are listed below.

Funerary objects – The four **shrines**★, which fitted one inside the other around the outer sarcophagus, are made from gilded stuccoed wood, as are the three **funerary beds**★★ decorated with animals such as cats, cows and hippopotami. Protected by four representations of the goddess

Serket, the **chapel of canopic containers**★★ was kept in the treasure chamber. This originally housed the canopic jars used to store the small sarcophagi containing the viscera of the deceased.

The most remarkable object in the collection is the gold-plated **throne**★★★ studded with coloured glass, semi-precious stones and silver leaf *(Room 35)*, the arms of which are winged serpents wearing the double crown of Egypt. The **ceremonial chair**★★ *(Room 25)*, embellished with ebony, ivory, gold and faience, is another of the museum's masterpieces; note how the seat of this finely crafted piece is moulded to take a cushion.

Other funerary objects exhibited here include naos statuettes, chests, a *senet* table *(senet* was a game played during the Old Kingdom and was not unlike draughts), perfume vases, pots for cream, and royal *shabti* statues.

Sculpture – Thirty-two statuettes were discovered in the naos, the most elegant of which is **Tutankhamun harpooning fish**★ *(Room 40)* portraying the Pharaoh in the typical loincloth of the time. Two **life-size statues of the king**★ *(Room 45)* in gilded and bitumenised wood once guarded the funerary chapel and represent Tutankhamun's *ka*. The extremely life-like **model of the king**★★ *(Room 15)* is thought to have been used to design the Pharaoh's clothes and neckpieces. Admire also the varnished black wood statue of **Anubis**★ *(Room 9)* which once stood in the passage between the funerary chapel and the treasure.

Goldwork – *Room 3.* As well as two sarcophagi, this room houses precious items found on the mummy or in the treasure chamber; the chests stored here were packed full of precious items. The **gold mask**★★★ is undoubtedly the most beautiful of the funerary masks discovered to date. Although over 3 000 years old, the mask is so perfectly finished that it looks as though it was made yesterday. Comparison with portraits of the young king suggest that his actual features are represented on the mask. The mummiform **inner sarcophagus**★★★ (110.4 kg/243lb of 22-carat gold), which protected the mask-covered mummy, is solid gold and is decorated with a vulture whose wings are made from coloured stones. The **middle sarcophagus**★★, carved from wood and covered with gold leaf and semi-precious stones, is also mummiform in shape, and has the most lifelike face of the entire collection.

The complete panoply of goldwork techniques (cloisonné and filigree work, setting of jewels and engraving) is represented in this collection of royal jewels, which comprises necklaces, broad collars, pectorals, pendants, earrings, bracelets and even a dagger. The **scarab pectoral**★★★ is a good example of the fine craftwork of the time: in the

WORTH SEEING
Don't miss the Fayum Portraits★★ in Room 14 and the north side of Room 13. It is also worth spending some time admiring the many statuettes and amulets in Room 19 where a number of Egyptian gods are featured *(for identification of the different gods see the Insight and Images section of the guide).*

TUTANKHAMUN'S MASK

This life-size mask is made of gold, cornelian, lapis-lazuli, quartz, obsidian, turquoise and coloured glass. It weighs 11kg/24lb and is 54cm/21in tall. The Pharaoh wears the *nemes* headcloth and a false beard, as well as the royal *uraeus* and the vulture's head of the goddess Nekhbet.

This tender portrayal of the royal couple, depicted on the back of the throne, bears the hallmarks of the Amarnian style.

VISITING THE MUSEUM

The museum collection is arranged in 23 rooms, organised according to theme. Exhibition rooms not mentioned in the detailed museum description opposite are as follows:
Room 1: new acquisitions. *Room 2*: Umayyad, Abbasid, Fatimid and Ayyubid art. *Room 10*: patio. *Room 19*: manuscripts. *Room 22*: Persia. *Room 23*: temporary exhibitions.

centre, a bird struck by a scarab beetle made of chalcedony holds a lily and a lotus in its claws; the beetle pushes a celestial bark containing the sacred eye beneath the eternal image of Tutankhamun.

ISLAMIC ART MUSEUM★★★

Midan Ahmed Mahir; entrance on Sheraa Bur Sa'id. Metro: Muhammad Nagib. Open daily 9am-4pm (closed 11am-1.30pm Fri). E£16; students E£8.

The museum was created in 1883 and established itself in this building 20 years later. Initially conceived to safeguard the ancient treasures uncovered during archaeological excavations around Egypt, it now contains some 70 000 exhibits, making it one of the leading museums of its kind in the world.

Mameluke period – *Room 5*. Exhibits of note include an impressive bronze-plated door, printed textiles, pottery, lamps (also in bronze), and a delightful fountain from the mosque of the Sultan Qalaoun.

Woodwork★★ – *Rooms 6 and 9*. The decorative mastery of the sultans' craftsmen is clearly evident in this section of the museum, where *mashrabiyas*, the **cenotaph of Soliman el-Kasim★** (1433), the doors from the Al-Ashraf Mosque, the coffered ceilings, and the *koursis* (the dais from which passages from the Koran were read) all bear witness to their great skill. Further evidence of their expertise can also be seen in a 13C *mihrab* from the Al-Azhar Mosque, the **door** from the mosque of the Sultan Qalaoun, and the **cenotaph★★** of Al-Husayn, also 13C, ornamented with verses from the Koran written in Kufic script.

WORTH SEEING
The sculpted **wood panels★★** in Room 4 are from the *maristan* (hospital) of Qalaoun. The scenes they portray (hunting, musicians and dancers) are extremely rare as Islamic art did not encourage the depiction of the human form.

Metalwork★ – *Room 11*. Exhibits on display include delicately crafted vases, incense burners, lamps and chandeliers inset with gold and silver, in addition to Persian and Turkish **astrolabes★**.

Weaponry★★ – *Room 12*. Artistry was not excluded from weapons of warfare as is demonstrated here by the 16C-17C Iranian pistols inlaid with gold, the sword adorned with an ivory handle, and an assortment of Mameluke daggers.

Ceramics★★ – *Rooms 13-16 and Room 20*. This extensive collection encompasses several centuries, including the 10C-12C *Fayum* ceramics, and the terracotta pieces from the excavations at **Fustat**, which illustrate the full technical range of this art form. Note the dominance of white and turquoise in the extensive array of **vases**, spanning the 10C-14C, as well as the fact that many of these bear the signature of artists or the name of the sultan who commissioned the work. Various elegant designs also adorn the different pieces. The collection is enhanced by examples from elsewhere in the Islamic world, including the Spanish region of Andalucia, in addition to pieces of Turkish faience and Chinese porcelain.

PERSIAN TILES
Enamelled tiling is a Persian rather than an Egyptian speciality. The magnificent **wall tiles★★** on display are from Syria, Tunisia, Turkey, but above all from Iran.

Textiles – *Room 17*. The high quality of some of the fragments of different types of cloth from Egypt, the Yemen and Iran is a clear indication that these articles were destined for extremely wealthy clients.

Lapidary art★ – *Room 18*. The introduction of the Arabic alphabet as a decorative feature is reflected not only in the evolution of calligraphy but also in the variety of styles employed.

Glasswork★ – *Room 21*. The outstanding **collection of michkats**★★ is unique in the world. These enamelled, blown-glass lamps were a Mameluke speciality and were attached to chains via their handles and suspended from the ceilings of *iwans*; a small globe placed on the chain prevented mice from feeding on the oil. A large proportion of these originated from Syria, although the finest specimens (mid-14C) were taken from the mosque of the Sultan Hassan.

The similarities in style between Umayyad and Byzantine art are clearly evident. It wasn't until the Tulunid Dynasty that Islamic art adopted its own specific characteristics.

COPTIC MUSEUM★★

Coptic Quarter (see section on Old Cairo). Metro: Mary Girgis. Entrance through the Roman towers. Open daily 9am-5pm. E£16; students E£8. Camera permit E£10; video permit E£100. Established from a private collection assembled in the early part of the 20C, this museum was nationalised in 1931. It continued to expand and in 1947 acquired the Coptic collection belonging to Gaston Maspero. The museum highlights the widespread artistic importance of the early Christians in the Nile Valley, although it is hoped that in the future the museum will have the funds necessary to display its exhibits in a more favourable light.

The old wing of the museum is currently being renovated. As a result, several rooms remain closed to the general public.

Lapidary art★ – *Rooms 1 to 8*. Numerous fragments from monuments dating back to the 6C-4C BC illustrate the evolution of this art form since Greco-Roman times, as well as the development of motifs from their early secular form to decidedly Christian-inspired art.

Painting★★ – *Rooms 3, 9 and 13*. Among the superb **frescoes**★, several originate from Omm el-Bregatt in the Fayum region *(Room 9)*. A number of religious **icons**★★ from various churches and monasteries catch the eye, including a **Madonna** *(no 3367)* and a **Virgin Carrying the Crucified Jesus** *(no 3472)*. Most date from the 18C and 19C, although several are from as early as the 15C and 16C, a period from which few examples remain. Note also the collection of ivories displayed in Room 13.

Textiles★★★ – *Rooms 10 to 12*. It is in this field that the Copts developed an unsurpassed originality. Using weaving techniques inherited from the Pharaonic period they incorporated ornamental features (embroidered with linen, wool and silk) inspired by Greek mythology or Sassanid naturalistic art, and gradually Christianised them, through the integration of motifs such as ansate crosses, fish, lambs, doves, ciboria, saints and apostles. The workshops, located in Middle Egypt (Antinoe and Akhmim) and in the Babylon of Egypt quarter of Old Cairo, mainly produced tunics, shrouds, sacerdotal vestments and sanctuary curtains. One of the finest examples of the latter on display is a 4C **curtain**★★ representing the façade of a sanctuary, whose arches are inscribed with the *ankh* cross *(Room 11, no 2023)*.

Metalwork – *Rooms 14 to 16*. Religious and domestic pieces take pride of place in these rooms, including several delightful articles of **jewellery**★ and a magnificent **bronze eagle**★★ from the 4C *(Room 15)*.

Woodwork – *Room 8 and Rooms 22 to 25 are currently inaccessible*. Not only were the Copts gifted wood sculptors, they also produced exquisite inlaid and marquetry work, some of which is on display throughout the museum.

Manuscripts – *Rooms 10 and 17*. The collection covers the period between the 4C and the 13C and includes one of the oldest biblical manuscripts in existence: a 4C parchment **psalter**★★ with its original wood binding, and entirely written in the Coptic language *(Room 10)*.

ROOM 6
The superbly sculpted series of 12 capitals★★ (6C) from the Monastery of St Jeremiah *(Deir Apa Jeremia)* in Saqqara is without a doubt the highlight in Room 6.

ROOM 10
The two papyruses of the Gospel according to St Thomas★★ (3C and 4C) combine pagan teachings with the recognition of Christianity.

Dahshûr ★

Part of the long chain of pyramids that runs from Cairo to Fayum, Dahshur is a pearl in the middle of the desert plain. This archaeological site, opened in 1996, is much less visited than Saqqara or Giza, but is nonetheless impressive in its beauty and peaceful setting. Its two superb stone pyramids, one rhomboidal in shape and the other red in colour, make this site well worth a visit.

Location
45km/28mi S of Cairo, 11km/7mi S of Saqqara, on the left bank of the Nile. Access: the easiest way from Cairo or Saqqara is by taxi; another option is the microbus running from both Giza and Saqqara.

Name
The origins of the name Dahshur remain shrouded in mystery. The site comprises a number of pyramids of all colours, including red, black, white and pink.

Transcription: دهشور

Famous People
The Egyptian archaeologist Ahmed Fakhry (1905-73) excavated the Rhomboidal Pyramid in 1952 and established beyond doubt that it was the Pyramid of Sneferu. Other archaeologists who subsequently worked on the site include the Frenchman Jacques de Morgan.

In October, on the road to Dahshur, visitors will see dates spread out on the ground to dry in the sun.

History
The royal necropolis of Dahshur, situated in the 21st nome of Upper Egypt, was used by Sneferu, the first Pharaoh of the 4th Dynasty, as well as by Senusret III and Amenemhat II and III, kings of the 12th Dynasty.

background

An important landmark – Built after Djoser's Step Pyramid at Saqqara and before the better-known massive pyramids of Khufu (Cheops) and Khafra (Chephren) at Giza, two of the five pyramids at Dahshur, built during the reign of Sneferu, represent a crucial evolutionary step in pyramid construction.

Sneferu had just built what is usually refered to as the "False Pyramid" at Meidum, which he abandoned to build a double rhomboidal pyramid – also known as the "South" or "Bent" Pyramid – and then a regular pyramid – known as the "North" or "Red" Pyramid – here at Dahshur. It was therefore at Dahshur that the transformation between the step pyramid and the true pyramid took place. Although several historians consider the structure at Meidum to be the first real Egyptian pyramid, other experts suggest that the Red Pyramid at Dahshur has a stronger claim, as it was designed and built on a square plan with a single-angled slope.

An inaccessible site – The site was classified as a military zone in 1967 and was subsequently off-limits to the general public for a number of years. When the site eventually re-opened to the public in 1996 the military zone was moved to a nearby location to the west, where its barbed wire fences make it easily distinguishable. The major advantage that Dahshur has over other pyramid sites such as Saqqara and Giza is that it is far less visited. The site is not overrun with tour groups and you will not be pestered by souvenir sellers, allowing for a pleasant, relaxed visit. All in all, Dahshur is remarkably peaceful and unspoilt.

highlights

The Site

Open all year 8am-5pm. E£10; students E£5; camera permit E£5; video permit E£25. Only the Red Pyramid is open to the public.

Altogether the site has five pyramids, arranged in two parallel lines that separate the oldest structures from the most recent. On this north-south axis stand the Pyramid of Senusret III, the North Pyramid, the Pyramid of Amenemhat II, the Pyramid of Amenemhat III and the Rhomboidal Pyramid. The site is the southernmost extension of the necropolis at Saqqara and originally included mastaba tombs of important people and even a small town.

Rhomboidal Pyramid★★

Closed for restoration.

Sneferu – It is thought that the founder of the 4th Dynasty, probably the natural son of Huni, married his half-sister, Hetepheres, who bore him a son, the immortal Khufu. Sneferu, regarded as the model of the perfect king by many of his successors, enjoyed a long and peaceful reign, despite a number of military expeditions abroad. No fewer than three pyramids are attributed to him (the "False Pyramid" at Meidum, and the Rhomboidal and Red Pyramids at Dahshur).

Pyramid – In ancient times the splendid Rhomboidal Pyramid was given the name "Sneferu is resplendent in the south". Many consider this to be the most beautiful of the pyramids, possibly because of its unusual and distinctive shape.

The shape of the pyramid has been widely discussed and interpreted. The most common theory holds that the original angle of the pyramid (54° on its 189m/620ft sides) would have made it the highest pyramid in Egypt at 140m/459ft. However, the weight of the construction threatened its stability so the builders chose to modify the angle to create a more gentle slope, in order to avoid the risk of collapse. By reducing the angle to 43° from a height of 45m/147ft, they obtained a structure which stood almost 100m/328ft high. The German archaeologist Ludwig Borchardt has suggested that the sudden death of the Pharaoh may have accelerated work on the pyramid. A third opinion is that the shape of the pyramid was intended to emphasise the double nature of the building, which had two entrances (north and west), a unique characteristic. If this were the case, then the structure fully deserves its other name of the "Double Pyramid".

At a height of 12m/39ft, the north entrance leads into a 79-m/259-ft long corridor which descends 25m/82ft to reach a corbelled room. The second entrance, probably blocked because of dangerous cracks, led to another room. A satellite pyramid can be seen to the south, a mud-brick funerary temple to the north-east and the ruins of an altar-table flanked by steles to the east.

Neither the pyramid at Meidum nor those at Dahshur have revealed the sarcophagus of **Sneferu**. Although it is believed that the Pharaoh's tomb would have been in the Red Pyramid, it is possible that it was housed elsewhere as the site once contained 11 pyramids.

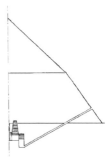

North-south section. The adjective rhomboidal is used to describe a diamond shape. The shape may also be described as truncated.

The harmonious, regular shape of the Red Pyramid is thought to be the prototype for the Giza pyramids.

North Pyramid★

Situated to the north of the Rhomboidal Pyramid, Sneferu's second pyramid has lost its limestone slab casing. The limestone slabs used for this structure have given it the nickname the "Red Pyramid", although it was known in Ancient times as "Sneferu is resplendent".

The sides slope at an angle of 43°, less than the Giza pyramids; were this not the case the pyramid would have been even more impressive, with sides measuring 219m/718ft and a height of 102m/334ft. In 1981 the German Archaeological Institute of Cairo discovered the pyramidion which crowned the structure, the only one from the Old Kindgom which can still be seen today; this has now been placed on the east side.

Entrance is to the north. As with other 4th Dynasty pyramids, the situated at a height of 30m/98ft with 125 steps, the entrance leads into a 60-m/196-ft long corridor which in turns leads to three 16-m/52-ft high corbelled rooms.

The Rhomboidal Pyramid was built with limestone blocks faced with slabs of polished limestone.

In 1895, Jacques de Morgan discovered several tombs inside the pyramid complex; these belonged to Queen Keminebu and to the daughters of Amenemhat II.

MAGNIFICENT JEWELLERY

Jacques de Morgan discovered items of jewellery in Dahshur, now on display in the Egyptian Museum in Cairo. These items include pectorals once worn by Mereret (Senusret III's daughter) and necklaces worn by Khnemet (Amenemhat II's daughter), made of gold, turquoise and lapis lazuli. They are on display in Room 4 on the first floor of the museum.

WADI GARAWI

At Wadi Garawi, on the right bank of the Nile, opposite Dahshur, the remains of the oldest dam in the world, the Sadd el-Kafara or "dam of the pagans", can be seen. The dam dates from the 4th Dynasty and is 110-m/360-ft long. Its central section once stood at a height of more than 50m/164ft.

Pyramid of Amenemhat II

Amenemhat II – The son of Senusret I, this Pharaoh inherited a prosperous kingdom and organised trade expeditions to destinations as far afield as Asia.

Pyramid – This is the first of the three Middle Kingdom pyramids on the site. Built in light limestone (hence its nickname, the "White Pyramid"), the pyramid was known as "Amenemhat is powerful". Its sides are estimated to have been 50m/164ft long (since the pyramid is now in ruins) and the entrance is to the north. As the exact angle of the walls is not known, it is impossible to calculate its original height. One of the two funerary chambers had a ceiling with blocks of limestone shaped to form the letter A.

Pyramid of Senusret III

Senusret III – Senusret III was considered the greatest Pharaoh of the 12th Dynasty. He greatly reduced the power of the nomarchs, solidified Egyptian control of Lower Nubia, drained the marshes of the Fayum region and launched military operations as far away as Palestine, to the southern part of the region then known as Canaan.

Pyramid – Built in mud-brick originally covered with limestone slabs, which have since disappeared, this pyramid is not unlike a small volcano in appearance. It was originally 78m/255ft in height (now 30m/98ft), with 105-m/344-ft long sides and an angle of 56°. The entrance was to the west. A shaft leads to a funerary chamber painted in white. Although the chamber has been pillaged, it still contains a granite sarcophagus with a palace-façade decor.

The pyramid complex also contains mastaba tombs, two of which, to the north, were accessible by an underground gallery. De Morgan discovered sarcophagi and magnificent items of jewellery here; to the south he found two solar barks, now in the Egyptian Museum in Cairo and the Natural History Museum in Chicago.

Pyramid of Amenemhat III

Amenemhat III – This Pharaoh inherited a powerful Egypt from his father, Senusret III, and was responsible for the completion of a complex irrigation system in Fayum. He extended the Egyptian border as far as the third cataract, in Nubia, developed trade relations with Syria and Phoenicia and exploited the turquoise mines of the Sinai.

Pyramid – Also built from mud-brick covered with stone, this pyramid, often referred to as the "Black Pyramid" (because of the black basalt stone), was intended to resemble the Pyramid of Senusret III. The entrance, to the east, was unusually situated on the outside, and led to a complex arrangement of funerary apartments built for the queens.

A magnificent wooden statue found in one of the tombs to the north represents the *ka* of the ruler Awibra Hor and is now housed in the Egyptian Museum in Cairo. The painted stucco which covered the statue turned to powder when the statue was exhumed.

Giza★★★

The Great Pyramid of Khufu (Cheops), one of the Seven Wonders of the Ancient World, is situated on the plateau of the Giza Desert, to the west of Cairo, in an area fast being encroached upon by the city's suburbs. The pyramids of Khafra and Menkaura, and the Great Sphinx, which has stood guard over the pyramids for 4 500 years, are also part of this magnificent site, easily the most famous in Egypt, and usually the first stop for most visitors to the country.

Location

12km/7.5mi W of the centre of Cairo, on the left bank of the Nile. The pyramids stand at the end of the Avenue of the Pyramids, which runs through the densely populated suburb of Giza. Access: from the city centre by taxi (E£25), by air-conditioned bus no 355 (E£2, from behind the Egyptian Museum), or by microbus (E£1) from Midan Rameses or from in front of the Nile Hilton (ask for Al-Ahram).

Transcription: الجيزة

Name

The Giza Plateau takes its name from the old rural settlement of *Al-Djiza*, founded in the 7C. Egyptians often refer to the area as *El-Ahram*, which simply means "the pyramids".

Famous People

Numerous renowned Egyptologists have worked at this extraordinary site, including Europeans such as the Italian Prospero Alpino, the Frenchman Auguste Mariette and the Englishman Sir William Flinders Petrie. Perhaps less well known is the contribution made by Egyptian archaeologists, such as Selim Hassan (1886-1961), who led work on the old German section of the site and excavated the temples and complex of the Pyramid of Queen Khentkawes, as well as the temple of Amenhotep II. Other Egyptians who have worked here include Kamal el-Malakh (1919-87), who discovered Khufu's boat pits, which are now open to the public, and Abdel Aziz Saleh (1921), who excavated the area around the causeway of Menkaura, which led to a greater understanding of the ancient techniques used for transporting materials.

History

The royal necropolis of the 4th Dynasty was situated in the nome of the "white wall". Architectural features from the 1st, 2nd, 5th and 6th Dynasties can also be seen here.

AÏDA

The pharaonic opera, Aïda, performed for the first time at the Cairo Opera House in 1871, was composed by Giuseppe Verdi at the request of the Khedive Ismail Pasha. It is a little-known fact that the Egyptologist Auguste Mariette was responsible for the stage design of this first production. The opera is sometimes performed on site, behind the Pyramid of Khafra.

The German **Karl Richard Lepsius** (1810-84) was the first to enter the Pyramid of Khufu, while the American **George Andrew Reisner** (1867-1942) worked from 1902 until his death at the "Harvard Camp" to the west of the pyramids, in so doing establishing the record for the longest excavation of the site.

Reconstruction of the Giza Plateau.

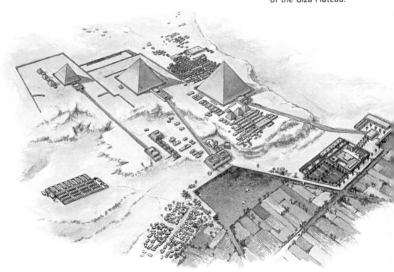

background

Giza Plateau – The Giza Plateau extends for more than 1.2km/0.7mi from north to south and approximately 1.5km/0.9mi from east to west. This geographical feature is unique in the annals of Egyptian archaeology and has made possible the almost complete survival of the monuments built here. The pyramids of three pharaohs from the same dynasty stand proudly at the edge of Egypt's rapidly expanding capital city, displaying a wonderful historical and archaeological coherence and providing one of the most tangible expressions of the eternal quality of the pharaohs of Ancient Egypt.

The site – The pyramids at Giza have been described by numerous travellers and historians from Antiquity through to modern times. In the 5C BC, Herodotus was particularly fascinated by these impressive monuments, as were Diodorus Siculus and Strabo four centuries later. The pyramids were then forgotten for many years until Arab scholars of the Middle Ages made reference to them in their work, following the example of Ibrahim Ibn Wasif Shah. Once again, it was the size and geometric forms of the pyramids that intrigued writers and led to a number of extraordinary hypotheses. In the past two centuries Europeans have become increasingly interested in these colossal structures, intially offering unlikely explanations as to the purpose of their construction, but later becoming more concerned by practical details, such as the plan and measurements of the site. Napoleon himself once calculated that by using the blocks from all three pyramids, the whole of France could be surrounded by a wall just over 3m/10ft in height.

> **A**lthough few of these studies have taught us anything about the mystery surrounding the construction of the pyramids, they do at least provide proof that they existed during Antiquity.

A camel ride offers a unique way of seeing the pyramids.

GETTING TO THE PYRAMIDS

Most visitors on holiday in Egypt as part of an organised tour will arrive at the pyramids directly from their hotel in the comfort of an air-conditioned coach, and will receive a general introduction to the site from a local guide. Others may arrive in a small group, having taken a taxi from Midan el-Tahrir, the Coptic Quarter or Saladin's citadel. The more adventurous, independent traveller may take one of the overcrowded microbuses from the city centre, or even walk to the site, if not staying too far away. One thing is certain – although these travellers come from many different walks of life and may be experiencing different facets of this fascinating country, none can fail to be impressed by their first glimpse of these world-famous, magnificent monuments.

Pillaging of the pyramids – The pyramids have been systematically plundered over the centuries in the hope of finding hidden treasure. Although it is uncertain who was the first to ransack the site, we do know that Saladin's son dug a shaft on the western side of Menkaura's Pyramid in an attempt to plunder treasure hidden within it. Stone was also removed from the pyramids over the years and used for the construction of other buildings; as a result, although the protective outer casing was still in existence at the time of Herodotus and Strabo, this had been lost by the Middle Ages.

Excavations – Excavation of the pyramids and the mastaba tombs which surround them began as early as 1815. These initial digs involved the excavation of the Sphinx and the entrances to the pyramids, the study of the mastaba tombs and funerary complexes surrounding the pyramids, and subsequently the measuring of the monuments and the formulating of various hypotheses regarding their construction. The first person to put forward serious scientific theories was the archaeologist and scholar Sir William Flinders Petrie in 1880. At the beginning of the 20C the necropolis was divided into a

BATTLE OF THE PYRAMIDS

On 21 July 1798, 29 000 of Napoleon's soldiers defeated the Mameluke cavalry of Murad Bey and Ibrahim Bey, bringing an end to three centuries of Ottoman domination. This battle took place 15km/9mi north of the site. The following day Napoleon took control of Cairo.

directory

SOUND AND LIGHT SHOW

Two or three shows are held opposite the Sphinx in different languages every evening *(6.30, 7.30 and 8.30pm in winter; an hour later in summer).* Contact your hotel reception to book tickets.
An impressive display of lights and lasers against a truly magnificent backdrop.

WHERE TO STAY

• *Moderate*
Cataract Pyramids Resort – *Saqqara Road – ☎ (02) 384 29 01 – 400 rooms: $180.* This large, well-located hotel caters mainly for business customers with its conference hall and Internet access. It also offers guests a number of sporting options, as well as a swimming pool and a free shuttle bus to the pyramids and city centre.
Pyramids Inter Continental Resort – *on the Alexandria road, 5min from the pyramids – ☎ (02) 383 86 66 – 470 rooms: $135/$160.* This pleasant resort hotel has numerous bungalow chalets grouped around a large swimming pool. Avoid the rooms overlooking the main road.

WHERE TO EAT

• *Budget*
Andrea – *1.5km/0.9mi N of Pyramids Road (a E£2 taxi ride from the site).* This restaurant specialises in chicken dishes. E£20 will get you a main dish and a selection of hors d'oeuvres. Pleasant garden.
Alezba – *Open 10am-11pm. Marioteya Road (8km/5mi S of Pyramids Road).* The **Alezba** has an attractive garden and offers a full buffet for E£30. A convenient stop between the Giza pyramids and Saqqara.
• *Moderate*
Mena House Oberoi – This opulent hotel has a wonderful location at the foot of the pyramids, Oriental-style decor and a delightful tea-room. Cakes start at E£15, while tea, espresso or Turkish coffee will set you back E£8.

number of different sections which were then explored in turn. The large West cemetery was divided into three sectors: the Italian section led by Ernesto Schiaparelli, the German section led by Ludwig Borchardt and the American section led by George Reisner.

highlights

THE GIZA PLATEAU

⌖ *Open daily, 7am-7.30pm. Entrance to the site: E£20. Each pyramid E£20 (two open and one closed on a rotation system), except Khufu, E£40 (limited to 150 people at a time). The chambers are open 8.30am-4pm. Camera permit E£10; video permit E£100.*
The Giza Desert Plateau, which is becoming increasingly threatened by the encroaching Cairo suburbs, was levelled during the Pharaonic period and has since been home to three monumental pyramids, which are laid out according to size and the date of their construction.

▶ **T**he Ancient Egyptians referred to the site as *Imentet* (the West) or *Kher Neter* (the necropolis).

Pyramid of Khufu (Cheops)★★★

Khufu – The son of Sneferu and Hetepheres is immortalised by his pyramid, but has left very little information about himself. According to Herodotus, who paints

The three pyramids (from left to right, Khufu, Khafra and Menkaura) seen from the viewpoint to the west of the plateau.

him in a cruel light, he was much more authoritarian than his father. He was a popular figure during the Roman occupation, corresponding exactly to the type of ruler portrayed in Oriental legends of the time. Only a tiny statue of this Pharaoh who built the largest of all Egyptian pyramids now remains.

Pyramid – *See also ABC of Architecture in the Insights and Images section of this guide.* In Ancient Egypt, the pyramid's classical name was "Khufu is the one belonging to the horizon", although the monument is now referred to simply as the Great Pyramid. It stood 146.59m/480ft high (its present height is 138.75m/455ft) and 230.37m/755ft wide, with an estimated volume of 2 521 000m3/89 029 115cu ft. To fully comprehend the monumental scale of this pyramid, it was not until the construction of the Cholula Pyramid in southern Mexico and the "modern" Gothic spires of the cathedrals of Cologne and Ulm in Germany that buildings of a greater height were attempted. A total of 2 300 000 blocks of limestone were used in its construction, the average weight of which was on average 2.5t. These were then placed on 201 superimposed bases and the structure was faced with white limestone slabs, which have since disappeared.

THE KEY TO AN OLD MYSTERY

How did the architects of the pyramid manage to align it perfectly with magnetic north, without the use of a compass or reference to the present polar star, which would not have been visible from Giza at the time of its construction?

A British Egyptologist, Kate Spence, appears to have solved this conundrum. Her theory suggests that Egyptian astronomers used two stars as reference points: Kochab (the constellation of the Great Bear) and Mizar (that of the Little Bear). These stars would have been perfectly aligned with the north in 2467 BC, even though as a result of the precession phenomenon this is no longer the case. This argument is all the more persuasive as pyramids built after this date show an increasing drift in their orientation which corresponds with the slowly increasing gap between these stars and the north. This suggests that architects were unaware of the phenomenon and continued to use the stars as reference points. As the calculations of astrophysicists are accurate to almost five years, this theory should enable the pyramids to be dated more accurately than carbon 14 dating or Manetho's chronology currently allow.

The original entrance was to the north, from where a 77m/252ft gallery descends to an unfinished burial chamber. Here the architects changed their plan, probably for technical reasons, and constructed a 39m/127ft ascending gallery 19m/62ft from the entrance. This gallery opens into a horizontal gallery which then leads into a second unfinished burial chamber, with herringbone vaulting and air shafts. This ascending gallery was extended by the addition of a **great gallery**★★, 46m/150ft long and 8.5m/27ft high. The walls of this architectural masterpiece are adorned with perfectly finished corbelled foundations. The antechamber, originally enclosed by three granite portcullises, leads into the 10.5m/34ft-wide royal chamber, the ceiling of which is surmounted by five further rooms (the last bears the cartouche of Khufu), whose purpose was to relieve the weight of the masonry on the royal chamber. The granite sarcophagus can still be seen in the chamber, but the mummy has since disappeared.

Pyramid of Khafra (Chephren)★★

Khafra – It would appear that the second son of Khufu, who succeeded his brother Djedefra (buried at Abu Roash, 9km/5.5mi north of Giza) to the throne, enjoyed a glorious reign, although less is actually known about him than about his father. What is certain, however, is that he followed his father's tradition in having a pyramid built for himself on the Giza Plateau. The three triad statues dedicated to this Pharaoh *(see Egyptian Museum, CAIRO)* depict him with gentle features which would appear to correspond with what is known about his character.

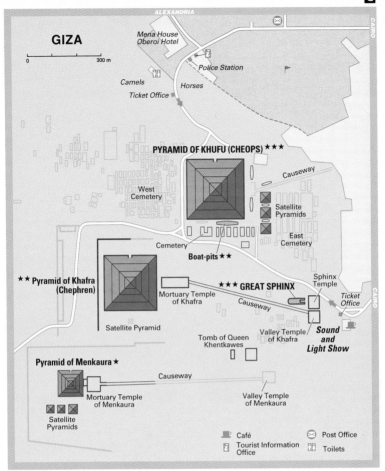

GIZA

0   300 m

Mena House
Oberoi Hotel

ALEXANDRIA

Police Station

Camels

Horses

Ticket Office

PYRAMID OF KHUFU (CHEOPS) ★★★

Causeway

West
Cemetery

Satellite
Pyramids

East
Cemetery

Cemetery

Boat-pits ★★

★★ **Pyramid of Khafra
(Chephren)**

Mortuary Temple
of Khafra

★★★ **GREAT SPHINX**

Causeway

Sphinx
Temple

Ticket
Office

Satellite Pyramid

Valley Temple
of Khafra

*Sound
and
Light Show*

Tomb of Queen
Khentkawes

Pyramid of Menkaura ★

Causeway

Mortuary Temple
of Menkaura

Valley Temple
of Menkaura

Satellite
Pyramids

Café

Post Office

Tourist Information
Office

Toilets

Pyramid – This pyramid was called "Great is Khafra" in Ancient times and is sometimes referred to as the Second Pyramid. Originally 143.5m/470ft high (nowadays 136.4m/447ft) and 215.25m/706ft wide, it has a more acute incline (53°) than the Pyramid of Khufu (51°). Its volume is estimated at 1 659 200m3/58 594 648cu ft.

This monument was built more quickly than its larger neighbour and with less precision in terms of the arrangement of its blocks. The interior was explored for the first time in 1818 by **Giovanni Belzoni**, although the building had already been violated in Antiquity. The original entrance is to the north. A 32m/104ft-long descending gallery leads to a horizontal corridor which opens into the royal chamber. The second entrance leads into a descending gallery which provides access to an unfinished burial

The Pyramid of Khafra still retains a section of its original limestone facing at the top of the monument.

PYRAMID CONSTRUCTION

According to Herodotus, pyramids were built by means of levees, although this claim is not supported by any text or iconography. As evidence to counter this claim, at a number of sites archaeologists have found mud-brick ramps which were used to haul the blocks, as the Ancient Egyptians did not use lifting techniques. Transported on a type of sleigh pulled by men with the aid of ropes, the blocks were added layer by layer from platforms built on the ramp, which was raised as the work advanced. Consequently, two construction sites existed, one for stone, the other for brick, with specialist labourers employed on each. However, this arrangement tells us more about the organisation than it does about the expertise of the Egyptian architects. The quality of the foundations demonstrates that they were aware of the laws of statics, but we still do not know how these pyramids were prevented from sliding.

chamber; from here the same horizontal corridor is reached via an ascending gallery. A phrase on one of the walls reads "Discovered by G. Belzoni on 2 March 1818", although when Belzoni discovered the granite sarcophagus it was empty. It should also be noted that the Italian found a 12C inscription written in charcoal by the son of Saladin, which made the same claim!

Pyramid of Menkaura (Mykerinos)★

Menkaura – This son of Khafra was obliged to fight bitterly for his succession and in order to retain his throne. The Greek historian Herodotus portrays him in a favourable light, unlike his predecessors.

Pyramid – In Ancient Egypt this pyramid was called "Menkaura is Divine". It measures 66m/216ft in height and 108m/354ft in width and is built of larger blocks than the other two pyramids.

Opened by Richard Vyse and John Perring in 1837, the pyramid has a complex internal structure, with its entrance to the north. A 32m/104ft-long descending gallery leads to an antechamber which itself runs into a 13m/42ft-long horizontal corridor, access to which was originally blocked by three portcullises. This, in turn, leads into the original burial chamber, which overhangs the final chamber housing the king's sarcophagus; the coffin itself is made from basalt and decorated in the palace façade style.

LOST AT SEA
This sarcophagus was removed from Egypt by Vyse, but was lost at sea when the ship transporting it sank off the Spanish coast.

The Pyramid Complexes

The necropolis is home to other monuments in addition to the three stone pyramids of Khufu, Khafra and Menkaura. The site is divided into two sections: one contains the pyramids and the mastabas which surround them, and the other houses the valley temples, the Sphinx and a few private tombs.

The Khufu Pyramid Complex – As is the case with all pyramids, the Khufu Pyramid was originally just one part of a much larger funerary complex. To the east of the pyramid are remains of the floor of the cult temple, two pits which once housed a royal boat (plus a third a little further away) and three satellite pyramids, the southernmost of which is attributed to Henutsen, Sneferu's daughter and Khufu's sister-in-law.

The cult temple was linked to the valley temple, discovered in 1991, by a 800m/880yd-long causeway. The funerary port would have been near this temple, and it is possible that the royal palace would also have stood near here. In 1994, a basalt wall thought to have been part of the port was unearthed during construction work on a modern building site. To the south of the pyramid are two further pits, where two large dismantled boats were discovered (see Worth a Visit below). To the west lies the West Cemetery, with its regular streets leading to the tombs and mastabas, one of which belonged to the king's vizier, Hemiunu.

The necropolis to the east of the pyramid was used by the royal family and important court officials. The mastaba tombs (some open to the public) follow a regular layout. The tomb of the Pharaoh's mother, Hetepheres, was discovered here in 1925.

WORTH SEEING
The reconstructed pyramidion block which once crowned the pyramid can be seen on the east side of the monument.

The Khafra and Menkaura Pyramid Complexes – Like the Great Pyramid, both these complexes were surrounded by a small wall. The ruins of a satellite pyramid (scale 1:10) are visible to the south of the Khafra complex, while three additional satellite pyramids can be seen to the south of the Menkaura complex; the pyramid furthest to the east is attributed to the royal wife, Khamerernebty II.

Both pyramids were part of a funerary complex which extended to the east and included a cult temple, a causeway and a valley temple. The original structure of the complex is more easily visible in the Khafra complex than in that of Menkaura. Only a few ruins remain from the cult temple – larger than that of Khufu – as for several centuries the temple was plundered for its stone.

Excavation work has revealed that the temple comprised two sections; one reserved for the priests, the other accessible to ordinary worshippers. The 500m/550yd-long causeway, discovered by Auguste Mariette in 1852, linked the cult temple with the valley temple and was situated to the west of the landing stage. It was probably originally lined with four sphinxes, in addition to the Great Sphinx which can still be admired today.

WORTH SEEING
The valley temple of Khafra is the best-known example of this type of monument. The centre of the temple probably once housed a naos containing the statue of the king. This building stood next to the temple of the Sphinx, which also had a central courtyard.

Dug out of the sand in 1925, the Sphinx was last restored in 1999.

Great Sphinx★★★

The unique, colossal statue of the Great Sphinx of Giza, partly carved from an outcrop of rock, faces the rising sun and sits alongside the causeway leading to Khafra's mortuary temple. This impassive creature acts as the narrator during the sound and light show held at the pyramids.

The "Terrible One" – The origin of the word "sphinx" is the Ancient Egyptian *shesep ankh*, meaning "living image". In Egypt the word described a sculpture with the head of a man or beast and the body of a lion, which represented the sovereignty of the king through the evocation of his strength and spiritual power. The Arabs later used the phrase *Abu el-Hol*, or "terrible one", to describe the Sphinx. Over the centuries, particularly in the 18C and 19C, the monument has been a symbol of amazement and mystery to hundreds of travellers. Back in their native Europe, which as yet had little experience of archaeology, such travellers often produced fanciful interpretations of the monument, which appealed to those interested in esoteric ideas. The beginnings of science fiction could perhaps be seen in some of these unusual interpretations which attempted to reveal the true nature of the Sphinx. One such theory suggested that the monument was the work of a civilisation that had disappeared several thousand years before the construction of the pyramids. Even today, a small group of archaeologists believes that the monument is the work of extraterrestials. If nothing else, the Sphinx has stimulated man's imagination for hundreds of years.

The symbol of Egypt – The Sphinx is carved from an outcrop of rock, measures 57m/187ft in length and 20m/65ft in height, and wears the *nemes* headcloth and the royal *urœus*. This strange beast is thought to represent Khafra – although some archaeologists suggest that it may portray Khufu or the god Horus – standing guard at the beginning of the causeway leading to his pyramid. The statue remains the ultimate symbol of Ancient Egypt and can be seen reproduced on souvenirs and postcards all over the country.

Damage and restoration – The damage caused to the Sphinx has often been blamed on the armies of Napoleon, although this is now known not to be the case. The Emperor's scholars merely took samples of the statue and cleared the sand away from the stele of Pharaoh Thutmose IV, the first ruler to carry out any sort of restoration of the Sphinx, which was later once again covered by sand. This explains why none of the Greek historians – Herodotus, Strabo or Didorus Siculus – make any mention of the monument, and it is not until the

▶ **T**he false beard of the Sphinx is on display at the British Museum in London; fragments of its nose can be seen at the Egyptian Museum in Cairo.

▶ **I**n Greek mythology the Sphinx was a winged lion with the head and bust of a woman. This legendary monster was said to kill travellers unable to solve its riddles.

INITIAL RESTORATION
The stele which stands between the front paws of the Sphinx tells how Thutmose IV had the Sphinx restored after his ascension to the throne. The Pharaoh is said to have dreamt that he would be made a ruler by the Sphinx if he cleared away the sand engulfing the monument.

Roman period and Pliny the Elder that a Classical writer makes any reference to it. It was restored again under Marcus Aurelius and Septimus

◄ Severus, but was subsequently engulfed by sand once more. In 1817 it was excavated by Giovanni Caviglia who found its false beard, then Mariette started to clear the monument of sand in 1853, followed by Maspero in 1858. In 1925, Émile Baraize carried out work on the head-piece and brought to light the temple which stands next to the valley temple. The monument was completely restored by Selim Hassan in 1936. Various archaeological teams have been working for the past two decades in an attempt to save the Sphinx, which despite – and perhaps as a result of – the many attempts to restore it in the past, is still gradually deteriorating.

THE NOSE
During the Mameluke period the Sphinx was covered with sand up to its neck. It was at this time that the monument's famous nose was damaged by cannon fire during military exercises.

worth a visit

Boat Pits★★
S of the Pyramid of Khufu. ◉ *Open daily, 9am-4pm (5pm in summer). E£20.*
In 1954, the archaeologist Kamal el-Malakh and the inspector Zaki Nour discovered two large pits dug along the southern side of the Great Pyramid. Contained within these were hundreds of pieces of wood from two solar barks. The 1 224 pieces of boat in the east pit have been reassembled in a modern building overlooking the pit.

Vessel of Ra or of the Pharaoh – According to the *Pyramid Texts*, the soul of the deceased king took its place in the solar bark to join his father Ra. It is probable that the boat reconstructed here is such a vessel, although its precise role has not been defined with any certainty. It is unclear whether this boat actually took to the waters or whether it was used to transport the Pharaoh's mummy. What we do know is that no smaller model of the boat has been found among the funerary objects, and that the boat still buried in the second pit is the same kind of vessel. The boat has provided experts with important information on boat-building techniques in Antiquity.

The restoration process – Ahmed Yussef Mustapha ded-
◄ icated 10 years to restoring and rebuilding this gigantic puzzle made from cedar of Lebanon. The vessel is 43.4m/142ft long, 5.9m/19ft wide at its centre, and has a draught of 1.5m/5ft.

Its timbers are held together by a skilful arrangement of wooden pegs and by ropes which became swollen on contact with water, thus increasing buoyancy. The stern has two steering oars; a 9m/29ft-long cabin stands in the centre of the boat, five pairs of oars provide the necessary propulsion and there is a little cabin in front of the prow. The only ocean that this boat would have been capable of tackling would have been the ocean of eternity.

According to its restorer, the boat has undertaken at least one voyage. Might this have been on pilgrimage to Abydos, the traditional domain of Osiris?

The construction of these boats varied depending on their use. With no mast or sail, and with its raised stern, the silhouette of Khufu's boat is similar in style to the papyrus vessels built during the Old Kingdom.

outskirts

Birqash Camel Market
27km/17mi N of the Pyramid roundabout. Held daily from 6am-2pm. In theory there is no charge for entrance, although occasionally visitors are asked to buy a ticket (E£3). Access: the easiest method is by taxi (E£50 round trip); it is possible to get here by microbus, but the journey is longer and more uncomfortable.
This is the most important *souk al-gamaal* or camel market in Egypt. A total of 2 000 camels are brought here every week from Somalia and the Sudan, via Daraw (*see KOM OMBO*) where they must spend time in quarantine in order to be vaccinated. Others are brought here from the Sinai. The most sought-after camels are the *baladis* breed from the Sudan; these are generally used for rides at tourist sites. Most of the remaining animals will be sent to the abattoirs in Cairo and then re-sold to butchers. In order to stop the camels from escaping one of their legs is tied, although this does not always stop them attempting to run away.

BEST TIMES TO VISIT
The markets on Friday, Saturday, Sunday and Monday have the liveliest atmosphere, although make sure that you arrive fairly early (preferably before 9.30am) if you want to watch bargains being struck between Nubian traders. Don't forget to ask permission if you want to take photos.

Saqqarah★★★

The necropolis at Saqqara is of fundamental importance to the understanding of the history of Ancient Egypt. This vast site, in the heart of a desert plateau, is situated close to Memphis, for so long the most important city in Egypt, and offers visitors the peace and quiet that can no longer be found at Giza, which lies so close to the encroaching suburbs of Cairo.

Location

25km/15mi S of Cairo, on the left bank of the Nile. Access: taxi is the best option from Cairo or Giza (approx E£80 round trip), although you can also catch a microbus from the Saqqara Road stop in Giza, and then another to the site itself (the site and not the village).

Name

The name Saqqara is thought to originate from the name of the god Sokar, who was worshipped in the area around Memphis.

Transcription: سقارة

Famous People

The French architect Jean-Philippe Lauer (1902-2001) came to Saqqara in 1926 to work with the British archaeologist Cecil Firth. Known as "The Egyptian", Lauer dedicated the rest of his life to his work here.

History

Almost all the major periods of Egyptian history are represented at Saqqara, from Ancient times to the Coptic era, with the exception of the Roman period. In fact, no other necropolis in Egypt provides such a detailed picture of the development of Egyptian architecture.

background

The largest necropolis in Egypt – The necropolis at Saqqara, to the west of Memphis, extends for almost 8km/5mi, with a width varying from 800m/880yd to 1 800m/1 980yd. The site was divided into two sections in the 19C: **North Saqqara**, stretching towards the site of Abusir; and **South Saqqara**, extending in the direction of Dahshur. The two sections combine to create an impressive site in the middle of the desert.

SAQQARAH

0 — 1km

★★★ Ty   Mereruka ★★

★★ Serapeum

★★★ Djoser

Unas ★★

Great
Enclosure

Sekhemkhet

MEMPHIS

Pepy I

Merenra

Isesi

Pepy II   Ibi

El-Faraun
Mastaba

Khendjer

Pyramids of
the 13th Dynasty

► **S**aqqara was both the burial place for kings and the necropolis for the city of Memphis.

Step Pyramid of Djoser, built by Imhotep.

VISITING SAQQARA
The site at Saqqara
opens at 8am. If you
plan on visiting other
monuments in addition
to the complex of
Djoser, make sure that
you start your visit early
in the morning,
because of the searing
heat later in the day,
particularly in summer.

IMHOTEP MUSEUM
The imminent opening of
the Imhotep Museum
will provide a showcase
for artefacts that Lauer
was unable to place back
in their original position,
as well as a model of the
Djoser funerary complex,
a copy of which is kept
in the Musée du
Cinquantenaire in
Brussels.

An empty horizon – Beyond the ticket office, the path leaves the greenery of the palm groves and heads into the desert, climbing up towards the limestone plateau on which the site is built. It leads first to the impressive Step Pyramid and the funerary complex of Djoser. From here there is an excellent view of the rest of the necropolis, although little stands out apart from the pyramids at Giza, far in the distance. The necropolis is, in fact, built on a series of levels and the mastaba tombs and pyramids are hidden below the horizon. However, despite inauspicious first impressions, the Saqqara necropolis is packed with hidden treasures.

New discoveries – Although nowadays archaeological discoveries are not an everyday occurrence in Egypt, scarcely a year passes without new findings being made somewhere in the country. Saqqara is no exception. The site is subject to systematic, patient excavation work which means that only a small part of it is open to the public. A number of monuments are currently being studied, rebuilt or restored, such as the **Bubasticion** tombs, where the goddess Bastet was worshipped and which prove the importance of the necropolis during the New Kingdom period.

highlights

Site open all year, 8am-5pm. E£20; E£10 (student); camera permit E£5; video permit E£25.

FUNERARY COMPLEX OF DJOSER★★★
The Complex★★
Imhotep *(see below)* laid out a 15-ha/37-acre enclosure around the pyramid, surrounded by a 10.5-m/34-ft stone wall. Decorated in the palace-façade style, the enclosure,

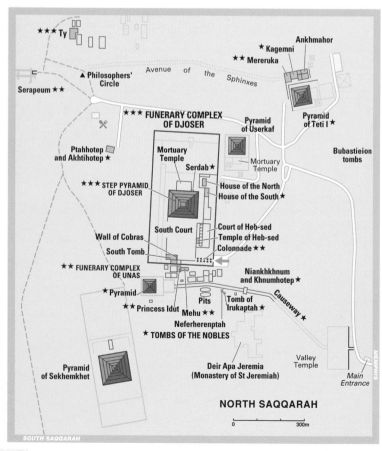

NORTH SAQQARAH

The colonnade's 40 ribbed columns, 6.6m/21.6ft high and unique in Egypt, are supported by a palm-tree ceiling.

which has been partially rebuilt, symbolises the fictitious world which the architect has created here. It once had 14 false doors and one actual entrance, which is still used today. The entrance leads into a very narrow passage with a long **colonnade★★** or hypostyle hall, which in turn leads into a vestibule opening onto the southern courtyard.

The fact that the colonnade can be admired today is down to the Herculean efforts of Jean-Philippe Lauer, who managed to restore and reassemble a gigantic puzzle of 2 000 pieces of column, using the anastylosis method. Lauer believed that the columns represented fluted wooden posts or bundles of palm stems.

South Court – The **South Tomb** is identifiable by an innovative decorative feature designed by Imhotep and known as the **"wall of cobras"**. This wall is adorned with a frieze decorated with the *uraeus* of the goddess Wadjit over the false doors. Only the soul of the deceased could use these doors, which were used for offerings. A 28-m/91-ft shaft leads to the funerary chambers which it is thought were intended to house the canopic jars of the Pharaoh. The chamber walls are decorated with blue faience tiles.

To the east, the **Temple of Heb-sed** (or Temple T) housed the royal *ka*. Follow the curved wall to reach the **Court of Heb-sed** which is surrounded by chapels, reproductions of festival shrines built of wood, reeds and adobe during the Predynastic period. With the exception of those situated at each end and in the centre, the chapels on the west side were ornamented with three small engaged columns with capitals which are unique in the history of Egyptian architecture: the cubic abacus is flanked by leaves bearing a hole which was made to hold a banner bearing the divine or royal emblem.

House of the South★ and House of the North – These houses differ in their decorative elements, which are typical of Upper and Lower Egypt respectively. Above the entrance to the House of the South is a *kheker* frieze depicting bundles of knotted reeds used in wooden architecture to secure the walls. The proto-Doric columns, now 3m/9.8ft high, once measured almost 12m/39ft. Inside, hieratic graffiti left by "tourists" from the 28th Dynasty can be seen; one of these grafitto inscriptions contains the first reference in Saqqara to Netjerykhet by the name of Djoser. The papyrus-shaped capitals on top of the capitals of the House of the North are typical of the architectural style of Upper Egypt.

Serdab★ – The oldest Egyptian life-size sculpture, that of King Djoser, seated in regal splendour, is on display in the Egyptian Museum in Cairo. This **statue★★** was discovered in the *serdab* situated to the west of the House of the North. Peering through the holes in the façade, through which the king was able to see and receive offerings, note the plaster copy of this statue. Sculpted 23 centuries before the birth of Christ, the statue is evidence of the level of artistic skill achieved during the 3rd Dynasty, marking the beginning of a new era in both sculpture and architecture.

ANASTYLOSIS
This type of restoration involves setting out in their original position whatever identifiable parts of a structure are available. It enables almost entirely ruined monuments to be rebuilt. Missing sections are made either with the same material or with a synthetic substance.

The **Sed Festival** (*Heb-sed* = Royal Jubilee) enabled the Pharaoh to regenerate his strength through magic, thereby avoiding death. The presence of the Heb-sed buildings enabled him to do this even in the afterlife.

CORNICHE DECORATION
In his House of the South Imhotep used three types of decorative cornice for the first time in Egyptian architecture. These included the torus (full, rounded cornice), the Egyptian groove (a leaf-shaped hollow cornice) and the roll (a rolled plait).

Saqqarah

Cartouche of Djoser.

The open hole to the south of the pyramid was part of a tunnel hollowed out during the 26th Dynasty, either for the purpose of excavating or pillaging the pyramid. It is believed that almost 1 000m3/35 315cu ft of rubble was removed during its construction.

SON OF RA
From the reign of Userkaf onwards pharaohs were referred to as the "Son of Ra". From the 2nd Dynasty Ra was associated with the sun, or more specifically with the sun at its zenith; the rising sun was called **Khepri** and the setting sun **Atum**.

Mortuary Temple – The ruins of this temple, the first of its kind, can be seen to the north of the pyramid. The entrance to the pyramid was situated in the paving.

Step Pyramid of Djoser★★★

Djoser – Not much is known about the second Pharaoh of the 3rd Dynasty. The name Djoser was only used for the first time during the 12th Dynasty and during his reign the Pharaoh was referred to as Horus Netjerykhet. He led expeditions into the Sinai, and the so-called "famine" stele on the island of Sehel in Aswan attributes the conquest of Lower Nubia to him. Given the important architectural changes that occurred through the work of Imhotep *(see below)*, it seems safe to assume that this Pharaoh was a charismatic leader of men.

Pyramid – *No longer open to the public because of the risk of collapse.* The appearance of this forerunner of Egyptian pyramids has changed significantly since the time of its completion, as the limestone slabs which originally covered the pyramid have since disappeared. The monument cannot be considered a true pyramid, as it was not built to a square plan: the north and south sides measure 123m/403ft, whereas the east and west are only 107m/350ft. It consists of six mastaba tombs built one on top of the other and, as a result, does not have the same regular shape of the Red (or North) Pyramid at Dahshur, which is the first perfect example of its type. In addition, the top (60m/196ft high) was crowned with a terrace rather than a pyramidion. The monument is, in fact, a composition of mastaba tombs, one stacked on top of the other; Imhotep constructed the building from one initial mastaba which was extended by the addition of two further mastabas and by three steps of the same shape. Although the structure of these buildings differs slightly, its stepped form is consistent with its purpose of easing the ascension of the king's soul to heaven. This pyramid, the result of calculations made by Imhotep, is one of the oldest monuments in the world.

The interior of the building, whose entrance was situated to the north, housed a maze of underground apartments built around a granite burial chamber; a 3t block of stone sealed off the entrance to this underground world. Although the galleries and apartments have been plundered, thousands of vases and containers, as well as two alabaster sarcophagi, were discovered here. The remains of Djoser himself, however, have yet to be found.

worth a visit

Description of the main sights, some of which may be temporarily closed. If you plan to visit the whole site, or most of it, make sure that you bring bottles of water with you.

NORTH OF THE FUNERARY COMPLEX OF DJOSER

Pyramid of Userkaf

Userkaf – According to legend, Queen Khentkawes, the wife of Shepseskaf, the last king of the 4th Dynasty, was mother to the first three kings of the 5th Dynasty, the oldest of whom was Usir Kaf or Userkaf. His reign was marked by the first contact between Egypt and the Aegean world.

Pyramid – In 1928, Cecil Firth identified this pyramid, which was built of roughly hewn blocks of limestone (the facing has disappeared). The pyramid was used as a quarry, which explains its present condition, and was once 49m/160ft high. The complex contained a mortuary temple, which unusually faced south as a result of the steep slope to the east, and a satellite pyramid, to the south-west, of which some ruins remain.

Close to this pyramid, in mastaba C8, Auguste Mariette discovered the famous **statue of Sheikh el-Beled**, now on display in the Egyptian Museum in Cairo.

Pyramid of Teti★

Teti I – The first king of the 6th Dynasty, Teti married one of the daughters of Unas, the last king of the 5th Dynasty. Although the pharaohs of the 6th Dynasty are often associated with a period of decadence, Teti's policy of maintaining peace between Upper and Lower Egypt, his work as a legislator and his trade relations with Nubia all contradict this notion.

Pyramid – The ancient name of this pyramid, which originally reached a height of 52.5m/172ft and is scarcely in better condition than that of Userkaf, was "The sites of Teti are long-lasting". The layout of the complex is of the usual type, with the entrance to the pyramid to the north and the mortuary temple to the east. A satellite pyramid is situated to the south-east and remains of two small pyramids attributed to Queens Iput and Kawit, two of the wives of Teti I, stand to the north-west.

The descent into the heart of the pyramid leads to a burial chamber still with its original black sandstone sarcophagus, which was built in situ and was the first to be engraved with hieroglyphs. The ceiling is decorated with astronomical designs and stars, representing the soul of the deceased.

Mastaba of Mereruka★★

Mereruka, the vizier of Teti and husband of Seshseshet, the Pharaoh's daughter, was buried in the most complex and one of the most beautiful mastaba tombs in Saqqara. The tomb comprises 32 chambers, and was one of the largest built during the Old Kingdom. This superbly decorated family tomb is divided into three sections: Mereruka's apartments, those of his wife and his son. To the south, the only entrance leads into the chambers of Seshseshet *(west)* and Mereruka *(east)*; the section dedicated to their son is situated to the back of the mastaba, beyond the chamber with six pillars.

The **low-reliefs**★ which cover the walls of half of the chambers are perhaps not the finest in Egypt, but their detail and originality make them particularly attractive. Lively scenes can be seen throughout the mastaba, depicting everyday activities such as hunting or fishing, the transport of harvested crops and life in the harem. In the Chamber of Six Pillars the southern wall is decorated with a scene of lamentation, rare for the period, in which women can be seen mourning the death of the vizier. A niche overhanging an altar-table in the same room houses a **statue of Mereruka**★.

Mastaba of Kagemni★

The tomb of Kagemni, who was vizier at the beginning of the reign of Teti, was discovered by the German Karl Lepsius in 1843. Although it is almost as large as the previous tomb, this mastaba has far fewer chambers. The **low-reliefs** here show typical sepulchral scenes of the period, depicting themes such as agriculture, hunting, fishing and making offerings to the gods; although they are more finely rendered, these low-reliefs are not as well preserved as those in the mastaba of Mereruka.

Mastaba of Ankhmahor

This mastaba of another vizier of the 6th Dynasty is better known as the "Doctor's Tomb". The name refers to a number of medical scenes which depict surgery on a toe ▶ and a thumb, and circumcision.

Mastaba of Ty★★★

Ty was the overseer of the pyramids of Neferirkara and Nyuserra, kings of the 5th Dynasty, at Abusir. This mastaba, excavated by Mariette in 1865, is the most

---

INSCRIPTIONS
The major attraction of the pyramid is its inscriptions★ (extracts from the *Pyramid Texts*) which decorate the chamber walls, according to a custom started in the pyramid of Unas. Carved in vertical columns, the texts contain magic formulae, whose purpose was to encourage the king's survival in the afterlife.

Discovered by Jacques de Morgan in 1892, the mastaba of Mereruka houses a life-size statue of the deceased, dressed in a short loincloth.

Circumcision was carried out at the age of about 10 and, although not compulsory, was used as a form of identification. After battles with the Libyans the Egyptians would castrate the uncircumcised dead in order to count the number of enemies killed.

Saqqarah

A PINNACLE OF ACHIEVEMENT

First used during Sneferu's reign in the Old Kingdom (4th Dynasty), the art of low-relief reached its zenith here. The sculptors demonstrated strong observational qualities, even if the figures depicted are still somewhat severe in form. A far larger percentage of surfaces were decorated during this period.

APIS

The Apis bull, a divinity of fertility, has been associated with a number of gods. In Memphis, he was worshipped as the incarnation of Ptah and then Osiris. Under Ptolemy II Philadelphus (the Greco-Roman period) he was identified with the god Serapis. His mortuary temple then became known as the Serapeum, the Latin form of the Greek *serapeion*.

ANIMAL WORSHIP

The worship of sacred animals is known as zoolatry and was one of the major characteristics of Egyptian religion. From the Old Kingdom onwards, each nome venerated a particular species. In Saqqara, a number of animal necropolises contained thousands of mummies of ibises, hawks, baboons and dogs.

beautiful of the entire necropolis. To admire the mastaba's magnificent series of **low-reliefs★★★**, cross the courtyard of pillars and follow the corridor leading to the south. These works represent some of the finest examples of private low-reliefs dating from the Old Kingdom.

The first room or chapel of offerings is dedicated to representations of offerings, including food and drinks such as beer; a series of detailed and amusing scenes in the second room or main chapel depict everyday life in Ancient Egypt. Starting at the east wall, note the life-size figures of Ty and his wife in the centre, and illustrations of work in the fields to the left. The wall is also decorated with the famous boat-building scene.

A slit in the south wall opens into the *serdab*, where a copy of the statue of Ty can be seen. Wild animals and cattle are depicted in the centre, between two portraits of the deceased, while the north wall bears a remarkably delicate relief in which Ty, portrayed in his boat, is taking part in a hippopotamus hunt in the Delta marshland. The bottom of this painting is beautifully engraved with reeds and papyrus; the magnificent carving of a fight between a crocodile and hippopotamus is of particular interest.

Serapeum★★

◄ **The Sacred Apis Bull** – In Egypt sacred animals were mummifed after death. The Apis bull, who was considered to be a living god as he was chosen from the herd by the priests, was venerated in Memphis, where he was worshipped with offerings, took part in parades and provided oracles. Herodotus described Apis as "black, with a white triangle on his forehead and a scarab-shaped mark under his tongue". From the New Kingdom onwards, he was embalmed and buried in a sarcophagus in the underground galleries of his temple, the Serapeum. After a period of mourning which lasted for 60 days, a new Apis bull was selected.

The Necropolis of the Sacred Bulls – Horemheb, the last Pharaoh of the 18th Dynasty, and the pharaohs of the 19th Dynasty, buried the first Apis bulls in the Serapeum. Extended during subsequent dynasties, the sacred cemetery was enlarged further under the 30th Dynasty, and again under the **Ptolemies**, who transformed it into a monumental architectural structure. The famous semicircular monumental ramp linking the cultivated land with the sanctuary dates from this period. Known as a *dromos*, this sacred way lined with sphinxes was built under Nectanebo I.

Serapeum – *Be wary of the extreme differences in temperature between the heat outside and the cool inside.* The Serapeum once consisted of a vast underground complex. Several of its large galleries can still be seen, although the surface structures have not stood the test of time. The large gallery, 340m/1 115ft long, is barrel-vaulted and contains a number of niches housing sarcophagi. Each of these 24 sarcophagi is cut from a single block of stone up to 4m/13ft high and 5m/16ft wide, with an average weight of 70t. Three of them are inscribed with the names of kings: Ahmose (26th Dynasty), Cambyses (27th Dynasty) and Khababash (an Egyptian king who ruled during the second period of Persian domination). Once the Apis bull was buried, the niche was walled in and a stele embedded in the wall. There is no doubt that the Serapeum is one of the most extraordinary sights in Saqqara.

Philosophers' Circle

Built under Ptolemy I, this structure houses, from left to right, statues of Plato, Heraclitus, Thales, Protagoras, Homer, Hesiod, Demetrius of Phalerum and Pindar.

196

Mastaba of Ptahhotep and Akhtihotep★

Akhtihotep was a judge and vizier at the end of the 5th Dynasty; his son, Ptahhotep, occupied the same positions at the beginning of the following dynasty. This is, in fact, a double mastaba, but because of the beauty of the polychrome low-reliefs in the section containing the tomb of Ptahhotep, the mastaba is referred to mainly by his name.

The entrance to Ptahhotep's chapel is situated to the south of the chamber with four pillars. The east wall is of particular interest, with two symmetrical scenes of nine registers. On each of these the deceased is represented standing up, in a series of paintings which depict rather unusual subjects for the time and in startlingly realistic style. The scenes include portrayals of sports, a lion attacking a cow and a hedgehog catching a cricket.

SOUTH OF THE FUNERARY COMPLEX OF DJOSER

Pyramid of Sekhemkhet

Sekhemkhet – Little is known of this Pharaoh beyond the fact that he was the successor to Djoser (3rd Dynasty).

Pyramid – Excavated in 1954 by the Egyptian Zakaria Goneim, this unfinished pyramid was surrounded by an enclosure similar to the one built around Djoser's Pyramid. Although only 7m/22ft high, had it been completed it would have reached a height of 70m/229ft. Unlike Djoser's Pyramid, it is built on a square plan and therefore marks an important stage in the brief evolution of pyramid construction.

The entrance is 40m/131ft to the north and leads into a burial chamber housing an alabaster sarcophagus. Although the sarcophagus was closed when discovered, it was found to be empty, suggesting that the king was never buried here. The descending passage into the pyramid also leads into another corridor which opens into a gallery of 132 chambers.

Funerary Complex of Unas★★

Unas – Unas was the last Pharaoh of the 5th Dynasty, and is remembered for his military campaigns in Asia and Libya. It was during his reign that the funerary texts known as the *Pyramid Texts* first appeared.

Pyramid★ – *Closed for restoration.* Originally 43m/141ft high, this pyramid is badly damaged. Excavation work carried out by the Italian Alessandro Barsanti at the beginning of the 20C identified a mortuary temple and the valley temple, as well as a shaft leading to three tombs known as Persian tombs, which at 25m/82ft are among the deepest in Egypt.

The entrance is to the north. A descending passage leads into a second horizontal corridor with three granite portcullises, which opens into an antechamber and the burial chamber where the sarcophagus is found. The ceilings are decorated with stars, but the pyramid is best

The pyramid's structural similarity to Djoser's Step Pyramid is such that it had long been suspected that a South Tomb also existed. In 1956 Jean-Philippe Lauer discovered this tomb, whose excavation proved that Sekhmekhet was never buried on this site.

HOREMHEB AND MAYA TOMBS

These tombs of Tutankhamun's army chief (Horemheb) and his nurse (Maya) to the south of the Pyramid of Unas are closed to the public. The superb reliefs here include a long, extended hand, typical of the Amarnian style of the 18th Dynasty.

THE PYRAMID TEXTS

Unas was the first king to have the walls of his burial chamber engraved with hieroglyphic prayers and magic formulas, whose purpose was to guarantee the survival of the Pharaoh. These texts followed a ritual and describe the Pharaoh's ascension to heaven and his transformation into Osiris, while at the same time allowing him to overcome the many obstacles to his survival. These texts were to assume greater importance with the kings of the 6th Dynasty, such as Pepy II, the last Pharaoh of the dynasty, whose pyramid contains twice as many of these texts as the Pyramid of Unas.

It was long believed that these texts were employed for pharaohs only, but recent discoveries *(see below)* prove that this is not the case. This pharaonic ritual was gradually extended to other individuals; texts have subsequently been found in the pyramids of queens and, more rarely, in the *Sarcophagus Texts* of wealthy Egyptians.

known for the **inscriptions**★ taken from the *Pyramid Texts* adorning the walls, which were used here for the first time. These were discovered by Maspero in 1881.

Causeway★ **and pits** – The causeway is approximately 650m/715yd long and was discovered by the Egyptian archaeologist Selim Hassan. It once linked the valley temple to the pyramid and was decorated and covered with a roof of star-shaped slabs, which allowed daylight to filter through along its entire length.

Two large boat-shaped pits measuring more than 40m/131ft lie side by side to the south side of the causeway, about 150m/165yd from the pyramid. Egyptologists are still uncertain whether these pits were a symbol of the royal barks taken by the pharaohs on their final journey or whether they were once actually used to store the royal boats.

Tombs of the Nobles★

South of the causeway of Unas. Special ticket E£10. Access from the main entrance.

A remarkable number of tombs dating from the 5th Dynasty have been found to the east of the pyramid and more continue to be discovered. To the north of the causeway lie the tombs of Queens Khenut and Nebet, Iynefert (Unas's minister) and Unas-Ankh (the king's son), as well as the **mastaba of Princess Idut**★★, richly decorated with animal scenes, the tomb of Khenu and the **mastaba of Mehu**★★ *(currently closed for restoration.)*

◄ **Mastaba of Niankhkhnum and Khnumhotep**★ – This tomb is shared by two of the leading royal wig-makers, who were either friends or brothers. The hall where the two deceased are depicted leads into two rooms, the first of which is decorated with low-reliefs restored by Ahmed Moussa and representing scenes such as a funerary procession, craftsmen, hygiene, market and hunting scenes. Note also the chapel carved into the rock to the south of the courtyard. Between the two doors leading into the room of offerings is a beautiful relief portraying the two deceased facing each other and engaged in an affectionate embrace.

Tomb of Irukaptah★ – This hypogeum contained the body of the master of the royal abbatoirs, hence its other name "the Butcher's Tomb". Ten engaged polychrome statues, plus four unpainted statues, are aligned in the chapel, a technique that is only otherwise found in Giza. These statues represent the relatives of the deceased: the last three each have a moustache, a feature showing that they are young men. The evocative scenes adorning the tomb depict the slaughtering of animals, hunting in the marshland, trapping and boat building.

◄ **Mastaba of Neferherenptah** – This small tomb is of particular interest because it is adorned with paintings rather than engravings. This finely crafted decoration portrays a series of agricultural themes, including milking a cow, a servant pouring milk, the birth of a calf, the harvesting of grapes and the planting of lettuces. One of the scenes depicts a flight of birds and is the source of the mastaba's alternative name, "the Tomb of the Birds".

Tomb of Nefer – Traditional reliefs depicting offerings, hunting and fishing can be seen in the tomb of Nefer, the "Head of the Choir", although the tomb also contains more unusual scenes such as the harvesting of papyrus, gathered in bundles.

Deir Apa Jeremia

◄ It is surprising to find the ruins of the monastery of St Jeremiah, less than 500m/550yd from the Pyramid of Djoser. Founded c 430, the monastery was built with mud-brick and blocks of stone taken from the necropolis, which was by then in ruins. The complex includes a basilica, a mortuary chapel, a refectory, monks' cells, workshops and wells, all of which were protected by defensive walls. A large number of fragments from the monastery are now on display at the Coptic Museum in Cairo.

PRIVATE RELIEFS

The appearance of private reliefs under the 5th Dynasty must be understood as a reflection of the development of royal reliefs, not many of which survive. Although these reliefs were fewer and their execution less sophisticated, they nonetheless bear witness to the high quality of art during this period.

These four tombs built during the 5th Dynasty are found in a sector which comprises mainly cave tombs and which was excavated by the Egyptian **Ahmed Moussa**. These tombs are characterised by the use of colour and by the good condition of their decor.

COPTIC RELIGION

The monastery would have been founded in the traditional way. A hermit would have settled at the edge of the desert, taking refuge in an ancient tomb. In time he would have been joined by followers, establishing a small community, and leading to the founding of a monastery.

SOUTH SAQQARA

The necropolis of South Saqqara, about 2km/1.2mi from North Saqqara, covers a greater area than its northern counterpart but contains fewer sights. Visitors to the site will be offered a range of transport options, such as camel, donkey or horse, although the site is also accessible by car via the village of Saqqara.

Pyramid of Pepy I

Pepy I – Pepy I, son of Teti, was the second Pharaoh of the 6th Dynasty (if Userkara, who reigned before him, is considered to be his regent).

Pyramid – Because much of the pyramid's stone has been removed, its initial identification is far from easy. Once known as Men-Nefer-Pepi – Men-nefer is the equivalent of the Greek name Memphis, meaning "balanced and perfect" – the pyramid was once 52.5m/172ft high. Now only 12m/39ft in height, it is so badly damaged that Mariette was at first convinced that this was a mastaba and not a pyramid. The excavations carried out by Lauer and Jean Teclant revealed 2 500 blocks of *Pyramid Texts*★, which have been restored by anastylosis and in which previously unknown passages were discovered. This restoration technique was also used to rebuild the satellite pyramid to the south-east. Archaeologists have also used modern technologies such as electromagnetism, electric sounding and radio frequencies on this site to discover the remains of the Queens' Pyramids, also known as the West, Centre and East Pyramids.

Pyramid of Merenra

Merenra – Pepy I's son inherited a kingdom threatened by increasingly independent nomarchs and ruled for only six years, under the authority of Queen Nit.

Pyramid – In 1881 Gaston Maspero discovered Merenra's mummy, the oldest royal mummy ever found, in this pyramid which, sadly, is badly damaged and measures just 26m/85ft in height compared with its previous 52.5m/172ft. The monument was also decorated with *Pyramid Texts*.

Pyramid of Pepy II

Pepy II – It is believed that Pepy II, the brother of Merenra, enjoyed the longest reign in Egyptian history: a period of 94 years. However, the length of his reign weakened his power and led to a period of decadence.

Pyramid – Although the exterior of this pyramid does not appear to be in good condition, this is actually one of the best preserved pyramids of the necropolis. It was excavated in 1932 by Gustave Jéquier, who also discovered the valley temple and the ramp that connected it to the pyramid. The pyramid was 52.5m/172ft high, like the previous monuments, and in keeping with Djoser's

---

ANKHENESMERIRA II
In April 2000, the French Egyptologist Audran Labrousse discovered the sarcophagus of this queen, one of the wives of Pepy I, at the bottom of the pyramid. The sarcophagus was accompanied by *Pyramid Texts*, a tradition which had previously been reserved only for pharaohs.

A SLENDER PROFILE
The king's pyramid is built at a 53° angle, compared with the 55° (Iput II), 61° (Nit) and 65° (Wedjebten) of the Queens' Pyramids. This more slender style was later used at Abydos during the Middle Kingdom and at Deir el-Medina during the New Kindgom.

Reconstruction of the funerary complex of Pepy I.

Pyramid had six steps covered with limestone facing.
It is surrounded by the pyramids of three queens:
Wedjebten to the south-east and Iput II and Nit to the
north-west. All three pyramids are smaller copies of
Pepy II's Pyramid and all contain *Pyramid Texts*.

El-Faraun Mastaba

◄ This mastaba, the only royal tomb of the 4th Dynasty to
be discovered at Saqqara and known locally as the "Seat
of the Pharaoh", is that of Shepseskaf, the son of
Menkaura. The mastaba is unusual because the mortuary chapel was built against the east wall, and this king
was the only one from the 4th Dynasty to build a
mastaba rather than a pyramid to house his tomb.

outskirts

ABUSIR

*2km/1.2mi N of the Serapeum and 5km/3mi from the site
of Saqqara by road. Currently closed for restoration.*

The Site

◄ The funerary complexes of a number of 5th Dynasty kings
are found at Abusir, between Giza and Saqqara. Although
the pyramids of this dynasty are smaller than those at
Giza, this is more than compensated for by the appearance
of a new architectural monument: the sun temple.

The Sun Temple of Nyuserra

This temple, in the north-west of the site, was excavated
by a German team led by Friedrich von Bissing and
Ludwig Borchardt in 1902, and is the only religious temple to have survived from the Old Kindgom. The temple
is surrounded by an enclosure and comprises a courtyard preceded by what archaeologists consider to be the
forerunner of the New Kingdom obelisks: a base in the
form of a truncated pyramid, 20m/65ft high, supporting
a colossal obelisk with a height in excess of 50m/164ft.
These measurements are estimates as the temple is now
in ruins.
Although it bore some of the same characteristics as the
pyramidal funerary complexes, the main difference
between the two was that the sun temple was not a
burial chamber but a place of worship, in which the
meteorological power of the sun god Ra, who controlled
the seasons, was praised.

Pyramid of Sahura

Sahura – Sahura succeeded his brother Userkaf to
become the second Pharaoh of the 5th Dynasty. He
waged war against the Libyans and exploited the diorite
mines in Nubia.

◄ **Pyramid** – This pyramid, the furthest to the north and
the best preserved, was originally 47m/154ft high, but
now measures only 36m/118ft. The ruins of the valley
temple and the mortuary temple, linked by a causeway,
stand at the bottom of the pyramid to the east. The mortuary temple contains two palm-shaped columns and
fragments of beautiful reliefs covering an area
of 150m²/1 614sq ft. These reliefs once covered 10 000m²/107 630 sq ft of wall and depicted mainly
war scenes, with particular emphasis on the surrender
of the Libyans, shown kneeling before the king.

MEMPHIS

3km/1.8mi E of the Saqqara site.

The Former Capital

Origins of the name – This, one of the oldest cities in
Egypt, was known to the Greeks by the name *Mennofra*,
and to the Egyptians as *Hout-ka-Ptah*, which translates as
"here the god Ptah created the world". The city was said
to have been founded by the legendary King Menes and

Sculpted from a block of limestone, the Colossus of Rameses II was discovered in 1820.

called *Ineb-Nedj*, the "white walls", a reference to its fortifications. Under **Djoser**, the town became the capital, but was then abandoned by the 4th Dynasty. When Pepy I had his pyramid built at Saqqara, he named it *Men-Nefer-pepi* or *Mennofra*, which gradually became adopted as the name of the town.

Contrasting fortunes – Memphis was at its peak during the 4th and 6th Dynasties, an era which is often referred to as the "Memphite period". The town lost its position as capital during the First Intermediate Period, although it remained the capital of the nome and retained an important role as a result of its geographical position on the Delta; it was at Memphis that the waters of the Nile were first seen to rise. The town then entered a period of decline, only returning to pre-eminence during the reign of **Rameses II**, when it became the most cosmopolitan city in Egypt. According to Maspero "Memphis was to the Greeks of the 19th Dynasty what Egypt is for us today, the Oriental city par excellence".

Final decline – The foundation of Alexandria in 332 BC dealt a heavy blow to Memphis, as the new city attracted many of the foreign residents who had settled here. However, centuries were to pass before the town would finally collapse into ruins. It was not until the 13C that the city's fate was sealed, when the dikes surrounding the town collapsed, reducing what was left of its buildings to rubble.

Museum★

🔲 *Open all year, 8am-5pm. E£14; E£7 (students); photo permit E£5; video permit E£25.*

A modern building to the right of the entrance to this open-air museum houses the **Colossus of Rameses II**★★, a statue originally 13m/47ft high and which, even now, without its lower legs, stands at a height of 10.3m/34ft. The name of the Pharaoh is engraved on the right shoulder of the statue. A second colossus of Rameses II was erected in Rameses Square in Cairo in 1955. The museum houses fragments of sculptures, as well as a superb **alabaster sphinx**★ dating from the time of Amenophis III. This sculpture stands 4.25m/14ft high and 8m/26ft long, and has an estimated weight of 8t.

The museum is situated near the southern wall of the enclosure surrounding the temple of Ptah, where a number of statues were found. A large granite slab depicting the god Ptah as a demiurge (creator of the universe) was discovered in this temple and is now displayed in the British Museum in London. The inscriptions on this slab allowed Egyptologists to identify the third cosmogony of Egyptian religion, after those of Heliopolis and Hermopolis.

VISITS
You may well be advised to visit Memphis before Saqqara. However, by arriving here later in the day, you will miss the morning rush of tour groups and will be able to take advantage of more shade. Taxi is the recommended mode of transport here as the train journey from Cairo can be unbearable!

MELTING POT
Syrians, Phoenicians, Greeks, Jews and Arameans were all attracted to the town of the god Apis, with its temples to Asian gods such as Baal and Astarte.

A number of carpet merchants, who describe themselves as "carpet schools", line the road between Giza and Memphis. A better option, perhaps, is the **Ramses Wissa Wassef Art Center**, based in the village of Harania, 1km/0.6mi S of the ring-road. This centre was founded in 1942 to revive the art of Egyptian weaving *(open daily, except Fri, 9.30am-5pm)*.

The Oases
and the Desert

Bahariya★

The Oasis road from Cairo enters the Libyan desert, which extends under a blazing sun as far as the eye can see. Bahariya, the first oasis after a drive of approximately four hours, is a haven of greenery, date palms and shade, a welcome reward for those bold enough to venture into a part of Egypt which seems to belong to another world.

Location
360km/225mi SE of Cairo, 185km/115mi N of Farafra, at the heart of a 2 000km²/772sq mi depression. Access: via the oasis road only; by car or by bus (E£12.5-E£15) from the oases' bus station at Midan al-Turguman in Cairo (departures at 7am, 8am and 6.30pm; return at 7am, noon, 3pm and midnight).

Name
The full name of the oasis is El-Wahat el-Bahariya, which translates as "the northern oasis". During Roman times it was referred to as "the small oasis" to distinguish it from the oasis of Kharga.

Transcription: البحيرة

Famous People
According to Coptic legend, St Bartholomew was buried close to the source of the Aïn Ris, 40km/25mi south of here.

background

A SMALL OASIS
Although Bahariya measures 94km x 42km/59mi x 26mi and has a population of around 40 000, the oasis is a mere drop in the ocean compared with the immensity of the surrounding desert.

A number of mummies wore cardboard masks decorated with gold powder.

◄ **On the caravan route** – Caravans have passed through the Bahariya oasis since time immemorial. Unlike the caravans stopping at Farafra which transported slaves to Siwa to sell to the Greeks or Mediterranean Arabs, the more peaceful caravans travelling through Bahariya carried olives, dates, salt and oil for sale in the Fayum region or Cairo. Other travellers who have stopped here include pilgrims from North Africa on their way to Mecca.

A pasture in the middle of the desert – Already an active oasis during the New Kingdom, Bahariya has long been an important staging post as a result of its pasture and its springs, which were harnessed and canalised by the Romans. A Christian community, attracted by this favoured location, settled near Bahariya in the 4C; the settlement then became a bishopric in the 12C and the oasis has prospered ever since, despite occasional attacks by Bedouin tribes. This rich history explains the presence around the oasis of the ruins of wells and small forts, and even a church with a basilical plan not far from El-Heiz, a little further south.

The valley of the mummies – In 1999 it was reported that a huge necropolis of Greco-Roman mummies had been discovered in the sand of the Bahariya oasis. More than 200 mummies were unearthed after 2 000 years, when a donkey belonging to a local peasant put his hoof through the roof of the cave where they were buried. These mummies, which can now be admired by visitors, continue to fascinate Egyptian archaeologists, as although similar necropolises had previously been discovered, notably in the Kharga oasis and at Hawara, in Fayum, the Bahariya necropolis was completely untouched, providing specialists with a wealth of information. Specialists were also surprised by the discovery of masks adorned with headdresses bearing the *uræus*, the raised cobra usually reserved for royalty, as well as pictures of ibis, an image not usually associated with mummies.

exploring the oasis

Bawit

As the few ancient buildings of the oasis are virtually enveloped by sand and therefore practically inaccessible, the main attraction of the "capital" of the oasis is its vernacular architecture. The town is now inhabited by descendents of Bedouins who settled here and has managed to retain its original feel despite the gradual development of low-key tourism. By exploring the areas away from the main street, visitors will discover a world that has changed very little over the centuries.

Springs – Bawit has a choice of several springs close to the town, all of which provide a refreshing refuge from the desert. The closest, and most popular, with fine views of the pink-tinged desert, are at **El-Bishmu** (30°C). Nearby (2km/1.2mi), the baths at **Bir el-Ramla** will appeal to those who prefer sulphurous hot springs, while those at **Bir el-Muftella** (3km/1.8mi) are perhaps the least attractive. The less busy **Bir el-Matar** springs (literally, the "well of the airport"), 8km/5mi from the town and best reached by taxi, have a constant temperature of 30°C, a heavier sulphurous odour and run from an aqueduct. Those at **Bir el-Ghaba** (the "well of the forest"), a longer taxi ride away, have the best location of all, at the edge of the desert, in the evening shadow of the "pyramid mountain".

worth a visit

The famous tomb of the governor discovered by Ahmed Fakhry at Abu Gharisi is no longer open to the public.

Bawit Tombs

Combined ticket for all sites E£30; camera permit E£10. On the other side of the main road, near the office.

The tombs of Zed Amun Yuf Ankh and Baen-Netyu are open to the public. They contain beautiful paintings representing Thoth, the god who protected caravans travelling at night and was therefore much venerated in the oases.

Oasis Heritage Museum

1km/0.6mi N on the Cairo road. No charge.

This small private museum is dedicated to the work of artist Mohammed Eed and depicts everyday life in the oasis. The originality of the statues lies in the technique of baking the clay with wood-fired stoves (the colour of the statue varies according to the type of wood used).

outskirts

El-Qasr

W of Bawit.

El-Qasr was the capital of the oasis during the 26th Dynasty. Four chapels, two of which are open to the public, have been excavated in a small necropolis here by the Antiquities Department. ▶

Temple of Alexander the Great

SW of Bawit, behind the Ahmed Safari Camp.

It was here that the archaeologist **Ahmed Fakhry** found a cartouche bearing the name of Alexander; sadly the temple is now in ruins.

Gebel al-Ingleez

Take the Cairo road, then head towards Bir el-Matar. Continue uphill by foot for approx 1hr.

TRADITION

Tradition ensures that law and order is maintained in the oases, especially in Bahariya. Not long ago, anyone found guilty of theft was paraded through the village on the back of a donkey, to the overwhelming shame of their family. As a result, honesty is second nature here.

PRACTICALITIES

In the first four springs men bathe during the day and women (in full-length clothing) in the evening. Men and women can bathe together at Bir el-Ghaba; as there is no food for sale here you will need to take your own picnic.

TICKETS

Tickets can be bought in the office of the Antiquities Department (El-Mathaf Street, behind the police station); open 9am-3pm. A few **mummies**, discovered in the valley of the same name, can be seen here.

APRIL FESTIVITIES

The festival of *Sham en-Nessim* celebrates the arrival of spring, a time when groups of locals take to the streets singing and dancing.

The desert is not always composed of vast yellow sand dunes, as these mountains of the Black Desert testify.

Visitors walking on Gebel al-Aswad ("the Black Mountain"), also known as Gebel al-Ingleez, will notice that the hill is marked from bottom to top with reddish traces; these marks are, in fact, the sandstone beneath the outer rock, which have been revealed by the footsteps of previous walkers.

The ruins of a structure built during the First World War can be seen on this hill, which is reached by a pleasant walk. From the top admire the ever-changing hues of the sandy desert, which vary from pink to dark brown, according to the time of day.

The British Captain Williams, after whom the mountain is named, manned the look-out post here alone and monitored the movements of the Senussi tribe in Libya.

Black Desert

Follow the Farafra road for 20km/12.5mi.

The road from Bahariya to Farafra crosses a range of dark mountains, which have been eroded by time. Over the years this erosion has covered the desert floor with fine black specks of basalt, hence the name "black desert".

directory

PETROL

There is only one petrol station between Cairo and Bahariya. If the station has run out of petrol, which often happens, then petrol can be bought in jerrycans from the Rest House (180km/112mi from the oasis).

SAFARIS

All the hotels organise desert safaris, as do Reda Abd al-Razzoul, known as "the desert fox", ☎ (011) 80 29 34, and Peter Wirth, ☎ (011) 80 23 22. Prices vary according to the type of safari. Rolou Abd al-Raouf (speaks English and French) organises hiking treks (10-15 days) in the white desert.

SHOPPING

New Nashwa Handicrafts – *Souvenirs sold here include old silver jewellery, traditional oasis basketwork and stones from the desert.*

WHERE TO STAY

• *Budget*

Oasis Panorama Hotel – ☎ *(011) 80 27 00 – 32 rooms. E£100 + breakfast. This recently opened hotel has a wonderful location.*

Ahmed Safari Camp – ☎ *(011) 80 20 90 – 20 rooms. E£50 + breakfast. Rooms, huts and space to pitch your tent.*

Alpenblick Hotel – ☎ *(011) 80 21 84 – 14 rooms. E£56 + breakfast. Beer can be bought at the hotel bar. The hotel also has a "traditional" camp site 17km/10.5mi from the oasis at Bir el-Ghaba.*

• *Moderate*

International Hot Spring Hotel – ☎ *(011) 80 30 14 – 35 rooms. $60 + breakfast. This German-run hotel, with its own hot spring, is located at the edge of the desert.*

WHERE TO EAT

• *Budget*

Cafeteria al-Rahma – *In the main street, next to the police station. Oriental and Western dishes.*

Rashed Restaurant – *In the main street. An attractive new restaurant.*

Dakhla★★

It is well documented that the Ancient Egyptians had a profound fear of the desert. And even today, despite travelling by comfortable bus, minibus or 4WD jeep, the immensity of the desert continues to inspire awe in modern visitors. Yet, despite the monotonous nature of this oasis road, it is a journey well worth taking, especially to Dakhla, the largest and most populated of the oases. The rich landscape here is breathtakingly beautiful and dispels any slight anxiety you may feel as you embark upon your journey.

Location
675km/421mi SE of Cairo, 315km/197mi SW of Farafra and 195km/122mi W of Kharga. Access: along the oasis road by car or by bus (£E30, £E35 or £E40) from the oases' bus station at Midan al-Turguman in Cairo (departures at 7am, 6.30pm, 7pm and 8pm; return at 6am, 6pm, 7pm and 8pm). By plane with Egyptair (Weds at 6am).

Name
El-Wahat ed-Dakhla, to give the settlement its full name, means "the inner oasis". The town is also known as El-Wahat el-Gharbi, which translates as "the western oasis".
Transcription: الواحة الداخلة

Famous people
The French naturalist and explorer Théodore Monod (1902-2000) visited the oasis on a number of occasions in his search for Libyan glass, which was long considered to be of extraterrestrial origin.

background

The arid desert – The average annual rainfall here barely reaches 0.2mm a year and when it does rain, it is quite possible not to even notice! It rains so infrequently at the edges of the Libyan Desert that the courageous nomads who venture into this isolated part of the world occasionally come across old tracks in the rocky desert which were left by travellers several decades ago.

The desert takes on magnificent hues at dawn and dusk.

The effect of the wind – The high dunes which are the most attractive feature of a number of deserts are the direct result of the action of the wind. In the Libyan Desert, where the wind usually blows north-north-west, the dunes have formed parallel to its direction and the plains revealed by it are constantly battered by the wind, resulting in the creation of *regs* (desert made up of rocks), the only objects not to be borne away by the wind.

Marks of passage – As these *regs* are made up of stones, gravel and rock fragments lying on the desert floor, they are easily marked by anything heavy enough to leave an imprint on them. Consequently, travellers who have ventured into the desert are able to make out the tracks of camels or vehicles which have passed the same way. In one of his books, Théodore Monod describes how in 1993 he saw, between Asyut and Dakhla, tracks left by tyres whose unusual markings proved to belong to a make of Citroen used in 1928 by Prince Kemal.

El-Qasr and the 12C minaret of the Nasr el-Din mosque, typical of Ayyubid Islamic architecture.

> ### THÉODORE MONOD, "THE DESERT MADMAN"
> "I first visited the desert at five years of age and I have not left it since." This is how Théodore Monod described the birth of his fascination with the desert during a visit to the Natural History Museum in Paris.
> Monod was a scholarship student at the museum, and then an assistant there after completing his geology studies, and was sent to Mauritania on a research project. Instead of returning to Paris as planned, he followed a caravan leaving Dakar on foot and fell in love with the desert. He later became an expert on this subject, which he once described as his "diocese".
> As a botanist, an old-fashioned naturalist and an indefatigable walker, he combined his scientific research with a spiritual quest, making him a true humanist, and there is hardly a single desert in Africa which he failed to visit in his search for a flower which he never found. In the course of his wanderings, he immersed himself in the enthusiastic study of the desert, prehistory, rocks, insects and plants. At over 90 years of age, this convinced ecologist was still travelling through the desert in the same basic conditions that he employed as a young man: with provisions of one and a half litres of water, some rice and a handful of dates.

worth a visit

Mût

Mût, the capital of the oasis, has an old town of narrow winding streets and mud houses overlooking its modern quarter. The view of the old mosque and old town from the ruins of the citadel is particularly memorable. A little further to the south of the old town is the "Tourist Village", designed by the famous Egyptian architect **Hassan Fathy**, whose buildings are inspired by traditional architecture.

> **AIR CONDITIONING**
> Hassan Fathy has incorporated the old principle of the Nubian vault in his designs. A double roof and a wall adorned with openwork create natural air conditioning in which the rooms are constantly ventilated.

Ethnographical museum – *Open by appointment 8am-2pm, except Thur and Fri: contact the Cultural Office (Kasr el-Sakafa) between the El-Iseaf and El-Tahrir squares. £E2.* This modest little museum was built in typical oasis style and provides an interesting introduction to life here.

Springs – Like Bahariya, Dakhla has several springs. The most popular *(3.5km/2mi N on the El-Qasr road)* is the one at **Mût Talata** (42˚C/107˚F; £E5). The water here is so rich in iron that it may stain your clothes.

Balat

35km/22mi E of Mût.

> **THE OLD QUARTER**
> As you wander around the old abandoned district with its covered alleyways, you will undoubtedly be struck by its eerie atmosphere.

The old district overlooks the modern quarter, providing a contrast between the new concrete buildings and the white mud-brick of more traditional dwellings. Sadly, the taste for modern architectural styles emanating from Cairo has resulted in the demise of the old part of town, which dates from the 14C.

Aïn Asil – *2km/1.2mi S. Accessible by 4WD only.* It was after a violent windstorm (the *khamsin* – a dry, hot wind from the south) that the ruins of the old capital of the Dakhla and Kharga oases were discovered in 1972, the oldest of which date back to the Old Kingdom period. In the necropolis at **Qila el-Dabba**★ *(1km/0.6mi SW; open 8am-5pm; £E20; camera permit £E5; video permit £E25),* the Egyptian archaeologist **Ahmed Fakhry** excavated six mastaba tombs of governors who held office during the time of Pepy II. A sculpture of the governor Ima-Pepy and his wife Isut was discovered in the tomb of this governor (no 2), while wall paintings in the tomb of Khentika (no 3) evoke the life of the deceased.

The intact tomb of Prince Medu Nefer (no 5) revealed a sarcophagus, wall paintings illustrating the agricultural life of the oasis, funerary objects and magnificent gold jewellery. This major discovery confirmed the links that existed between the oases and the centre of power at Memphis, largely as a result of the similarities between these scenes and those discovered in the Nile Valley.

▶ **O**nly tomb no 3 is open to the public. The stone chapel which once stood over this brick mastaba has been rebuilt 30m behind it.

Ezbet Bashindi - *8km/5mi W on the Kharga road, then left for 2.5km/1.5mi.* This old village of mud-brick houses untouched by the passing of time is known for two particular crafts: the production of kilims (woven rugs) and basketwork, made from dried palm fibres. A stroll through the village will reveal women dressed in blue selling their craftwork outside their houses, the floors of which are often covered with a layer of sand as an indication of their poverty. Barbers plying their trade on a mat in the street are also a typical sight, as are groups of men sitting on the floor playing siga, a type of draughts which dates back to Antiquity.

The name of the village derives from "Pasha Hindi", a sheikh who came here from Constantinople in the 11C. He is now worshipped as a saint in a marabout, whose walls are covered with the imprints of henna-stained hands; these marks were made by women who came to the tomb to pray for a child.

El-Qalamûn
10km/6mi NW of Mût.
This old fortified Mameluke town was built on the top of a hill. For the best view, walk up to the cemetery.

El-Qasr★★
30km/19mi NW of Mût. Open 8am-5pm.
The first impression of El-Qasr as you enter the village is that of walking straight into the Middle Ages, as this large settlement, founded in the 11C, has changed very little since the days when the caravans stopped here. Its network of partly covered narrow alleyways form a huge, slightly neglected labyrinth and the silhouette of the **Nasr el-Din mosque**★ recalls the time when crowds milled through the streets of the town.

This photographer's paradise is a typical Arab town, and therefore has fewer characteristics asociated with the oasis settlements. A number of the houses are decorated with *mashrabiyas*, traditional Arab balconies screened with lattice-work.

▶ **OLD TRADITIONS**
In the Badoura district, 10 clay ovens are still used to bake the pottery produced in the village. Among the jars note the oval pitchers known as *segas*. These jugs are typical of the village and their production dates back over a thousand years.

Amheida – *4km/2.5mi SW. At present closed to the public.*
The decoration of one of the 3 000 tombs at the Roman town of Trimithis may well be familiar to those interested in archaeology. Its mythological scenes illustrate the legend of Perseus, who succeeded in decapitating the Gorgon Medusa, whose appearance was said to be so hideous that all who gazed directly at her turned into stone.

El-Muzawwaka – *9km/5.6mi SW.* The site of the "hill of colour" *(currently closed for restoration)* provides an introduction to Egyptian religious imagery interpreted in a Greco-Roman style. The ceilings of the two beautiful tombs of the governors **Petosiris** and **Petubastis** are decorated with remarkable images of the zodiac.

The wide-rimmed straw hat is a speciality of Dakhla and is unique in Egypt.

Deir el-Hagar★ – *12km/7.5mi N. Open 8am-5pm. £E20.* This temple – literally the "stone monastery" – was an important staging post for caravans, as it was home to the last freshwater spring before heading into the vast emptiness of the desert. The monument, dedicated to Amun, is situated in the middle of the ruins of Set Uha, a town built during the reign of Nero, finished under Domitian (1C) and destroyed by an earthquake. Low reliefs and graffiti bear witness to the cults of the gods Khons and Thoth. Inscriptions refering to Roman emperors such as Titus, Vespasian, Domitian and Nero can be seen in the temple. Careful inspection also reveals inscriptions carved into the stone by **Gerhard Rohlfs'** expedition *(see FARAFRA)*. Information panels have been laid out in a modern building to the right of the entrance.

EXCAVATIONS
The Dakhla oasis was first excavated by Ahmed Fakhry, who made some extraordinary finds at Qila el-Dabba. The area has also been dug by Canadian archaeologists as part of the Dakhla Oasis Project, as well as by an Australian team who restored the sandstone temple of Deir el-Hagar in 1992.

directory

SAFARIS
Most of the hotels organise safaris, as does Anwar Mishal at the Anwar Restaurant, ☎ (092) 94 11 51.

SHOPPING
Local craftwork can be bought in most places, especially in Bashendi, well known for its kilims. Other good shopping areas include El-Guedida, 22km/14mi N of Mût, where a German-Egyptian project started in 1995 sells furniture and decorative objects. Pottery can also be found at El-Qasr.

WHERE TO STAY
• *Budget*
Mebaz Tourist Hotel – *Mût.* ☎ (092) 94 15 24 – 33 rooms: £E68.
Anwar Hotel – *Opposite the central telephone office.* ☎ (092) 82 00 70 – 14 rooms: £E50 + breakfast.
El Forsan Tourist Hotel – *Mût.* (092) 82 13 43 – 9 rooms: £E45 + breakfast. Camping is also possible here.
Naser's Hotel – *Sheik Wali village.* ☎ (092) 82 27 27 – 7 rooms: £E20 + breakfast. A typical hotel built of cob.

• *Moderate*
Mût Resort Hot Spring – *Mût Talata.* ☎ (092) 82 15 30 – 14 rooms: $105. Mût Talata's hot springs double as the hotel swimming pool. Five of the 14 rooms are chalets.

WHERE TO EAT
• *Budget*
Arabi – *Mût.* A modest, but reasonable restaurant which serves beer and rice flavoured with "*libsane*", a herb which grows in winter and is unique to the oases.
Moderate
Mût Resort Hot Spring – *Mût Talata.* The restaurant of the hotel mentioned above. Serves alcoholic drinks and wine.

Farafra ★

The smallest and least populated of the oases in the Libyan Desert is one of Egypt's 26 provinces in its own right, and is the only one situated in the middle of a plain rather than a depression. It is considered as *the* oasis *par excellence*, with its relaxed air and isolated position far from anywhere, surrounded by the white sand of one of the world's most unusual deserts.

Location
545km/340mi SE of Cairo, 185km/115mi S of Bahariya, and 315km/197mi NW of Dakhla. Access by the oasis road only, either by car or bus from the oases' bus station at Midan al-Turguman in Cairo (departures at 7am and 6.30pm; return journeys at 9am and 9.30pm; E£25 or E£27).

Name
At Edfu, an old inscription *(Ta-iht)* refers to Farafra as the "land of the cow", probably a reference to the goddess Hathor, the divinity of faraway lands.

Transcription: الفرافرة

Famous People
The German, Gerhard Rohlfs (1831-96) was the first European explorer to venture into the Libyan Desert when, in 1873, he reached Farafra accompanied by local guides and 250 camels. During his expedition he reported that he experienced a rainstorm in the middle of the desert that lasted for two whole days!

background

King Cambyses – In the spring of the year 525 BC, the Persian king, Cambyses, crushed the Egyptian army and seized almost all of the country, which was to become a province of the Persian Empire. Converging on Thebes (modern-day Luxor) following the surrender of the Nile regions of Egypt, he decided to seize the line of oases running from Kharga as far as Siwa, which was then known as Ammonium. This action enabled him to control all the routes which provided a link with the Mediterranean other than along the Nile, and to demarcate Egypt's western border.

The legend of the lost army – According to Herodotus, the Persian king gave the order to one of his army corps to march towards Ammonium from Thebes. In his writings, this Greek historian tells of how the 50 000-strong force reached Kharga after seven days, but that all trace of the army was subsequently lost. His explanation was that the troops were buried by a violent sandstorm blowing from the south. But if this was the case, where exactly did the troops disappear? If we are to believe Herodotus, this disaster occurred halfway between Kharga and Ammonium, in the area around the Farafra oasis.

Clues to the mystery – In 1991, credence was briefly given to this Greek – and consequently anti-Persian – version of events, when a German, Carl Bergman, discovered what Gerhard Rohlfs had noted down in his expedition diary: namely a large quantity of fragments which, according to him, were the remains of pitchers used to carry water for an army. Unfortunately, carbon-14 dating analysis of these fragments revealed that they were from a later period. However, even if doubt is attached to Herodotus's account of events, his theory was written less than 100 years later and it is still conceivable that an army of just 1 000 soldiers was deliberately led astray by Bedouin guides in the area.

According to a number of historians, Herodotus's history is technically unreliable. Why, for example, would the Persians, themselves used to the desert, have sent 50 000 troops into an area where only small, highly mobile groups could survive? And why did they not make their way to Siwa via the Delta route?

Fantastical effects of erosion in the White Desert.

highlights

The White Desert★★

Take the Bahariya road and continue for 20km/12mi to the first rock formations.

"The Great Sand Sea" – This was how the explorer Gerhard Rohlfs described this vast undulating ocean of dunes separating Siwa from the south-west of the country. In this extremely arid desert, which receives no more than 5mm/0.2in of rain a year, compared with 100mm/4in in the Sahara, signs of life are rare, apart from the occasional gazelle, fennec fox and gerbil, which attempt to survive in this harshest of environments.

Limestone formations – The dazzlingly white limestone formations of the White Desert *(Sahara el-Beida)* rise up across a small area on the edge of this extraordinary landscape of sand and stony *regs*. Erosion over the millennia has sculpted these rocks into mysteriously shaped sculptures that now resemble huge white mushrooms. The play of light on these rocky formations is an unforgettable sight, particularly at sunset when these incredible rocks turn from white to pink and then to orange, before disappearing quickly into the starry Saharan night sky.

> **VISITING THE WHITE DESERT**
>
> A 4WD safari vehicle is essential, otherwise you can venture no further than the desert edge. Either that or head out on foot, but make sure you have suitable equipment and a guide with you.

> **ROHLFS' FAMOUS CAVE**
>
> Based on information given to him by his guides, Gerhard Rohlfs visited a vast underground cave between Farafra and Dakhla, which was known locally to be a traditional water source, during the course of his 1873 expedition. As a result, Rohlfs entered the cave, whose entrance was blocked by sand, and reached a spacious cavern almost 40m/131ft by 30m/98ft, whose ceiling rose in places to a height of 10m/33ft. He was staggered by the sight of enormous stalactites hanging down from the top of the cave, which confirmed what his guides had told him: that a spring once existed in this cave.
>
> The discovery, which may seem somewhat insignificant, is further proof of the gradual drying-up of springs in the Libyan Desert, where the supply of water remains of vital importance, despite the lakes that exist here. In 1991, Carl Bergman rediscovered the entrance to the cave, which Théodore Monod then visited two years later. It was Monod who discovered engravings on the walls depicting hoofed mammals, which proves that animals migrated to this area in search of water.

exploring the oasis

Qasr Farafra

This oasis perched on a small hill leads a quiet, isolated area between the rocky escarpments of two mountainous plateaux. Sadly, there are no longer any vestiges of Ancient monuments to provide an insight into its history; even the protective wall that originally surrounded it has since disappeared. However, the modern settlement is in itself visually impressive, with its palm grove, traditional mud houses, basket-makers, knitted wool garment-makers, kilim rugs hanging from the walls, and carts pulled by indefatigable donkeys. Walking around Qasr Farafra, it is clear that this oasis was never more than a place of passage.

Bir Sita – *3km/2mi towards the military barracks, then turn right.* Spring no 6 in Bir Sita, situated in an arid area at the foot of the mountains, provides an opportunity for visitors to bathe in its hot ferruginous waters. A channel transports this 36°C/97°F water into a narrow basin before it is used to irrigate the surrounding plantations.

> **MISTER SOCKS**
> "Socks", as this unmistakable local character is known (his real name is Gaafar Abdullah), heads back and forward across the oasis on his motorbike, stopping occasionally to show visitors whatever he has to sell on the day. Items can include clothes made from camel hair, as well as his famous socks – hence his nickname.

worth a visit

Badr Museum

Next door to the post office. No charge.
This mud-brick building displays naïve paintings and sculptures relating to life in the oasis by a local artist, Badr Abd El-Moghny.

directory

SAFARIS IN THE WHITE DESERT
Al-Badawia Safari – ☎ *(020) 377 46 00.*
This company organises excursions across the desert, by jeep, camel or on foot.
Hussein Abu Bakr (Nice Time Coffee Shop) – ☎ *(020) 377 46 01.* Jeep, motorbike and hiking trips to the White Desert and the hot springs.

TRACTOR EXCURSIONS
The only bar on the road leading to Dakhla *(in the village of Abu Minqar, situated 85km/53mi S of the oasis),* organises short trips by tractor across the surrounding sand dunes.

SHOPPING
Sculptures and paintings are on sale at the Badr Museum – not forgetting Mister Socks!

ENTERTAINMENT
Bedouin flute music – The musician Abd al-Mogdi does the rounds giving flute renditions in bars along the way. Well worth listening to if you get the chance.
Zikrs – In Qasr Farafra, these religious ceremonies are an opportunity for visitors to discover local traditions.

WHERE TO STAY
• *Budget*
El-Badeya Hotel – ☎ *(020) 345 85 24 (reservations in Cairo) – 15 rooms: E£100 plus breakfast.* A basic hotel in a mud-brick building.
Two other hotels are currently under construction.

Mister Socks

Kharga★★

Kharga is the most developed and most accessible of all the oases in the Libyan Desert. Capital of the New Valley, a modernisation project started under Nasser, Kharga is noticeably less wild in appearance than other oases and as such makes a good starting point for visitors unfamiliar with oasis life.

Location
202km/126mi E of Dakhla, 233km/145mi SW of Asyut and 280km/175mi W of Luxor. Access: from Cairo along the oasis or Nile roads; by car or by bus (departures at 6am, 9pm, 10.30pm and 11pm; return at 6am, 6pm, 7pm and 8pm; E£25/E£40); by plane with Egyptair (Weds and Sun at 6am); by bus from Luxor (departures at 7am, noon and 2.30pm; E£5/E£10). The oasis is also now accessible via a direct route across the desert.

Name
The origins of the name Kharga are unknown. Herodotus referred to the area simply as "the oasis". The capital, of the same name, was once called *Hibis*, which means "plough" and probably refers to the intense agricultural activity in the local area.

Transcription: الواحة الخارجة

Famous People
The Egyptian, Ahmed Fakhry (1905-73), was one of the first archaeologists to undertake a comprehensive study of the oasis in the 1970s and 1980s.

background

Origins – The Greek word *oasis* comes directly from the Egyptian *ouhat.* The term commonly refers to an area of agricultural land in the desert where vegetation grows as a result of the presence of water. However, linguistic scholars have shown that the word originally referred to different areas of the Egyptian desert. Studies of etymology suggest that the word meant "place of abode" during the Old Kingdom, but for many centuries the desert to the west of the Nile was considered particularly inhospitable and was no more than a collection of isolated settlements grouped around the rare water sources. Today, Kharga is proof of the fact that the definition of an oasis has changed.

The miracle of water – The fact that water could be found in the middle of the desert was long considered to be a gift from the gods. Nowadays, the potential of such sources of water is extended by the use of deep drilling,

An excursion into the desert is an unforgettable experience.

directory

GETTING AROUND

Local transport in Kharga is provided by pick-ups *(25-50pt)*. Taxis parked by the bus station in Midan Showla also offer reasonably priced tours to nearby sites. Two buses a day connect the town with Baris and El-Dush *(7am and 2pm)*; Baris can also be reached by microbus *(E£5)*.

WHERE TO STAY

• **Budget**

Kharga Hotel – *Gamal Abdel Nasser Street.* ☎ *(092) 92 49 40 – 30 rooms: E£84.* The hotel has a pleasant terrace and also serves beer. An adequate overnight stop for those on the road.

• **Moderate**

Pioneer Hotel – *Gamal Abdel Nasser Street.* ☎ *(092) 92 79 82 – 102 rooms: $168.* The Pioneer is proof that luxury in Egypt's oases can and does exist! Opened in 1998, the building has a pleasant design and includes a swimming pool with a bar service. Easily accessible, especially by air, as it is located just 5 minutes from Kharga's airport.

---

which enables hitherto unattainable levels to be tapped. However, besides the gradual drying-up of resources in the Libyan Desert, the disadvantage of this technique is ▶ that it causes the groundwater level to rise and can cause waterlogging. It is for this reason that the current trend is to remove from the network those valleys that have developed over time into caravanserai oases, in other words those whose hydraulic capacity can only meet limited water needs.

The "New Valley" – In 1959, **Gamal Abdel Nasser** launched a vast desert colonisation programme, in which Farafra, Dakhla and Kharga were grouped together within the same governorate with the title "New Valley", covering a surface area of 460 00km?/177 606 sq mi. The aim of this programme was to release the pressure on the Nile Valley, which had become seriously overpopulated, by intensively developing agricultural (with a target of 3 million hectares) and industrial (mining, brickworks, flour mills) resources in the oases. Although landless peasants and urban dwellers were offered incentives to settle in the desert, figures have shown that the New Valley has failed to achieve its goal, as the population of the governorate only increased from 120 000 in 1959 to 143 000 in 1996. As a result, the agricultural targets set at the beginning of the project have not been met.

> **DEEP WATER**
> Between them, the oases involved in the project had over 3 000 water sources and wells with a maximum depth of 80m/262ft. The governorate had a further 300 dug, from which water could be pumped from a depth of between 500m/164ft and 1 500m/4 920ft.

worth a visit

The Kharga oasis occupies a depression 190km/119mi long and 30km/18mi wide and is home to the majority of archaeological remains visible in Egypt's oases.

Qasr Kharga

The capital of the Wadi el-Gedi ("New Valley") has developed into a modern town and bears witness to the efforts made by the governorate to create a prosperous settlement in the middle of the desert. To find traces of what Qasr Kharga was like at the time when the town was a staging post on the "Forty Days Road", head to the atmospheric old town, which was fortified in the 11C.

Oases Museum★ – *Gala Abdel Nasser. Open daily 8.30am-5pm (9am-6pm in summer); closed Fri 11.30am-1.30pm. E£16; students E£8. Camera permit E£10; video permit E£120.* Housed on two floors, this museum displays finds from Egypt's Prehistoric, Pharaonic, Greco-Roman, Coptic, Byzantine and Islamic periods discovered during excavations undertaken in the New Valley. Several pieces stand out, such as the Khentika stele; cartonnage masks; the polychrome limestone group of Ima-Pepy II and his wife Isut; the sarcophagus of Badi Bastet; a fine collection of *ba*-birds; fabrics dating from the 7C-9C; as well as 18C icons.

> **FORTY DAYS ROAD**
> Darb el-Arbaïn, as this road was known, was once the busiest route in the Libyan Desert, linking Darfur, in the Sudan, with Asyut, across a distance of 1 700km/1 062mi. The caravans following this route would have passed through Kharga loaded with spices and elephant tusks, bringing with them slaves, who were then sold to the north of Asyut, provided that the latter were able to survive the journey, which often lasted 50 rather than 40 days.

The Oases Museum's architecture is based on a modern interpretation of the Bagawat tombs.

Temple of Hibis★

2km/1.2mi N. Open daily 8am-5pm. E£20; students E£10. No charge for camera permits. Likely to be closed in the near future in preparation for its relocation to the N of the Bagawat necropolis.

This temple dedicated to the god Amun is one of the few Persian monuments in Egypt, even though it was enlarged by Nectanebo II and completed under the Ptolemies. It is preceded by a *dromos* and measures 42m/138ft by 20m/65ft. Its main interest lies in the **sculpted decor** on the walls of the sanctuary which provides an interesting overview of typical embellishments found in an Egyptian pantheon.

The best-preserved of the temples in the oasis was built by Darius I on foundations dating back to Psamtek II. In former times it stood alongside a lake and as a result is still at risk from water seepage.

Temple of Nadura

Opposite the Temple of Hibis. No charge.

The ruins of the temple stand on top of a hill, from where the **views**★ of the desert are delightful, particularly at sunset. The temple dates from AD 138 and was erected during the reign of the Roman emperor, Antoninus Pius. The Turks built a fortress on the site in the 18C.

Bagawat Necropolis★★

3km/2mi N. Open daily 8am-6pm (5pm in winter). E£20; students E£10. No charge for photography.

The 273 mud-brick tombs here were built at the time of the heretical leader Nestorius, who was exiled to Kharga in 434. They encircle a 4C church and are all crowned by a dome, hence the name of the site, which is a contraction of the Arabic term *al kiblat*, meaning "dome". The atmosphere of this necropolis, with its backdrop of desert and mountains, is quite unforgettable.

The Nestorian heresy was outlawed by the Council of Ephesus in 431; Nestorius himself was condemned and banished. Today, the Church named after him still has several thousand followers around the world.

Decoration – Several tombs within the necropolis house chapels adorned with impressive palaeo-Christian **frescoes** depicting scenes from the Old and New Testaments, as well as graffiti left by pilgrims and travellers through the ages.

The Chapel of Peace (chapel no 80) enjoys an isolated location in the middle of the desert.

Chapel of Peace★ – *No 80.* The chapel's 5C cupola has immortalised Adam and Eve, Abraham and Isaac, Peace and its key to life, Daniel in the Lions' Den, Justice and its scales, Noah's Ark, the Annunciation, and St Thecla, all of which are flanked by red peacocks and vine branches.

Chapel of the Exodus – *No 30.* Paradoxically, the oldest (4C) tomb in the necropolis contains Bagawat's best-preserved frescoes. The cupola rising above the chapel with its typically Alexandrian style of architecture (imitation mosaics and marble) relates the exodus of the people of Israel guided by Moses and pursued by the army of Rameses II. In particular, note the Calvary cross beneath the *ankh* cross, the Egyptian sign of life.

> ► **C**hapels 23, 24 and 30 are also well worth seeing. The latter is known to its custodian as the "Chapel of Grapes" because of its abundance of vegetal decoration.

Ein Mustapha Kashif
1km/0.6mi N of the necropolis. Entrance via the Bagawat necropolis; same ticket.
A fine view extends across the oasis from the ruins of a 5C monastery bearing the name of a former governor of the oasis during the Mameluke period. It is said that a Roman-Byzantine fortress was also built on this strategic site.

outskirts

FROM KHARGA TO EL-DUSH

Qasr el-Ghueita
20km/12mi S of Kharga. Open daily 8am-5pm; E£16; students E£8. The "Palace of the Beautiful Garden" was a strategic site upon which Darius erected a temple dedicated to the Theban Triad (Amun, Mut and Khons). The temple, which dominates the desert plain and nowadays stands close to the road leading to Thebes, was later embellished by the Ptolemies. The hypostyle hall has been preserved, although its roof has failed to withstand the test of time.

Qasr ez-Zayan
5km/3mi S of Qasr el-Ghueita. Same admission times and charges.
The ruins of this Roman temple are considerably less impressive than those at Qasr el-Ghueita.

Baris
72km/45mi S of Kharga.
This town, whose name derives from *Per-esit,* or the "Town of Isis", is of limited interest to visitors, with the exception of New Baris, a village built by **Hassan Fathy** in 1967 but never inhabited. This underrated Egyptian architect was a great advocate of modern dwellings that sought inspiration in the past, through a combined traditional and contemporary use of space.

El-Dush★★
23km/14mi SE of Baris. Open daily 8am-5pm. E£16; students E£8. No charge for photography.
This former border stronghold was erected at the crossroads of a number of caravan routes, including the legendary "Forty Days Road". This remarkable site is known for its fortress, which encloses a **temple** dedicated to Isis and Osiris-Serapis. Initiated by the Emperor Domitian, and completed under Trajan and Hadrian, the building repeats the classical plan of the temples in the Nile Valley. Since 1976, the French Institute of Oriental Archaeology has been painstakingly excavating this fascinating site.

The massive 4C Roman **fort**, built under Domitian, is protected by a wall 6m/20ft-12m/40ft high and with sides 50m/164ft long. During excavation of the extrados of a vault here in 1989, archaeologists discovered the famous **"Treasure of Dush"**, a 1.2kg/2.5lb cache of gold artefacts, including two bracelets, a large necklace, a solid gold crown and votive panels in honour of Serapis, all of which were concealed inside an earthenware jar.

> ► **NORTH OF KHARGA**
> The impressive walls of the Roman fortress of El-Deir rise dramatically out of the desert 32km/20mi north of the oasis. This military outpost was used by the British during the First World War.

The beautiful Ptolemaic capitals at the temple of Qasr el-Ghueita.

> **OTHER SITES**
> Prior authorisation is required from the Antiquities Office *(opposite the Oases Museum; open 8am-2pm)* for visits to any other site not mentioned above.

Siwa★★

Set back from the road linking it with its four fellow oases, Siwa is without doubt one of the most picturesque sights in the whole of Egypt. Because of its isolation, it is a place to travel to rather than through, but visitors who make it to this desert outpost will not be disappointed by its astonishing range of landscapes and images, particularly at night, when the stars seem to be within touching distance.

Location
720km/450mi W of Cairo, 590km/369mi SW of Alexandria, 300km/186mi SW of Mersa Matruh, and 380km/237mi NW of Bahariya (on a tarmac road only suitable for 4WD vehicles because of the encroaching sand dunes). Access: by car or West Delta bus services from Alexandria (E£15-E£25; journey time: 8hr) or Mersa Matruh (E£8-E£10; journey time: 4hr).

Name
During the Old Kingdom, Siwa was known as *Tehenou*, or the "land of the olive"; the Greeks simply referred to it as Amun, because of the oracle. In the 15C it adopted the name *Santarieh* (the "place of the acacias"), and only became known by its modern title of Siwa in the 18C, after the local Siwanese tribe.

Transciption: سيوة

Local Tribes
The Siwanese, descendants of the Zanata tribe of Berbers, are one of the major aspects of interest in the oasis and are the only Berbers of Egypt.

background

The oasis of the Oracle – Before the 16th Dynasty, Siwa was unaware of Pharaonic Egypt, although under its Libyan domination it had contact with Sudanese caravans which travelled here to buy and sell goods in the land the Egyptians referred to as the *Tehenou*. A temple dedicated to Amun was built here around 550BC by Ahmose I; the Oracle of Amun, based at the site, was widely consulted and its renown grew quickly, to such an extent that Croesus, the immensely wealthy king of Lydia, dispatched his representative to Siwa to glean information on the plans of his Persian enemy, Cyrus. Under the influence of Cyreneica (a Hellenised town in Eastern Libya), the god became identified with Zeus. From this time on, the Temple of Siwa became a place of pilgrimage for Greeks, including Alexander the Great, who journeyed here in 331 BC.

Alexander the Great in Siwa – When he came ashore at the port of *Parætonium* (modern-day Mersa Matruh), this Macedonian conqueror was just 25 years of age. He had already been king of Macedonia for five years, ruled over Greece, defeated Darius III, occupied Syria and Phoenicia, and initiated the conquest of Asia. Aware that the priests at the temple of Amun were lucid and spoke Greek, he decided to make his way to the oasis for consultation and to obtain confirmation of his divine nature. Escorted by just a few men, Alexander took five days to cross the desert, enduring a sandstorm that almost cost him his life. The risks were worth it, however, as the gods welcomed him as a son and predicted that he would become "master" of the world.

A Berber oasis – Visitors hoping to exchange a few basic words of Arabic or the odd simple greeting in English with the local population will perhaps be surprised to learn that the inhabitants of the oasis speak the almost incomprehensible *Siwi*, the dialect of the Siwanese tribe. This people, the most eastern of all Berber tribes in

---

Following his defeat by Cyrus, Croesus was condemned to the pyre. However, his victor spared him this fate following consultation with the Oracle.

BERBERS OF SIWA

Siwa's inhabitants are reserved in character and respect the ancestral customs that set them apart from the rest of Egypt. Yet despite this initial distance, provided you stay for a day or two you will soon become aware of the warm hospitality of this desert people. The Siwans are, however, wary of the effects of tourism on their haven of peace and tranquillity.

The stone and mud-brick ruins of the Temple of the Oracle.

North Africa, have continually resisted incursions by rival Bedouins. The oasis is an interesting melting-pot made up of the black descendants of Sudanese slaves who settled here, and the Berbers, with their fair hair and light-coloured eyes. The reserve and even distrust is immediately discernible in the latter, who remained beyond the realms of Egyptian authority until 1820. Even then the army had to resort to the cannon to bring the Berbers under the yoke of the State.

exploring the oasis

Although there's not a great deal to do in Siwa, it is the **atmosphere**★★ of this verdant oasis that appeals to visitors. Despite the immense desert around it, the true wealth here lies in the fields of olive trees, fruit and vegetables, and more importantly, its dates, reputed to be the best in Egypt.

The village and fortress

The jagged outline of **Shali** (the "town" in Berber) dominates the centre of the oasis. This fortress was built in the 7C, but was rebuilt six centuries later with blocks of salt and the clay-like render known as *karshif*, following a Bedouin attack. With the exception of its minaret, which is still used by the *muezzin* to call the faithful to prayer, it was subsequently abandoned. The **view** from the top of the fortress, encompassing the surrounding palm groves, the village with its souk and shops at its feet, and the modern districts to the north and east, is particularly memorable.

House of Siwa Museum – *Theoretically open 10am-noon, except Fri. In the street to the S of the tourist office.* Exhibits in this small museum include traditional tools and clothes.

Temple of the Oracle

2km/1.2mi E. Open daily from dawn until dusk.
A series of stone and *karshif* ruins stand on the summit of the Aghormi Hill. The stones are those from the Temple of Amun, which became known as Ammon under the Greeks, where a priest, hidden in a false ceiling, would act as an oracle for the god. This spiritual site, stripped bare over the years by local inhabitants searching for treasure, had a village built over it, from which just the walls and a minaret survive. The temple was discovered in 1852 and only excavated in 1971 by the archaeologist Ahmed Kakhry.

> The best way of exploring the oasis and its surrounding area is by bicycle, enabling you to venture out along dirt roads and shady tracks through palm groves to discover the very soul of this tranquil "land of the olive". Bikes can be rented either from the Abdu Restaurant or from the Arouss al-Waha and Palm Trees hotels *(cost: E£3/half-day; E£6/full day).*

> **I**n Greek, the word for "Libyan" is *ammôniakos*, which comes from the temple near to which Libyans extracted ammonium chloride. This is the origin of the modern word "ammoniac."

In 1926, torrential rain reduced the four floors of the Shali fortress to a state of ruin.

Already known in former times for its olive groves, the oasis still produces a delicious olive oil that is on sale in the town's shops.

Although the hill is just 25m/82ft high, the **view**★★ from the top takes in the modern village, a sea of palm trees and the extensive Zeytun Lake; the Gebel al-Mawta is visible to the north and the Gebel Dakrur to the south. The ruins (including the remains of reliefs) of the **Temple of Umm Ubayda** can also be seen 300m/330yd away; this sanctuary dedicated to Amun by Nectanebo II was devastated by an earthquake in 1811.

Springs

Of the thousand springs said to exist in Antiquity, 281 remain today; these are dotted around Siwa and are harnessed to irrigate the crops of the oasis. Because of the traditional use of these springs, it is not as easy to swim here as it is in other oases. Furthermore, to get an idea of the conservatism of the local population, only recently has a sign been removed proclaiming that "Women are asked to respect our customs and traditions by keeping their arms and legs covered. Alcohol and affection are forbidden in public". Although this notice has been removed, the sentiment still remains.

Cleopatra's Baths – The name is something of a misnomer as the queen never bathed here; the actual name of this circular pool is *Aïn el-Guba*, or "Jupiter's spring" and is a popular bathing spot for locals. Reference is made to this spring in the Koran (surah 26, verse 86): "When Dhu el-Qarnaïm [Alexander the Great] reached the west he saw the sun disappear in a boiling fountain". This spring, which is also evoked by Herodotus, Aristotle and St Augustine, is located at the heart of a palm grove and is a pleasant end-point for a stroll.

Mount Dakrur

To the S. The Festival of the *Sihaya* is held on this mountain during the October full moon. This three-day event celebrating the fertility of the oasis is an opportunity for locals and visitors from around Egypt to enjoy a period of feasting and merriment. Outside this period, it's well worth coming here anyway just to admire the wonderful **view**★★.

Lake Siwa

To the W. The oasis stands at 24m/78ft below sea-level and is littered with either lakes or dry beds surrounded by sand dunes which appear to have once belonged to an evaporated sea. Sunset on Fatnas Island in the middle of the lake is a wonderfully calming experience.

Gebel al-Mawta

To the N. Tombs accessible 7am-2pm (noon on Fri). Entrance fee as yet unspecified, although a baksheesh is expected. The "Mountain of the Dead" is a limestone massif occupied by numerous tombs, some of which can be visited.

Tomb of Si-Amun★ – *26th Dynasty.* The Egyptian-style paintings show clear Greek influence, quite probably as a result of the Cyreneican origins of the deceased. The impressive ceiling bears a representation of the goddess Nut.

Tomb of Niperpathot – *26th Dynasty*. The outline drawings in this tomb pay homage to Osiris and not Amun as local worshipping practices would normally have dictated.

outskirts

The "Great Sand Sea" – The first dune formations are clearly visible from the top of Mount Dakrur. The area is accessible by 4WD, but only with a local guide (*see below*).

directory

SAFARIS
Every hotel and even some of the restaurants in Siwa are able to organise desert trips ranging from a short donkey ride in the surrounding dunes to a week-long safari across the Great Sand Sea to the Libyan border. A typical one-day excursion is to the Bir Wahid spring (*approx. E£50, including lunch*) which some believe to be the location of Alexander's tomb.

SHOPPING
Oasis specialities include silver jewellery, rugs and palm-leaf baskets. Beautiful black veils embroidered with red and orange thread are also widely on sale in the town's shops.

WHERE TO STAY
• Budget
The oasis has several hotels, most of which are poorly maintained and lacking charm. This situation is slowly changing, however, with the influx of more tourists, although it is hoped that any new construction will be in keeping with the natural setting.
Amun Hotel – *Mount Dakrur.* ☎ (03) 590 21 75 – *16 rooms: E£20.* ✉ 🖥 very basic hotel hardly worthy of the name, although it does offer sand immersion treatment for those suffering from rheumatism.
Arouss al-Waha – ☎ (046) 460 21 00 – *20 rooms: E£75.* ✉ 🖥 Despite its rather ugly appearance, this friendly hotel is generally well-maintained. Easy to find opposite the tourist office.

Siwa Inn – ☎ (046) 460 04 05 – *10 rooms: E£106/E£160.* Simple but scrupulously clean with meals prepared from produce from the organic garden. The fresh fish on the menu is collected from Mersa Matruh, although guests should advise the inn ahead of time if they wish to eat in. Not the easiest place to find, but once you've found it you won't want to leave! Another attraction is the natural spring in the garden. The hotel is also able to organise safaris.
• Moderate
Siwa Safari Paradise – ☎ (046) 460 22 89 – *78 rooms: E£250/E295, including half-board.* Somewhat basic for the price, but the setting in a palm grove on the outskirts of the town is idyllic. The hotel has its own secluded spring to help cool you down at the end of a hot day in the desert, and like its competitors also offers a range of safari options.
• Expensive
Gafar Village – *10km/6mi W.* ☎ (046) 736 78 79 – *30 rooms: $400.* This exclusive hotel set in the middle of nowhere is a series of stone and mud-brick buildings which blend in with the rock of the white mountains around it. Although the design is based on simplicity, the overall effect borders on the luxurious, with superb attention to detail: Peace and quiet guaranteed and fabulous views. A unique experience for nature-lovers.

WHERE TO EAT
• Budget
Abdu Restaurant – The best-known and easiest restaurant to find in town. Meals are served on the terrace and include *fuul* (*E£2*), omelettes (*E£2*), chicken with salad (*E£10*) and good pizzas (*E£9-E£13*). Don't bother asking for a beer as alcohol is prohibited in the oasis.
Fatnas Island – *Lake Siwa.* A popular place from which to view the sunset and enjoy a mint tea. If you give Mr Abbas Ahmed Mohammed 24 hours notice, he will rustle up a *mechoui* which will set you back no more than E£20 per person.

The Sinai and the Red Sea

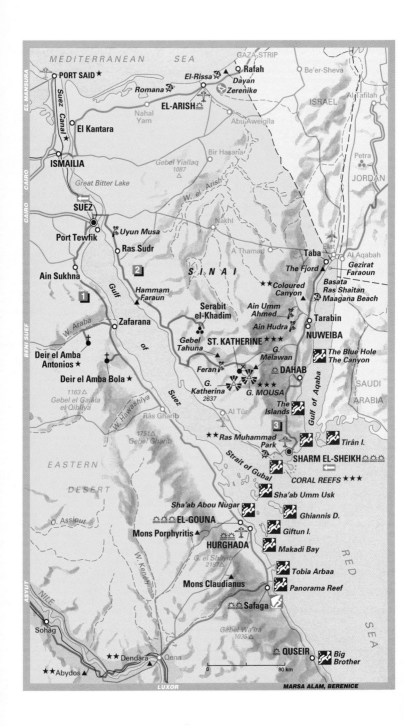

MEDITERRANEAN SEA

GAZA STRIP

PORT SAID ★
Romana ☆
El-Rissa
Rafah
Be'er-Sheva
Dayan
Zerenike
EL-ARISH ☆
Nahal Yam
Abu Aweigila
ISRAEL
Al Tafilah

Suez Canal

El Kantara

ISMAILIA

Great Bitter Lake

Gebel Yiallaq 1087 △

Bir Hasana

Petra

JORDAN

SUEZ

Port Tewfik

Uyun Musa

Ras Sudr

Nakhl

A' Thamad

Taba
Elat
Al Aqabah

The Fjord ▲
Gezirat Faraoun

Ain Sukhna

Gulf

Hammam Faraun

S I N A I

★★ Coloured Canyon

Basata
Ras Shaitan
Maagana Beach

Zafarana

Serabit el-Khadim

Ain Umm Ahmed

Ain Hudra

Tarabin

NUWEIBA

Deir el Amba Antonios ★

Gebel Tahuna

ST. KATHERINE ★★★

G. Melawan

The Blue Hole
The Canyon

Deir el Amba Bola ★

Feran

G. Katherina 2637

DAHAB

SAUDI
ARABIA

1163 △ Gebel el Galâla el Qiblîya

W. Hawashiya

G. MOUSA

Rås Gharib

Al Tûr

The Islands

Gulf of Aqaba

1751 △ Gebel Gharib

★★ Ras Muhammad Park

Tirân I.

EASTERN

DESERT

SHARM EL-SHEIKH ♨♨♨

Strait of Gubal

CORAL REEFS ★★★

O. Assiout

Sha'ab Umm Usk

Sha'ab Abou Nugar

EL-GOUNA ♨♨♨

Ghiannis D.

Mons Porphyritis ▲

HURGHADA ♨♨

Giftun I.

Makadi Bay

G. el Shâyib 2187 △

RED

Mons Claudianus ▲

Tobia Arbaa

Panorama Reef

W. Kenêh

NILE

Safaga ♨♨

Sohâg

Gebel Wa'îra 1035 △

SEA

QUSEIR ♨

Big Brother

★★ Dendara

Qena

★★ Abydos ▲

0   80 km

LUXOR

MARSA ALAM, BERENICE

EL MANSURA   CAIRO   CAIRO   BENI SUEF   ASYUT

Dahab ☼

For years cosmopolitan Dahab has been a centre for hippies and alternative travellers, although much of the beach resort has recently been modernised in an attempt to attract more conventional tourists.

Location
On the Gulf of Aqaba, 103km/64mi NE of Sharm el-Sheikh, and 72km/45mi W of Nuweiba. Access: see Sharm el-Sheikh, from where taxis and buses (departures at 7.30am, 9am and 3pm; journey time: 1hr 30min) operate to Dahab bus station.

Name
The word *"dahab"* is the Arabic for gold and refers to the colour of the resort's sandy beaches.

Transcription: **دهب**

exploring Dahab

The Bedouin village which once contributed much of the traditional charm to Dahab has moved to Assalah, to the north of the town. The palm-fringed bay is now lined by hotels, bars and restaurants; shops and other services tend to be concentrated within the town of Dahab itself.

outskirts

Diving Sites★★
The Canyon – This site is teeming with glass catfish.
The Blue Hole – *8km/5mi N of Dahab.* This 80m/262ft-deep hole is situated only a few metres from the shore. A tunnel at a depth of 60m/196ft is reserved for experienced divers only.
The Islands – *17km/10mi S of Dahab.* The main attraction of this site is its magnificent labyrinth of coral.

SMOKING IN DAHAB
Dahab is a notorious resort for drugs. Visitors should be aware that the possession of drugs is illegal in Egypt and that the penalties if caught are severe. If you want to try smoking the traditional shisha or hookah pipe, make sure that you know what type of tobacco you are smoking!

---

directory

WHERE TO STAY
• Budget
Ganet Sinai Hotel – *Next to the Hilton –* ☎ *(069) 64 04 40 – 50 rooms: $60, $150.* ⌷ The rooms are small and a little overpriced, but the hotel has a good windsurfing school, as well as a beach and diving centre.
Sphinx Hotel and New Sphinx Hotel – *Shat El-Mashrabey –* ☎ *(069) 64 04 94 – 40 rooms: E£120/E£150/E£180.* Two hotels outside Dahab run by the same management, with a reasonably priced diving centre and private beach. Opt for one of the newer rooms, which are larger and closer to the pool.
Dyarna Dahab Hotel – *At the entrance to the resort –* ☎ *(069) 64 01 20 – 42 rooms: E£110/E£125.* ⌷ Friendly service, but does not serve alcohol. Facilities include a beach and billard room.

• Moderate
Hilton Dahab Resort – ☎ *(069) 64 03 10 – 163 rooms: $140/$180; 24 suites: $220.* The most luxurious hotel in the resort, with beautiful domed rooms. The hotel has a beach, diving centre and surfboarding school but the night-club has closed.
Swiss Inn Golden Beach – *Next to the Hilton.* ☎ *(069) 64 04 71 – 76 rooms: $130/$180.* Ideal for those who want both comfort and diving or windsurfing facilities. More reasonably priced than the Hilton next door. Private beach.
Helnan Dahab Hotel – ☎ *(069) 64 04 30 – 180 rooms; $96/$160.* This hotel is further away fom the centre, but has its own beach and bars and is soon to open its own diving centre.

NIGHTCLUBS
El-Zar – A well-known nightclub, situated close to the Dolphin Camp. Loud rock music.
Black Prince – E£5. Another local favourite, but one that does not serve alcohol.

El-Arish ⌂

Long renowned for its magnificent palm groves, the capital of the North-Sinai region has developed into a lively summer resort popular with visitors from Cairo. Situated on the old military road used in former times by pharaohs, Persians and Christian crusaders, El-Arish now derives most of its income from the tourist industry.

TOURIST OFFICE
Fuad-Zikry Street.
☎ (068) 34 05 69.
Open daily 9am-2pm
and 4-8pm.
Located on the ground
floor of the Sinai Beach
Hotel.

Location
On the shores of the Mediterranean, 315km/197mi NE of Cairo, 160km/100mi E of Port-Said, and 41km/26mi from the Israeli border and Gaza Strip. Access: by air from Cairo (Mon and Thur) with Air Sinai; by bus from Cairo (departures at 7am and 4pm; journey time: 5hr) and Ismailia (departures at 11am, noon and 1pm; journey time: 3hr).

Name
At the time of the pharaohs, the town was known as Rinclora. The name changed to Al-Orche during the Moorish conquest, and later to El-Arish.

Transcription: العريش

Although King Baudouin I (1058-1118) was laid to rest in Jerusalem, he died in El-Arish, where his entrails are buried at the so-called Tourbet el-Bardaouil (Tomb of Baudouin).

Famous People
The Holy Family on their flight to Egypt, and King Saint Louis in pursuit of his divine mission and dreaming of new horizons, would all have passed this way.

exploring El-Arish

Beaches
In recent years, the development of tourism has seen the fine, white sandy beaches of the resort lined by numerous hotels and apartment blocks. Despite this feverish construction, El-Arish has still managed to preserve parts of its old town.

Spoilt for choice – The resort's most popular beach is undoubtedly at El-Rissa (4km/2.5mi on the Rafah road), one of the region's most attractive resorts with its little palm-clad hill descending to the azure waters of the Mediterranean. This beach is free of charge, as are the neighbouring beaches of **El-Nakhil** and **El-Massaïd**, 5km/3mi west; and **Romana**, a further 20km/12mi away. **Sama El-Arish** and **Coral Beach** are reserved for residents of nearby tourist villages and for those who have paid an entrance fee.

Old Mercedes and American limousines from a bygone era ply the route between the seafront, the bus station, and the residential district of El-Masa.
Cost: approx. 25pt.

The white-tailed eagle is a familiar sight in the skies of the Northern Sinai.

The Dayan Rock – This huge rock, brought here from the Southern Sinai by the Israelis, sits on top of the hill of Sheikh Zowayeid. Engraved on it are the names of 10 Israeli generals who perished during a spying mission in 1973. The Camp David Agreement of 1979 stated that "this rock should be preserved for ever". This menhir-like rock is said by some to be shaped like a map of Palestine.

Town and Souk
The remains of a 16C Ottoman fortress occupied by Napoleon's troops but destroyed during the First World War can still be seen in the old town. On Thursday mornings a Bedouin market is held near the ruins (*Souk el-Khamis road*), where men come to sell camels and rugs, and women clothes and jewellery.

> **O**ne of the main attractions of the Thursday souk is watching veiled women selling their gold and silver. The best quality products, however, are generally set aside for traders from Cairo.

worth a visit

Sinai Heritage Museum
Along the coast road towards Rafah. Open Sat-Thur, 9.30am-2pm; E£2; fee for photographic equipment: E£5; fee for video equipment: E£25.
This museum, opened in 1991, is dedicated to the Bedouins (desert nomads) of the Northern Sinai. Exhibits include re-creations of local weddings and exquisite silver jewellery (bracelets, earrings and pendants), probably of Yemeni origin.

outskirts

Zerenike Park
35km/22mi E of El-Arish. Open daily from dawn to dusk. $5. Cafeteria.
This nature reserve covering 200km²/77sq mi was created in 1985 to protect and provide shelter for migratory birds.

Rafah
45km/28mi E of El-Arish. Access: by bus from El-Arish (departures at 7.15am and 10am; journey time: 45min) and via the Egyptian border post. Just 4km/2.5mi from the Israeli border and Gaza Strip, this small town is surrounded by fields of crops and greenery as a result of the highest rainfall in the Sinai region. Salaheddine Street, a long souk of stalls selling exotic spices, is particularly worth a visit. There are no hotels in Rafah.

Crossing the Border – *Check locally beforehand.*
Following a passport check on the Egyptian side, travellers will need to hire a minibus to reach the Israeli side (*tax: E£20*).

DESERT FORTS
As Egypt's gateway to the Orient, the Northern Sinai has several forts around El-Arish. The largest is at Farama, 35km/22mi west of the town. Built in the year 239 of the Hegira by the Caliph Al-Motawakel Ala Allah, it was sacked by Baudouin I in the year 510 of the same calendar.

TOURIST OFFICE
El-Mena.
☎ *(068) 30 12 26.*

directory

WHERE TO STAY
• *Moderate*
Egoth Oberoi – *El-Fateh Street* – ☎ *(068) 35 13 21 – 226 rooms and bungalows: E£85/E£115.* Own beach. One of the few places to enjoy a beer.
Semiramis Arish – *El Fariq Fouad Zekri Street* – ☎ *(068) 34 41 67 – 125 rooms.* Two sections: the first by the beach; the second facing the road. Large swimming pool.

WHERE TO EAT
• *Budget*
Aziz Restaurant – *Tahrir Street. Almost opposite the mosque.* Specialities include *fuul* (purée of fava beans, garlic and oil) and koftas. Breakfast also available.
• *Moderate*
Maxim – *Between Fuad Zikry Street and the beach. Open in summer.* Fish specialities in a setting of palm trees.

Hurghada

Over the past 20 years, Hurghada has been transformed from a tiny fishing village into the most popular resort on the Red Sea, as witnessed by the numerous holiday complexes that have sprung up here. While the coastline is deserving of its reputation for its underwater treasures, the town itself is a somewhat disappointing mass of concrete.

Location
On the Red Sea, 536km/335mi SE of Cairo, 406km/254mi S of Suez, and 277km/173mi N of Luxor. Access: by plane from Cairo on Egyptair, or on bus services operated by Upper Egypt Bus (E£40-E£55; journey time: 6hr) and Superjet (E£50).

Name
At the time of the Ptolemies this area was known as Myos Hormos and acted as an important transit point for goods. Transcription: الغردقة

Modern Hurghada
Once no more than an isolated fishing port Hurghada has exchanged its fisherman for tourists who come here to relax on the beach or to make the most of the superb diving opportunities on offer in the Red Sea.

exploring Hurghada

It has to be said that there is not a great deal to do in Hurghada apart from underwater diving and heading off to the beach. The cheaper hotels tend to be found in the centre of the downtown tourist area *(Dahar)* to the north; the more upmarket area of Sigala to the south sees the start of a long line of luxury hotel complexes hemmed in between the main highway and the sea.

Red Sea Aquarium – 🖼 *Open all year, 9am-10pm (closed during Friday prayers). E£5; camera permit: E£2; video permit: E£10.* This sadly neglected aquarium on the ground floor of the marine biology station provides a limited insight into marine life in the Red Sea.

Sindbad Submarine★ – 🖼 *Information available from the Sindbad Hotel and most other hotels; capacity: 44 passengers; E£180 per person, E£90 for children under 12.* This submarine takes passengers on a 2-hour tour of the nearby coral reefs. The dive itself lasts 50 minutes, reaching a depth of 22m/72ft and providing a rare and unforgettable experience for those on board.

The yellow submarine – a regular sight in the Red Sea!

outskirts

Diving in the Red Sea★★★
Sites – Although the coastline here has suffered extensive damage as a result of urbanisation and the overuse of close-meshed fishing nets, according to Mahmoud Hanafi, the Director of Natural Reserves in the Red Sea region, "the coastal waters of the Red Sea are one of the world's richest ecosystems". Since 1995, 22 islands in the Strait of Gubal have been designated nature reserves, and with the exception of Giftun, between the Southern Sinai and the African coast, have been declared off-limits to protect the numerous migratory birds from divers who have been accused of causing excessive damage to the reefs. At present, there are no signs indicating that these reserves exist.

As in Sharm el-Sheikh, the major downside of diving in Hurghada is the sheer number of divers! Most boats leave at the same time (around 8am) and drop anchor

---

CONVOYS
To get to Luxor by road, convoys travel under military escort from Safaga, departing at 6.15am, 9.15am and 5.15pm. Convoys heading north to Cairo leave at 4.15am, 11.15am and 5.15pm.

STRAIT OF GUBAL
This extension of the Gulf of Suez is considered by sailors to be a treacherous stretch of water because of the strong winds in this area and the numerous reefs hidden below the surface of the water.

at buoys placed immediately above the same diving sites; and because of Hurghada's reputation as one of the world's diving centres, there is an unavoidable scrum of vessels around those islands nearest the coast. Although this rise in popularity has resulted in the migration of fish to calmer waters, the underwater world of the Strait of Gubal remains a unique and unforgettable sight, with its magnificent reefs, multicoloured fish and the numerous wrecks resulting from the increase in shipping since the opening of the Suez Canal in 1869.

The following is a list of some of the best diving sites:

Sha'ab umm Usk – *Between the islands of Gubal and Shadwan.* This large, horseshoe-shaped barrier reef encloses a lagoon accessible via a channel to the west. Dolphins are a frequent sight here.

The Wreck of the *Ghiannis D* – *N of the island of Shadwan.* This 100m/328ft-long cargo vessel sank in 1983 after hitting the Abu Nuhas reef, and is the best preserved in the area. The ship's stern and imposing funnel are popular with parrot-fish, although divers should take care to avoid the razor-sharp sheets of metal.

Sha'ab abu Nugar – *Between El-Gouna and Hurghada to the S of the island of Sha'ab El-Erg.* This reef is well protected from the wind and as such is a perfect environment for divers to discover its rich resources of varied coral.

Umm Gamar – *N of Giftun Island.* The plateau 30m/98ft below the surface leads to a wall with a 70m/230ft drop, providing a wonderful observation deck for the numerous pelagic fish here. The eastern section of the site has an abundance of multicoloured coral.

Carless Reef – *NE of Giftun Island.* Although recognised as one of the best dive sites in Hurghada, this area should only be explored in fine weather. The incredible array of sea life visible here ranges from whitetip sharks to sea horses, although the most impressive sight is undoubtedly the giant moray eel that inhabits the nooks and crannies among the coral.

El-Fanadir – *N of Giftun Island.* The vertical wall in the shallows of El-Fanadir is covered with coral. The poisonous stonefish and scorpionfish inhabit the waters here.

Giftun Seguir – *Just to the E of Giftun Island.* The smallest of the two Giftun islands is home to a superb vertical wall whose English name, Gorgonia Reef, bears witness to the presence of abundant gorgonian coral.

> **LOCAL CORAL**
> The waters around Hurghada are home to two main types of coral: hard species, such as Acrobora and Boraites; and softer, more colourful coral, such as Zenia and Sarcobhyton. The two main threats to these formations are anchors and starfish.

> The giant moray eel *(Gymnothorax javanicus)* is relatively common in the Red Sea. This impressive fish reaches a maximum length of (2.5m/8ft), but despite its size it appears to enjoy contact with divers, although it should not be forgotten that it is still a predator.

Comatulids or "feather stars" on gorgonian sea fan, a type of soft coral.

DIVING CENTRES

Almost all the hotels in Hurghada have their own diving centre, all offering similar packages. Some may be better than others, so it's worth shopping around to find the one best suited to you.

Blue Club – An offshoot of the Blue Sea Diving Centre in Sharm el-Sheikh, this SSI-, PADI, CMAS- and FFSSEME- approved centre is excellent for beginners and experienced divers alike.

Red Sea Diving Center – PADI, SSI and CMAS-approved, with an excellent reputation and standard of equipment and facilities.

Aquanaut Red Sea – This founder-member of the Hurghada Quality Dive Club is PADI-approved and specialises in dive cruises. High-quality safety provisions and facilities.

INTERNET CAFES

Internet Café and Coffee Shop – In the same building as the Princess Palace Hotel *(on the right-hand side)*. First and foremost a café with a few computer terminals to send and check your e-mails over a drink. E£8/30min.

SAFARIS

Most of the resort's hotels are able to organise excursions to the Mons Porphyrites and Mons Claudianius mountains *(you will need a guide to visit these two sites)*, as well as day trips to Luxor.

HURGHADA-SHARM EL-SHEIKH BY BOAT

The Amco company operates fast catamaran services *(1hr 30min; E£40)* between the two towns, although these are not daily and the timetables change frequently. Contact your hotel reception desk to book seats.

WHERE TO STAY

• *Budget*

Princess Hotel Palace – *6km/3.5mi S of Hurghada* – ☎ *(065) 44 77 01 – 256 rooms: $60 (palace); E£40 (village).* The clientele here is mainly Russian and the staff predominantly Italian! The hotel is divided into two sections: the palace *(on the beach side)*, and the village. Good value for money with lots of sports activities for guests.

Three Corners Empire Hotel – *Dahar* – ☎ *(065) 54 92 00 – 396 rooms: $42.* This smallish old building popular with the Scandinavians and Dutch has its own beach despite being set back from the sea. Unusually for Egyptian hotels, it has a "no food or drinks" policy; as a result the counter behind reception is lined with the drinks of customers who pick them up on their way out !

Sea Horse – *Dahar* – ☎ *(065) 54 87 04 – 44 rooms: E£80/100.* This well-kept hotel reasonably close to the sea has its own beach and diving centre 1 5.km/1mi away. Popular with German visitors.

El-Gezira – *Dahar* – ☎ *(065) 54 87 08 – 34 rooms: E£93.* A no-frills hotel close to the Sea Horse. Free access to the beach of the Sand Beach Hotel, with its overpriced rooms.

• *Moderate*

Marriott – *Hurghada* – ☎ *(065) 44 69 50 – 283 rooms: $114.* All the rooms have views overlooking the Red Sea. You can swim to the hotel's private island from the beach. Numerous sports activities available including squash, waterskiing, windsurfing and parasailing. Nightclub open from 9.30pm to 3am (E£20 for non-guests).

Sindbad Hotel – *Hurghada* – ☎ *(065) 44 32 60 – 259 rooms: $130/$167 (half-board).* Mainly frequented by Germans and Russians, this hotel is famous for underwater trips aboard its own submarine.

The Grand Hotel – *Hurghada* – ☎ *(065) 44 74 85 – 549 rooms: $179 (standard)/$215 (superior).* A huge hotel with an extensive beach, good facilities and numerous sports options. The comfortable rooms overlook colourful bougainvillea and hibiscus. Peace and quiet hard to come by here when the hotel is full, however. Nightclub open from 9pm until late.

Hilton – *10km/6mi S of Hurghada* – ☎ *(065) 44 21 16 – 276 rooms: $114/$173.* An efficient, well-maintained and very comfortable hotel. Sporting and leisure activities centred around the beach. Night-club open 10pm to 3am (E£20 for non-guests).

Sofitel Hurghada – *14km/9mi S of Hurghada* – ☎ *(065) 44 72 16 – 312 rooms: $140.* Opened in 1995, the Sofitel is keen to promote an image of sport and relaxation with its 800m? pool and long private beach. It offers a huge range of activities, including parasailing, and is one of the best-run hotels in the city. Night-club open from midnight to 3am. The only drawback is the fare-paying shuttle bus (E£10) into Hurghada.

Grand Azur – *10km/6mi S of Hurghada* – ☎ *(065) 24 25 64 – 185 rooms: $120.* This new hotel, where all activities are included in the price (excluding alcohol and massage sessions), is part of the Best Western chain and was opened in 2000. Piano-bar from 5pm to 2am (no nightclub).

Le Méridien – *Makadi Bay – 40km/25mi S of Hurghada – ☎ (065) 59 05 90 – 813 rooms: $206.* A brand-new hotel with an almost holiday-village feel. Because of its huge size, the general atmosphere is somewhat impersonal, although the hotel is luxurious and attractively laid out around a magnificent pool. All rooms enjoy pleasant views. The half-board restaurant leaves a lot to be desired, which is unusual for this hotel chain.

WHERE TO EAT
• Budget
In general, guests have lunch and dinner at their hotel as most visitors are on organised packages. For those who want to venture beyond their hotels, there are a number of inexpensive restaurants in both Hurghada and Dahar, although the cuisine on offer can be less than tempting. The few exceptions to the rule are:

Felfela – *Open 9am-midnight.* On the Corniche between Hurghada and Dahar (Sheraton Road), with a terrace overlooking the turquoise waters of the Red Sea. Visitors who have been to Cairo might be familiar with the name, which has an excellent reputation for its good-quality Egyptian cuisine. Specialities include *taamiya, fuul,* squid tagine and grilled fish.

Pronto – *Open noon-midnight.* Located next door to the booking office for the Sindbad Hotel submarine. A surprising menu which combines Italian and Russian cuisine. Views of the sea, as well as the chefs at work. The Italian side of things is run by an Egyptian, and the Russian part by a female Russian chef.

Sha'ab Abu Ramada – *To the S of Giftun Island.* The cool, shallow water at this site, nicknamed "the aquarium", makes it ideal for diving without the need for oxygen tanks. The site abounds with fish: grouper, flutemouth, emperor fish, red mullet and trigger fish are all a permanent feature here, ensuring an unforgettable visual experience for divers and snorkellers alike.

Makadi Bay – *To the S of Hurghada.* This impressive barrier of coral shelters numerous species of fish, such as sergeant majors and fierce longfin bannerfish.

El-Gouna◊◊◊
22km/14mi N of Hurghada.

The Marina – The splendid marina of El-Gouna, which is often referred to as the "Little Venice of Egypt" or the "Little Venice of the Red Sea", was built around 10 years ago by developers who have harnessed the potential of the waterways along this coast – El-Gouna means "lagoon" – to create this tourist complex. Although comparisons with Venice may be exaggerated, El-Gouna is an attractive resort, with its network of canals which criss-cross the town and flow into small lagoons of turquoise water.

The marina of El-Gouna – a haven of greenery on the edge of the desert.

TWO IN ONE
El-Gouna does, in fact, have two marinas: **Abydos**, the oldest, to the south; and **Abu Tig**, opened at the end of 2000, to the north. The latter, a modern marina incorporating tradtitional Yemenite architecture, was designed by the Italian, Alfredo Freda.

BEACHES
Zeytuna Beach is located on an island restricted to inhabitants and guests and is accessible via two bridges. Mangroovy Beach, near Abu Tig, will soon have an impressive camp site to add to its facilities.

A sophisticated development – Visitors expecting an inexpensive resort with lots going on are likely to be disappointed with El-Gouna. This attractive town appears to have stepped straight out of the pages of an upmarket magazine and has little in common with other Egyptian resorts, including Sharm el-Sheikh, which is largely dominated by hotel complexes. In El-Gouna, there is no medina, no rubbish and none of the urban structures that tend to disfigure other modern coastal developments. Here, the design and construction of the resort have been undertaken from a highly functional and environmentally conscious viewpoint, to the delight of residents and tourists who come here to enjoy the excellent services and facilities on offer. This unique setting on the Red Sea may not be of great interest to travellers keen to discover the "real" Egypt, but for those seeking isolation and comfort, luxurious El-Gouna is certainly the place, providing a new image of Egypt to visitors.

Sport and leisure – Like other Egyptian resorts, El-Gouna has broken with the Egyptian tradition of archaeological tourism, offering a number of diving centres and excellent sports facilities, including a world-class golf course designed by Gene Bates and Fred Couples. It is almost possible to imagine that you are in the Seychelles or on a remote Pacific island, but with the bonus of being able to transport yourself back to the time of the pyramids.

Mons Porphyrites

41km/25.5mi from El-Gouna. Difficult to visit apart from on an organised tour (check with your hotel in El-Gouna or Hurghada).

These porphyry quarries, which produce a dark red volcanic rock mixed with white crystals, used to decorate temples in Rome, have been worked since Roman times. The mysterious vestiges of columns, that once belonged to temples dedicated to Isis and Serapis, and ruined dwellings stand in the heart of an area of outstanding natural beauty.

directory

GETTING ABOUT
The best way of getting to El-Gouna from Hurghada is by taxi (around E£50), although hotels offer shuttle services. Boats operate inside the marina.

LEISURE
Activities and facilities on offer here include water sports, karting, golf, tennis, squash, horseriding, microlight flights, fitness centres etc. Information on all of these can be obtained from your hotel.

WHERE TO STAY
• *Budget*
El Khan – ☎ *(065) 54 56 00 – 25 rooms: $75.* Part of the Swiss Inn chain. No pool (although guests can swim at another hotel) or diving centre, but the hotel does have its own beach, where windsurfing is an option. El Khan is full of charm, with its Nubian-style architecture and typical rustic Egyptian rooms, albeit with European creature comforts.
• *Moderate*
LTI Paradiso Beach – ☎ *(065) 54 79 34 – 239 rooms: $100/$143 (half-board).* When it was opened in 1992, the Paradiso Beach (originally the Sonesta Paradiso) was the best hotel in Hurghada. Now part of a German hotel group, it still offers comfort, charm and excellent service. The hotel has its own diving centre and a yacht, the 8-cabin *MS Galatea*, which runs regular cruises (9am-5pm; $50).
• *Expensive*
Sheraton Miramar – ☎ *(065) 54 56 06 – 338 rooms: $162 + breakfast.* The American architect Michael Graves designed this colourful architectural gem which successfully combines Arab traditions with modern features. The sea here seems to be even more turquoise than elsewhere, providing a haven for those seeking peace and quiet and a range of sporting activities. All the spacious, luxurious rooms have a terrace overlooking the artificial lagoons and colourful displays of bougainvillea.

BARS AND CAFES
The Boat Bar – *Open 9am-1pm – Sheraton Miramar.* Enjoy a quiet beer or cocktail on the bridge of the *Samir 2* (open to non-guests).

The spines on the dorsal fin of the flying scorpionfish are best avoided!

Safaga☺☺
22km/14mi S of Hurghada.

The development of the resort – Not long ago, Safaga was the main Egyptian port on the Red Sea. Nowadays, however, although the port is still used to export phosphates mined nearby and at Abu Tartur in Middle Egypt, and by pilgrims heading to Mecca by sea, Safaga has seen its maritime activities decrease considerably while its revenue from tourism has rocketed, significantly altering the appearance of the town.

Windsurfing – Because of the northerly wind that is a regular feature here throughout the year, Safaga has become Egypt's most popular resort for surfboard and funboard enthusiasts. It has also seen an increase in the number of divers who come here in preference to busier centres such as Hurghada.

Diving sites – One of the latest diving areas to develop in popularity is **Tobia Arbaa**, to the south of the cape of Ras Abu Soma. The site is ideal for night diving, with its seven ergs of coral, 12m/39ft high, all of which contain formations of incredible beauty. **Panorama Reef**, marked by a small red lighthouse, encircles a small island to the east of the port, and is unquestionably one of the most spectacular diving sites along the coast, with its wide coral plateau and a 35m/115ft vertical wall plummeting to the depths of the Red Sea. One part of the site referred to as "Anemone City" is home to an incredible concentration of multicoloured polyps.

Mons Claudianus
61km/38mi from Safaga. Difficult to visit except by organised tour (check with your hotel in El-Gouna or Hurghada). In Roman times, this arid site surrounded by desert mountains was home to a fortress and a caravanserai. In Arabic, it is known as *Umm Diga*, or "the mother of columns", as it was here that granite was extracted. Convicts imprisoned here would extract the granite, which would then be transported to *Myos Hormos*, modern-day Hurghada, for shipment to Rome.

A NATURAL GULF
The resort stands alongside a wide natural basin, lined by a succession of delightful beaches, between Ras Abu Soma, to the north, and a barrier reef to the south.

SALEM EXPRESS
The wreck of this ferry sits at a depth of 32m/105ft to the southeast of the port. It sank en route from Jeddah, Saudi Arabia, on 15 December 1991, resulting in the death of hundreds of pilgrims returning from Mecca. Nowadays, it has become a site for divers.

This archaeological site contains innumerable amphorae and pieces of crockery that have still to be analysed and listed.

---

directory

Ismailiya

A hint of nostalgia pervades the streets of Ismailiya as a result of the colonial architecture dating from the city's creation in the second half of the 19C. Despite its rapid growth and the reputation of the delicious mangoes grown in the surrounding area, the city's livelihood is still dominated by the Suez Canal alongside which it was built.

THE MUSLIM BROTHERHOOD
Founded by Hassan el-Banna in Ismailiya in 1928, this organisation originally campaigned for the moral regeneration of Egypt, before forming terrorist cells and becoming more radical in its beliefs.

Location
Just north of Lake Timsah, 120km/80mi NE of Cairo and 80km/50mi S of Port-Said. Access: by train from Cairo and via Zagazig (5 departures daily; journey time: 2hr 30min); by bus from Cairo on services operated by the West Delta Bus Company (hourly from 6am to 6.30pm; journey time: 2hr).

Name
The city takes its name from the Khedive Ismail Pasha, who founded the city in the 1860s.

Transcription: الإسماعيلية

Famous People
The great-grandson of Mohammed Ali, Ismail Pasha (1830-95) became Khedive, or Viceroy of Egypt, in 1867.

exploring Ismailiya

A PLACE OF PIGRIMAGE
The European cemetery is the resting place for those who worked for the Suez Canal Authority. Although poorly maintained, it remains an impressive site.

The city centre, built on a grid system, has retained the atmosphere of the original European quarter. Here, the former offices of the Suez Canal Authority (*next to De Lesseps' house*) and the villas of the company's agents, with their attractive gardens, exude an old-fashioned charm. Several parts of the city, such as Mohammed Ali Street, which runs alongside the freshwater canal, the area around the church, and Champollion Square, show strong similarities with European spa towns. Although the gardens and beaches along Lake Timsah are popular with locals, the major interest here is the canal, a large expanse of blue water running between banks of golden sand and separating Africa from Asia.

The Canal★
Follow directions to Ferry no 6, not the Ferdan Ferry Boat, which is reserved for lorries and military personnel.
If you're hoping to watch shipping negotiating its path along the canal you may have to be patient as vessels travel along the canal in convoy, either from north to south, or south to north (the only points where vessels can pass each other are at Ballah and on Great Bitter

The extraordinary sight of a boat in the middle of the desert.

Lake). However, the sight of enormous tankers gliding through the calm waters of this narrow canal is an impressive one and well worth the wait.

Ferdinand de Lesseps' House

Mohammed Ali Street. Only open to guests of the Suez Canal Authority.

The architect of the famous Suez Canal *(see SUEZ)* lived in this chalet-style villa until the completion of his project.

Lake Timsah

The "Crocodile Lake" is located to the south-east of the city.

The garden of Ferdinand de Lesseps' house.

worth a visit

Ismailiya Museum

Mohammed Ali Street. Open daily 9am-4pm (5pm in summer). E£6; students E£3; camera permit E£5; video permit E£100.

The design of this neo-Classical-style building is of interest in itself; unfortunately, the museum's contents and old-fashioned presentation are somewhat less impressive.

Egyptian Antiquities – The Egyptian collection contains a sandstone head dating from the 19th Dynasty, Coptic papyrus texts, and gold jewellery discovered in the wrappings of mummies.

Greco-Roman Antiquities – Artefacts on display include glass phials (including 10 small bottles symbolising honesty and sadness, which were used to collect tears), and a marble statue of Venus.

Islamic Collection – The pottery oil bombs and two 14C copper incense burners from the Mameluke period are of particular interest in the museum's Islamic collection.

> **WORTH SEEING**
> The large mosaic (late-4C) represents a single mythological scene in three registers: Phaedra sending a love letter to Hippolytus; Dionysus on his chariot; and the virtue of Herakles.

outskirts

El-Qantara

28km/17.5mi N of Ismailiya.

The town, which was almost completely destroyed in 1973 during the war with Israel, takes its name from a bridge, the *Qantara el Khasna*, which was levelled at the time of the construction of the canal.

An important river crossing – The huge suspension bridge under construction to the south of the city bears witness to the importance of this crossing point between the Nile Delta and Palestine over the past 5 000 years.

directory

LEISURE TIME

Beaches – *On Lake Timsah, to the south of the city.* The beaches along the lake either belong to luxury hotels or private clubs. The normal entrance fee is around E£20, which entitles guests to have lunch by the lakeside.

TRANSPORT

Ferries – Ferry no 6 operates between the Asian and African sides of the canal to the east of the city (users of the Ferdan Ferry Boat, 4km/2.5mi NW of Ismailiya, require a special permit). The service operates from 6am-midnight and is free of charge.

WHERE TO STAY

• *Moderate*

Mercure Coralia – *Forsan Island –* ☎ *(064) 33 80 42.* 152 rooms: E£147/E£130. A luxury hotel with excellent facilities. The Coralia is the only hotel with a superb view of the lake.

WHERE TO EAT

• *Moderate*

George's Place – *11, Sultan Hussein Street* – ☎ *(064) 33 73 27.* Fish and prawn specialities and a pleasant bar for an aperitif (alcohol available).

Nuweiba

This bustling port on the Gulf of Aqaba also acts as a transit point between Jordan and Egypt. It is situated at the mouth of the Wadi Watir, a delta that dries up for 10 months of the year. Although the landscape around the town is attractive, the resort here is disappointing in comparison with others along this stretch of coast.

Location
475km/297mi from Cairo, 165km/103mi NE of Sharm el-Sheikh, and 70km/44mi from the Israeli border. Access: see Sharm el-Sheikh, from where the best option is by bus (departure at 9am to the Nuweiba ferry terminal) or taxi.

Name
The town is named after a local Bedouin tribe.
Transcription: نويبع

Famous People
Abdallah, a young deaf and dumb Bedouin boy from the village of Mizena *(1km/0.6mi N of Nuweiba)*, recently became a local hero when he miraculously discovered the ability to talk after befriending a dolphin which he named "Olin". Now large numbers of visitors come to Nuweiba in the hope of swimming with this gentle dolphin.

For E£10, the residents of the village who feed Olin allow visitors to swim at Dolphin Beach, which is situated 5km/3mi south of the port. Those who take up this option should not forget that this mammal is untamed and in its natural environment.

exploring Nuweiba

Nuweiba City
This settlement, situated 8km/5mi north of the port and the ferry terminal providing links with Aqaba, was originally a simple Bedouin village. Nowadays it is a small town with souvenir shops and a disappointing souk. Despite its proximity to superb coral reefs and magnificent arid mountains, the town has a tourist-trap feel to it, with expensive accommodation generally offering poor value for money.

Tarabin
4km/2.5mi N.
Tarabin is easily accessible by foot *(15min)* along Nuweiba Bay. This Bedouin village, dominated by an 18C Turkish citadel and with a beach lapped by the warm waters of the Gulf of Aqaba, can be likened to a miniature Dahab. During the Israeli holidays, Tarabin becomes very busy and noisy although Israeli visitors have become increasingly rare in recent times.

TAXIS
To get from the port to Nuweiba City, expect to pay an exorbitant E£15 for a collective taxi. If you're arriving by bus from Sharm el-Sheikh, you'll need your best bargaining skills to get this price down – otherwise, your only other option here is on foot.

outskirts

The coast★ between Nuweiba and Taba
With its mountains plunging down to the sea and those of Saudi Arabia visible in the distance, this stretch of coastline is undoubtedly one of the most attractive on the Sinai. Although many of the touristy villages along the coast road have had a negative effect on the wild beauty of the area, there are still several unspoilt beaches here.

Maagana Beach – *8km/5mi N of Nuweiba*. The bay is close to colourful rock formations and coral reefs. A campground which also has accommodation facilities is also located nearby.

Ras Shaitan – *11km/7mi N of Nuweiba*. The shape of this rocky headland, which translates as "Devil's Head", has lent its name to this beach, which is perfect for swimming. Four camp sites are situated close by.

EXCURSIONS
Nuweiba's strong point is that it is an excellent starting-point for jeep or camel safaris to the mountains on the Sinai. For detailed information on particular excursions, and to make reservations, contact your campsite, hotel or diving centre.

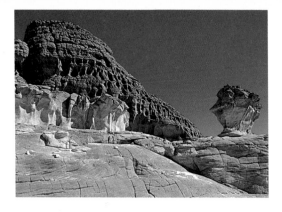

The best way to appreciate the amazing rock formations of the Coloured Canyon is on foot.

Basata – *29km/18mi N of Nuweiba*. The beach is part of a campground designed with respect for the environment in mind. If you're not staying at the camp, an entry fee of E£10 is payable. Diving with breathing apparatus is prohibited here.

Coloured Canyon★★
35km/22mi NW of Nuweiba.

If it's peace and quiet you're after, the Coloured Canyon is for you – provided you come here outside the times popular with tour groups. Sheltered from the wind, this gorge was created by the erosive effects of water and owes its name to the colourful strata, which range from sandy hues to shades of blue and green, and provide natural decoration to the cliffs here. This geological attraction provides a wonderful climax to a walk that normally takes around two hours if you're reasonably fit.

> **A**n impressive 700m/770yd-long stretch of canyon may prove difficult for those visitors who are not used to hiking.

Ain Hudra – *47km/29mi W of Nuweiba.*
In the Bible, Miriam is said to have been struck down with leprosy here for having criticised Moses. This small oasis situated close to the Gebel Ghlim (1 230m/4 034ft), is home to a Bedouin camp, numerous palm trees, as well as surrounding **scenery**★ that is worth several hours' exploration in its own right.

Ain Umm Ahmed – *50km/31mi W of Nuweiba.* This second oasis is quite delightful. When the hot sun is shining in the spring and summer it is hard to imagine that its water course occasionally freezes in winter.

directory

Port Said★

With its status as a duty-free port, Port Said is the most prosperous place on the Suez Canal. Established in 1859 as part of the development of the canal, Port Said has become one of the world's busiest maritime cities. The city has been designed according to a Western grid system, and has more in common with the modern business world than with the Egypt of the pharaohs.

Location

180km/112mi NE of Cairo, on an area of raised land at the northern tip of the African side of the Suez Canal. Opposite, on the Asian side, stands the port of Port Fouad. Access: by train from Cairo and via Zigazag (departures at 6.20am, 9.15am and 11.30am; journey time: 4hr); by Superjet and Charq Al-Delta bus from Cairo (hourly from 6.30am to 8pm; journey time: 3hr).

TOURIST OFFICE
Palestine Street,
☎ *(066) 23 52 89.*
Open daily except Fri, 9am-1.30pm and 3-8pm.

Name

The port owes its name to Mohammed Saïd Pasha, the son of Mohammed Ali and a friend of Ferdinand de Lesseps, who founded the town around an encampment of shacks built on stilts. The earth excavated to make way for the canal was used as landfill for a small section of Lake Manzana.

Transcription: بور سعيد

Famous People

In 1935, Mikhail Fedorovitch Larionov (1881-1964), the artist associated with the renowned Ballets russes, designed the set for the ballet *Port Said* performed at the London Coliseum, although it is unclear whether he ever actually set foot in the city.

NASSER'S PRESTIGE
Nasser initially nationalised the Suez Canal to finance the Aswan Dam, after the Americans and Europeans had refused him funds.
This process, along with his purchase of arms from Communist countries and his refusal to "align himself" with Western theories, rapidly turned him into a hero for the Arab cause.
Consequently, the Nasser myth was born.

background

The Suez Canal affair – On 26 July 1956, **Gamal Abdel Nasser** nationalised the Suez Canal, guaranteed freedom of movement between the Mediterranean and the Red Sea, and replaced French and British pilots with Egyptians and Russians. Paris and London were concerned that Nasser was about to prevent their access to lucrative oil reserves; Washington was worried about possible military action. Meanwhile, Israel, which was prohibited from using the canal, saw this as an opportunity to dent Nasser's political ambitions. As a result, Britain and France decided to mount a large-scale offensive.

On 29 October, Israel invaded the Sinai with French planes whose markings were camouflaged with the Star of David.

The official opening of the Suez Canal in Port Said.

THE STATUE OF DE LESSEPS

European visitors, particularly those from France, who make their way to Port Said come here to reflect on the work of Ferdinand de Lesseps, who designed the Suez Canal. His imposing statue used to stand at the entrance to the port, to the north of the quayside promenade along Palestine Street. However, all that is left of it today is the plinth bearing his name.

Having become a symbol of the Anglo-French attack in 1956 and the oppression of workers who dug the canal, the statue was dynamited on 24 December 1956. For many years it lay in pieces in a Canal Company warehouse.

Today, the statue is back in one piece and waits patiently at the Port Fouad arsenal, opposite its original location, while a decision is made on its future.

The statue of Ferdinand de Lesseps, now on display at the Port Fouad arsenal (closed to the public).

Paris and London immediately demanded the withdrawal of Israeli and Egyptian troops from the canal. As agreed, Israel accepted what was unacceptable to the Egyptians. From this point on, France and Britain had a pretext to mount a military attack, referred to by the code name "Musketeer". Nasser then seized the initiative, blocking the canal by sinking 47 old vessels.

On 5 November, 1 000 French and 600 British soldiers, landed in Port Said and occupied the town, which although now rebuilt, still shows traces of the conflicts of 1956, 1967 and 1973. While the British troops were preparing to close in on Ismailiya, the Soviet Union, through Bulganin, began to threaten the use of nuclear arms, which the recently elected Eisenhower countered with a call for moderation and the UN with the announcement of a ceasefire. In December, France and Britain withdrew from Egyptian territory, an act that Israel belatedly followed on 14 March 1957. It was only then that Nasser reopened the canal to shipping.

A freeport – The definition of a freeport or urban area with a special administrative or tax status where the transit of goods is free, in other words where the customs authorities are only interested in them if they leave the customs area. The major advantage of this status is the speeding up of ship turnarounds by reducing customs formalities, as is also the case in Gibraltar and on the island of Malta. The drawbacks are few and far between although some people view the system as an incitement to smuggling given that security checks are almost non-existent. Port Said has been a freeport since 1975.

> ▶ **DON'T FORGET YOUR PASSPORT**
> Since Port Said is a freeport, you will need to pass through customs when you enter and leave the city. Make sure your passport contains a stamp for your video camera if you have one.

exploring Port Said

The City

In summer, Port Said's commercial quarter *(Al-Togari)* is ▶ very popular, particularly with visitors from Cairo who come here to shop. This district borders the quayside *(Palestine Street)* and is the oldest part of the city with an attractive mix of somewhat dilapidated late-19C colonial architecture. After strolling through this miniature version of Hong Kong, head for the new elevated promenade lining the quayside from the fishing port to the Commerce Basin. On the north side, note the plinth upon which a statue of Ferdinand de Lesseps once stood.

> **W**ith its numerous stores selling clothes and the latest gadgets from South-East Asia, the shopping district has a bazaar-like feel to it.

The beach – Although the Mediterranean is not at its cleanest here, the beach is nonetheless fronted by numerous clubs and apartment buildings. However, it remains less lively than Alexandria and less popular with tourists. In the evening, the long Tarh el-Bahr Street continues to attract customers who come here to frequent the numerous bars, restaurants and clothes shops that stay open late into the evening.

The old lighthouse, 53m/174ft high, stands above the buildings on Palestine Street.

The Port

The port area is the backdrop to the incessant to-ing and fro-ing of container ships, ferries and barges.

Facts and figures – The channel has a width of between 200m/656ft and 600m/1 968ft. The western jetty (a breakwater inaccessible to pedestrians) is 7.3km/4.5mi long, and the eastern jetty 1.9km/1.2mi long. The pier-heads are a further 900m/2 950ft away. The light from the original lighthouse was visible 37km/23mi away (the new building is along the beach). In 1998, some 14 500 vessels loading between 15 000t and 26 000t passed through the port at a rate of almost 90 ships per day.

The Suez Canal Company★ – *Closed to the public.* This magnificent building at the far end of Mustafa Kamel Street, between the Arsenal and Commerce Basins, was completed in 1869 in readiness for the opening of the canal. To appreciate its impressive white façade fronting the canal to best effect, take the free ferry linking Port Said and Port Fouad.

Port Fouad

The residential quarter of Port Said stands on the Asian continent, on the opposite bank of the canal.

Founded in 1925 to provide accommodation for the employees of the Suez Canal Company, the suburb was named in honour of King Fouad I, the third son of the *Khedive* Ismail Pasha. With its marina, calm atmosphere and small houses with gardens full of white jasmine, Port Fouad offers a complete contrast to its neighbour on the opposite bank.

worth a visit

Port Said National Museum

Palestine Street (on the north side of the quay). Open daily 9am-5pm (ticket office closes at 4pm). E£12; students E£6; camera permit E£10; video permit E£100.

The exhibits on display in the garden are from the museum in Ismailiya. The collection inside is of relatively little interest, even though it contains some 2 500 artefacts displayed in five sections (Pharaonic, Greco-Roman, Coptic, Islamic and Modern) on two levels. Highlights include leather and papyrus sandals (5th Dynasty), the phaeton (coach) used by the family of Mohammed Ali, and unusual Coptic icons, including one dating from the 15C representing Christ in Glory surrounded by apostles, angels, the Devil, and Adam and Eve (the 1191 date refers to the Copts).

Military Museum

July 23 Street. Open 9am-2pm and 6-8pm. E£2; camera permit E£2; video permit E£20.

The museum's finest exhibit is a life-size limestone "reserve head". This type of idealised, albeit already realistic, sculpture would have been used as a die for moulds, which explains why on most of them the ears have been broken off (during the mould-removal process).

Opened by Nasser in 1964, this small museum displays exhibits ranging from models and dioramas to iconographic documents (photographs and paintings) mainly relating to the 1956 conflict as well as to the Egyptian-Israeli wars of 1967 and 1973. The museum is mainly of interest to Egyptians and amateur military historians, although explanations in English are useful to visitors with a more general interest in the subject. At the entrance to the museum note the three central display windows exhibiting an impressive collection of armour from the 12C-16C.

directory

BOAT TRIPS

Noras I – Departures from gate no 1 (opposite the Port Said National Museum). A short cruise on the Mediterranean and the entrance to the canal. *Departures at 3pm and 8pm; E£10, including one drink.*

TRANSPORT

Ferry services – *No charge for pedestrians.* Services every 10min between Port Said and Port Fouad (boarding just north of the Suez Canal Authority building).

SHOPPING

Shops – The most popular buys in this duty-free port are clothes and shoes (beware of the many fake goods on sale) and all the latest gadgetry. Don't forget to bargain! The main shopping areas are along Al-Gomhuriya (parallel to Palestine Street), El-Nahda, and the beachfront.

LEISURE TIME

Beaches – Parasols can be rented for E£4 per day on the long beach to the north of the city. Apart from the occasional private hotel beach, all the beaches in Port Said are public.

Bike rental – The shop on the south side of Hafez Ibrahim near the Tourist Office rents bicycles for E£3/hour.

INTERNET FACILITIES
– E-mails can be sent and checked at the Internet desk on the first floor of the Panorama Hotel. E£3/hour *(open to non-guests).*

WHERE TO STAY

• *Budget*

Panorama Hotel – *Al-Gomhuriya Street* – ☏ *(066) 32 11 02 – 64 rooms: E£170.* This pleasant hotel on the north side of the street is perhaps a little too close to the mosque for an undisturbed night's sleep.

Palace Hotel – 19, *Ghandy Street* - ☏ *(066) 23 94 50 – 84 rooms: E£105.* Simple and clean, with a billiard table for those inclined.

Savoy Hotel – *Mohammed Ali Street* – ☏ *(066) 33 00 57 – 45 rooms: E£73.* Basic but clean.

• *Moderate*

Sonesta Port Said – *Sultan Hussein Street* – ☏ *(066) 32 55 11 – 110 rooms: E£150/E£200.* Overlooking the entrance to the canal with a superbly located swimming pool, a fitness centre and rooms with Internet connections for laptop users.

Helnan Port Said Hotel – *Corniche* – ☏ *(066) 32 08 90 – 203 rooms: E£130/E£170.* This comfortable hotel, with a night-club, sauna and jacuzzi, is well located between the beach and the entrance to the canal. The best rooms are those overlooking the canal and fishing port.

Noras Beach Hotel – *Atef El-Sadat Street* – ☏ *(066) 33 98 34 – 198 rooms: E£110/E£175.* Because of its "hotel-village" label, the Noras beach is restricted to a 3-star Egyptian rating although the comfort and facilities here are undoubtedly higher. The hotel offers both lunch and dinner cruises on the Mediterranean. E£10 will buy non-guests a drink here.

WHERE TO EAT

• *Budget*

El-Ektesad – 19, *Safeia Zageia Zaglhoule.* Customers continue to frequent "The Economy" for the warm welcome and to sample its rice with liver, kebabs and *koftas* (meatballs). If you order a *mehalabeya* (Egyptian cream) for dessert, the chances are you'll see one of the waiters hop on his bicycle to buy one at the nearest shop! No alcohol served.

Pizza Pino – *Al-Gomhuriya Street.* The pizzas here are some of the best in the city.

• *Moderate*

El-Borg – *Tahr el-Bahr Street* – ☏ *(066) 32 34 42.* "The Tower" is a recognised name in Port Said and beyond, and is worthy of its excellent reputation. Fish is the mainstay here (you can choose your fish and the way you want it cooked), including specialities such as fish soup with crab and shellfish, and the delicious pumpkin and coconut cream dessert.

El-Bagaa – *Tahr el-Bahr Street* – "The Pelican" also enjoys a good reputation for its fish dishes, especially its rice with seafood and its fish *tagine.* The restaurant does not serve alcohol.

The green dome of the Suez Canal Company building is almost as well known as the canal itself.

Quseir ☲

Despite its label as a new tourist destination on the future Egyptian "Riviera", the town of Quseir has a long history behind it and is one of the oldest ports on the Red Sea. The pleasant sea breeze here is welcomed by visitors, as it was by the numerous adventurers who plundered this coastline in days of old.

Location
On the Red Sea, 860km/537mi SE of Cairo and 85km/53mi SE of Hurghada. Access: by bus from Cairo (E£65; journey time: 11hr); Hurghada (E£15); and Safaga (E£8); or by taxi.

Name
The town owes its name to its ancient port. Its founder, Mentuhotep II, named it *Toua*, while the Ptolemies referred to it by the name of *Leukos Limen* ("white port"). This harbour, situated 8km/5mi south of the modern town, has now silted up.

Transcription: القصير

Famous People
◄ Queen Hatshepsut (18th Dynasty) launched an expedition here in search of the mysterious "land of Punt".

> **H**atshepsut's temple at Deir el-Bahri is adorned with painted low reliefs which record the chronology of her expedition.

background

The ancient secrets of the Red Sea – The early Egyptians referred to this body of water by the same name they used for the Mediterranean, and to them it was a sea full of mystery. Up until the 12th Dynasty, not a single port had been founded on its western shoreline, and only boats from Byblos were prepared to risk sailing in its waters. The famous *Tale of the Shipwrecked Sailor*, which relates the astonishing story of a passenger who set sail aboard a ship destined for the mines of the Sinai, dates from this period. This marooned traveller was washed ashore on the island of Ka, in the middle of the Red Sea, whose coastline was believed to be inhabited ◄ by the gods. Over the centuries the Red Sea was to develop an aura of spirituality and a sense of the unknown, particularly along the coast around Quseir.

> **THE BLUE SEA!**
> The Red Sea does in fact owe its name to a blue algae *(Trichodesmium erythræum)* which turns red when it dies.

Punt – From the time of the Old Kingdom, Egyptians sent maritime expeditions to Punt (the "land of the god"), ◄ a region that was thought to exist "somewhere" on the shores of the Red Sea. To confuse matters further, its location varied in references found in documents from the reigns of Hatshepsut and Horemheb. To some scholars, this land was situated in modern-day Saudi Arabia, to others in Abyssinia (Ethiopia).

> **T**he French archaeologist Maspero suggested that Punt was located near Cape Guardafui, to the north of Somalia.

exploring Quseir

The old town – Before the opening of the Suez Canal, Quseir was the main port for pilgrims from Egypt and North Africa heading for Mecca. The construction of the canal brought about a rapid decline for the port, which only managed to survive thanks to the export of phosphates, developed in the local area by an Italian company during the 20C. In the afternoon, all activity seems to come to a standstill because of the heat, although this ◄ is the best time to discover the **architecture**★ of the town. It is dominated by a small Ottoman fort built in the 16C by Sultan Selim, and its narrow streets have houses adorned with screened balconies *(mashrabiyas)*.

> **WORTH SEEING**
> Some of the old houses along the seafront have been constructed using coral, the building material most readily available in the area.

Modern Quseir – Today, the town is an expanding resort, as witnessed by the development underway in the old quarter.

directory

WHERE TO STAY
• *Moderate*
Mövenpick Sirena Beach (Mövenpide resort El Quseir) – *7km/4.4mi N of Quseir – ☎ (065) 33 21 00 – 175 rooms: $85/$175.* A prestigious hotel built in the Nubian style, which blends in well with the surrounding landscape. With its delightful setting, the hotel is a perfect place to unwind. Facilities also include the Subex diving centre.

outskirts

Diving
The coastal reef is dotted with diving sites which are home to a magnificent array of underwater fauna. These areas are still relatively free from tourists – and as such under very little threat – and are considered to be the most complete of any along Egypt's coasts. It is hoped that the lessons learned from the destruction of the reefs in Hurghada will protect those in Quseir.

Big Brother – The waters off this island contain high concentrations of fish and coral and a succession of steep walls, and are renowned for their excellent visibility. Further out to sea, divers are able to view sharks and shoals of barracuda.

> **DUGONG**
> Some divers may be lucky enough to catch a glimpse of this sea mammal, which is threatened with extinction. Also known as the "sea cow", it can grow to 3m/10ft in length.

Marsa Alam
145km/90mi S of Quseir.
This small, tranquil fishing port is now starting to witness the development of tourism through the arrival of small numbers of divers who come here to explore the turquoise waters of its delightful coves. As yet, however, very few specialist dive boats have established their activities in Marsa Alam.

Berenice
145km/90mi S of Marsa Alam. A military pass issued in Cairo is currently required to visit here.

Historical outline – The port of Berenice was founded around 275 BC by Ptolemy I, who named it after his mother. For over 500 years it enjoyed intense commercial activity and developed into a port for the precious silk and wood imported from East Africa, Persia and India.

Temple of Semiramis – The excavations carried out on the ruins of the temple at the end of the 19C brought to light several representations, including one of Tiberius making an offering to the god Min.

Mining – Emerald mines were once exploited in the Wadi Sakait, close to Berenice. Although appreciated by the Egyptians, as well as by sultans during the Mameluke period, their production ceased under Mohammed Ali.

> **LANDMINES**
> Never visit a beach without a guide as not every beach has been cleared of these deadly mines.

> **B**etween 1500 BC and the mid-20C, olivine, a semi-precious stone, was extracted from mines on the island of Zabargad.

The best way to get a close look at the weird and wonderful emperor fish is to don a mask and flippers.

Sharm el-Sheikh ☳☳☳

In just a few years the most attractive of Egypt's coastal resorts has experienced tremendous growth and is now the largest in the Sinai. The nearby Ras Mohammed National Park and the impressive Tiran Strait enhance the natural beauty of Sharm el-Sheikh, which has developed a worldwide reputation for diving, and although it is undoubtedly the most expensive resort in the country, it is also the most appealing.

> The East Delta bus station is situated behind the Mobil petrol station, between Sharm el-Sheikh and Naama Bay.

Location
500km/312mi SE of Cairo and 380km/237mi S of Suez, at the southernmost tip of the Sinai between the Gulfs of Suez and Aqaba. Access: by plane from Cairo on Egyptair, by road, or on bus services operated by the East Delta Company (E£40-E£65; journey time: 7hr) and Superjet (E£55).

Name
Sharm el-Sheikh came to worldwide attention when it hosted the Middle East peace summit between Presidents Mubarak, Clinton, Barak and Arafat in October 2000.

Transcription: شرم الشيخ

Famous People
Divers who come here to indulge in their exhilarating underwater sport will use oxygen bottles, an invention they owe to Jacques Cousteau (1910-97) and Emile Gagnan, who developed the automatic aqualung.

exploring Sharm el-Sheikh

Sharm el-Sheikh☳☳ and Naama Bay☳☳☳
Two resorts in one – **Sharm el-Sheikh**, to the west, has expanded around its small natural harbour (Sharm el-Moya), which sits attractively at the foot of a cliff. The occupation of the peninsula by the Israelis from 1967-82 was the catalyst for its early growth, since when it has continued to develop to the extent that it now extends as far as Naama Bay, 7km/4.5mi away. A small medina set back from the beach is a maze of souvenir shops and tiny stalls serving local specialities such as fried aubergines, and cold drinks. The port area to the east of the beach is the departure point for ferry services across to Hurghada.

Naama Bay, with the mountains of the Sinai Peninsula in the distance.

Little Italy – The resort of **Naama Bay** is situated on the magnificent long bay from which it takes its name. Although created no more than 20 years ago, this town has developed into an attractive and charming village-like resort with a relaxed atmosphere and lively nightlife, and has now surpassed its friendly rival and neighbour in popularity. The hotels here have attempted to outdo each other in terms of comfort, facilities and grandeur, and are complemented by a number of casinos, although these tend to be frequented solely by foreign visitors. Originally Naama Bay was dominated by German tourists, although nowadays the main influx of visitors tends to come from Italy. As a result, Italian is widely spoken and understood throughout the hotels and restaurants of the resort.

For those wishing to escape briefly from the resort's consumerism, the desert extends inland just behind the town, a line of stark, steep mountains providing an impressive backdrop on the horizon. This is the land of the Bedouin tribes, who live in brightly coloured tents and whose lifestyle provides a striking contrast with the comfort and modernity of the two neighbouring resorts.

Beaches – Almost all the beaches here are private, owned by the hotels built between the sea and the main road leading to the airport. There are, however, a number of clearly signposted public beaches, namely Sharm el-Sheikh, Naama Bay and Shark's Bay, with very little on them apart from sunshades *(E£15 to rent)* which provide some relief from the hot sun. The private beaches are far more refined, with deck-chairs, parasols, bars and other facilities. If you have a car, you may wish to visit some of the other beaches along the coast, although you will need to take provisions with you for a picnic as well as a parasol, as shade among the rocks is hard to find.

> A pedestrian promenade fronted by restaurants and diving centres runs parallel to the beach along the horseshoe-shaped Naama Bay. A second pedestrianised street, lined with numerous shops, runs parallel to the beach for a similar distance through the village.

The mangroves within the park are the most northerly to be found anywhere on the planet.

highlights

Ras Mohammed National Park★★
12km/8mi SW of Sharm el-Sheikh. There are two entrances to the park: one to the NW, the other to the NE. Divers can also reach the park from the sea. Land entry is not permitted for visitors with a Sinai visa only (eg those arriving from Israel). Open 8.30am to 5pm. E£5; vehicles E£10. A map of the park comes with the entrance ticket.

The Ras Mohammed National Park occupies a strip of land on the southern tip of the peninsula (*ras* means "cape"). It was created in 1983 and became a national park five years later. Although the landscape here is not particularly spectacular unless you head underwater, the main feature of the park is its wild, unspoilt scenery.

A total of 829km²/320sq mi of wilderness – Because of the protected status of the park, which extends out to sea as far as Tiran Island, the coast of the Southern Sinai has partially resisted the overtures of property developers (just 10% of the overall area is open to visitors). As a result, the land section of the park, characterised by creeks, bays, dunes and mangroves (to the south of the cape), is home to migratory birds such as storks, white-tailed eagles and spoonbills. Several species of animal, such as the gazelle and the fox, have also been re-introduced into the reserve, the aim of which is to protect and preserve both marine and land flora and fauna. Unauthorised camping is strictly prohibited here.

The Park's Beaches – The park has several beaches, each marked by a coloured arrow on signposts. **Khashaba Beach** *(pink arrow)* on Marsa Bay, does not perhaps have the best location, but you are almost certain to be on your own here.

> **▶ PARK REGULATIONS**
> Visitors to the park are asked to respect the park environment, not to drive beyond track boundaries, not to feed the fish and not to venture into prohibited areas marked by a white sign with a red line through it.

Yolanda Bay, at the extremity of the Ras Muhammed National Park, is famed for its translucent water.

PROVISIONS
Make sure you take sandwiches and mineral water with you as there are no shops or drink stands within the boundaries of the park.

A BLAZE OF COLOUR
A multitude of colourful fish (wrasse, parrotfish, grouper, emperor fish, red mullet, triggerfish, butterfly fish, double-saddled butterfly fish, clown fish etc) inhabit the gorgonians and yellow, blue, white, mauve and pink coral found within the park.

The attractive **Old Kay** beach *(green arrow)*, facing directly west, is renowned for its turquoise waters and its views out to the horizon; **Observatory Beach** *(orange arrow)*, near an interesting viewpoint overlooking the park, is lapped by the waves and is not particularly conducive to sunbathing. **Main Beach** *(blue arrow)* is particularly pleasant, and is popular with snorkellers, who come here to admire the vertical wall of coral.

Yolanda Bay *(red arrow)* is unquestionably the most beautiful beach within the park, and as a result attracts tour groups on guided visits. Despite this, the small cove stands in a perfect location where children can paddle safely because of the shallow water here.

The deep indentation of **Hidden Bay**, an old barrier of fossilised coral, stands impressively between Yolanda Bay and the mangroves. Although swimming is prohibited in the bay, this attractive beach is well worth a stop.

Diving – The maritime section of the park is a favourite site for divers because of its unpolluted waters, which offer perfect conditions for underwater exploration. Apart from the fact that it is teeming with fish, it is particularly renowned for its magnificent, multicoloured **coral reefs**★★★ which many divers consider to be the most beautiful to be found anywhere in the world; in total, 137 species of coral have been identified in the park. All we know about coral is that it is hard or soft, that it is a multicellular animal, and that it has existed on our planet for some 450 million years; the word also describes its calcareous skeleton, which is used in jewellery. The clarity of the water here is such that even from a boat it is possible to see to a depth of 15m/49ft. Because of its clear waters and diverse fish and coral species, diving in Ras Mohammed has been compared to swimming in a giant natural aquarium.

THE RED SEA

The Red Sea owes its name to a blue algae which turns a ruby colour when it dies. Despite this less-than-enticing explanation, the waters of the Red Sea are a paradise for swimmers, snorkellers and divers alike. However, before rushing into the water, it is best to be aware of dangers that lurk in the depths. Firstly, do not swim away from the shore if you have an open wound as the blood may attract sharks, even if they are for the most part inoffensive creatures. Secondly, if you are unsure about anything, consult the booklets available from staff at most of the private beaches to find out which fish are a danger to humans, such as the scorpionfish, with its poisonous spines, and in particular the stonefish, which turns red when disturbed and can deliver a fatal sting. In addition, do not investigate crevices and cracks as the giant moray eel has powerful jaws, and do not touch the coral as contact with the skin can be unpleasant; in any case it is against the law to touch the coral in the Red Sea.

worth a visit

Aquascope Submarine★

Six departures daily starting at 8am; last departure at 3.30pm; capacity: 24 passengers; E£150. Advanced booking recommended (either at the dock or at your hotel; pick-up at your hotel possible upon payment of a supplement). Embarkation at the Sharm el-Sheikh beach.

Despite its name, this vessel is not a submarine, but a small boat with a bottom consisting of two glass walls in between which passengers can view the coral reefs close to Sharm el-Sheikh. The excursion lasts 1hr 30min and enables non-divers to get an insight into the secrets of the Red Sea. The thickness of the glass makes viewing slightly fuzzy, although the overall sensation is amazing because of the huge quantities of fish and coral that are visible.

The aquascope may look like a submarine, but it stays above rather than below the surface.

outskirts

Diving sites★★★

Transparent turquoise waters – The body of water between the **Ras Mohammed National Park** and **Tiran Island** offers divers some of the best diving they are ever likely to experience. The crystal-clear waters separating these two land masses are home to an incredible diversity of coral and multicoloured fish, mainly as a result of the currents circulating in the Tiran Strait, which flows into the Gulf of Aqaba.

Although there is a huge number of diving sites within the park, we have selected the main ones, described from west to east. Despite the fact that the number of boats authorised to carry divers in this area is limited, these sites attract close to 50 000 divers every year, a figure that is likely to increase in the future.

Ras Mohammed – This is by far the most famous diving site, comprising 20 separate dive sectors. Because of its protected park status, access is restricted *(see above)*. In addition to its magnificent coral, divers can also visit the wrecks of the *Dunraven* (a British vessel that sank in 1876 en route from Newcastle to Bombay) and the *Thistlegorm* (another British ship which went down here during the Second World War); the latter is the most famous wreck in the Sinai and was discovered by Jacques Cousteau.

Ras um Sid – *Access for hotel guests via the private beaches run by them; otherwise head to the left of the lighthouse on the promontory.* This site, located between Sharm el-Sheikh and Naama Bay, is renowned for the outstanding beauty of its coral garden. In the past this area was home to myriad species of coral, although some of these have been badly damaged by overly zealous divers. Note also the gorgonians slightly away from the centre of the site at a depth of 20m/65ft.

According to some sources, 25% of visitors to Sharm el-Sheikh are divers. If you're among them, make sure you bring your diving qualifications with you.

PHOTOGRAPHY
The boutiques and sports shops in Naama Bay all sell disposable underwater cameras to capture your discoveries on film. More sophisticated photographic equipment can be rented for E£20/day from opposite the Red Sea Diving College along the pedestrian promenade.

The Thistlegorm.

RECOMMENDATIONS
Divers should be aware that the islands of Tiran and Sinafir are out of bounds. Elsewhere, dropping anchor is prohibited, so buoys have been placed around dive sites. It is forbidden to feed the fish for fear of destabilising the marine life's ecological balance. As a general rule, do not remove anything from the area in which you are diving.

The Tower – *Opposite Naama Bay, 15m/50ft from the beach.* The Tower consists of a large abyss over 30m/98ft in depth which is better known for its relief than its fish, which are less numerous here. Not for beginners.

Near Garden – *To the NE, 10min from Naama Bay.* Another beautiful site, which is ideal at night, when phosphorescent plankton are visible if you turn off your lamp. Beware of the numerous glass-bottomed boats that come here during the daytime.

Middle Garden – *To the E of Naama Bay.* This sandy, so-called "easy" site does not exceed 12m/39ft in depth and is teeming with fish of every possible description.

Far Garden – *To the E of Naama Bay, just to the north of Middle Garden.* This site, which at no point descends below 15m/49ft, is best explored slowly in order to appreciate the numerous species of small fish here, including the poisonous scorpion fish.

Shark's Bay – *6km/4mi NE of Naama Bay, opposite Beit el-Irsh.* Manta rays can often be seen in the waters around this 20m/65ft fault. Shark's Bay is an ideal site for beginners.

Ras Nusrani – *To the N of Shark's Bay.* Close inshore, this site is full of small fish such as the glass catfish. Beware of the current here.

Woodhouse Reef – *Between Tiran Island and the coast, just to the SW of Jackson Reef.* Of greater interest for its blue water than its limited variety of fish.

The walls of this fault are recognised as being some of the most spectacular in the Sinai.

Jackson Reef – *Between Tiran Island and the coast, 1hr15min from Naama Bay.* This site is solely for experienced divers because of the sharks in this area and the currents in the strait, which are often violent. The reef's vertical wall descends to between 25m/82ft and 40m/131ft. The western section of Jackson Reef is of greater visual interest because of its cooler water.

BASIC DIVING RULES

Recreational diving can be enjoyed by anyone in good physical condition, but because of the weightlessness experienced and the fact that sensations are different under water, a minimum level of training is required. In this respect safety is of vital importance. Equipment problems are extremely rare nowadays, provided you and your diving partner have an efficient supply of oxygen. The main situations that occur tend to be physical in nature, such as: problems with your ears; a feeling of breathlessness or cold; and an increased state of narcosis (particularly below 30m/98ft). If you do experience any of these symptoms, your diving partner should escort you to the surface. Finally, do not go diving if you have had a lot to drink the night before, if you are suffering from heavy jet lag or if you are not feeling on top form.

directory

GETTING ABOUT

By minibus – All the major hotels located outside Naama Bay provide a free shuttle service for guests. The drop-off point is generally at the resort car park at the western end of the pedestrian promenade. Make sure you note down return times as, unusually for Egypt, these buses are normally on time.

By taxi – As in Luxor, taxi prices are very high compared with Cairo. Allow E£20 to get back to your hotel, even if it's relatively close.

By collective taxi – These old minibuses (white with a green stripe) depart from Sharm el-Sheikh and run along the main road as far as the last hotel. They are a far cheaper option than normal taxis (50pt) but

do not operate to the airport. Be sure to give the driver plenty of warning of where you want to get off.

LEISURE ACTIVITIES

As is the case all along this coast water sports take pride of place here, although in Naama Bay these are not for those on a tight budget. As a general guideline, expect to pay the following rates: windsurfing – E£45/hour; snorkelling equipment – E£20-E£30/hour; waterskiing – E£50-E£60/trip; sailing – E£60-E£80/hour; pedaloes – E£35/hour; paragliding – E£120/one person, E£200 for two; banana boat – E£25/hour.

GLASS-BOTTOMED BOATS

The aquascope (see Worth a Visit) is not the only excursion option, even though it's by far the most impressive.

Several other cheaper boats offer 1hr trips from Naama Bay (book at least 1hr in advance). Some of these stop at the most spectacular reefs for 15min to enable those with a snorkel and mask to take to the water.

DIVING CENTRES

Most, if not every hotel in Sharm, has its own diving centre offering generally similar packages. However, although this is an easy option for visitors, not all the diving centres are of the same level in terms of quality and the sites they visit, with some having a conveyor belt-type feel. Exceptions to the rule include the **Subex Centre** (run by the Mövenpick Jolie Ville), and **Sinai Divers**, which is part of the Ghazala Hotel. You are best advised to check out a few centres and compare what they offer before making your decision.

Blue Sea Diving Center – Sharm el-Sheikh (opposite the Iberotel). SSI-, PADI-, CMAS-AND FFSSEME-approved. This centre has decided to use its website for information and direct bookings, mainly to avoid dealing with tour operators: bluesea.sharm@skynet.be. For beginners, including children over 8, the centre offers a stress-free, PADI-approved introductory course which starts off in a swimming pool, before moving on to the beach, taking to the water in a small boat, and finally visiting the sandy White Knight site (1 day, lunch provided at sea). For experienced divers the options are endless, including a visit to the wreck of the Thistlegorm. Contact the centre by e-mail for further information.

Red Sea Diving College – Naama Bay – ☎ (069) 60 01 45; college@sinainet.eg. This PADI-approved school is run by a Belgian diver and Red Sea expert, Alain Sobol, along with a team of 20 divers with a range of languages, including English. Initial instruction is in the sea rather than in a swimming pool. "Junior open water" courses are run for children aged 10 and over.

African Divers – Naama Bay. This long-established and highly respected SSI-, PADI-, NAUI- and CMAS-approved centre offers a more individual approach for participants. For further details, e-mail the centre at: african@sinainet.com.eg/

Camel Dive Club – Naama Bay. SSI-, PADI-, NAUI- and CMAS-approved. A centre run by the renowned Egyptian diver, Hisham Gabr. Particularly recommended for those with disabilities who wish to get involved in this exciting sport.

SHOPPING

With the exception of a few Bedouin arts and crafts, the resort's souvenir shops sell little that is truly local, although there's plenty of choice if all you're after is an expensive T-shirt or a few postcards.

SAFARIS

As with diving, all the hotels are able to organise safaris by minibus or four-wheel drive to places of interest in the surrounding area. Because these excursions have been running for a long time, unpleasant surprises are rare these days, although some of the Bedouin dinners on offer lack an authentic feel. Other less popular, but equally enjoyable options include the following:

Buggy trips – These three-wheel vehicles can be hired for E£75/hr for two people. The excursion includes a stop for mint tea halfway. Departures from near the Ghazala Hotel (bookings possible here) and opposite the Marriott on the side facing the main road.

Horse and camel rides – San Marino, Naama Bay (pedestrian promenade). Excursions include 2hr treks by Arabian horse (E£25), sunset trips by camel (E£20), and visits to Tiran Island (E£30), where nervous swimmers and children can enjoy the calmer waters of the Blue Lagoon (lunch included).

SHARM EL-SHEIKH–HURGHADA BY BOAT

The AMCO company operates fast catamaran services (1hr30min; E£40) between the two towns, although these are not daily and the timetables change frequently. Contact your hotel reception desk to book seats.

INTERNET FACILITIES

Neam Internet – At the end of the shopping street running parallel to the beach. Open 10am-3am. Plenty of computer terminals where you can check and send e-mails. E£20/hr.

WHERE TO STAY IN SHARM EL-SHEIKH
• Moderate

Iberotel Palace – ☎ (069) 66 11 11 – 255 rooms: $200. This luxury hotel near the medina overlooks its private beach. Facilities include three swimming pools, one of which is indoors.

Seti Sharm – ☎ (069) 66 08 70 – 277 rooms: E£255/E£290. Standing next to the Iberotel Palace, the Seti Sharm offers similar services but is kinder on the pocket!

Partner Aida – ☎ (069) 66 07 20 – 149 rooms: $75/152. No direct sea views, but with two beaches reached via a shuttle bus. The hotel has its own diving centre and organises excursions for guests.

WHERE TO STAY AT NAAMA BAY
• Budget

Tropicana Sharm – Along the main road (after the Marriott). ☎ (069) 60 06 52 – 52 rooms: $90/$170. Although the Tropicana is set back from the sea, it has its own private beach (Delta Sharm). The hotel pool enjoys pleasant views of the Sinai mountains.

Pigeon House – Next to the Tropicana Sharm. ☎ (069) 60 09 96 – 40 rooms: E£95 (standard); E£170 (superior). ⊿ The latter are preferable as the standard rooms share a bathroom. The hotel has its own diving centre, but no private beach, although a pool is planned for the near future. A pleasant, inexpensive hotel built in Bedouin style.

• *Moderate*

Mövenpick Jolie Ville – *Opposite the Sharm Conference Center.* ☎ *(069) 60 01 00 – 356 rooms: $270/$290.* In effect a luxury village which extends at right angles to the beach. The hotel can cater for almost all needs, with facilities including tennis courts, a casino, four restaurants and the obligatory dive centre. Accommodation is in bungalows between the road and the beach.

Ghazala Hotel – ☎ *(069) 60 01 50 – 256 rooms: $230; 2 suites: $520.* Next door to the Mövenpick, but with a more family-orientated atmosphere. An attractive hotel with fewer facilities than its neighbour but which makes a fuss of its younger guests. The diving centre here organises excursions.

Sanafir Hotel – ☎ *(069) 60 01 97 – 72 rooms: $116.* Located slightly away from the sea, but with its own beach. The hotel's style is more in keeping with the traditional architecture of the Sinai and as such has less of an international feel about it. Diving school and excursions available.

WHERE TO STAY TO THE EAST OF NAAMA BAY

• *Moderate*

Pyramisa Resort – *Shark's Bay.* ☎ *(069) 60 10 91 – 720 rooms: $120/$180.* This massive complex has gone for the "largest pool in the Middle East" carrot to tempt guests away from Naama Bay. The pool is in fact three separate ones, including one indoors. Facilities include an Internet desk, sauna, squash courts, three beaches and a diving centre.

Le Meridien – *White Knight Beach.* ☎ *(069) 60 24 60 – 408 rooms: $120/$180.* The brand-new, superbly appointed Meridien has been built like a village with the attention to detail befitting a hotel of this standard. The split-level pool has three sections, including a waterfall, and overlooks the White Knight diving site with its rich collection of coral.

When not full of groups, the restaurant's half-board menu is quite remarkable. Other facilities include beach volleyball, tennis, squash, billiards and a dive centre.

• *Expensive*

Jolie Ville Golf Club – *Um Marikha Bay.* ☎ *(069) 60 32 00 – 288 rooms: $210 (mountain view); $230 (sea view); 16 suites: $530; 2 presidential suites: $1 800.* This sumptuous hotel has hosted Presidents Clinton and Mubarak – the latter a regular visitor here – and the King of Jordan. Impeccable service in a magnificent setting, including the most beautiful swimming pool in Egypt, an 18-hole, par-72 golf course, and numerous diving possibilities…but no nightclub!

WHERE TO EAT

• *Budget*

Most visitors generally have lunch and dinner on the beach of their hotel, although there are also a number of independent restaurants behind the beach. These include the following:

Mashy – *Open 24hr a day. Along the main shopping street.* This excellent Lebanese restaurant specialises in seafood, although it also serves *shawerma*, steak and *shish taouk* (chicken with garlic), washed down with a beer or glass of wine. Breakfast is also available. The terrace is large and preferable to the back room.

Andrea – *Open 11am to 2am. Between the Hard Rock Café and Planet Hollywood.* This well-known Egyptian chain serves excellent grilled meats. E£20 for half a chicken with salad and vine leaves. Pitta bread at extra cost. Beer served here.

Safsafa – *In the Asia shopping centre in Sharm el-Sheikh.* E£40 will buy you a delicious fish soup, followed by a healthy serving of spaghetti with seafood or a plate of grilled fish. No beer served here.

BARS AND CAFÉS

Hard Rock Café – *Open 1pm to midnight; disco open midnight to 3am.* Opened in 1998, this was the first HRC in Egypt. The same concept as others around the world, with its rock 'n' roll ambience and items of memorabilia on the walls. Local "Stella" beer on draught, plus a choice of cocktails including the Hard Rock Hurricane. The emphasis in the à la carte restaurant is on American-style cuisine.

Planet Hollywood – *Open 1pm to 3am. Mall 8 in Naama Bay.* Another Western import, with a bar and terrace, American restaurant and free disco. The decor is distinctly Uncle Sam-orientated throughout, with big-screen costumes worn by the likes of Michelle Pfeiffer and Ben Kingsley by the entrance.

Bus Stop – *In the Sanafir Hotel.* You may be asked to pay an entrance fee of E£20. Drinking and dancing in a lively atmosphere.

Bar Fishawy – *Open 9.30am to 3am. Between the resort's two pedestrianised streets.* A good place to enjoy a hot anise, a mint tea or to smoke a hookah pipe away from the crowds.

Tiran Hotel Bar – *On the western end of the beach. Non-guests welcome (E£20 to access the hotel beach).* Delicious fresh fruit juices (melon, mango, strawberry, melon, banana, orange and guava) for E£4 to E£10. Whisky (E£15-E£30) and champagne (E£500) also available.

Café Bedouin – *At the western end of the pedestrian street, near the car park.* This café, a mix of small cushioned niches on several levels, is almost lost in the natural surroundings of the cliff. Fresh fruits, mint tea and fine views of the bay.

excursions

③ ALONG THE GULF OF AQABA

232km/145mi from Sharm el-Sheikh to Taba.
Leave Sharm el-Sheikh on the main road to the airport, pass the Esso petrol station, then head back on yourself to take the road to the right leading to Dahab and Nuweiba.

Dahab♿ *(see DAHAB)*

At km 130 you come to the road leading to St Catherine's Monastery (police checkpoint).

Nuweiba *(see NUWEIBA)*

Taba

Years of diplomatic efforts were needed between Israel and Egypt to settle the problem of the Israeli-built Hilton Hotel. The Sinai was, in fact, returned to Egypt in 1982, although it wasn't until 1989 that the enclave of Taba readopted its role as a border post. Nestling almost at the end of the Gulf of Aqaba, just a stone's throw from Eilat, Taba has little to offer apart from the facilities at the Hilton, and as such acts as no more than a place of transit.

GETTING AROUND THE SOUTHERN SINAI

This desert region of stunning beauty and often merciless drought is criss-crossed by several tarmac roads linking the main permanent settlements. Collective taxis are not as common in the Southern Sinai as in the rest of the country and are not as accustomed to taking foreigners. Bus services do exist, although trying to find out where they're going is harder than you might expect. Also bear in mind that although the region has been cleared of mines, it is unwise to venture away from the main roads. A preferred option might be to sign up for excursions organised and led by Bedouins, if you want to visit sights away from the coastal strip.

A safari on horseback is just one of the memorable excursions organised by hotels in the Sinai.

Pharaoh's Island.

Gezirat Faraoun – *5km/3mi S of Taba. Access by boat between 9am and 5pm: E£13.5; tickets can be purchased from the hotel next door. Entry to the citadel: E£20; tickets can be purchased on the island.* Pharaoh's Island, as it is known to Egyptians, or Coral Island, to Israelis, stands just 250m/275yd off the coast, and is dominated by the ruins of a Crusader fortress and enlarged by the sultan Salah al-Din-Ayyuses, better known as **Saladin** (1138-93). The north-east of the island, in particular, is renowned for its banks of white coral, although they are considered less spectacular than those close to Sharm el-Sheikh.

The Fjord

9km/5.5mi S of Taba. This tiny, well-protected inlet is a popular spot for sun-worshippers, despite its proximity to the road.

THE SIX-DAY WAR: 5-10 JUNE 1967

Sensing a threat from Nasser's pan-Arab policies, combined with the consolidation of military alliances between Egypt, Syria and Jordan, and by the departure of United Nations troops stationed on the borders of the Sinai since the war in 1956, Israel decided to instigate a so-called "preventative" war against Egypt and Jordan in the early hours of 5 June.

Egyptian aircraft on the ground were destroyed by early-morning air attacks by the Israelis, who targeted both the Sinai Peninsula and the West Bank. Their ground troops seized control of Gaza on 6 June, and encircled the Arab sector of Jerusalem, Jericho and Nablus the following day.

The entire West Bank was occupied in two days, and on the evening of 7 June Jordan accepted the ceasefire proposed by the United Nations. On the same day, the "Zionist" offensive reached Sharm el-Sheikh, followed by the east bank of the Suez the day after. Egypt was forced to withdraw from the conflict on the evening of 8 June. On 9 June, Syria's Golan Heights and the town of Kuneita came under repeated attack. A ceasefire was agreed on the afternoon of 10 June. Israel retained possession of its conquered territories until 1973. A fourth Arab-Israeli war, known as the Yom Kippur War in Israel and the War of 6 October 1973 in Egypt, provided evidence of Egypt's renewed military presence and pan-Arab solidarity, particularly during the European oil embargo.

---

directory

WHERE TO STAY

• *Moderate*

Hilton – *Taba Beach (just before the border post).* ☏ *(069) 53 01 40 – 410 rooms: $198.* The Jordanian resort of Aqaba is visible from the rooms facing north-east. Numerous sporting activities on offer, including windsurfing and sailing. Sadly, the current political situation in the Middle East has transformed the Hilton into a transit hotel.

Salah El Deen Beach Resort – *5km/3mi S of Taba, opposite Pharaoh Island.* ☏ *(069) 53 03 40 – 114 rooms: $93.* A superb view and a relaxing beach, part of which is set aside for children. The hotel organises safaris to St Catherine and the Coloured Canyon.

CROSSING THE BORDER

Taba is located just 200m/220yd from Israel and performs the role of border post for the Southern Sinai. At present it is a preferable crossing to Rafah, in the Northern Sinai, which is too close for comfort to the Gaza Strip. A departure tax is payable for those who have travelled outside the Sinai. Israeli immigration will issue a visa free of charge, although the validity can vary from one person to the next. For reasons of diplomatic incompatibility between certain countries, some visitors will not want to have an Israeli stamp in their passport, in which case ask for a "flying visa" – in effect, a separate piece of paper attached to it. Also be aware that the unavoidable Egyptian "Taba Crossing Point" in your passport may cause a problem if you enter the Lebanon or Syria as it shows that you have travelled through Israel.

If you are (re-)entering Egypt from Israel, you cannot obtain an Egyptian visa at the border; this has to be done at the Egyptian Consulate in Eilat, which will issue it within 24hr at a cost of $18. If you're only planning to visit the Sinai (between Taba and Sharm el-Sheikh), a 14-day entry stamp will be issued free of charge. For visitors entering the country from Aqaba, in Jordan, a visa will be issued on the spot in return for 17 Jordanian dinar and a passport photo. If you plan on leaving Egypt and then coming back into the country, ask for a multiple-entry visa.

The border is open 24hr a day, except on Friday and Saturday nights.

St Katherine★★★

The monastery of St Katherine stands in a tranquil, mountainous setting in the heart of the Sinai, at the foot of Mt Sinai where the prophet Moses is said to have received the Ten Commandments. This is primarily a pilgrimage site, visited by pilgrims from three religions who come here to celebrate their faith. An extraordinary sense of fraternity pervades the monastery, which is bathed in the striking light of this mythical and mystical desert.

Location
310km/194mi SE of the Suez Canal, 220km/137mi SW of Nuweiba, in the Sinai Mountains. Access: from Cairo, by bus (E£45; journey time: 9hr); excursions are also organised from most of the hotels in Sharm el-Sheikh, Dahab and Nuweiba.

Name
The monastery is dedicated to St Catherine of Alexandria.

Transcription: سانت كاترين

background

Moses and the Sinai – It was at the foot of one of the mountains of the Sinai Peninsula that the founder of the religion and nation of Israel had his vision of the Burning Bush. On this mountain, now Mt Sinai, Moses later received the Ten Commandments during the Exodus, an episode of the Old Testament which describes Moses leading the people of Israel out of Egypt. For 40 years the Israelites followed what are referred to as "the oldest roads in the world", until the prophet led them into the Promised Land.

Saint Catherine – A popular figure in the Middle Ages, St Catherine was martyrised in Alexandria at the beginning of the 4C by the Emperor Maxentius. Catherine had suggested engaging in a philosophical discussion with this persecutor of the Christians, who sent 50 philosophers to debate with her; she soundly demolished their arguments and was then martyred on the wheel and decapitated for daring to defy the emperor. The emperor's wife was forced to undergo the same torture for speaking up in favour of the young 18 year-old. Legend says that when the executioner cut off the martyr's head, milk, not blood, flowed from her veins. Angels are supposed to have then transported her body to the present-day Mt Catherine in the Sinai and a monastery was later built in her name in the valley.

> **THE EXODUS**
> It is thought that the people of Israel travelled through the Eastern Delta, Amers lakes, the Suez isthmus, the east bank of the Gulf of Suez and the Feran oasis to Mt Sinai.

> **B**efore converting to Christianity and being baptised by a Syrian monk, Catherine's name was Dorothy.

The Monastery of St Katherine was built on the exact spot of the Burning Bush.

ASCENT OF MT SINAI

By camel – A large part of the climb can be undertaken by camel *(hire cost: E£35)*, with the exception of the last 750 steps, which must be tackled on foot. Usually the descent is made on foot, although if you are too tired you can head back down by camel (for an additional E£35). Camel rides are guided by Bedouins.

SHOPPING

Isis Bazaar – The usual tourist souvenirs, as well as carpets made by Bedouin tribes, are on sale in this shop situated next to the post office. The cheapest are made from cotton *(E£10)*; the most expensive from undyed camel wool *(E£95/E£130)*.

WHERE TO STAY

As most visits to St Catherine include an ascent of Mt Sinai, hotels usually offer half-board, enabling visitors to relax after their climb.

• Budget

Morgan Land – *5km/3mi from the monastery, at the entrance of the monastery road junction* – ☎ (069) 47 04 04 – *220 rooms: $55 (old)/$83 (new).* ⌨ The old rooms are a little basic and not as attractive as the newer ones, which overlook a lovely swimming pool. Desert safaris available.

Daniela – *In the village* - ☎ (069) 47 03 79 – 74 rooms: $60.* ⌨ This hotel has a friendly atmosphere and a reasonable level of comfort, and is popular with independent travellers.

• Moderate

Catherine Plaza – *In the village* – ☎ (069) 47 02 89 – 120 rooms: $120.* This pleasant hotel offers clean, comfortable rooms in bungalow chalets. Wine and beer are served at the bar, and the hotel even has Internet access. Camel and mountain-bike safaris can be booked at the hotel.

St Catherine Tourist Village – *At the entrance to the village – 118 rooms: $110.* ⌨ The style of the hotel's chalets is in keeping with the setting (the monastery is visible from the hotel), although the cleanliness of the rooms leaves a little to be desired. Popular with tour groups.

WHERE TO EAT

• Budget

Panorama Restaurant – *In the village, just before the Isis Bazaar.* Simple setting and food, but the only place to eat apart from in the hotels. Pizzas from E£8-E£12, chicken with vegetables E£10, fish E£15. The locals play dominoes and smoke hookah pipes on the terrace.

highlights

Monastery of St Catherine★★

The monastery belongs to the Greek Orthodox Church and has been protected since the time of Muhammad to the present day. As such it has never been conquered nor destroyed.

◀ **Foundation** – The monastery was built in the mid-6C by Emperor Justinian in order to protect the monks who had settled around the Burning Bush. Half a century later, guided by a dream, the monks are said to have discovered the body of the martyr, which they placed in a sarcophagus. The monastery was then dedicated to the saint.

Sunrise over Mt Sinai.

Monastery – *Open all year, 9am-noon, except Fri, Sun and during festivals. No photos or videos allowed inside the building.* The monastery's fortress-like appearance dates back to its foundation when Justinian had the defensive walls built to protect the building from Bedouin tribes. Although the monastery has been rebuilt over the centuries, it has retained its original appearance. It consists of a number of structures dating from different periods, including a 10C mosque, a treasury, a museum, a charnel house, the Chapel of the Burning Bush and a well-stocked library *(not open to the public)* containing the oldest translation of the Gospels, the *Codex Syriacus*.

A document believed to have been signed by Muhammad and a facsimile signed by Napoleon (both evoking the special protection which the monastery enjoys), are on display near the entrance.

Church★★ – This 6C granite church is decorated in Byzantine style and retains two very rare old **doors**★: the first is Fatimid and dates from the 11C; the second is Byzantine, from the 6C. Inside the basilica, the walls are literally covered with icons. Two of these, hanging in the narthex, are particularly worthy of note: a **St Peter**★ (early 6C), whose realistic style brings to mind the Fayum portraits; and a Byzantine-style **Christ Pancrator**★ (7C). The mosaic of the Transfiguration in the apse is the oldest in the Orient, and depicts Christ flanked by Moses, Elijah, Peter, John and James. The sarcophagus of the saint stands to the right of the choir. Opposite the entrance to the church is Moses' well.

The **Burning Bush**★★ still grows in the chevet of the church, having been transplanted from its original site to the chapel of the same name. It is said that no cutting from the bush has ever been successfully propagated.

Gold and silver lamps in profusion inside the church.

Gebel Musa★★★

S of the monastery.

Mt Sinai – Mt Sinai, also known as Mt Moses, the Holy Summit, or Mt Horeb in the Bible, is one of the highest mountains in the 40 000km²/15 444 sq mi of arid desert occupied by the Sinai Peninsula. At an altitude of 2 285m/7 494ft, it is lower than the nearby Mt Catherine (2 637m/8 649ft), as well as the peaks of Umm Shumar (2 586m/8 482ft) and Thabt (2 438m/7 996ft), but far surpasses these in biblical importance, as the Bible states that it was here that God appeared to Moses 1 300 years before the birth of Christ.

It is a tradition in the Muslim, Christian and Jewish faiths to climb Mt Sinai, preferably at night in order to watch the sunrise from the summit and to enjoy the magnificent panoramic **view**★★ over the mountainous expanse stretching interminably eastward. There are two possible routes up to the summit; note that the mountain that can be seen from the monastery is not Mt Sinai.

Ascent of Mt Sinai by the camel path – *The Bedouins and their camels can be found just beyond the monastery.* This route was created by Ibrahim Abbas Pasha in the mid-19C and can be followed either by camel (the easier option) or on foot. Leaving Mt Jethro to the left, and then the valley of Wadi Isbaiyah (an old caravan route linking Palestine to Cairo), the path joins the second route for the last 750 steps to the top of the mountain *(allow 2hr each way by foot or camel)*.

Ascent by the Steps of Repentance – This is the traditional pilgrims' route, which starts 200m/220yd south of the area where camels can be hired, and has 3 700 steps. The path passes a Byzantine chapel, then heads through the Gate of Absolution, where pilgrims of old would confess their sins and receive a certificate as proof of their ascent. It's a strenuous climb, and you need to be reasonably fit. Many visitors follow the camel path to the summit and then take the steps back down to the monastery.

> ## CLIMBING MT SINAI
>
> If you intend to climb the mountain at night, it is best to leave at 3am. Take water and something to eat with you, or you may prefer to buy tea and a snack from the Bedouin stalls that you will pass on your climb. Make sure you are dressed warmly as it can get cold at night, but don't forget a sunhat for the descent to protect against the hot midday sun.

The magnificent view at sunrise more than compensates for the cold, tiring climb up Mt Sinai.

Mt Catherine – A small chapel dedicated to St Catherine has been erected on the summit of this mountain, situated to the south-west of the monastery. The ascent *(4hr 30min one way)* requires a certain level of fitness, although a hut at the top is available for walkers wishing to stay overnight. The views from this point are breathtaking.

outskirts

Gebel Melawan
10km/6mi N of the monastery.
In 1980, President Sadat commissioned a work of "land art" from the Belgian artist Jean Vérame. The artist covered an area of 15km²/5.79sq mi with blue paint, hence the name "Blue Sinai" often given to this area.

Feran Oasis
61km/38mi NW of the monastery.
This 4km/2.5mi-long oasis makes a pleasant stopping-off point on the magnificent road leading to the Monastery of St Catherine. Planted with palm trees, acacias and tamarisk trees, the oasis is inhabited by Bedouins who grow dates, corn and wheat.

A biblical mountain – Gebel Tahuna, the mountain overlooking the oasis, is thought to be the biblical Rephidim, where Moses is said to have observed the victory of the Israelites over the Amalekites. The oasis, believed to be earliest Christian stronghold in the Sinai, was occupied by hermits in the 1C AD, became an episcopal see in the 4C, but saw its monasteries destroyed in the 7C.

The hermitage which is still standing at the entrance to the palm grove is a dependency of the Monastery of St Catherine. The ruins of two churches dating from the 12C can also be seen.

Although the Bedouins lead a more sedentary way of life nowadays, they still retain many of their old traditions.

Suez

The town of Suez is synonymous with the gulf and canal of the same name and is the only settlement along the canal with its roots in Antiquity. From its pharaonic origins, the city became a port for mail between Britain and India as well as a major oil terminal. Following its almost complete destruction during the wars with Israel, it has since been rebuilt and nowadays gives the impression of a city in a state of constant change.

Location
150km/94mi E of Cairo and 92km/56mi S of Ismailiya, at the southern entrance of the Suez Canal. Access: by train from Cairo (3 departures daily; journey time: 3hr); by West Delta bus from Cairo (every half-hour from 6am-8pm; journey time: 2hr).

Name
For many Muslim pilgrims from North Africa, the name Suez symbolises an important step on their route to Mecca.

Transcription : السويس

Famous People
The city and canal are indelibly linked with the name of Ferdinand de Lesseps (1805-94), who finally realised a dream that had existed for two thousand years.

DE LESSEPS
The son of the French consul in Egypt, Mathieu de Lesseps, Ferdinand himself was appointed French consul in Cairo from 1831-38. He left the diplomatic service in 1849 and, with the support of his cousin, the Empress Eugénie, and the viceroy, Mohammèd Said, began the task of digging a canal to link the Red Sea with the Mediterranean.

background

The pharaohs' canal – Nekau, a pharaoh of the 26th Dynasty and son of Psamtek I, began the task of digging a canal linking the Red Sea with Bubastis *(see ZAGAZIG)*, from where ships could sail along the Nile to the waters of the Mediterranean. This "Canal of the Pharaohs", which was completed by the Persian, **Darius I,** at the end of the 6C BC, began at Klymsa; the site of this canal is marked today by the tell which is visible at the entrance to today's canal.

Although maintained by the Romans, this waterway ► gradually silted up during the Byzantine period and was finally abandoned for strategic reasons by the Caliph Mansur in the 8C, despite the fact that maintenance work had been carried out by the caliph Omar during the previous century.

A canal through the Suez Isthmus – We will never know for certain who had the initial idea of digging a canal through the desert between the Red Sea and the Mediterranean. What we do know, however, is that General Amr, who served under the Caliph Omar; the Venetians; the philosopher Leibnitz and the sultans of the Ottoman Empire all contemplated the possibility before **Bonaparte,** the commander in chief of the Eastern army, thought seriously about the question, going so far as to entrust the engineer Lepère with an analysis of the canal's technical feasibility.

The pioneer: Ferdinand de Lesseps – Lepère had envisaged two canals: one towards Alexandria, the other towards Persia *(to the SE of Port-Said)*. He had calculated ► a 10m/33ft gradient between the two bodies of water which would have required the construction of locks; however, the preparatory work undertaken by Bourdaloue in 1847 for the Indian Mail established the difference in level to be almost non-existent.

Armed with this knowledge and the result of research carried out by the Saint-Simonians, De Lesseps decided to move heaven and earth to conquer the desert and build the first canal in the world linking two seas. A friend of **Mohammed Saïd Pasha,** whom he had known

If Herodotus is to be believed, at least 120 000 men began work on Nekau's canal. However, the pharaoh halted the project once an oracle predicted that "he would be working for the benefit of the Barbarians".

SAINT-SIMONIANS
Today, a project such as the Suez Canal would be considered straightforward, yet in the 19C a great leap of faith was required to get it off the ground. The Saint-Simonians, a French movement of social reformers, provided this impetus, completing research carried out during the expedition to Egypt.

The final digging work before the meeting of the waters.

during his career as a diplomat, he obtained a treaty of concession granting him authorisation to finally start work on the canal, despite British objections to the plan.

From dream to reality – Digging started in earnest in 1859 in the area of the future Port Said, and De Lesseps quickly proved himself to be a great leader of men and a talented engineer. His faith in the project overcame one obstacle after another, and on 17 November 1869 the waters of the Red Sea met those of the Mediterranean for the first time under the salvo of a 21-gun salute. The same evening, Emperor Franz-Joseph of Austria and Prince Friedrich-Wilhelm of Prussia made their way to the canal to see the Khedive Ismail Pasha and **Empress Eugénie** officially open the waterway to maritime shipping on board the imperial vessel, *The Eagle*. The sceptics were finally won over, and the distance of 11 696km/7 310mi between London and Calcutta via Cape Town was suddenly reduced to 8 019km/5 012mi.

A military and diplomatic success – Administered until 1956 by the Universal Suez Maritime Canal Company founded by Ferdinand de Lesseps, the waterway would continually act as the backdrop for countless intrigues and battles, mainly because it controlled the route to India.

The decree signed in 1856 granted the company a 99-year concession from the day on which the canal opened to navigation; this concession was to last until 1968. In 1956, in response to the West's refusal to advance loans to finance the Aswan High Dam, **Gamal Abdel Nasser** surprised the world by nationalising the canal, resulting in the halting of maritime traffic for a period lasting four months *(see PORT SAID)*. Shipping was prohibited from using the canal once again on 5 June 1967, during the war against Israel, on this occasion until 5 June 1975, when **President Anwar el Sadat** reopened it less than two years after the end of the War of 6 October (Yom Kippur War) and following extensive mine clearance (730 000 explosive devices in the canal itself and 690 000 along its banks).

Since this period, the waterway linking Suez and Port Said has enjoyed a more peaceful existence.

exploring Suez

Founded in the 15C near the hill of Kom el-Koulsoum, upon which a settlement was built during the Pharaonic period, Suez nowadays exists predominantly as a place of transit. The city's major sights are its bay and the channel into the canal which enables shipping to enter at low tide.

Port Tawfiq

The residential district of Suez, at the entrance to the waterway, is built on an artificial peninsula created from the earth dug from the canal.

FACTS AND FIGURES
This lock-free ship canal is 173km/108mi long. At its widest it measures 200m/242yd with a minimum depth of 20m/65ft. The maximum authorised draught is 16.2m/53ft. Distances are measured from the lighthouse at Port Said, and the journey through the canal takes approximately 15 hours.

Before creating the Statue of Liberty, destined for the harbour in New York City, the sculptor Frédéric Auguste Bartholdi (1834-1904) sketched the colossal statue used as a lighthouse in the city of Suez. However, the project never made it past the initial draft stage.

TOURIST OFFICE
Port Tawfiq,
☎ *(062) 22 35 89.*
Open daily 8am-8pm except Fri (8am to 2pm).

excursions

① THE GULF OF SUEZ VIA THE WEST

Leave Suez along the Corniche. The road runs past the foot of the Gebel Ataqa and close to the small port of Adabiya. It then continues through Ras Ghuba, Bir Odeib and Ghabet el-Bos before reaching Ain Sukhna.

Ain Sukhna

This small town whose name translates literally as "hot spring" occupies a pleasant location that is gradually being transformed by the building of holiday villages.

Zafarana

This stopping-point on the Hurghada road (its name literally means "saffron") is predominantly visited by Egyptians who come here for the weekend.

Follow the road to the left which heads towards Beni Suef across the Arabian desert. After 33km/17mi, turn left at the blue sign and continue for a further 14km/9mi.

Deir el Amba Antonios★

Open all year 9am-4pm (closed during Coptic Holy Week – dates vary). No accommodation available.

Monastery of St Antony – The monastery is dedicated to the first anchorite in Egypt, who had a profound influence on Coptic Christianity. Born in 250 AD, Antony devoted his life to asceticism and headed into the desert, where he lived until the age of 105. Shortly after his death, disciples established a monastery at the foot of the mountains that had sheltered this pious monk during his lifetime. Between the 17C and 19C, the patriarchs of Alexandria and the metropolitans of Jerusalem were chosen from the monastery.

A magnificent setting – Around 30 monks still live in the monastery, which is enclosed by a perimeter wall 1km/0.6mi long and 12m/39ft high and where contemplation is at one with surrounding nature.

The 6C tower at the centre of the monastery is testimony to the continual threat once posed by Bedouin invaders. Access to the tower is via a drawbridge at first-floor level; an old pulley-operated lift fulfils a similar function at the entrance to the monastery. The building contains a series of magnificently coloured **frescoes★★**, some dating from the 7C and 8C, others from the 13C, that are considered to be the most complete of their kind in the Coptic world. Painted on dry plaster, and recently cleaned by Italian restorers, they illustrate the life of the martyrs – most of whom are depicted on horseback – as well as miraculous episodes from their lives. In the choir of the 12C church dedicated to St Antony stands the tomb of the saint surrounded by representations of saints dating back to the 14C; the 13C icons on display have been restored by a team of Russian experts. The palm grove of the 15C St Mark's Church is the place of rest for the allegedly miraculous relics of this saint.

The cave in which St Antony led his reclusive life stands 300m/330yd above the monastery and is accessible via an occasionally steep footpath *(45min round trip)*. The **view★** of the desert plain from the terrace is particularly memorable.

Return via the coast road, which you rejoin to the right. Turn right after 25km/15.5mi and continue for a further 13km/8mi.

Deir el Amba Bola★

Open all year 9am-4pm (closed during Coptic Holy Week – dates vary). No accommodation except by prior arrangement on ☎ (02) 590 02 18.

Monastery of St Paul – This monastery nestles at the foot of a steep-faced rocky depression on the southern side of the Gebel el-Galala which separates the two

Nestling at the foot of the mountains, the Monastery of St Antony is the oldest in Egypt.

> **WORTHY OF NOTE**
> West side: the warrior-saints represented with their martyrdom in the background; south side: the Chapel of the Apocalypse, depicting a bleeding Christ flanked by the Virgin Mary and John the Baptist; east side: the ascetic saints of Egypt (Pachomius, Bishuy, Antony, Maximus, Moses the Black etc).

The Monastery of St Paul was restored in the 18C by the patriarch John XVI following devastating attacks by Bedouin tribes.

monasteries. A cave here sheltered the person referred to by St Jerome as the very first monk; born in 228 AD, Paul of Thebes spent much of his reclusive life here, dying at the venerable age of 113. According to Jerome, he survived on nothing more than a diet of a single piece of bread brought to him every day by a crow.

A protected site – The monastery is similar in layout to the Monastery of St Antony, with a high surrounding wall which once protected the monastic buildings from Bedouin attacks often so fierce that the buildings became known as the "Monastery of the Tigers". Probably founded at the end of the 6C, the monastery has two churches with unusual plans: the south end of the first, which is dedicated to St Paul, has been dug into the cave once inhabited by the saint; the second church, erected above the cave, is dedicated to St Mercurius. The 6C tower, with its drawbridge, houses a wooden-domed chapel dedicated to the Virgin.

From here, you have three choices: either continue along the coast road towards Hurghada, retrace your steps to Beni Suef and the Nile Valley, or return to Suez along the eastern side of the Gulf of Suez.

② THE GULF OF SUEZ VIA THE EAST

Driving tour approximately 780km/483mi.

Pass through the tunnel under the canal (taxis: E£1.5; cars: E£2; minibuses: E£4.5) to the N of the city. All distances below are measured from here.

The road (no 34) soon connects with the coast road, passing three police checkpoints before reaching the turn-off to St Catherine's Monastery.

Uyun Musa
Between the road and the gulf, at km 29.

This tiny oasis nicknamed "Moses' Springs" is of biblical interest because of the two circular wells (the third had dried up), one hot spring with brackish, non-drinkable

It was at Uyun Musa that Moses struck the waters of a stagnant spring with his staff to purify them.

water, and a few palm trees, some of which were topped during the Sinai wars. Small, colourful bracelets and necklaces can be bought here from Bedouin children dressed in attractively embroidered robes.

Ras Sudr

At km 61.

At a distance of 15km/9.5mi beyond Uyun Musa the first holiday village at Ras Sudr comes into view, although the town itself starts at km 66. Sadly, the beach is somewhat blighted by the oil tanks of the nearby refinery and the drilling platforms out in the Gulf of Suez.

This resort is still under construction, with some holiday villages complete.

Hammam Faraun

At km 114.

The "Baths of the Accursed Pharaoh" are located close to a large limestone rock facing the gulf. A spa resort dealing with rheumatism and respiratory problems is to be built in the near future next to this sulphurous spring (70°C/158°F), whose waters flow into the sea creating a cloud of vapour. The name of the spring was given to it by the Bedouins following the legend in which the Pharaoh's army was following Moses, only to be swallowed up in its waters.

From here the coastline improves considerably as the road climbs into the foothills of the Sinai before rejoining the shores of the gulf.

Serabit el-Khadim

Turn left at km 136 and continue for a further 40km/25mi. Only accessible to 4WD vehicles.

The "Heights of the Servant" is home to an old turquoise mine that has been exploited since the Old Kingdom. One temple, which dates from the 12th Dynasty, is dedicated to the goddess Hathor, "she who sews turquoise to create stars"; the second sanctuary is dedicated to Soped, a hawk god who watched over the eastern frontier and protected the track leading to the mine.

At km 207 you can either turn left along the road to St Catherine's Monastery (see ST CATHERINE) or continue straight on towards Sharm el-Sheikh.

③ SHARM EL-SHEIKH

See SHARM EL-SHEIKH – Gulf of Aqaba driving tour 460km/285mi.

WHERE TO STAY EN ROUTE

The Moon Beach Hotel is located 38km/24mi south of Ras Sudr, alongside the gulf.
☎ *(069) 40 15 00 – 71 rooms: $90 (half-board).*

Apart from the good beaches here, this part of the coast is a popular destination for windsurfers.

VISITING THE TEMPLES

To visit these you will need to head for the village of Sheikh Barakat (at km 40, follow the track to the left by the white dome). From here, hire a guide to take you to Serabit el-Khadim, located a further 7km/4.5mi away.

directory

WHERE TO STAY

• **Budget**

White House – *El-Geish Street* –
☎ *(062) 33 15 50 – 45 rooms: E£75.*
Although some features are in need of attention, this clean, centrally located hotel is popular with young travellers.

• **Moderate**

Red Sea Hotel – *13, El-Riad Street* –
☎ *(062) 33 43 02 – 81 rooms: E£259/293.*
This is the best hotel in Suez, with rooms overlooking the entrance to the canal and Asia. The restaurant on the sixth floor enjoys a fine view of the gulf. No alcohol served.

Green House Hotel – *Port Said Street* –
☎ *(062) 22 33 30 – 48 rooms: E£260.*
Located to the east of the city on the corner of the Corniche running along the bay, this pleasant hotel (notwithstanding the dreadful entrance hall) has a number of rooms overlooking the gulf as well as a circular swimming pool to the rear.

Summer Palace Hotel – *Port Tawfiq* –
☎ *(062) 22 44 75 – 70 rooms: E£200.*
Sadly, the only palatial feature of this hotel is its name, as apart from its excellent position along the bay, the prices are far too expensive for dusty rooms that have seen better days.

WHERE TO EAT

• **Budget**

Abu Ali – *El-Geish Street (on the corner of El-Hareem Street).* Unpretentious decor, but good food, where E£55 will buy you squid, prawns, crab and dessert. Beer on sale except during religious festivals.

Fish Restaurant – *As-Salaam Street (near El-Geish Street).* An eatery serving large portions of freshly caught fish.

The Nile Valley
and its Ancient Sites

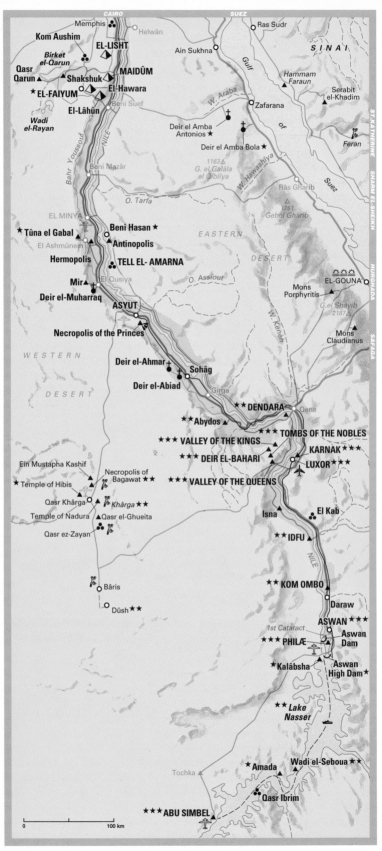

Abu Simbel★★★

As a result of the extraordinary salvage operation led by UNESCO in the mid-1960s, Abu Simbel has become famous across the globe. This magnificent Ancient site, situated close to the border with the Sudan, stands in splendid isolation on the banks of Lake Nasser. The Great Temple of Abu Simbel, carved directly into the rock-face, is one of the most unforgettable sights of Ancient Egypt.

Location
1 195km/746mi S of Cairo, 253km/158mi S of Aswan, on the left bank of Lake Nasser. Access: by road from Aswan (re-opened in 2001), by cruise ship or by plane (daily flights operated by Egyptair).

Name
The name Abu Simbel is a corruption of the Ancient Egyptian *Ipsambul.*

Transcription: أبو سمبل

Famous People
Rameses II was deified in a temple hewn "for eternity" from the rock of the Libyan mountains.

History
The site dates from the 19th Dynasty of the New Kingdom.

> **AERIAL VIEWS**
> For a good view of the site when landing at Abu Simbel, make sure that you ask for a window seat on the left side of the plane.

background

The Aswan High Dam – The Aswan High Dam was built between 1960 and 1971 and involved the flooding of all the inhabited areas of Lower Nubia between Aswan and the Sudanese border. Among the many temples threatened by the creation of this man-made lake, those at Abu Simbel presented the greatest technical headache.

A herculean task – In 1963, just a few years before the flooding, Egypt and UNESCO entrusted a group of French, German, Italian, Swedish and Egyptian companies with the task of dismantling, transporting and rebuilding the two rock-temples at Abu Simbel. The temples were to be rebuilt block by block, 65m/213ft higher than their original location. This was the simplest and least expensive of the many solutions that had been put forward since 1960.

> **AN UNKNOWN SITE**
> Before the salvage operation, the Abu Simbel temples were completely unknown to the general public. It was the Egyptologist **Christine Desroches Noblecourt** who brought them to the attention of the international community and UNESCO.

The operation was supported by 50 countries and cost in the region of $40 000 000. For almost five years, some 1 000 people worked here in average temperatures of 50°C. Specialists included Italians from Carrara, the home of the world-famous marble.

NILOMETER
Although the most famous nilometer is at Aswan, the one at Abu Simbel is the most accurate, as it is situated downstream of the dam. Installed during the salvage operation, it is the only Nilometer that still measures the flooding of the Nile.

Ramesside architecture is built on a gigantic scale. Among the rock temples built by Rameses II in Nubia, this is undoubtedly the most impressive.

Saved by high technology – The site was protected from the floodwaters of the Nile by the construction of a temporary dike 350m/1 148ft in length. At the same time, the hills above the temples were levelled, removing 300 000t of rock. In order to protect the temples from vibration, the façades were covered with sand, leaving a passageway to the interior. The next stage was the most delicate of the whole operation, as the pink Nubian sandstone had become very crumbly over the years. The whole complex had to be cut into more than 1 000 blocks, each of which was attached with epoxy resin to copper bars so that it could be lifted and then moved to the top of the cliff by travelling crane. Altogether 15 000t of rock was moved, with the Great Temple itself weighing 11 500t; the latter was reassembled around a concrete frame, following the same orientation as on the original site. This remarkable operation was completed in 1968 and scarcely a blemish is visible on the Ancient structures.

The site – Though it is possible to stay overnight, most visitors come here in groups on day visits by plane and are consequently rather rushed. Abu Simbel is a photographer's paradise, but if you do move away from your group, make sure you keep a careful eye on the time!

highlights

⊙ *Site open all year, 7am-5pm. E£36; students E£19.5; camera permit E£5; video permit E£25.*

A broad esplanade stretches down to the banks of Lake Nasser in front of the two temples.

Great Temple★★★
It was probably for a combination of political and economic reasons that Rameses II built this temple so far from his capital at Thebes. At that time Egypt imported goods from the African hinterland, including gold mined in the Nubian desert, quartz from Wadi el-Alaki, and diorite from the area to the west of Abu Simbel. By building this temple, the Pharaoh hoped to pacify a region of economic importance, while symbolically protecting the borders of his kingdom.

Façade★★★ – The façade, cut in the form of a pylon into a cliff 33m/108ft high and 38m/124ft wide, faces east and is preceded by a terrace decorated with alternating statues of the king and the falcon-headed god Horus. A niche above the entrance gate houses the statue of Ra-Horakhty (the sun at its zenith, represented by a falcon-headed figure) flanked by low-reliefs depicting the king; a hieroglyphic rebus states that the temple is dedicated to the deified god. The façade is surmounted by a cornice decorated with 22 jackal-headed monkeys.

The Colossi of Rameses II during the salvage operation of the Great Temple.

The **four colossi**★★★ represent Rameses II, who is seated and looking towards the rising sun. The Pharaoh is depicted wearing a *nemes*, *pschent* and a false beard, and the royal cartouche is engraved into the stone, under the chest and on the arms. Carved directly into the rock the statues measure 20m/65ft high and are therefore larger than the Memnon colossi to the west of Luxor (forehead 0.59m/1.93ft; nose 0.98m/3.20ft; eyes 0.84m/2.75ft; mouth 1.1m/12.64ft; hands 2.64m/8.65ft). The statues are realistic in style, as though the artist was attempting to emphasise the impression of an all-powerful god, while giving a sense of unity and calm. Despite their size, the statues are perfectly proportioned. Smaller statues can be seen next to and between the legs of the larger statues; these represent figures such as Queen Tuya (mother of Rameses II), Nefertari (his wife) and Princess Meritamun (his daughter). On the approach to the statues, note the many inscriptions in different languages, carved by visitors ranging from Greek soldiers during the Saite Period to modern-day European travellers.

THE BATTLE OF QADESH

The Syrian town of Qadesh, situated on the upper reaches of the Orontes, was twice the subject of a political struggle between Egypt and its Eastern neighbours: once when the town was seized by Thutmose III, and again in the fifth year of the reign of Rameses II. Muwattali, the King of the Hittites, had just established the largest-ever coalition against Egypt, whose eastern borders he was threatening. Rameses II reacted swiftly, marching on Syria at the head of four army divisions. Believing, wrongly, that the enemy had withdrawn to Aleppo, Rameses camped at the gates of Qadesh with just a single division. Muwattali attacked this division and succeeded in routing the Egyptians. The inscription known as the *Poem of Pentaur* recounts that it was the personal courage of Rameses II that reversed the situation, leading the Egyptians to a glorious victory. However, history is more circumspect and we know that on this occasion Rameses was neither victor nor vanquished, and that he owed his good fortune to the last-minute reinforcements provided by one of his delayed divisions. Muwattali even retained Qadesh, although a large number of the Syrian elite were killed during the battle.

EGYPTIAN ARMS

Composed mainly of mercenaries, the army of Rameses II had at its disposal a selection of bows, spears, curved two-edged swords, and leather shields and breastplates covered with bronze scales. The two-wheel chariot was driven by an officer, who was flanked by a soldier, and pulled by two horses (the Hittites' chariots carried three men).

Interior★★★ – Dedicated to Amun-Ra, the Great Temple of Abu Simbel is a *speos*, the term given to a temple cut into a rock-face. The temple is 62m/203ft deep and follows the traditional plan of open-air temples.

Decorated with vultures with outstretched wings symbolising the sky, the ceiling of the **pronaos** is supported by **eight Osirid pillars**★, typical elements of a temple courtyard, representing Osiris with the features of Rameses II (those to the south wear the crown of Upper Egypt, those to the north the *pschent*). The low reliefs on the walls illustrate military achievements, with the north wall depicting the famous **Battle of Qadesh**★★. The scenes represented on the lower register include the king seated on his throne, holding counsel, his chariot and guard, and Hittite spies being beaten; the Egyptian camp with horses and soldiers setting up camp; and the departure of the troops. On the upper register, the king is depicted on his chariot firing arrows at the enemy, with the citadel of Qadesh and the Hittites also depicted. A middle register shows the cavalry engaged in combat; the end of the battle can be seen in the top right-hand corner, with the king standing in his chariot, watching the victims being counted, the hands and sexual organs of whom have been cut off. Opposite, on the south wall, scenes of religious offerings can be seen above scenes of war, one of which is a lively representation of the king and his three sons at the head of their army.

Rooms on both sides of the pronaos have unfinished decor and are surrounded by benches once used for offerings. A door leads to two chapels decorated with scenes of offerings, which in turn lead to the **naos** where

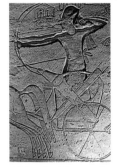

A triumphant Rameses II on his chariot during the Battle of Qadesh.

four statues have been carved into the rock; they are, from left to right, Ptah, Amun-Ra, Rameses II and Ra-Horakhty. Rameses II is represented as an equal of the gods, as is proclaimed on the rebus in a niche on the temple façade, next to the divine triad. An unusual feature of this temple is that twice a year, on 20 February (the date of the king's birthday) and 20 October (the date of his coronation), the rays of the sun shine directly on to three of the four statues (with the exception of Ptah, whose statue is uncrowned). This shows the precision with which the temple was built, although this phenomenon now occurs a day later than originally planned.

Temple of Hathor★★

To the right of the Great Temple dedicated to the king (to the north) stands the Small Temple or Temple of Hathor devoted to Queen Nefertari. This temple also faces east, albeit a little out of line, and is dedicated to the cow-goddess, who was believed to give birth to the sun every morning.

Façade★★ – Less imposing than the Great Temple, but also cut in the shape of a pylon, the façade consists of a remarkable succession of seven buttresses rising up to the cliff, with six 10m/32ft-tall **colossi★★** carved into the rock between them. From left to right, these figures represent: Rameses II wearing the crown of Upper Egypt; Nefertari dressed as Hathor and crowned with horns in the shape of a lyre (with two tall plumes encompassing the solar disc); a deified Rameses II wearing the crown of Upper Egypt; a deified Rameses II wearing the *pschent* crown; and Nefertari and Rameses II wearing the *nemes* headcloth crowned with the solar disc. Note that Rameses and Nefertari both stand with their left leg thrust forward, indicating that they are both alive. A frieze of cobras (the *uræus* of the goddess Wadjyt), similar to the one in the southern courtyard of Djoser's funerary complex at Saqqarah, protects the entrance to the temple.

Interior★★ – This *speos* is smaller than that of the Great Temple and the ceiling of the **pronaos** is supported by **six Hathor-headed pillars**. The low reliefs on the north and south walls depict scenes of offerings, showing Hathor conferring eternity on the king; Nefertari presenting the sistrum (the musical instrument of the goddess Hathor) to Anuket, the goddess of the cataract; and the king offering papyrus. The queen's cartouches protected by vultures can be seen above the doorway of the vestibule, situated to the rear of the room; the vestibule in turn leads into the naos. It is here between two Hathor-headed pillars that the statue of the goddess Hathor (in poor condition) appears to emerge from the rock to protect Rameses II, who is thus made immortal.

MAKING THE DESERT BLOOM
An ambitious project is currently under way at Tochka, 70km/44mi west of Abu Simbel, in the middle of the desert. In this landscape of scorpions and soaring temperatures, 7 000 workers are digging an artificial oasis with a view to increasing the country's percentage of cultivated land (5% of the country along the banks of the Nile) to 25%. Called "Mubarak", the world's largest pumping station is being built here to open up a canal that will supply water to this isolated oasis.

directory

SOUND AND LIGHT SHOW
Without a doubt, the most spectacular of all the sound and light shows in Egypt, although it can only be enjoyed by cruise passengers or visitors staying overnight.

WHERE TO STAY
• *Moderate*
Nefertari – ☎ (069) 40 05 08 – 100$. This hotel enjoys an excellent location overlooking Lake Nasser and has a good restaurant (E£40). Campers can pitch their tents nearby.

Aswan★★★

Aswan, the southernmost city in Egypt, enjoys a superb location on the border with Nubia, overlooking the River Nile and downstream of the first cataract. Visitors are attracted to the city by the archaeological site of Philae, as well as by the town's clean air, friendly welcome and tranquil atmosphere, a refreshing contrast to the noise and chaos of Cairo.

Location

913km/570mi S of Cairo, 213km/133mi S of Luxor, on the right bank of the Nile, just N of Lake Nasser. Access: most tourists arrive by cruise ship from Luxor, but the city is also accessible by plane with Egyptair from Cairo or in convoy by road from Luxor (see LUXOR for more details). Bus services also operate to Cairo (12hr), Luxor (5hr), Esna (3hr) and Kom Ombo (1hr).

> **C**ruise ships are moored next to each other on the right bank of the river, bringing with them a feeling of modernity to this peaceful, Ancient setting.

Name

The Ancient Egyptians referred to the city as Swenet ("the market"); the Greeks later knew it as Syene (the root of the word "synesite", once used to describe the famous rose granite of Aswan and now used for another stone). The Copts called the city Souan, which then became Aswan in Arabic.

Transcription: أسوان

Famous People

Aswan has long been popular with the British, having been frequented by distinguished visitors such as Shelley, Winston Churchill and Agatha Christie, many of whom would have enjoyed the peace and colonial grandeur of the hotel situated opposite Elephantine Island.

CLIMATE

Aswan partly owes its reputation to its clear blue skies and healthy climate, which have attracted visitors to the city since the early 20C. Although temperatures can easily climb above 40°C/104°F in summer, the heat is usually bearable as the climate is remarkably dry.

background

From ivory to granite – The city was founded by the pharaohs and originally consisted only of **Elephantine Island**, the capital of the 1st nome of Upper Egypt. The name of the island comes from the word *yeb*, meaning "elephant" in Egyptian, which suggests that ivory from the African hinterland was perhaps brought here. It is extremely likely that the city was of major economic

Feluccas on the Nile near Kitchener Island.

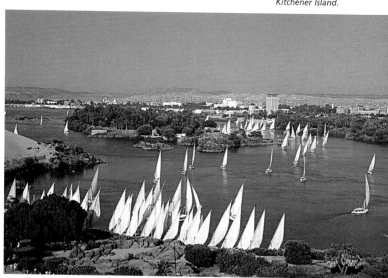

importance, as goods arriving from Nubia by caravan were traded in Aswan before being transported downriver. Goods included gold, iron, semi-precious stones such as obsidian, ebony, spices, Arabic gum, ostrich eggs and feathers, tiger skins, hunting dogs, monkeys and giraffes.

An eventful history – Most port activity took place around the aristocratic Elephantine Island, where a large garrison was stationed to watch over this strategically important point.

Under the Greeks, the city developed on the right bank of the river and took the name Syene. During the Roman period, disgraced generals were sent here, while in the Christian era the city became a bishopric. In subsequent years the city that would later become known as Aswan was fought over by various Nubian and Upper Egyptian tribes, and experienced centuries of unrest before its fortunes were revived at the time of the construction of the High Dam.

The Nubians – As the name suggests, the Nubians are descendants of the Nubae, a large Libyan tribe that once dominated the area of present-day Ethiopia and which the Egyptians referred to as "the land of the Kush" *(see Nubian Museum below)*. With the construction of the two dams upstream of Aswan, the lands occupied by the Nubians in Lower Nubia were flooded as part of the Lake Nasser project, and they were forced to leave the date palms and *sakiehs* (waterwheels) which symbolised their culture and of which they were so proud. Moved to land between Aswan and Luxor, they have recreated their world in the outlying areas of Aswan and Kom Ombo, where they were invited to settle en masse by the Egyptian government. Today, Nubians can be seen in all of the country's large cities, including Alexandria, where their *gamma'iyyat*, a kind of Nubian club, provides a solid support network for Nubian newcomers.

exploring Aswan

ALONG THE NILE

Aswan is undeniably the most attractive city in Egypt, with on one bank of the Nile administrative buildings, travel agents and hotels, and, on the other, the desert landscape of the left bank and the long, green Elephantine Island situated in the middle of the Nile.

More than anywhere else in Egypt, this is the perfect setting for Egypt's most famous waterway, showing the country at its most picturesque. Tamed by the dam, the sparkling blue river flows smoothly and slowly, dotted here and there with the white sails of feluccas. Sitting and watching the sunset at Aswan, with the feluccas silently weaving in and out of the islands on the river, is one of the most memorable experiences of a trip to Egypt.

Corniche★★

Most visitors fresh off their cruise ship will make their way along the corniche. The difference in topography between the north and south of the country is immediately striking: from Luxor the Nile winds its way through a wide fertile valley which only starts to narrow just before Aswan. Suddenly the landscape changes as tall, granite cliffs close in on the river; the faster waters of the first cataract are not far from here. Both the landscape and the atmosphere of the city with its Nubian inhabitants are unmistakeably African.

Feluccas are often besieged by local children, who offer to sing for tourists in exchange for a few piastres.

Felucca Boat Trips★★★

A trip on the Nile in a traditional felucca is one of the highlights of any holiday in Aswan – or Egypt, for that matter. The slow, lazy rhythm of the boat is a welcome contrast to the frenetic pace of modern life or the often rushed itinerary of an organised tour. Feluccas glide gen-

TROPIC OF CANCER

During a lunar eclipse in the 5C BC, the Greek Anaxagorus noticed the circular shape of the shadow made by Earth. Two centuries later, his compatriot Eratosthenes, a librarian at the Mouseion in Alexandria, took the first measurement of the circumference of our planet at Syene, now Aswan. Noticing that the walls of a well in Syene were lit perpendicularly during the summer solstice, he measured the angle of the sun's rays during the same solstice at Alexandria and, calculating a distance of 5 000 stadia (the measuring unit used in Ancient Greece) between the two towns, arrived at a circumference of approximately 250 000, ie almost 44 000km/27 500mi, within 10% of the actual measurement. His observation of the sun's rays at Syene led experts to long believe that the city stood on the Tropic of Cancer, which is, in fact, situated approximately 50km/31mi further south.

tly and silently along the river, allowing passengers to sit back, relax and do nothing but enjoy the scenery, occasionally sipping the tea offered by the boat's Nubian crew. A felucca is a small, narrow boat with elegant white sails ▶ which can be either sailed or rowed. In Aswan, the boats are moored along the Corniche and a range of excursions are on offer, ranging from a short trip around the Corniche to Kitchener Island or Elephantine Island, to a longer trip as far as Sehel Island. It is even possible to hire a felucca for several days, sailing upstream to Kom Ombo and Edfu *(see Directory)*.

> **A**lthough there is an official hourly rate for renting a felucca, don't be afraid to approach a number of different boats and haggle before deciding on a trip. Feluccas can carry between one and eight passengers *(see Directory)*.

Elephantine Island★★

Opposite the Corniche. Access by boat for 25pt.
Not much remains of the rich past of this fertile island. The temples of Thutmose III and Amenhotep III – destroyed by the Turks in 1822 – are now little more than ruins. The island has been excavated by a German archaeological team since the 1970s.

Antiquities Museum – *Open Sun to Thur, 8am-5pm. E£10; students E£5. A baksheesh is recommended if visiting the garden.*
This charming, if slightly old-fashioned museum was founded in a colonial villa in 1912 to house material rescued from the construction of the first Aswan dam; its collection includes items ranging from the Predynastic Period to the Late Period, discovered in Aswan and Lower Nubia. Exhibits include a number of interesting artefacts, such as a **mummy of a ram** in a sarcophagus, statues of nomarchs of Elephantine, amulets and **schist palettes**, one of which is in the shape of a rhinoceros, an animal unknown in Egypt at that time.

> **L**ate afternoon is the perfect time for a stroll★ on the island. As the sun starts to set over Aswan, turning the sky a glorious palette of pinks and reds, the views of the museum's garden, the Nubian village and the ruins of the Ancient city provide an unforgettable sight.

Nilometer – *To the S of the island.* Mentioned by Strabo in the 1C, this nilometer was probably built during the Ptolemaic period. Discovered in 1822, it has a long staircase which leads down a shaft to a graduated ladder once used to measure the Nile inundation: when the water covered 24 marks the country was sufficiently irrigated for a successful harvest. The device also enabled officials to calculate the tax to be levied on the harvest.

Temple of Khnum – *Currently under restoration.* Only parts of the foundation and a few columns remain from this temple built for the most part during the reign of Nectanebo II (30th Dynasty), although it was added to ▶ by Alexander II. The ruins have been painstakingly excavated by a team of German archaeologists to reveal a courtyard, a hypostyle hall and a large granite doorway decorated with scenes of offerings.

Temple of Satet – *Currently under restoration.* Recently excavated and partially rebuilt, this New Kingdom temple dating from the 18th Dynasty was dedicated to Khnum's wife, the protector of granite quarries. The walls consist of the original blocks bearing fragments of decoration and blocks which have been added to complete the scenes, giving a much clearer idea of how the original decor would once have appeared.

> **KHNUM**
> This ram-god was worshipped on Elephantine Island during the Old Kingdom. Represented pouring water from a vase, he was believed to be the guardian of the source of the Nile.

The majestic royal palm trees on Kitchener Island provide an oasis of greenery and birdsong.

Kitchener Island★★

Between Elephantine Island and the left bank of the Nile. Access by boat (NB: there is no ferry at the Botanic Garden landing stage; a ferry operates a shuttle service on Friday (E£1) near the Hotel Abu Simbel on the Corniche). Private motor boats are available and ply the route for E£5 to E£15 – remember to haggle! Open all year from 8am-6pm (5pm in winter).

Earl Kitchener of Khartoum – The island is named after **Horatio Herbert Kitchener** (1850-1916), commander-in-chief of the Egyptian army. In 1898, Kitchener avenged the defeat of the Sudanese expedition led by General Gordon. After a British ultimatum issued to the French, he obtained the retreat of the general and explorer, Jean-Baptise Marchand de Fachoda, whose official mission had been to place France in a position of power on the Nile.

Botanical Garden★ – This peaceful and attractive oblong-shaped island is more generally and aptly known as the Island of Flowers. The botanical garden here dates from 1898 and was started by Lord Kitchener, who was presented with the island after his successful military campaign in the Sudan. This haven of greenery, with its plants from the Far East, India, and equatorial and sub-equatorial Africa, sits amid a delightful landscape, providing a soothing contrast to the stark cliffs on the left bank of the river.

◄ Plant-lovers will note a number of different species of sycamore, palm, ebony, teck, eucalyptus, kapok and tamarisk trees in the lush gardens, as well as medicinal plants and a multitude of colourful bushes such as bougainvillea and jasmine.

REST IN THE SHADE
A peaceful haven away from the heat of the midday sun, the island is the perfect place for a leisurely **stroll**★, except on Fridays when it is packed with locals from Aswan who come here for a picnic.

Mausoleum of Aga Khan III

On the left bank, opposite the southern part of Elephantine Island. Not open to the public since the Begum's death.

Mohammed Shah, Aga Khan III, the 48th imam of the Ismaili sect of Shi'ite Muslims, chose to be buried on the left bank of the city where he came to spend a few months each winter, drawn here by the mild climate of the region. His mausoleum is perfectly in tune with its peaceful setting and is built on a barren hillside with a magnificent **view** of Aswan and the river below.

Mausoleum – The domed mausoleum is reminiscent of a small fortress, and is similar in design to the Fatimid tombs of Cairo, taking particular inspiration from the El-Guyushi Mosque on the Moqattam Hill in the capital. Built in granite and pink sandstone, it houses a Carrara marble sarcophagus decorated with inscriptions taken from the Koran. Although the Aga Khan was a man who demonstrated extravagant and luxurious tastes during his lifetime – during anniversary celebrations it was his custom to have himself weighed in gold, platinum or diamonds – his mausoleum is a building of delightful and harmonious simplicity.

THE BEGUM'S ROSE
The Begum (the title is equivalent to Princess), the Aga Khan's wife, lived in the white villa below the mausoleum. When in residence it was her custom to lay a red rose on the tomb of her husband every morning. She died in 2000.

The mausoleum of Aga Khan III overlooking Aswan.

Deir el Amba Samaan

On the left bank, 1km/0.6mi NW of the mausoleum. Access from the Tombs of the Nobles. Open daily, except Mon, 7am-4pm. E£12; students E£6.

Perched on a hill overlooking the desert valley and protected by sand dunes, the fortress-like **Monastery of St Simeon** occupies an evocative site inhabited by anchorites since the beginning of Christianity. Originally dedicated to Amba Hadra, a local saint, the building, which is now in ruins, dates back to the 7C and was attacked in 1173 by Sultan Salah al-Din al-Ayyubi, better known as Saladin. Subsequently pillaged by Bedouin tribes, the monastery was finally abandoned in the 13C as a result of water shortages.

> **T**he ruins blend in perfectly with the surrounding desert landscape. The stone and mud-brick fortifications are damaged, but still standing, and are punctuated at intervals by tall defensive towers.

Ruins – The main entrance, to the east, leads into the ruins of a cruciform church where damaged paintings can be made out on the central apse (Christ Pantocrator flanked by angels in the cul-de-four and the Apostles on the north wall). On the west side of the church, cells formed naturally in the rock were used by the first anchorites who settled here. One of these is decorated with paintings that predate the construction of the monastery. The ruined monastery building has retained many features intact; still visible are the monks' cells, the refectory, a kitchen, an oven, a wine-press, and two basins, one used for water, the other for salt.

Tombs of the Nobles★

On the left bank. Access by boat (ferry) for E£1 from the N of the Corniche. Open daily, except Mon, 7am-4pm (5pm in summer). E£12; students E£6; camera permit E£5; video permit E£30. A visit early in the day is advisable.

There are approximately 40 of these tombs cut into the cliff-face and staged in terraces. The tombs date back to the Old and Middle Kingdoms and are the final resting place for both nomarchs and other dignitaries from Elephantine. Although most of the tombs are badly damaged and difficult to reach, five of them are open to the public and are well worth a visit, as much for the splendid views of Aswan and the river as for the tombs themselves.

Sirenput II was commander of the "southern country" garrison during the reign of Amenemha I (12th Dynasty).

Tomb of Sirenput II – *No 31.* 12th Dynasty. The corridor separating the two chambers is flanked by two rows of three niches, each housing a mummiform statue of the deceased sculpted into the rock. In the first chamber, the six pillars and walls are decorated with *trompe-l'oeil* horizontal stripes in black, grey, yellow and red imitating the natural striation of the cliff. In the second chamber, the four pillars are painted with portraits of the deceased, showing him in scenes with his son and his wife, the priestess of Hathor.

Tomb of Mekhu and Sabni – *Nos 25 and 26.* 6th Dynasty. This double tomb was built for the king of Upper Egypt's chancellor during the reign of Pepy II, and his son. The painted decor is interesting and includes hunting and fishing scenes; one scene in particular provides an insight into the different species of fish found in the Nile.

Tomb of Harkhuf – *No 34n.* 6th Dynasty. The four-pillared room in this tomb is also adorned with *trompe-l'oeil* paintings imitating the rock stratum. Inscriptions relating to expeditions taken by the deceased on behalf of the Pharaoh Merenra can be seen on either side of the door.

Tomb of Sirenput I – *No 36.* 12th Dynasty. This is the largest of the tombs and also the best decorated. Finely sculpted doorjambs and six pillars decorated with low reliefs remain from the doorway which once led into the courtyard preceding the tomb.

> **DETAIL**
> The deceased, the high priest of Satet, is represented to the left and right of the tomb entrance (with his harem to the right). The badly damaged paintings in the four-pillared chamber depict nautical scenes.

Tomb *no 34f*, which was transformed into a chapel during the Christian period, is also open to the public. The tombs of Khunes *(34h)*, Sekta *(34g)* – unusually containing decoration from the First Intermediary Period – and Heqa-Ib *(35d)* are currently closed.

Sehel Island★

5km/3mi SW of Aswan. Access by boat from the Corniche. See Directory. Bring water and a sun hat, and make sure that you are appropriately shod as the rocks and sand can be very hot.

Much less visited by tourists than the two islands described above, Sehel Island makes for a pleasant excursion by felucca or motor boat. Although the island's archaeological remains may not be of great interest, its friendly Nubian village and wild landscapes provide a complete contrast to Aswan. Local children often accompany visitors on their walk through the island, offering necklaces and rag dolls for sale; the older villagers are more reserved, but seem to take the influx of tourists in their stride.

Famine Stele★ – *Open 7am-5pm (6pm summer); E£20.* The climb to the top of the hill with the sun beating down on the granite rocks of the island is challenging, but the magnificent **view★** of Aswan, with the Libyan Desert in the distance, and the famous **first cataract** at the foot of the hill, believed in Ancient times to be the source of the Nile, makes the effort worthwhile.

The stele known as the "famine stele" stands among the rocks and is surrounded by blocks of stone covered with inscriptions dating from the Middle Kingdom to the Ptolemaic period, many of which record expeditions south beyond the first cataract, or offer prayers of gratitude for a safe return. The famine stele was engraved in 187 BC and therefore dates from the reign of Ptolemy V Epiphanes of the Ptolemaic Dynasty. The text on the stele attributes the conquest of Nubia to King **Djoser** (3rd Dynasty), stating that the ram-god Khnum intervened and put an end to a period of unrest at that time: "[...] we had little to eat, everyone was frustrated by their harvest. We could no longer walk, children cried, men were beaten and the old were sad at heart; [...] Even the courtesans had nothing, the temples closed and sanctuaries turned to dust. Everything that was alive suffered."

The stele recounts how Egypt suffered a seven-year famine as a result of the failure of the annual Nile inundation during the reign of Djoser.

The typically Nubian dwellings on Sehel Island form a picturesque sight in the clear light of southern Egypt.

THE FIRST CATARACT

The first of the six cataracts – or waterfalls – of the River Nile is situated just beyond Sehel Island. The cataract is no longer the impressive sight it once was, as the construction of the Aswan High Dam has reduced it (and the other five cataracts) to little more than a series of small rapids, where granite boulders block the course of the river. The cataract once formed the natural border of the Egyptian kingdom, and although the pharaohs temporarily conquered Nubia, it remained a psychological barrier to which the borders of the country retracted time and time again.

OLD TOWN

Although Aswan has experienced a sharp increase in population over the past decade, the city has managed to retain much of its original charm. As there are no bridges crossing the Nile here, Aswan has developed on the right bank of the river, parallel to the Corniche which runs alongside it.

This colourful capital of the governorate of Aswan has always attracted a melting-pot of nationalities, and acted as a centre for trade and cultural exchange between the Arab world and black Africa. Situated at the point where Upper Egypt meets Lower Nubia, modern Aswan has absorbed a large Nubian population since the construction of the High Dam, maintaining its ethnic mix of peoples and adding to the exotic atmosphere of its market. The best way to explore the city is to take a leisurely stroll through its streets, soaking up the gentle charm of this cosmopolitan and typically Nubian town.

The colours and exotic scents of the souk.

Souk★★

Situated approximately 100m/110yd from the river, the souk runs along a street parallel to the Corniche, extending from Abbas Farid Street to the railway station.

Indigo blue and paprika red – Although the souk has become very geared to tourists, it is still one of the highlights of Aswan. A huge selection of items are on sale here, including multicoloured pigments; clothes ranging from garish T-shirts to pearl-embroidered *galabiyyas*; cotton materials; spices; hookah pipes made from glass and tinplate; wool carpets; dried plants and flowers; bread, sometimes even displayed on bike frames; stacks of baskets made from plaited palm leaves; souvenirs made from alabaster and granite; keyrings; sea-shells from the Red Sea; pyramids of fruit and vegetables, including the obligatory dried or fresh dates; perfumes and incense; fresh meat hanging on butchers' hooks; fried fish; and even small crocodiles captured from Lake Nasser, hidden in the quietest corners of the bazaar. In between the colourful market stalls, tired donkeys pull rickety carts, while the loud strains of old transistor radios from the small shops compete with the ever-present cacophony of car horns.

> **TIPS IN THE SOUK**
> If you want to take a photo of a market trader and his stall, make sure you ask his permission to do so. If you're planning on buying something, have a good look around to compare prices. The best time to visit the souk is without a doubt in the evening.

Fatimid Cemetery

To the SE of the park running alongside the Corniche, behind the Nubian Museum. The Unfinished Obelisk can be reached by crossing the cemetery.

Although most of the tombs in the cemetery are recent, some date back to the 10C, providing an interesting overview of the development of funerary architecture. The small mausolea, built in the Southern Egyptian style, are characterised by a dome built over a kind of flared drum. Built from brick and dressed stone, these tombs are similar in style to the fountain of ablutions in the Ibn Tulun Mosque in Cairo, the work of the sultan of the same name.

A number of tombstones were uprooted by torrential rain towards the end of the 19C and are now on display in the Islamic Museum in Cairo.

One of the tombs in the little-visited Fatimid Cemetery.

Unfinished Obelisk

Behind the Fatimid Cemetery, 1km/0.6mi from the town. Open 7am-5pm (6pm summer). E£10; students E£5; camera and video permits not required.

A monumental ambition – This 41.5m/136ft obelisk, the weight of which has been estimated at 1 200t, would have been the largest obelisk in the world if it had been completed. However, the monument developed a flaw in the stone and as a result was abandoned in its granite bed, where workers had been carving it directly from the rock. Three of its sides have been finished, although it bears no inscriptions.

Cutting and transporting an obelisk – Once the outer face had been cut and polished, the sides of the obelisk were cut using a hammer made of diorite, a rock which is harder than granite. In order to cut the inner face, grooves were made into which wooden levers were inserted; these were then soaked in water so that they became swollen, creating fissures in the rock. The task was completed using copper or bronze shears.

Once finished, the obelisk was hauled out of its bedrock using beams and rolled to the river. The transport vessel (80m/262ft long in the case of some of Hatsheput's obelisks) was positioned parallel to the monument and loaded with ballast in order to be able to take its weight. Once the obelisk was safely in position the ballast was removed and the ship assumed a suitable buoyancy level for it to be transported to its erection site.

worth a visit

Nubian Museum★★

Behind the Old and New Cataract Hotels. ⊚ *Open 9am-1pm and 5-9pm. E£20; students E£10; camera permit E£10.*

Museum – Opened in 1997, this magnificent museum was designed by the Egyptian architect **Mahmoud el-Hakim**. The building is highly successful, both in terms of its design and technical features; the museum blends harmoniously with its surrounding rocky landscape, and the works on display are protected from the extreme heat and light of Aswan.

Collections – These include exhibits ranging from the Prehistoric era to the modern day. Nubian culture and art are presented in a series of small sections, which are grouped by theme rather than chronology. The varied exhibits provide an insight into the unique Nubian heritage and traditions, paying homage to a region that made such huge sacrifices during the construction of the Aswan High Dam.

◀ **Prehistory** – Tools, pottery and paintings bear witness to the period when mankind hunted for food along the Nile Valley. Traces of Nagada I and Nagada II (Neolithic period) have been found at Abu Simbel.

Pharaonic Nubia – The history of Nubia during the Pharaonic era generally divided into three periods: Group A, from 3100 to 2700 BC; Group B, the Old Kingdom; Groups C1 and C2, from 2140 to 1539; and Group C3, from 1539 to 1069. The Nubian works displayed are generally more recent than those produced by the Egyptians. During the Old Kingdom, the latter began to extend their control further south, almost as far as the second cataract.

From the time of Senusret I (12th Dynasty), Ancient texts refer to Upper Nubia as **Kush**, a prosperous region which acted as a trade link between Egypt and Central Africa. During the Second Intermediate Period, Kush became more powerful, representing a real threat to the Egyptian kingdom. Its first capital, **Keram**, was at that time the largest commercial centre in equatorial Africa. During the New Kingdom, the pharaohs made efforts to secure their borders. As Kush was allied with the Hyksos, the southern part of the Nile Valley was annexed to Egypt and by the 18th and 19th Dynasties the Egyptian occupation of Nubia and Sudan was complete. Subsequently, Nubia suffered the effects of the collapse of the New Kingdom and little is known about events over the following three centuries.

◀ **Kushite Era** – After a long period of Egyptian domination in Nubia, the Egyptians saw the rise to power of **Piy**, a strong and ambitious ruler who was to conquer all of Egypt. His rule laid the foundations for the 25th Dynasty, also known as the Kushite Dynasty, whose most important Pharoah was **Taharqo**.

One of the most remarkable features of this period of Nubian domination was the respect the Nubians held for their former occupier: their leaders bore Egyptian titles, spoke the Egyptian language, adopted its writing and religion and absorbed its artistic style, in so doing respecting the Classicism of the Third Intermediate Period.

Meroitic Period – The term Meroitic refers to the relatively unknown period from 593 BC to AD 350. When the Persians arrived in Egypt in 525 BC, **Cambyses** attempted to conquer Nubia, with little success; later attempts by **Ptolemy II** also met with failure. Situated between the fifth and sixth cataracts, Meroe was the capital of a kingdom which had its own culture but which was later absorbed by the Ethiopian kingdom of Aksum. Meroitic art continued to be influenced by Egyptian styles during this period, but was also influenced by other trends as a result of the numerous trade links maintained by the country.

Roman and Christian Nubia – A treaty was signed between Meroe and the Romans, who inherited Lower Nubia. However, as a result of attacks by desert tribes such as the **Blemmyes** and the **Nobades**, in AD 296 the Romans were forced to withdraw their border as far north as the first cataract, effectively sounding the death knell for the Meroe kingdom. Riots subsequently broke out in the region in 380 when **Theodosius** proclaimed Christianity as the state religion. The rebellion was crushed by the Romans, who nonetheless conceded the right of local people to continue to worship the goddess Isis at Philae. Under **Justinian** (527-565), Emperor of the Eastern Empire, Christianity spread throughout Nubia and soon split into two separate traditions, Coptic Christianity and Byzantine Christianity.

Islamic Nubia – The Arab Muslim presence in Nubia gradually increased under the **Abbasids**. Many Nubians converted to Islam under the **Fatimids**, and a powerful Arab principality controlled by the Rabia tribe was soon established in the region. The war against the crusaders had little effect on the **Ayyubids** of Nubia, who continued to enjoy local support in the region. Under the **Mamelukes**, Nubian kings were nominated by the Sultan of Egypt, to whom they were expected to pay homage and by whom they were considered to be subjects of his Islamic State. In 1305, Sultan Nasser Mohammed ibn Qalaoun defeated the last rebel Nubian king, whom he forced to convert to Islam. Islam finally replaced Christianity as the dominant religion in Nubia as late as the 16C.

The museum houses exhibits relating to both art and daily life.

► **H**ighlights of the museum include a model of the Temple of Philae, the statue of Rameses II and the reconstruction of an Islamic tomb.

outskirts

OLD ASWAN DAM

8km/5mi S of the city (no photography).

The old dam stands just upstream of the first cataract ► and was built from Aswan granite by the British in 1902. It is 2 440m/8 003ft long (1 960m/6 428ft of which is directly over the Nile) and 30m/98ft high (it was increased to 35m/114ft in 1912 and then 45m/147ft in 1934); at the time, the dam was the largest structure of its kind in the world. The initial capacity of the reservoir (1 billion m³/35 billion cu ft) soon proved to be insufficient and this was increased to 5 billion m³/176 billion cu ft. This expansion had a dual purpose: firstly, an increase in the area of cultivated land by ensuring the provision of water from the spring onwards; and secondly, the supply of hydroelectricity to the whole country. The dam was no longer needed after the construction of the High Dam *(see below)* was completed.

TEMPLES OF PHILAE★★★

Situated on Agilqiyya Island, 10km/6mi S of the town. Access by boat from the landing stage at Shellal, to the SE of the old dam; approx. E£20 round trip during the day, slightly more expensive for the sound and light show in the evening.

TEN MONTHS UNDERWATER
Construction of the old dam resulted in the partial flooding of Philae Island for almost 10 months of the year. Visits to the island during this time took place by boat.

HISTORICAL CONTEXT
The oldest monuments at Philae date back to the 30th Dynasty, although blocks engraved with the name of Taharqo, a Pharaoh of the 25th Dynasty, were found on the site when it was dismantled.

Site

Open all year, 7am-4pm (5pm summer). E£20; students E£10; no camera or video permits required; tickets can be bought at the Shellal landing stage.

Saved from the waters – Known as the "Pearl of Egypt", this island dedicated to the goddess Isis – or more accurately to her patrimony – was saved from the rising waters of Lake Nasser during the construction of the Aswan High Dam. Under the aegis of UNESCO, the temple ruins were transferred to the nearby island of Agilqiyya, which was not under threat from the artificial flooding of this section of the Nile, and which was considered by the Ancient Egyptians to be the gateway to Egypt.

The salvage operation – From 1972-74, the island of Agilqiyya, to the north-west of the island of Philae, was flattened with dynamite; 300 000m³/10 594 500 cu ft of granite was then removed from the island, in order to give it the same topographical appearance as Philae. The temples were then carefully dismantled stone by stone and rebuilt on their new site, which stood on ground 20m/65ft higher than Philae. Construction was started in 1977 and completed in March 1980, at a total cost of 30 million dollars, half of which was paid by the Egyptian State.

Temples and Monuments

The description below starts from the landing stage to the S of the island, at the passenger disembarkation point.

Hall of Nectanebo I – This hall, dating from the 30th Dynasty, comprises a small portico supported by 14 campaniform columns, the dado of which bears an effigy of the goddess Hathor on all four sides. The goddess's triangular-shaped face and her crown are in the shape of the sistrum, her favourite instrument.

A temple to the north of the hall, dedicated to a Nubian god, Arensnuphis, was built by Ptolemy IV Philopator.

SOUND AND LIGHT SHOW

A sound and light show★★ is held every evening in a number of different languages opposite the kiosk of Trajan. Shows run at 6pm, 7.30pm and 9pm in winter, and at 8pm, 9.30pm and 11pm in summer *(exact times should be checked)*. E£33 + E£25 for the boat trip; E£30 for a video permit. If taking a taxi to the show, make sure that you book your return trip.

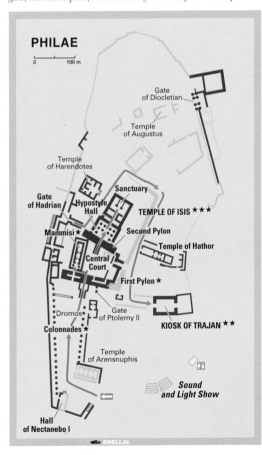

PHILAE

0   100 m

Gate of Diocletian
Temple of Augustus
Temple of Harendotes
Sanctuary
Gate of Hadrian
Hypostyle Hall
TEMPLE OF ISIS ★★★
Mammisi ★
Second Pylon
Temple of Hathor
Central Court
First Pylon ★
Dromos
Gate of Ptolemy II
KIOSK OF TRAJAN ★★
Colonnades ★
Temple of Arensnuphis
Sound and Light Show
Hall of Nectanebo I
SHELLAL

The Temple of Isis, seen from the west.

Colonnades★ – Two colonnades stand either side of a dromos along the terrace overlooking the Nile. The colonnade to the east is unfinished, whereas the one to the west has 31 columns, each decorated with a different capital. These colonnades form a propylaeum, a kind ▶ of open-air vestibule leading up to the temple.

Temple of Isis★★★ – This, the main temple on the island, was started by Nectanebo I, replacing a temple built by Ahmose II during the 26th Dynasty. The temple was added to by the last Egyptian pharaohs and was not completed until the Roman period. It is the southernmost of the Ptolemaic temples in Upper Egypt and acted as a model for the architects of the kingdom of Meroe.

Once flanked by two obelisks (now at Kingston Hall, England) and two granite lions (which, although badly damaged, are still visible here), the **first pylon**★ is ▶ 45m/147ft wide and 18m/59ft high; unusually for Egypt, a staircase leads up to it. The two façades of the pylon are decorated with low reliefs depicting Ptolemy XII in a ritual pose for this type of monument: seizing his enemies by the hair before killing them. The gods depicted are Isis, Horus and Hathor. Traces of the gateway of Ptolemy II Philadelphus can be seen to the right of the eastern tower.

The **central court** is bordered by the two pylons, as well as by a mammisi to the west, and by a porticoed building with 10 columns leading into the temple's chambers, to the east.

The free-standing **mammisi**★ was completed under Tiberius and is similar in style to those at Edfu and Dendera. Surrounded by a crown of columns with composite and Hathor-headed capitals, it contains three chambers preceded by a pronaos. The scenes decorating the building depict the birth and education of Horus, showing the god in the form of a falcon in the middle of the Delta marshland.

The **second pylon** (32m/104ft by 13m/42ft) is lower and narrower than the first by almost one-third; it is also adorned with large low reliefs representing Ptolemy XII taking part in scenes of massacre.

A doorway leads into the **hypostyle hall** of the temple. As demonstrated by the Coptic crosses engraved on the walls and columns, the hall was transformed into a church dedicated to St Stephen in 557, shortly after the Egyptian temples were closed by Justinian. The ceiling is covered with paintings of vultures symbolising Upper and Lower Egypt (*centre*), solar barks, and representations of the celestial vault (*sides*). The scenes decorating the walls have been badly damaged by alluvium from the Nile.

> **DECOR**
> The columns and back wall are decorated with scenes of offerings and the cartouches of Augustus, Tiberius, Caligula, Claudius and Nero.

> **TEMPLE LAYOUT**
> This temple is far more compact than the Temple of Horus at Edfu and was designed to take account of the uneven nature of the ground. Note that the second pylon is at a slight angle to the first.

Can you identify this goddess?

FORBIDDEN BIGA

The partly submerged island of Biga to the south of the island of Agilqiyya was regarded as the final resting place of Osiris and was therefore strictly off-limits. However, monuments on the island bear a number of inscriptions, and a temple here dating from the Ptolemaic period was even transformed into a church.

CONVOYS TO ABU SIMBEL

The road from Aswan to Abu Simbel has recently been reopened, leaving Aswan just before the airport and the High Dam. Convoys make the trip under military escort, with departures from outside the Nubian Museum at 4.30am and 10.30am. It is also possible to travel from Abu Simbel to Aswan by taxi, without an escort. Allow 3hr 30min for the 275km/171mi journey.

The **sanctuary** houses the naos and has 12 rooms decorated with liturgical scenes. A staircase leads to the terrace where the chapel of Osiris, adorned with scenes relating to the embalming of Osiris, to his cult and to the rites which guaranteed his survival, can be seen.

The cult of Isis is believed to have survived on the island of Philae until well into the Christian era and the temple was not finally abandoned until the time of Justinian (6C).

Gate of Hadrian – With its low reliefs illustrating the cult of Osiris, this gate has often been mistaken for the chapel of Osiris. It was begun under Hadrian and completed under Marcus Aurelius and originally led, at least symbolically, to the island of Biga, now to the south of the temples of Philae, but previously to the west and opposite this structure. The previous orientation of the gate explains the presence of the scene on the north wall representing Happy, the god who personified the Nile inundation. The river god is depicted kneeling in a cavern hollowed out of the cliff holding two vases from which flow the waters of the Nile – a reference to the belief in Greco-Roman times that the source of the river was at the foot of the cliffs at Biga.

Temple of Hathor – This temple, built by Ptolemy VI for the goddess Aphrodite, houses the remains of a colonnade whose columns are adorned with musical scenes; note the harpist, flautist and monkey playing the lyre.

Kiosk of Trajan★★ – From an architectural point of view, this is the most attractive monument on the island. It is built in the form of a portico, suggesting that the processions which arrived on the island approached it from the foot of this elegant building. The monument is adorned with 14 campaniform columns bearing magnificently carved capitals which give the building a light, elegant feel. The capitals and the architrave of the dados are unfinished; like those in the hall of Nectanebo I, these were intended to be carved with representations of the goddess Hathor.

OPEN-AIR MUSEUM

Turn right off the road leading from the landing stage for Philae. Carry straight on for 600m/660yd, then turn left (unmarked road) and continue for a further 500m/550yd to the top of the hill. No charge.

This rarely visited museum stands in an isolated position in the middle of a rocky, lunar landscape exposed to the full heat of the midday sun. Although its collection of works from exhibitions held by the Aswan Sculpture Symposium is not of major interest, the strange, silent setting of the museum lends it a certain appeal.

The sculptures on display at the Open-air Museum were created in Aswan by both Egyptian and foreign artists. Other examples are exhibited in the city.

Close-up of the Kiosk of Trajan

ISIS AND OSIRIS

One of the most important and probably the most popular Egyptian goddess, Isis enjoyed an influence which extended beyond the country's borders. The cult of this goddess-mother originated in the Delta and became firmly established along the Nile Valley, subsequently spreading to the Greek islands, where she was identified with Demeter, and even as far as Rome, where she was assimilated with Fortuna of Praeneste. The tale of Isis and Osiris is undoubtedly one of the most popular of all mythological legends and is responsible for the image of Isis as a loving goddess and devoted mother.

Osiris, who was married to his sister Isis, was invited to a feast by his brother Seth who, having made a casket to fit Osiris's measurements, stated that he would make a gift of the casket to whoever it fitted. As soon as Osiris climbed into the casket, Seth closed it and disposed of it in the Nile. Isis searched for her husband's body, which she found at Byblos, and hid it in the Delta. Seth discovered the hiding place and cut the body into 14 pieces, which he scattered throughout the country. The determined Isis managed to reassemble the body of her husband, which she then had embalmed by Anubis. Taking on the form of a bird, the goddess breathed life back into Osiris by flapping her wings, and 10 months later gave birth to Osiris' son Horus. Horus succeeded in avenging his father, who was resurrected in the kingdom of the dead.

Osiris

ASWAN HIGH DAM★

15km/9mi S of the town. Open 6am-5pm (6pm summer). E£5. Photos allowed without a zoom lens; no videos.

Signposted to the **Memorial to Friendship between the Soviet Union and Egypt**, the High Dam (*Sadd el-Ali* in Arabic, which literally translates as "high dike") is a colossal structure built between 1960 and 1964, although the project was not finally completed until 1971.

A national necessity – Egypt covers an area of approximately 1 million km²/386 100sq mi, but before the construction of the dam the country had little more than 50 000km²/19 305sq mi of land suitable for cultivation. It soon became obvious that this growing area had to be increased if it was to feed its increasing population. It had also become apparent at the beginning of the 1950s that the old dam was no longer able to control the unpredictable floods caused by the Nile.

Nasser's dream – On 26 July 1956, President **Gamal Abdel ▶ Nasser** nationalised the Suez Canal in order to finance construction of the Aswan High Dam, following the refusal of Europe and the United States to contribute towards the cost of the project. The Suez crisis hardened Nasser's resolve and the canal was only reopened to maritime traffic in 1957. However, the Soviet Union agreed to finance the dam project – plans for which had been drawn up as early as 1952 – and offered to provide engineers for its construction. This impressive structure measures 3 600m/11 808ft in length, 110m/360ft in height and with a thickness of 980m/3 214ft at its base and 40m/131ft at its highest point; 40 000 000t of granite and clay were used to build it – 17 times the amount of materials used for the Khufu Pyramid at Giza. A power station producing 40 billion mW is situated on the top of the dam. ▶

The largest artificial lake in the world – The lake created by the dam – named after Nasser himself – holds 155 billion m³/5 473 billion cu ft of water. It covers an area of more than 5 200km²/2 007sq mi and stretches from Aswan to the Sudan, extending for more than 300km/187mi over the Sudanese border (the total length of the lake before the construction of the High Dam was no more than 225km/140mi). The average annual flow of the Nile is close to 84 billion m³/2 966 billion cu ft, which is shared between Egypt (55.5 billion m³/1 959 cu ft) and the Sudan (18.5 billion m³/653 billion cu ft). A total of 30 billion m³/1 059 million cu ft of its total capacity will, over a 500-year period, fill up with silt, 35 billion m³/1 235 billion cu ft will act as the lake's reserve, while 6 billion m³/211 billion cu ft will be lost to evaporation.

PROS

As a result of the construction of the dam, Egypt has increased its surface area of cultivated land by 30%, doubled its energy resources, improved its irrigation methods, developed its rice fields, and stabilised the river, thus enabling traffic to use the Nile all year round

---

CONS

The disadvantages resulting from the dam include the loss of some 20 temples; the displacement of around 100 000 Nubians from their homes; the depletion of fertile alluvium resulting in an increased use of chemical fertiliser; climate change (more rain in Cairo); and an increase in the amount of salt in the waters of the Delta.

In 1978 President Sadat authorised the resettlement of a certain number of Nubians above Lake Nasser. A few thousand of these now live in small public-housing projects located some distance away from the villages that were flooded as part of the scheme.

En route to Kalabsha.

The first of the Nubian temples to be moved, Kalabsha was originally situated 40km/25mi south of its present location. The operation to transfer the temple was financed by West Germany.

LAKE NASSER★★

Looking out at the clear blue waters of Lake Nasser it is difficult to imagine that this is a body of water created by man. Surrounded by the shifting golden sand of the desert and an empty, uninhabited shoreline – settlements are forbidden as a result of the fluctuating water level – the lake is striking for its immense size and sober beauty. The only way to fully appreciate its huge scale is to either take a plane or boat to Abu Simbel from Aswan, as no roads run around the lake.

Lake Cruises★★★

Also see Directory.

Five boats run between Aswan and Abu Simbel (a maximum of six is permitted) and this is without doubt the best way to reach the famous temple built by Rameses II. The return journey takes eight days and seven nights, with stops to visit some of the temples saved from the waters of the lake. Visitors can, if they wish, travel by boat in one direction and by plane in the other, in which case the best arrangement is to take the boat from Aswan to Abu Simbel and to fly back. Approaching the temple of Abu Simbel at sunrise by boat is one of the highlights of any trip to Egypt.

Kalabsha★

1km/0.6mi SW of the High Dam. Open 9am-5pm in winter and 7am-6pm in summer. E£12; students E£6. Landing stage to the right just before the Soviet-Egyptian Memorial (approx. E£20 there and back by motor boat).

This is the only site on the lake, with the exception of Abu Simbel, which can be visited without having to join a cruise. The site includes the temple of Kalabsha, dedicated to Madulis, a Nubian avatar of the god Horus, and the temples of Kertassi and Beit el-Wali.

Temple of Kalabsha★ – From the landing stage, a flight of steps leads to this temple, which was built by Emperor Augustus on the site of an older temple by Amenhotep II (18th Dynasty). The 14m/46ft-high **pylon** stands at a slight angle to the main building and has two staircases leading to a platform, from where is a magnificent **view** of the lake and desert. The **porticoed court**, with columns bearing composite capitals, leads into a **hypostyle hall** originally supported by 12 campaniform columns (the column to the right of the entrance still bears a text in Meroitic writing). The hall is decorated with scenes of offerings and worship of the gods Min, Khnum and Mandulis. Beyond the hall, the next three rooms of the **naos** are adorned with representations of Augustus; each of these rooms is slightly smaller than the previous one. A nilometer, small mammisi and large relief depicting the god of the temple can be seen in a kind of ambulatory located outside the temple but inside the temple enclosure.

Temple of Kertassi – Similar in style to the kiosk of Trajan at Philae, this temple originally stood 30km/18mi south of its present location. The building is not as well

The MS Eugénie, one of the luxurious cruise ships operating on Lake Nasser.

TEMPLES AROUND LAKE NASSER

The construction of the High Dam directly threatened a number of Ancient monuments in Lower Nubia, resulting in the launch of an international appeal by UNESCO in 1960 for financial and technical help to save some of these monuments from the rising waters of Lake Nasser. A number of countries responded to this appeal and sent archaeological teams to Nubia. Fourteen temples were dismantled and reassembled on higher ground, with every attempt being made to respect the topographical layout of the original site. Other sites were excavated and studied in detail before disappearing beneath the waters for ever; these included seven fortresses from the Middle Kingdom situated close to the second cataract. All the temples saved were erected on islands or on the left bank of the Nile (with the exception of the Temple of Derr) so that they would face the rising sun.

The temples that were saved were divided into four geographical groups: 1) Kalabsha, Beit el-Wali and Kertassi; 2) Dakka, Meharaqqa and Wadi el-Sebua; 3) Amada, Derr and the tomb of Penut; 4) the two Abu Simbel temples, Abu Oda and the niche from the tomb of Pasar. In addition, the temples of Dabod, Dendur and Tiffa were saved and donated by Egypt to foreign countries. The temples at Philae, situated between the old and new dams at Aswan, were also moved and rebuilt to protect them from the fluctuating water levels.

DONATIONS

Egypt donated a number of monuments to those countries that provided most assistance with the temple salvage operations. The Temple of Dabod now stands in Madrid, the Temple of Dendur in New York, the Temple of Tiffa at Leyde, the first speos of the New Kingdom in Turin, a colossus of Amenhotep IV in Paris, and a Ptolemaic gate discovered in Kalabsha in Berlin.

---

preserved as the one in Philae, with only two Hathor-headed columns and four composite columns link by corbelled constructions still standing.

Stele of Psamtek II – This stele was discovered in 1964 during excavation work carried out at Shellal, the landing stage for Philae. It is decorated with text describing an expedition that Psamtek II undertook in the third year of his reign (26th Dynasty) in the land of the Kush (Nubia), which was led by his general-in-chief Ahmose.

Temple of Beit el-Wali – This small speos, dating from the reign of Rameses II and rebuilt by the Egyptian Antiquities Service, originally stood 1.5km/1mi from the temple of Kalabsha. Dedicated to the god Amun-Ra, the temple was later transformed into a church and referred to as the "house of the saint". The court in front of the temple is decorated with beautiful **polychrome scenes** depicting the Pharaoh's victories over the Libyans, Asiatics and the Kushite tribes. Painted plaster casts of these lively and expressive scenes are on display at the British Museum in London.

Wadi el-Sebua★★

Can only be visited as part of a cruise. E£30.

Temple of Wadi el-Sebua★ – Moved 2km/1.2mi from its original location by the Egyptian Antiquities Service in an operation financed by the United States, this temple comprises a damaged first pylon, a court, a second pylon, a pronaos, and a naos. The naos leads into a speos consisting of a kind of 12-pillared hypostyle hall, the walls of which are decorated with scenes of offerings; the speos was converted into a church during the paleo-Christian period and an image of St Peter can still be made out on the distemper. To the back of the room, a niche is adorned with three gods: a deified Rameses II, to whom the temple is dedicated, stands in the centre and is flanked by Amun and Ra-Harmakhis, to whom the temple is consecrated. The long side room was also used as a sanctuary and once housed a bark of the sun-god.

Temple of Dakka★ – Originally located 40km/25mi further north from its present position, this temple, dedicated to the god Thoth, unusually faces north. Work on the temple began under Ptolemy II Philadelphus, continued during the Ptolemaic period and finished during the reign of Emperor Augustus. The pylon is in perfect condition and is decorated with scenes of offerings in which Ptolemy VIII is represented. The most interesting part of the temple is the **sanctuary** designed by Ergamen, a Meroitic king. The walls are adorned with representations of the king making offerings to the gods, as well as two ibises of the god Thoth, and the goddess

The sun over Kalabsha. The eyes of the god Mandulis were believed to be the incarnation of both the sun and the moon.

DODEKASCHOINOS

This was the name given to the area stretching from Aswan to Meharraqa, so-called because the region measured 12 schoinoi, or 360 stadia. This area was considered neutral land by the Meroitic kings of the Sudan and the Ptolemies of Egypt, and was violated only once, by King Ergamen who ruled from 218 to 195 BC.

Tefnut in the form of a lioness. In the temple's most recent sanctuary, built under Augustus, the Roman emperor is portrayed as a Pharaoh.

Temple of Meharaqqa – This smaller, unfinished temple was originally situated 10km/6mi from the Temple of Dakka. It dates from the Roman period and was dedicated to Isis and Serapis (an Alexandrian god). It now comprises a hypostyle hall which still bears traces of its original decor (scenes of offerings) and a spiral staircase – very unusual in Egypt – which leads up to the terrace.

Amada★

Can only be visited as part of a cruise. E£30.

Temple of Amada – The French archaeological team responsible for the removal of this small temple succeeded in pulling off a technical tour de force. Because of the fragile nature of its low-relief **paintings★**, the temple could not be dismantled and had to be transferred to its new site in one solid block, weighing 900t. It was wrapped and moved a distance of 2.5km/1.5mi and an altitude of 65m/213ft by means of a railway built especially for the purpose.

The temple is preceded by a courtyard with 12 pillars and four proto-Doric columns; to the back of the building a stele is dated from the reign of Amenhotep III, although the temple was actually built during the reigns of Thutmose III and Amenhotep II. In the north chamber, paintings on the walls illustrate ceremonies relating to the founding and consecration of the temple to Ra-Horakhty.

Temple of Derr – The only Nubian temple built on the right bank of the Nile originally stood 11km/7mi to the south-west of its present location. This rock-cut temple was built by Rameses II and dedicated to the god Amun-Ra. In the first room, the walls are decorated with scenes depicting one of the Pharaoh's military campaigns in Nubia; only a few paintings remain in the second room. According to Champollion, the badly damaged seated statues in the sanctuary represent Amun-Ra flanked by Ptah *(left)*, Rameses and Ra-Harmakhis *(right)*.

Tomb of Penut – This hypogeum, which was moved 40km/25mi by the Egyptian Antiquities Service, is the tomb of an important official under Rameses VI. The tomb is well preserved and is adorned with scenes evoking everyday life *(right side)* and life in the kingdom of the dead *(left side)*.

Qasr Ibrim

Not open to the public, although boats makes a 15min stop for passengers to enjoy the view of the castle from their upper decks.

This fortress still stands on its original site, occupying a strategic position overlooking the Nile from a height of 70m/229ft. The site was for many years a bastion of paganism and converted late to Christianity; it subsequently became an important Christian stronghold, resisting conversion to Islam until the 16C. The Egyptian monuments, Coptic churches and mosques in the castle bear witness to its eventful and varied history.

Note the roughly sculpted camels at the top of the façade; these are thought to have been carved by travellers during the Middle Ages.

Scenes of offerings adorn three sides of the pillars in this room. In the middle Rameses II is represented opposite various gods.

The Egyptians, Nubians, Romans, Byzantines and Mamelukes all maintained a garrison in the fortress, which was abandoned at the beginning of the 19C. It is thought that the border between Egypt and the kingdom of Meroe was located here.

Thutmose III makes offerings to Amun in the Temple of Amada.

The 10-sphinx dromos standing in front of the Wadi el-Sebua temple gave it its name: the "valley of the lions".

directory

INTERNET

Golden Dream Net – Abtal el-Tahrir Street at the back of a café courtyard, on the right as you approach from the station. Open 10am-midnight. Four computers for internet access. E£15/hr.

GETTING AROUND

Horse-drawn carriages – Like Luxor, Aswan can be explored by horse-drawn carriage. A 2hr tour costs approx. E£35 and a short trip from E£5-E£10. Try to avoid stops at souvenir shops.

Taxis – Taxis are cheaper in Aswan than Luxor, but are not really used within the city – it is easier to take a horse-drawn carriage. Allow E£40 for a round trip to Philae (the driver will wait for you). If you are not on an organised tour, you can hire a taxi to Abu Simbel for around E£200.

Collective taxis – Journeys cost 50pt each. All white in colour, like private taxis, these vehicles are easily recognised by their poor condition.

BOAT RIDES BY FELUCCA

Feluccas run short trips from Aswan across to Kitchener and Elephantine Islands. Signs giving the official rate for felucca trips are few and far between; those that can still be seen along the Corniche are barely visible and, in any case, very little attention is paid to the official rate! In other words, bargaining is necessary. It is difficult to give a precise idea of price, as rates vary depending on the season and will increase with inflation. For two people, allow around E£20 for a 1hr trip and E£40 for a 3hr trip. It is advisable to shop around.

The second option is to spend a whole day on a felucca, sailing down the Nile and heading back to Aswan when the wind rises in the late afternoon. Lunch and tea are taken on board. Once again, fierce bargaining is required.

The third option is a two-day trip to Kom Ombo with one night on board, or a three-day trip to Edfu, the furthest point that you can go, with two nights on board. Avoid booking through small hotels (they get a commission and don't always offer the best value for money) and don't be put off by the insistent offers that you are bound to receive. The trip is well worth the trouble it takes to organise, as long as you check certain details thoroughly: eg the condition of the boat, provision of blankets, meals served on board, the exact number of passengers, luggage security provisions and the exact destination. Allow at least E£70 per person, not including food, and add E£5 for registering with the police. If you are asked for your passport, refuse and produce a photocopy instead.

CRUISES ON LAKE NASSER

Traditional Cruises – Of the five cruise boats that currently operate on Lake Nasser, two, the *Eugénie* and the *Qasr Ibrim,* come highly recommended. Both are air-conditioned, have charming decor and offer excellent service and a wide range of organised events and entertainment, including concerts and the magnificent sound and light show upon arrival at Abu Simbel. Contact your local travel agent *(see Practical Information at the beginning of the guide)* for specific information on cruise packages. Visitors travelling independently can contact Belle Epoque Travel in Cairo ☎ (02) 518 18 57.

Hydrofoil Cruises – The two hydrofoils run by the Blue Stars company (☎ (097) 30 29 09; reserve 24hr in advance) operate between Aswan and Abu Simbel at speeds of 70kph/43mph and take 4hr. Departure at 5.30am, return 11hr later. $90, including transfers and two light meals.

Sailing Cruises – Hermes Travel (☎ (02) 303 51 05) operates a yacht with five double cabins. This cruise explores the more secluded corners of the lake as far as Wadi el-Allaqi, from where it is possible to reach Berenice, a small resort on the Red Sea, by 4WD. Allow $60 per day per person.

HENNA TATTOOS

In a number of towns in Upper Egypt and in the resorts along the Red Sea, temporary henna tattoos are all the rage. However, this technique is a particular speciality of Aswan and the Nubian villages. Women who wish to be tattoed can have their hands painted by Nubian women in the village just to the north of the Tombs of the Nobles. Between E£20 and E£30, depending on the design.

WHERE TO STAY

• **Budget**

Hotel Kalabsha – Abtal el-Tahrir Street – ☎ (097) 30 29 99 – 120 rooms; $60. The Kalabsha overlooks the Old Cataract hotel and has some rooms offering views of the first cataract. Somewhat lacking in charm. Facilities include a tiny swimming pool.

• **Moderate**

Aswan Oberoi – Elephantine Island – ☎ (097) 30 34 55 – 244 rooms; $148/$230. This hotel is easily recognisable by its huge concrete tower. It has a panoramic restaurant (currently closed), and spacious, attractive rooms, each with a fine view of either the large swimming pool, the garden or the town. The setting is particularly impressive at the end of the day, when the hotel is literally surrounded by feluccas.

Isis Island Hotel – On an island to the S of Elephantine Island – ☎ (097) 31 74 00 – 447 rooms; $155. This pink concrete hotel has a splendid setting close to the granite rocks of the first cataract and has some of the best facilities in town.

Basma Hotel – Opposite the Nubian Museum – ☎ (097) 31 09 01 – 188 rooms; $130/$141. A pleasant hotel, with a relaxing atmosphere and friendly staff. Its Nile Terrasse bar (open to non-guests who must spend more than $20) overlooks a beautiful swimming pool and, like most of the rooms, offers lovely views of the surrounding area as a result of the hotel's hillside position.

New Cataract – Abtal el-Tahrir Street – ☎ (097) 31 60 00 – 144 rooms; $128 (Nile view). This modern white building dominates the Old Cataract and the Nile. The riverside rooms on the upper floors have wonderful views of Elephantine Island, although those to the back are generally not as good value for money. The staff here tend to be less friendly than other hotels.

Isis Hotel – El Nile Corniche – ☎ (097) 31 51 00 – 100 rooms; $112. ☐ This hotel enjoys a good location overlooking the Nile, opposite the Aswan Oberoi. The hotel is part of the Pyramisa chain, which also runs the Isis Island Hotel. Guest accommodation is in chalets.

• **Expensive**

Old Cataract – Abtal el-Tahrir Street – ☎ (097) 31 60 00 – 131 rooms; $272 (minimum). Like the Cecil in Alexandra and the Winter Palace in Luxor, this is one of Egypt's legendary hotels. A large hotel, surrounded by gardens, it enjoys the perfect location opposite Elephantine Island and offers guests a real taste of the past, as the decor has changed little since 1899. Many famous names have stayed here, including Tsar Nicholas II and Jimmy Carter. As yet, non-guests are prohibited from enjoying the sunset over an aperitif at the hotel's La Terrasse bar. If you decide to stay here, insist on a riverside room.

WHERE TO EAT

• **Budget**

Nubian Restaurant – Open 10am-midnight – Essa Island (free ferry from the S of the Corniche, next to the ferry for Amun Village). This typical restaurant, situated to the south of Elephantine Island, stages a Nubian show at 8.30pm. Tagine (a type of North African stew) is the house speciality.

El Masry – El-Mattar Street – open noon-midnight. This small, popular restaurant is very clean and serves a number of different dishes, such as kebabs, kofta and stuffed pigeon, all served with salad and tahina. Customers are mainly Egyptians and tourists travelling independently. No alcohol.

El-Madina Restaurant – Open 11.30am-midnight – Saad Zaghloal Street (the same street as the souk), to the left as you approach from the station. This small, pleasant restaurant serves koftas, stuffed pigeon and excellent fish accompanied by rice and salad.

CAFÉS AND BARS

Nubian House – 700m/770yd from the Nubian Museum, after the Hotel Basma. Open 9am-1pm. Enjoy a fruit cocktail (E£7) or a non-alcoholic beer (E£7) in front of the finest view in Aswan, from a hilltop overlooking the Nile. Snacks such as kofta are also available. A typical Nubian house has been built to the rear of the restaurant.

Asyut

This industrial and university town is the largest in Upper Egypt and is often in the news because of the ongoing religious conflict in the region. It is also a major crossroads for trade and an important centre for handicrafts. Asyut stands at the centre of the Said region, of which it is the capital, and has a large Coptic community.

Location
380km/237mi S of Cairo, 320km/200mi N of Luxor, on the left bank of the Nile. Access: the journey by car from Cairo is not advisable, as the region is occasionally beset by problems between fundamentalists and the police; the best option is by train from Cairo or Luxor, although Asyut also has good bus services between the two cities.

Name
In Ancient Egypt the name of the town was Djawty, while the Greeks adopted the name Lycopolis, which translates as "the town of the wolf"; by the Greek period the local jackal-god, Wepwawet, had been transformed into a wolf.

Transcription: أسيوط

Famous People
The neo-Platonist Plotinus (c 205-70) was born in Asyut. He left his native city for Alexandria, and then Rome, where he taught philosophy.

History
Asyut was the capital of the 13th nome of Upper Egypt.

background

The brief independence of the princes – Towards the end of the reign of Pepy II (6th Dynasty), the nomarchs took the title of vizier in order to assert their autonomy from the Pharaoh. This marked the beginning of the First Intermediate Period and with it over a century of conflict, during which Middle Egypt seceded and was ruled by the princes of **Herakleopolis** (south of Fayum). Around 2130 Asyut experienced a period of prosperity under Khety I (9th Dynasty), who declared himself king of both Upper and Lower Egypt. During this period Herakleopolis was a powerful town in direct conflict with **Thebes** (Luxor), whose nomarch had also declared himself king of Upper Egypt. Eventually, Thebes won this power struggle and Asyut became a part of the Theban empire.

An important crossroads – The town was founded during the Pharaonic era at a meeting-point of caravan routes. Although its geographical location afforded it a strategic role in Egypt's history, Asyut was never to become of national importance. Today the town is a stopping point for visitors following the oasis road.

exploring Asyut

With the exception of its old district built along the Nile, an area also referred to as Gezirat al-Moz ("Banana Island"), Asyut has few features of interest, apart from its traditional craftwork, including cloth, pottery and ivorywork, which is sold all over Egypt.

The town's **dam**, 800m/2 624ft long, is used as a bridge and was built by the British in the 19C to regulate the Ibrahimiyya canal that irrigated the valley north of the town.

WARNING
Visitors here are usually escorted by police, creating a tense atmosphere made worse by the fact that the police themselves are often the main target of attacks by fundamentalists.

TOURIST OFFICE
Ath-Thawra Street (first floor) ☎ *(088) 31 00 10). Open daily, except Fri, 8.30am-2pm.*

THE DIVISION OF EGYPT
The terms Upper and Lower Egypt correspond to the northern and southern kingdoms of the Pharaoh. However, during the Middle Kingdom a third political division, known as Middle Egypt, was created, extending from Abydos to Memphis and which included Asyut.

ARRIVING IN ASYUT
In many ways, Asyut is more typical of a town in the Middle East than one in Africa, with a character more akin to the Lebanon or United Arab Emirates. As the region is under the strong influence of Islamic fundamentalists, street signs are exclusively in Arabic. Visitors would be well advised to refrain from wearing shorts in the town.

*The village of Zauët
el-Meïtin near Asyut.*

outskirts

*Visitors are advised to check the opening times given below
with the tourist office in Asyut as some of the sites may occasionally be temporarily closed to tourists.*

Tombs of the Princes
*5km/3mi SW of the town. As the site is situated in a military area, special authorisation is required to visit it. No
charge.* A number of hypogea have been cut into the
rock-face here, and once contained interesting funerary
artefacts which are now housed in various museums.
The **view**★★ of the valley from the platform is particularly impressive.

◀ **Tomb of Djefahapy** – The tomb of this prince of Asyut
dates from the reign of Senusret (12th Dynasty) and is
one of the largest hypogea (40m/131ft, with three large
chambers) of the Middle Kingdom. The prince was not
buried here as he died in Nubia, an area over which he
governed.

Tombs of Khety II, Mesehti and Nakhti – Although
badly damaged, these tombs bear inscriptions relating to
the wars of the Herakleopitan period.

> **INSCRIPTIONS**
> The tomb's wall
> inscriptions highlight the
> contract made between
> the deceased and the
> priests, to ensure the
> continuation of his
> funerary cult.

Deir el-Muharraq
9km/5.5mi SE of El-Qusiya. Open 9am-4pm.
Founded around 350, the Monastery of the Virgin is the
largest in Middle and Upper Egypt and home to around
100 monks. An important centre of the Coptic religion, the
monastery's theological college plays a major role in the
heart of the Egyptian Christian Church. From 21-28 June
each year, thousands of pilgrims come here to commemorate the consecration of the Church of the Virgin.
The defensive tower dates from the 8C-12C and still
retains its traditional drawbridge entrance on the first
floor. In the centre, the 12C Church of the Virgin
(*Al-Adhra* in Arabic) houses a stone altar-table dating
from 747 which was used as a funerary stele before the
construction of the church.

> **COPTIC TRADITION**
> According to tradition the
> **Holy Family** stayed on the
> site where the monastery
> was built for three years,
> six months and ten days,
> until an angel said to
> Joseph: *"Rise, take this
> child and his mother and
> go to the land of Israel"*
> (Matthew, II-20).

Mir
*8km/5mi NW of El-Qusiya. Open 8am-5pm. E£16; camera
permit E£10; video permit E£150.*
This village gave its name to its necropolis, in which the
nomarchs of the Middle Kingdom are buried. The most
interesting of the nine tombs open to the public is that
of **Ukhhotep**, the priest of Hathor, containing lively
reliefs depicting everyday scenes of provincial life. Note
that some of the faces of the gods are missing: at the
beginning of the Christian era these were erased by
Copts who occupied the tombs at that time.

Tell el-Amarna (*see TELL EL-AMARNA*)

Hermopolis
*9km/5.5mi from Mallawi, as you leave the village of
El-Ashmunein. This site is currently closed.*

During Antiquity, this was one of the small hills believed by religious tradition to have emerged from the primordial waters, making this the place where the Ancient Egyptians believed that the world was created.

The site – At the entrance to the site, two 4.5m/14ft statues of the god Thoth bear the cartouche of Amenhotep III (18th Dynasty). With the exception of the Greek agora and the paleo-Christian basilica, the site lies in ruins and it is difficult to make out the few remains of the first temple of Thoth – the foundation of which dates back to the time of Khufu (4th Dynasty) – and the four jackal-headed colossi, from the reign of Amenhotep III.

> **MUSEUM**
> A small museum in Mallawi exhibits a collection of artefacts found at Hermopolis and Tuna el-Gebel *(open daily, 9am-4pm (noon on Fri); E£6).*

Tuna el-Gebel★

7km/4mi W of Hermopolis. Open 8am-5pm. E£12; students E£6.

Just before arriving at this rarely visited site, note the cliff where one of the border-steles of Akhetaten is situated *(see Tell el-Amarna)*.

Tomb of Petosiris – In addition to three interesting necropoli of sacred animals, including ibises and baboons, this site contains the late-4C BC tomb of Petosiris, the high priest of Thoth, whose sarcophagus is on display in the Egyptian Museum in Cairo. Excavated in 1920, this tomb heralded a new artistic style in Egypt, as its low reliefs are an amalgam of both the flat Egyptian and Greek models; this is particularly noticeable in the vestibule. Next to his tomb was that of Isadora, dating from around AD 120, housing the mummy of this young girl, who met her death through drowning.

Antinopolis

Opposite El-Roda (6km/4mi N of Mallawi), on the right bank of the Nile.

At the time of Napoleon's expedition to Egypt, the ruins of present-day El-Sheikh Abada were still impressive; but sadly they were later used as a quarry for the construction of a sugar refinery. Antinopolis or Antinoe was founded by Hadrian around 130 in honour of his favourite Antinous, who drowned close to the site. An earlier temple, the vestiges of which include fragments of pylons, a courtyard and a hypostyle hall, dates back to the time of Rameses II (19th Dynasty). The city was the capital of the Thebaid region under Diocletian.

Beni Hassan★

24km/15mi N of Mallawi, on the right bank of the Nile. Open 7am-5pm. E£12; E£6.

This town, which takes its name from an Arab family who once lived here, is home to a necropolis dating from the 11th and 12th Dynasties. The necropolis is of particular interest because its tombs were those of provincial princes, unlike most other sites which contained royal tombs or tombs of important state officials (with the exception of Saqqara and Giza). Beni Hassan is one of the oldest settlements in Egypt and it is thought that the pharaohs **Sneferu** and **Khufu** were both born here.

The mummy of an ibis discovered at Tuna el-Gebel.

Decoration of the hypogea – Twelve of the hypogea's 39 tombs are decorated with paintings depicting scenes of hunting, fishing, farming, athletic competitions, acrobatic dances, and – new for the period – aspects of military life, all of which are divided horizontally on a number of registers. Because of the famous biographical inscriptions they contain, these rock-tombs have taught scholars much about the history of Ancient Egypt; all are situated 20m/65ft above the level of the Nile.

Tomb of Amenemhat (no 2) – The walls of the chamber are decorated with lively scenes, including one depicting cooking; the best examples are on the south wall.

Tomb of Khnumhotep III★★ (no 3) – This tomb has an open door (a characteristic of Beni Hassan), leading into a chamber decorated with a number of famous scenes ; one shows the feeding of antelopes, another depicts a caravan of Asians. An inscription of 222 vertical lines recounts the history of Khnumhotep's family.

Dendara★★

All that remains of the city of Dendara that prospered during Antiquity is a village, a few architectural vestiges and, most importantly, a magnificent temple which still conveys the full grandeur of a time when it played host to kings and emperors. Despite its isolated, neglected appearance today, the site was one of the cradles of Ancient Egypt.

Location
69km/43mi N of Luxor and 6km/3.5mi N of Qena, on the left bank of the Nile. Access: most visitors visit Dendara as part of an organised tour; otherwise the easiest option is by shared taxi from Luxor.

Name
The city was first known as *Iunu*, then *Iunet Tantaré* (the "pillar" of the goddess), then *Tentyris* under the Greeks. Transcription: دندرة

Local Gods
Dendara was the principal cult centre of the goddess Hathor, the "divine mother of the pharaohs", and "protector of women". Every year, a pilgrimage lasting several days was held between Dendara and Edfu to celebrate her divine marriage with Horus.

History
Dendara was the capital of the 6th nome of Upper Egypt. Although it is highly probable that a temple was erected here under Khufu, the city's zenith was the period from the 30th Dynasty until the arrival of the first Roman emperors.

worth a visit

Site
Open all year 7am-6pm. E£12; students E£6.

The sacred complex – The site was enclosed by a mud-brick wall 280m/918ft long, 2m/6.5ft thick and 12m/39ft high, and included several constructions in addition to the **Great Temple**. Today, only the west section has remained more or less intact; the pylon to the north of the main courtyard was never completed. The line of buildings to the west of the temple consisted of the **Roman mammisi** *(level with the esplanade)*, the **mammisi of Nectanebo I** (30th Dynasty), a **sanatorium** and a **sacred lake**. To the south, just behind the temple, stood the **Small Temple** dedicated to Isis. A series of buildings to the east were devoted to Harsomtus (an infant Horus represented naked and holding a sistrum). The site also comprised a number of mud-brick mastabas dating from the Old and Middle Kingdoms, as well as catacombs in which the mummies of animals have been discovered. A small stone chapel

---

HATHOR
The literal meaning of her name is the "house of Horus". In Dendara she was, in effect, the wife of this god, although she was regarded as his mother according to the legend of Isis. The situation is further complicated by the fact that Horus and his son were the very same god!

THE SACRED COW
Despite the presence of cow sepulchres, resulting from Hathor's association with this animal, not a single mummified cow has ever been found.

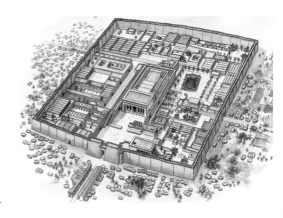

A re-creation of the site.

built during the time of Mentuhotep I (11th Dynasty) and embellished by Merenptah (19th Dynasty) has been dismantled and reconstructed in front of the Egyptian Museum in Cairo. The main entrance to the entire complex stood to the north, and was carved from sandstone. A **dromos**, of which just the outline is now visible, linked the Great Temple with a dock on the banks of the Nile.

Mammisi of Nectanebo I – This "birth-house" is the oldest monument of its kind still standing in Egypt. Its decoration evokes Hathor bringing her son into the world.

Roman mammisi★ – Built by Nero or Augustus, this mammisi was subsequently decorated by Trajan, Hadrian and Antoninus Pius. Its two sides are flanked by a portico comprising composite columns connected by wall-screens: as in the mammisi at Edfu, their dados are not effigies of Hathor but are decorated with representations of the god Bes. Inside, the scenes evoke the birth and suckling of the divine child born of Horus and Hathor.

Sanatorium – This building received the sick who came to this sacred site in search of a cure through the magical formulae prescribed here. To ensure recovery, patients would drink or bathe in the miraculous water that flowed from a statue.

Sacred lake – The lake is one of the best preserved in Egypt and has flights of stairs on each of its four sides.

Temple of Isis – This temple was erected by the Emperor Augustus.

> ► **COPTIC CHURCH**
> A 5C Christian church, built from reused stone, was erected between the two mammisis at the Temple of Dendara.

PRIMITIVE HEALTH CARE

Because early civilisations believed that illnesses were the result of evil spirits, all forms of Ancient medicine, involving a combination of prayers and divination, were initially prescribed by priests inside temples. From the 12th Dynasty onwards, two papyruses, one dealing with veterinary care, the other with gynaecology, opened up the path towards medical science. The latter, known as the "Berlin Papyrus", described several methods of contraception and provided advice on how to combat sterility and how to find out the sex of a future baby. Six dynasties later, around 1 500 BC, the "Edwin Smith Papyrus" served as a treatise on surgical matters, describing lesions and injuries and providing a list of appropriate treatments. Doctors, known as *sinw*, could either exercise their art as a priest or carry out their functions as a civil servant. Rich patients would pay them for their services, those of poorer means would receive free treatment. Medicine gradually became a lay affair, a process completed by Hippocrates in the 5C BC.

The splendid columns in the inner hypostyle hall.

Great Temple of Hathor★★

Architecture – This temple stands at right angles to the Nile and was probably built during the reigns of Ptolemy XII and Ptolemy XIII. Although similar in appearance to the temple at Edfu, it differs in its absence of a pylon and colonnade. To the south of the courtyard stands the façade of the outer hypostyle hall, erected under Tiberius, but of later construction than the inner hypostyle hall with its six Hathor-headed columns. The hall of offerings and the pronaos precede the naos, while a corridor around the sanctuary gives onto 11 small chapels. The 12 crypts built into the walls can be reached from the south-west corner, although only crypt no 4 is open to the public. A small **kiosk** in the south-west corner of the terrace was where the procession consisting of the Pharaoh and his priests (as depicted on the walls of the stairs) would celebrate the ceremony of the "union of the solar disc", involving the exposure of Hathor's statue to the sun's rays. Note also the small **chapel** to the north-west, comprising three rooms ornamented with representations tied in with the myth of Osiris. It was here that one of the tombs attributed to him in Egypt was located.

Decoration – The most striking feature on the exterior is the **façade★** of the hypostyle hall, on which six columns crowned with Hathor-headed capitals are connected at mid-height by a series of wall-screens. The sculptures here depict the consecration of the temple by Tiberius.

NEW YEAR FESTIVAL
Horus "inhabited" Edfu and Hathor Dendara. Every year a solemn procession took place on New Year's Day, when Horus would visit his wife, who by this time had benefited from the "Union of the Disc" ceremony. The New Year festival was by far-the most important in the Dendara calendar.

On the south wall of the temple is the only known low relief of Cleopatra VII on which she is making an offering to Hathor.

OUTER HYPOSTYLE HALL
In addition to a colony of bats, the last bay of the hall's ceiling contains a superb representation of the goddess **Nut**, in which she is depicted swallowing the sun, which she returns to the world to enable its rays to illuminate the Temple of Dendara.

On the inside, the ceiling of the outer hypostyle hall is adorned with astronomical figures (stars, vultures, diurnal and nocturnal hours); the decoration on the walls commemorates the temple's consecration (note the proliferation of Roman emperors dressed as pharaohs). The inner hypostyle hall evokes the rituals relating to the foundation of the temple, including a priest with a censer. The paintings in the naos define (from left to right) the rituals of daily worship to be fulfilled by the Pharaoh, such as the breaking of the seals, the adoration of Hathor, and the offering of incense.

Dendara is the only temple of its kind in which crypts are decorated; the themes of their low reliefs, accompanied by cartouches of Ptolemy IX and Ptolemy XIII, have led experts to conclude that they were used as "safes".

outskirts

The aim of every Ancient Egyptian was to embark upon a pilgrimage to Abydos, where a stele or an ex-voto would be left to mark this momentous event. Many of these are now on display in museums around the world.

ABYDOS★★
100km/62mi W of Dendara. Open all year 8am-4pm. E£12; students E£6.

Today, the ruins at Abydos are an important place of pilgrimage.

The early necropolis – During the Old Kingdom, the kings established their capital at Memphis and their necropolis at Saqqara, thereby repeating what their ancestors had done with their respective choices of Thinis and Abydos as the capital and necropolis of the Thinite monarchy. Consequently, Abydos is one of the oldest necropolises known to man.

With the development of the Osirian cult, several Egyptian kings erected a tomb at Saqqara and a cenotaph at Abydos.

A place of Osirian worship – These historical foundations resulted in Abydos becoming the main cult centre for the funerary worship of Osiris. According to the Osirian myth, Seth had his brother Osiris cut into 14 pieces; the Ancient Egyptians believed that the head of the god was buried at Abydos, an event that turned the site into the principal reliquary of the Osirian cult. It was during the 12th Dynasty that the cult of Osiris finally replaced that of the local jackal-god, Khentimentiu, known as the "master of death".

Site – The site stands on the edge of the desert and comprises monuments from several periods. These include a cemetery and the ruined temple of Osiris to the north, Thinite cemeteries and tombs in the centre, and buildings erected during the 19th Dynasty *(see below)* to the south.

Temple of Sety I★★
Seven temples in one – This magnificent structure was built on a slope and deviates from the classical plan of Egyptian temples. Another of its peculiarities is that it is flanked by a side wing.

The temple had seven entrances which, with the exception of the middle one, were turned into niches by Rameses II. These opened into two hypostyle halls divided into seven bays leading to seven chapels, each devoted to a divinity (Amun in the centre; Osiris, Isis and Horus to the right; and Ra-Horakhty, Ptah and the king himself to the left).

Ramesside reliefs – The reliefs in the hypostyle halls enable a comparison to be drawn between two periods of Ramesside art: the first under Rameses II, the second under Sety I. The quality of execution during the reign of the latter is considered to be vastly superior. It is generally thought that Rameses II built to excess and that the decoration of his works was too hasty. At Abydos, it is in the chapels that the renewal of the Egyptian style is most evident, following the period of Amarnian art under the 18th Dynasty. These **reliefs**★★★, sculpted during the reign of Sety I, bear witness to the revival of piety initiated by an anti-Amarnian reaction, as well as to the return of the academicism that preceded the Amarnian period. The silhouettes of the king and gods here have rediscovered the rigour prevalent under Amenhotep III, and show the deference of the king before the god. Yet, under the guise of academicism, the art of Sety I is nonetheless influenced by the Amarnian period. It is precisely this merging of styles which constitutes the great originality of the Ramesside style, and which is characterised in particular by the appearance on the royal profile of the long curved nose which originally perhaps was an ethnic trait.

> **T**hese outstanding reliefs have retained their original colour and are divided into 36 sections. The images painted on them depict the ceremonies celebrated by the king.

The Osireion – Another feature of the temple is the cenotaph *(to the rear)* which has been interpreted as a kind of symbolic tomb for Osiris. The central room, constructed of granite, was designed to represent an island surrounded by a canal. A chamber to the right of this room is decorated with finely chiselled astronomical **reliefs**★.

Temple of Rameses II

The most prolific builder of the New Kingdom also erected a funerary temple at Abydos. Smaller and in a poorer state of repair than that of his father, Sety I, its layout comprises a court with three staircases leading to a terrace. A portico leads to the two hypostyle halls, both with remarkably well-preserved low reliefs, and to three chapels built from alabaster and probably dedicated to the Osirian triad.

SOHAG

150km/94mi NW of Abydos.

This important textile-producing town is also one of Egypt's main Coptic centres. The Sohag region is home to around 10 monasteries, the most interesting of which are located within the immediate vicinity of the town.

> **GETTING TO SOHAG**
> As in Asyut, foreign visitors are escorted by police who generally prohibit them from leaving their hotel in the evening. As a result, the best way of visiting Sohag and its monasteries is on a guided full-day excursion from Luxor.

Deir el-Abiad

Visitors should make their way to the entrance of the monastery.

Shenoudi, the iron abbot – The **"White Monastery"** owes its renown to this abbot, born around AD 348 in Akhim, who became a monk here at the age of just seven, and whose saintly reputation quickly attracted a large number of disciples. Shenoudi imposed rigorous discipline and was a fervent opponent of pagan cults, but despite his authoritarianism, he extended great charity towards the poor. He is also considered one of the greatest writers of Coptic literature, as well as one of the key figures in the Coptic Church following the role he played at the Council of Ephesus in 431.

Church of St Shenoudi★ – Although little remains of the long nave in this 5C basilica, the vestiges of columns (taken from various Roman buildings) enable visitors to visualise the original scale of the church. Separated from the nave by a high wall added at a later date, the choir has a cloverleaf plan and as a result has three apses. These are adorned with niches flanked by columns; their culs-de-four are decorated with fine 11C-12C wall paintings by Armenian and Egyptian artists.

> **THE WHITE MONASTERY**
> The monastery takes its name from the white limestone used in its construction and has been known by this title since the time of Arab domination. Certain architectural features within the walls are engraved with hieroglyphs and were removed from Ancient temples.

Deir el-Ahmar

5km/3mi N. Visitors should make their way to the entrance of the monastery.

The **"Red Monastery"** owes its name to the colour of its brick. It probably dates from the second half of the 5C and is similar in plan than its "White" counterpart, albeit with smaller dimensions.

El-Fayum ★

The "Garden of Egypt", as the Fayum region is known, could hardly be more different from Cairo, just an hour to the north. The area is renowned for its roses and jasmine, while its flourishing fields of crops provide an impressive contrast with the arid landscape of the desert. Its inhabitants are particularly welcoming to visitors, although their religious fundamentalism may come as something of a shock.

Location

110km/69mi SW of Cairo between the Nile and the Gebel Gatrâni, at the centre of a depression extending over an area of 18 000km²/6 950sq mi. Access: by bus from Cairo (E£6; 3hr), although it is far easier by taxi. The train is not recommended as it is extremely slow.

Name

The name Fayum has evolved from *Peiom* or Pa Yom, meaning "lake" in Coptic. Nowadays, the name refers to the whole province.

Transcription: الفيوم

Local god

> **CROCODILOPOLIS**
> Under the Greeks, the regional capital was first known as "the city of the crocodile" and every settlement had a temple dedicated to the crocodile god.

◄ Although the lake no longer harbours any crocodiles, in former times it was home to a multitude of them as this is the land of the god Sobek. This god of water fertilising the earth, portrayed as a man with a crocodile's head, was venerated to such an extent in the Fayum that a Pharaoh from the 13th Dynasty took the name of Amenemhat Sobekhotep I.

History

The Fayum came to the fore in Egyptian history during the 12th Dynasty when the pharaohs established their capital at nearby El-Lisht. However, it was the Greco-Roman period that was to have a more profound effect on the region.

background

Election day in Qasr Qarun.

A false oasis – Although the Fayum depression is generally considered to be an oasis, this is a false interpretation as its vegetation benefits from the waters of Nile via a branch canal known as the **Bahr Yussef** or "Joseph's Channel", which supplies water to the Birket el-Qarun (Lake Fayum).

Lake Fayum – The origins of the word Fayum, which translates simply as "lake", date back several million years when this region was nothing more than a huge expanse of water. However, it wasn't until the time of the 12th Dynasty that the pharaohs undertook work to limit the flow of water into the lake. In order to irrigate surrounding land, they built levées, as well as a lock at El-Lahun. During the Ptolemaic period, these levées were removed as the lake had receded, so the task then was to dry out the swamps that had appeared and to build new levées, which nowadays mark out the approximate boundaries of the lake. Towns were established and the region flourished until the 3C AD, when it gradually fell into a period of neglect and decline.

Arsinoe or Arsinoes? – From the 4C BC onwards, Egypt became Hellenised. At the end of this century, the Ptole- ◄ maic Dynasty came to the fore, founded by Ptolemy I, "the Saviour". His successor, Ptolemy II Philadelphus ("the lover of his sister"), was the second protector of the Fayum, following on from **Amenemhat II** (12th Dynasty). Having repudiated his first wife, Arsinoe I, he married his own sister, Arsinoe II, in line with a typically Egyptian tradition; and given that this king adored the Fayum, he named the capital of the province after his betrothed. It is for this reason that the ancient Shedyet, which was briefly known as Crocodilopolis, became Arsinoe, a name that it retained until the end of the Roman period.

> **C**ontrary to the theory put forward by Edgar P. Jacobs in *The Mystery of the Great Pyramid*, it was Ptolemy II, and not Ptolemy I, who commissioned Manetho to write a history of Ancient Egypt.

These creaking norias or waterwheels in the centre of the city are a legacy of the Greeks. The buckets attached to them raise water in the canals from one level to the next.

highlights

Medinet el-Fayum

The old settlement of Arsinoe is today the capital of the Fayum province, having formerly been the capital of the 21st nome of Upper Egypt. Often abbreviated to El-Fayum or "the city of the Fayum", it is well worth a detour, mainly because of its bridges and lively atmosphere, even though it has scant remains from the city of Arsinoe apart from an obelisk attributed to Senusret I. This red-granite monument, in the middle of a roundabout to the north-east of the city, is the only example of its type to be topped by a rounded crown.

Souk – *On the main street, in the centre of the city.* This colourful market is proof of El-Fayum's role as an important producer of fruit and vegetables such as aubergines, cabbages, bananas, oranges and fresh dates sold by peasants dressed in black.

Qaitbay Mosque – *To the N of the city.* This 15C building is one of a number of mosques in this bastion of Islamic fundamentalism, which came to the fore here around 1990. The main entrance gateway, created from ruins removed from neighbouring Ancient sites, is particularly impressive.

The "hanging mosque", built above Coptic capitals, and the slightly dilapidated El-Roubi mosque, with its fine minaret *(closed to the public)* are also worthy of interest.

> **DUST AND NOISE**
> Despite the province's general well-to-do air, Medinet el-Fayum is a somewhat dusty and animated city, with streets heaving with people, carts and drivers intent on making maximum use of their car horn.

Birket el-Qarun

Known locally as the "lake of horns" because of its shape, the extensive Lake Qarun measures 52km/32.5mi in length, 10km/6mi across and stands at 44m/144ft below sea-level. Although it has an average depth of 5m/16ft, parts of the lake descend to 18m/59ft.

The level of salinity in the lake is high, as are the concentrations of fish (despite its allegedly high pollution), providing work for several fisheries along its banks.

Kom Aushim

To the E of the lake.

Site – *Open all year, 9am to 4pm. E£16; camera permit: no charge; video permit: E£100.* The site of Kom Aushim contains the ruins of Ancient Karanis, the city founded under the Ptolemies. All that remains of the **Southern Temple** (dedicated to the god Sobek) is the entrance gateway, built under Commodus, on which a Greek inscription *(on the bay lintel)* evokes Nero. It is thought that the city, which also contains the remains of a sacred lake, was abandoned in the 5C.

Museum – *Open all year, 9am to 4pm; E£6; camera permit: E£10; video permit: E£100.* The collection includes ceramics, glass and mummies, as well as several sculptures discovered at El-Lahoun, Karnak and Tanis. Coptic art and the Fatimid period are highlighted on the first floor.

Shakshuk

On the south side of the lake.

An attractive corniche road runs alongside this fishing village nestling at the end of a small bay. Its colourful fishing boats are adorned with phrases intended to encourage miraculous fishing exploits.

Qasr Qarun

4km/2.5mi W of the lake.

Ptomelaic settlements – Arsinoe and Karanis weren't the only towns founded by the Ptolemies in the Fayum; they also established Bacchias, Soknopaiou Nesos and Philadelphia, among others. The ruins of the latter form the site of Qasr Qarun.

> **THE TEMPLE CRYPT**
> Underground passageways lead to the rarely visited crypt, where a small torch would come in very handy.

◄ **Temple of Dionysus** – *Open all year, 9am to 4pm (5pm in summer); E£16 (E£8 students); camera permit: no charge; video permit: E£25.* The unusual feature of this temple is the first floor, which was used for bedrooms. Note the representations of the local god, Sobek, particularly in the sanctuary's central chapel. Make sure you climb to the top of the monument to enjoy the fine view over the surrounding fertile fields and desert.

Wadi el-Rayan

30km/19mi SW of Lake Qarun. E£5 + E£5 for a vehicle. No public transport available. Under the presidency of Sadat, two large artificial lakes were created in this large ◄ 675km²/260sq mi depression situated 42m/138ft below sea level. This was the first stage of an extensive plan to irrigate this desert landscape via the Bahr Yussef channel, which supplies the Fayum with water from the Nile.

> **S**mall waterfalls link the lakes, conferring a bucolic atmosphere on this nature reserve dominated by the Gebel Rayan. Several species of migratory birds can be spotted here.

El-Hawara

11km/7mi SE of Medinet El-Fayum. Open all year, 9am to 4pm (5pm in summer); E£16 (E£8 students); camera and video permits: no charge.

This town has preserved the remains of the Pyramid of **Amenemhat III** (12th Dynasty) in addition to those of a funerary temple, also referred to as the "Labyrinth".

Amenemhat III – After his father, Senusret III, had ensured the country's military safety, Amenemhat III undertook the task of developing the nation's economy. He was the first protector of the Fayum and was buried in the region.

> **WHAT DAY IS IT?**
> The Fayum region is characterised by an unusual tradition: if a child is born on a Thursday or Friday, the parents name him or her after the day and month of his/her birth. As a result, their children carry the name Friday Ramadan or Thursday Ragab!

Pyramid – As the thin outer layer of limestone has disappeared, all that is now visible is a mound of mud-bricks. In its full glory, the pyramid measured 58m/190ft in height with sides 100m/328ft long; the entrance is on the south side, but is now under water.

The Funerary Temple – Without doubt, this temple was one of the most astonishing structures in Ancient Egypt. Located to the south of the pyramid, its remains served as a quarry during the Roman period. Sadly, what the Greeks referred to as the **"Labyrinth"** is no longer recognisable – according to Herodotus, this was a complex of 1 500 rooms above ground and a similar number beneath

---

THE SO-CALLED "FAYUM PORTRAITS"

Westerners are familiar with this region through the famous funerary portraits exhibited in major museums around the Western world. The portraits were created after the conquest of Egypt by Rome and have since been referred to as the Fayum Portraits as of the 700 or so discovered, the vast majority originate from the Fayum region.

Executed in encaustic or tempera on wood panels, linen or papyrus, they were placed on the face of a mummy, reproducing the exact features of the deceased. This was in fact a late adaptation of the funerary traditions from the time of the Pharaohs, with the portrait – created used techniques developed as a result of the hellenisation of Northern Egypt –replacing the mask.

Given that none of these portraits can be seen in the Fayum nowadays, visitors will have to make their way to the Egyptian Museum in Cairo in order to appreciate these outstanding works.

it. While Strabo viewed this monument as a symbol of the geography of Egypt, numerous archaeologists concur that this is the Pharaoh's mortuary temple, at the same time recognising that its surface area (300m/984ft x 245m/803ft) and the layout of its rooms are contrary to other known funerary temples in Egypt. Others have suggested that the site harbours the remains of a palace and administrative centre.

outskirts

El-Lahun

11km7mi SE of Medinet el-Fayum. Open all year, 9am-4pm (5pm in summer); E£16 (E£8 students); camera and video permits: no charge.

The Pyramid of **Senusret II** (12th Dynasty) stands a short distance from the village on the edge of the desert.

Senusret II – No much is known about the son of Amenemhat II except that like his father he embarked upon trade expeditions in the Mediterranean.

Pyramid – *The interior is closed to the public.* This square, mud-brick pyramid, built on a rocky core, was faced with limestone slabs and crowned by a small granite pyramidion, part of which was discovered by Petrie in 1889. Its sides measured 107m/351ft in length, and its probable height was 48m/157ft. The entrance, on the south side, led to a well dug into the rock, which in turn led to the funerary chamber where the Pharaoh's sarcophagus was discovered.

The Fayum Portraits are strikingly realistic in style.

Kahun – The remains of this settlement extend for several hundred metres to the north of the pyramid. To the west stood the quarters for labourers building the pyramid; more luxurious dwellings, some in excess of 50 rooms, were located to the east. It is possible that a royal palace also existed here as Kahun was Senusret I's main residence.

directory

SHOPPING

A small pottery school set up by a Swiss artisan, Evelyne Bouret, in Tounès, to the south of the lake, towards Qasr Qarun, displays and sells the delightfully naïve pieces produced and decorated by children in the village.

WHERE TO STAY

• *Budget*

Safari Camp – *Wadi el-Rayan – Huts: E£40; 16 bungalows: E£50.* 🚭 This camp on the edge of the lake is ideal for those wishing to get away from it all without worrying too much about creature comforts. Little to do apart from swimming and watching the lake gradually change colour.

• *Moderate*

Auberge du Lac – *Shakshuk –* 🕾 *(02) 354 23 56 – 5 suites and 67 bedrooms: $114/$157.* This former hunting lodge used by King Farouk has a good location on the edge of the lake. All the charm of an old residence, but with bedrooms that have seen better days. Superb views at sunset from the pool area and bar.

Panorama – *Shakshuk –* 🕾 *(084) 71 17 57 – 34 apartments, 3 suites and 23 bedrooms: E£130/E£190.* Also by the lake. Better

facilities than the Auberge du Lac, but with a less welcoming ambience. Attractive new pool which is preferable to the somewhat dirty beach.

WHERE TO EAT

• *Budget*

Goharet Shakshuk – *Shakshuk.* 🚭 The "Jewel of Shakshuk" is better known by the name "Mofreh", after its owner. Specialities include prawns, fried fish and duck couscous (E£20). Sadly, the toilets leave a lot to be desired.

El-Lisht

This small village between Dahshur and Meidum has two pyramids situated on the edge of the Gebel Qatrani. Although in poor condition and less impressive than other Egyptian pyramids, the site is an interesting stop between Cairo and the Fayum oasis.

Location
74km/46mi S of Cairo on the left bank of the Nile. Access: the only option is by taxi, although the site is somewhat difficult to find.

Name
Itjtawy *(see below)* translates as "the seizer of the two lands". The lands in question are those of Upper and Lower Egypt, although El-Lisht is situated in Middle Egypt.
Transcription: برنشت

Although in theory close to El-Lisht, the site of Itjtawy has yet to be discovered.

History
El-Lisht was the burial site for Itjtawy, the capital of Egypt under Amenemhat I and Senusret I during the 12th Dynasty.

highlights

Site currently closed for restoration.

The Muslim cemetery at El-Seoudeya, near El-Lisht.

Pyramid of Amenemhat I
Amenemhat I – While civil war was raging under Mentuhotep IV (11th Dynasty), his vizier, Ammenemes, seized power under the name of Amenemhat I. He quickly established law and order, abandoned the capital at Thebes and established a base between Fayum and Memphis. He was able to reconcile Memphite administrative affairs and Theban religion, but was assassinated after a reign of 30 years.

Pyramid – The most northerly of the two pyramids at El-Lisht is 20m/65ft high, although it originally measured 55m/180ft in height with sides 79m/259ft long. Built close to the temple of Mentuhotep II at Deir el-Bahri, the pyramid occupied a terrace overlooking a mortuary temple on a lower terrace to the east. A gallery *(almost always flooded)* facing the north side of the pyramid leads to the burial chamber.

MASTABA TOMBS
Among the mastabas spread around the pyramid, the largest is that of Senusret-ankh, the chief priest of Ptah. The tomb is located about 200m/220yd to the east of the outer enclosure wall.

Pyramid of Senusret I
Senusret I – Unusually, the son of Amenemhat I played an active role in running the country. As the man responsible for military affairs and expeditions, Senusret I would seem to have had no difficulty in suppressing the initial conspiracy that was to ultimately lead to the assassination of his father. Having learnt his lesson, he reigned as co-regent with his own son, who had to wait a further forty-five45 years before coming to the throne. Although a product of military training, Senusret I reigned over what was a relatively peaceful kingdom.

Pyramid – Similar in design to that of Amenemhat I, in other words in keeping with the style of funerary temples of the 6th Dynasty, it originally measured 61m/200ft high with sides 105m/344ft long. Here also, the funerary temple opens to the east, and the family members are buried inside the enclosure demarcated by a double wall. The pyramid uses a system of construction unheard of at the time, perhaps motivated by financial constraints, with thick walls of limestone blocks with gaps filled by loose stones, brick and sand.

These white, perfectly preserved limestone statues were discovered in 1894 as part of the excavations carried out by the Swiss Egyptologist, Gustave Jéquier, in the courtyard preceding the temple.

A magnificent collection of 10 almost identical **seated life-size statues** of the Pharaoh can be admired in the Egyptian Museum in Cairo *(Room 22)*.

Idfu★★

Idfu is situated at the crossroads of a number of old caravan routes and has become the main stopover point for Nile cruise ships. The town is an agricultural and sugar-producing centre and owes its popularity to the Temple of Horus, the best-preserved temple and one of the most visited monuments in Egypt.

Location
130km/81mi S of Luxor, 115km/72mi N of Aswan, on the left bank of the Nile. Access: if you are not on a cruise ship, the site can be reached by road from Luxor or Aswan, either by bus (between E£5 and E£8) or by taxi as part of a military convoy. The train is not recommended as the railway station is quite a distance from the temple.

Name
The Romans named the town *Apollinopolis Magna*; the Copts referred to it as *Artbô*. Other names visible on the temple walls are Ayn, Hebenu, Mesen and Behdet.

Transcription: إدفو

Local gods
The god Horus, represented either in the form of a hawk or a winged sun, was worshipped in his celestial form in the temple at Idfu.

History
Idfu was the capital of the 2nd nome of Upper Egypt and was known as the "seat of Horus".

worth a visit

Temple of Horus★★
Urban and Ptolemaic – Although an inscription on the temple states that its architect was "Imhotep the Great, son of Ptah", the same architect who built Djoser's pyramid at Saqqara, the edifice was actually constructed during the reign of several of the **Ptolemies** (IV, V, VIII, XI and XII). The explanation for this lies in the fact that blocks which were previously part of an older building, still standing during the reign of Thutmose III, were reused to build the temple here.

It is the second largest temple in Egypt (137m/449ft x 79m/259ft), after the one at Karnak and is still in excellent condition, as a result of being covered in sand up to its capitals for many centuries; this natural protection was removed by Mariette in 1860. The temple stands in the centre of town and is lined to the east by modern houses.

> **T**he journey from the river to the temple is by horse-drawn carriage – needless to say, there's plenty of choice!

> **HORUS**
> This god was also known as the "Lord of the Two Lands", as he was the son of both Isis and Osiris.

> **WHERE TO EAT**
> New Egypt – *Opposite the post office.* Reasonably priced roast chicken and broad beans, provided you double-check the exact price before ordering.

> **T**his inscription also reminds us that the cult of Horus already existed during Djoser's reign.

The first pylon of the temple, both sides of which bears reliefs of Ptolemy II facing Horus.

This urban location has the advantage of placing a pharaonic temple back in its original context. In Ancient times the area around the temple would also have been crowded with people, as ordinary citizens were not allowed access to the temple itself – only the "divine fathers" or priests had the right to see the statue of the god. However, the public was able to watch processions, whose rituals can be seen carved on the temple walls.

Layout – The west side of the temple leads to an imposing **pylon**★, with 36m/118ft-high towers decorated with images of Ptolemy XII sacrificing prisoners to Horus and Hathor. Openings show that these towers are divided into floors with individual chambers (a staircase leads to the terrace). Two falcons representing Horus are carved on either side of the gate entrance, as if to stand guard over the temple.

The **court**, known as the "Court of the People", is flanked on three sides by a **colonnade**★: each column has a different capital, which is echoed in the opposite wing.

The first hypostyle hall is in semi-darkness and is one of the few to have retained its roof; it is decorated with a large number of scenes of offerings, organised into registers. The second hypostyle hall, surrounded by three small offering chambers, leads into the **offering hall**, flanked by flights of steps leading to the terraces. A vestibule leads into the sanctuary, whose **naos** is built from a 4m/13ft-tall granite block, recycled from the original temple.

The corridor around the sanctuary opens into 10 small chapels, whose purpose is explained by inscriptions: the second to the left, for example, is the "chamber of linen"; the one situated in line with the temple houses a replica of the stuccoed wooden solar bark on display in the Egyptian Museum in Cairo.

A long ambulatory, adorned with low reliefs, runs between the temple and the wall enclosing the covered sections of the building. The low relief on the west side of the ambulatory portrays a famous scene illustrating the final episode in the myth of Isis and Osiris: armed with a harpoon, their son Horus is depicted killing Seth, who is represented in the form of a hippopotamus.

Mammisi – The ruins of the mammisi, which dates from the time of Rameses III and is situated opposite the temple, still bear traces of the original plan of two rooms surrounded by a peristyle. The dados of the portico pillar capitals are decorated with the god Bes, whose symbolic role here was that of the protector of childbirth. The columns in the forecourt are adorned with gods playing musical instruments, such as the sistrum.

outskirts

El-Kab
18km/11mi N of Idfu, on the right bank of the Nile. Neither the cruises nor the convoys between Idfu and Luxor stop at El-Kab. As a result you will need to obtain special authorisation to stop here or else hire a taxi.

Nekhbet – El-Kab was once Ancient Nekheb, a name that had been in use since the 2nd Dynasty. This important religious centre, known to the Greeks as *Eileithyiapolis*, is now little more than a collection of ruins. The site was dedicated to the goddess Nekhbet ("she who comes from Nekheb") who was depicted in the form of a vulture. The remains of thick mud-brick walls of a temple built during the reign of Thutmose III, a second temple dating to the time of Amenhotep II, and a sacred lake are still visible here today.

Necropolis – The rock-tombs of the nobles of El-Kab date back to the beginning of the 18th Dynasty. The tomb of Paheri, the governor of Nekheb, is decorated with colourful scenes taken from daily life depicting activities rang-

A superb pschent-crowned hawk★ stands guard at the entrance to the naos.

A flight of steps to the east of the temple leads to the **nilometer**.

On the way back from the temple, you will pass through the souk district, with its multitude of horse-drawn carriages. If you are on a cruise, you're unlikely to have time to stop here.

EXCAVATIONS
It was at Idfu that the Belgian archaeologist Jean Capart (1877-1947) made his name. He led an expedition for the Fondation Reine-Élisabeth and was responsible for work at the site from 1939-45. The house in which he lived is located between the railway line and the Nile.

The magnificent ceiling in the hypostyle hall of the Temple of Khnum at Esna.

ing from farming and family life to hunting and funerals. That of Ahmose (no 5), an admiral who fought against the Hyksos, is adorned with decorations and inscriptions evoking his glorious life.

Isna

61km/38mi N of Idfu, on the left bank of the Nile. Neither the cruises nor the convoys between Idfu and Luxor stop at Isna. As a result you will need to obtain special authorisation to stop here or else hire a taxi.

The first sights as you approach Esna are an elegant Fatimid minaret and a 875m/2870ft long lock-bridge, built in 1905 and modernised in 1995. This small agricultural town is now also a centre for the textile industry.

Temple of Khnum★ – *Open all year, 6am-5.30pm (6.30pm in summer). E£8; camera permit E£4; video permit E£25.* Only the **hypostyle hall★★** still survives from this temple started during the reign of Ptolemy VI and finished under the Emperor Vespasian. Like the temple of Horus in Edfu, this beautiful example of Greco-Roman architecture has retained its impressive ceiling. Its 24 columns with composite capitals (all different) support architraves decorated with astronomical scenes; cartouches of Ptolemy VI can be seen on the central section of the back wall, which is part of the earlier temple built under Ptolemy VI.

The rest of the room dates from the reigns of Tiberius, Claudius and Vespasian and depicts scenes which prove beyond doubt the participation of several Roman emperors, including Domitian, Nerva, Hadrian, Septimus Severus and Caracalla, in pharaonic rituals. The inscriptions in the temple are considered to be among the most difficult to decipher in Egypt; some of the pictorial symbols here are unusually complex, and the task is made even more difficult by the use of unusual hieroglyphs and spelling mistakes. The temple was partly cleared by Mariette in the 19C, although much of it remains buried under the modern town.

> ### KHNUM AT ISNA
> The main centre for the worship of the ram-god Khnum was Elephantine Island in Aswan, although some of the most beautiful ceremonies took place here. Scenes on the temple walls depict the annual festival, during which an icon of the god was borne across the city and then displayed to the sun to soak up its energy.

> ### TOYS IN ANCIENT EGYPT
> In Ancient Egypt childless couples were often accused of being selfish. For this reason, orphans were quickly adopted and their new parents were expected to raise them as if they were their own flesh and blood. Children were brought up to respect their elders and honour their mother and father, but there is no doubt that they were much loved and cherished nonetheless .
> Little girls were given a collection of dolls, some made from rags, and others carved from wood with movable joints and often painted with bright colours. Boys, on the other hand, played with miniature weapons made by craftsmen who were skilled in producing realistic toys.
> As they grew up, young girls would play games such as *"zenet"* (similar to draughts) or "serpent" (not unlike snakes and ladders); young men took part in sporting events such as running or the throwing of weights.

Kom Ombo★★

The temple of Kom Ombo, dedicated to the crocodile-god Sobek, enjoys a superb position on a hillock overlooking the Nile. One of the legendary sites of Ancient Egypt, the temple is particularly breathtaking at sunset and is a popular stopping point on Nile cruises. This is romantic Egypt at its best.

Location

LUXOR TO ASWAN BY ROAD
Vehicles travel between Luxor and Aswan in convoy. As Kom Ombo is not one of the scheduled stops en route, police authorisation is required before stopping here.

190km/118mi S of Luxor, 45km/28mi N of Aswan, on the left bank of the Nile. Access: by cruise ship or taxi from Luxor or Aswan; collective taxis (E£2) run between the two towns and drop off 1km/0.6mi N of the temple; the long train journey is best avoided.

Name

The name Kom Ombo comes from the prehistoric site on which the temple was built: the site was known as *Nubyt* in Ancient Egyptian, *Embo* in Coptic and *Ombos* in Greek. Transcription: كوم أمبو

Local gods

The temple at Kom Ombo was associated with the crocodile-god, Sobek. As a result of the construction of the Aswan Dam, crocodiles, once so numerous in this area, are no longer found in the Nile north of Aswan.

The crocodile was venerated through Sobek, the god of water who fertilised the earth. The main cult centres of this god were in the Fayum; during the New Kingdom Sobek was worshipped in Kom Ombo as Hathor's husband and the father of Khons.

History

A dependency of the 1st nome of Upper Egypt, whose capital was situated on Elephantine Island in Aswan, it is thought that Kom Ombo became an independent province during the 18th Dynasty. The temple visible today dates from the Ptolemaic period.

highlights

Temple★★

Open all year, 8am-4pm. E£10; students E£5; camera permit E£5; video permit E£25.

Started by Ptolemy VI, the temple was finally completed in the 3C AD.

The temple stands in a picturesque setting of maize and sugarcane fields, its white stone providing a sharp contrast with the blue sky and green, fertile countryside. Although much of the building is in ruins, it is still an impressive sight which conveys perfectly the image of Ancient Egypt.

Sobek and Haroeris – The temple is dedicated to **Sobek** and the falcon-headed **Haroeris.** The latter was none other than Horus, son of Ra, a god of the sky assimilated in the New Kingdom with the Heliopolitan god Shu, the god of air, who, with his wife Tefnut, formed the first divine couple. Other gods worshipped in the temple included Hathor, Amun, Ptah, Min, Thoth, Khum, Nephthys, Isis and Osiris.

Kom Ombo – a popular stopping point for cruise ships.

A unique plan – Although the temple bears an obvious resemblance to the temple of Horus at Edfu (a courtyard, two hypostyle halls, one of which is a pronaos, three vestibules – as opposed to two at Edfu – and a naos), the plan of the temple at Kom Ombo is unique, as it is the only temple of Ancient Egypt to have two entrances and two parallel galleries around the sanctuary. This unusual feature lends the temple a mysterious air and is explained by its dedication to two gods, combining two sanctuaries in one.

Mammisi – The mammisi, built by Ptolemy VIII, can be seen to the left and in front of the temple.

Hypostyle halls – The **façade**★ of the temple (or the external wall of the first room) has a double door, on either side of which Ptolemy XIII is depicted; to the left, the Pharaoh is shown being purified by Horus and Thoth, and, to the right, by Sobek and Haroeris.

The ceiling of the first room, which acts as a pronaos, is decorated with astronomical scenes. The campaniform columns are adorned with scenes of offerings, and also bear the name of Ptolemy XIII; the names of Ptolemy VIII, Ptolemy XII and Cleopatra II can be seen on the walls, alongside paintings of scenes of ritual.

The walls of the second room are decorated with scenes of offerings and the names of Ptolemy VI and Ptolemy VIII.

Sanctuary and galleries – As is the case with the façade, the decoration of the three vestibules is dedicated to Ptolemy VIII and Cleopatra II; the naos is divided into two chapels dedicated to Haroeris *(left)* and Sobek *(right)*. The internal gallery surrounding the sanctuary bears the cartouches of Nero and Vespasian and is decorated with scenes of offerings. The external **gallery**★ is more interesting: on the external wall, in line with the naos, surgical instruments such as tongs, knives, scissors and trepans can be seen; the internal wall is adorned with an image of the lionness-goddess Sekhmet. This goddess was believed to be the divine incarnation of the "eye of Ra" and was said to be used by Ra to punish those who rebelled against him. She was able to bring illness or death upon mortals and as a result held a stranglehold over matters of health. It was for this reason that the priests of Sekhmet included doctors and veterinary surgeons.

EXCAVATIONS
The temple was cleared of debris by the Egyptian Antiquities Department led by Jacques de Morgan.

Deeply carved reliefs are a typical feature of Ptolemaic art.

outskirts

Daraw
8km/5mi S of Kom Ombo. Access: by taxi or collective taxi from Kom Ombo (25pt) or Aswan (E£1.5).

Camel market – *Souk al-Gamaal, 2km/1.2mi from the village; follow the crowd in the direction of the Nile. Tues, 7am-2pm; also Sun in winter*. This colourful market, organised by a local character by the name of "Sheikh Badawi", brings together animals from Sudan, brought here by nomads of the Bishari tribe, both in traditional caravans ► and by lorry.

Other markets held nearby include a fruit and vegetable market and a livestock fair selling a range of animals, including cows and goats, and where stall-holders are often seen carrying their animals over their shoulders.

► **T**ry to visit the market on a Sunday before 11am as this is when more than 1 000 camels are brought here to be sold.

directory

WHERE TO EAT
• *Budget*
Venus – *Open 24hr a day. On the banks of the Nile (between the temple and the taxi stand.* ✉ Feta sandwiches and excellent ice-cream with raisins. A pleasant patio.

Al-Noba – *On the main road.* ✉ This snack bar sells takeaway chicken, *kofta* and vegetables.

Luxor★★★

Champollion claimed that "Thebes is the greatest word that exists in any language".

The former capital of Egypt, built on the site of Ancient Thebes, has long been an important tourist centre because of the high concentration of Ancient temples and tombs in the surrounding area. These include the magnificent temple of Karnak and the necropolises of the two royal valleys, which provide a fascinating insight into the pharaohs of the New Kingdom and the gods of Ancient Egypt.

Location
707km/442mi S of Cairo, 235km/147mi N of Aswan, on the right bank of the Nile. Access: by plane, either charter or Egyptair, from Cairo or Aswan; by bus from Cairo (journey time: 11hr, E£55) or Aswan (5hr, E£10); by road, as part of a convoy from Hurghada or Aswan; or by train from Cairo (10hr, E£315); the best option is the night train.

Name
At the time of the pharaohs, the city had three alternative names: *Waset*, meaning the "village of the sceptre"; *Niut*, the "town"; or *Het Amun*, the "castle of Amun". The present village of Luxor was called *Ipet Reset*, the "harem of the south". The Greeks referred to it as *Diospolis Magna*, as well as Thebes, either after the Thebes in Boeotia or because of phonetic confusion. The present name is a corruption of the Arabic *El-Qusur*, a reference to the *castrum* or camp built here by the Romans.

Transcription: الأقصر

Famous People
Famous Egyptologists who have worked here include Howard Carter, who discovered Tutankhamun's tomb, the Frenchman Auguste Mariette, who began the first excavations of the Temple of Karnak, and Gaston Maspero, who unearthed the Temple of Luxor.

History
During the First Intermediate Period, Thebes was the capital of the 4th nome of Upper Egypt. The town became the capital of Egypt during the Middle Kingdom, although it temporarily lost this role under the Hyksos during the Second Intermediate Period.

The Sphinx at the Temple of Luxor.

background

From a village to a capital – During the Old Kingdom, when Memphis was the glittering capital of Egypt, Thebes was no more than a large village, which then became a centre for the cult of the god Montu from the 6th Dynasty onwards. The First Intermediate Period, which saw the nomarchs of Herakleopolis (near Asyut) gain in strength, brought increasing importance for the village when its own nomarch, Intef I, founded the 11th Dynasty and became ruler of Egypt. Shortly after, Mentuhotep II made the village the capital of his empire.

Thebes enters the history books – After the Hyksos domination during the Second Intermediate Period, Thebes increased in size and became an important metropolis during the 18th and 19th Dynasties. The town amassed hitherto unparalleled wealth, from booty won through war and as a result of its trading links with Central Africa and the Persian Gulf. It was divided into a number of districts (Medamut and Karnak to the north; Tod and Ermant to the south) and boasted houses, tall buildings, magnificent residences surrounded by gardens, royal palaces and temples. Never before had Egypt known such splendour.

In the shadow of the Delta – The constant threats from Asia forced the Rameses pharaohs to reinforce their military positions in the Delta for strategic reasons. The Delta town of Piramesse even became the capital of Egypt, although in many ways Thebes remained the most important city in the empire. However, gradually this situation began to change and the first four dynasties of the Second Intermediate Period all had their origins in the Delta. Under the 25th Dynasty, the Kushite kings raised the profile of the city once again, but Luxor's golden age had passed and the town's fate mirrored that of Egypt, as the country slowly fell into decline.

Metropolis and necropolis – From the time of Intef I, the west bank of the Nile opposite the city was used as a burial ground for several kings, with the river separating the world of the living from that of the dead. Within the walls, Theban temples were built at Karnak and on the site of present-day Luxor to the glory of the god Amun; beyond the boundaries of the city there developed a world dedicated to the afterlife. Here, hewn into the rock, the pharaohs built mortuary temples and a number of tombs for both kings and private individuals, a huge enterprise that required a legion of workers who lived on site. Consequently, Thebes was a huge agglomeration clearly divided into two distinct sections by the Nile.

The Theban necropolis and its temples are an endless source of fascination for archaeologists. Here, at the Ramesseum, workers use traditional methods.

AMUN,
THE GOD OF STATE
Originally Thebes was a centre of the cult of the god Montu, as well as for a more obscure god by the name of Amun. From the 12th Dynasty, the latter, whose names means "the hidden one", became the offical state god. He was worshipped as the most important of all Egyptian gods for many years, although he was briefly replaced by Aten during the reign of Amenhotep IV.

exploring Luxor

Souk and Corniche★ – Before embarking on a Nile cruise south to Aswan, most visitors will explore the lively and colourful souk situated behind the Temple of Luxor. Although not as impressive as its counterpart in Aswan, the souk is still a fascinating introduction to Egypt for visitors fresh from Europe. Independent travellers may wish to buy fresh fruit and vegetables here, preferably in the morning. Those travelling as part of an organised tour group will have no choice: their visit to the souk will take place at night, when the market is at its liveliest.

The Corniche stretches from the Novotel to the Temple of Karnak, passing the Temple of Luxor en route. Feluccas are moored along the southern stretch of the Corniche; the large cruise ships can be found to the northern end. The former offer short boat trips to Banana Island, a lush island planted with palm trees 5km/3mi upriver from Luxor, or across the river to the west bank, a means of transport considerably more expensive than the public ferry *(see Directory)*.

FELUCCA TRIP
A **boat trip**★★ on the Nile provides the perfect end to the day, as the sun dips behind the mountains overlooking the royal valleys on the west bank.
Alternatively, you may prefer an early morning **hot-air balloon ride**★★★ above the magnificent Theban Valley.

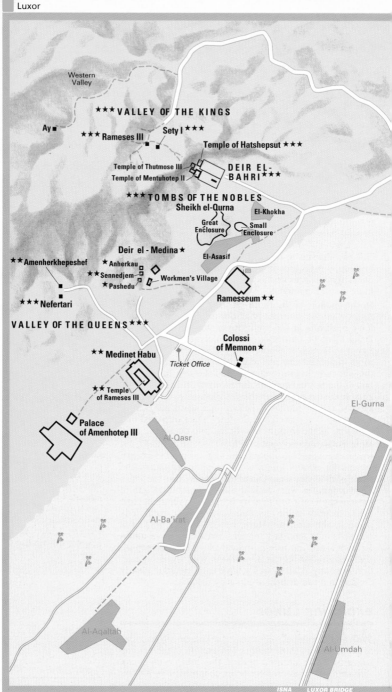

Plantations ★ – Luxor has so many archaeological sites and architectural ruins to tempt visitors that the modern town has little to offer in comparison, with the exception of its souk and the Corniche. However, a pleasant excursion at the end of the day is a bike ride or trip by horse-drawn carriage through the surrounding plantations. The dirt tracks on the outskirts of the town head into dense banana, palm and sugar-cane plantations, providing glimpses of a quiet, rural world where agricultural activity is still intense. As is so often the case in Egypt, whether you are cycling or in a carriage, you are

TOURIST OFFICE
Tourist Bazaar, south of the temple of Luxor, on the El-Karnak road (☏ (095) 37 32 94). Open daily, 8am-8pm (1pm Fri).

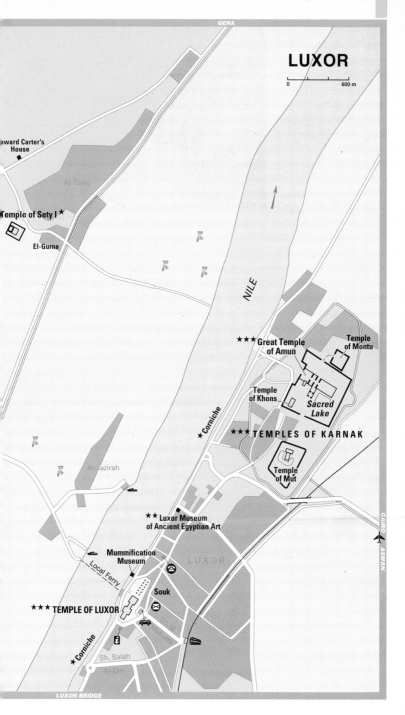

sure to be followed by dozens of children keen to catch a glimpse of foreign visitors.

highlights

TEMPLES OF KARNAK★★★

1.5km/0.9mi N of the town (3km/1.8mi N of the Temple of Luxor). Open all year 6am-5.30pm (6.30pm in summer). E£20; students E£10; camera permit with tripod E£20; other cameras and videos no charge. Open-air museum E£10; students E£5. The ticket office is situated on the square in front of the temple.

The Corniche, between Karnak and Luxor.

Site

Enclosures – The temple complex of Karnak covers an area of 123ha/303 acres and comprises three distinct sections: the temple precinct of the god **Montu**, to the north; the Great Temple precinct of the god **Amun**, in the centre; and the temple precinct of the god **Mut**, to the south. Of these, the Great Temple precinct is by far the richest in archaeological ruins. Built in mud-brick, this immense quadrilateral enclosure has a circumference of 2 400m/7 872ft and once had eight doors; the magnificent temple and the ruins of other buildings stand within this enclosure, alongside the ruins of other monuments both contemporary to the temple and built during later periods.

Thousands of blocks of stone are still strewn around the site. To make matters worse, in 1899, 11 columns of the hypostyle hall collapsed, although these have been rebuilt by architects from the Egyptian Antiquities Service.

◄ **A continual restoration process** – In the year 27 AD, an earthquake destroyed part of the hypostyle hall of the Great Temple of Amun. In the centuries that followed, the site was plundered under Constantine, parts of the temples were transformed into churches after the closing of all pagan temples by Theodosius, and stone from the monuments was removed and used to feed lime kilns; as a result, by the time Napolean's archaeologists arrived here the site was little more than dust and sand. However, around 1860, the Khedive **Ismail Pasha** commissioned Auguste Mariette to protect the site, and since the beginning of the 20C it has been painstakingly excavated and rebuilt by archaeologists. Although only a quarter of the area has been examined to date, thanks to the enthusiasm of the many experts who have worked here much of the splendour of this magnificent Ancient site has been restored, and excavation work continues to this day.

The ram represented the god Amun, hence the ram-headed sphinxes lining the avenue to the temple.

Great Temple of Amun★★★

The building dates mainly from the 18th and 19th Dynasties, although some sections were added during the 22nd, 25th and 30th Dynasties, as well as during the Macedonian period. The temple faces east-west and follows the daytime trajectory of the sun; the "propylaea" (from the 7th to the 10th pylons) stand parallel with the Nile.

Avenue of Sphinxes – Previously preceded by a pit which once housed the sacred barks and which was linked to the Nile by a canal, this avenue is flanked on either side by 20 ram-headed sphinxes, each of which holds a small statue ◄ of Rameses II between its front paws.

First Pylon – This pylon, 113m/370ft wide, 15m/49ft thick and 30m/98ft high at its southern side, was built during the 30th Dynasty, probably by Nectanebo I. It was never completed and has no decoration on its walls. Inscriptions carved on the pylon in the 19C give an idea of how much sand covered the temple at that time.

Great Court★★ – This is the largest of all internal Egyptian courts, measuring 100m/328ft in width and 80m/262ft in length. The processions of sacred barks

Barks and ships
During the time of Rameses II the sacred bark of Amun measured 67m/219ft. These sacred boats all had their own distinctive symbol: Amun was represented by a ram, Mut by an effigy of a goddess, and Montu by a hawk's head.

would have taken place here during the reign of Rameses II. Two **porticoes** run along the side walls: the northern portico is lined with 18 columns bearing papyrus bud capitals; the southern portico is interrupted by the temple of Rameses III, and runs into the **Bubastite Portal**, so-called because it was built under the 22nd Dynasty, the capital of which was at Bubastis in the Delta. In the centre, the ruins of the **kiosk of Taharqo** (25th Dynasty) have retained just one of the 10 large bell-shaped columns which once surrounded it; this column was largely rebuilt in 1928 as it leant to one side, in much the same way as the famous Leaning Tower of Pisa.

The **Temple of Sety II** in the north-west corner was used as a shelter for sacred barks. It comprises three adjoining chapels dedicated, from left to right, to the Theban

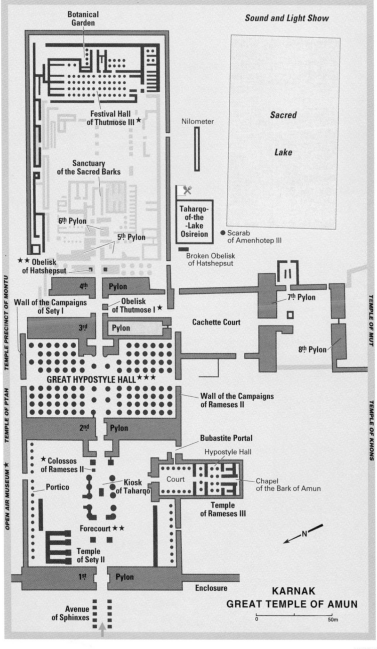

Botanical Garden

Sound and Light Show

Festival Hall of Thutmose III ★

Nilometer

Sacred

Lake

Sanctuary of the Sacred Barks

6th Pylon

5th Pylon

Taharqo-of-the-Lake Osireion

● Scarab of Amenhotep III

★★ Obelisk of Hatshepsut

Broken Obelisk of Hatshepsut

TEMPLE PRECINCT OF MONTU

4th Pylon

7th Pylon

Wall of the Campaigns of Sety I

Obelisk of Thutmose I ★

Cachette Court

3rd Pylon

TEMPLE OF PTAH

GREAT HYPOSTYLE HALL ★★★

8th Pylon

Wall of the Campaigns of Rameses II

2nd Pylon

Bubastite Portal

Hypostyle Hall

★ Colossos of Rameses II

Court

Chapel of the Bark of Amun

OPEN AIR MUSEUM ★

Portico

Kiosk of Taharqo

Temple of Rameses III

Forecourt ★★

N

Temple of Sety II

1st Pylon

Enclosure

KARNAK
GREAT TEMPLE OF AMUN

0   50m

Avenue of Sphinxes

TEMPLE OF NUT

TEMPLE OF KHONS

Hatshepsut, whose two obelisks were erected by the queen on the occasion of her jubilee or Festival of Heb-Sed. It is thought that these obelisks were covered with pure gold. An inscription tells us that the obelisks took seven months to complete.

gods, Mut, Amun and Khons. The **Temple of Rameses III** is a smaller version of the great temples built during the New Kingdom period and has the same layout, with a pylon preceded by colossal statues, a porticoed court, a hypostyle hall decorated with offering scenes, and a naos divided into three chapels to house the sacred barks.

Second Pylon – Built by Horemheb, this pylon has a portal flanked by colossal statues of Rameses II, only one of which has survived. The upper section of the portal, restored under the Ptolemies, is decorated with Ptolemaic reliefs.

Great Hypostyle Hall★★★ – It is worth making a journey to Luxor to see this hall alone. Its 134 colossal columns form an unforgettable forest of stone, creating an overall impression of surreal beauty and breathtaking grandeur. The hall is at its most atmospheric either early in the morning or late in the afternoon, when diagonal shadows increase the effect of the massive columns.

The hall is 102m/334ft wide, 53m/173ft long and 23m/75ft high. It was started by **Sety I** and finished by **Rameses II**, although it is likely that the 12 bell-shaped columns of the central avenue – the upper section of their capitals has a circumference of 15m/49ft – were built under **Amenhotep III**. The hall is lit by clerestory windows between the central avenue and the side aisles, so that when the roof of the temple was still intact, only the central columns would have been suffused with light.

The decoration on the walls and column-shafts evokes honours bestowed upon the three Theban gods by the Pharaoh. On the inner wall of the left side of the pylon the king is depicted kneeling, offering a statue of Maat to Amun-Ra and Mut; also visible is a procession of sacred barks carried on poles by priests, identifiable by their shaven heads. On the external wall, to the north, the **wall of the campaigns of Sety I** portrays the military exploits of the king in Syria, Palestine *(east section)*, and against the Libyans and Hittites *(west section)*. To the south, the **wall of the campaigns of Rameses II** depicts the battle of Qadesh *(east section)* and the Pharaoh's exploits in Palestine *(west section)*.

Third Pylon – This pylon stands at the end of the great hypostyle hall and acts as the façade of the Temple of Amenhotep III, which is no longer standing, hence the presence of a **portal**. This is followed by a narrow court, where four pink granite obelisks once stood; only the **obelisk of Thutmose I★**, 23m/75ft in height, with an estimated weight of 143t, has survived.

Fourth Pylon – Built by Thutmose I, this pylon acted as the façade of a temple constructed at the beginning of the New Kingdom around an old temple dating from the 12th Dynasty. Of this king, only the colossal statues along the wall remain, wearing the white crown *(to the south)* and the red crown *(to the north)*, remain of this king. Two obelisks once stood in front of the pylon but today only the **obelisk of Hatshepsut★★** survives. It measures 30m/98ft in height and has an estimated weight of 380t; its pyramidion was added by Thutmose III, who also surrounded the obelisk with casing.

Fifth Pylon – Little remains of this pylon, which was also built by Thutmose I.

Sixth Pylon – The last of the pylons was built by Thutmose III. Although it is now half of its original height, its famous list of peoples vanquished by the Egyptians can still be seen, with the names of the defeated towns and peoples inscribed in cartouches.

Sanctuary of the Sacred Barks – Built by Philip III, the half-brother of Alexander the Great, this sanctuary consists of two rooms decorated with religious scenes. It was once used to house the sacred barks and was originally surrounded by a corridor. A sanctuary dating from the Middle Kingdom once stood beyond the building, although nothing remains of this construction today.

The sacred lake and obelisks of Thutmose I and Hatshepsut.

Festival Hall of Thutmose III★ – In a break from tradition, the entrance to this hall is situated to the right, rather than along the central axis of the building. Known as "Akhmenu", this hypostyle hall, with its 32 pillars and 10 columns built in Archaistic style, was in fact a jubilee temple in which the Pharaoh participated in rites in order to regenerate his temporal strength and spiritual power. To the north, a flight of steps leading up to a platform marks the spot where he made his offerings to the sun.

The rear section of the Akhmenu comprises a number of solar halls and an area popularly referred to as the **botanical garden**. The walls of this small room, an antechamber to the sanctuary, are decorated with plants discovered by the king during his campaign in Syria.

A small temple with a façade of six Osirid pillars, and the ruins of a temple attributed to Rameses II can be seen behind the Akhmenu.

> **A**lthough this decor may seem unusual for an Egyptian temple, its purpose is more symbolic than decorative: plants contribute to the regeneration of the universe and so these motifs can be seen as an analogy of the Pharaoh's regeneration and the rites that took place in this temple.

PYLONS

Karnak was the first temple to use pylons, a type of monumental gateway built in two symmetrical sections which marked the entrance to the building. Their origins remain unclear, although it is possible that they evolved from the massive structures adorned with a horizontal crown that were used in temples erected during the Middle Kingdom. Both structures had grooves used to hold masts.

These two massive forms flanking the entrance to the temple represented the two mountains between which the sun rose, usually depicted on the cornice. This symbolism was completed by the movement of the oriflamme masts, representing the breath of the divine.

North of the Great Temple

Temple of Ptah – This temple is situated close to the precinct wall, at the end of a path littered with debris. It was built by Thutmose III and later restored and decorated by the Ptolemies. The building is divided into three chapels, dedicated to Nefertem, Ptah and Sekhmet, each of which have retained their roofing.

Open-air Museum★ – *A special ticket should be purchased at the entrance.* Thousands of blocks of stone adorned with magnificent reliefs have been gathered here as attempts are made to discover their provenance within the site. Some have been reconstructed using the anastylosis method *(see SAQQARAH)*, such as the altar with horns, the calcite chapel of Thutmose IV, the **white chapel** of Senusret I (the first to be built at Karnak) and the **red chapel** or sanctuary of the bark of Hatshepsut, rebuilt by masons from the Compagnons de France organisation.

> **WORTH SEEING**
> In the last chapel, almost hidden in the darkness, is a **statue of a lioness**★, the emblem of the goddess Sekhmet. The statue is illuminated by a shaft of sunlight which falls through an opening in the ceiling, with breathtaking results.

Amenhotep III's granite scarab at the north-west corner of the lake. Walking around once is said to bring good luck, three times marriage and seven times a first child.

ANASTYLOSIS
In the coming century this method of restoration should make it possible to rebuild a range of buildings which are currently in ruins or have disappeared, such as pylons, the kiosk of Taharqo, and the many Osirid chapels on the site.

The list of monuments that need rebuilding is a long one. The various sections have to be classified, documented and preserved in order that certain monuments, many of which are still being excavated, can then be rebuilt. This research laboratory has already reconstructed five statues of Sekhmet, the west section of the ninth pylon, and the temples of Sety II and Rameses III, among others.

Precinct of the Temple of Montu – A Ptolemaic gateway, once preceded by an avenue of sphinxes, leads to the ruins of this temple, built by Amenhotep III.

South of the Great Temple

Sacred lake – This lake, the walls and steps of which have been rebuilt, measures 120m/132yd by 77m/85yd.

Taharqo-of-the-Lake Osireion – This sacred structure was built with blocks taken from an earlier kiosk built by Shabaka, another Pharaoh of the 25th Dynasty.

Cachette Court – In 1901, 779 stone statues and close to 170 000 bronze statues, dating mainly from the Late Period, were discovered here. They are now part of the collection of the Egyptian Museum in Cairo.

Built by Horemheb, the 9th and 10th pylons were constructed from thousands of "talatat" blocks (blocks of engraved sandstone) taken from a temple built in Karnak by Amenhotep IV and dedicated to Aten *(see Museum of Ancient Egyptian Art).*

Seventh, Eighth, Ninth, and Tenth Pylons – These pylons formed the propylaeum leading from the Great Temple of Amun to the Temple of Mut. Two obelisks built by Thutmose III once stood in the first court. Only the base remains of one of these; the other is now in Istanbul.

Temple of Khons – This well-preserved temple was built by Rameses III. Decorated by the Ramesside rulers, with a fine **gateway** added by Ptolemy III, it provides an interesting synthesis of the architecture of the late New Kingdom and early Greek periods. The eight-columned hypostyle hall leads into the hall of the bark, which is adorned with beautifully coloured Ramesside reliefs. The best examples of these can be seen in the chapel to the right of the naos, where Rameses IV is depicted offering bouquets to Khons.

A small unfinished temple built by Ptolemy VIII and dedicated to the god Opet stands to the west.

Temple of Mut – *Closed to the public.* Two avenues of sphinxes lead to this temple, which was built by Amenhotep III and is surrounded on three sides by a sacred lake.

EXTRACT FROM THE GREAT HYMN TO AMUN
"Praise be yours, who dwell in contentment,
lord of a joyful heart, glorious in power,
Possessor of the Crown, with towering double plumes,
with splendid diadem, tall in the White Crown.
The sight of you is cherished by the gods –
the Double crown firm on your brow,
With love of you spreading throughout the Two Lands
and your sunbeams glorious in the eye."
Taken from an 18th Dynasty papyrus dating from the reign of Amenhotep IV; from "Hymns, Prayers and Songs – An Anthology of Ancient Egyptian Lyric Poetry" translated by John L. Foster (Scholars Press, Atlanta, Georgia) .

worth a visit

Mummification Museum

On the Corniche, N of the Temple of Luxor, opposite the Mina Hotel. Open all year, 9am-1pm and 5-10pm. E£20; students E£10.

Although the explanations are not quite thorough enough for a full understanding of the mummification process, this museum has an interesting and comprehensive collection of utensils, funerary objects, sarcophagi, and, more importantly, mummies, including a ram, cat, crocodile and baboon, in addition to the mummy of Maserhati, an important official from the 21st Dynasty. Sarcophagi were used to protect the mummy, as the Ancient Egyptians believed that it was essential for the body to retain its physical form in order to survive in the hereafter. These sarcophagi were used from the 1st Dynasty onwards, and were usually placed in a north-south direction in the tomb, so that the deceased, lying ▶ on his or her left side, was facing the rising sun.

> This explains why two large eyes can often be seen painted on the left side of the coffin.

Luxor Museum of Ancient Egyptian Art

On the Corniche, beyond Nefertiti Street, heading in the direction of the Temple of Karnak. Open all year, 9am-1pm and 4-9pm (5-10pm in summer). Last entry 30min before closing time. E£38; students E£19; camera permit E£10; video permit E£100.

This small museum, opened in 1975, houses a collection of statuary, steles, pottery, jewels and furniture discovered in the temples and tombs of Thebes. All the items, only a fraction of which are on display, date from the Middle and New Kingdoms.

Cachette Room – *Ground floor, immediately to the right.* This room is so-called because it houses a display of statues discovered in 1989 in the cache under the Temple of Luxor *(see Temple of Luxor)*. The most impressive statue is that of **Amenhotep III**★★ *(to the rear)*, the car- ▶ touches of which have been destroyed, probably by his son Amenhotep IV. The Pharaoh stands with his left foot thrust forward, indicating that he is alive; the text behind extols his virtues.

> **O**ther highlights of the museum include the **Sphinx of Tutankhamun**; the three statues of **Horemheb**, one of which depicts him with two jars in front of Aten; and **Amun and Mut**★ (second room of the cachette), the divine couple of Thebes, sculpted during the reign of Rameses II.

Entrance – The magnificent red granite **Colossal Head of Amenhotep III**★★ comes from El-Qurna on the west bank. The right side of the face shows the rough material used by the Ancient Egyptian sculptors and helps us to understand the skill required to produce such fine works of art. The head is just over 2m/6.56ft high and is an excellent example of the Classical art of this period.

Ground Floor – The **Head of King Senusret III**★, unearthed in 1970 beneath the fourth pylon of the Great Temple of Amun at Karnak, demonstrates the realism of the Middle Kingdom; note the lines on the face. Senusret is depicted here as a person rather than a Pharaoh and his face seems to portray the anxieties and concerns that he must bear as king. One of the highlights of the museum, **Thutmose III**★★★, is a remarkable work of art, both because of its technical perfection and as a synthesis of the art of the New Kingdom. The Pharaoh's name (Menkheperra), which translates as "the stable prosperity of Amun-Ra", is written in hieroglyphs in the cartouche of his belt: a scarab beetle *(kheper)*, a sun *(ra)* and a bar *(mn)*. The face is of outstanding beauty, partly explained by the idealising Classicism of the period, although Thutmose III was renowned for his physical elegance. The statue of **Amenhotep III with a clenched fist**★ demonstrates a move towards greater realism. The unusual stance (a clenched fist on the left knee) of this statue discovered near the pylon of the Temple of Luxor suggests that perhaps it once stood in front of a gateway alongside its counterpart (a clenched fist on the right knee). Also worthy of note is the sculpture of Amenhotep III with the god Sobek (crocodile head), whose royal cartouche (depicted on the calf) was usurped by Rameses II – a particular habit of this Pharaoh.

Sculpted in dark green schist, the statue of Thutmose III was discovered in 1904 in the cache at Karnak.

Other exhibits worthy of note include the **head of the goddess Meheturet**★ (cow-headed) in gilded wood, copper and lapis-lazuli, from the tomb of Tutankhamun, and the **Osirid statue of Senusret I**★, discovered in Karnak in 1971 and originally covered in painted plaster.

First Floor – The first-floor displays include a collection of jewellery, coins (Greek or Roman, as the Ancient Egyptians did not use coins), votive statuettes and low and high reliefs. The entire collection is worthy of note, although a few items are of particular interest. These include the statue of **Amenhotep son of Hapu**★, an architect and favourite of Amenhotep III, who was responsible for much of the Temple of Luxor. Deified under the Ptolemies, he is shown here in the typical seated position of a scribe. The statue was found at Karnak in 1913. Also worthy of note is **Amenhotep IV wearing the double crown**★, which comes from a temple dedicated to Aten and was built by Amenhotep IV in Karnak; the temple was later destoyed by Horemheb in order to reintroduce the cult of Amun. The treatment of the face on this Osirid statue is very evocative of the brutal rupture which occurred when Amenhotep IV took the name Akhenaten. Note also the 17m/55ft-long **wall of talatat blocks from the temple of Amenhotep IV**★★, also from Karnak. "Talatat" blocks are blocks of sandstone of a standard size, carved with low reliefs. Although many of these blocks can be seen at various museums around the world, this wall is the only successful reconstruction.

TALATAT
This unusual word comes from a unit of measure used in Islamic architecture. In archaeology it is used to describe carved stone blocks which are typical of the Amarnian period.

Temple of Luxor★★★

Entrance from the Corniche. Open all year, 6am-9pm (10pm in summer). E£20; students E£10; tripod camera permit E£20, otherwise no charge for cameras and videos.

The "southern harem of Amun" – The Temple of Luxor or "harem of the south", a dependency of the Great Temple of Amun at Karnak, is situated on the site of the old quarter of *Ipet Reset*. It stands close to the Nile on bedrock which protects it from flooding. Originally linked to the site of Karnak via a triumphal way which ended at the beautiful colonnade, it was later closed by Rameses II as part of his expansion project.

At 260m/852ft in length, the Temple of Luxor is smaller than the temple at Karnak as its main purpose was as a suitable setting for the annual procession of the god Amun (the Festival of Opet). This festival celebrated the sexual union between Amun, in his ithyphallic form of Min, and his wife, Mut.

Construction – Started but not completed by Amenhotep III and his architect Amenhotep, the temple was abandoned by Amenhotep IV, who moved to Middle Egypt (Tell el-Amarna) to build a new capital dedicated to the god Aten. Tutankhamun, thought to be the son of Akhenaten/Amenhotep IV, and who died very young, finished the colonnade with reliefs that would later be usurped by Horemheb. Rameses II added a porticoed court, preceded by a monumental pylon, but preserved the bark shrine dating from the time of Thutmose III, which was situated outside the temple built by Amenhotep III. Subsequent modifications were made to the sanctuary by Alexander the Great.

Dromos★★ – An avenue of human-headed sphinxes was added to Amenhotep II's triumphal way by Nectanebo I (30th Dynasty), although some of these date from the time of Amenhotep. More than 700 of these mythical creatures once stood in line with the first pylon, which was built in the style of the façade of the Great Temple of Amun at Karnak. Although much of this avenue now lies under the modern city of Luxor, it is not difficult to imagine its former magnificence.

View of the Corniche and the Temple of Luxor.

First Pylon – *See also ABC of Architecture in the Insights and Images section.* As you stand and admire this imposing structure marking the entrance to the temple, it is worth trying to imagine how what is now little more than a ruin would have appeared in Ancient times. The two sections would have been covered with a white casing, itself adorned with brightly coloured engravings, often decorated with precious metals. The Battle of Qadesh was represented on the left of the upper register, in the centre of which Rameses II was depicted in his chariot pursuing the Hittite enemy. To the right of the upper register, the Egyptian camp could be seen, with the Pharaoh being spied upon. The lower register contained hieroglyphs of the *Poem of Pentaur (see ABU SIMBEL)*. Four coloured oriflamme masts stood in the grooves of the two towers; two obelisks flanked the entrance gate. Six colossal statues of the king (four standing and two seated) completed this stone tableau, and the entire structure was painted. Although it is little more than a ruin today, the first pylon was once a true work of art.

Court of Rameses II – 50m/164ft long and 57m/187ft wide, this court was originally flanked by a double row of columns. The eastern section of this colonnade is now occupied by the **Abu el-Haggag Mosque**, built on a thick bed of backfill which was only cleared in the 19C. The bark ▶ shrine of Thutmose III in the north-west corner is dedicated to the Theban triad and is therefore divided into three chapels. The court stands at a slight angle to the axis of the colonnade of Amenhotep IIII, probably in order to incorporate this earlier shrine in the temple building.

The walls are decorated with reliefs: the east wall *(south side)* is adorned with a procession of personifications of the mining districts; the south wall *(west side)* depicts the procession celebrating the inauguration of the pylon and its two obelisks, including a parade of offerings.

Colonnade★ – The colonnade is 52m/170ft long and comprises two rows of seven smooth-shafted columns, each of which is 15.8m/52ft tall and bell-shaped in style. Under Tuthankhanum and Horemheb, the east and west walls were decorated with scenes which were still strongly influenced by the Amarnian art of Akhenaten. They show a procession, which runs all the way around the room from the inner west side of the pylon: note the voyage of the sacred barks from Karnak to Luxor *(west wall)*, accompanied by priests, standard bearers, musicians and dancers, and welcomed by soldiers and musicians; and the return from Luxor to Karnak *(east wall)* after the Festival of Opet. Two limestone groups at the entrance to the colonnade bear the cartouches of Rameses II; possibly dating from the period of Tuthankhamun.

Court of Amenhotep III★★ – The court, which was also known as the "solar" court, measures 48m/157ft in ▶ length and 52m/170ft in width and is surrounded on three sides by a portico with a double row of papyrus-shaped columns. It was originally enclosed by walls on both sides. On the upper part of the capitals, all references to Amun were effaced by Amenhotep IV, who even removed the Amun cartouches of his father. During the Festival of Opet, the boats were carried across the court in the direction of the naos.

Hypostyle Hall★★ – The 32 papyrus-shaped columns (four rows of eight columns) of this court form an impressive and harmonious ensemble with the previous court. A series of cartouches depict Rameses IV, ▶ Rameses VI and a third Pharaoh by the name of Sobekhotep II (13th Dynasty), to whom reference is rarely made. He is probably mentioned here as a result of stone being reused.

The east wall is decorated on three registers and depicts Amenhotep bringing animal offerings to Amun, carrying sceptres and accompanied by his *ka*. These scenes were restored at the beginning of the 19th Dynasty after they had been damaged by Amenhotep IV; inscriptions in the hall indicate that Rameses II was responsible for

---

OBELISK

Only one of the two obelisks of Rameses II, both of which were offered to France by Mohammed Ali in 1831, can be seen in front of the first pylon. It took three years to transport the first obelisk to Paris and erect it in the middle of Place de la Concorde. The event will never be repeated as France gave up its rights to the second obelisk in 1980.

STATUES

Eleven statues of Amenhotep III in pink granite (one in black granite) between the columns of the second pylon were usurped by Rameses II. Two black granite statues of Rameses II stand on either side of the entrance.

A HIDDEN CACHE

In 1989, an American mission from the Institute of Chicago discovered a cache of 25 beautiful sculptures here. It is still not known why these statues were buried. Was it part of a religious rite or as protection against pillaging? *(see Museum of Ancient Egyptian Art).*

The best time to visit the temple, and the court in particular, is at night, when the site takes on an even more spectacular appearance.

VISITING ANCIENT THEBES

In order to make the most of a visit to Luxor and its surrounding area, visitors are advised to spend at least three days here; those with more time may wish to extend their stay to six or seven days. The itinerary suggested below is for a five-day stay, and includes visits to the main monuments, as well as time for relaxation and exploration of lesser-known sights:

Day 1: A morning visit to Karnak, a stroll along the Nile, and an evening felucca trip.

Day 2: In the morning, cross the Nile and rent a bike to visit the Colossi of Memnon, the Ramesseum, the site of Deir el-Bahri and the temple of Sety I; in the evening, explore the souk and the surrounding area.

Day 3: In the morning, cross the Nile and cycle to the Valley of the Kings, the Tombs of the Nobles and the site of Deir el-Medina; in the evening, visit the illuminated Temple of Luxor.

Day 4: A morning hot-air balloon trip, followed by an afternoon trip by bike or horse-drawn carriage along the Corniche and into the plantations; in the evening, attend the sound and light show at Karnak.

Day 5: In the morning, cross the Nile and cycle to the Valley of the Queens, the site of Medinet Habu, and the colourful village of El-Qurna; later, enjoy an afternoon visit to the Luxor Museum.

repairing the temple. It is interesting to note that the bases of the central columns were reduced in size during the reign of Rameses II in order to accommodate the procession of the sacred barks, as the boats would have been carried by a larger number of bearers at this time.

Pronaos – The pronaos is decorated with liturgical scenes (Amenhotep III in front of Amun and Min) and is reached via a vestibule which was first transformed into a Roman chapel (note the paintings of four emperors), and then into a church in the 5C.

Naos – Although the naos was built during the reign of Amenhotep III, the bark shrine was rebuilt under Alexander the Great, who is shown on the walls, facing the god Amun.

The temple guards will be only too happy to point out reliefs to visitors, but will expect a baksheesh for their trouble!

The sanctuary houses a number of chapels, including the **chamber of the birth of Amenhotep III**★, situated to the east of the pronaos and containing scenes in which the Pharaoh claims divinity as the son of Amun. The west wall, which is divided into three registers, illustrates the divine conception of the king. The first scene depicts the conception, with Khnum modelling Amenhotep on his potter's wheel, while Amun embraces Queen Mutemwiya. The pregnancy scene portrays Thot announcing the birth of a son to the queen in the presence of Taweret and Bes who preside over the birth. The final scene shows the birth, with Amenhotep and his double *(ka)* being suckled by Hathor, and then depicts the Pharaoh taking possession of his throne.

Temple Exterior – *Leave the temple by the west door of the hypostyle hall.* Although much of the external decor of the temple has been destroyed, fragments are still visible in places. The west side of the temple still retains sections of Rameses II's military triumphs, such as the capture of the cities of Tunip and Dapur from the Hittites.

A street scene in Luxor.

directory

INTERNET

A number of shops have signs offering Internet facilities, but all too often their main purpose is to entice tourists into the jewellery shops they front. Although they often have a computer linked to the Internet, you are likely to be hassled until you show some interest in the goods on sale in them.

Rainbow Net – *19, Yussef Hassan Street (near the souk). Open 9am-10pm.* A useful address for checking and sending e-mails. E£5/30min.

Internet Service Center – *Corniche el-Nile (just before the Mercure Hotel) – Open 8am-2pm and 6-10pm (closed Fri).* The town's official Internet provider. E£10.40/hr.

GETTING ABOUT

By calèche – With the exception of Aswan, Luxor has more horse-drawn carriages than any other Egyptian city. Consequently there's never a problem tracking one down – it's more a question of fending them off! A comprehensive two-hour tour will set you back around E£40, a much shorter trip between E£5 and E£10, although you may wish to test your bargaining skills. Make sure your driver doesn't stop at souvenir shops.

By taxi – Taxis tend to be on the expensive side in Luxor – a morning trip to the Valley of the Kings is likely to cost between E£40-E£60 for the three sites, although the driver will more than likely drop you off and wait for you outside a shop where he picks up a commission. For taxis around town, allow E£10-E£15. For visitors not on an organised tour, a taxi to Dendera can be hired for E£100 and E£150 should get you to Abydos.

By collective taxi – An inexpensive way of getting around Luxor (50pt/E£1), although they are prohibited from using the Corniche. Given that most of the sites in Luxor are along here, you're unlikely to make too much use of them.

Public ferry – These ferries *(baladi)* operate a 24hr service between the two banks of the Nile. The embarkation point is by the Temple of Luxor.

By bicycle – A great way of seeing the sites, particularly in winter *(see Leisure Activities overleaf)*.

By donkey – Only recommended for those with an iron constitution. Best avoided for longish trips to the Theban necropolis or between individual sites. If you are still keen, you'll find plenty of choice at the ferry point on the opposite bank of the river *(see Leisure Activities overleaf)*.

CONVOYS

All non-Egyptians travelling by road to Hurghada or along the Nile must go by convoy. This applies to organised coach tours, rental vehicles or privately hired taxis. These convoys congregate in the un-named road by the youth hostel known locally as "Convoy Street". Convoys depart as follows, although it's best to confirm these times with the tourist office:
– Hurghada: 8am, 2pm and 6pm
– Dendera and Abydos: 8am and 2pm
– Aswan: 7am, 11am and 3pm.

EXCURSIONS TO THE OASES

Provided the local police are advised ahead of time (for further information contact the tourist office), foreigners can now take the direct road from the river's west bank to Kharga, thus avoiding the long detour via Asyut. If you're planning on hiring a vehicle, you're best advised to do this through your hotel reception desk. A possible alternative is **Samuel Adly** (Flash Tour) who speaks English and has a number of air-conditioned minibuses (☎ *(012) 347 72 51)*.

FELUCCA TRIPS

Boats are lined up along the Corniche. As in Aswan, you'll need to negotiate a price: as a general guideline, allow E£10-E£15/hr or E£3-E£5 per person. The basic rule is to never show any initial interest whatsoever!

NILE CRUISES

See below. Around 250 boats ply the stretch between Luxor and Aswan. If you're planning on taking one (90% of visitors to Egypt do so), you are strongly recommended to book your cabin via a tour operator *(see the PRACTICAL INFORMATION at the beginning of the guide).* Although you may be able to book a cruise on the spot, there's always the chance that the boats will be full. By booking ahead of time with a reputable company, you'll at least have the reassurance of a company rep in the event of a delay, change to the itinerary, downgraded cabin etc. You'll often find that contrary to popular belief it's also cheaper to book ahead of time than at the very last minute.

Reliable Cairo-based companies operating Nile cruises include the following: Misr Travel (☎ *(02) 383 34 44)*; Abercrombie & Kent (☎ *(02) 394 77 35)*; Thomas Cook (☎ *(02) 574 39 55)*; Seti First Travel (☎ *(02) 341 98 20)*; Tivoli Travel (☎ *(02) 259 07 58)*.

LEISURE ACTIVITIES

Hot-air ballooning – Hod-Hod Soliman (☎ (095) 37 01 16) organises balloon trips lasting between 45min and 1hr over the west bank of the Nile and the Valley of the Kings. Cost: E£200. You will be picked up from your hotel by motor-boat at 5.15am and dropped off at the end of the excursion.

Balloons Over Egypt (☎ (010) 56 85 29 40) have desks at the Hilton and Sheraton Hotels and operate trips of a similar length. The price of $250 includes two meals, one before and one after the flight. Minibus transfers are included (departure time: between 5-5.30am). Your hotel will be happy to book this excursion for you.

Bicycle hire – Plenty of choice on the east bank, although bike quality varies. The general rate is E£8 per day, plus you're supposed to leave your passport as collateral, although we advise against this. Children's bikes are hard to find *(ask your hotel if they can find one for you)*. **Ahmed Youssef**, on the west bank, rents bikes for E£7 for a morning, which gives you enough time to visit the Valleys of the Kings and Queens. Take the public ferry across the Nile, then continue along the road for around 100yds: you'll find him on the left-hand side *(see also El-Nady below)*. Always check that your bike is in good working order before you set out.

Excursions by horse, donkey or camel – **Nobi Mahmoud Omar**, on the west bank, offers accompanied Arabian horse and camel trips for E£20/hour *(by the Mobil petrol station just past Ahmed Youssef)*. Also on the west bank, **El-Nady** (☎ (010) 51 54 652 - mobile) rents out bikes *(E£10 for a morning)*, as well as organising accompanied excursions by donkey *(E£15 for a morning)*, camel *(E£17)* and horse *(E£17)*. He will also come and pick you up from your hotel by motorboat if required (included in the cost).

WHERE TO STAY

After the drastic downturn in business following the tourist attack at the Temple of Hatshepsut in 1997, the construction of large luxury hotels has recently regained its momentum, with several hotels, such as the Meridien and a second Mercure at the foundation stage. Given the rapid nature of building work in Egypt, these are likely to be open by the time this guide is published.

• Budget

Marsam Hotel – West Bank – ☎ (095) 37 24 03 – 23 rooms: E£45. 🗗 🖾 This hotel, which is also known as Abd al-Rasul and Sheikh Ali, occupies buildings previously used as a base by archaeologists. At this price, creature comforts are at a minimum although it is a perfect base from which to explore the Theban necropolis.

Flobater – Khaled Ibn el-Walid Street – ☎ (095) 37 04 18 – 40 rooms: $28/$35. 🗗 Simple comfort and architecturally uninspiring, although the terrace restaurant overlooking the Nile is particularly pleasant.

St Joseph Hotel – Khaled Ibn el-Walid Street – ☎ (095) 38 17 07 – 75 rooms: $30/$35. 🗗 Wonderful views of the west bank from the pool on the seventh floor. Excellent value for money.

Philippe Hotel – Dr Labeb Habashy Street – ☎ (095) 37 22 84 – 70 rooms: $35/$45. 🗗 The most comfortable rooms of any hotel in this price range. Close to the city centre, with 8 rooms overlooking the Nile. Often full.

Gaddis – Khaled Ibn el-Walid Street – ☎ (0095) 38 28 28 – 55 rooms: $92. A small friendly hotel set back from the Corniche. A tiny pool in which to cool after visiting the main sights.

• Moderate

Novotel – Khaled Ibn el-Walid Street (south of the Corniche) – ☎ (095) 38 09 25 – 185 rooms: $120. A superb pool, delightful views and the service and high standard expected from this international chain. The hotel offers 2-hr cruises as well as longer trips towards Dendara (E£170, guide and lunch included) on its private cruise boat.

Mercure – Corniche – ☎ (095) 38 09 44 – 314 rooms, including 8 suites: $155. A good location, with 163 rooms overlooking the Nile. Negatives include the disappointing buffet, rooms at the back which look out at a wall, and the less than impressive daily dance show.

Sheraton Luxor Resort – South of Khaled Ibn el-Walid Street – ☎ (095) 37 49 55 – 290 rooms: $161 + breakfast (Nile view); 6 suites: $325 + breakfast. The Sheraton is located on the banks of the Nile, albeit slightly out of town. The rooms on the recently added fourth floor are slightly superior to those on the floors below. Facilities include an attractive circular pool with plenty of shade. The hotel organises cruises to Dendara on its own boat, the Meri Ra.

Sonesta St George – Khaled Ibn el-Walid Street – ☎ (095) 38 25 75 – 270 rooms: $180/$270. A wonderful experience for those guests with views of the Nile, less so for those without. Apart from its abundance of marble, the hotel has a fitness room, an Oriental restaurant and a circular pool.

• Expensive

Old Winter Palace – Nile Corniche – ☎ (095) 38 04 22 – 102 rooms: $218 (standard room - garden view); $248 (executive room – Nile view); 6 suites: $1 108 (royal). Add a further $50 between 23 Dec and 6 Jan and 8-21 Apr. Built in 1886, to accommodate the guests of King Farouk, the building was converted into a hotel in 1899. It enjoys a superb location on the banks of the river and has a magnificent garden to the rear.

Now part of the Sofitel chain, the hotel accommodates mainly American and French guests, although in days gone by it was graced by the likes of Agatha Christie, Winston Churchill and the Aga Khan. The Old Winter Palace's restaurant, the 1902, is the height of elegance and refinement, with an atmosphere that takes you back to the time of the very first tourists to the city.

WHERE TO EAT

• Budget

Salt & Bread Cafeteria – *El-Mahatta Square (opposite the railway station)*. The E£5 menu includes a choice of stuffed pigeon or an omelette.

El-Houla – *El-Television Street*. Clean, with the added bonus of tablecloths. El-Houla serves typical dishes costing no more than E£10.

Tutankhamun – *West Bank*. The only cheap restaurant near the ferry dock serving reasonable, inexpensive food. The chicken with rosemary and the varied vegetable dishes are the pick of the menu.

New Sunrise – *Open 11am-1am. Khaled Ibn el-Walid Street*. Egyptian-style stuffed pigeon, Indian tandoori and English "home steak" all feature on a menu that has something for every taste. A meal here will cost you around E£30. Pleasant balcony.

• Moderate

The best mid-range restaurants generally belong to the city's better hotels such as the **Mövenpick Jolie Ville** (Crocodile Island), the Lotus Boat at the **Novotel**, and the Japanese restaurant at the **Sonesta St George**.

Sinouhe – *Khaled Ibn el-Walid Street*. The menu here includes dishes from all four corners of the world for E£35-E£40. Sinouhe also has its own nightclub, the *Red Lion*.

BARS AND CAFÉS

Oum Kolsoum Café – *Open 24hr a day*. Behind the Temple of Luxor, near the souk. Tables outside. Good tea and Turkish coffee.

Esquire of Luxor – *Open 10am-1am. Ali Ibn Abi Taleb Street (off Khaled Ibn el-Walid Street)* – ☎ *(095) 37 00 76*. A modern pub with a European atmosphere and satellite TV. Grilled meats and pizzas available (E£17).

The King's Head – *Open 10am-3am. 1, Khaled Ibn el-Walid Street (2nd floor)* – ☎ *(095) 37 12 49*. Another modern English-style pub serving a range of cocktails and a choice of Egyptian and international cuisine for around E£20. The Indian buffet (E£25) is a regular Thursday event here.

SHOPPING

You'll find a gamut of traditional Egyptian souvenirs either in the souk, in the Tourist Bazaar *(just south of the Temple of Luxor)* and at the entrance to the royal valleys, particularly the Valley of the Kings; at the latter, be aware that you're likely to be accosted by locals selling "Ancient" artefacts. In addition to plastic busts of Nefertiti and Luxor and Egypt T-shirts, stallholders will also tempt you with clay *tajine* pots known as *tawagen* (E£5 and upwards), carpets and attractive tablecloths in the national colours. For good quality products, head for the boutiques beneath the entrance to the Old Winter Palace, where prices can be very high.

Adel Estafanos *(on the corner of Cleopatra Street and the souk road; open 10am-2pm and 5pm-10pm except Sun)* will make made-to-measure *galabiyyas*, shirts and even suits for visitors in just a day or two.

The nearby Nabil Agaiby **Shopping Center** sells just about everything, including a good selection of reasonably priced postcards.

outskirts

CRUISE ON THE NILE★★★

Also see Directory.

A long tradition – It is not known whether the pharaohs' solar barks actually sailed on the Nile; what is certain, however, is that the Nile has seen a constant stream of commercial and pleasure craft on its waters over the centuries, ranging from the papyrus boats of Ancient times to enormous modern cruise ships. In the Middle Ages, this magnificent waterway was used by upwards of 30 000 craft. Some of these ships were veritable floating palaces, with domes on their upper bridges to enable their rich owners to relax and enjoy the views of the surrounding countryside on their return from purchasing slaves or gold in Cairo.

The advent of tourism – Thomas Cook launched paddle steamers on the Nile in 1869 and pioneered the concept of the package holiday, offering cruises for an all-inclusive price. A winter cruise on the river was soon to become a fashionable way for wealthy travellers to escape the cold of Europe, allowing them to enjoy the exotic sights of Egypt in comfort.

Cruising today – To say that cruising has become a popular way to travel would be an understatement. Unfortunately the threat of terrorism put a stop to cruises between Cairo and Luxor in the 1990s, although some 250 boats still ply the route between Luxor and Aswan, albeit under tight guard. Although the romantic image of a cruise paddle-steamer is now confined to the pages of *Death on the Nile*, a Nile cruise is still a wonderful way of seeing the sights of Egypt. The pleasant routine of relaxing on board, interspersed with visits to fascinating sites, on-board lectures by qualified guides, and the constant views of delightful scenery from the ship's deck is now the favoured form of travel for tens of thousands of visitors to the country each year. Most cruises last for two or three days, with morning stops at Edfu and Kom Ombo. The majority of these floating hotels have a swimming pool and most cabins have a private bathroom.

RITUALS ON BOARD
Don't be surprised if you occasionally hear the boat's siren going off for no apparent reason, or if you catch a crew member throwing salt into the river. These rituals are believed to bring the boat good fortune.

WEST BANK

To get to the west bank from Luxor, either cross the bridge situated 7km/4mi S of the town (open from 6am), or catch the local ferry. Once you reach the west bank, you can either rent a bike, catch a minibus (25pt to El-Qurna), or take a taxi from one sight to the next. Taxis are cheaper on this side of the river, although a certain amount of bargaining is always required.

The road heading from the Nile towards the distant cliffs of the Libyan mountains visible on the horizon passes a fertile area of sugar-cane plantations dotted here and there with colourful houses. Two colossal sandstone statues soon come into view, with the uneven silhouettes of mortuary temples visible further in the distance. These statues mark the beginning of the necropolis of Ancient Thebes, a staggering collection of tombs and temples scattered around this stark desert landscape, providing an unforgettable insight into the beliefs and traditions of the Ancient Egyptians.

It may not be the height of luxury, but the public ferry will take you across the Nile for E£1.

Colossi of Memnon★

This famous pair of statues mark the border between the cultivated land close to the river and the desert beyond. The statues stand to the right of the road which then leads to an intersection at which a number of routes diverge towards the monuments on the west bank.

Remains of a temple – These two monolithic quartzite blocks weigh 720t each and once stood in front of the mortuary temple of Amenhotep III. The temple was destroyed in Ancient times and plundered for its stone by other pharaohs. The statues represent Amenhotep III, who is seated in the most typical of royal poses and wears the *nemes* headcloth.

The statues are flanked on either side of the throne by smaller statues representing Queen Mutemwiya, the king's mother, and Queen Tiy, his wife.

ARCHITECTURE
To the right of the main road stands the mud-brick village built by the architect **Hassan Fathy**, indicated by a sign saying "Hassan Fathy Cultural Palace" *(no charge)*. By involving villagers in his work, Fathy has attempted to reintroduce this type of cheap, traditional dwelling in order to slow down the rate at which the country is being covered in concrete.

These 16.6m/54ft-tall statues appear to guard the entrance to the necropolis.

The temple of Rameses III at Medinet Habu is the largest Theban temple after Karnak.

Singing at dawn – It is thought that the two colossi were damaged in an earthquake in 27 BC. The statue to the right was badly affected and subsequently became prey to a phenomenon upon which a legend was founded. After the humidity of the night and with the warmer temperatures of dawn, the statue began to emit a sort of plaintive murmur. The Greeks saw this as the reincarnation of Memnon, a hero of the Trojan War; this interpretation was reinforced by the fact that the Egyptians referred to the statues as *memnou*, a word used to describe any religious monument. According to Greek legend, Memnon, who had been killed by Achilles, was granted immortality by Zeus as a result of the intervention of his mother Eos, the goddess of the dawn. The Ptolemies believed that as the sun rose every morning, Memnon plaintively greeted his mother who, in response, covered him with dew, which represented her tears. It has been suggested that the "singing" may have been caused by the expansion of the stone or the effect of the wind, although the exact cause remains unknown. Given the legend, only the statue on the right should strictly be referred to as the colossus of Memnon.

Restoration work – Both Greeks and Romans undertook pilgrimages to visit this "living" statue; this is confirmed by the many inscriptions visible on the colossus. One of these, on the legs of the colossus, was made by a Roman poetess named Julia Balbilla, who accompanied Hadrian when he came to Luxor to listen to the statue. The statue was repaired by Septimius Severus, after which time it was never heard to "sing" again.

Medinet Habu ★★

See map of Luxor. S of the Valley of the Queens. E£12; students E£6. No charge for cameras and videos.

From an ancient city to a quarry – During the 20th Dynasty, this desert site was the administrative centre of western Thebes. As such, it gradually attracted *fellahin* and workers from the surrounding area and developed into a bona-fide city in the Christian period. During the Arab invasions, the local Coptic population took refuge in Esna, resulting in the abandonment of the mud-brick walled town of Medinet Habu, which was then used as a quarry by locals, who until fairly recently would still remove stone known as *sebakh* from the site.

Royal Pavilion – Unlike many other New Kingdom sites, the entrance to this pavilion is marked by a triumphal gateway which is military in style. A guardroom decorated with a representation of the Pharaoh offering incense to Amun precedes the pavilion. A passageway housing two statues of the goddess Sekhmet and decorated with scenes of prisoners symbolising the victories of Rameses III (the Pharaoh responsible for building the pavilion) leads into the enclosure.

The interior of this two-towered building is thought to have housed the royal harem, as all the rooms are decorated with images of the king surrounded by women.

A representation of the unification of Upper and Lower Egypt can be seen on the base, where the god of the Nile, Hapy, who is depicted twice, can be seen binding the lotus of Upper Egypt and the papyrus of Lower Egypt around the hieroglyph *sma*.

TICKET OFFICE
Tickets for all the Theban sites can be bought at the ticket office situated at the intersection of roads leading to the different monuments *(see map of Luxor)*. The ticket office is open all year from 6am-5pm (6pm in summer).

SEBAKH
The Arabic word *sebakh* refers to a block of cut stone taken from a temple, as well as to the earth created from the rubble from archaeological sites. This rubble was either used in lime kilns or as fertiliser in the fields: an ignominious end for such magnificent Ancient ruins.

Esplanade – The **temple**★ to the right dates from the 18th Dynasty and was started by Amenhote I. Work on the building continued under Thutmose I, and it was subsequently enlarged under Thutmose II and Thutmose III. The project was finally completed by Shabaqo, Nectanebo I, Ptolemy IX and Ptolemy XII, with the addition of an avant-corps during the reign of Antoninus Pius. Despite the many modifications that ensued, the building, with its harmonious proportions and elaborate plan, has retained the elegance that is so typical of the 18th Dynasty. The Roman court with its Ptolemaic pylon are followed by the colonnade of Nectanebo I and the pylon of Shabaqo (25th Dynasty). This then leads to a court, a peristyle and the naos, preceded by six chapels, all adorned with scenes of offerings, which are unfortunately somewhat difficult to identify because of the dark conditions here.

To the left, the **Temple of the God's Wives of Amun** is divided into two buildings: the chapel of Amenirdis (25th Dynasty), the naos of which contains the oldest vault built from dressed stone; and the chapels of Shephenwepet II, Mehitenwesekhet and Shephenwepet III (also known as Nitocris; 26th Dynasty), decorated with scenes of offering to the god Amun.

Nilometer – *NE of the temple.* The flight of steps in this small room leads 20m/65ft underground. The cartouches in the room bear the name of Nectanebo I.

Temple of Rameses III★★ – Like other mortuary temples, the purpose of this superb masterpiece of Rameses III was to celebrate the cult of the Pharaoh. The building is impressive both for the unity of its architecture, which was respected by successive pharaohs, and for its size: a total of 7ha/17 acres of decorated surface. The building was inspired by the Ramesseum of Rameses II *(see below)* and provides an insight into how the Ramesseum, now in ruins, might once have looked. The temple consists of two porticoed courts both preceded by a pylon, in addition to a sanctuary divided into three hypostyle halls and a naos with rooms on either side. The left portico of the first court once led to the royal palace – the foundations of which can still be seen – and acted as its façade. An opening in the wall, known as the "window of appearances", stands 2m/6.5ft above the ground. The second court is in better condition than the first and is lined with porticoes; two of these are decorated with eight Osirid pillars; the other two are adorned with five columns each. Beyond the hypostyle hall, in which only the bases of the 24 columns which once supported the ceiling have survived, the temple is in ruins, mainly as a result of having been plundered for its stone over the centuries. All three hypostyle halls have chambers. The last room leads to the naos, divided into three chapels dedicated to the Theban triad of gods, Amun, Khons and Mut. The middle chapel lies in line with the temple axis and is open, having once served as a bark shrine.

The god Ra is represented on one of the pillars of the entrance to the hypostyle hall.

The external walls of the two pylons depict scenes celebrating the Pharaoh's military successes against the Libyans and the Philistines; the inner walls are decorated with religious scenes. Similar reliefs are also visible on the walls of the courts; in addition to these, representations of the major religious festivals of the gods Sokar and Min can be viewed in the second court. Note, in particular, the scenes of offerings depicted on the pillars of the end portico. The functions of the various rooms and chapels in the sanctuary can be ascertained by their decor. As an example, the five rooms adjoining the first hypostyle hall to the left once housed the treasure, as shown by the portraits of vases and precious chests offered by Rameses III to Amun.

OTHER SIGHTS

The external decoration on the temple walls portraying the military campaigns of Rameses III is well worth seeing, as are the expressive hunting scenes★ on the south-west side of the first pylon, remarkable for their realism and sense of drama.

Palace of Amenhotep III – *At Birket Habu, to the SW.* Amenhotep III's monuments on the west bank include a mortuary temple and a tomb cut in the Valley of the Kings, as well as his palace, built next to an artificial lake, linked to the Nile via a canal.

VALLEY OF THE QUEENS★★★

See map of Luxor.

The Valley of the Queens, the southernmost of the necropolises built on the west bank, sits in a deep and narrow gorge of the Libyan range of hills known in Arabic as *Biban el-Harim* (the "Gates of the Ladies").

A Royal Domain

This valley was chosen during the 18th Dynasty to house the tombs of royal princes and princesses, as well as high officials of the court. Under the 19th Dynasty, beginning with the burial of Satra, the wife of Rameses I and mother of Sety I, it was decided that the pharaohs' queens would also be buried here. During the following dynasty, Rameses III also took the decision to bury some of his sons at the site. The valley had already been pillaged before the onset of the Third Intermediate Period, when the necropolis was opened to the burial of non-royal citizens; during the period of Roman domination, it became an ordinary cemetery.

The valley – It was the famous French Egyptologist Jean-François Champollion who named this necropolis the Valley of the Queens. The Egyptians referred to it as *Ta set Neferou*, which translates as "the place of perfection" or "the place of the king's sons", perhaps a more accurate description. Close to the Theban summit overlooking the Valley of the Kings, where the valley starts to narrow, is a grotto with a sacred reputation. In Ancient Egyptian times the opening to the grotto was referred to as the womb of the goddess Hathor, probably as a result of its shape.

There are no monuments in the two royal valleys, simply discreet entrances to the tombs. Above: the entrance to the tomb of Nefertari.

ERNESTO SCHIAPARELLI (1856-1928)

Schiaparelli, an Italian Egyptologist who ended his career as Curator of the Egyptian Museum in Turin, studied with Gaston Maspero and led 12 separate archaeological digs in Egypt, including two in the Valley of the Queens. In 1903 and 1904, assisted by the Egyptologist Francesco Ballerini, he discovered the most important tombs in this valley, including those of Sethherkhepeshef, Khaemwaset and Amenherkhepeshef, as well as the burial chambers of the sons of Rameses III. However, his most exciting discovery was undoubtedly the tomb of Queen Nefertari, which is generally considered to be the most outstanding of all the tombs in Ancient Thebes.

Tombs

Tickets should be bought from the main ticket office (see map of Luxor): open all year from 6am-5pm (6pm in summer). E£12, students E£6; Nefertari's tomb: E£100, students E£50 (in theory visits are limited to 150 people a day). No camera or videos. Visits restricted to 10min per tomb.

Tomb of Nefertari★★★ – *No 66.* This tomb was reopened in 1995 after painstaking restoration work thought to have cost in the region of $2 million. Such was the high level of technical expertise required that a number of international experts were called in to participate in the project. The tomb once housed the sarcophagus of Nefertari, wife of Rameses II, known as "the most beautiful, the favourite of Mut". The layout of the tomb is similar to that normally used for the tombs of the pharaohs. The first room, illustrating Chapter 17 of the *Book of the Dead*, is decorated with painted reliefs, typical of the refined, mannerist style of the period. Characters are portrayed as slim and svelte, but are realistic in appearance. The celestial vault is dotted with stars, and both the vestibule and the chamber known as the room of "fabrics" (the deceased is depicted offering fabrics to the god Ptah) are adorned with colourful images of the queen in the presence of various gods, including Isis, Osiris, Nephthys, Maat, Khepri, Serket, Hathor, Nekhbet and Thoth *(see the table of gods in the Insights and Images section).*

Tombs are numbered in the order in which they were discovered and listed here in chronological order, with the exception of the tomb of Titi. Those that are badly damaged, unfinished, closed or under excavation, are not described. Some tombs are occasionally closed to visitors.

RELIEFS

One of the most evocative reliefs can be seen in the first room and depicts Nefertari playing *senet* (draughts) against an invisible opponent. The scene symbolises the challenges that the deceased faced as they entered the world of Osiris.

HENTY-REKI

Henty-Reki was the naked genie who guarded the fifth gate of the kingdom of Osiris. He was known as "he who chased the enemy" and is depicted in the centre of the east wall. Nefertari was required to speak to each of the guardians before continuing her journey.

The walls of the second staircase are decorated with symmetrical scenes depicting Nefertari offering two *nou* vases to the gods Isis, Nephthys and Maat *(left)* and Hathor, Selket and Maat *(right)*. Anubis, the patron of embalmers and creator of the first mummy, Osiris, is represented under the *uraeus*.

The sarcophagus chamber (90m²/968sq ft) is supported by four pillars adorned with representations of Osiris, who is dressed in the same red-belted tunic worn previously by Nefertari, demonstrating that the deceased has undergone changes since her appearance in the earlier rooms. On the pillars, note also the image of the *djed* of Osiris, symbolising his vertebral column and flanked by cartouches of Nefertari. The stone sarcophagus once stood opposite the pillar; unfortunately only a portion of the sarcophagus lid has been found. The south wall was also inspired by the *Book of the Dead,* in this case, Chapter 164, and shows Nefertari talking to the guardian of the first gate of Osiris *(left)* and the three guardians of the second gate *(right)*.

Khaemwaset★ – *No 44.* The tomb of the eldest son of Rameses III is a smaller version of a royal tomb, with remarkably well-preserved decoration. In the antechamber, Rameses III, followed close behind by the prince, is depicted with the gods Thoth, Anubis and Ra-Horakhty *(left)*; the same image can be seen in the sarcophagus chamber *(right)*, where a representation of a cat (called *myou* by the Egyptians) can also be seen. As in the tomb of Nefertari, much of the decor is inspired by the *Book of the Dead* and the prince is also shown addressing the guardians of the gates of Osiris. Osiris himself is represented in the annexe to the rear, on the left-hand side, his face painted green as a symbol of regeneration.

Amenherkhepeshef★★ – *No 55, visit restricted to 5min.* This prince, who commanded the king's chariots and was referred to as a "hereditary prince", was also a son of Rameses III and was no more than 16 years old when he died. His tomb was discovered in excellent condition. Inside it, the young prince is represented several times in the company of his father, who is portrayed paying homage to the gods so that they will welcome his son into their kingdom. The reliefs decorating the sarcophagus chamber evoke Chapters 145 and 146 of the *Book of the Dead*. Here, Amenherkhepeshef, accompanied by his father, can be seen addressing the guardians of the fifth, sixth, seventh and eighth gates of the kingdom of Osiris: Heneb-Reku (a black dog), Sematy (a ram), Lukenty (an ox) and Qutqetef. The granite funerary urn is now kept in the annexe to the rear of the tomb.

Titi – *No 52.* This tomb belongs to a wife of one of the Rameses pharaohs. It consists of a long corridor leading to a small chapel, with further smaller chambers on either side. The decor on the walls of the descending corridor is badly damaged in parts and as a result is now protected by glass. Note the portrait of the queen wearing a sidelock of hair, a symbol of childhood. Once again, the tomb is embellished with representations of Egyptian gods, including Thoth, Ptah and Horus *(for identification, see the table of gods in the Insights and Images section).*

DETAIL

The splendid reliefs in this tomb are brightly coloured and well preserved. Note the fine detail in many of the portraits, such as the gold circles on the helmet and the opulence of the ceremonial robes.

Cartouche of Nefertari.

"SERVANTS AT THE PLACE OF TRUTH"

Under the Rameses pharaohs, the royal tombs were built and administered by the "great and noble tomb of millions of years". This organisation was founded during the reign of Thutmose I (18th Dynasty) and brought together the builders and craftsmen who were involved in the building of a royal tomb, including unskilled workers, plasterers, designers, sculptors, painters, site managers and scribes. The site team was divided into two groups, each working on one side of the tomb under the management of a team leader, architect and scribe. All the workers were recruited by the king's vizier from families who passed on their crafts from one generation to the next. Like the priests, these men were among the first to learn of the death of a Pharaoh, an event which signified the end of one project and the beginning of the next.

DEIR EL-MEDINA

See map of Luxor. W of the Ramesseum. Temple and tombs: E£12; students E£6. Tomb of Peshedu: E£10; students E£5. No photography or video cameras.

The road to Deir el-Medina passes through a desert landscape of sand and rocks, dotted here and there with small settlements of brightly coloured houses. The scene is bathed in the golden light of the desert, and is set against the cloudless blue backdrop of the Egyptian sky. After a while the road starts to climb, before suddenly plunging into a greyer landscape, devoid of any signs of habitation.

The Workers' Village

This small valley is home to the remains of a village once inhabited by the workers who built and decorated the tombs in the Valley of the Kings between the early 18th Dynasty and the late Ramesside period. On the valley floor are the foundations of around 50 small houses, modest dwellings comprising one main room, a bedroom and a kitchen, which could also be used for storage. The workers' tombs can be seen on the western side of the hill. Founded in the time of Thutmose I, the village was at its most prosperous during the 19th and 20th Dynasties. It was placed under the protection of Ptah, the god of the craftsmen, and was linked to the Valley of the Kings by a footpath which crossed the mountain.

Anherkhau★ – *No 359, 20th Dynasty*. Anherkhau was the "chief workman of the Master of the Two Lands in the Place of Truth" (in other words, the foreman of the site) during the reigns of Rameses II and Rameses IV. His tomb is remarkable for the quality of its decoration (which is more ornate than that usually found in private tombs) rather than as a typical example of the style of the period. The most beautiful paintings, depicting extracts from the *Book of the Dead* and the *Book of Gates*, can be seen in the burial chamber. In total, the walls are covered with 31 scenes, with more space given to the images than to the text. Anherkhau himself is represented here with a shaven head and dressed as a priest.

Sennedjem★★ – *No 1, 19th Dynasty*. This worker was known as the "servant in the Place of Truth" and was an official in the necropolis during the reigns of Sety I and Rameses II. Discovered in 1886, the tomb of Sennedjem originally housed a number of interesting artefacts which are now on display in the Egyptian Museum in Cairo *(first floor, Room 17)*. The colourful paintings, set against an ochre background, are renowned for their beauty and are typical of the Ramesside period, which was characterised by the wide range of styles employed in the decoration of private tombs. Lively and picturesque in style, these murals depict the subjects that are so often found in Ancient Egyptian funerary art. The most famous painting in the tomb, located on the wall to the right of the burial chamber, illustrates Chapter 60 of the *Book of the Dead*. It is divided into four registers and shows Sennedjem and his wife engaged in a series of agricultural tasks in the afterworld, also known as the Fields of Iaru or Fields of Reeds (to "pass through the field of reeds" was a Egyptian metaphor for death). On the upper register, note the child in a papyrus boat (it is presumed that their child died before them) and a priest performing the opening of the mouth ceremony.

Peshedu★ – *No 3, 19th Dynasty*. This tomb belonged to Peshedu, yet another "servant in the Place of Truth" under Rameses II, and has recently been opened to the public. A barrel-vaulted corridor, adorned with a representation of Anubis, holding the *nekhakha* flail in his back paws, leads into the burial chamber. Immediately to the right note the famous scene showing Peshedu praying under a palm tree by the side of a lake; to the left, friends and relatives of the deceased are portrayed wearing copious garments with stylised folds, similar to those represented in the statuary of the period. The walls of the chamber are decorated with inscriptions taken from the *Book of the Dead*.

ORIGINS

The name Deir el-Medina ("the monastery of the village") dates back to Coptic times when a **temple** built nearby by the Ptolemies IV, VI and XI was transformed into a monastery. The temple was protected by an enclosure and originally dedicated to Hathor and Maat.

Anherkhau with three of his grandchildren.

WORKERS' TOMBS

The workers' tombs were usually small and built on two levels. The upper level comprised a court housing the statue of the deceased and a chapel; the burial chamber was found on the lower level. The chapel was surmounted by a small pyramid.

A small bookstall is situated on a terrace nestling in the middle of the tombs. It sells an excellent selection of good-quality literature, including a wide range of specialist works which can be quite difficult to find outside Egypt.

RAMESSEUM★★

See map of Luxor. On the right-hand side of the road lead-ing to the Valley of the Kings. E£12; students E£6. No charge for cameras or videos.

3 500 years of history

On the edge of cultivated land and at the foot of the mountains of the Libyan hills stand a number of mortu-ary temples built by pharaohs from the New Kingdom. Although some of the original temples have disappeared and others are barely identifiable, the scattered ruins of some still remain. From south to north stood the tem-ples of RamesesIII, Ay and Horemheb, AmenhotepII (guarded by the colossi of Memnon), Merenptah, ThutmoseIV, RamesesII, AmenhotepII, Thutmose III, Rameses IV and Sety I. This vast area is now an immense archaeological site where teams of archaeologists rebuild monuments once new discoveries are made. Gradually colonnades, façades and annexes are reconstructed to reveal these temples, once known to the Egyptians as "the million-year-old castles".

To the glory of Amun and Rameses II

The mortuary temple of Rameses II is similar in plan to a state temple. Described in glowing detail by Ancient Greek writers such as Diodorus Siculus and Strabo, the temple still shows remarkable unity of style, although much of it now stands in ruins. Started during the Pharaoh's lifetime and finished after his death, the temple was dedicated to the god Amun, to whom the Great Temple in Karnak was already dedicated. Once a year, during the Beautiful Festival of the Valley, the statue of the god (husband of Mut and father of Khons) was brought here from the Great Temple in Karnak on the east bank of the Nile to visit his ancestors and the deceased king.

Site – The site covers approximately 5ha/12 acres and once comprised a port, enclosures, a royal palace, a mammisi and the temple itself, which stands on a south-east/north-west axis. This building, built entirely during the reign of Rameses II, allows the visitor to appreciate the size and grandeur of the temples built during the Ramesside period.

First Pylon – This 68m/223ft-wide pylon, which has par-tially collapsed, is decorated with carved reliefs of battle scenes on its inner walls, including the Battle of Qadesh, which is also depicted at Abu Simbel and Karnak.

First Court – A double colonnade once stood on the south side of this court, measuring 56m/184ft in width and 52m/170ft in length. It originally preceded the royal palace, of which nothing but the foundations now remain. The north side comprised a portico with Osirid pillars rep-resenting the king dressed in a loincloth and flanked by two of his children; two **colossal statues** stood to the west side. The collapsed and fragmented remains of one of these, approximately 16m/52ft in height and representing Rameses II, now lies on its back on the ground. The other, approximately 9m/29ft high, was of Mut-Tuy, the Pharaoh's mother.

ORIGINAL NAME

Champollion coined the term Ramesseum for the temple of Rameses II on his visit here in 1829. The temple's Ancient name was "the castle of millions of years of King Usermaatra Setepenra who united the city in Thebes with the domain of Amun to the west." (Usermaatra and Setepenra were the first names of Rameses II).

EXCAVATIONS

Since 1991, the Ramesse-um has been the subject of excavation work led by the Institute of Theban Egyptology at the Louvre Museum in Paris. Other teams working on the site include the Association for the Protection of the Ramesseum, led by Profes-sor Leblanc, which is exca-vating the annexe section of the site.

Before the construction of the Aswan High Dam, the Nile flood used to reach the first pylon of the Ramesseum.

Second Court – This court is situated beyond the second pylon, which is almost completely destroyed but which still bears reliefs of the Battle of Qadesh and the Festival of the god Min. The court is surrounded to the east and the west by a row of eight Osirid pillars; the row to the west is paralleled by a row of papyrus-shaped columns which also once ran along the north and south sides. Note on the west side of the court a magnificent **head of Rameses II**★, carved from blue-tinted granite, which once belonged to one of the two colossal statues which flanked the staircase leading to the hypostyle hall; the bust of the statue to the left, the torso of which is still intact, was removed from the site in 1816 by Belzoni and is now in the British Museum in London.

Hypostyle Hall★ – Three ruined doors lead into the hypostyle hall, enclosed to the east by a wall. The roof of the hall was once supported by 48 white sandstone columns, 29 of which still remain. The **polychromy**★ of the central row of columns, with scenes depicting Rameses in the company of various gods, has been partially restored. The east wall is decorated with carved reliefs highlighting the capture of Dapur in Syria by Rameses II; note how the artist has succeeded in portraying the series of events, from the royal attack to the surrender of the enemy. A double procession of the sons and daughters of Rameses adorns the lower part of the west wall on both sides of the doorway; his successor, Merenptah, stands 13th in line; when he ascended to the throne, his loincloth was restored, a tunic was added, and an *uræus* attached to his forehead.

Boat Chamber – This hypostyle chamber is the first of the two remaining rooms to the rear of the building. Its most outstanding feature is a magnificent **astronomical ceiling**★ depicting a calendar divided into 12 months and 36 decans, probably used to determine the dates of cultural festivals.

Chamber of Litanies – This chamber is similar in architectural structure to the one preceding it. The reliefs on its east wall, which glorify the principal gods of Memphis, suggest that the chamber was used to pay tribute to the main temples in Egypt. The rest of the sanctuary has collapsed.

Temple annexes and storerooms – This mud-brick complex is spread out around the temple and was once known as "Joseph's granaries". It is currently being excavated and researched and it is hoped that work being carried out here will enhance our knowledge of what is considered to be the bext example of its type from the Pharaonic Period. It is already known that the Theban clergy transformed these storerooms into a necropolis in the 22nd Dynasty.

TOMBS OF THE NOBLES★★★

See map of Luxor. N of the Ramesseum. Tickets should be purchased from the main ticket office (see map of Luxor); open all year from 6am-5pm (6pm in summer).

This complex stretches from Deir el-Medina to Deir el-Bahri and contains close to 500 private tombs spanning a period from the 6th Dynasty to the Greco-Roman era. Far less visited than the tombs in the two royal valleys, these tombs of high officials in the Pharaoh's court in Thebes are nonetheless interesting for the insight they provide into everyday life of the period between the 18th and 20th Dynasties. The best preserved and most beautiful of these tombs take their rightful place among the masterpieces of New Kingdom art.

Sheikh el-Qurna

Tombs of Nakht and Menna: E£12; students E£6. Tombs of Rekhmira and Sennefer: E£12; students E£6. Tombs of Ramose, Userhet and Khaemhat: E£12; students E£6. Tombs of Khons, Userhet and Benia: E£12; students E£6. No cameras or videos.

All the private tombs in Sheikh el-Qurna are more or less identical in structure, with the exception of the vestibule, which is open in some tombs and closed in others. The

---

ACCESS
The visitors' entrance to the Ramesseum is through this court, whose sandstone flagstones have been replaced.

WORLD VISION
The Ramesseum was decorated with the aim of emphasising the authority of the king, who was still alive when it was built. Through the military and cult scenes and the portrayals of political and family life, the Pharaoh demonstrates that he has succeeded in defeating the enemy, honouring the gods, ensuring the continuation of his dynasty and providing proof of his ability to lead his people.

DECORATIVE THEMES
The decor of these tombs is less religious in tone than in the royal valleys; consequently, the deceased is more commonly depicted in scenes of everyday life. Family and agricultural scenes are popular themes, as is the funerary banquet, attended by musicians and dancers.

standard layout comprises an external courtyard, a vestibule, a mortuary chapel with a niche for statues of the deceased, and a gallery or shaft leading to the burial chamber.

The hill of Sheikh el-Qurna is divided into three sections: the great enclosure (on the hillside), the small enclosure (surrounded by a low wall) and the village, around which a number of tombs are scattered.

◀ **Nakht**★★★ – *No 52, Small Enclosure, 18th Dynasty*. Nakht was the "royal scribe and astronomer of Amun", although the paintings and reliefs in the tombs make no reference to this position. We also know that his wife was a chantress of Amun; the name of the god was carefully removed during the reign of Akhenaten. The portraits of Nakht are often defaced, acts presumably carried out during the same period.

In addition to the traditional scenes of offerings and funerary rites, the walls of the tombs are also adorned with brightly coloured scenes taken from everyday life. These include working in the fields *(left)*, the false door *(left wall)*, the funerary banquet *(to the left of the door to the chapel)*, hunting and fishing, the production of wine *(to the right of the door to the chapel)*, Nakht and his wife feasting and making offerings *(right wall)*, and the purification of these offerings *(right)*. One of the scenes depicting the funerary banquet is of such beauty and elegance that it is often included in books on Ancient Egyptian art; it represents three **young musicians** playing the double flute, the lute and the harp respectively. What is considered unusual is that the lute player is depicted naked, a representation not seen in any other Egyptian tomb. Their presence in a funerary scene was not intended to enliven proceedings, but rather to accompany the solemn rites of the cult by playing music and singing to the glory of the gods. When portrayed in an entirely different setting the harp was considered to be a gentle allusion to love, as it was often used as a symbol of eroticism.

Menna★★★ – *No 69, Great Enclosure, 18th Dynasty*. Menna was the "scribe of the fields of the Lord of the Two Lands of Upper and Lower Egypt" during the reign of Thutmose IV and for this reason many of the paintings depict country life. The tomb's design and iconography combine to provide a fine example of a private Theban tomb.

The scenes depicted in the vestibule include working in the fields *(left)*, Menna and his wife Henuttawy before Osiris *(left wall)*, the funeral banquet *(to the left of the door to the chapel)*, the couple receiving offerings *(to the right of the door to the chapel)*, people praying in front of a stele *(right wall)* and the couple's children *(right)*. The agricultural scenes are divided into four registers and provide vivid detail of the measuring of the harvest under the watchful eye of the scribes, and the workers surveying the land with a piece of string. In the chapel, the funeral
◀ *(left)* is depicted opposite hunting and fishing scenes, and a pilgrimage to Abydos *(right)*; the latter is represented in the upper register by a procession of boats. The lower register has paintings of various rituals performed in front of the mummy of the deceased.

RESTORATION
Part of this tomb was restored using an unusual technique in which the vestibule walls (the only ones actually painted) were partially insulated with crystal. This method proved so laborious, however, that it was decided not to employ it elsewhere in the tomb.

PAPYRUS
Forests of papyrus once covered much of the Nile Delta. In Ancient Egypt, this plant was used to make a range of articles including rope, matting, sails, loincloths, sandals, boats and "paper". The literal meaning of its Egyptian name (wadj) was "youth".

THE DAUGHTERS OF MENNA
These girls are represented in the hunting and fishing scenes adorning the chapel walls: one is shown picking lotus flowers; the other is carrying birds and fish. Menna himself can be seen standing in a papyrus boat, fishing with a harpoon.

Offering bearers depicted in the chapel of Menna's tomb.

Rekhmira★★★ – *No 100, Great Enclosure, 18th Dynasty.*
Rekhmira was the "governor and vizier of the town of
Thebes" under Thutmose III and Amenhotep II. His
important position explains the imposing size of his
tomb (although it has a very simple T-shaped layout), the
varied iconographic themes represented, and the considerable amount of wall space adorned with decoration
(approximately 300m?/3 228sq ft). Although badly damaged in places, the paintings here are of exceptional
quality and will hold a particular fascination for those
visitors with a passion for New Kingdom art; unfortunately it is impossible to describe them in exhaustive
detail within the context of this guide. Another interesting feature of the tomb is the absence of a shaft and
burial chamber; this omission suggests that the deceased
may have been buried in a hypogeum in the Valley of
the Kings which has yet to be discovered.

The walls of the vestibule are literally covered with vivid
scenes relating to agriculture and to the administrative
role of the deceased. To the left of the door to the chapel
note the **presentation of tributes from foreign lands**, ▶
a ceremony which was always attended by the governor
of Thebes. These delightful scenes are divided into five
groups and provide additional information relating to
trade of the time. The envoys depicted come from the
land of Punt (*see QUSEIR*; dressed in short garments),
the land of Kefti (Crete; curly hair and embroidered loincloths), the land of Kush (Nubia; panther-skin loincloths), Retenu (Syria; short robes and tight sleeves) and
elsewhere, including parts of Central Africa.

The narrow chapel is adorned with a number of paintings
in excellent condition, with both walls divided into three
scenes which are further subdivided into several registers.
To the left, the first painting shows Rekhmira supervising
the harvest and the distribution of grain to workers from
the temple of Amun; the second depicts him overseeing ▶
work on the temple; the third represents the funeral. To
the right, the first painting is of two boats sailing towards
Amenhotep II; the second portrays a banquet presided
over by the deceased and his wife, Merit, with music provided by instruments including the lute, harp, cittern, tambourine and flute; the third illustrates scenes from the *Book
of the Opening of the Mouth*. The banquet is, in fact, the
funerary meal which preceded the separation of the
deceased from the land of the living, at which men and
women sit separately. As is the case with most wall paintings, several of the characters depicted wear a small cone
on the top of their head; fixed in place by their slaves, this
scented pomade melted in the heat, in so doing soaking
the wig with a very distinctive aroma.

Sennefer★★★ – *No 96, Great Enclosure, 28th Dynasty.*
Sennefer was "mayor of the city of Thebes and overseer
of the gardens of Amun" during the reign of Amenhotep II.
The burial chamber in this tomb is decorated, a feature
which is unique in the private tombs of the Theban
necropolis. Furthermore, the iconography of the tomb
focuses entirely on the deceased, with repeated portraits
of Sennefer, his wife, sister and daughter, rather than on
the gods of the afterworld, who are here relegated to a role

> The tributes portrayed
> here include ebony, ivory,
> ostrich feathers,
> monkeys, leopards and
> baboons from Punt;
> goldwork, cups and
> vases from Kefti; ostrich
> eggs, leopards, monkeys,
> dogs and giraffes from
> Kush; and chariots,
> weapons, amphorae,
> horses, bears and
> elephants from Retenu.
> Every gift presented was
> duly noted down by the
> scribes.

> **WORK ON THE TEMPLE
> OF AMUN**
> This painting is of
> particular interest for its
> depiction of workers
> such as carpenters, wood
> sculptors, goldworkers
> and masons employed in
> the construction of the
> temple, as well as the
> techniques they used to
> build it.

◄ of secondary importance. In the 19C, this hypogeum became known as the "tomb of vines" after the painted arbour of grapes and vines depicted on its ceiling.

This unusual decorative feature recurs in the antechamber, 12m/39ft underground, where the artist has taken advantage of the highly irregular surface of the rock on the ceiling to paint large bunches of grapes supported by red branches, thereby creating an effective illusion of depth. The deceased is shown beneath this arbour of vines receiving offerings brought by priests in the presence of his daughter, Mut-Tuy, who can be seen offering him a heart-shaped amulet.

The burial chamber evokes the afterlife of the deceased and his wife. The ceiling, decorated once again with vines, in addition to the geometric motifs so typical of the 18th Dynasty, is supported by four pillars; on three sides of these Sennefer is depicted receiving gifts from his wife, Merit. The remaining three sides are embellished with different funerary scenes, such as the ritual of the opening of the mouth *(right pillar)*. The decoration on the walls highlights the journey of the deceased's soul, which eventually leads to his regeneration; this journey begins with offerings made to Osiris and Hathor, followed by the funeral, in which the sarcophagus can be seen pulled by four oxen. A nautical scene on the rear wall relates the pilgrimage to Abydos, the sacred town of the tomb of Osiris; this god was responsible for weighing the soul of the deceased against the feather of Maat.

Khaemhat★★★ – *No 57, village, 18th Dynasty.* Khaemhat was a "royal scribe and inspector of the granaries of Upper and Lower Egypt" during the reign of Amenhotep III. Here, paintings give way to magnificently sculpted reliefs carved in the typical style of the period. A number of unusual themes, the symbolism and significance of which are still unclear, can be identified alongside the usual funerary scenes.

Khaemhat himself is depicted in the vestibule flanking the doorway to the tomb, his arms raised in worship; the litanies which accompany this unusual image tell us that he ◄ is worshipping the sun-god, Ra. Note also the complete set of instruments used for the opening of the mouth ceremony. In the chapel, most of the religious scenes (such as the funeral and the pilgrimage to Abydos) and inscriptions are taken from episodes recounted in the *Book of the Dead*; these scenes can be seen on either side of the niche housing the statues of the deceased and his parents.

Khons – *No 31, village, 18th Dynasty.* Khons was the "first prophet of Menkheperra", better known as Thutmose III. This tomb is once again decorated with paintings, in this instance providing details of religious rites through the representation of the Festival of the god Montu, who was worshipped in the region of Thebes from the 6th Dynasty onwards.

Ramose★★★ – *No 55, village, 18th Dynasty.* Ramose was the "vizier and governor of the town of Thebes" under Amenhotep II and IV. The tomb was dug and decorated shortly after that of Khaemhat, but was not completed as this important official would have been obliged to follow Amenhotep IV (Akhenaten) when the court moved from Thebes to Tell el-Amarna, where undoubtedly a new tomb would have been built; however, this tomb was never discovered. The decoration on the magnificent reliefs in this tomb is of a very high quality and is similar to that of the tomb of Khaemhat, although it differs in its representation of the political and religious unrest of the period preceding the Amarnian revolution.

Only the court and the hypostyle hall (the 32-columned antechamber) are decorated. Visitors familiar with the characteristics of Akhenaten's art will have no difficulty in distinguishing the characters depicted in the "Classical" manner from those which already show features typical of the Amarnian period. This new art, the beginnings of ◄ which are already visible in this private tomb, tended to accentuate facial features and to distort the proportions of

The characters represented in the tomb of Ramose have been sculpted with great skill and finesse from the limestone rock.

the body. The increasing attention paid to aesthetic appearance in art during the reign of Amenhotep III has moved the emphasis in many of these scenes from a pre-occupation with perspective to a concern for spatial aware-ness. This aspect was developed further under Akhenaten, and is manifested here in the treatment of various char-acters depicted in the paintings, as well as in the many details of the fashion of the time, which was becoming increasingly sophisticated.

Benia – *No 343, village, 18th Dynasty.* Benia was an "inspec-tor of works" and although his tomb is highly colourful, it appears somewhat archaic alongside the artistic treasures in the tombs which surround it. The finest scenes *(to the left and right of the chapel entrance)* depict the deceased in front of a table of offerings and a banquet.

Userhet – *No 56, village, 18th Dynasty.* Userhet was a "royal scribe" during the reign of Amenhotep II. His tomb is painted in predominantly pastel shades, with lively scenes that show a spontaneity in the treatment of certain details that is in marked contrast with more traditional scenes.

Userhet★ – *No 51, village, 19th Dynasty.* This second Userhet, also known as Neferhebef, was the "first prophet of the royal *ka* of ThutmoseI" under SetyI. Although the magnificent decoration of this tomb is hardly original in theme, it is of interest for the quality of its colour.

El-Asasif and El-Khokha

Tombs of Kharuef and Ankhhor: E£12; students E£6. Tomb of Pabasa: E£12; students E£6. Tombs of Neferronpet, Nefersekheru and Dhutmosi: E£12; students E£6. No cam-eras or videos.

Kharuef★ – *No 192, El-Asasif, 18th Dynasty.* Kharuef was the "intendant of the great royal wife Tiy" during the reigns of Amenhotep III and Amenhotep IV. This large, badly damaged tomb is particularly interesting for the decoration on the west wall of the large courtyard, on either side of the door. The king can be seen to the left of the door, seated under a canopy next to Hathor and the queen, and is depicted participating in his jubilee festival and dressed in his festival costume. The first reg-ister contains lively scenes of dancers, musicians and wrestlers (the larger figures), one of whom wears a zoomorphic mask. To the right of the door, Kheruef can be seen offering precious necklaces to the royal couple, who are once again depicted under a canopy, on this occasion as part of the *djed* pillar festival; the last reg-ister highlights the king's participation in the festivities.

Ankhhor – *No 414, El-Asasif, 26th Dynasty.* Ankhhor was the "great intendant of the divine worshipper Nitocris". His tomb dates back to the Saite period and acts as a use-ful introduction to the art of this dynasty, which was both Classical and African in style.

Pabasa – *No 279, El-Asasif, 26th Dynasty.* Pabasa was the "great major-domo of the divine worshipper Nitocris" under Psammtek I. Also dating from the Saite period, this tomb is decorated with beautiful hieroglyphs and elegantly represented figures.

> **WORTH SEEING**
> It is worth spending a few moments admiring the scene on the right wall, which represents the deceased and his wife in front of a sycamore tree, accompanied by their human-headed *ba*-bird souls.

> **WORTH SEEING**
> Pabasa, seated and dressed in a beautiful pleated robe, is depicted opposite the entrance to the antechamber; a gazelle beneath his chair is holding a lotus flower in its mouth.

EL-QURNA

Perched on a hillside, the houses of the old village of El-Qurna are built over a vast quantity of tombs dug into the soft limestone of the foothills of the Libyan mountains. As early as the 19C, the local authorities suspected villagers of breaking into the tombs, plundering them of their contents and damaging them and, in some cases, destroying the paintings on the walls. Towards the end of the 19C the Abdel Rassoul family made a name for itself by flooding the black market with antiquities taken from a shaft in which mummies had been hidden; these are now on display in the Egyptian Museum in Cairo. Villagers are adamant that such pillaging has long stopped, and that their presence deters any further attempts, although rumours of unofficial finds persist.

Neferronpet – *No 178, El-Khokha, 19th Dynasty.* Neferronpet, also known as Kenro, was the "scribe of treasure in the lands of Amun-Ra" under Rameses II. Although the decorative style within the tomb is generally simplistic in nature, a delightful scene in its antechamber depicts the deceased and his wife drinking from the lake in their garden, surrounded by lotus flowers, ducks, palm trees and bushes with nesting birds.

The badly damaged tomb of Dhutmosi (no 295) is accessible via a small passage.

◀ **Nefersekheru** – *No 296, El-Khokha, 19th and 20th Dynasties.* Nefersekheru was the "scribe of divine offerings in charge of the treasure of the city of Thebes". Thematically similar to the tomb of Neferronpet, this tomb has an attractively decorated antechamber.

DEIR EL-BAHARI★★★

See map of Luxor. E£12; students E£6. No charge for cameras or videos.

The valley was once known as Nefer-Neferu, which translates as "the most sublime of the sublime".

◀ This site owes its name, "the northern monastery", to the monastery built in the temple of Hatshepsut by Christians in the 6C and 7C. The temple hit the headlines on 17 November 1997 when a terrorist attack by a commando division of the *Gama'at al-Islamiya* resulted in the deaths of a number of tourists here. The temple and its surrounding area has since been subject to continual surveillance, along with many other tourist sites around the country. Since the massacre, *Gama'at* has ordered a complete and unconditional end to such violent attacks.

It is worth climbing the Theban hills to appreciate how the temples of Mentuhotep and Hatshepsut blend in perfectly with their surroundings.

Temple of Hatshepsut★★★

A famous temple – The temple of the female Pharaoh
Hatshepsut was built by the architect **Senenmut**, who
was also the Pharaoh's chancellor and favourite courtier,
and is one of the most striking sites of the west bank,
sitting in a natural amphitheatre dug deep into the rock ▶
at the foot of steep ochre-coloured cliffs. Senenmut was
evidently inspired by the terraces and porticoes of the
older and neighbouring temple of Mentuhotep II and
deserves widespread acclaim for his role in the construction of this temple, the harmonious proportions and
quality of which have immortalised Senenmut's name.

First Terrace – A sphinx-lined avenue preceded by a
canal linked to the Nile connects the valley temple to
the mortuary temple. To the west of this terrace, which
was once planted with incense trees, stands a portico
consisting of two rows of 11 rounded pillars and
11 columns. An access ramp in the centre of the portico
leads to the upper terrace. Two Osirid colossi of the
queen once stood either end of the portico.

Second Terrace – Lined to the north by an unfinished portico of 15 proto-Doric columns, this terrace is flanked to
the west by a second portico comprising two rows of 24 pillars. This portico, decorated with **low reliefs**, also has an
access ramp in the centre leading to the third terrace.

The left side of the portico is adorned with carved reliefs
depicting a maritime expedition to the land of Punt (*see
QUSEIR*), shown here in the form of a narrative. It is possible for visitors to follow the events of this peaceful campaign, which was led by Nehesy with the purpose of
bringing back to Egypt a range of exotic goods such as
ivory, ebony, wild cats, resin and incense trees, referred
to by the priests of the time as the "perfume of the gods".
The Queen of Punt is also represented here twice and is ▶
recognisable by her obesity (this is a moulding; the original relief is now exhibited in the Egyptian Museum in
Cairo). The scenes to the right show the birth, education
and coronation of Hatshepsut.

To the south of this portico, the chapel of Hathor, in
effect a *speos* within a *speos*, consists of a series of interlinked rooms preceded by two hypostyle halls. The first
of these is dominated by two rows of beautiful Hathor-
headed columns; the second is attractively decorated
with representations of soldiers on parade at festivals
held in honour of the goddess.

The chapel of Anubis, to the north of this portico, is
another *speos*, and is reached via the entrance to its
hypostyle hall, which shows a remarkable harmony of
style with the portico. A splendid celestial ceiling can be
seen inside the chapel.

Third Terrace – *Not open to the public.* The portico, once
formed by 22 columns preceded by Osirid pillars, leads
into an inner court (40mx26m/131ftx85ft). This court
leads in turn into a number of rooms, including the sanctuary which once housed the sacred bark.

Temple of Mentuhotep II

*See ABC of Architecture in the Insights and Images section
of this guide.*

This temple was constructed at the beginning of the
11th Dynasty almost six centuries before Hatshepsut's
reign and was used as a prototype for many of the monuments built on the west bank of Thebes. Very little of
the temple has survived to the present day.

A pivotal building – The temple symbolically belongs to
the Old Kingdom, because of its role as both a mortuary
temple and a tomb, although its design of staggered terraces prefigures the style of the New Kingdom. Organised
around a mastaba tomb which housed a cenotaph and was
probably crowned by a pyramid, the temple was
approached via a processional avenue and a ramp, and
consisted of two porticoed terraces, both of which led to
an ambulatory around the mastaba. A peristyle set against
the cliff to the rear of the building led to a hypostyle hall,
a sanctuary built in the rock and six tombs intended for
the princesses and royal wives of the Pharaoh.

SPEOS
This architectural term is
given to a sanctuary or
temple built into the
rock.

WORTH SEEING
On the right-hand side of
the west portico, note
the scene where
Hatshepsut's mother is
depicted embracing the
god Amun, who has
taken the place of her
husband, Thutmose I.
Their union is
represented by an
entanglement of legs.

TOMB OF SENENMUT
A few yards to the north-
east of the first terrace
stands the unfinished
tomb of the architect of
the temple, who was actu-
ally buried in the Valley of
the Nobles. A wall of one
of the small chambers
inside the tomb bears a
portrait of Senenmut
along with an inscription
of his name.

EXCAVATIONS
The temple was discov-
ered in the mid-19C by
Lord Dufferin and exca-
vated by the Swiss Henri
Édouard Naville and the
American Herbert Eustis
Winlock. Howard Carter
later discovered the only
surviving statue of the
11th Dynasty, represent-
ing Mentuhotep II, in a pit
at the base of the masta-
ba. The statue is now displayed in the Egyptian
Museum in Cairo.

Detail from the astronomical ceiling in the burial chamber of Rameses IV.

Temple of Thutmose III

In 1961 a third, unfinished temple, that of the Pharaoh Thutmose III was discovered between the temples of Mentuhotep and Hatshepsut by the Polish Archaeology Centre. It is currently being studied with a view to its future restoration.

VALLEY OF THE KINGS★★★

Along with the pyramids at Giza and the temples of Luxor, the Valley of the Kings is the most visited archaeological site in Egypt. Opposite the town of Luxor, the valley, known in Arabic as *Biban el-Molouk* (the "Gates of the Kings"), is the result of erosion in the limestone relief of the Libyan mountains. The valley stretches for several miles, but offers few visible signs of its monuments, as the 58 tombs that have been discovered so far are all built underground.

Domain of the Pharaohs

It has been suggested that the pyramid shape of the mountain overlooking the valley inspired the Pharaohs of the 18th, 19th and 20th Dynasties to dig their tombs along this stretch of sunburnt desert. But it is also true that the valley is isolated and difficult to reach and would therefore have been easy to protect and control. Despite their isolation, these tombs, separated from their mortuary temple since the time of Amenhotep I, have been systematically plundered since the 20th Dynasty.

Construction – Work began as soon as the Pharaoh had chosen the site of his tomb. Labourers cut into the limestone rock and layers of flint using wooden mallets and metal chisels, in accordance with precise instructions given by the architect. As their work progressed, plasterers covered up any irregular surfaces in the rock wall by applying stucco, on top of which they then applied a thin coating of white chalk. At this stage, the designers of the tomb made their contribution to the project, marking out the surfaces to be decorated in red ochre. Once they had finished their drawings and hieroglyphs, the sculptors took over, carving out designs to produce low reliefs which were in turn coloured by painters according to a strict classification system determined by rites.

Layout – Each tomb has a slightly different layout, though certain features, such as the flight of steps, the descending corridor and the rooms around the burial chamber, are common. The descending corridor in 18th Dynasty-tombs usually forms a right angle and is cut in two by a shaft, whereas 20th Dynasty-corridors form a straight line. The **decoration** in the tombs focuses solely on the afterworld and the Pharaoh's journey to the kingdom of Osiris. This is in marked contrast to the natural scenes depicted in many of the private tombs, as the overriding concern of the royal tombs was the survival of the Pharaoh's soul.

A DOUBLE VALLEY
The valley is, in fact, divided into two: the eastern valley, or Valley of the Kings, and the western valley, or Valley of the Monkeys. The latter contains just four tombs.

CARTER'S HOUSE
The lower of the two houses visible as you enter the Valley of the Kings is that of the archaeologist Howard Carter, who discovered the tomb of Tutankhamun. Plans are under way to open a museum in the house.

PRACTICAL ADVICE
Visitors are advised to start their visit in the early morning to avoid the hottest part of the day and to take plenty of water with them. The valley can either be climbed on foot or by a little train (E£1).

Entry into the tomb – Although considered divine, the Pharaoh was, of course, mortal. After his death, it took 70 days to carry out the mummification of his body and to wrap it in bandages before he was ready to start his journey to eternal life. The cortege of priests and mourners led the body in its wooden sarcophagus to the threshold of his tomb. Next came the opening of the mouth ceremony (a ritual which was believed to give life to the deceased), followed by the carrying of the Pharaoh to the burial chamber where a monumental sarcophagus had been built. Once the Pharaoh had been enclosed in his sarcophagus and the lid placed on top, the tomb was secured by fixing the royal seal on the entrance door.

Visiting the Tombs

Tickets available at main ticket office (see map of Luxor): open all year, 6am-5pm (6pm in summer). Three tombs E£20, students E£10; tomb of Tutankhamun E£40, students E£20; tomb of Ay E£10, students E£5; tomb of Hatshepsut E£12, students E£6. Camera permit E£5 per tomb, with the exception of Tutankhamun (available from the ticket office at the entrance to the valley); no videos. Visits limited to 10min per tomb.

Thutmose I – *No 38*. Thutmose I was the first Pharaoh to build a tomb here. Its layout, with a cartouche-shaped burial chamber, set the tone for many subsequent tombs.

Hatshepsut – *No 20*. Once on the throne, Queen Hatshepsut assumed the male attributes of the Pharaoh; this explains why she abandoned work on an earlier tomb started in the Valley of the Queens to build a new one here. This 200m/656ft-deep tomb, which was never completely finished and is devoid of ornamentation, originally housed her sarcophagus in addition to that of Thutmose I.

Thutmose III★★ – *No 34*. This tomb is located at the end of a narrow gorge and was discovered in 1898 by the French archaeologist Victor Loret. The shaft leads into a vestibule decorated with paintings representing 765 deities. From here, a staircase leads to the burial chamber, which has a large empty sarcophagus built from red quartzite at its centre; the mummy was discovered by Maspero in a secret cache in Deir el-Bahri in 1881. The walls imitate the decoration of papyrus texts, and illustrate the *Book of Amduat*. This magical text described the journey of the sun-god through the hours of darkness; the painting is divided into 12 sections, corresponding to the 12 hours of the night. The pillars are adorned with extracts from the *Litanies of the Sun*, on which the king is depicted as the sun.

Amenhotep II★★ – *No 35*. The tomb of Amenhotep II was also discovered by Loret in 1898 and is one of the deepest in the valley. Steps descend into its huge chamber, which is supported by six pillars and adorned with images of the king in the presence of various gods. The walls are decorated with scenes from the *Book of Amduat* in the same style as the tomb of Thutmose III. A red quartzite sarcophagus dominates the burial chamber. The Pharaoh's mummy was exhibited here until 1934, but is now on display in the Egyptian Museum in Cairo. When the mummy was first discovered, it still wore a garland around its neck and a small bouquet of mimosa was still in place on its heart.

Tutankhamun – *No 62; guides are not allowed to accompany visitors into this tomb*. The most famous of all the tombs in the valley came to light on 4 November 1922, when it was discovered by **Howard Carter** and his patron Lord Carnarvon. However, despite the magnificent treasure found inside it, the tomb may prove a disappointment to visitors as the entire collection has been moved to the Egyptian Museum in Cairo. The only features that remain are the sarcophagus and the **external coffin★**, which still contains the mummy of the king. The tomb is small, reflecting the Pharaoh's short reign, and the burial chamber is the only decorated part of it; even then the paintings are generally poor in quality. Tutankhamun's tomb has come to symbolise the magnificent wealth of Egyptian art, and it is this spirit of discovery and adventure that continues to draw visitors here.

The tombs are numbered in the order in which they were discovered and are listed in chronological order from the 18th to the 20th Dynasty. Those which are unfinished, closed, badly damaged or currently being restored have not been included. Tombs may occasionally be closed to visitors.

Note the absence of relief decoration in this tomb, which is typical of the 18th Dynasty. The deities are depicted as stick figures, and are drawn in black or red on a grey background.

Loret discovered nine royal mummies still in their sarcophagi, in one of the four rooms adjoining the burial chamber. These mummies, which included those of Amenhotep III, Rameses V and Rameses VI, had been hidden here at the end of the 20th Dynasty to protect them from tomb-robbers.

With the financial backing of Lord Carnarvon, Carter had already discovered the tomb of Amenhotep I, before making the discovery that was to bring him international recognition. After five years' work, Lord Carnarvon was on the point of withdrawing his support when Carter uncovered a step cut in the rock beneath the entrance to the tomb of Rameses VI.

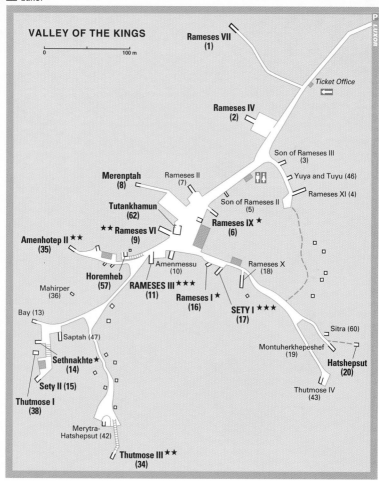

VALLEY OF THE KINGS

0 _____ 100 m

Rameses VII (1)

Ticket Office

Rameses IV (2)

Son of Rameses III (3)

Merenptah (8)

Rameses II (7)

Yuya and Tuyu (46)

Rameses XI (4)

Son of Rameses II (5)

Tutankhamun (62)

Rameses IX ★ (6)

★★ Rameses VI (9)

Amenhotep II ★★ (35)

Amenmessu (10)

Rameses X (18)

Horemheb (57)

Mahirper (36)

RAMESES III ★★★ (11)

Rameses I ★ (16)

SETY I ★★★ (17)

Bay (13)

Sitra (60)

Saptah (47)

Montuherkhepeshef (19)

Sethnakhte ★ (14)

Hatshepsut (20)

Sety II (15)

Thutmose IV (43)

Thutmose I (38)

Merytra-Hatshepsut (42)

Thutmose III ★★ (34)

> **T**his tomb marks a change in layout: the descending corridor now runs in a straight line, rather than at a right angle, and low reliefs appear for the first time.

◄ **Horemheb** – *No 57*. When British archaeologist Edward Ayrton discovered this tomb in 1908, he was first obliged to clear away piles of stone and debris which had been swept down over the centuries by torrential rain from the Libyan mountains. The paintings in this tomb are damaged in places, but nonetheless provide an interesting example of the techniques used by artists of the time, in particular the square patterns on the wall used by designers to outline their work.

Rameses I★ – *No 16*. The small dimensions of this tomb, discovered by Giovanni Belzoni in 1817, can be explained by the fact that this Pharaoh ruled for only two years. Despite its modest size, the wall decoration, which is similar in style to that in the tomb of Horemheb, is of fine quality and depicts scenes taken from the *Book of Gates*. The fourth hour of the book is represented on the southern wall: note the nine mummies in the upper register and

---

AND THEN THERE WAS LIGHT

The antechamber had previously been broken into by tomb-robbers and was covered in shards of pottery and other objects when the tomb was first discovered. Two large statues of the king stood against the north wall, almost as though they were keeping guard. Howard Carter and Lord Carnarvon made an opening into the burial chamber and found four chapels of gilded wood, one inside the other. In the last chapel stood a coffin containing three mummiform sarcophagi in gilded wood; the last of these revealed a stunning solid gold sarcophagus which was opened on 28 October 1925. Inside they found the magnificent gold death mask of Tutankhamun, untouched since the day the priests had placed it over the mummy and locked it away from the eyes of the world.

the enormous serpent, Apophis, flanked by 12 goddesses symbolising the 12 hours of the night in the lower register. It was believed that Apophis attacked the sun every morning and every evening and that only ritual sacrifices organised in the temples allowed the sun-god Ra to triumph in this perpetual conflict.

Sety I★★★ – *No 17; also see ABC of Architecture in the Insights and Images section*. Although this tomb has been closed since 1991, it deserves mention both for its construction and decoration, and is arguably the finest of all the tombs in the valley. Discovered by Belzoni, the tomb is 120m/132yd in length, with a complex layout. Its walls and ceilings are adorned with low reliefs and paintings which combine to produce an almost magical effect. Scenes portrayed include the *Litanies of Ra* in the first corridor and the journey of the sun-god from the *Book of Amduat* in the burial chamber itself. Belzoni removed the fine alabaster sarcophagus of Sety I from Egypt and sold it to a collector, John Soane, the architect of the Bank of England. The sarcophagus can now be seen in the Sir John Soane Museum in London.

Merenptah – *No 8*. This 115m/126yd-long tomb was one of the first to be built with descending corridors constructed with higher ceilings. The tomb is decorated with beautiful reliefs of a high quality, which subsequently give way to low reliefs which are technically quite poor. It is possible that Merenptah, who only became Pharaoh in his sixties, ordered that work on his tomb should be finished quickly so that it would be completed in time for his death.

Sety II – *No 15*. This tomb was used by Howard Carter to house and restore the treasures that he found in the tomb of Tutankhamun. The descending corridor is decorated with extracts from the *Litanies of Ra*, and the vestibule is covered with representations of the funerary deities.

Sethnakhte★ – *No 14*. This tomb was originally built and designed for Queen Tawsert, wife of both Merenptah and Sety II, but was usurped by Sethnakhte, the first king of the 20th Dynasty. The Pharaoh had the many representations of the queen painted over; however, since the tomb has been restored some of these can now be glimpsed in the corridor *(immediately to the left)*. In the eight-pillared hall, the king is represented with an erect phallus, as a symbol that he is still alive. Note the serpent Apophis, often portrayed as the incarnation of evil, depicted below him.

Rameses III★★★ – *No 11*. When James Bruce explored this tomb in 1768, he named it the "tomb of the harpists" after the two superb representations of these musicians that can be seen in the tomb. The tomb is 125m/137yd long and complex in layout, with a dead-end passage where workers accidentally broke into the neighbouring tomb of Amenmessu (currently being excavated by Otto Schaden). The decoration illustrates the funerary texts of the *Litanies of Ra*, the *Book of Amduat* and the *Book of Gates*. The most unusual feature of the tomb is the eight side chambers which lie off the second corridor. The scenes portrayed here are extremely uncommon for a tomb in this valley, as they depict food preparation, boats on the Nile, cereals, the personification of the Nile, royal weapons (bows, helmets and chariots), the personification of the nomes of Egypt, furniture and vases, the king's double, agricultural tasks and two harpists playing to the gods Shu, Atum and Onuris (the god of hunting and war). In the four-pillared room the four human races known to the Egyptians of the period are also represented, along with scenes of offerings to Ra-Horakhty, Khepri and Atum (all various forms of the sun-god). The eight-pillared burial chamber is not open to the public. The red quartzite sarcophagus is now on display in the Louvre Museum in Paris; its lid forms part of the collection of the Fitzwilliam Museum in Cambridge, in England.

Rameses IV – *No 2*. This tomb contains the valley's largest sarcophagus (3.3m/10.82ft long, 2.12m/6.95ft wide and 2.75m/9.02ft high), the sides of which are engraved with

GRID SYSTEM

In order to produce a low relief or a painting, a large grid was traced on to the wall from a previously prepared design. This grid usually had a height of 21 squares, which could be further subdivided. This technique allowed the designers, who worked almost without light, to respect the proportions of their subject.

The god Osiris in the tomb of Rameses I.

HUMAN FIGURES

The human figure is represented descriptively, so that as many features as possible could be portrayed. This explains why the face, although viewed from the side, nonetheless bears the features normally seen from the front, such as the eyebrows, eyes and part of the mouth. The shoulders are viewed from the front in order to show the arms; the stomach is not quite in profile so that the belly-button is visible; and the legs are drawn in profile, with the big toe shown on both feet.

scenes of hell. The ceiling of the room where it is on display is painted a magnificent blue and is decorated with astronomical symbols surrounding the goddess Nut. In the 5C, this tomb was used as a Christian place of worship.

Rameses VI★★ – *No 9*. This tomb was built for Rameses V, but was actually used by his successor, probably for economic reasons. Its magnificent iconography, painted in a mix of reds and yellows, is particularly complex. Scenes from the *Book of Caverns* and *Book of Gates* decorate the walls up to the four-pillared room, providing information on the geography of the afterlife; the ceiling is adorned with astronomical images. Between this room and the burial chamber, the scenes displayed are taken from the *Book of Amduat* and the *Book of the Dead*. Each of these funerary texts was considered to have a magical power over the world of the deceased, guiding and protecting him or her with magical spells so that they would overcome the forces of evil that they encountered. Some of their evil foes are depicted in the burial chamber, in the form of figures who have been decapitated.

Rameses VII – *No 1*. The burial chamber in this tomb is decorated with extracts from the *Book of Caverns*; note also the attractive ceiling adorned with astronomical images. A fine portrait of the deceased can be seen at the entrance.

Rameses IX★ – *No 6*. The decoration in this tomb follows the same themes as those found in the tomb of Rameses VI; it also represents scenes from the *Litanies of Ra*, which described the 75 changes which the god and the Pharaoh underwent during their nocturnal journey. Various deities from the afterworld are also depicted in the second and third corridors. The ceiling of the burial chamber is decorated with astronomical scenes, including Nut swallowing the sun. A scene on the south wall illustrates the birth of the sun, with the scarab of the god Khepri, who symbolised the morning form of the sun-god.

Ay – *No 23, in the west valley, 2km/1.2mi from the Valley of the Kings.* Ay, the successor to Tutankhamun, reigned for just three years, which perhaps explains why his tomb is unfinished. Discovered by Belzoni in 1816 (his name is engraved on a stone by the entrance), the tomb has the linear layout later adopted by the pharaohs of the 20th Dynasty. The beautiful hunting scene of the kind normally seen in private tombs is of particular note.

TEMPLE OF SETY I★

See map of Luxor. E£12; students E£6. No charge for cameras or videos.

This is the northernmost building on the west bank of Thebes and was once known as the "Temple of Qurna" because of its proximity to the village of the same name. The Ancient Egyptians referred to this mortuary temple as **"Glory to Sety in the west of Thebes"**. It is considered to be the best preserved of the "million-year-old temples", and is situated on the edge of cultivated land.

Enclosure – The temple precinct included a royal palace to the south, and warehouses where the harvest was stored to the north, as well as the temple itself. The warehouses are the first examples of their kind to be built within the royal enclosure itself; this model is repeated later in the Ramesseum *(see Ramesseum)*. The royal palace stood within the enclosure and had a ritual role: during festivals a statue placed in the throne room allowed the deceased king to appear before his people.

Temple – *Entrance through the north enclosure*. A processional avenue leads to the first courtyard. Originally preceded by two pylons and two courtyards, the building has retained its attractive **portico** with its papyrus-bud columns within the hypostyle hall. The low reliefs date mainly from the reign of Rameses II, as Sety I did not live long enough to see the building decorated. The goddesses Mut and Hathor are represented here suckling the king. In the sanctuary, the chapels are adorned with beautiful reliefs, including a splendid ram's head crowned with the solar disk, the symbol of the sacred bark of Amun.

THE GODDESS NUT
This goddess appears twice on the ceiling of the burial chamber: once with the solar disc (day), and a second time with the stars (night). Nut was said to swallow the sun in the evening and give birth to it in the morning.

COLOURFUL LANGUAGE
Black (charcoal or soot) symbolises death and eternal life; red (iron oxide), fire; yellow (arsenic sulphide), gold or the resurrection; white (gypsum), silver; green (copper salts), regeneration; and blue (a combination of copper salts, calcite and sodium salts), the sky.

Columns in the Temple of Sety I.

Maidum

Maidum is a small, peaceful village situated close to the remains of one of the first (if not the very first) of the pyramids. For this reason, the village, which is also famous for its frieze of painted geese, is an important stop for those interested in unravelling the mystery of the great Egyptian pyramids.

Location
92km/57mi S of Cairo, 44km/27mi E of Medinet el-Fayum, on the left bank of the Nile. Access: the only feasible option is, by taxi, as the microbus via El-Wasta and Maidum involves a walk of several miles, with no roadsigns.

Name
Literally, Maidum means "the pyramid is stable". The ▶ Arabs named the pyramid *Ahran el-Kaddah* or "the false pyramid".

Transcription: ميدوم

▶ **T**he pyramid is described as false because of its resemblance to a mastaba crowned with a two-storey tower.

Famous People
Prince Rahotep and his wife Nofret have survived the passing of time. Their painted statues discovered in Maidum are now exhibited at the Egyptian Museum in Cairo.

History
Sneferu, the first pharaoh of the 4th Dynasty, chose Maidum as a necropolis because he wanted to break all ties with the preceding dynasty.

background

The oldest pyramid in Egypt? – Despite its Arabic name *(see above)*, many historians consider the pyramid at Maidum to be the first "true" pyramid. Although it has certain features in common with the pyramidal structures of the 3rd Dynasty, it differs in other characteristics, such as the square plan, the entrance to the north and its interior layout, all of which are unique to the 4th Dynasty.

The pyramid was built in three stages: the first consisted of a mound built at an angle of 2°, and the second of a stepped structure at an angle of 8°. It was the third stage that made this the first real pyramid in Egyptian history: once all cavities had been plugged with backfill, a smooth limestone facing was added to the structure. All that remains today is the first stage of the structure.

Graffiti – For a long time experts believed that this pyramid may have been that of Huni, the last pharaoh of the 3rd Dynasty and the father of Sneferu. However, engraved inscriptions dating from the New Kingdom and referring to Sneferu have been found on the walls of the mortuary temple, proof that the Egyptians of that period believed Sneferu to be responsible for construction of the pyramid. Some historians suggest that the pyramid may have been started by Huni and finished by his son.

The pyramid's strange silhouette stands out on the edge of the desert, near the irrigation channels of the alluvial plain.

worth a visit

Pyramid of Sneferu
9km/5.5mi from the village of Maidum.
Open all year, 8am-5pm. E£16; students E£8; camera permit E£5; video permit E£25.
Sneferu - It is thought that the founder of the 4th Dynasty, probably the natural son of Huni, married his half-sister, Hetepheres, who gave him a son, the immortal Khufu. Sneferu, who was portrayed as the

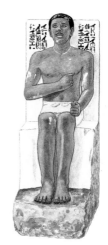

A statue of Prince Rahotep discovered at Maidum

The beautiful geese of Maidum, now exhibited in the Egyptian Museum, Cairo.

model of the perfect king by many of his successors, enjoyed a long and peaceful reign, despite a number of military expeditions abroad. The technique of coloured mosaics was used for the first time during his rule, and no fewer than three pyramids are attributed to him (Maidum, the Rhomboidal Pyramid and the Red Pyramid).

The site – Situated between the desert and the alluvial plain of the Nile, the site comprises the pyramid and mastaba no 17 in the southern section, and the necropolis, including the princes' mastabas, in the north.

The magnificent sculptures of Rahotep and his wife Nofret were discovered in the **mastaba of Rahotep**, while the **mastaba of Nefermaat** (no 16) is of great significance for art history of the Old Kingdom period. Excavation work carried out by Mariette in 1871 revealed the famous frieze of the **Maidum geese**, as well as paintings created using the new procedure of colour mosaics, which was unfortunately too fragile to be employed by subsequent dynasties.

The funerary complex – Maidum is a good example of a typical Egyptian funerary complex. Below, on the edge of the cultivated land, stood the valley temple (the first of its kind), also known as the reception temple, which was a place of purification, often under the protection of a female deity. From the temple, a long, narrow causeway led towards the pyramid. This causeway represented the point of passage between life and death, was usually painted or even covered and led to the mortuary temple, also known as the temple of worship, which faced the rising sun. The temple of offerings was situated further up the site, at the foot of the pyramid.

Pyramid – The pyramid, which now measures 65m/213ft in height, was originally 93.5m/307ft high, with a base measuring 147m/482ft on each side. To the north, an entrance 18.5m/61ft above the ground leads into a gallery (1.5m/5ft high) which leads down into the burial chamber. No sarcophagus has ever been found in this corbelled chamber and it is thought that the tomb was probably pillaged.

The present condition of the pyramid may be the result of the collapse of the exterior limestone casing while the Rhomboidal Pyramid was being built at Dahshu. Alternatively, it may be that the outer casing never existed and that the pyramid was, in fact, never completed.

EMPTY MASTABAS

Unfortunately, there is nothing of interest in these two mastabas, which have now been colonised by bats. However, mastaba no 17 contains a sarcophagus, reached via a narrow passageway.

LAYOUT

Before Maidum, funerary complexes were built along a north-south axis; Sneferu was the first pharoah to build on an east-west axis, enabling the difference in elevation between the valley and the desert floor to be exploited and the deceased to move from the world of the living (the valley) to that of the dead (the desert).

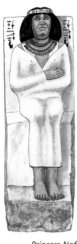

Princess Nofret, now with her husband in the Egyptian Museum in Cairo

THE MAIDUM GEESE

Only a few examples of painting have survived from the Old Kingdom, and the frieze discovered in the mastaba of Nefermaat is of great historical importance. Known as the "Maidum Geese", it is a lively composition, painted on a dry coating (unlike the fresco technique), and is an excellent example of the high artistic standards of decorative art during the Old Kingdom.

27cm/10in high and 172cm/67in long, the panel depicts three pairs of geese. The colours and outline of the geese are very true to life; the artist has chosen to represent four white-fronted geese and two barnacle geese with red necks, easily identified by their plumage.

Tell el-Amarna

Although the site of Tell el-Amarna in Middle Egypt was occupied for no more than 30 years, it saw the rise and fall of the Armanian revolution, arguably one of the most important episodes in the history of Ancient Egypt. It was here that Amenhotep IV founded his short-lived capital, Akhetaten, in a 12km/7.5mi-long natural semicircle situated between the Arabian cliffs and the right bank of the Nile.

Location
305km/190mi S of Cairo, 79km/49mi N of Asyut, on the right bank of the Nile. Access: difficult, as the region is troubled by clashes between fundamentalists and the authorities; from Mallawi take a collective taxi to the ferry which crosses the Nile to At-Till, on the east bank (50pt or E£4 by tourist boat).

Name
The villages of El-Amarna (whose name comes from the Bedouin tribe of the Amrân) and El-Tell (a *tell* is an artificial hill formed by ruins) combine to form the name Tell el-Amarna.

Transcription: تل العمارنة

Famous People
The site of Tell el-Amarna is associated above all with the Pharaoh Amenhotep IV, whose name translates as "Amun is content", and who later changed his name to Akhenaten ("glory of the sun disc").

History
The capital city Akhetaten was occupied for just a brief period during the 17 years of Akhenaten's reign. It was built in 1348 BC during the 18th Dynasty.

Cartouche of Amenhotep IV

background

The break with Thebes – Four years after ascending to the throne of Egypt, **Amenhotep IV** broke with the clergy of Thebes (Luxor). No texts remain to shed light on the cause of the dispute, although we do know that conflict already existed in the Middle Kingdom and that in the second year of his reign Amenhotep IV replaced the state god Amun-Ra with **Aten**. It would appear obvious that the Pharaoh wanted to free himself from the power of the priests of Amun, but at the same time his actions were to result in such radical change and such a complete break with tradition, that historians now refer to the period as the "Amarnian revolution".

The cult of Aten – The main contribution of the Amarnian revolution from a religious point of view was the abandonment of polytheism in Egyptian temples. Henceforth only one god was to be worshipped – Aten, the solar disc, who until this time was merely an aspect of the Heliopolitan sun-god Ra and not represented in human form. Amenhotep IV subsequently ordered the destruction of all images of other gods throughout his kingdom. Despite this revolution, the Egyptian people ► continued to follow traditional religious practices and the cult of Aten remained essentially a cult of the royal court, replacing mythology with an emphasis on nature and human life.

Akhetaten, a new capital – In the fourth year of his reign, Amenhotep IV decided to leave Thebes and his temple at Karnak, which was dedicated to Amun. The site that he chose for his future capital, "revealed by Aten himself", was in Middle Egypt and had no historical significance. He moved there with his wife, the beautiful Nefertiti, a close confidante in both his personal and political affairs. Here he founded a city which he called Akhetaten ("Horizon of the Disk"), of which only the

A NEW PHILOSOPHY
Akhenaten's reforms reflected a new mindset and philosophy, which affected all of Egyptian society, including its language. This profound and dramatic change, which perhaps was too radical for the time, was followed by a violent "counter-reformation".

The only god to survive the destruction ordered by Akhenaten, often referred to as the "heretic king", was Osiris. Although the traditional funerary cult disappeared, Osiris himself did not, as is shown by the Osirid colossi which represented the king.

foundations now remain, the buildings having been destroyed on the orders of Horemheb after the death of Amenhotep IV.

This new capital was the centre of a society which endeavoured to free itself from tradition and which was similar in many ways to the Romantic movement in Europe in the 18C and 19C, with its emphasis on sentimentality, nature, the importance of the individual, and the role of women. To emphasise this new era, the Pharaoh changed his name to Akhenaten in the sixth year of his reign.

◄ **Amarnian Art** – This religious revolution, which was even felt in the political arena through administrative centralisation, was most evident in the economy and in art. The art of Tell el-Amarna without a doubt represents one of the greatest moments of artistic activity in Ancient Egypt. The word "Amarnian" was coined following the discovery of the first traces of this art at Tell el-Amarna, although several of its features were apparent under Amenhotep III. Akhenaten was perhaps inspired by some of the characteristics of this earlier trend (for example, the bent head and pensive eyes) to create a completely new and unrealistic style. Although very few examples of architecture remain from this period, the impressive sculpture and paintings that still exist bear witness to a remarkable wave of artistic freedom. In fact, the effects of the spiritual Amarnian revolution were to prove most lasting in its art, which was to have a strong influence on the originality of the later Ramesside period.

> **In** order to fully appreciate the qualities of Armanian art, a visit to the Egyptian Museum in Cairo is a must. Superb artefacts from this period are displayed in Room 3. The full impact of the period can be admired in the treasure of Tutankhamun, which was produced at Tell el-Amarna.

The city of Akhetaten today.

AKHENATEN, THE CONTROVERSIAL PHARAOH

To some Egyptologists, Akhenaten was a brilliant Pharaoh; to others he was a weak-minded ruler. Either way, he and his wife, Nefertiti, have intrigued scholars for centuries. In one of his books, Sigmund Freud, who considered Akhenaten to be an important visionary, wrote "If Moses was an Egyptian who passed his own religion on to the Jews, then his religion was that of Akhenaten, the religion of Aten". Some historians even claim that the true origins of monotheism can be traced to Tell el-Amarna.

Sculptures of the period portray the royal couple with bodies that are out of proportion: they have elongated heads, a slim torso, wide hips and a bulging stomach. Some historians consider these details to be symbolic, while others suggest that maybe the Pharaoh was ill. Although the style cannot easily be explained, Armanian art also expressed feelings and family intimacy for the first time.

The Armanian revolution was brought to an abrupt and mysterious end, perhaps as a result of illness or murder, or the enigmatic and heretical Akhenaten's neglect of his empire. However, although this revolutionary reign was short-lived, modern experts are still arguing over its true impact.

worth a visit

TOWN AND NECROPOLIS★

Usually open all year, 7am-4pm. Site: E£12. Add an extra E£3.75-E£12, depending on the tombs visited.

Site

The ruins of the site extend along the Nile in the heart of a fertile area 10km/6mi long and 25km/15mi wide, stretching from one desert to the next. A number of bor- ◄ der-steles marked the territory of the nome founded by Akhenaten (11 have been found on the right bank); these large stone inscriptions depict the royal family worshipping the solar disc. Many of the steles are badly damaged and difficult to read, with the exception of those at Tuna el-Gebel, on the left bank *(see TUNA EL-GEBEL)*.

Town

The town was situated to the north (the cultivated area was to the south) and comprised a number of buildings which are difficult to make out today. The town centre was crossed by an avenue which ran north-south and which separated the palace from the two temples.

> **ENIGMA**
> The text on the border-steles contains a sermon instructing people not to stray beyond the borders of the nome. The exact meaning of this sermon is unclear. Although it seems unlikely, it has been interpreted by some as a pronouncement by the Pharaoh that he would never leave Akhenaten.

Palace – The royal residence was divided into two sections connected by a covered passage which spanned the main avenue, from where the king and queen appeared to the people. The first section, overlooking the Nile, consisted of the throne room, a hypostyle hall, two harems, a garden, a court and ceremonial rooms. The second section housed the king's apartments.

Great Temple – The great temple was, of course, dedicated to Aten and hardly differed from the great Theban temples. Surrounded by a huge 800x275m/2 624x902ft enclosure, it housed a number of sacred areas. Behind the entrance pylon stood a hypostyle hall which led into a number of courtyards separated by pylons. Various altars once stood in the courtyards. The last room was dedicated to Aten.

Necropolis

The necropolis has a total of 26 tombs hollowed out of the rock. Tombs nos 1 to 6 are to the north, tombs 7 to 25 to the south, and the royal tomb to the east.

Tomb of Huya★ (No 1) – Huya was the intendant of the royal harem and Queen Tiy's chamberlain. The first of the three interlinked rooms is decorated with scenes depicting Akhenaten, Nefertiti and the princesses. In the third chamber, a niche houses the badly damaged funerary statue.

Tomb of Meryra (No 2) – Construction of the tomb of this royal scribe, who was also a chamberlain of Queen Tiy, was started under Akhenaten and completed under Smenkhkara. It also comprises three rooms and is adorned with several scenes portraying Akhenaten, including one on the right wall of the first room where the king is shown receiving a foreign delegation.

Tomb of Meryra★ (No 4) – This Meryra was the high priest of the disc. Two of the three rooms in this tomb are highly decorated; the second houses a painting of a rainbow, the only one of its kind in Egypt, as well as a plan of the palace which has enabled experts to understand the function of those ruins which were completely destroyed.

Tomb of Tutu (No 8) – The tomb of Tutu, another chamberlain, has a similar layout to the Theban tombs, with a large 16m/52ft room, the ceiling of which is supported by two rows of papyrus-shaped columns. The low reliefs represent the deceased in the company of the king and queen.

Tomb of Ay (No 25) – Ay, Queen Tiy's brother, was the vizier of Tutankhamun, whose widow he married and whom he succeeded to the throne. His tomb was started under Akhenaten, although he was in fact buried at Thebes (Luxor). One of the best-preserved texts of the *Hymn to Aten*, thought to have been written by Akhenaten himself, was discovered here.

Royal Tomb (No 26) – The king's tomb is badly damaged and access is difficult. Although the mummy of this controversial Pharaoh has yet to be found here, a team of British archaeologists is currently excavating tomb no 56, which was originally opened in 1908. Early findings suggest that the tomb may be the final resting place of the queens.

Akhetaten was a large town of 40 000 inhabitants with streets, temples, elegant houses belonging to the nobility, districts for its workers, warehouses and tombs.

There is a good view of the desert plain from the top of the necropolis, although you'll need to use your imagination to envisage the past splendour of the town.

RELIEFS
The scenes painted on the walls of this tomb are of interest for two reasons: firstly, they bring this ruined city back to life, and secondly, they provide examples of the two different styles found in Amarnian art.

MYSTERIOUS NEFERTITI

Nefertiti's cartouche appears 164 times in Karnak (Luxor), demonstrating the influence of this queen, who was much more than a royal consort. The origins of Nefertiti, whose name means "a beautiful woman has come", have long been the subject of debate among historians. Was she a daughter of Amenhotep III – and therefore sister to her husband Amenhotep IV? Or could she have been the daughter of Ay who later became Pharaoh and whose wife Tiy is described as the "nurse of Nefertiti"? A third theory suggests that she was the Asiatic princess Taduchepa, who was sold to Amenhotep III in exchange for pure gold. Towards the end of Amenhotep IV's reign, the king and queen separated. It has been suggested that Nefertiti subsequently ruled jointly with Amenhotep's successor, Smenkhkara; a more novel theory claims that Smenkhkara was none other than Nefertiti herself.

The bust of Nefertiti, found by Borchardt. Finely carved, it contrasts with the caricatural style popular in the early Amarna period.

Index

Abou Simbel..City, town, region, other point of interest or subject.
Alexander the Great.................. ....Personal name.

The best-known pyramids are shown under the heading Pyramids, others are listed under the name of the pharaoh.

Photo credits

p. 1 : B. Pérousse/MICHELIN
p. 4 : Musée du Caire/M. Elba-Studio Vart/MICHELIN
p. 4 : Hany Aziz/MICHELIN
p. 5 : A. Soubre/Visa Productions/MICHELIN
p. 5 : Fr. Soreau/MICHELIN
p. 16-17 : B. Kaufmann/MICHELIN
p. 18 : S. Sauvignier/MICHELIN
p. 21 : M. Magni/MICHELIN
p. 23 : S. Sauvignier/MICHELIN
p. 25 : Hany Aziz/MICHELIN
p. 26 : J.-L. Blanchon/Visa Productions/MICHELIN
p. 27 : S. Sauvignier/MICHELIN
p. 28 : Hany Aziz/MICHELIN
p. 30 : A. Soubre/Visa Productions/MICHELIN
p. 32 : Hany Aziz/MICHELIN
p. 33 : J.-L. Gallo/MICHELIN
p. 34 : Fl. Joalland El Abd/MICHELIN
p. 37 : B. Dumas/MICHELIN
p. 38, p. 40 : Hany Aziz/MICHELIN
p. 42-43 : Fr. Soreau/MICHELIN
p. 43-44 : R. Mattes/MICHELIN
p. 44 : Collection AL-ALAHRAM
p. 45 : Fr. Soreau/MICHELIN
p. 46 : Collection H. Youssef
p. 47 : Musée du Caire/Abou Ghazala/MICHELIN
p. 47 : Musée du Caire/M. Elba-Studio Vart/MICHELIN
p. 47 : © Collection VIOLLET
p. 48 : H.-P. de Girardier
p. 48 : Collection M. Wassef
p. 48 : B. Kaufmann/MICHELIN
p. 49 : B. Pérousse/MICHELIN
p. 49 : S. Sauvignier/MICHELIN
p. 49 : B. Pérousse/MICHELIN
p. 50 : Collection M. Wassef
p. 50 : Fr. Soreau/MICHELIN
p. 51 : B. Kaufmann/MICHELIN
p. 51 : Collection M. Wassef
p. 52-53 : Abou Ghazala/MICHELIN
p. 52 : R. Mattes/MICHELIN
p. 53 : M. Elba-Studio Vart/MICHELIN
p. 52-53 : Abou Ghazala/MICHELIN
p. 54 ht et bs : Ch. Roth/MICHELIN
p. 55 : J.-L. Blanchon/Visa Productions/MICHELIN
p. 55 : R. Mattes/MICHELIN
p. 56 : B. Kaufmann/MICHELIN
p. 57 ht et bs : B. Pérousse/MICHELIN
p. 58-59, p. 58 : Hany Aziz/MICHELIN
p. 59 : J.-P. Michel/MICHELIN
p. 59 : B. Pérousse/MICHELIN
p. 58-59 : A. Soubre/Visa Productions/MICHELIN
p. 60 : Fr. Soreau/MICHELIN
p. 60-61, p. 61, : B. Pérousse/MICHELIN
p. 62 : M. Guillou/MICHELIN
p. 62 : J.-Cl. Boulais/MICHELIN
p. 63 : M. Guillou/MICHELIN
p. 63 : A. Soubre/Visa Productions/MICHELIN
p. 63 : J.-L. Blanchon/Visa Productions/MICHELIN
p. 64-65 : Hany Aziz/MICHELIN
p. 64 : Musée du Caire/M. Elba-Studio Vart/MICHELIN
p. 65 : B. Pérousse/MICHELIN
p. 66 : Hany Aziz/MICHELIN
p. 66 : Musée du Caire/G. Mesmin/MICHELIN
p. 67 ht et bs : Hany Aziz/MICHELIN
p. 68 : Fr. Soreau/MICHELIN
p. 68 : Hany Aziz/MICHELIN
p. 68 : M. Guillou/MICHELIN
p. 69 : R. Dechamps/MICHELIN
p. 69 : Fr. Soreau/MICHELIN
p. 70-71 : Hany Aziz/MICHELIN
p. 71 ht et bs : © Collection VIOLLET
p. 72-73 : Collection AL-ALAHRAM
p. 72 : M. Guillou/MICHELIN
p. 73 : H. Ruiz
p. 73 : Hany Aziz/MICHELIN
p. 74 : Musée du Caire/M. Elba-Studio Vart/MICHELIN
p. 75 : Musée du Caire/ B. Kaufmann/MICHELIN
p. 75 : Musée du Caire/M. Elba-Studio Vart/MICHELIN
p. 76 : J.-P. Michel/MICHELIN
p. 77 : Hany Aziz/MICHELIN
p. 77 : J.-L. Blanchon/Visa Productions/MICHELIN
p. 78-79, p. 78 : M. Elba-Studio Vart/MICHELIN
p. 79 : Musée du Caire/ B. Kaufmann/MICHELIN
p. 79 : Musée du Caire/M. Elba-Studio Vart/MICHELIN
p. 80, p. 81 : Hany Aziz/MICHELIN
p. 81 : A. Mouraret/MICHELIN
p. 82, p. 83, p. 84, p. 85 : M. Guillou/MICHELIN
p. 86-87, p. 86 : J.-L. Blanchon/Visa Productions/MICHELIN

p. 86 : G. Blot/RMN
p. 87 : Hany Aziz/MICHELIN
p. 88-89 : B. Kaufmann/MICHELIN
p. 89 : R. Holzbachova, Ph. Benet/MICHELIN
p. 90-91 : © Collection VIOLLET
p. 90 : Y. Tierny/MICHELIN
p. 91 : Abou Ghazala/MICHELIN
p. 92, p. 93, p. 94, p. 95, p. 96, p. 97 : M. Guillou/MICHELIN
p. 98 : R. Dechamps/MICHELIN
p. 98 : Musée du Caire/M. Elba-Studio Vart/MICHELIN
p. 99 : J.-P. Michel/MICHELIN
p. 99 : Musée du Caire/B. Kaufmann/MICHELIN
p. 100 : Musée du Caire/M. Elba-Studio Vart/MICHELIN
p. 100 : B. Kaufmann/MICHELIN
p. 101 : Musée du Caire/B. Kaufmann/MICHELIN
p. 102 : J.-L. Blanchon/Visa Productions/MICHELIN
p. 102 : G. Mesmin/MICHELIN
p. 103 : R. Holzbachova, Ph. Benet/MICHELIN
p. 103 : A. Mouraret/MICHELIN
p. 104-105 : Musée du Caire/M. Elba-Studio Vart/MICHELIN
p. 104 : Fr. Soreau/MICHELIN
p. 105 : Musée du Caire/M. Elba-Studio Vart/MICHELIN
p. 106 : M. Guillou/MICHELIN
p. 107 : Musée du Caire/M. Elba-Studio Vart/MICHELIN
p. 107 : S. Sauvignier/MICHELIN
p. 108 : Fr. Soreau/MICHELIN
p. 108 : R. Mattes/MICHELIN
p. 109 : B. Kaufmann/MICHELIN
p. 109 : R. Mattes/MICHELIN
p. 110-111 : B. Kaufmann/MICHELIN
p. 111, p. 110-111 : G. Mesmin/MICHELIN
p. 112-113 : B. Kaufmann/MICHELIN
p. 114 : B. Kaufmann/MICHELIN
p. 115 : M. Guillou/MICHELIN
p. 116 : G. Mesmin/MICHELIN
p. 118 : Abou Ghazala/MICHELIN
p. 119 ht et bs : B. Pérousse/MICHELIN
p. 120, p. 121 : B. Kaufmann/MICHELIN
p. 124 ht et bs, p. 126 ht et bs, p. 127, p.128, p.130 : R. Dechamps/MICHELIN
p. 131 : © IMAPRESS
p. 132 : R. Dechamps/MICHELIN
p. 133 : © Éditions Albert et René
p. 135, 136 : R. Dechamps/MICHELIN
p. 137 : M. Guillou/MICHELIN
p. 139 : Musée du Caire/M. Elba-Studio Vart/MICHELIN
p. 141 : Fl. Joalland El Abd/MICHELIN
p. 141 : R. Dechamps/MICHELIN
p. 143 : Haras Rih el-Janoub/S. Sauvignier/MICHELIN
p. 144-145 : B. Pérousse/MICHELIN
p. 147 : Fr. Soreau/MICHELIN
p. 149 : J.-L. Blanchon/Visa Productions/MICHELIN
p. 150 : R. Dechamps/MICHELIN
p. 151 : A. Soubre/Visa Productions/MICHELIN
p. 152 : Hany Aziz/MICHELIN
p. 153 : B. Kaufmann/MICHELIN
p. 154 : M. Guillou/MICHELIN
p. 155 : Hany Aziz/MICHELIN
p. 155 : B. Kaufmann/MICHELIN
p. 160 : B. Pérousse/MICHELIN
p. 161, p. 162 : B. Kaufmann/MICHELIN
p. 163 : Hany Aziz/MICHELIN
p. 164 : R. Dechamps/MICHELIN
p. 165, p. 166 : B. Kaufmann/MICHELIN
p. 168 : B. Kaufmann/MICHELIN
p. 169 : J.-L. Blanchon/Visa Productions/MICHELIN
p. 171 ht et bs, p. 172, p. 173, p. 174 ht et bs, p. 175 : Musée du Caire/M. Elba-Studio Vart/MICHELIN
p. 176 : Musée du Caire/B. Kaufmann/MICHELIN
p. 177 : Musée du Caire/G. Mesmin/MICHELIN
p. 177 : Musée du Caire/B. Kaufmann/MICHELIN
p. 178 : B. Kaufmann/MICHELIN
p. 180 : R. Dechamps/MICHELIN
p. 181 : M. Guillou/MICHELIN
p. 181, p. 182 : B. Kaufmann/MICHELIN
p. 183 : M. Guillou/MICHELIN
p. 184 : G. Mesmin/MICHELIN
p. 185 : Cl. Rigault/MICHELIN
p. 187, p. 189 : J.-L. Blanchon/Visa Productions/MICHELIN
p. 190 : R. Jarry/Visa Productions/MICHELIN
p. 191 : R. Dechamps/MICHELIN
p. 193 : B. Kaufmann/MICHELIN
p. 194 : M. Guillou/MICHELIN
p. 195 : B. Kaufmann/MICHELIN
p. 197 : R. Dechamps/MICHELIN

p. 199 : EDF
p. 201 : J.-Cl. Boulais/MICHELIN
p. 202-203, p. 204 : Hany Aziz/MICHELIN
p. 206 : Abou Ghazala/MICHELIN
p. 207, p. 208, p. 210, p. 212, p. 213 : Hany Aziz/MICHELIN
p. 214 : M. Guillou/MICHELIN
p. 216 ht et bs, p. 217 : Hany Aziz/MICHELIN
p. 218, p. 219 : Fr. Soreau/MICHELIN
p. 220 : Fr. Soreau/MICHELIN
p. 221 : R. Dechamps/MICHELIN
p. 222-223 : K. Tigrine/MICHELIN
p. 225 : B. Kaufmann/MICHELIN
p. 226 : M. Guillou/MICHELIN
p. 228 : R. Dechamps/MICHELIN
p. 229, p. 230 : K. Tigrine/MICHELIN
p. 231 : R. Dechamps/MICHELIN
p. 233 : K. Tigrine/MICHELIN
p. 234, p. 235 : Association Ferdinand de Lesseps
p. 237 : B. Kaufmann/MICHELIN
p. 238, p. 239 : Association Ferdinand de Lesseps
p. 240, p. 241 : R. Dechamps/MICHELIN
p. 243 : K. Tigrine/MICHELIN
p. 244 : B. Kaufmann/MICHELIN
p. 245, p. 246, p. 247: R. Dechamps/MICHELIN
p. 247 : K. Tigrine/MICHELIN
p. 250 : R. Dechamps/MICHELIN
p. 251 : B. Pérousse/MICHELIN
p. 252 : R. Dechamps/MICHELIN
p. 253, p 254, p. 255 : B. Kaufmann/MICHELIN
p. 255 : Hany Aziz/MICHELIN
p. 256 : J.-Cl. Boulais/MICHELIN
p. 257, p. 258 : Association Ferdinand de Lesseps
p. 259 : R. Dechamps/MICHELIN
p. 260 : G. Mesmin/MICHELIN
p. 261 : R. Dechamps/MICHELIN
p. 262-263, p. 265 : B. Pérousse/ MICHELIN
p. 266 : H. Ruiz
p. 267 : B. Kaufmann/MICHELIN
p. 269 : Cl. Rigault/MICHELIN
p. 270, p. 272 : R. Dechamps/MICHELIN
p. 272 : B. Kaufmann/MICHELIN
p. 273, p. 274 : R. Dechamps/MICHELIN
p. 275 : B. Kaufmann/MICHELIN
p. 275 : R. Dechamps/MICHELIN
p. 277, p. 279 ht et bs, p. 280 : B. Kaufmann/MICHELIN
p. 281 : M. Guillou/MICHELIN
p. 282 : R. Dechamps/MICHELIN
p. 282 : R. Dechamps/MICHELIN
p. 283 : R. Dechamps/MICHELIN
p. 284, p. 285, p. 288 : B. Kaufmann/MICHELIN
p. 289 : Fl. Joalland El Abd/MICHELIN
p. 290 : M. Guillou/MICHELIN
p. 291 : B. Kaufmann/MICHELIN
p. 292 : Hany Aziz/MICHELIN
p. 294, p. 295 : R. Dechamps/MICHELIN
p. 297 : J. Liepe/AGYPTISCHES MUSEUM
p. 297, p. 298 : R. Dechamps/MICHELIN
p. 299 : B. Kaufmann/MICHELIN
p. 300 : A. Mouraret/MICHELIN
p. 301 : B. Kaufmann/MICHELIN
p. 302 : Cl. Rigault/MICHELIN
p. 303 : J.-L. Blanchon/Visa Productions/MICHELIN
p. 304 : B. Pérousse/MICHELIN
p. 305 : R. Dechamps/MICHELIN
p. 308 : B. Kaufmann/MICHELIN
p. 308 : B. Kaufmann/MICHELIN
p. 310, p. 311 : B. Kaufmann/MICHELIN
p. 312 : Hany Aziz/MICHELIN
p. 313 : B. Kaufmann/MICHELIN
p. 314 : Fr. Soreau/MICHELIN
p. 316 : B. Pérousse/MICHELIN
p. 316 : A. Soubre/Visa Productions/MICHELIN
p. 317 : R. Holzbachova, Ph. Bénet/MICHELIN
p. 319 : B. Pérousse/MICHELIN
p. 320 : R. Dechamps/MICHELIN
p. 320 : B. Pérousse/MICHELIN
p. 321 : B. Kaufmann/MICHELIN
p. 322 : A. Mouraret/MICHELIN
p. 323 : R. Dechamps/MICHELIN
p. 324 : M. Guillou/MICHELIN
p. 325 : B. Kaufmann/MICHELIN
p. 326 : B. Pérousse/MICHELIN
p. 328-329 : M. Guillou/MICHELIN
p. 331 : B. Kaufmann/MICHELIN
p. 332 : R. Mattes/MICHELIN
p. 333 p. 334, p. 337, p. 338, p. 339 : B. Kaufmann/MICHELIN
p. 339 : M. Guillou/MICHELIN
p. 340 : Musée du Caire/M. Elba-Studio Vart/MICHELIN
p. 340, p. 341 : M. Guillou/MICHELIN
p. 342 : Fl. Joalland El Abd/MICHELIN
p. 343 : M. Büsing/AGYPTISCHES MUSEUM